JAMES THE BROTHER OF JESUS AND THE DEAD SEA SCROLLS I

The Historical James, Paul the Enemy, and Jesus' Brothers as Apostles

Robert Eisenman

James the Brother of Jesus and the Dead Sea Scrolls
I

The Historical James, Paul the Enemy, and Jesus' Brothers as Apostles

The Way Publishing

ISBN: 9781793388988
3rd Edition

Redaction work by Dennis Walker
Cover Design: Robert Eisenman

Images - Bottom: Mausoleum of the Righteous Teacher at Qumran Left: Christian wall painting of Balaam pointing at the Messianic Star Top Right: Interior of Qumran Cave IVthe Scroll Library

James the Brother of Jesus and the Dead Sea Scrolls I: The Historical James, Paul the Enemy, and Jesus' Brothers as Apostles

1.James, Brother of the Lord,Saint. 2. Christianity-Origins. 3. Paul, Apostle, Saint. 4. Dead Sea Scrolls - Criticism, Interpretation

For:

Monobazus and Kenedaeos, the two grandsons of the 'Ethiopian Queen', Freedom Fighters and Converts, who gave their Lives at the Pass at Beit Horon

Jesus son of Sapphias, the Leader of the 'Galilean' Boatmen and 'the Party of the Poor', who 'poured out' their blood until 'the whole Sea of Galilee ran red'

and

Orde Wingate and Jonathan Netanyahu

Contents

PART IV THE DEATH OF JAMES

PART V THE BROTHERS OF JESUS AS APOSTLES

PART VI JAMESIAN COMMUNITIES IN THE EAST

Once Perfection comes, all imperfect things will disappear.
When I was a child, I spoke as a child, I thought as a child,
I reasoned as a child; but when I became a man,
I put aside childish things. For the moment we see as
through a glass darkly, but in time face-to-face.

1 Corinthians 13:11-12

Our Lord and Prophet, who has sent us, declared to us that the Evil One, having disputed with him for forty days, but failing to prevail against him, promised He would send Apostles from among his subjects to deceive them. Therefore, above all, remember to shun any Apostle, teacher, or prophet who does not accurately compare his teaching with (that of) James … the Brother of my Lord … and this even if he comes to you with recommendations.

Pseudoclementine *Homilies* 11.35 (Peter preaching at Tripoli)

Introduction

James the brother of Jesus, usually known as James the Just because of his surpassing Righteousness and Piety, is a character familiar to those with some knowledge of Christian origins. He is not so well known to the public at large, an inevitable if peculiar result of the processes described in this book.

James is not only the key to clearing up a whole series of obfuscations in the history of the early Church, he is also the missing link between the Judaism of his day, however this is defined, and Christianity. Insofar as the 'Righteous Teacher' in the Dead Sea Scrolls occupies a similar position, the parallels between the two and the respective communities they led narrow considerably, even to the point of convergence.

In the introduction to an earlier book on this subject, I wrote with specific reference to James as follows:

> In providing an alternative historical and textual framework in which to fit the most important Dead Sea Scrolls, it is to be hoped that most of the pre-conceptions that have dominated Scrolls research for so long will simply fade away and new ideas will be brought into play and previously unused sources given their proper scope. When this is done, individual beings, the facts of whose lives tradition has distorted beyond recognition or who have been otherwise consigned to historical oblivion, will spring immediately to life and a whole series of associated historical fabrications and accusations evaporate.[1]

It is to the task of rescuing James, consigned to the scrap heap of history, that this book is dedicated. James the Just has been systematically downplayed or written out of the tradition. When he suddenly emerges as the leader of the '*Jerusalem Church*' or '*Assembly*' in Acts 12:17, there is no introduction as to who he is or how he has arrived at his position. Acts' subsequent silence about his fate, which can be pieced together only from extra-biblical sources and seems to have been absorbed into the accounts both about the character we now call '*Stephen*' and even Jesus himself, obscures the situation still further.

Once the New Testament reached its final form, the process of James' marginalization became more unconscious and inadvertent but, in all events, it was one of the most successful rewrite – or overwrite – enterprises ever accomplished. James ended up ignored, an ephemeral figure on the margins of Christianity, known only to aficionados. But in the Jerusalem of his day in the 40's to 60's CE, he was the most important figure of all – '*the Bishop*' or '*Overseer*' of the Jerusalem Church.

Designated as '*the brother*' of Jesus, James the Just is often confused or juxtaposed, and this probably purposefully, with another James, designated by Scripture as '*James the brother of John*', the '*son of Zebedee*', thus increasing his marginalization. This multiplication of like-named individuals in Scripture was often the result of the rewrite or overwrite processes just remarked.

There is a collateral aspect to this welter of like-named characters in the New Testament – even going so far as to include 'Mary the sister of' her own sister Mary (John 19:25). These instances are all connected with downplaying the family of Jesus and writing it out of Scripture. This was necessary because of the developing doctrine of the supernatural Christ and the stories about his miraculous birth.

James

The leader of the 'Jerusalem Assembly', James met his death at the hands of a hostile Establishment before the events that culminated in the Uprising against Rome and the destruction of the Temple (66–70 CE). To have been 'Bishop' of the Jerusalem *Ecclesia* (Church, Assembly, or Community) was to have been the head of the whole of Christianity, whatever this might have been in this period. Not only was the centre at Jerusalem the principal one before the destruction of the Temple and the reputed flight of the Jamesian community to a city beyond the Jordan called Pella, but there were hardly any others of any importance.

Because of James' preeminent stature, the sources for him turn out to be quite extensive. In fact, extra-biblical sources contain more reliable information about James than about Jesus. There are also strong parallels between the Community led by James and the one reflected in the Dead Sea Scrolls. This is particularly true when one considers the relationship of James to the person known in the Scrolls as 'the Teacher of Righteousness' or 'Righteous Teacher'. This book will present an alternative way of viewing the Scrolls; so many doctrines, allusions, and turns of phrase in these texts are common to both traditions that the parallels become impossible to ignore.

The research I am presenting here was originally completed under a National Endowment for the Humanities Fellowship at the Albright Institute in Jerusalem in 1985–6, where the Scrolls were first photographed in 1947. It was during the tenure of this award that the insights became clear to me that led to the struggle for open access to the Scrolls, and the final collapse of the scholarly élite controlling their publication and, even more importantly, their interpretation.

But the subject of the person and teaching of James in the Jerusalem of his day is not only more important simply than his relationship to the Scrolls, it is quite independent of it. Even without insisting on any identification of James with the Righteous Teacher of the Scrolls, the Movement led by James – and it does seem to have been a 'Movement' – will be shown to have been something quite different from the Christianity with which we are now familiar. James' relationship to the Scrolls is only collateral not intrinsic to this.

One of the central theses of this book will be the identification of James as the centre of the 'opposition alliance' in Jerusalem, involved in and precipitating the Uprising against Rome in 66–70 CE. The Dead Sea Scrolls, while important, only further substantiate conclusions such as this, providing additional insight into it.

In the course of this book, it will become clear that it was James who was the true successor to his more famous brother Jesus and the leader of what we now call 'Christianity', not the more Hellenized Peter, the 'Rock' of the Roman Church. Peter may not be as historical as we think he is, and the role we attribute to him may possibly be an amalgam of that of several individuals, one a martyred cousin of both Jesus and James and their reputed successor in Palestine, Simeon bar Cleophas.

Roman Power and its Effects

It is a truism that the victors write the history. The period before us is no exception. Paul would have been very comfortable with this proposition, as he makes clear in 1 Corinthians, where he announces his *modus operandi* of making himself 'all things to all men' and his philosophy of 'winning' and 'not beating the air' (9:24–27). So would his younger contemporary, the Jewish historian Josephus (*c.* 37–96 CE), who in the introductions to his several works also shows himself to be well aware of the implications of this proposition without being able to avoid its inevitable consequences.

There is in this period one central immovable fact, that of Roman power. This was as elemental as a state of nature, and all movements and individual behavior must be seen in relation to it. But the unsuspecting reader is often quite unaware of it, when inspecting documents that emanate from this time or trying to come to grips with what was actually a highly charged and extremely revolutionary situation in Palestine. This is the problem we have to face in this period, not only where individuals are concerned, but also in the documents that have come down to us. For example, in the Gospels, probably products of the end of this period, one would have difficulty recognizing that this highly charged situation existed in the Galilee in which Jesus wanders peacefully about, curing the sick, chasing out demons, raising the dead, and performing other 'mighty works and wonders'.

But in the parallel vocabulary of a key Dead Sea Scroll text treating the final apocalyptic war against all Evil on the earth, led by the Messiah and the Heavenly Host, these same Messianic 'mighty works and wonders' are the battles God fights on behalf of His people and the marvelous victories He wins. In this document, known as the *War Scroll*, we are in the throes of an apocalyptic picture of Holy War, with which the partisans of Oliver Cromwell's militant Puritanism in seventeenth-century England would have felt comfortable.

On the other hand, where the Gospels are concerned, we are in a peaceful, Hellenized countryside, where Galilean fishermen cast their nets or mend their boats. Would it were true. The scenes in the New Testament depicting Roman officials and military officers sometimes as near-saints, or the members of the Herodian family – their appointed custodians and tax collectors in Palestine – as bumbling but well-meaning dupes also have to be understood in the light of this submissiveness to Roman power. The same can be said for the scenes featuring the vindictiveness of the Jewish mob. These are obviously included to please not a Jewish audience but a Roman or a Hellenistic one. This is also true of the presentation of the Jewish Messiah – call him 'Jesus' – as a politically disinterested, otherworldly (in Roman terms, *ergo*, harmless), even sometimes pro-Roman itinerant, at odds with his own people and family, preaching a variety of Plato's representation of the *Apology* of Socrates or the *Pax Romana.* Josephus, whose own works suffer from many of these same distortions, was himself a defector to the Roman cause. Much like Paul, he owed his survival, as well as that of his works, to this fact. Both, it seems, either had or were to achieve Roman citizenship, Josephus in the highest manner possible – adoption into the Roman imperial family. His works were encouraged by persons previously high up in the Roman Emperor Nero's chancellery (54–68 CE) and equally favored later under Domitian (81–96 CE), with whom Paul also seems to have been in close touch.

Josephus sums up this obsequiousness to Roman power in his preface to his eyewitness account of this period, the *Jewish War*, a work based in part on his interrogations, as a defector and willing collaborator, of prisoners. In criticizing other historians treating the same events, Josephus notes that all historical works from this period suffer from two main defects, 'flattery of the Romans and vilification of the Jews, adulation and abuse being substituted for real historical record'.[2] Having said this, he then goes on to indulge in the same conduct himself. That historical portions of the New Testament suffer from the same defects should be obvious to anyone familiar with them. But the Dead Sea Scrolls do not suffer from such defects, and were probably hidden in caves for this reason. The fact of Roman power was probably the principal reason why no one ever returned to retrieve them. No one could have, because no one survived. It was that simple.

Jesus

The quest for the historical Jesus has fascinated sophisticated Western man for over two centuries now, but the quest for the historical James has never been pursued. Rather than be disconsolate that the material regarding James is so fragmentary and often presented from the point of view of persons like Paul who disagreed with him, it is the task of the historian to revive him, to rescue him from the oblivion into which he was cast. This is not so difficult as it might seem, because materials about James exist – quite a lot of them. It remains only to place them in a proper perspective. This would be much more difficult to achieve for James' brother Jesus. But is Jesus as well-known as most people think? Experts, lay persons, artists, writers, political figures from all ages and every place constantly assert the fact of Jesus' existence and speak of him in the most familiar way, as if they had certain knowledge of him. Unfortunately, the facts themselves are shrouded in mystery and obscured by a cloud cover of retrospective theology and polemics that frustrates any attempt to get at the real events underlying them. Most who read the documents concerning him are simply unaware of this.

Questions not only emerge concerning Jesus' existence itself, but also regarding the appropriateness of his teaching to his time and place. Where the man 'Jesus' is concerned – as opposed to the redeemer figure 'Christ' or 'Christ Jesus' Paul proclaims and with whom, via some personal visionary experience, he claims to be in contact – we have mainly the remains of Hellenistic romance and mythologizing to go on, often with a clear polemicizing or dissembling intent. In fact, Paul, portrayed as appearing on the scene only a few years after Jesus' death, either knows nothing or is willing to tell us nothing about him. Only two historical points about Jesus emerge from Paul's letters: that he was crucified at some unspecified date, and that he had brothers, one of whom was called James (Gal. 1:19). In fact, taking the brother relationship seriously may turn out to be one of the only confirmations that there ever was a historical Jesus.

Where the Gospels are concerned, Jesus is largely presented in the framework of supernatural storytelling. Hellenistic mystery cults were familiar over a large portion of the Greco-Roman world where Paul was active. They would certainly have provided fertile ground for the propagation of competing models among a population already well-versed in their fundamentals.

One attitude, particularly important in determining the historicity of Gospel materials, is the strong current of anti-Semitism one encounters lying just below the surface. This anti-Semitism was already rife in Hellenistic cities such as Alexandria in Egypt and Caesarea in Palestine, and ultimately led to the destruction of the Jewish populations there.

One can assert with a fair degree of confidence that while Messianic agitation in Palestine could be sectarian, it would not be anti-Jewish or opposed to the people of Palestine. Of course, there was internecine party strife, often vitriolic and quite unforgiving, but for a popular Messianic leader to be against his own people would be *prima facie* impossible and, one can confidently assert, none ever was – except retrospectively or through the miracle of art. The reader may take this as a rule of thumb.

Nor can we say that in the Gospels we do not have a composite recreation of facts and episodes relating to a series of Messianic pretenders in Palestine in the first century, familiar from the works of Josephus, interlaced or spliced into a narrative of a distinctly Hellenistic or non-Palestinian, pro-Pauline cast. This includes some light-hearted – even malevolent – satire where events in Palestine are concerned. Josephus displays a parallel, but inverted, malevolence, calling examples of the charismatic Messianic type of leader 'religious frauds' or 'impostors more dangerous than the bandits and murderers', and 'deceivers claiming divine inspiration leading their followers out into the wilderness there to show them the signs of their impending Deliverance'.[3]

The Gospel of Matthew, even more than the other Gospels, has long been recognized as a collection of Messianic and other scriptural proof-texts taken out of context and woven into a gripping narrative of what purports to be the life of Jesus. In describing an early flight by Jesus' father 'Joseph' to Egypt to escape Herod – *à la* Joseph in Egypt and Moses' escape from Pharaoh in the Bible – not paralleled in the other Gospels – Matthew utilizes the passage, 'I have called my son out of Egypt' (2:15). Whether this passage applies to Jesus is debatable. In its original context (Hos. 11:1), it obviously refers to the people Israel as a whole. However, it does have very real relevance to a character in the mid-50s, whom Josephus – followed by the Book of Acts – calls 'the Egyptian', but declines to identify further. This Messianic pretender, according to the picture in Josephus, first leads the people 'out into the wilderness' and then utilizes the Mount of Olives as a staging point to lead a Joshua-style assault on the walls of Jerusalem.[4] But the Mount of Olives was a favorite haunt, according to Gospel narrative, of Jesus and his companions. We will note many such suspicious overlaps.

For his part, Josephus, predictably obsequious, applauds the extermination of the followers of this Egyptian by the Roman Governor Felix (52-60 CE). Acts, too, is quick to show its familiarity with this episode, including Josephus' tell-tale reticence in supplying his name. Rather it somewhat charmingly portrays the commander of the Roman garrison in the Temple as mistaking Paul for him (21:38).

Another example of this kind is the so-called 'Little Apocalypse' in the Gospels (Mt 24:4-31 and pars.). In Luke's version, Jesus is depicted as predicting the encirclement of Jerusalem by armies, followed by its fall. All versions are introduced by reference to the destruction of the Temple and generally refer to famine, wars, and sectarian strife, along with other signs and catastrophes. This probably has very real relevance to a section in the *Antiquities of the Jews*, in which Josephus describes in gory detail the woes brought upon the people by the movement founded by 'Judas the Galilean' around the time of the Census of Cyrenius in 6–7 CE. This is contemporaneous with Jesus' birth according to the Gospel of Luke, and is also referred to in Acts (5:37). Josephus calls this movement the 'Fourth Philosophy', but most now refer to it as 'Zealot'. Here, as in the Little Apocalypse, Josephus portrays this movement – the appearance of which, again, is contemporaneous with the birth of Christ in Luke – as bringing about wars, famine, and terrible suffering for the people, culminating in the destruction of the Temple.

These 'woes' also have relevance to another Messianic character whom Josephus calls 'Jesus ben Ananias'. This man, whom Josephus portrays as an oracle or quasi-prophet of some kind, went around Jerusalem directly following the death of James in 62 CE for seven straight years, proclaiming its coming destruction, until he was finally hit on the head by a Roman projectile during the siege of Jerusalem and killed just prior to the fulfillment of his prophecy.

The applicability of this story to the Historical Jesus (and in a very real way the Historical James) should be obvious. In fact, 'Jesus ben Ananias' was set free at the end of Josephus' *Jewish War* after having originally been arrested. The release of such a Messianic double for Jesus is also echoed in Scripture as it has come down to us in the release of another 'double'. One Gospel calls him 'Jesus Barabbas' – the meaning of this name in Aramaic would appear to be 'the Son of the Father' – a political 'bandit' who 'committed murder at the time of the Uprising' and is released by Pontius Pilate (Mt 27:26 and pars.).

Variant manuscripts of the works of Josephus, reported by Church fathers like Origen, Eusebius, and Jerome, all of whom at one time or another spent time in Palestine, contain materials associating the fall of Jerusalem with the death of *James* – not with the death of Jesus. Their shrill protests, particularly Origen's and Eusebius', have probably not a little to do with the disappearance of this passage from all manuscripts of the *Jewish War* that have come down to us. As will also become clear, other aspects from the biography of James have been retrospectively absorbed into the biography of Jesus and other characters in the Book of Acts in sometimes astonishing ways.

In fact, in what suggests that the Gospels and some Dead Sea Scrolls are virtually contemporary documents – and that the authors of the former knew the latter – it will be shown that fundamental allusions from the Scrolls have been absorbed into Gospel presentations of Jesus' relations with his disciples. It will be shown that the presentation of the disciples as peaceful fishermen on the Sea of Galilee incorporates a play on key ideological usages found in the Dead Sea Scrolls. This is the language of *casting down nets* familiar from Gospel accounts of Jesus' appearances to his disciples along the Sea of Galilee both before and after his resurrection and in parallel notices in the Dead Sea Scrolls and Revelation. This language of *casting* or *throwing down* will also be shown to be integral to presentations of the death of James in virtually all traditions we are heirs to.

The 'Galilean' language in these and like episodes can also be thought of as playing on the name of the movement developing out of the activities of Judas *the Galilean*, the founder of the Zealot Movement mentioned above. Changing terms with ideological connotations into geographical place names tends to trivialize them. This is certainly the case with confusions relating to whether Jesus came from a place in Galilee called '*Nazareth*' (never mentioned in either the works of Josephus or the Old Testament) or whether, like James, he followed a '*Nazirite*' life-style or was a '*Nazrene*' or '*Nazoraean*', which have totally different connotations in the literature as it has come down to us.

These are complex matters and will doubtless be perplexing at first, but it is necessary to elucidate them to describe the true situation behind some of these highly prized scriptural re-presentations. It is hoped that the reader will soon get used to the kind of word play and evasions at work. The evidence, which might at first appear circumstantial, will mount up, allowing the reader to appreciate the validity of the explanations provided. This is not to say that the Jesus of history did not exist, only that the evidence is skewed and that the problem is more complex than many think.

The Study of James

The situation with regard to James is quite different and clearer, probably because except for the Gospels and the first eleven chapters of the Book of Acts it has not been so overwritten. Here, too, materials do exist outside the tradition of Scripture. Even scriptural materials regarding James, where not theologically refurbished, are very helpful. Where rewritten or overwritten, they can by comparison with external materials be brought into focus and sometimes even restored.

But one can go further. It is through the figure of James that one can get a realistic sense of what the Jesus of history might have been like. In fact, it is through the figure of James, and by extension the figure of Paul, with whom James is always in a kind of contrapuntal relationship, that the question of the Historical Jesus may be finally resolved.

The same is true with regard to 'the brother of Jesus'. In the Gospels, Paul's letters, and Josephus, no embarrassment whatsoever is evinced about this relationship with Jesus, and James is designated without qualification as Jesus' brother. There are no questions of the kind that crop up later in the wake of the developing doctrine of the supernatural 'Christ' and stories about his supernatural birth, attempting to depreciate or diminish this relationship. These stories about the birth of 'Christ' are, in any event, not referred to by Paul and appear first in the Gospels of Matthew and Luke, thus leading in the second century to embarrassment not just over Jesus' brothers, but the fact of Jesus' family generally, including sisters, fathers, uncles, and mothers.

Embarrassment of this kind was exacerbated by the fact that Jesus' brothers ('cousins', as Jerome would later come to see them at the end of the fourth century) were the principal personages in Palestine and Jesus' successors there, important in Eastern tradition. What exacerbated the problem of their relationship to Jesus even further in the second century was the doctrine of Mary's *'perpetual virginity'* and with it the utter impossibility – nay, inconceivability – that she should have had other children. This even led Jerome's younger contemporary, Augustine, in the fifth century, to the assertion reproduced in Muhammad's Koran in the seventh, that Jesus didn't have any father at all, only a mother![5]

To the ideologue, it was simply impossible that Jesus should have had a father or brothers, Gospel notices and references in Paul notwithstanding. Nor could Joseph have had *any* children by Mary. These had to have been by another wife. All such theological considerations will be set aside and all family designations treated naturally. If a person was said to have had a brother, then he was a natural brother, conceived by natural generation, not a half-brother, stepbrother, 'cousin', or 'milk brother'.

The wealth of extra-biblical sources relating to James has already been noted. If we include with these those in the Book of Acts, where not adulterated, and notices in the letters of Paul, then there is a considerable amount of material relating to James. He is also mentioned in the Gospels, but here the material is marred by doctrinal attempts either to defame the family and brothers of Jesus or to disqualify them in some manner.

Though a parallel process is at work in the early chapters of the Book of Acts, as one moves into chapter 12 where James is introduced and beyond, the character of the material changes and quickens. For some reason Acts assumes that we already know who James is, as opposed to another James it calls 'the brother of John', whom it conveniently disposes of at the beginning of chapter 12 just before introducing the real James. It is possible to read through this material in Acts to the real history underlying it and the real events it transmogrifies.

The same can be said for Paul's letters, which provide additional straightforward witness to 'James the brother of the Lord' and *know no other James*. The Historical James can also be reconstructed from the underlying circumstances to which remarks in these letters are directed. These, plus a myriad of extra-biblical materials, such as Josephus, apocryphal gospels, non-canonical acts including the 'Pseudoclementines', the Gnostic manuscripts from Nag Hammadi in Upper Egypt, and the mass of early Church literature all constitute sources about James. The documentation is that impressive.

The Historical Jesus and the Historical James

It is through documentation of this kind that we can recover the person of Jesus as well. The proposition would run something like this: let us assume that a Messianic leader known as 'Jesus' did exist in the early part of the first century in Palestine. Furthermore, let us assume that he had brothers, one of whom was called James.

Who would have known Jesus better? His close relatives, who according to tradition were his legitimate successors in Palestine, and those companions accompanying him in all his activities? Or someone who admits that he never saw Jesus in his lifetime, as Paul does, and that, on the contrary, he was an *enemy* of and persecuted Jesus' followers, and came to know him only through visionary experiences that allowed him to be in touch with a figure he designates as 'Christ Jesus' in Heaven?

The answer of any reasonable observer to this question should be obvious: James and Jesus' inner circle knew him best. But the answer of all orthodox Church circles has always been that Paul's understanding of Jesus was superior and that he knew him better than Jesus' own family or companions. Furthermore, it is claimed that the doctrines represented by James and the members of Jesus' family generally were defective in their understanding of Paul's 'Christ Jesus' and inferior to boot. Given the fact that the Christianity we are heirs to is largely the legacy of Paul and like-minded persons, this is just what one would have expected.

Moreover, the 'Pauline' view of these matters has been confirmed by the picture of Jesus that has come down to us in the Gospels. This is particularly evident in the description of the disciples in the Gospels as 'weak' (Mt 14:31 and pars.), a term Paul repeatedly uses in his letters, almost always with derogatory intent, when describing the leaders of the community, particularly in Jerusalem, and their directives (Rom. 14:1–2 and 1 Cor. 8:7–9:22). Occasionally he parodies this, applying the term to himself to gain sympathy, but most often he uses it to attack the leadership, in particular those keeping dietary regulations or relying on Mosaic Law – even those who, as he puts it, 'only eat vegetables', like James.

In the Gospels, reflecting Paul, when an Apostle as important as Peter 'sinks' into the Sea of Galilee for lack of 'Faith' or denies Jesus three times on his death night, the implications are quite clear. They are 'weak' in their adherence to the Pauline concept of 'Faith', a concept opposed to the more Jamesian one of salvation by 'works'. In addition, they have a defective understanding of Jesus' teaching, particularly of that most important of all Pauline doctrines, the *Christ*. This is the situation that has retrospectively been confirmed by eighteen hundred years of subsequent Church history too – however unreasonable or in defiance of real history it might appear.

Here, two aphorisms suggest themselves: 'Poetry is truer than history' and 'It is so, if you think so'. The first has a clear connection to the development of the documents that have come down to us. If the Gospels represent the 'poetry', and truly they are perhaps the most successful literary creations ever written both in terms of their artistry and the extent of their influence, then their authors were the poets. It was Plato, who, comprehending the nature of the ancient world better than most, wished to banish the poets from his ideal state – not without cause, because, in his view, it was the poets who created the myths and religious mysteries, by which the less critically-minded lived. For Plato, this was a world of almost total darkness.

Where the second is concerned, one can say with some justice that it does not matter what really happened, only what people *think* happened. In essence, this is the theological approach of our own time, and, in the court of public opinion at least, the decision has long ago been rendered, not only for Christians themselves, but also for the world at large, including Jews and Muslims, because for all these people the Jesus of Scripture is real too.

This is why the study of James is so important, because the situation is for the most part just the opposite of what most people think it is. The reader will, undoubtedly, find this proposition preposterous. How could so many people, including some of the greatest minds of our history, have been wrong? The answer to this question has to do with the *beauty* of the concepts being disseminated, however uncharacteristic of the Palestine of the period they might be, ideas epitomizing the highest ideals of *Hellenistic* Civilization.

Like Plato's picture of his teacher Socrates, Jesus refused to answer his interlocutors or avoid his fate. At least as far as his chroniclers are concerned, he met an end more terrible even than Socrates' – but then Socrates was not dealing with the might of Imperial Rome, only of Athens. Of course, the very terribleness of this end is what makes the drama and its symbols so attractive.

It was Plato's pupil Aristotle who informed us how the most successful tragedy inspires terror and pity. Indeed, much of the legacy of Plato and Socrates is incorporated into the materials about Jesus, including the notions of non-resistance to Evil and a Justice that does not consist of helping your friends and harming your enemies – all doctrines absolutely alien to a Palestinian milieu, such as that, for instance, represented in native Palestinian documents like the Dead Sea Scrolls.

Beauty and artistry are two reasons for the abiding appeal of these documents, but so too, for instance, is the attractiveness of a doctrine such as Grace, not something anyone would have any need or desire to resist. Along with these, however, goes the lack of any real historical understanding of this difficult period, and so oversimplifications, artifice and disinformation are preferred. In turn, these have operated on the level of general culture worldwide in an almost hypnotic fashion. It is this phenomenon that has been generalized to describe religion as 'the opiate of the people'. This is not true for all religions. Some operate in exactly the opposite manner.

The End Result

It will transpire that the person of James is almost diametrically opposed to the Jesus of Scripture and our ordinary understanding of him. Whereas the Jesus of Scripture is anti-nationalist, cosmopolitan, antinomian – that is, against the direct application of Jewish Law – and accepting of foreigners and other persons of perceived impurities, the Historical James will turn out to be zealous for the Law, and rejecting of foreigners and polluted persons generally.

Strong parallels emerge between these kinds of attitudes and those of the Righteous Teacher in the Dead Sea Scrolls. For instance, attitudes in the Gospels towards many classes of persons – tax collectors, harlots, Sinners, and the like – are diametrically opposed to those delineated in the Dead Sea Scrolls, but in agreement with anti-Semitic diatribes of the time in Greco-Hellenistic environments.

At the centre of the agitation in the Temple in the mid-50s, hostile to Herodians, Romans, and their fellow-travelers, James will emerge as the pivotal figure among the more nationalistic crowd. In his incarnation of 'the Perfect Righteous' or 'Just One', he will be at the centre of the Opposition Alliance of sects and revolutionary groups opposed to the Pharisaic/Sadducean Establishment pictured in Josephus and the New Testament.

The election of James as leader of the early 'Church', missing from Acts, will be shown to be the real event behind the election of Matthias to succeed Judas *Iscariot* in his 'Office' (*Episcopate*). James' death too, in 62 CE, will be shown to be connected in the popular imagination with the fall of Jerusalem in 70 CE in a way that Jesus' some four decades before could not have been.

Two attacks on James also emerge in our sources – both physical – one paralleling the attack on Stephen in the 40's related in Acts, and the other in the 60s, described by Josephus and in early Church sources, ending in his death. The stoning of Stephen, like the election of Judas *Iscariot*'s replacement that precedes it in Acts, will turn out to be totally imaginary – or rather dissembling – yet written over very real materials central to the life of James.

The *modus operandi* of New Testament accounts such as those in Acts, some merely refurbishment of known events relating to the life of James, will be illumined. Once the aim and method of these substitutions are correctly appreciated, it will be easy to see that the Hellenized Movement that developed overseas which we now call Christianity, was, in fact, the mirror reversal of what actually took place in Palestine under James. It will be possible to show that what was actually transpiring in Palestine was directly connected with the literature represented by the Dead Sea Scrolls, which in its last stages was either equivalent to or all but indistinguishable from that circulating about and normally associated with James.

Paul, on the other hand, will emerge as a highly compromised individual, deeply involved with Roman officials and Herodian kings – a proposition given added weight by the intriguing allusions to a parallel character in the Dead Sea Scrolls called 'the Lying Spouter' or 'Scoffer' – even to the extent of actually being a member of the family of King Herod. His contacts will go very high indeed, even into the Emperor Nero's personal household itself (Phil. 4:22). Appreciating this context will help rescue Jesus' closest relatives and his religious and political heirs in Palestine from the oblivion into which they have been cast either intentionally or via benign neglect.

This book, which is the first of a two-part series and represents a compression of the earlier *James the Brother of Jesus* (1997-98), is written for both the specialist and the non-specialist alike – particularly the latter where interest is generally even more keen. Readers are encouraged to make judgments for themselves and, where possible, to go to the primary sources directly and not rely on secondhand presentations. Because of this, secondary sources will not prove particularly useful, except in so far as they supply new, previously overlooked, data, because writings or materials later than 500 CE are for the most part derivative. Later writers too – even modern researchers – sometimes forget the motives of their predecessors, adopting the position and point of view of the tradition or theology they are heirs to. In the controversy regarding the Dead Sea Scrolls, a struggle developed with just such an academic and religious élite, not only over the publication of all the documents but even, more importantly, over their interpretation.

I have done my best to make the Dead Sea Scrolls, which have come along as if miraculously to redress the balance or haunt those who would adopt an a historical approach, available across the board to a wider populace. The matters before us are not for those who docilely accept biblical writ or scholarly consensus as the final word. The criticism we are doing is historical and literary criticism, looking at the way a given author actually put his materials together and to what end. It is the weight of the gradual accumulation of detail and textual analyses of this kind that ultimately renders the presentation credible.

To follow the arguments, as well as to make sure the materials are being correctly presented from the sources, the reader is urged to have a copy of the New Testament, the works of Josephus and a translation of principal Dead Sea Scrolls at his or her disposal. Nothing more is really required. Even though all necessary quotations from these sources are provided in the book, it is still very useful to see them in their original context and to follow the sequencing and order surrounding a specific historical or legal point.

It is important to look into the original contexts of passages used in scriptural and scholarly debate, because the ambience of such materials is important in determining the frame of mind and intent of the original, not its derivative application. References are confined as far as possible to primary sources, the trends implicit in secondary ones often ebbing and flowing with the times and one generation's consensus being overturned by the next's.

For this reason, readers are advised to go directly to the ancient sources themselves. It is in the ancient sources that the data is to be found and this is where the battle must be joined. What is required is a critical faculty, sensitivity to language, and simple common sense. These, one hopes, are shared by everyone.

Fountain Valley, California
April 30th, 2012

Author Robert Eisenman at the entrance to Qumran's Cave 4 in 1992

PART I:

PALESTINIAN BACKGROUNDS

Chapter 1
James

The Downplaying of James in Christian Tradition

In the period of Palestinian history ending with the destruction of the Second Temple, one of the most under-esteemed and certainly under-estimated characters is James the brother of Jesus. James has been systematically ignored by both Christian and Jewish scholars alike, the latter hardly even having heard of him, his very existence being a source of embarrassment to them both. Muslims, too, have never heard of him, since their traditions were bequeathed to them by Christians and Jews.

This silence surrounding James was not accidental. Augustine (354–430), writing to his older contemporary Jerome (348–420), expressed his concern about problems between Peter and Paul signaled in Paul's Letter to the Galatians. Clearly, these were directly connected to James' leadership in the early Church and his directives. But, curiously, neither Augustine nor Jerome even mentions James in this exchange. The early Church theologian Eusebius (260–340) had finalized the process of the downplaying of James, questioning the authenticity of the Letter of James. Martin Luther a thousand years later felt that this letter should not have been included in the New Testament anyhow.[1]

It is not surprising that these arbiters of Christian opinion in their day should have felt the way they did, because it is hard to consider the Letter of James as 'Christian' at all, if we take as our yardstick the Gospels or Paul's letters. If we widen this interpretation somewhat to include the Eastern sectarian tendency referred to in early Church literature as '*Ebionite*' (a word deriving from an original Hebrew root meaning 'the Poor') and other parallel currents like the Essenes, Nazoraeans, Elchasaites, Manichaeans, and even Islam, we discover a different story. For its part, the Letter of James in its essence resembles nothing so much as the Dead Sea Scrolls.

Origen (185–254) railed against traditions giving James more prominence than he was prepared to accord him, namely those connecting James' death – not Jesus' – to the fall of Jerusalem. The normal scriptural view and popular theology to this day connects Jesus' death not James' to the destruction of the Temple. Origen's view of the tradition connecting the fall of Jerusalem to the death of James, which he credited to Josephus, is probably not a little connected with its disappearance from these materials as they have come down to us.

Eusebius contemptuously alluded to the poverty-stricken spirituality of the Ebionites, who held James' name in such high esteem. He did so in the form of a pun on the Hebrew meaning of their name, 'the Poor', thereby showing himself very knowledgeable about the meaning and consideration of James' person.[2] 'The Poor' was already in use as an honorable form of self-designation by the community responsible for the Dead Sea Scrolls, as it was among those in contact with James' Jerusalem Community, most notably Paul. The usage also figures prominently in both the Sermon on the Mount in the Gospel of Matthew and in the Letter attributed to James.[3]

The group or movement associated with James' name and teachings in Jerusalem is usually referred to as 'the Jerusalem Church' or 'Community', an English approximation for the Greek word *Ecclesia*, which literally means 'Assembly'. It is also possible to refer to it as *Palestinian Christianity*, which would indeed be appropriate. But an even more popular notation one finds in the literature is *Jewish Christianity*.

Jewish and Christian Sectarianism

Sects such as these were at a very early time pronounced anathema by the Rabbis – the heirs of the Pharisees pictured in the New Testament – who took over Judaism by default seven and a half years after James' judicial murder. After the destruction of the Temple theirs was the only Jewish tradition the Romans were willing to tolerate in Palestine. The legal tradition they inherited has come to be known as *Halachah*, the sum total of religious law according to the traditions of the Pharisees. It is preserved in the literature of the Rabbis known as the *Talmud*. This includes what is also known as 'the Oral Law' and consists mainly of a document compiled in the third century called the *Mishnah*, a number of commentaries on it, and further traditional compilations, together known as either the 'Babylonian' or 'Jerusalem *Talmud*', depending on whether they originated in Iraq or Palestine.

The Movement headed by James from the 40's to the 60s CE in Jerusalem was the principal one of a number of groups categorized in the *Talmud* by the pejorative terminology *minim*. This has now come to mean in Jewish tradition 'sectarian'. With the gradual production of this rabbinical literature, a new form of Judaism was formulated no longer predicated on the Temple. This became dominant in Palestine only after the Romans imposed it by brute force.

Because of its palpably more accommodating attitude towards foreign rule and, at least while the Temple was still standing, to High Priests appointed by foreigners or foreign-controlled rulers, it was really the only form of Jewish religious expression the Romans were willing to live with. The same was to hold true for the form of Christianity we can refer to as 'Pauline', which was equally accommodating to Roman power. For his part, Paul proudly proclaimed his Pharisaic roots (Phil. 3:5).

This form of Judaism must be distinguished from the more variegated tapestry that characterized Jewish religious expression in Jesus' and James' lifetimes. This consisted of quite a number of groups before the fall of the Temple, some of which were quite militant and aggressive, even apocalyptic, that is, having a concern for a highly emotive style of expression regarding 'the End Time'. Most of these apocalyptic groups focused in one way or another on the Temple. They were written out of Judaism in the same manner that James and Jesus' other brothers were written out of Christianity.

'Christianity', as we know it, developed in the West in contradistinction to the more variegated landscape that continued to characterize the East. It would be more proper to refer to Western Christianity at this point as 'Pauline' or 'Gentile Christian'. It came to be seen as orthodox largely as a result of the efforts of Eusebius and like-minded persons, who put the reorganization program ascribed to Constantine into effect. It can also be usefully referred to as 'Overseas' or 'Hellenistic Christianity' as opposed to 'Palestinian Christianity'.

Its documents and credos were collected and imposed on what is now known as the Christian world at the Council of Nicaea in 325 CE and others that followed in the fourth century and beyond. These formally asserted the divinity of Jesus and made it orthodox. Eusebius, Constantine's bishop and personal confidant, had a major role in the organization and guidance of the Council of Nicaea. The development of this genre of Overseas Christianity was actually concurrent and parallel to the development of Rabbinic Judaism. Both were, not only willing to live with Roman power, they owed their continued existence to its sponsorship.

To put this proposition somewhat differently: it was the fact of the power and brutality of Rome was operating in both traditions to drive out and declare heretical what many now refer to as 'Jewish Christianity' – '*Ebionitism*' would perhaps be a better description of it in Palestine. In Judaism, what was left was a legalistic shadow of former glories, bereft of apocalyptic and Messianic tendencies; in Christianity, a largely Hellenized, otherworldly mystery cult, the real religious legacy of three hundred years of Roman religious genius and assimilation. This surgery was necessary if Christianity in the form we know it was to survive, since certain doctrines represented by James were distinctly opposed to those ultimately considered to be *Christian.*

James the Real Successor to Jesus, not Peter

In the literature, James' place as successor to and inheritor of the mantle of his brother was largely taken over by the individual known, in the West, as 'Peter'. This was a logical end of the legitimization of certain claims advanced by the now Hellenized and largely non-Jewish, Gentile Church at Rome following the destruction of the Jerusalem centre in the wake of the Uprising against Rome. It is an interesting coincidence that 'the Jerusalem Community' of James the Just and the Community at Qumran disappeared at about the same time – though perhaps this is not so coincidental as it may seem.

The 'Rock' terminology reflected in Peter's name and the imagery related to it were actually in use contemporaneously in Palestine in both the literature at Qumran and in what were probably the documents of the Jerusalem Church.[4] In the latter, a version of it was applied to James, as well probably to his successor - a man identified in the tradition as Jesus' (and therefore James') *first 'cousin'*, Simeon bar Cleophas. We shall see that Simeon bar Cleophas is very likely *the second brother of Jesus*, an individual called '*Simon*' (and sometimes even 'Simon *the Zealot*'/'*Zealotes*') as presented in Gospel Apostle lists - Christianity in Palestine developing in something of the manner of an Islamic Caliphate (and a Shi'ite one at that), that is, one centered on the *family* of Jesus and familial succession.

James is not only the key to a reconstruction of Jewish Christian history, he is also the key to the Historical Jesus. The solution to this problem has evaded observers for so long primarily because they have attempted to approach it through the eyes and religious legacy of James' archrival and sometime religious 'Enemy', Paul.[5] It is through James that we are on the safest ground in approaching a historically accurate semblance of what Jesus himself, in so far as he actually existed, might have been like.

Of all the characters in the early stages of Christianity, Paul alone is known to us through first-hand autobiographical documents, that is, the genuine letters attributed to him. They reveal his life, character and thought in the most personal manner possible. All others, even Jesus and most of those generally called 'Apostles', we know only by second- or third-hand accounts, if we know them at all. We have Gospels or letters purportedly written about them or in their names, but these must be handled with the utmost care.

It is also not generally comprehended that this is the sequence in which we should take the New Testament. Paul's genuine letters and a few other materials – possibly including the Letter of James – come first and are primary. The rest come later and are secondary. The Gospels themselves are probably even tertiary. Biblical scholars have not come to a consensus on which aspects of this legacy can properly be considered historical. Nor have they succeeded in giving us a very real picture of what might have occurred at this formative moment in human history or of the events surrounding and succeeding the life of the individual called, in the Hellenistic world, 'the Christ'.

When it comes to the person of Jesus' brother James, however, we are on much firmer ground, not least because he has been so marginalized. We have a number of facts concerning James' life attested to by a variety of independent observations within and without Christian tradition.

It should not be surprising that the existence of an actual brother of Jesus in the flesh was a problem for the theologian committed to ideas of divine sonship and supernatural birth. In Roman Catholic doctrine it has been the received teaching since the end of the fourth century that James was the brother of Jesus, not only by a different father, an obvious necessity in view of the doctrine of divine sonship, but also by a *different* mother – the answer to the conundrum presented by the perpetual virginity of Mary. That is, James was a cousin of Jesus. We shall take this for what it is, embarrassment over the existence of Jesus' brothers and bids to protect the emerging doctrine of the supernatural Christ. This started gaining currency in the second and third centuries, but was totally absent from contemporary documents relating to the family of Jesus that survived the redaction processes of the New Testament.

There is also sufficient evidence to show James as a normative Jew of his time, even one referred to by the most extreme terminology 'Zealot' or '*Sicarii*', this in spite of his being the most important of the Central Triad of early Church leaders, whom Paul denotes as 'Pillars' (Gal. 2:9). What a normative Jew might have been in these circumstances before the fall of the Temple will require further elucidation. For the purposes of discussion we are on safe ground, however, if we say that such a concept at least encompassed an attachment to the Law. It also consisted of a feeling for Temple and Temple worship, regardless of attitude towards the Herodian, pro-Roman Priesthood overseeing it. At some point in the mid-40's, Cephas and John, two of those Paul designates as 'Pillars' in Galatians 2:9, along with another James, 'the *brother* of John' as distinct from James the subject of this book, disappear from the scene, probably in the context of conflict with Herodian kings such as Agrippa I (37–44 CE) or his brother Herod of Chalcis (44–49 CE). Thus, James was left to occupy the 'Christian' leadership stage in Palestine alone for the next two decades. At least this is what can be gleaned from the materials in Acts, however imprecise or mythologized they may be.

The Direct Appointment or Election of James

Whether James succeeded to this leadership by direct appointment of Jesus, or he was elected by the Apostles, is disputed in the sources. However he emerged, such a succession seems to have been connected with the sequence of the post-resurrection appearances of Jesus to his Disciples, as depicted in the literature, or, as Eusebius puts it, following Clement of Alexandria, the order in which 'the tradition of Knowledge' was accorded individual leaders.[6]

There are lost resurrection traditions that accorded precedence even in this to James, despite attempts to obliterate them. One of these, found in the first post-resurrection appearance episode in the Gospel of Luke, depicts Jesus as appearing to '*Clopas*' – that is, Simeon bar Cleophas or his father – together with an unnamed companion, possibly James, on the Emmaus road outside Jerusalem. A second is certainly to be found in 1 Corinthians 15:7, where Paul confirms an appearance to James and 'last of all' himself. In the former at least, if not in the latter, we have unassailable evidence of a tradition according precedence in the matter of the first appearance to a member or members of Jesus' family – '*Clopas*', according to extant tradition, being, at the very least, *Jesus' uncle*. Interestingly enough, this appearance takes place in the environs of Jerusalem, not in Galilee as most other such Gospel renditions.

In addition, other early traditions actually speak in terms of a *direct* appointment of James by Jesus.[7] As opposed to this, early Church traditions via Clement mention an election of James. Whatever the conclusion, there can be no doubt that James was the actual successor in Palestine.

Finally, there is the Letter ascribed to James in the New Testament, which Eusebius considered spurious. Despite its Jewish apocalyptic character and in spite of its purportedly late appearance on the scene, it was evidently imbued with such prestige that it could not be excluded from the canon. It can be shown to be a direct riposte to points Paul makes in his

Letters to the Romans, Corinthians, and Galatians. Even if this is not sufficient to consider it authentic, its doctrines are enough like those of the Historical James, reconstructable from other sources, to contend that it at the very least represents authentic Palestinian tradition.

The antiquity of its materials can also now be confirmed by reference to its many parallels to doctrines in the Dead Sea Scrolls, not available previously. It also lacks the Gnostic tendencies so prevalent in later documents featuring the person of James. In it, too, the Temple would seem to be still standing and the catastrophe that was soon to overwhelm Jewish life in Palestine has seemingly not yet occurred. At present, opinions concerning it show a greater flexibility in their willingness to come to grips with at least the possibility of its authenticity.

Given its manifest parallels with the documents from Qumran, with which it makes an almost perfect fit, and doctrines attributable to the person of James from other sources, it has to be considered a fairly good reflection at least of the 'Jamesian' point of view. In fact, apart from the Pauline corpus and the 'We Document', on which – as we shall see – the second part of Acts is based, and a few worrisome phrases such as 'the Perfect Law of Freedom' (Jas. 1:25 and 2:12), it is one of the most homogeneous, authentic, and possibly even earliest pieces in the New Testament corpus.

There are also two Apocalypses attributed to James in the Nag Hammadi corpus, as well as an additional riposte from James to Peter in the prelude to the version of the Pseudoclementines known as the Homilies. In this last there are also letters, reputedly from Clement to James and Peter to James. There is also a Gospel attributed to James, usually referred to as the 'Infancy Gospel' or the Protevangelium of James, averring, of all things, the perpetual virginity of Mary! As will be seen, its author might more appropriately have applied this doctrine to James' lifestyle. Who else to give a better testimony to 'facts' relating to the infant Jesus than the person represented as being his *older* brother? But it is most certainly spurious.

Finally there is a now-lost work, known to the writer Epiphanius (367-404), called the *Anabathmoi Jacobou* or *The Ascents of James* after the lectures James is pictured as delivering to the Jerusalem masses from the Temple steps. Epiphanius even quotes from this work, further concretizing James' role at the centre of agitation in the Temple opposed to the Herodian Priesthood and decrying its pollution.

It was around this *Perfectly Holy* and *Righteous* 'Just One' in the Temple that in our view all parties opposing the Herodian/Roman Establishment, from the more violent and extreme to the less so, ranged. In this role as Bishop, James was also High Priest of the Opposition Alliance – thus, in effect, the *Opposition High Priest.* Ultimately we shall place James at the centre of the alliance of all the groups and parties opposing foreign rule in Palestine and its concomitant, foreign gifts and sacrifices on behalf of foreigners in the Temple. The opposition of this Alliance to Herodian Kings and the Herodian Priesthood led directly to the Uprising against Rome. This forms the mirror image of the way Christian tradition portrays the Messianic individuals it approves of, who are pictured as sympathetic – or at least not antipathetic – to Rome. This kind of inversion will be shown to be a consistent aspect of the portraiture and polemics of this period.

Judea Capta coin depicting Emperor Vespasian on obverse and suppliant captive Judea under Palm Tree on reverse

Chapter 2
The Second Temple and the Rise of the Maccabees

The Maccabean Priesthood

With the coming of Alexander the Great in 333 BCE, two successor states under Hellenistic kings – descended from his generals – arose in Asia: 1) the Seleucids in Syria and 2) the Ptolemies in Egypt. Judea or Palestine, consisting primarily of the region around Jerusalem proper, swung back and forth under the control, first of the former – then of the latter. As a rule, relations with the more tolerant Greek Ptolemies in Egypt were more cordial than those with the Seleucids at Antioch. This is important because the Independence War, which broke out in 167 BCE, was pointedly waged against Seleucid Hellenization and intolerance.

The war against the Seleucids was led by Judas Maccabee and his real or imagined father, Mattathias. Judas, like Jesus, had three brothers, John, Eleazar (Lazarus), Simon, not to mention Judas himself - all names familiar in New Testament usage as well. This war is celebrated in Jewish ritual by *Hanukkah* festivities to this day. *Hanukkah* literally means 'Rededication', that is, the rededication of the Temple, which was considered polluted by the Seleucids. The struggles surrounding this war went on for some thirty more years until the rise of Simon's son John Hyrcanus (134–104 BCE) to power.

With the attainment of independence, problems associated with being independent – if only for a hundred years – developed, and the groups and parties that came into prominence and form the substance of Gospel accounts come into focus. In this period, too, the Romans are extending their influence into the eastern Mediterranean after their victories over the Carthaginians, a Semitic people along the coast of North Africa and Spain. 1 Maccabees makes much of Judas' friendly correspondence with the Romans. This correspondence is probably authentic, as is another with the Spartans, which proudly proclaims that the Jews and the Spartans are related and therefore 'brothers'![1]

At first, the Maccabees seem to have affected only the title of 'High Priest'. At some point in the first or third generations, however, the title 'King' was adopted. Though the Maccabees were from a priestly family, the question has been raised in the debate relating to the Dead Sea Scrolls, whether they 'usurped' the High Priesthood. There is no indication whatsoever of such a usurpation, and the Maccabees seem to have occupied what appears to have been a very popular priesthood indeed. Josephus, for instance, at the end of the first century in Rome, evinces no embarrassment at the Maccabean blood he claims flows in his veins. On the contrary, he would appear to be most proud of it (*Vita* 1.2–6).

The Book of Daniel and Apocalyptic

The appearance of the Romans in the eastern Mediterranean would appear to be referred to at an important juncture of the Book of Daniel, where their victory over the Syrian fleet in the eastern Mediterranean is mentioned (11:30–35; 190 BCE). This seems, in fact, to trigger the predatory activities upon the Temple by the Seleucid King Antiochus Epiphanes, the villain of both Daniel and the Maccabee Books. Here, too, the Book of Daniel uses the key terminology of 'the *Kittim*,' which the Dead Sea Scrolls use to refer to foreign armies invading the country, to refer to the *Romans* (11:30). This is important for sorting out chronological problems at Qumran.

Along with Ezekiel and Isaiah, Daniel is perhaps the most important scriptural inspiration for much of the apocalyptic ideology and symbolism of the Dead Sea Scrolls, as well as for the literature of Christianity. Daniel is also, chronologically speaking, one of the latest books in the scriptural canon, except perhaps for Esther.

Daniel's clear association with the Maccabean Uprising in Palestine was doubtlessly one of the reasons why the Rabbis, following the uprisings against Rome, downgraded it from its position among the 'Prophets', placing it among the lesser 'Writings'. No doubt, the Rabbis saw Daniel as a representative of a new, more vivid, style of prophetic expression, which we now call apocalyptic. This style, which they downplayed because of its association with the movement that produced both the Maccabean Uprising and the Uprising against Rome, is very much admired in the documents from Qumran, as it is by New Testament writers. In Daniel, prophetical and eschatological motifs – concerned with the End Times – are combined amid the most awe-inspiring and blood-curdling imagery.

For instance, Daniel is the first document to refer to what might be described as a 'Kingdom of God'. God is not only described as 'enduring forever', 'working signs and wonders in Heaven and on earth', and 'saving Daniel from the power of the lions' (that is, death), but as having a 'sovereignty which will never be destroyed' and a 'kingship that will never end' (6:26–28). Daniel also evokes the 'Son of Man coming on the clouds of Heaven', one of the basic scriptural underpinnings for the Messiahship of Jesus and a title often applied to him. This passage will also loom large below in the materials relating to James' activities in the Temple and the proclamation he makes there.

For Daniel, 'the Holy Ones' (*Kedoshim*) make war on a foreign invader who has violated and pillaged the Temple. This foreigner, who has 'abolished the perpetual sacrifice', is clearly Antiochus Epiphanes (7:13–8:12) - the villain of Jewish *Hanukkah* festivities ever since. Daniel uses additional terms that became popular, particularly at Qumran but also in the New Testament and the Koran – namely, 'the Last Days', 'the Wrath', 'the Time of the End' and, of course, the Resurrection of the Dead (12:2–13).

The way Daniel refers to the Resurrection of the Dead is particularly significant: 'Of those who lie sleeping in the dust of the earth, many will awake, some to everlasting life … cleansed, made white, and purged … [they] will rise for [their] share at the End of Time'. Aside from ambiguous allusions in Psalms and a similar reference in 2 Maccabees in the context of Judas Maccabee's military activities (12:43–44), this is the only overt reference to this doctrine of Resurrection of the Dead in the entire Old Testament.

In Daniel and 2 Maccabees, such references are normally associated with a kind of apocalyptic Holy War also outlined in Daniel. The reference in 2 Maccabees is presented in the context of the Maccabean Uprising against Hellenization and foreign rule in Palestine. Parallel descriptions in 1 Maccabees raise the banner of '*zeal for the Law*' or *taking one's 'stand on the Covenant*' (2:27). We shall have occasion to refer to allusions like these with regard to James, as well as to the Zealot Movement taking its inspiration from them.

It was apocalyptic literature of this kind that was seen by the Rabbis as the impetus behind the unrest that led to the disaster represented by the First Jewish Uprising against Rome (66–70 CE) and the destruction of the Temple and the State, not to mention the Second Uprising (132–6 CE). It encouraged an extreme *zeal for the Law*, that zealotry associated with Holy War, and a willingness to undergo martyrdom rather than to submit to foreign kingship, as well as an associated impetus towards Messianism.

Since these ideas were all seen as stemming from the party or parties opposed to what the Pharisee predecessors of the Rabbis had represented – that is, seeking accommodation with Rome and foreign powers generally at all costs – they were considered reprehensible. It is therefore understandable that in the version of Jewish history that the Rabbis transmitted and in the collection of documents they finally declared to be Holy Writ at the beginning of the second century CE, books like the Maccabees were set aside and Daniel given the lowest priority.

The Jewish Historian Josephus

Josephus (37–96 CE) is important for a consideration of this whole period; without him, we would be almost completely ignorant of events. With him, we have a marvelous insight into – and almost encyclopedic reportage of – what transpired.

From 62 CE onwards, the year of James' death as recorded in the *Antiquities*, Josephus was a mature observer relying on his own experience and eyewitness reporting. His personal experiences are, in fact, incorporated in great detail into the book called the *Jewish War*, which he wrote directly after the events of 66–73 and which ends, significantly enough, with a description of the triumphal parade in Rome of Titus, the son of the new Roman Emperor Vespasian (69–79). Josephus, as a member of the latter's staff, witnessed this event. The commemorative Arch of Titus still stands in the ruins of the Roman Forum today, a chilling reminder of these age-old cataclysms.

But Josephus was also a turncoat, a traitor to his people. When reading him, this should always be kept in mind. It was on the basis of this betrayal that he was allowed to live and was not put to death like others who played a role in the events he describes. For Josephus *did* play a role in these events. Originally, by his own testimony, he was military commander of Galilee – 'commissar' might be more accurate – responsible for its organization and fortification in the early days of the Revolt. Later, after his desertion, he was an interrogator of prisoners.

His popularity among his fellow countrymen can be deduced from the following episode which he describes in *The Jewish War*. Deputized by the Romans, presumably because he spoke the native language, to call up to the defenders on the walls of Jerusalem during its siege and ask for their surrender, he was hit on the head by a projectile thrown by someone on the battlements. When he fell, a spontaneous cheer erupted among those watching from the walls. Their enemy Josephus had been wounded (*War* 5.541–7). With military commanders or commissars like Josephus, the Jews had no need of enemies, and the military catastrophe that overtook them was inevitable. Later he uses the prestige his priestly status allowed him in the eyes of the Romans to appeal to their credulity and the exaggerated awe they felt for such augurs or foreign oracles (*War* 6.310–15).

It was to his role as a fortune-telling Jewish priest, supposedly held in high esteem by his own people, that his survival can be credited. He and several companions had taken refuge in a cave after the collapse of the military defense of Galilee, for which he was ostensibly responsible. The Romans were taking this time-honored route on their way to lay siege to Jerusalem, and Josephus betrayed the suicide pact that he and a few companions had made – the normal 'Zealot' approach in such extreme circumstances. Instead, he and another colleague, after dispatching their comrades, surrendered to the Romans, an episode he relates quite shamelessly.

Ushered into the Roman commander Vespasian's presence, Josephus proceeded to apply the Messianic 'Star Prophecy' to him, prophesying that Vespasian was the one foretold in Jewish Scripture, who was going to come out of Palestine and rule the world. This was the prophecy that was of such importance to resistance groups in this period, including those responsible for the documents at Qumran and the revolutionaries who triggered the war against Rome, not to mention the early Christians.[2] The following year Vespasian was to replace Nero (54–68 CE) as Emperor.

Of course, Josephus was not the only turncoat to whom sources attribute reversing the sense of the Messianic Prophecy, applying it to the destroyer of Jerusalem instead of to its liberator. The Rabbis, who became the Roman tax collectors in Palestine after the fall of the Temple, claim the same behavior for the progenitor of the form of Judaism they followed, Rabbinic Judaism-to-be, Rabbi Yohanan ben Zacchai. Rabbi Yohanan seems also to have been involved in the process of fixing the Jewish Canon at the end of the first century. Like Hillel and Shammai before him with Herod, Rabbi Yohanan's behavior with the Romans has become paradigmatic. He is described in rabbinic sources as applying the same 'Star Prophecy', the most precious prophecy of the Jewish people at that time, to the conqueror of Jerusalem, Vespasian, who was elevated to supreme ruler of the known civilized world after his military exploits in Palestine.

As the rabbinic presentation of this story goes, Rabbi Yohanan, after having himself smuggled out of Jerusalem in a coffin – quite appropriately, as it turns out; besides, it was the only exit possible at the time – had an arrow shot into Vespasian's camp, attached to which was a note claiming that 'Rabbi Yohanan is one of the Emperor's friends'.[3] Doubtless this was true, but the camp had to have been Titus', because Vespasian, the founder of the new Flavian line of emperors, had already gone to Rome at this point to assume his crown, leaving Titus behind to wind things up in Palestine. Rabbi Yohanan, as Talmudic materials present him, then had himself ushered into Vespasian's presence to proclaim the very same thing Josephus recounts *he* did, that Vespasian was the Ruler prophesied to come out of Palestine and rule the world.

Whether Josephus was a cynical opportunist or not, his account is the more credible, though both may be true. If so, Vespasian must have become very impatient of all these Jewish turncoats obsequiously fawning on him and proclaiming him the Ruler foreseen in Jewish Scripture, who was to come out of Palestine to rule the world (or maybe he didn't). For his part, the Romans accorded R. Yohanan the academy at Yavneh, where the foundations of what was to become Rabbinic Judaism were laid; whereas Josephus was adopted for services rendered – writing the *Jewish War* being one of them – into the Roman imperial family itself.

In Josephus' case, the contacts for his treachery had already been laid some time before. As he recounts it, he knew someone in the Roman camp, someone he had met on a previous mission to Rome on behalf of some obscure priests who, he contends, were being held on a 'trifling' charge of some kind.[4] These priests, like Paul according to Acts, had appealed to Nero, and were probably connected in some manner to the 'Temple Wall' Affair. In this affair, which in our view led directly to the death of James, a wall had been built – presumably by 'Zealot' priests – to block Agrippa II (49–93 CE) from viewing the Temple sacrifice while reposing and eating on the balcony of his palace (*Ant.* 20.189–90).

In his autobiographical excursus appended to the *Antiquities* called the *Vita*, Josephus describes how as a young priest he went to Rome on a mission to rescue those who had gone there and been detained as a result, presumably, of the 'Temple Wall' Affair. Somehow he had gained access through a well-connected Jewish actor to Nero's wife, Poppea, whom he elsewhere describes as being interested in religious causes, Jewish or otherwise. It will be remembered that Nero, too, enjoyed the company of people of the theatre. So pleased was Poppea with the young Josephus that he apparently attained all he wished of her – and perhaps more – for he proudly brags that she sent him away laden with gifts. One wonders what else the artful young priest managed to achieve during his stay, apart from the contacts he made in Roman intelligence circles that served him so well when Roman armies finally did appear in Galilee three years later.

Josephus was obviously, then, very well placed to produce his accounts of the history of Palestine and matters such as the rise of the Flavians and their qualifications either for Jewish Messiahship or divine honors, as the case may be, for which he was duly rewarded. In writing the *Jewish War*, for instance, he was putting the Flavians on the same level as the forerunner of the previous dynasty, the divine Julius. The only difference was that, whereas Julius Caesar wrote his own histories, Josephus, an adoptee and a captive, wrote theirs.

Josephus is inaccurate when it comes to matters having a direct bearing on his own survival; in particular, his questionable relations with revolutionaries, apocalyptic groups, and sedition, as well as his attempts to ingratiate himself with his new masters. But his meticulous reproduction of the minutiae of day-to-day events is unparalleled. For this reason, we have an encyclopedic presentation of events and persons in Palestine in this period without equal in almost any time or place up to the era of modern record-keeping and reportage.

Coin of Antiochus Epiphanes, c. 167 BC, Daniel's 'Eleventh Horn' who provoked the Maccabean Uprising

Presumed bust of the Jewish historian Josephus.

Right: Pompey who stormed the Temple in 63 BC

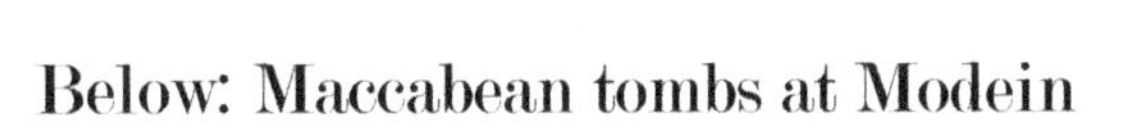

Below: Maccabean tombs at Modein

Chapter 3
Romans, Herodians, and Jewish Sects

The Sects in the Second Temple Period

Josephus describes the Jewish sects of this period in a tendentious manner. The *Talmud* presents an equally tendentious picture of a Rabbinic Judaism opposed to all other groups, lumped together as *minim* – '*sects*'. Sometimes these last are even called 'Sadducees' without further elucidation as to who they really are.

In the Dead Sea Scrolls from Qumran, these Sadducees are '*the Sons of Zadok*', evoking the term as employed in the vision of Ezekiel (chapters 40–48) of the reconstructed Temple of the Last Days. Related to it is the '*Righteousness*' ideology expressed in the root letters *Z–D–K* of the Hebrew word underlying the Greek rendering '*Sadducee*'. The Sons of Zadok or Sadducees depicted in the Qumran materials have little in common with those in the New Testament or Josephus. Where these opposing groups of Sadducees – Herodian (Establishment) or separatist (Purist) – are concerned, there are common approaches to legal minutiae that so obsess the authors of Talmudic tradition. However, in the broad lines of hostility towards the 'fornication' of the Establishment (incest, polygamy, divorce, etc.), there is almost nothing in common between them. Moreover, the second group is characterized by an *antagonism to foreign rule*, including foreign-appointed kings, foreign-appointed High Priests, and foreign gifts and sacrifices in the Temple, which does not characterize the first group at all.

The same issues are fundamental to '*the Zealots*', those who follow the demands of the *zeal* -oriented Covenant of Phineas (Num. 25:6–13). Where the relationship of the Scrolls to so-called 'Zealots' is concerned, it is interesting to point out that Phineas, portrayed in Numbers as functioning in the wilderness at the time of Moses, is accorded the High Priestly Covenant in perpetuity because of the 'zeal' he displayed in killing backsliders who were marrying foreigners, thereby deflecting *pollution* from the camp of Israel. 1 Maccabees 2:26 raises this Covenant on behalf of Judas Maccabee's father, Mattathias, and presumably all of his descendants succeeding to him. But this Phineas, who was Aaron's grandson, was also the High Priestly ancestor of the '*Zadok*' of David's time, an important connection between the '*Zealot*' and '*Zadokite*' ideologies. This idea of '*pollution*' in the camp of Israel in the wilderness as relating to the issue of *mixing* with foreigners has important ramifications in the Qumran documents and is the focus of the '*Zealot*' ethos.[1]

Sadducees, Essenes, and Zealots

The group called 'Essenes' also have much in common with Qumran *Sadducees* – not to mention with the so-called Zealots and Palestinian Christians following James – but, as with Opposition or Purist Sadducees, they have nothing in common with Establishment *Sadducees* of the Herodian period as pictured in Josephus and the New Testament.

There is an even better description of these Essenes, which includes several important points linking them closely with James' followers in Palestine, in a work called the *Refutation of All Heresies*, attributed to Hippolytus, an early third-century Church writer in Rome (160–235). This description is possibly an even earlier version of Josephus' description of the Essenes in the *Jewish War*. In it, 'Zealots' and their more extreme counterparts, the '*Sicarii*' ('Assassins' – so styled because of the Arab-style dagger they concealed under their cloaks), are seen only as *Essenes* less prepared to compromise (9.21). This clarifies the sectarian situation in Palestine considerably.

At the end of the fourth century, Epiphanius, whose *Panarion* (*Medicine Box – Against Heresies* in Latin), has the greatest difficulty distinguishing Essenes from a group he calls 'the Jessaeans' (followers, according to him, of David's father Jesse or of Jesus himself).[2] This is not surprising, because even modern confusions relating to the term 'Essene' are legion.

Philo of Alexandria, the first-century Jewish philosopher referred to their expertise in health or medicinal matters, including presumably curings.[3] For its part, the New Testament does not refer to Essenes at all, nor does the *Talmud*, not at least *qua* Essenes. This may be explained by the fact that all groups of this kind are simply being referred to retrospectively as *minim* ('sects') or *Saddukim* ('*Sadducees*') after the Pharisees took control of Jewish life in the wake of the failed Uprising against Rome. In using these notations, no attempt was made to draw fine distinctions, if in fact these were even appreciated by the time the Talmudic materials were finally redacted in the second and third centuries CE.

The *Talmud* does refer to '*Zealots*' as *Kanna'im* ('*those jealous*' or '*zealous*'), but not really as a group – rather simply as avenging priests in the Temple. This will have relevance to the way James' death is portrayed in early Church sources.[4] This avenging zeal is not surprising in view of how the ethos of this group is explained in terms of 'the zeal of Phineas'. 1 Maccabees 2:28, as noted, evokes this slogan in describing how the progenitor of the Maccabean family, Mattathias, acted against those who would abrogate the traditions of the Forefathers and collaborate with foreign rule. He slays them on the altar at Modein, the family place of origin.

One of the problems with Josephus' picture of the sects is that, since he is covering a chronological time frame of some two hundred and fifty years, one does not really know to which period his points apply. His accounts are usually derivative and accurate only for the period in which he lives. Even here he often dissembles, because of his own embarrassing relations with sectarian groups and his pre-Flavian, revolutionary past. As one can see in his *War* or his *Vita*, he was under tremendous pressure to explain his past and justify actions that enabled him to survive, and he constantly defends himself against attacks on his behavior and his loyalty to Rome.

It is quite likely that Josephus fell foul of Titus' younger brother and successor, Domitian (81–96), who was considered to be as mad, unpredictable, and sadistically violent as Nero had been. Indeed, the mercurial Domitian seems to have executed his secretary, Josephus' publisher Epaphroditus, who had also been Nero's secretary and someone with whom Paul appears to have been extremely intimate.[5] In addition, this Epaphroditus, as is clear from Josephus' introductions, encouraged Josephus in all his works, particularly his *Antiquities*, which was published in 94 CE just a little before both disappeared from the scene. Like Epaphroditus, Josephus just drops from sight around this time and may or may not have been executed in the course of Domitian's often brutal or sadistic reign. Trajan (98–117), whose father had been commander of the Tenth Legion in Palestine under Vespasian and Titus, then proceeded to have his difficulties with Messianic agitation and unrest, particularly in the eastern portions of his empire.

Sectarian terminology thus tends to slide around a good deal, depending on who is doing the observing, what vocabulary he is employing, and what his own misunderstandings or prejudices might be. For instance, in his *Vita* Josephus suddenly tells us about a 'wilderness' sojourn he made during a trial he says he was conducting of all the sects. There he meets a teacher he calls '*Banus*' – not a name, but a title or cognomen of some kind, probably having something to do with *bathing* – without telling us that this teacher is almost indistinguishable from Jewish Christians or Essenes, the group heading his list of Jewish sects.

There is indeed a bewildering plethora of these groups. This diminishes only when one appreciates the verbal acrobatics involved where subversive or threatening sects or a given writer's own embarrassing relations with them are concerned. In order to sort these various groups out, it is better simply to group them according to whether they supported the Roman -Herodian Establishment or opposed it. Likewise, it is often more edifying to look at groups in terms of who their common enemies were. Seen in this way, James' Jerusalem Community, Ebionites, Essenes, Zealots, and the group responsible for the documents found at Qumran all can be thought of as opposed to the reigning Establishment.

The Qumran documents, for example, are not simply a random collection of disparate sectarian writings. The same ideology, nomenclature, and dramatis personae move from document to document regardless of style or authorship. For instance, one never encounters a document approving of the contemporary Establishment, which in the writer's view must be seen as the Herodian one.

For this reason, it is proper to refer to the authors of these documents as comprising a Movement of some kind which is always, at its core, anti-Establishment. Its precise name for the moment must be left indeterminate, but 'the Way', 'the Sons of Zadok', 'the Poor', 'the Simple', 'the Meek', 'the Perfect', 'the Sons of Light', 'the Holy Ones' or combinations such as 'the Zealots for the Day of Vengeance', 'the Poor Ones of Piety', 'the Zealots for Righteousness' and 'Perfect of the Way' are all terms cropping up in their repertoire as self-designations.

To add to all these groups, one has the bewildering assortment referred to by Church heresiologists of the third to the fifth centuries, like Naassenes, Nazoraeans, Sampsaeans (*'Sabaeans'* as we shall see) and Elchasaites, most located on the other side of the Jordan extending on up to Syria and Northern Iraq and holding James' name in particular reverence – some, like the Ebionites, in absolute awe. Where the relationship of these groups to the Qumran documents, or for that matter to the New Testament, is concerned, their location across the Jordan in that 'Damascus' region so important to both is particularly significant. All of these groups too can be considered as allied or related in some way, all being anti-Establishment and having common enemies.

Where the first century CE is concerned, it is also useful to consider the opposition groups in terms of their various degrees of *zeal*, extending from the more pacifist to the more violent. This is how Hippolytus discusses his Essenes, who range by degrees to the most extreme *Sicarii,* namely those Josephus describes as committing suicide on Masada in the last installment of the War against Rome. If one keeps one's eyes firmly fixed on support of or opposition to the Roman-Herodian Establishment, one will never go far astray. Those supporting this Establishment can be described (echoing language found in the Dead Sea Scrolls) as 'seeking accommodation with foreigners', which the Herodians and their Roman overlords were most certainly considered to be.

These are the kinds of distinctions that will prove useful in considering the best-known Establishment Party, the Pharisees, who in their current embodiment of Rabbinic Judaism still constitute the Establishment among Jews today. This is a vivid reminder of just how enduring these traditions can be. Whether in their present-day Orthodox, Conservative, Liberal, or Reform embodiments, all not only claim to be heirs to the Pharisaic legacy but in addition – and, as we shall see, even more astonishing – that the Pharisees were *the popular party of the first century* CE. For this reason, many Jews, even secular ones, are unable to grasp the true import of their own *Hanukkah* festivities, which are basically a celebration of Maccabean, anti-foreign, non-accommodationist, priestly zeal. This is because this tradition, too, which is diametrically opposed to the inherited one, has been downplayed, trivialized and virtually written out of Talmudic literature, where most references to the Maccabees are negative for the same reason that they are in Christianity.

It is no wonder that many scholars, Christian and Jewish alike, thought that the Maccabeans could have been candidates for 'the Wicked Priest' of the Dead Sea Scrolls when these documents appeared. Thus, the view was widely disseminated that the Maccabees had 'usurped' the High Priesthood from a previously more legitimate one. This was not only to misunderstand the essence of the Maccabean Uprising, but the Qumran position with regard to such matters.

Zealots, Anti-Nationalist Pharisees, and the Messianic Roots of the Uprising

But the Pharisees were not the popular party of their time and place, despite Josephus' attempts – and those of Rabbinic Judaism thereafter – to prove otherwise. To clarify and highlight this, I have in my work generally redefined Pharisees as those 'seeking accommodation with foreigners'. In the Scrolls, these appear as 'the Seekers after Smooth Things', clearly a hostile designation. In terms of political attitudes, Pauline Christians are not very different from Pharisees. This puts the proposition in the broad brushstrokes that have meaning for the period before us, dispensing with the kind of legal hair-splitting usually discussed.

The Establishment groups, quite simply put, were the Pharisees, accommodationist Sadducees, and Herodians, the last being those members of the Herodian power structure and their associates not encompassed under the preceding two designations.

Pauline Christianity and Rabbinic Judaism develop in conjunction with each other and both follow an accommodationist policy towards Rome, which is why no doubt both survived. In this context, the main difference is that one is pro-Law and the other against it. But the points of accommodation here are not the minor ones belabored in Rabbinic tradition, such as those connected with dietary regulations, sexual purification or Sabbath observation, though these played a part. Rather, they are the broad lines of accommodation with foreigners in a political sense.

That the Pharisees are the popular party in this period, which the New Testament too is anxious to promote, is repeatedly and definitively gainsaid by Josephus, despite his attempts, pro-Roman and Pharisee fellow-traveler that he is, to promote it. Over and over again, Josephus presents, often unwittingly, the people as opposing the *anti-nationalist* policies of the Pharisees. Predictably, *the people*, as in most times and places, are predominantly nationalist. They may have been forced to go along with the Pharisees and the Rabbinic Party that succeeded them after the fall of the Temple and the elimination of all serious opposition groups, but before this they most often opposed them.

It is a curious coincidence that Josephus launches into both his descriptions of the Jewish sects in the *War* and the *Antiquities* at just the point he comes to describe the Movement founded by Judas *the Galilean*. This he calls a new 'philosophy which our people were before unacquainted with' (*Ant.* 18.10). At present, it is sufficient to point out that this group or movement arises at just the moment one would expect it to, when the previous leadership had been eliminated by Herod and new leadership principles, including the *Messianic*, emerge.

Eleven years after the death of Herod the Romans annexed the country and, in anticipation of direct taxation by governors or procurators, imposed a census. This is the 6–7 CE 'Census of Quirinius', by which the Gospel of Luke dates the birth of Jesus (2:1). The Gospel of Matthew, by contrast, has Jesus being born some time before the death of Herod, more than a decade earlier; so that Herod can attempt to chase him down and kill all the Jewish children - as did Pharaoh at the time of *the birth of Moses*. The two accounts are, of course, irreconcilable.

This is 'the Census' - essentially a tax assessment - which the Zealots oppose and, against which, Judas the Galilean and *Saddok* preach. It is supported by the Pharisees and, of course, the '*Herodian* Sadducees'. This issue is also a burning one in the Gospel narratives and Jesus' riposte to 'the Pharisees and the Herodians' concerning it (Mt. 22:21), 'render unto Caesar what is Caesar's and God what is God's', has now become proverbial – strange, because the Gospels picture 'Jesus' as adopting *the Pharisee policy* of 'paying the tax to Caesar' here.

There are, in fact, a plethora of revolutionary outbursts even at the time of the death of Herod, with which the unrest begins, by groups Josephus pictures as being *zealous for the Law* – Mosaic not Roman – and as having 'an inviolable attachment to liberty'. One of these, led by someone he calls Judas Sepphoraeus – probably identical with Judas the Galilean – broke into the arsenal at Sepphoris in 4 BCE, the principal town at that time in Galilee (*War* 2.56/*Ant.* 17.271).

There is no doubt about the popularity of the Movement, because Josephus, in his lengthy description of it and the woes the people suffered in consequence of their support for it, admits not only that 'our young men were zealous for it' but that 'the nation was infected by it to an incredible degree' (*Ant.* 18.6–10).

In addition to Jesus' birth being presented as coincident with its inception and the fact that its appearance triggers Josephus' discussion of the sects of his time, there is another interesting aspect to this Movement. At the end of the *Jewish War*, when describing the signs and wonders that presaged the fall of the Temple, of which people as superstitious as the Romans were so enamored, Josephus finally reveals something that he neglected for some reason to tell us earlier. He claims that 'the thing that most moved the people to revolt against Rome was an ambiguous prophecy from their Scripture that one from their country *should rule the entire world'*. For Josephus they had only themselves to blame for what ensued, because they interpreted this oracle 'to suit themselves and went so mad because of it' (*War* 6.312–14).

But this is precisely the Prophecy, '*the World Ruler*', '*Messianic*', or '*the Star Prophecy*', he has just finished applying to Vespasian – thus saving his own skin – as, one might add, did R. Yohanan and his 'Pharisee Party' along with him and does so again in this passage from the *War*. In the Scrolls, where it occurs at least three times even in the surviving texts, it receives a wholly other, completely uncompromising, nationalistic and fully 'Messianic' interpretation. In addition to remarking earlier how '*zealous*' the young men were for this approach, Josephus notes that 'the Jews thought this prediction applied only to themselves, and therefore, many of their most learned men had deceived themselves in this determination'.

But this is precisely the Qumran interpretation as well, the representatives of which would never have stooped to the cynical opportunism of applying it to the destroyer of Jerusalem Vespasian, whatever the short-term benefits. In revealing this, Josephus, of course, also reveals that Zealots and other parties displaying the '*zeal of Phineas*' were not simply political, but religious and *Messianic* as well.

This is proof that the Uprising against Rome, aside from being popular – which it was most definitely – was also *Messianic*. What is more, that since the Uprising was Messianic – and ethically and historically this is of the utmost importance – the Jews lost everything not because they *opposed the Messiah*, as early Church Fathers or the New Testament in their tendentious presentation of Christ's death and its meaning would have us believe, but, on the contrary, because they *were so uncompromisingly Messianic*. This is no mean proposition and constitutes an important reversal or inversion of historical invective as it has come down to us.

Not only was the Uprising aimed at burning the palaces of the High Priests and the Herodian Kings but the debt records as well, in order, as Josephus makes clear, 'to turn the Poor against the Rich' (*War* 2.425–9). Once again, this is the same genre of language evinced in the Letter of James and the Dead Sea Scrolls in their condemnation of 'the Rich'. It is also the language applied to the Movement led by James, by Paul (Gal. 2:10) and to the later Ebionites, so named because of it, as well as the nomenclature used by the Movement represented by the Scrolls to describe its own rank and file – called there as well 'the *Ebionim*' or 'the Poor'.[6]

Before leaving this subject of the outbreak of the Uprising in 66 CE, it is important to note that in a final moment of unparalleled candor Josephus tells us that it was 'the principal Pharisees, the Chief Priests, the men of power [by which he means Herodians], and all those desirous for peace' who invited the Roman army into Jerusalem 'to put down the Uprising'. This is what Josephus meant in the Introduction to the *War* about how the Romans were invited into the city by 'the Jews' own leaders' (1.10 & 2.418–19).

Here one comes to an even more startling detail provided by Josephus, if what he seems to be saying can be tied to characters we know in early Christian history. The intermediary in this process of inviting the Roman army into the city was a member of the Herodian family called Saul. He is the one who delivered the message from 'the peace coalition' to the Roman army camped outside Jerusalem to enter, and a final report even *to Nero's headquarters*, then in Corinth in Greece, a favorite haunt too of the religious activities of 'Paul'.

The anti-national, pro-Roman policy of the Pharisees should by now be clear. This is also the stance of the Pauline Gentile Christians, following the teaching of a person who describes himself as having been trained as a Pharisee and, according to the picture in Acts anyhow, vaunts a Roman citizenship, something not easily acquired in these turbulent times. Nor can the Pharisees in this period by any twist of the imagination be considered 'the popular party'. If anything, the Zealot and/or Messianic were the popular parties (as nationalist parties predictably are) at least until the fall of the Temple and the re-education policy undertaken by the heirs of the Pharisees under Roman suzerainty thereafter.

The Coming of the Romans and the Herodians

Then what is the key to events, as described in the above analysis? It is the rise of the Herodians and the coming of the Romans. This is the reason for the widespread disaffection being expressed in this period and most of the unrest. After the fall of the Maccabeans, Roman rule was imposed, sometimes through Herodian kings or sometimes more directly through Roman procurators. It is against the backdrop of the fall of the Maccabeans and the ascent of the Herodians in the first century BCE that the rise of various sects or movements, particularly nationalistic or Messianic ones, must be gauged. Again, if one keeps this and the fact of Roman power firmly before one's eyes, then almost all else follows comparatively easily.

The first appearance of the Romans in the Eastern Mediterranean came just prior to this period in the late stages of the Punic War. They actually made their presence felt in the 60s BCE, when they turned Syria into a Roman province, eliminating the last vestiges of Seleucid rule. Just as Caesar was making his inroads into Transalpine Gaul, the Rhine, Britain, and Spain in the West, Pompey was undertaking the siege of Jerusalem in 63 BCE. He was abetted in this by internal dissensions within the Maccabean family itself, but also by a half-Arab, Hellenized intermediary by the name of Antipater, the father of Herod.

Not only does Antipater successfully ingratiate himself with Pompey and his adjutants – the most well known of whom was Mark Anthony – but he ends up as the first Roman Procurator in Palestine and the ultimate arbiter of political events there. Mark Anthony, who distinguished himself in Palestinian campaigning, ultimately abets Antipater's son Herod in obtaining the Jewish Crown. Herod finishes the job of obliterating the Maccabean family. Those he doesn't execute he marries but, even these, he eventually butchers including his favorite wife Mariamme, the last Maccabean Princess, in the aftermath of his trip to Rome to get Octavius to reconfirm the crown Anthony had conferred on him (29 BCE). In the end, Herod even had his two sons by her – who had been brought up in Rome – put to death, presumably because he was jealous of their Maccabean blood and because the crowd preferred them to him. Here Herod really did *kill all the Jewish children* who sought to replace him, as Matthew 2:17 would have it, but these were rather his own children with Maccabean blood! This behavior shocked even his Roman sponsors, particularly Augustus, who upheld family values and was by all reports very displeased with it.[7]

But Herod survived all, got away with everything, including obliterating the Maccabean family and grafting his own family on whatever remained of it. This mostly-Idumaean, Greco -Arab line continued for three more generations until Titus, the man responsible for burning Jerusalem, made off with Bernice, a descendant of this line, as Caesar and Anthony had made off with Cleopatra – one of the last descendants of Alexander's ruling élite – before him. Nor does this give any more pleasure to the people of Rome – who do not appear to have wished to see an Herodian Princess as their Empress, than Caesar's and Anthony's actions had done previously. Bernice's fate is uncertain, but Titus seems to have put her away at some point prior to succeeding his father in 79 CE.

Herod also had the last Maccabean High Priest, Mariamme's younger brother Jonathan, put to death in 36 BCE when he reached the age of majority. Herod's marriage with the last Maccabean Princess, Mariamme, would appear to have been contracted by her mother, Hyrcanus II's daughter, on the basis that Jonathan would become the High Priest on reaching majority.

Josephus records the pathetic scene of how, when the boy at thirteen years of age donned the High Priestly vestments, the Jewish crowd wept when he appeared in the Temple (*War* 1.437/*Ant.* 14.50-56). For those who would still cling to the contention that the people considered the Maccabean family usurpers, this should provide vivid testimony to the contrary. Wild with jealousy, Herod then had the boy taken down to his winter palace in Jericho and drowned while he was frolicking in the swimming pool with some of his attendants. He was *the last Maccabean High Priest.*

After this, Herod is careful to maintain personal control over the High Priestly garments and appoints men, as Josephus himself observes, 'who were not of eminent families, some hardly priests at all' (*Ant.* 20.247). Once instituted, this was the policy followed by procurators such as Pontius Pilate after him (26–37 CE; *Ant.* 20.6–16) and kings such as Agrippa I, his brother Herod of Chalcis, and his son, Bernice's brother Agrippa II, until the Uprising against Rome. At this time 'the Zealots' elected their own High Priest, a lowly stone-cutter of the humblest origins whom Josephus calls 'Phannius', that is, *Phineas.* Such were the bloody origins of the Herodian High Priest class, tendentiously portrayed in the New Testament as the legitimate 'Chief Priests' and Sadducee party of the Jews!

At Herod's death, after he had indulged in all the cruelty and brutalities enumerated above and the total destruction of the national independence of the Jews and their previous royal priest line, revolutionary unrest began in earnest and continued for the next seventy years. This was possibly understood by exegetes like those at Qumran as the seventy-year period of 'Wrath' mentioned in Daniel 9:2. It continued until the outbreak of the War against Rome.

Actually, it continued for the next hundred and forty years until Hadrian crushed the Second Jewish Revolt in 132–6 CE and renamed Jerusalem Aelia Capitolina. He forbade Jews to enter Jerusalem or even to come within eyesight of it, except once a year to mourn its past glories. During this period, too, descendants of the family of Jesus and his brothers were involved in ongoing Messianic agitation and were martyred in their turn. This was the end of the earthbound Messianic hopes among the Jews, hopes that gradually turned more other-worldly, ethereal, or 'Gnostic'. This is what the imposition of Roman control really meant – destruction.

Chapter 4
First Century Sources Mentioning James

The New Testament and the We Document in Acts

The two most authentic testimonies to James' approach and role in the Jerusalem Church of his day are to be found in Paul's letters and in the second half of the Book of Acts, primarily in the document scholars refer to as 'the We Document'. Intruding variously after line 16:10, it seems to be a diary or travel document of some kind. For some, it is the only authentic material in Acts, though it is neither without problems nor continuous.

Had we to rely simply on Acts' presentation without Paul's definitive identifications, we would be in grave doubt as to just who this very powerful and popular James, described so reticently by Luke – the putative author of Acts – really was. James just appears out of nowhere in Acts 12, the same chapter that the more widely known other James, '*James the brother of John*', '*the son of Zebedee*', is conveniently disposed of. Later we shall see how this execution relates to a parallel and more convincing one Josephus mentions at this time, the beheading of someone he calls '*Theudas*'.[1]

James' identity and ideology are as solid as Paul's, because it is Paul who confirms them. What is more, Paul *never* mentions any *other* James. But Paul knows next to nothing about the person, ideology, and life of Jesus except as an individual in Heaven he considers himself to be in direct communication with via a mechanism he and Acts both – not to mention the Dead Sea Scrolls' Community Rule – refer to as the 'Holy Spirit'. This being, whom Paul calls 'Christ Jesus', often appears to be a carbon copy of Paul himself. So dubious did his claims regarding him appear to his opponents – and this *within the Church*, not outside it – that Paul was even mocked in his own lifetime as either a man of dreams or a 'Liar'. Aside from James, the only identifiable Apostle who emerges in any substantial manner from Paul's letters is '*Cephas*'. The portrait that emerges in these letters, not surprisingly, does not mesh with the one in Acts, to say nothing of the one in the Gospels.

Though there is continuing discussion among scholars about aspects of the Pauline corpus, there is general agreement on the authenticity of the main, particularly those letters of principal concern to us in this book like Galatians, 1 and 2 Corinthians, Romans, and Philippians. These give us insight of the most intimate kind into the mind of Paul and historical insight into this period, which no defender of the integrity of the early Church and its doctrines would have had the slightest interest in forging or, for that matter, even preserving.

Here, it is perhaps edifying to cite a general rule: one should treat very cautiously any material reflecting the known or dominant theological position of the final redactors of a given document. Where authenticity is concerned, one is often on safer ground settling on traditions that seem surprising or incongruous in some manner, or on traditions that would have a damaging effect on the theological consistency of that document. This is precisely the kind of material one would have expected to have been edited out or refurbished if it could have been, that is, had not the tradition behind its authenticity been widely disseminated, persistent, or very strong.

This is the case with the Letter of James. It is also the case with some of the severe character deficiencies that emerge where Paul is concerned, not only in his own letters, but also in the Book of Acts, accurate or not. These include his insubordination, jealousy, incessant bragging and vindictiveness. As an example of a tradition surprising in its content, one could cite Paul's attestation that Jesus not only had brothers, but that they traveled with women (1 Cor. 9:5).

In the Gospels, to cite an obvious example, there is the presentation of Jesus' Apostles as being *armed* at the time of his arrest (Mt 26:54). Jarring anecdotes such as these are just the kind of material that would have been remembered in contradistinction to lengthy speeches or parables. The treatment of Jesus' close family, including his mother and his brothers in the early parts of the Gospels – not to mention Jewish Apostles like Peter – verges on the slanderous. The material relating to James in Acts is of this kind as well. Were it not authentic and strongly supported, it is probable someone would have wished to delete it at some point. The downplaying of James in Christian tradition is important, not only where doctrine is concerned, but also because it is clear that James, as head of the Jerusalem Church and all that could be considered Christianity at the time, was superior to both Peter and Paul.

Paul, of course, repeatedly points out his personal disagreement with the rulings James makes and the instructions he receives from him. He even denigrates the authority of those he calls 'leaders', 'Pillars', 'Archapostles', 'who consider themselves important', or 'write their own references', and often displays his unwillingness to follow their views.[2] He never, however, contests James' legitimate right to exercise the position he occupies, nor the fact of his authority. In Galatians he makes it clear, too, that the character he calls either Peter or Cephas was subservient to James and not only obliged, but willing, to defer to James' leadership (Gal. 2:11–12).

Luke's reticence with regard to James in Acts contrasts markedly with the attitude of other groups relegated to sectarian status after the rise of Overseas Gentile Christianity to dominance. For these groups, James is the undisputed successor to Jesus and certainly the principal leader of all early Christianity. A particularly impressive example of this is to be found in the Gospel of Thomas. Here, in answer to the question by the Disciples, 'After you have gone who will be great over us?', Jesus replies, 'In the place where you are to go, go to James the Just for whose sake Heaven and Earth came into existence' (*Gos Th* 12).

This statement is at odds with the orthodox tradition of the succession of *Peter*; it represents nothing less than the lost tradition of the direct appointment of James as successor to his brother. It is upheld by everything we know about groups that were expelled from orthodox Christianity in the years prior to and following Constantine's adoption of it as the official religion of the Roman Empire in the fourth century. Many of these groups dispersed into a variety of sectarian groupings in the Syrian and Iraqi deserts, leading to a plethora of theological movements in the areas of Northern Mesopotamia and Syria. Some disappeared into Arabia only to re-emerge as Islam, in particular, as time went on, in its Shi'ite embodiment.

Pauline Christianity versus Jamesian: Anti-Semitism in the Gospels

In using the letters of Paul as our primary source material, we are on the firmest ground conceivable, for these are indisputably the earliest reliable documents of Christianity. They are patently earlier than the Gospels or the Book of Acts, which are themselves in large part doctrinally dependent upon Paul. Acts to some extent is dependent on Paul's letters for historical information as well.

The interrelationships between the four Gospels, particularly the three Synoptics (so called because of their use of a common source or sources), are probably far more complex than most conceive. Take, for example, the Synoptic most people consider to be the most Jewish, the Gospel of Matthew. It is considered the most 'Jewish' because of the amount of Law-oriented material it contains, particularly in the Sermon on the Mount (5:1–7:29), and because of its extensive evocation of biblical proof texts. Yet Matthew also contains a stratum of anti-Semitic material sometimes even more extreme than that found in the other Gospels – for example, the cry of the assembled Jewish masses, when Pilate hesitates to condemn

Jesus, 'his blood be on us and our children' (27:25). This has echoed down the ages, the famous – or infamous – 'blood libel' in Christian history.

Who could conceive of a crowd *en masse* uttering such an absurd statement? The answer is simple. No crowd ever did; it is based on a retrospective presentation of subsequent theology that certainly became concretized in the wake of the perspective exhibited by Paul and which by the time of Eusebius had grown to rich fruition, as the latter demonstrates over and over again in the viciousness of his invective.[3]

There are many examples of this kind in the Gospels, the relationships between which are so complex that no one will probably ever be able to sort them out to everyone's satisfaction. From internal textual considerations alone, however, it is possible to show that all the Gospels probably made their appearance after the fall of Jerusalem and the destruction of the Temple in 70 CE. This date, as has been explained, turns out to be a watershed for almost all the literary developments and movements that need to be discussed.

In reality, a far-reaching consensus has emerged among scholars on this issue – we are speaking here of the date of the actual documents themselves, not the various traditions many contend underlie them. This is no mean circumstance, for it explains many things about them, not the least of which being the paucity of sound historical material and in some cases the outright historical dissimulation and disinformation they contain.

The only serious remaining debate on this issue centers around the Gospel of Mark. From the same internal textual considerations already noted, it is possible to show that Mark, too, was written after the fall of the Temple in 70 CE. The whole nature of its anti-Jewish polemic and opposition to the family and brothers of Jesus, on the one hand, and its pro-Peter orientation, on the other, distinguish it as having appeared *after the destruction of the Jerusalem centre* – in particular, *after the attempt by the Roman Community* to represent itself as the legitimate heir to Jesus and 'the Messianic Movement' he represented, however absurd this might have seemed to any objective observer at the time.

What could be more suitable, heralded as it was by the massive triumphal procession through the streets of Rome to mark the glorious triumphs of Vespasian and his son Titus, commemorated in the works of Josephus and the Arch of Titus that still stands next to the Roman Forum today? Here, the surrender of the Jews to the *Imperium Romanum* was taken, as it were, in perpetuity.

There are, in fact, several veiled references to events of this kind in the Gospel of Mark, for instance, in the introduction to the Little Apocalypse, where Jesus is made to predict the utter destruction of the Temple (13:1–2) and in the Apocalypse itself, when the Pauline Mission is anticipated (13:9–10) – but, even more importantly, in the depiction of the rending of the Temple veil at his death (Mk 15:38 and pars.). This veil was more than likely damaged in the final Roman assault on the Temple or in the various altercations and the turmoil preceding this. Josephus specifically refers to it, along with its replacement materials, as having been delivered over to the Romans after the assault on the Temple. It was doubtless on display in Rome, damaged or otherwise, along with the rest of the booty Josephus describes as having been paraded in Titus' Triumph (*War* 7.121–62).

For his part, Jesus' meanderings about the peaceful Galilean countryside – at a time when Galilee was a hotbed of revolutionary fervor and internecine strife – doing miraculous exorcisms, cures, raisings and the like, while Scribes, Pharisees and synagogue officials murmur against him, resemble nothing so much as the incipient Paul traveling around the Mediterranean. In fact, Galilee, as referred to in the Gospel of Matthew, is a leitmotif for Gentiles – 'Galilee of the Nations'/'Galilee of the Gentiles' (4:15). It was also the seedbed of the Zealot Movement whose adherents were called by some 'Galileans'. These kinds of material, in particular, point to Mark as having been written, like the other Gospels, after the fall of the Temple and the destruction of Jerusalem.

It should suffice for the moment to say that when dealing with the authentic core of the Pauline corpus, we are dealing with the oldest and most reliable documents of Christianity, which have not failed to make their influence felt in the rest of the New Testament, despite the accident of their placement.

But a scholarly consensus of sorts has emerged even concerning the Gospels, which concedes that later religious history has made its influence felt, the only question being to what extent. Despite the last-ditch efforts by conservative scholars and fundamentalists to defend their historicity, based in part on a prior belief in the authority of Scripture, much material in the Gospels, even allowing for hyperbole, patently borders on the fantastic.

Even conceding the fact that the Gospel titles were not added until the second century, they are still representative of a genre of literature characteristic of the Second Temple Period and the Hellenistic world generally, called Pseudepigrapha – meaning books written under a false pen-name. For his part, 'Luke' admits from the start he is working from sources (1:1–4), but there still are questions about whether it is Luke or someone else doing the final redacting. These questions are too complex to be explored here, but they do not affect the nature of the conclusions we shall arrive at in this book.

Where the Book of Acts is concerned, the authorship by Luke is again taken as a given. Where Acts switches to the first-person-plural narrative of the 'We Document', it may be conceded that it is probably based on the travel notebooks or diary of a traveling companion of Paul named Luke (13:1). Here, as implied, we probably do have a genuine historical core, and fantastic raconteuring really does recede in favor of more matter-of-fact reportage and straightforward narrative. But what are we to make of much of what comes before in the first sixteen chapters of Acts, romantic legend and fantastic storytelling of the clearest sort?

The same considerations no doubt hold true, though in nothing like as clear a manner, for the records redacted under the names of Matthew, Mark and John as well. In fact, we will be able to show the kernels of real historical events beneath the surface of what can only, on occasion, be described as mythologization. Much information in the Gospels has been assimilated from other sources, including information, as we shall argue, about James, but also material from Josephus, Old Testament stories about heroes and prophets, and even episodes from the life of Paul.

Something that cannot help but strike the modern reader is the general flavor of Hellenistic anti-Semitism in the Gospels, in particular, when associated with the name of ostensibly *Jewish* witnesses such as Matthew, Mark and John. It is perhaps this attitude more than any other single characteristic that *marks them as having been composed by non-Jews* or makes it highly unlikely that in their present form they could have been redacted in a Jewish framework or been written by originally Jewish authors.

But what might strike the reader as more surprising still, the anti-Semitism of Gentile or Pauline Christianity is directed as much or even more towards the Jewish Apostles or the Jerusalem Church, particularly James, as it is towards Jews outside it. Paul is not so much concerned with Jews outside the Church, who are for him largely an irrelevant nuisance. It is against his Jewish opponents within the Church that Paul directs his bitterest attacks, most notably against those he calls 'some from James' or James' Jerusalem Church colleagues (Gal. 2:12).

It should be categorically stated that a Jewish document can be sectarian, that is, anti-Pharisee or even anti-Sadducee, as the Dead Sea Scrolls most certainly are and the Gospels at their most authentic sometimes are, but it cannot be anti-Semitic. This would be a contradiction in terms. It is possible to oppose persons of a different party or sectarian persuasion, nationalist or anti-nationalist, cosmopolitan or xenophobic, as Josephus does; but one cannot be against one's self – except abnormally. Paul sometimes exhibits this baffling characteristic, but, as we shall show, Paul is perhaps not really Jewish in the manner he thinks or advertises himself to be.

In Gospel criticism, therefore, we must set aside all such materials as incorporating a retrospective view of history and the anti-Semitism of Pauline or Overseas Christianity. These will include a large portion of the most familiar and beloved passages in the Bible, as, for instance, most of the parables, which are rarely very hard to decipher in this regard. They would also include the most oft-quoted and highly prized sayings of Jesus, many now commonplaces of Western historical parlance.

All of these are almost always directed against the people of Palestine, and are, therefore, anti-Jewish and pro the Pauline Gentile Mission – for instance: 'the First shall be last and the Last shall be first',[4] 'a Prophet is never accepted in his own land and in his own house',[5] 'who are my brothers and mother to me?',[6] 'Woe unto you Choraizin and Bethseida, had the miracles that were done here been done in Tyre and Sidon, they would have converted long ago and put on sackcloth and ashes',[7] sayings on behalf of 'publicans' (tax collectors), 'prostitutes', 'Sinners' (often meaning Gentiles), 'wine-bibbers', 'the good Samaritan', 'these Little Ones', 'the one lost sheep', 'gluttons' (people who do not keep dietary regulations), 'the Phoenician woman', etc. – all more or less connected to the priority of the Gentile Mission, the admission of Gentiles into the early Church, and related matters.

At this point, another shibboleth of latter-day scholarship will have to be jettisoned, that of the '*Judaization*' of early Christianity, which is the point of view propagated by Acts too (15:5). In line with its polemic, for Acts and modern scholarship thereafter, the original doctrines of Jesus and the Apostles, who supported Gentiles and the Gentile Mission, have been undermined by the 'Jamesian' Jerusalem Church. This is an absurdity and it must be stated categorically: there never was a '*Judaization of early Christianity*', only a progressively more rapid *Gentilization*.

This gathered momentum with the elimination of the Jerusalem center by the hand of Roman power after the Uprising of 66–70 CE. Only when principles of this kind are properly grasped and many favorite platitudes and historical clichés jettisoned, will it be possible to make any progress towards a resolution of the quest for the Historical Jesus.

To make an honest attempt to get at the truth of this period, therefore, one must be willing to part with the popular idea of the Gospels, for instance, as 'eyewitness' accounts. The only 'eyewitness' we have in this sorry spectacle – apart from the Dead Sea Scrolls – is Josephus himself, and we have already covered his flaws. This is not to say, however, that one must part with one's faith. The Gospel portrait is sacred history, and as such recommends itself, in particular, to one's faith, if not necessarily to one's sense of historical accuracy. In this kind of history, events are often represented retrospectively and entwined with the dominant religious point of view of the time.

Josephus' Testimonies to James and the 'Star Prophesy'

It is through the person of James, who is mentioned in a straightforward manner by his younger contemporary Josephus, that we have the most compelling testimony to the existence of his brother Jesus, whether one takes the name 'Jesus' symbolically or literally. Some consider even the reference to James found in the Twentieth Book of Josephus' *Antiquities* interpolated; but, aside from the fact that little could be gained by such an insertion, the reference is convincing enough and fits in with what we know about James ideologically and historically from other sources.

In addition, it provides previously unknown and seemingly reliable data about the circumstances of James' arrest and execution. It is consistent, too, with the pattern of other such notices in Josephus' *Antiquities* about persons not mentioned in the *Jewish War*. Though it is always possible that the notice is not complete in the form we have it, James does appear to have been mentioned at this point by Josephus.

Origen, the third-century Church theologian, and Eusebius, his successor in Caesarea in the next century, both claim to have seen a copy of Josephus different from the one we presently possess. This copy included a passage ascribing the fall of Jerusalem to the death of James *not to the death of Jesus* – a significant addition. This passage does not exist in the notice about James in the *Antiquities* available to us at the present time and there really is no place it could reasonably have been inserted in that document, except for the 62 CE notice of the circumstances surrounding James' death. Origen was outraged by what he saw and hastened to correct Josephus' version of the facts, insisting that he should have said Jerusalem fell on account of the death of Jesus. This in itself would probably explain the ultimate disappearance of this passage from all extant versions of Josephus' works – even the Arabic *Yusufus*.

Overtly anyhow, Josephus considers himself a Pharisee and, where Roman power was at issue, the behavior of two other self-professed Pharisees in this period, Paul and R. Yohanan ben Zacchai – the founder of Rabbinic Judaism – parallel his. Nor do the constraints under which he operated differ very much from theirs, especially when he tells those stories about popular Messianic leaders who had been crucified by Roman administrators.

Josephus' general view of the 'religious frauds' or 'magicians' he refers to in this period was that their influence over the people was more pernicious even than that of the 'robbers and assassins', and more dangerous. This was primarily because, as he puts it, they were scheming to bring about *both* religious reform *and* change in government, that is, they had a dual religious and political program (*War* 2.258–9 & 264–5). Therefore, by necessity if not inclination – in Josephus the two are often identical – the presentation of such 'impostors' or 'deceivers' was fashioned in an extremely negative manner, at least in versions of his work prepared for Roman circulation. As the censorship powers of the Church became absolute after Constantine, negative presentations of early Christian leaders, where recognizable, undoubtedly would have been replaced by more sympathetic testimonies or deleted altogether.

A similar conundrum bedevils Josephus' presentation of responsibility for the fall of the Temple. There can be little doubt that the Temple in Jerusalem was destroyed by an express Roman political decision, yet Josephus portrays the Jews as burning their own Temple down around themselves. The Romans, no doubt, perceived the Temple as being the seat of the pestilent Messianic Movement, which, Christian refurbishments notwithstanding, it was. The description of these events would have come in the famous, lost Fifth Book of Tacitus' *Histories*, or possibly the missing portions of the *Annals*, but Sulpicius Severus in the fifth century provides an account that was probably based on it.[8] He portrays the Roman war council on the eve of the final assault on the Temple, where the definitive decision was taken by Titus' staff to destroy it, no doubt with the enthusiastic support of individuals such as Bernice, Philo's nephew Tiberius Alexander, and Josephus himself. Another Roman historian, Dio Cassius, notes the Roman amazement at the Jews who in despair threw themselves into the flames (65.6.3).

For his part, Josephus is anxious to portray the Jews as burning down their own Temple and Titus as doing everything he can to quench the flames. In this manner he rescues Titus from the charge of impiety or Temple desecration, so important to a people as superstitious as the Romans. It is easy to recognize in Josephus' presentation of Titus the similar presentation of the behavior of Pontius Pilate and Herod towards Jesus and John the Baptist in the Gospels – not surprisingly, since all these documents were produced by similar mindsets under similar constraints. Though on the basis of the extant corpus, since he testifies that Jesus 'was the Christ', Josephus must be considered a Christian; elsewhere, as we have seen, Josephus informs us in no uncertain terms that he considers Vespasian to have been the one called from Palestine at this time to rule the world. Josephus' perversion of the 'World Ruler Prophecy' is comparable in its cynicism to the Hellenistic reformulation of it in the Gospels.

Rabbinic literature is equally cynical in its presentation of R.Yohanan ben Zacchai, the founder of Rabbinic Judaism, as making the same opportunistic interpretation of this Prophecy and applying it to Vespasian, presumably to save his skin. This is the kind of chicanery and sleight-of-hand typical of this period. Josephus might have been a secret Christian, depending on one's definition of 'Christian' in Palestine – if one wants him, one is welcome to him – but not on the basis of his description of Jesus. On this basis, so was Pontius Pilate and, indeed, apocryphal Gospels asserting this duly appeared in early Christian centuries. These absurdities have gone so far that there were even Josephinist cults in the Middle Ages and, as noted, the Josephus corpus accompanied the Greek Orthodox canon.

In England his first translators, like William Whiston in Isaac Newton's time, were convinced they were dealing with a Christian. History can attest to few more cynical people who have portrayed themselves so frankly. Indeed, besides the wealth of historical data he presents us, if he has a virtue, this is it. He is honest to a fault concerning his own shortcomings and flaws. In fact, he does not even seem to recognize them as flaws at all.

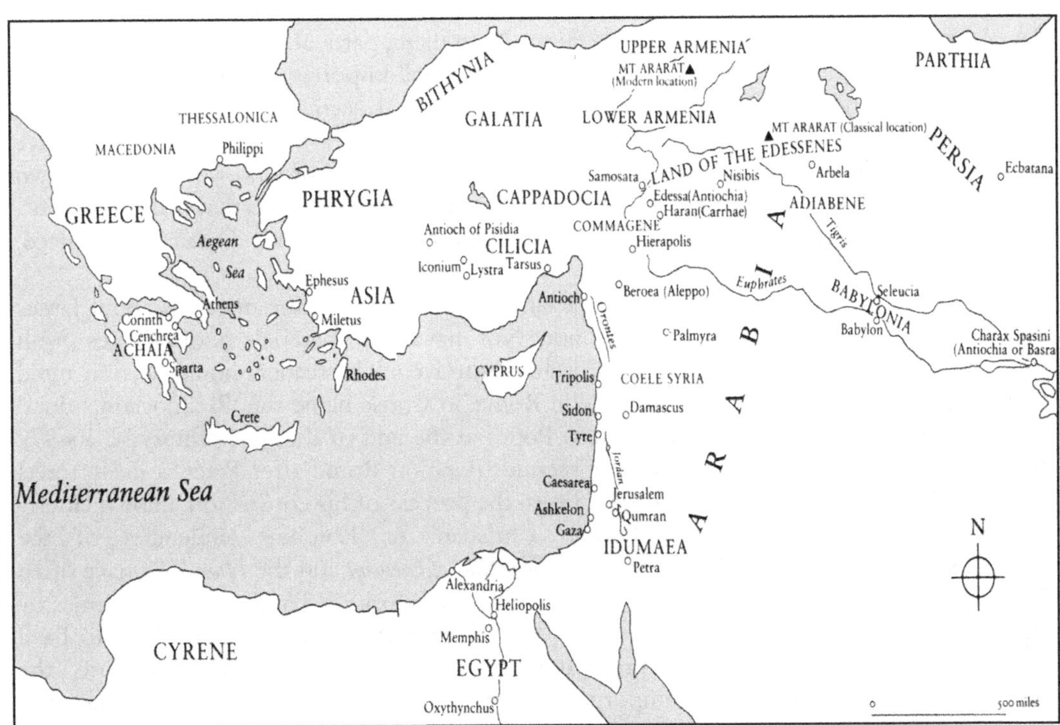

Map of Eastern Mediterranean World

Chapter 5
Early Church Sources and the Dead Sea Scrolls

Extra-biblical Sources Relating to James

The existence of James the brother of Jesus is not only confirmed in the Pauline Corpus, the Book of Acts, and by Josephus, it is also echoed in the Gospels, though downplayed. It is further enlarged upon in the literature of the early Church. The principal sources are Eusebius of Caesarea at the beginning of the fourth century (*c.* 260–340) and Epiphanius of Salamis at the end of it (367–404), both from Palestine. Their testimonies about James overlap, but with interesting differences and emendations. There is a much shorter notice in Jerome's *In Praise of Illustrious Men.* Jerome (347–420), whose principal work was also conducted in Palestine, most notably Bethlehem, was famous for his biblical scholarship, the basis of the Latin Vulgate Bible of today. His testimony overlaps with both Eusebius and Epiphanius, the latter his contemporary and, it seems, a Jewish convert to Christianity. While Eusebius and Epiphanius are more extensive, Jerome focuses on several aspects of the tradition that are extremely important for our understanding of James.

The greater part of these sources and testimonies is based on two earlier writers from the second century, both now lost. The first, Hegesippus (*c.* 90–180) was a second-century churchman, also from Palestine; the second, Clement of Alexandria (*c.* 150–215) was Origen's predecessor and teacher in Egypt. Their testimony, while not always in agreement, overlaps substantially, though Hegesippus' is more extensive. Eusebius is straightforward about his dependence on both and presents large sections from them, particularly Hegesippus. Without his verbatim quotations, we would be without these two all-important testimonies.

Hegesippus flourished within a century of James and seems to have been a 'Jewish Christian', whatever may be meant by this term in this time. As a young man he would have known persons whose memory spanned the time frame involved or who would have known people with personal knowledge of the events and individuals in question. His testimony, therefore, is to be highly prized, but it is regrettable that none of his works has survived, except these precious excerpts in Eusebius.

Though some works of Clement of Alexandria have survived, the materials about James used by Eusebius and Epiphanius did not. Nor have any materials about James from Clement, additional to those quoted in Eusebius, survived. The reader should keep in mind that there are two Clements. The first one in Rome, in whose name the 'Pseudoclementines' have been redacted, was one of the earliest Popes at the end of the first century (*c.* 30–97). Not only is he designated as the first or second 'Pope' in Rome after Peter, a lively travel literature developed in his name, associated with the process of his conversion, known latterly as the Pseudoclementines. The 'Jewish Christian' or Ebionite tendencies of the Pseudoclementines – comprising both the *Recognitions of Clement* and the *Homilies* – have often been remarked. The only real difference between the two works is that the attack on James by Paul in the First Book of the *Recognitions* and the surrounding material there seem to have been deleted from the *Homilies*, presenting a more sanitized version. Therefore, the *Recognitions*, in particular, provides important information for our consideration of James, not so much doctrinally, but historically.

The Clement on whose work some of the statements about James found in Eusebius and Epiphanius are based, however, is not this Clement but a second-century Alexandrian theologian by the same name. Though he was a younger contemporary of Hegesippus, the testimony he provides is neither as extensive nor as useful as Hegesippus' impressive legacy. From what has survived, it can be concluded that he had information about James' role as successor to Jesus and the circumstances of his death. Nor does Clement evince any embarrassment over James' 'brother' relationship with Jesus. But garbling of materials and mythologization have already begun to take place, even more than in Hegesippus' case, though he is only a little more than a century away from the events in question. Still, Clement of Alexandria is a useful link in the process of transmission and another firm testimony to James' importance in first-century Palestine and other areas in the East.

There are also important materials about James in two other writers from the second century, Papias (*c.* 60–135) and Justin Martyr (*c.* 100–165). Justin Martyr does not mention James specifically, but the data he records are extremely helpful as regards the substance of what early notions of Christianity might have been, particularly the Righteousness/Piety dichotomy, which he considers the essence of Christianity (*Dial.* 23, 47, & 93). He also provides interesting materials about what might have constituted Scripture in those days. Where Paul is concerned, though both come from Asia Minor, Justin doesn't mention him at all, but seems rather studiously to avoid him. If this is an indication of some second-century doctrinal rift, it is interesting information indeed.

Even more interesting for our purposes is Papias, whose works have survived only in fragments. Eusebius knows of Papias' works and once again here and there gives excerpts from these. However, there are some fragments purporting to come from Papias which came to light in the last century.[1] If authentic, these are of the utmost importance for studying the family of Jesus, particularly the relationship of Jesus' uncle Cleophas to Mary, and by extension, the relationship of Simeon, Cleophas' son, to Jesus and James. Even if only a later epitome, the information they provide is very penetrating. As these relationships are clarified, so too can the existence of a fourth, rather ephemeral brother of Jesus, which tradition insists on calling Joseph or 'Joses'.

Apocryphal Gospels, Apocalypses, Acts, and Anti-Acts

In these kinds of documents, too, we have important sources for the life, teaching, and person of James. In the Gospels – primarily the Synoptics – we have the testimony to the brothers of Jesus, however downplayed these may be.[2] No embarrassment is evinced about the fact of these brothers. Nor is there any indication that they may be half-brothers, brothers by a different mother, or any other such designation aimed at reducing their importance and minimizing their relationship to Jesus.

In these reports Jesus' mother and brothers come to him to talk to or question him. They are four in number, James, Simon, Jude, and Joses. One or more sisters are also mentioned – one specifically named Salome (Mk 15:40). Other than some sayings that imply a disparaging attitude towards those close to Jesus and his immediate family and additional material in Apostle lists, there is little else in the Gospels relating to them. This attitude of disparagement directed against what can only be called 'the Jewish Apostles' – in effect comprising the nucleus of what is called 'the Jerusalem Church' – is a retrospective one and part of the anti-family and anti-Jewish polemic of Pauline or Overseas Christianity, not a historical one.

The fact of these brothers – particularly James – also emerges in what are referred to as Apocryphal Gospels, those works in the gospel genre which for one reason or another did not get into the canon that emerged after Constantine. Principal among these are gospels that are known only through secondhand accounts from Church Fathers, notably Origen, Eusebius, Epiphanius, and Jerome. These include, in particular, the Gospel of the Hebrews, the Gospel of the Nazoraeans, and the Gospel of the Ebionites. None of these gospels, which were all said to have been based on the Gospel of Matthew, has survived (except in quoted fragments), nor is it clear that they were ever really separate gospels at all and not simply variations of each other. In several of the surviving notices, James plays a significant role, particularly in post-resurrection appearances of Jesus.

In addition, James plays a prominent role in the Gnostic Gospel of Thomas, recently discovered at Nag Hammadi. Unlike most other gospels, the Gospel of Thomas is simply a list of sayings ascribed to Jesus. Other materials from Nag Hammadi further reinforce the importance James was accorded in the early centuries of Christianity, particularly in the East. There can be no doubt that this is the James of this book and that he was viewed in the manner almost of a Supernatural Redeemer figure superseded in importance only by Jesus himself. This is very curious, and once again confirms that James' role in the East was one of over-arching importance. It will be the view of this book that this status was only a little exaggerated beyond his true role in the Palestine of his day. Among these documents from Nag Hammadi presenting James as being of such commanding stature are the First and Second Apocalypses of James. There is also the largely fictional Protevangelium of James, which claims to be an account of the infancy of Jesus, told from the point of view of James, his closest living relative. Regardless of the credibility of this gospel, and in it we have the doctrine of the Perpetual Virginity of Mary, the importance of James is again highlighted – this time in his role of unimpeachable witness.

Where Books of Acts are concerned, there are other lost materials like the documents referred to by scholars as the '*Kerygmata Petrou*', the 'Teaching of Peter', or another lost work, the 'Travels of Peter'. These are difficult to reconstruct with any certainty, but are thought to have been incorporated into the Pseudoclementines. It is difficult to overestimate the importance of these documents for a consideration of the person of James. Apart from doctrinal considerations, important for second-third-century groups known as 'Jewish Christians' or Ebionites', there are materials, particularly in the First Book of the *Recognitions*, that are important as a kind of anti-Acts. They present a picture of the early days of the Church in Jerusalem from the point of view not of a Luke or a Paul, but of a writer sympathetic to James – and with him, the whole of the 'Jerusalem Church' Establishment, including the Jewish Apostles.

It can be objected that the Pseudoclementines are not history but fiction – hence the prefixed 'pseudo'. But this is what we are dealing with in regard to most documents from this period, except those with outright historical intent like Josephus. On this basis, the Pseudoclementines do not differ appreciably from more familiar documents like the Gospels or the Book of Acts. The Pseudoclementines are no more counterfeit than these. The point is that there is occasionally reliable material in these accounts, particularly in the First Book of the *Recognitions*.

Here one might wish to apply the doctrine of incongruity, that is, when a fact is considered poorly documented for some reason or flies in the face of obviously orthodox materials, this is sometimes good grounds for taking it more seriously than one might otherwise have done. The physical attack by Paul on James, described in the *Recognitions*, is just such a piece of astonishing material. It will overlay lacunae and clearly counterfeit materials in the Book or Acts – for instance, about someone called 'Stephen' – so well that it will be all but impossible to discard.

The Pseudoclementines give a picture of the early Church in Palestine at odds with the one presented in Acts, yet meshing with it at key points. Though they have come down in several recensions, a case can be made for their being based on the same source as Acts – that is, the Pseudoclementines and Acts connect in a series of recognizable common joins, but the material is being treated differently in one narrative than in the other.

For the most part the Pseudoclementines are concerned with confrontations between Peter and Simon *Magus*. Acts is also concerned with this confrontation, but whereas it passes over it in a few sentences, the Pseudoclementines linger over its various metamorphoses *ad nauseam*. However these things may be, the basic treatment of the confrontation between Simon Peter and Simon *Magus* in Caesarea, where the Pseudoclementines correctly locate it, can be shown to be more historical than the patently more fantastic presentation of it in the Book of Acts. The *Recognitions* also clear up Acts' lack of precision about Simon *Magus*' place of origin, which is identified as '*Gitta*' in Samaria. This is also confirmed in Eusebius.[3] This is just one example of the superiority of the novelizing of the Pseudoclementines over the novelizing of the Book of Acts, and that all references to 'pseudo' in these matters are relative.

Because of its confusion over this, Acts places Peter's confrontation with Simon *Magus* in *Samaria* instead of Caesarea where it belongs. When this confrontation is joined with Josephus' picture of the Simon 'the Head of an Assembly' (*Ecclesia*) of his own in Jerusalem in the *Antiquities*, who also comes to Caesarea to meet with Agrippa I around 44 CE, then we shall be able to make some sense of all these overlapping and sometimes contradictory notices (*Ant.* 19.332–4).

Prefaced to the second cluster of Pseudoclementine materials, the *Homilies*, are two letters like those one finds in the New Testament, but purporting to be from Peter to James and Clement to James. Putting aside the question of their authenticity for the moment, that they are pointedly addressed to James as 'Bishop of Bishops' or 'Archbishop' shows that their authors had little doubt that James was the leader of the whole of Christianity in his time and that Apostles like Peter and Paul were subordinate to him.

In addition, these letters contain several important points for our consideration, for instance, that all overseas teachers required letters of introduction or certification from James and were required to send him back periodic reports of their activities – an assertion that makes sense. We would have had little trouble deducing this in any case from reading between the lines of Paul's shrill protests concerning his lack of such certification in his letters. But the fact of this requirement actually being present in these apocryphal letters prefacing an 'anti-Acts' is impressive. It is like finding a missing link. Had it not been present, we would have had to deduce it.

To sum up: it is our position that Acts and the Pseudoclementines are neither independent of nor dependent on each other; but parallel accounts going back to the same source: that is, the First and Second Books of the Pseudoclementine *Recognitions* do not go back to Acts, but to a common source both were using. But one can go even further than this. One can insist, however startling this may at first appear, that the *Recognitions* are more faithful to this underlying source than Acts. The points of contact between the two are clearly discernible as, for instance, the confrontations on the Temple Mount culminating in an attack led by Paul on someone, but so is the fact that Acts is changing the source on which both are based in a consistent and clearly discernible manner. At times this borders on what, in the jargon of today, might be called 'disinformation'.

These confrontations on the Temple Mount would also appear to be the subject matter of another lost work about James from which Epiphanius quotes several passages. Epiphanius calls this work the *Anabathmoi Jacobou* – the *Ascents of James*, a title that sets up interesting resonances with the Jewish underground mystical tradition, known as *Kabbalah*. The *Ascents of James*, which appears to relate to the discourses James gave in the Temple while standing on the Temple steps – hence the title – also relates to the picture in the early part of Acts of the Apostles going every day to the Temple as a group and, there, either talking to the Jewish crowd or arguing with the Temple Authorities. The same picture is represented in the *Recognitions of Clement*, and some believe materials from the *Anabathmoi* have ended up in the Pseudoclementines.

The materials that Epiphanius does excerpt are interesting in themselves and fill in some missing points about Paul's biography, as seen through the eyes of his opponents not his supporters, and place James at the centre of agitation in the Temple in the years leading up to the Uprising. Not only will this last assertion be shown to bear on how Temple service was being carried out by Herodian High Priests, but also to the rejection of gifts and sacrifices from Gentiles in the Temple by those Josephus calls either '*Sicarii*' or 'Zealots' three and a half years after the death of James, triggering the Revolt against Rome. Both will also be seen reflected in the Dead Sea Scrolls.

The Dead Sea Scrolls

The most controversial and debatable identifications we will make will concern the Dead Sea Scrolls. It will be asked, what have these documents to do with a study of James? The answer is simple. In the first place, they are parallel and, in some cases, contemporary cultural materials. Some may object that the Dead Sea Scrolls are earlier documents. Even if this proposition were proven for all the Scrolls, which it is not,[4] the ideas represented in much of the corpus have a familiar ring, particularly when one gets to know those ideas associated with James or takes an in-depth look at the letter associated with his name in the New Testament. So, initially, it is certainly permissible to say that the ideas in the Scrolls flow in a fairly consistent manner into the ideas associated with the Community led by James, regardless of the dating of the Qumran texts.

No one doubts that there are older documents among the Dead Sea Scrolls. But no one can contest the fact that there are also newer ones, the only question being how new? Some texts contain ideas and allusions that are all but indistinguishable from those represented by the Community led by James, and it is these that must be seen as contemporary. These documents are sometimes referred to as 'sectarian', meaning, in terms of our above discussions, non-Pharisaic or non-Rabbinic. These include, at the very least, all the *pesharim* at Qumran (Hebrew plural for *pesher*).

But what is a *pesher*? A *pesher* is a commentary – at Qumran, a commentary on a well-known biblical passage, usually from the Prophets. The important thing is that the biblical passage being interpreted was fraught with significance for the Scroll Community. Often this takes the form of citing a biblical passage out of context or even sometimes slightly altered, followed by the words, '*peshero*' or '*pesher ha-davar*', meaning 'its interpretation' or 'the interpretation of the passage is'. The text then proceeds to give an idiosyncratic interpretation having to do with the history or ideology of the group, with particular reference to contemporary events. These commentaries or *pesher*s have been found at Qumran in single exemplars only and none in multiple copies, which is not the case for most other documents found there.

The number of sectarian documents among the Scrolls reaches well into the hundreds. This is why the documents found at Qumran are so astonishing. They are not just a random sampling or cross-section of the literature from this period, as some have theorized, but very uniform and consistent in content. Of course there are variations having to do with the style or personality of individual authors or period of origin, but the same doctrines move from document to document, the same terms, the same *dramatis personae*.

The literature discovered in the caves – and it is a literature – is a wildly creative one, and different authors are expressing themselves, sometimes in a most creative or poetic manner. However one will never, for instance, find a document advocating compromise, nor one recommending accommodation with the powers-that-be or foreigners or those, the writers designate in their sometimes infuriatingly obscure code, '*the Seekers after Smooth Things*'. One will never find a text at Qumran denigrating the Law or advocating, for instance, 'niece marriage', 'polygamy', or 'divorce' – all of which this group considered 'breaking the Law'.

The same imagery, too, moves from document to document, the imagery of 'Righteousness', 'Perfection', 'zeal', 'the Poor', straightening 'the Way', the Community as Temple, 'Holy Spirit' baptism, the 'Perfection of Holiness', and the same personalities: 'the Righteous Teacher', 'the Wicked Priest', 'the Spouter of Lies', 'the Comedian', or 'the Traitors'.

There are multiple copies of some 'sectarian' or 'non-biblical' documents like the famous War Scroll, the Community Rule, the Damascus Document, the Qumran Hymns, '*MMT*' or 'the Letters relating to Works Righteousness',[5] and others. The precise date of these documents is still a matter of much controversy. It is not that these documents do not come from the Second Temple Period. They do. The problem is trying to date them with more precision than that.

Given the state of the archaeological and palaeographic data having to do with the Community responsible for these writings, I have said that one must make one's determinations on the basis of internal data – the allusions and perspective of the document itself. Take, for example, the Community Rule, which many Qumran specialists have attempted to date in the second century BCE or even earlier on the basis of handwriting that they consider 'older' relative to 'newer' fragments.

However in the Community Rule we have 'the Way in the wilderness' text from Isaiah 40:3, applied in the New Testament to the mission of John the Baptist, referred to twice, and an exposition of the passage consistent with the mindset of Qumran, applying it to the Community's own 'separation' and activities in the wilderness.[6] In addition, there is a plethora of other allusions like 'the Holy Spirit', baptism, the Community as Temple, and 'spiritualized sacrifice' imagery so familiar in the Pauline corpus.[7] Given the parallels with what we know to be first-century ideas, *this document is late* – meaning first century CE – regardless of dubious palaeographic estimations.

The same can be said for the Damascus Document. Again, on the basis of internal data, this document has a first-century ambience as well, regardless of arguments to the contrary based on external data. These internal considerations include the exegesis of 'the Star Prophecy' and other Messianic allusions – the first-century currency of which is indisputable – together with the ideology of 'Justification', the Commandment to 'love your neighbor', which the Letter of James calls 'the Royal Law according to the Scripture' and which Josephus designates as one of the fundamental parts of John the Baptist's 'Righteousness'/'Piety' dichotomy, and the 'Damascus' imagery one also finds in the Book of Acts. There are many more.

Similarly, all *pesharim* from Qumran must be seen as 'late'. This is not only because of formulae like '*the Last Priests of Jerusalem*' and Habakkuk 2:4, 'the Righteous shall live by his Faith', which we know was being subjected to exegesis in the first century CE; but also the searing description of the foreign armies invading the country, who 'sacrifice to their standards and worship their weapons of war' – Roman Imperial practice of the first century CE – and Roman 'tax-farming' and final 'booty- taking' in the Temple, which did not occur after any assault except that of 70 CE.[8]

Since they have been found in single copies only, they would appear to represent the latest literature of the Community, literature that did not have time to go into wide circulation or be reproduced in multiple copies. In addition, they are extremely personalized or idiosyncratic, filled with the ethos of events transpiring in the cataclysmic 'End Time' or 'Last Days' spoken of in Daniel and the New Testament.

It is also primarily in these *pesharim* that one comes upon all the dramatis personae of the Community and its history. For instance, in addition to the terms cited above, 'the Simple of Judah doing *Torah*', 'the Violent Ones of the Gentiles', 'the *Kittim*', 'the Additional Ones of the Peoples', 'the city built upon blood', 'the Poor', 'the Meek', and so on. These allusions are tied in an apocalyptic manner to prized biblical texts, the reason for whose choice becomes clear once one examines the vocabulary involved. The authors of these commentaries definitely felt they were living in some cataclysmic '*End Time*' and all the imagery, everything about their ethos, including the repetitive vocabulary they employ, points to the Roman Period – in fact, to be precise, to the Period of Imperial Rome.

We shall be able to link allusions – particularly from the *Pesharim*, but also from the Damascus Document, Community Rule, and War Scroll – to events of James' life. Not only this, but an additional effect will develop. When the events of James' life are superimposed on materials from Qumran, particularly those having to do with the destruction of the Righteous Teacher by the Wicked Priest, additional data can be elicited from them that one would not otherwise have known or suspected. Seeming *non sequiturs* or obscure readings are cleared up, and additional data thus elicited from the texts.

No other character from any time or place during the two or three centuries of Palestinian history we are studying produces anything like the same match one gets when one views James in relation to the Scroll documents. Reigning theories of Qumran origins generally evade this issue and often do not even attempt to develop the internal evidence involved. This is the safer way, but in these materials we have to do with a *major movement* within Judaism and dramatis personae of no slight importance. It is impossible that these people should have failed to make an impression on their time and place, nor appear in the wealth of sources we have available to us for this period.

There are other considerations, too, that need to be analyzed. Here we have two communities: 'the Jerusalem Community' led by a teacher called, in tradition, James 'the Just' – or, to follow the sense of the original Hebrew, James 'the Righteous One' – and the Community at Qumran led by an unknown teacher called 'the Righteous Teacher' or 'the Teacher of Righteousness'. Like James, he too appears to come to an unhappy end.

Whenever the details relating to the Qumran Teacher's life, teaching, and demise are being developed in a *pesher*, the allusion played on in the underlying biblical text is invariably 'the *Zaddik*' or '*Righteous One*'. This is so common that almost every available '*Zaddik*' text from the Bible is subjected to exegesis in some manner in the extant materials from Qumran. This amounts almost to a rule of thumb. Significantly, one will find the same or similar texts being applied to James' demise in early Christian writings.

It has been contended that the Scroll Community is at Qumran while the Jerusalem Community is in Jerusalem. Therefore, they are not identical however parallel their teachings. This might appear on the surface to be a fair statement except for the fact that a careful analysis of the Qumran texts often places the Righteous Teacher and his followers in Jerusalem. *Par contra*, materials in the Jamesian corpus definitively place James and all his Community following their flight from Jerusalem in the region of Jericho near the location of Qumran.[9]

With regard to the actual physical site at Qumran and the fortress-like settlement located there, references to the wilderness 'camps' in the Qumran documents are invariably in the plural. On the basis of internal data there is no indication whatsoever where these 'camps' might have been located, except for two references in the War Scroll to, firstly, '*the wilderness of the Peoples*' and, secondly, '*the wilderness of Judea*'. The former is probably synonymous with what goes by the name of '*the Land of Damascus*' or just plain '*Damascus*' in the Document deriving its name from that designation. And in this document, the figure known as 'the *Mebakker*' or '*Overseer*' or '*Bishop*', who is either synonymous with or parallels another known as '*the High Priest Commanding the Camps*', bears an uncanny resemblance to James and his role in the early Church.[10]

PART II

THE HISTORICAL JAMES

Chapter 6
The First Appearance of James in Acts

The Book of Acts as History

Historically speaking James first appears in a really tangible way in the Book of Acts. But the presentation is not a straightforward one. There are, as usual, puzzling lacunae. Materials known from other sources are left out and things that should logically have been covered are missing. To the perspicacious observer, however, the traces of these other data are still there, to be filled in by inference from what is said elsewhere or the underlying implications of the text itself. To the neophyte, this can be unsettling, but once he or she has grasped what is really occurring, it can be uplifting, approaching the joy of a discovery or enlightenment.

First, the reader should realize that the Book of Acts cannot be considered a historical presentation. There is too much mythologizing, too much that is out-and-out fiction, too much fantasizing. Important materials are left out, yet, underlying the presentation, the broad lines of a certain kind of history can be discerned.

For instance, how was the succession to Jesus managed? We hear about an 'election' of sorts, but then this turns out not to have been the election of Jesus' successor, which would have been the logical expectation at this point in a narrative purporting to cover the beginnings of the early Church, but rather clearly obscurantist material about the election of a Twelfth Apostle to succeed not Jesus but, of all people, 'Judas' his alleged 'betrayer'. This is the first bit of sleight-of-hand in Acts, and this election, as we shall see, will dovetail nicely with notices in early Church literature about a first election of James as *Bishop* or *Bishop of Bishops* of the early Church.

Questions like why there had to be 'Twelve Apostles' in the first place, or who – aside from the election of this inconsequential successor to Judas named Matthias – succeeded Jesus are passed by in silence. Then there are the questions about the identity of the majority of the Apostles or what a 'Bishop' or an 'Archbishop' actually was, not to mention how James came to be found in this position in the first place. Acts is normally thought of as being 'the acts' of the Apostles in general, that is, 'the Twelve', who are variously listed according to which account one is following, and yet the author clearly knows almost nothing about the majority of these Apostles.

At a very early stage the narrative moves over to the story of Paul – who is not really even an 'Apostle' at all – at least not one of the original ones (7:58) and, except as he comes in contact with one or another of these, the narrative completely loses interest in them. For instance, we know next to nothing about Peter after he conveniently leaves just in time to make way for the introduction of James in chapter 12. We are told nothing about his travels or experiences, and nothing about his death. Why not? We are not told about any of the other significant members of 'the Twelve' either, except James, and yet James is not supposed to be a member of 'the Twelve' or an Apostle.

But even when it focuses on Paul, the text tells us nothing about his early career. Again, we can learn more by looking at the first chapter of Galatians. We would have expected to have been informed of these things. All the text does is bring us to Rome with Paul. Then it leaves us. We do not know what happened to Paul in the end any more than we do Peter – or James for that matter. Acts is not history. It is not even particularly good narrative, romance, or fiction.

Nor does the text tell us about James' death, which, following even Acts' somewhat questionable time format, also occurred at exactly the point Acts ends about two years after

Paul's arrival in Rome. A lacuna of this magnitude is inexplicable, until one realizes Acts tells us about few, if any, of 'the other Apostles' except Paul. Of these presumed 'Twelve Apostles', Acts mentions John, but in little or no detail, and has one small more or less fictional episode about a 'Philip'. Peter is discarded almost completely after Paul makes his appearance. The first James – 'James *the brother of John*' – is eliminated from the scene at this point as well, just in time for the sudden eruption of the second James (James *the brother of Jesus*) into the narrative.

In fact, just about all the other Apostles that Acts so carefully lists at the beginning of its narrative are simply shadowy figures to flesh out the twelve-man Apostle scheme it is so intent on presenting. They are really only paper figures and the author of Acts really knows next to nothing about them or, if he does, he is not very forthcoming concerning them.

Indeed, it would be more accurate to say that Acts is really a narrative about the 'acts' of the Holy Spirit, not the early Church or Apostles at all. It traces the acts of the Holy Spirit in their various manifestations, and true history goes by the board almost from the beginning. When Paul argues with the Jerusalem Leadership of the Church – which he does – it is the Holy Spirit that in his view gives him equal status, even superior 'Knowledge' to them (Gal. 2:2). It is the Holy Spirit that not only certifies his credentials as an Apostle, but also his Mission generally. Not unmindful of this fact, the religio-historical narrative of Acts is careful to present the accoutrements of the descent of the Holy Spirit, such as *speaking in tongues* and *miracles*, raisings, curings, and the like (2:4).

James the Brother of Jesus and James the Brother of John

The first reference to James in Acts comes in a request by Peter to the servants at 'Mary the mother of John Mark's house' – whoever these may have been – after his escape from prison and before his departure to points unknown. It reads: 'Report these things to James and *the brothers*' (12:17).

Before proceeding to the problems presented by it, we must first distinguish this James from several other Jameses, particularly the more familiar Great James or '*James the brother of John the son of Zebedee*'. This James, as opposed presumably to '*James the Less*' (Mark 15:40 – our *James*) and another '*Justus*' who appears in Acts 1:23, is the James who occasionally appears along with James the Just, the brother of Jesus in the Gospels. He is the familiar James among the Apostles and the James most people think they are talking about when they speak of James. Few, if any, realize there was a second one even greater, and that the first is in all probability, if not merely a minor character, simply an overlay or gloss. The authors of Acts know nothing substantial about him and conveniently remove him at the beginning of chapter 12 just before the James we are speaking of appears. For his part, Paul never mentions a 'James *the brother of John*' and none of the Church Fathers knows anything else about him except apocryphally. Yet his existence is confidently asserted by almost all who talk with knowledge about Scripture. Such is the power of the written word. The same is true for his purported father 'Zebedee', another character again hardly more than simple fiction. For the present writer characters of this kind are simply meant as dissimulation to confuse the unsuspecting reader.

It is the '*brother*' theme, however, that will allow us to place in clear focus who this second James may have been, once we have dismissed the nomenclature 'Zebedee' as fiction. We will encounter several others of this kind, so by the end of the book the *modus operandi* behind such overwrites should become plain.

James – the real James – is never introduced or identified in Acts. He just appears. Actually he does not really appear here; this appearance is saved for chapter 15. He is alluded to parenthetically in Peter's request, 'tell these things [that is, Peter's miraculous escape and departure] to James and the brothers' after the alleged *other* 'James' has already disappeared from the narrative; but from what is said there, it is implied that our James – James the Just – was either mentioned earlier or we should know who he is. But how should we know who he is if in the present version of the document he was not mentioned previously or he was never introduced to us? Even this oblique mention of James, after the only other James we have ever heard of has been decapitated, does not tell us who he is.

Either one is willing to accept that a character as important as James could be just introduced into the text of Acts at this point in such an off-hand manner, or something is missing or has been discarded. He is obviously already the leader of 'the Jerusalem Church' and continues in this role for the rest of the book.

The actual episode occurs just after Peter, who has been having visions via the mechanism of the Holy Spirit and experiencing voices crying out to him from Heaven on the rooftop in Jaffa, goes to visit the household of a Roman Centurion named 'Cornelius' (Acts 9–11). All these episodes have as their root the admission of Gentiles or those who do not follow Jewish religious Law – 'the Law of Moses' – into the Church. Peter escapes from prison after having been arrested for some unexplained reason by 'Herod' (Acts 12:6). All these points need exposition. We are in the thick of the Jewish historical world in Jerusalem and along the sea coast of Palestine of the late 30s and early 40's CE.

The Herods

Setting aside for the moment the actual historicity of this curious Peter or Simon, involved in these kinds of activities along the Palestinian coast, and who he might have been – Josephus will tell us about a parallel 'Simon', the head of an 'Assembly' (*Ecclesia*) in Jerusalem in the same period, whom 'Herod' would have very good cause to arrest or execute – it would be important to grasp who all these characters designated in the New Testament as 'Herod the King' actually were. Acts has this particular Herod beheading James the brother of John at the beginning of the chapter and dying 'eaten by worms' at the end of the chapter (12:23).

Curiously, the next chapter, 13, in swinging back to Paul and describing the nature and composition of his Antioch 'Church' or 'Assembly' (*Ecclesia* again), begins with a reference to another 'Herod' – 'Herod the Tetrarch'. This notice is referring to the 'prophets and teachers of the Church in Antioch'. Aside from Barnabas and Saul, these include someone referred to as 'Manaen, the foster brother of Herod the Tetrarch'. This is not the same 'Herod' as in chapter 12. Whatever one might wish to say about him, the fact of a Herodian member of the founding Community for Gentile Christianity in Antioch is embarrassing enough. Ultimately, if one drops what is probably another nonsense name, 'Manaen', and transfers the descriptive phrase 'the foster brother of Herod the Tetrarch' to Saul or Paul, one might have a more accurate description of the truth of the matter. When speaking about this 'Herod the Tetrarch', though, there can be little doubt that Acts means *Herod Antipas* (7–39 CE).

Antipas was one of the several Herods, sons of Herod the Great. By this time the family was referring to its members, much like all the '*Caesars*' (whom it was aping in more ways then one), as '*Herods*'. This Herod, along with Herod Archelaus (4 BCE–7 CE) whom we have already mentioned above in connection with the 4 BCE disturbances and the Census Uprising, was the son of Herod's Samaritan wife. He is the Herod responsible for John the Baptist's death and the one King Aretas in Transjordan went to war with because he had divorced his (Aretas') daughter to marry his (Antipas') niece Herodias. He also appears in Luke interviewing Jesus.

Herod the Great had numerous sons by some nine or ten different wives, only a few of whom could by any yardstick be reckoned as 'Jewish'. This will be an important problem for our period, not only as far as the Dead Sea Scrolls are concerned, but also for the Jerusalem Church, that is, who will be Jewish and what effect this perception has on the Jewish mass. If we take the Rabbinic delineation of this problem, the matrilineal yardstick – if your mother was Jewish, then you were Jewish – Herod did have at least two *Jewish* wives, both daughters of High Priests and both called Mariamme ('Miriam' or 'Mary').

The first Mariamme carried within her veins the last of the Maccabean Priest line. On both sides of her family she was of the blood of the heroic Maccabees, the Jewish High Priest line defunct after Herod. This in itself is a tragic enough story. Herod married her, seemingly by force, when he was besieging the Temple in 37 BCE. Ultimately he had her executed on the charge that she had been unfaithful with his brother Joseph (the original 'Joseph and Mary' story?). In time, Herod also executed his two sons by her, who had been educated in Rome, because he feared the Jewish crowd would put them on the Throne in his place – presumably because of their Maccabean blood – though not before they had reached majority and produced offspring of their own.

In a similar manner years before, he also had her brother, a youth named Jonathan (Aristobulus in Greek, that is, Aristobulus III – the Maccabees often combined Greek with Hebrew names), killed for the same reason when he came of age and was able to don the High Priestly robes. It was the assumption of the High Priesthood by this Jonathan that probably explains Mariamme's willingness to marry Herod in the first place. In one of the most tragic moments in Jewish history as we saw, Herod, like some modern Joseph Stalin or Adolf Hitler, had Jonathan drowned while frolicking in a pool at his winter palace outside Jericho – this after the Jewish crowd wept when the boy donned the High Priestly vestments of his ancestors. The time was 36 BCE after Herod had assumed full power in Palestine under Roman sponsorship as a semi-independent King, the preferred manner of Roman government in that recently acquired part of their Empire.

Herod, not being of Jewish blood or origins, might have been able to secure his kingship from the Romans in replacing the Maccabees as Jewish kings, but he was unable to secure their High Priesthood as well, however he might have wanted it. There can be little doubt that in arranging the marriage with Herod, theoretically forbidden under Jewish law (certainly as advocated by 'the Zealots'), those left in the Maccabean family aspired to rescue whatever remained of the fortunes of their family after thirty years of civil strife and war with Rome had so destroyed it.

Grateful to a fault, Herod proceeded to decimate the remainder of the Maccabean family, even that part of it that survived by subordinating itself to him and accommodating itself to Rome: first Jonathan; then Mariamme herself – though Josephus portrays Herod, soap-opera style, as being both in love with and hating her at the same time; then Hyrcanus II, Jonathan's grandfather from the generation of the 60s when the fraternal strife that resulted in foreign occupation began.

This Hyrcanus had been Judas Maccabee's great-grandnephew and had first introduced Herod's father Antipater to a position of power as his chief minister and go-between with the Romans and Arab/Idumaean power across the Jordan and in Petra. It was he who probably arranged Herod's marriage with Mariamme in the first place. As noted above, Herod then executed his own two sons by her – again probably for the same reasons – because the crowd, being nationalistic and Maccabean in sentiment, preferred them to him. Finally he executed Mariamme's mother and Hyrcanus' daughter, the wily old dowager Salome, who was the last to go besides these.[1] When Herod was done, there were no Maccabeans left, except third-generation claimants in his own family, whose blood had been severely cut by his own over three generations of cleverly crafted marriages.

The Marriage Policy of Herodians

The Herodians in the third generation – the time of John the Baptist – descended from Herod and the last Maccabean Princess Mariamme, were one-quarter Jewish. The other blood line that flowed into them was carefully crafted and Idumaean/Arab. Herod himself was primarily what today we would call 'Arab' in origin. In fact his behavior, particularly where sexual mores and marital practices are concerned, is still very much that of what might be called a typical Middle Eastern chieftain or potentate.

Herod pursued the policy for his descendants of *niece marriage* or marriage to *close family relatives*, usually cousins. This marital policy, roundly condemned in the Dead Sea Scrolls, is probably the key datum of the kind we called 'internal' – as opposed to 'external' – for dating Qumran documents. So obsessed are the Qumran documents with this kind of sexual and marital behavior that we have used this to insist that key documents making such complaints must be referring to a *Herodian Establishment.* There is no indication that Maccabeans previously, that is, before they were '*grafted*' to Herodians, indulged in this kind of behavior. For Herodians from 60 BCE onwards, this kind of behavior – considered 'incest' at Qumran – was a matter of actual family policy preserving their mastery in Palestine and elsewhere in Asia.

It is this kind of sexual behavior that will provoke the ire of leaders – now considered 'Christian' – such as John the Baptist against Herodians. The popular picture of a Salome dancing at Herod's *Birthday Party* is just scriptural tomfoolery, although as always in these instances, not without a seed of historical reality – in this case, the seed is the problem of Herodian family morals and their sexual practices that were objected to by all these Messianic leaders like John the Baptist and after him, presumably Jesus, whoever he was.

The picture, therefore, that we have in the Gospels of a Jesus eating with '*tax collectors and Sinners*' or speaking favorably about '*harlots*' or '*prostitutes*' is again just part of this casuistry.[2] Herodian Princesses, as we shall see, will be seen by the Jewish nationalistic mass as nothing better than 'harlots' or 'prostitutes' – Herodias is a case in point, but there will be others – and this issue, '*zanut*' or 'fornication', dominates the mindset of those responsible for the Dead Sea Scrolls, as it does early New Testament documents like the Letter of James – so much so as to appear like an obsession. We will also be able show that other nationalist leaders like the Simon mentioned in Josephus above, 'the Head of an Assembly' or 'Church' of his own in Jerusalem, will confront the Herodians in the Hellenistic centre of Caesarea on the marital practices of Herodians, in particular Herodian Princesses.

In this next generation – the fourth after the original Herod in the 40's–60s CE and the period James held sway in Jerusalem – the principal representatives of this line, now one-eighth Maccabean or Jewish, are three Herodian Princesses, two of whom make an appearance in chapters 24–26 of the Book of Acts, Bernice and Drusilla. Both of these princesses have been divorced. Both ultimately took up with foreigners and deserted Judaism altogether. Bernice was not only divorced, she married her uncle as well, Herod of Chalcis, her father Agrippa's brother. Agrippa II, her brother who becomes king in the 50s and 60s just preceding the Uprising, also appears in Acts on her arm chatting amicably with Paul in prison (25:13). This is perhaps the original for the intervening interview in the Gospels between Jesus and Herod the Tetrarch (Luke 23:7–12), who really would have had no business in Jerusalem, his Tetrarchy – literally his 'fourth' of the Kingdom – being in Galilee and across the Jordan in Perea where John the Baptist was executed.

Here it is possible to lay another sexual-mores charge at the feet of these Herodian Kings and Princesses, 'incest', the basis in any event of the 'niece-marriage' charge so striking in the Scrolls. 'Niece marriage', on the other hand, has never been an infraction for Talmudic Judaism, nor is it in Judaism succeeding to it to this day. The Scrolls also pointedly condemn marriage with close family cousins on the basis of a generalization of the Deuteronomic Law of incest, and Josephus tells us that it was reputed that Bernice actually had an incestuous relationship with her brother Agrippa II.[3] The picture in Acts does not gainsay this. In fact, to some extent it reinforces it.

Both Claudius and Caligula were reputed to be great friends of Agrippa I, who had been brought up with them in Augustus' Imperial Household in Rome after his father, the second of Mariamme's two sons by Herod had been dispatched by him in 7 BCE. These third and fourth Julio-Claudians restored the Throne to this particular line which had been denied Herod's descendants in the aftermath of the uprisings from 4 BC to 7 CE – the period in which the Gospels date the birth of Jesus. Therefore, the various tetrarchs, ethnarchs, and governors in the period till Agrippa I's re-emergence in 37 CE. This was the line, of course, with the original Maccabean royal blood which, however diluted, was obviously both meaningful and significant to the Romans.

Agrippa I was restored to the Throne of Palestine following the death of Tiberius, who had put him in prison because of his too-friendly relations with Caligula and Claudius. Importantly, too, his restoration also followed the removal of Pontius Pilate from Palestine – after complaints like those of Philo's about his extreme venality and brutality – in the year 37 CE, not long after the death of John the Baptist according to the timeframe of Josephus' *Antiquities*.

In the previous generation, Herodias had first been married to one non-Maccabean uncle – supposedly named 'Philip' in the New Testament, but actually named 'Herod'. After divorcing him, she married another Herodian uncle, descended from a non-Maccabean, Samaritan blood-line. This one, as we saw, Herod Antipas (7–39 CE), was the Herod known as 'Herod the Tetrarch' in the New Testament (Lk 3:19 and Acts 13:1) and the individual both Josephus and the Gospels blame for the death of John the Baptist.

For his part, John is pictured in the Gospels as objecting to Herodias' divorce and remarriage on the basis of an obscure point in Mosaic law – violating the law of levirite marriage, a point that might have appealed to someone taking his view of the Jews in Palestine from books (Mk 6:17 and pars.). It was permitted to marry one's brother's or half-brother's wife, if that individual was childless and one were, so to speak, 'raising up seed unto your brother' which would be counted for your brother's inheritance or posterity. For the New Testament, this was not the case, but there is nowhere any external proof of this.

In fact, the New Testament has the situation totally wrong here. The man it is calling 'Philip' is rather only called 'Herod' in Josephus. Actually, he had at least one daughter by Herodias, the famous 'Salome' (though she is not identified by name in the New Testament even though most people think she is. One has to go to Josephus to for this). The 'Philip' in Josephus is the Tetrarch of Trachonitis in Syria a little south of Damascus. He is *not Salome's father, but rather her husband*! It is he, Josephus specifically remarks, who dies childless, making way for Salome's next marriage to *her mother's brother's* son Aristobulus. But the Gospels, as we presently have them, have conflated all these things, producing what we today perceive as truth. So ingrained has this picture become that it is now automatic as well to speak of *two Philips* and this *Herod* as '*Herod Philip*'.

Actually, however, to the non-Roman, non-Hellenistic native eye, there were all these other sexual and marital infractions sufficient to explain John's objections to Herodias, in particular, her relations with *not one uncle, but two*, and her *self-divorce*, which even Josephus admits 'violated the Laws of our country'. This is the kind of 'divorce' the Dead Sea Scrolls so protest against and, no doubt, John the Baptist as well.

It would be legitimate to query at this point, why among all these Herodian progeny – and the Herodian family was beginning to resemble a vast network like some royal families in the Middle East in our own time – was Herodias so desirable that two uncles were intent on having her, even to the extent of shedding John's blood and fighting a war with the Arabian King Aretas of Petra because of her?

The answer is twofold. The first is that of all the various Herodian lines, this Maccabean one was the 'Richest' – a factor further highlighted by the wealth that came to her brother Agrippa after his appointment as actual 'King' by his boon companion Caligula. Josephus specifically calls Agrippa I's daughter, Bernice, one of the 'Richest' women in Palestine and Herodias probably was not far behind her where this was concerned.

This is another important theme in our texts, 'the polluted Evil Riches' of the Establishment, a theme along with 'fornication' which is again paramount in both the Scrolls and the Letter of James. It is also prominent in the Gospels and in Josephus, all purporting to be first-century texts. This is certainly the principal reason behind Herodias' attractiveness to less fortunate, collateral Herodian lines, such as those of Herod (in the Gospels, 'Philip'), the son of Herod's second wife by the name of Mariamme, and Antipas, only the son of his Samaritan wife. It was also no doubt an important reason for the involvement of the future Roman Emperor Titus with Bernice, Herodias' niece, as it no doubt was a century before for the various parvenu paramours of Cleopatra.

But there is a second reason as well, royal blood – in Cleopatra's case, stemming from those connected to Alexander the Great; in Herodias', the blood of the Maccabees in her veins. Apart from her 'Riches', this is sufficient to explain all this interest in developing a progeny-bearing relationship with her. But John the Baptist certainly would have had quite a few other objections besides 'Riches' that would have met the Qumran criteria for condemnation as 'unlawful' (Matt. 14:4). Where *fornication* was concerned, 'divorce', 'polygamy', 'niece marriage', and 'incest' – including the marriage of close cousins – and the Herodian family could certainly be accused of practicing most or all of these.

When the Letter of James objects to 'fornication', all of these aspects of what was considered 'fornication' in this period by documents like the Dead Sea Scrolls should be uppermost in the reader's mind. Where, of course, those with royal blood are concerned, the Temple Scroll, drawing on the Deuteronomic King Law, adds another – marriage to a foreigner, insisting that the King should marry once and only once in the lifetime of his wife and this only to a Jewish woman.[4]

It is interesting that for Matthew 21:32, 'John came to you in *the Way of Righteousness*, and *you did not believe him* [note the Pauline thrust here] but *the tax collectors and the harlots believed him'*. 'The Way of Righteousness' is, of course, a favorite Qumranism, but the true situation as far as John is concerned is rather *the opposite*. Aside from the joke of having 'the harlots believing' John (not to mention the travesty), if one understands that at this point the Roman tax collectors in Palestine were the Herodians, then the farcical thrust of this saying ascribed to Jesus in this supposedly *most Jewish* of all the Gospels is actually quite amusing. Those who inserted it into the Jewish *Messiah's* mouth, no doubt, had a most macabre sense of humor. The saying of Jesus from the Pseudoclementines about being able 'to detect false coin from true' begins to develop the force of a hammer-like blow.

James the Brother of John and Theudas

Either Agrippa I, then, or his brother Herod of Chalcis, would appear to be the 'Herod the King' in Acts, portrayed as 'stretching forth his hands to ill-treat some of those of the Assembly' or 'the Church' (12:1). In the very next sentence in Acts, this 'Herod the King' puts 'James *the brother of John* to death with the sword', leading up to James' first appearance just a few lines further in the text in the same chapter!

This 'beheading' (which is what is meant by 'putting to death with the sword') parallels one mentioned in Josephus already alluded to somewhat obliquely in Acts 5:36 – the execution of '*Theudas*'. This was in the course of the suppression of these various seditious and charismatic leaders and Messianic pretenders that Josephus considers so dangerous. In fact, Acts 5:36 uses the same Greek word for 'put to death' in referring to him as Acts 12:2 uses in referring to the 'beheading' of 'James the brother of John'.

If one looks at the Talmudic enumerations of the various Jewish kinds of execution of this period found in Tractate *Sanhedrin* of the *Mishnah*, one will find that beheading was applied in Jewish religious Law to cases of subversion, treachery, insurrectionary activities, or the like. Some of the other kinds of execution described in *Sanhedrin* are quite gruesome, including pouring rocks down on someone or forcing burning pitch down his throat, but however tendentious Talmudic materials can sometimes be, crucifixion was not one of them. In fact, crucifixion or its Jewish equivalent, '*hanging upon a tree*', was quite specifically forbidden under Jewish Law (Deut. 21:23).

For his part, Josephus mentions at least four important beheadings in this period from the time of the Maccabees to the fall of the Temple. The first two are Maccabeans trying to regain their Kingdom following Herod's takeover in 37 BCE, both sons of Aristobulus II.[5] The other two are Herod the Tetrarch's beheading of John the Baptist and the beheading of Theudas in the period of Herod of Chalcis and the Roman Governor Fadus (*c.* 45 CE).

Apart from the impersonal mass of crucifixions by the Romans up to the fall of the Temple, Josephus mentions two that stand out: Jesus' (if not an interpolation) and that of James and Simon, the two sons of Judas the Galilean, the founder of 'the Zealot Movement', who were executed a year or two after Theudas.

Of stonings, Josephus really only mentions those of Honi or Onias the Righteous, just before the Romans first assaulted the Temple in 63 BCE presaging Aristobulus II's downfall; James in 62 CE; and another son or grandson of Judas the Galilean, one Menachem, in the events surrounding the outbreak of the Uprising in 66 CE. Puerile as these authors in the Roman period often were, had there been others, Josephus probably could not have resisted telling us about them.

Both 'James the brother of John' in Acts and '*Theudas*' in *Antiquities* are executed around the same time by either the same individual or set of individuals and, regardless of Acts' agenda, one would assume for similar reasons. As we saw, Acts 5:36 uses the very same Greek allusion 'put to death' in referring to Theudas' execution as Acts 12:2 does in referring to 'James the brother of John'.

Theudas is an otherwise unknown individual. The reference to his execution in a speech put in the mouth of Paul's Pharisee teacher Gamaliel gives rise to the well-known anachronism in Acts 5. This, in turn, is tied to another deletion or oversight, the crucifixion of Judas the Galilean's two sons, James and Simon, which follows almost directly thereafter in Josephus' *Antiquities*. In Gamaliel's speech, Theudas is represented as somehow being related to the activities of Judas the Galilean, but arriving on the scene before him.

Judas the Galilean seems to have flourished from around the time of Herod's death in 4 BCE to 7 CE, the time of the Tax Uprising that brought Herod's son Archelaus' crisis-ridden reign to an end. With the banishment of Archelaus, the Romans imposed direct rule, via governors who were obedient – and answerable – to the Emperor and Senate, until the time of Agrippa I's emergence in 37 CE. The period in between not only turns out to be a period when we have a paucity of historical data compared to the ones just preceding and following it, but also the time identified by most as precisely that of Jesus' lifetime. As the author of the Book of Acts has Gamaliel euphemistically describe Judas the Galilean's death: 'After this one [Theudas], Judas the Galilean arose in the Days of the Census and led many people astray. He perished and all of them scattered' (5:37); but neither he nor Josephus tells us how or under what circumstances. Rather Josephus in the *Antiquities* again turns to the subject of Judas the Galilean when discussing the execution of '*James and Simon*, the sons of Judas the

Galilean ... who caused the people to revolt when Cyrenius came to take an accounting of the estates of the Jews'. This would make 'James and Simon' quite old, since, as he describes it, their crucifixion appears to take place coincident with the Famine ca. 46–8 CE (*Ant.* 20.101–2).

The Census of Cyrenius and the Sects of the Jews

The Census of Cyrenius, imposed after a series of uprisings led by Judas and other 'Messianic' leaders, which Archelaus (4 BCE–7 CE) was unable to control, is the event seized on as well by the author of Luke – the author also credited with Acts – to fix the date of Jesus' birth. This, of course, makes the birth of Jesus coincident with the birth of sectarian strife generally – in particular, what Josephus is calling the birth of the 'Zealot' Movement and what we would call the 'Messianic Movement'. Though the point of Luke's approach is to get Jesus to Bethlehem to be born, so much does it fly in the face of the parallel one in Matthew that nothing of certainty can be said with regard to Jesus' birth at all, neither the place, the date, nor the political and social circumstances.

For Luke, if not Matthew, Jesus' parents are already living in Galilee. But since David came from Bethlehem, in his view Jesus should be born there as well. Perhaps this was the popular religion, but there is no known prophecy specifically delineating such a requirement. In fact, further information regarding this requirement in John 7:42 has the crowd doubting Jesus' Bethlehem birth and therefore specifically denying that he comes from there. However this may be, the Lukan author uses the patently artificial stratagem of a Roman-imposed census to get Jesus' family back to Bethlehem from Galilee and to develop his very popular 'no room at the inn' scenario. As a result, the Christ-child, like the Oriental mystery-religion god Mithra before him, is born in a manger, a favorite biblical folk tale without any historical substance whatsoever.

But the Census of Cyrenius, referred to by Luke both in his Gospel and Acts, does have substance. Cyrenius was Governor of Syria, to whom the task fell to take an evaluation of the property of Palestine for taxation purposes in advance of the imposition of direct Roman rule following the removal of the inept Archelaus. Josephus refers to this on three occasions in his works, the last, as we saw, when discussing the execution of James and Simon, the two sons of Judas the Galilean, in the *Antiquities*. It is this execution in the year 48 CE that explains the anachronism in the speech attributed to Gamaliel in Acts – better still would be to Josephus, once one realizes that Acts' author(s), like many a Roman historian thereafter, was dependent on the latter (not to mention a few other sources).

The sequence in Acts 5:36–37 of Theudas, his revolt, Judas the Galilean, and the Census would follow that of Josephus in the *Antiquities* precisely, if we simply assume that Luke has for some reason left out the mention of the execution of Judas the Galilean's *two sons*, James and Simon. This would restore the proper chronological sequencing to the text and give us the mention of Theudas, followed by the mention of the execution of Judas the Galilean's two sons, followed by the explanation of who Judas was, namely, that he perished in the Census Uprising. As far as Jesus' birth is concerned, it is totally irrelevant to the Census (except perhaps symbolically); and Luke's story connecting the two, fictional in any event. Even Acts' order as it currently stands follows Josephus exactly, the only thing lacking being a few minor details that have dropped out or been deleted in the process of transmission or rewriting. Why the author left out the crucifixion of Judas the Galilean's two sons in the first place we shall most likely never know.

What is interesting, though, is that Josephus uses the Uprising led by Judas the Galilean as the springboard to describe the Jewish sects in the first century in both the *War* and the *Antiquities*. It is edifying to compare the two descriptions of these sects found in them. In the earlier one – triggered by the appearance of Judas the Galilean and the mention of the imposition of direct Roman rule through a governor who 'had the power to impose the death sentence' – Josephus describes the normal three sects: 'Pharisees', 'Sadducees', and 'Essenes', and lingers in loving detail over the last, a group he was evidently well acquainted with.[6]

He also describes a *fourth group* owing its origins to the activities of Judas the Galilean and the teacher he identifies only by the puzzling sobriquet '*Saddok*'. Obviously it is in order to describe this 'Fourth Philosophy' of Judas the Galilean that he launches into his discussion of the sects at this point in the *Jewish War*. But though he promises to tell us about this group, he does not. Rather, he lingers over the Essenes in loving detail.

His descriptions of both Sadducees and Pharisees are cursory in the extreme, though they too have been picked up in the New Testament and used to characterize these groups. In the *Antiquities*, however, he makes good the omission, describing the ills associated with the Movement led by Judas and *Saddok* in great detail. This Movement, according to him, 'led our people to destruction', because 'our young people were zealous for it' (*Ant.* 18.10). As we have suggested, there can be little doubt that what he is describing is *the Messianic Movement* in Palestine. Others might call it 'the Zealot Movement', but Josephus never uses this terminology until after the Uprising and the killing of all the High Priests, particularly James' destroyer Ananus in 68 CE. In fact, he never names it at all, except tantalizingly as 'the Fourth Philosophy'.

What he does do, however, is sharply curtail his description of 'the Essenes' in the *War* and take part of it and add it to his description of the Movement initiated by Judas and *Saddok* in the *Antiquities*. This is the moment Luke chooses to date the birth of Christ. In line with his Establishment sensibilities and pro-Roman sympathies, Josephus rails against the leaders of movements such as this, as we saw too, as 'impostors and Deceivers', worse 'even than the bandits and murderers' that infested the country in this period – worse, because not only did they deceive the people, but they strove to bring about religious innovation and revolutionary change. Most often these disturbances took place at Passover time – probably because this could be looked upon as the Jewish National Liberation Festival when Moses led the ragtag group of former Jewish slaves out into the wilderness and not only gave them freedom and the Law, but produced a nation.

Judas the Brother of James and Theudas

It is precisely in this manner that Josephus describes – disapprovingly of course – the '*Theudas*' whose death parallels that of '*James the brother of John*' in Acts 12. Calling him an '*impostor*', in the sense of being a '*false prophet*' or '*Deceiver*', Josephus insists that he actually claimed to be 'a Prophet' and miracle-worker, and on this basis persuaded 'Many' (an important usage in the Dead Sea Scrolls) to follow him out into the wilderness, where he said he would part the Jordan River. In the Book of Joshua, Joshua is described as parting the Jordan River – just as Moses parted the Red Sea – when he led the people of Israel into the Promised Land 'dry-shod' (Josh. 3:13).

Evidently meant to be a Joshua *redivivus*, a Joshua brought-back-to-life or a Joshua incarnated, Theudas is reversing this and leading the people back out into the wilderness. When one appreciates that the name 'Jesus' is a Hellenized version of the name Joshua ('he who saves'), then one can appreciate that Theudas is a *Jesus redivivus* as well. Jesus goes out into the wilderness to confront the Devil or multiply loaves; Theudas, to part the Jordan River in reverse. For his troubles, his followers were decimated by Roman soldiers and he was *beheaded.*

The name 'Theudas' is a mystery. In the Greek – the only form in which we have it – it resembles the name 'Judas'. In our view, it is also a parallel to that character who in two

Apostle lists is called 'Thaddaeus'.[7] This character will turn out sometimes to be called 'Judas of James' or 'Judas the brother of James' and, as we shall further develop below, we would identify him as *the third brother of Jesus*, probably the person other sources call 'Judas Thomas'. The claim implicit in the name, 'Judas Thomas', is that he is a 'twin', '*thoma*' in Aramaic meaning 'twin'. The implication usually is that he is a twin of Jesus, his *third brother*, 'Jude' or 'Judas'. We would go further, considering 'Theudas' to be either a garbled form or conflation/contraction of the two names 'Judas' and 'Thomas'.

For the purposes of the argument or discussion, let us assume this to be the case. One can now see the importance of the 'brother' theme in the Book of Acts, only this time we are not dealing with a 'brother of John' or even another 'James' but, rather, the *third* brother of Jesus – that is, *Judas the brother of James* – seen here by the text as a Joshua or Jesus *redivivus*. Again, the theme of beheading and the chronology are approximately right. We are somewhere in the period of Agrippa I or Herod of Chalcis, around 44–45 CE.

Let us also for the purposes of argument assume that 'James', the so-called 'son of Zebedee', is an editorial gloss. Not only does Acts necessarily have to remove him at this point in order to make way for the appearance of James the Just the brother of Jesus, *the real James*, but what we have here in Acts are the faint traces of the real event just beneath the surface of the fictional one.

To put this another way, there *was* another brother of Jesus called 'Jude' or 'Judas'. In some texts this brother is alluded to as 'Judas Thomas', either evoking an actual twinship or the Joshua/Jesus *redivivus* theme of Josephus' narrative. And there *really* was a brother eliminated at this time, but this brother was not 'James the brother of John', but the lesser known, but probably more real, 'Judas of James' – 'Jude the brother of James' referred to in the letter by that name. That such a brother really did exist and produced offspring continuing down into the period of Vespasian, Domitian, and Trajan is also confirmed for us in Eusebius. Using Hegesippus, Eusebius refers to the offspring of one 'Judas called the brother of our Lord according to the flesh', one in the time of Domitian and one right before he describes the martyrdom of Simeon bar Cleophas – 'the cousin of our Lord' – in Trajan's time.[8] At this point Eusebius acknowledges that Simeon's mother was Mary and his father Cleophas, quoting Scripture. Still he cannot yet bring himself to admit that Simeon was a brother too, that is, Jesus' *second brother Simon*, but rather only 'of the family' or 'the relatives' of Jesus.

By the 90s these descendants of Jesus' third brother Judas are only simple farmers. Eusebius reports that Domitian (81–96), like his father Vespasian before him, attempted to round up all those people considered to be of the genealogy of David. Among these were the grandchildren of Judas. When questioned about the nature of 'Christ and his Kingdom', they replied it was not an earthly one, but celestial and Angelic – but that at the end of the world, he (the Messiah) would appear 'to give to everyone according to his *works*'. Thereupon Domitian purportedly dismissed them as simpletons. They were reported to have continued living until the time of Trajan (98–117).

There is one more link in this chain, and that comes in the documents from Nag Hammadi. Here in two previously unknown Apocalypses attributed to the person of James, an individual named '*Addai*', again obviously linked etymologically to the name of '*Thaddaeus*', is referred to, as well as another, '*Theuda*', paralleling him and referred to as 'the father' or 'brother of the Just One', that is, Jesus or even possibly James. We believe this also to be the implication of the author of the Book of Acts. Once one begins to appreciate Acts' working method and its evasiveness, much else becomes clear in the early history of Christianity.

The First Appearance of James

Acts portrays these kinds of seditious or subversive events, which lead up to the first appearance of James in 12:17, as occurring during 'the Days of the Unleavened Bread', that is, Passover time. 'Herod', who at this point beheads 'James the brother of John', goes on to imprison Peter, because the beheading of this other James 'so pleased the Jews' (*thus*), intending to put him on trial at the end of the Passover week (Acts 12:3). This is the kind of tendentious aside that so characterizes Acts and the Gospels.

In any event, Acts goes on to describe a miraculous escape by Peter from prison with the help of an Angel (12:5–10). This escape has interesting parallels with one later offered Paul (Acts 16:25–34). In this later episode, calculated to show the moral superiority of the Apostle to the Gentiles over this archetypically Jewish Apostle, Paul *refuses to escape* out of concern for the welfare of the guards, mindful of the fact that earlier those designated to guard Peter were executed after he escaped (12:19). However this may be, Peter's escape is used to explain why he no longer functions in Palestine or in Jerusalem. He is forced to flee, but not before James is, at last, introduced in 12:17 and Peter goes to a house in Jerusalem to inform him of his departure. This, at least, might bear some semblance of the truth.

The chapter ends with the death of this 'Herod', normally taken to be the death of Agrippa I in 44 CE (12:20–23). The indications are that because of Agrippa I's growing imperial ambitions in the East, which were unacceptable, his Roman overlords arranged to have him poisoned. Josephus portrays Agrippa, much like his patron Caligula, collapsing in a seizure while dressed in gold leaf – presumably like Apollo or the sun – and giving a theatrical performance of some kind (*Ant.* 19.343–52). Acts portrays him being struck down by an Angel because he looked so magnificent that people mistook him for a god.

The house in Jerusalem where Peter goes 'to leave a message for James and the brothers' is pictured as being that of 'Mary mother of 'John Mark', who is mentioned again in Acts as the man who deserted the mission of Barnabas and Paul in Pamphylia (15:37–39). In Acts 13:13 he is simply called 'John', and there is no hint of the bitterness evinced by Paul towards him in 15:39. Elsewhere, he would appear to be identified with the Gospel of Mark and Eusebius knows him as Peter's traveling companion.[9] We were not aware that he had a mother called 'Mary'. Nor that he had a 'house' in Jerusalem in which *Mary lived.* Plus, it would seem not a little strange to go to a house where 'Mary mother of John Mark' lived to leave a message for *James the brother of Jesus* and the *other brothers*. It is simpler just to think that the text originally said 'the house of Mary *the mother of Jesus*' or 'Mary *the mother of James the Just*' or 'Mary *the wife of Cleophas*', and that this somewhat enigmatic substitution has taken place – and so it has remained to be enshrined in seventeen–eighteen centuries of pious history.

But it will not stand up to investigation. One can simply dismiss it as either pious fiction or look at it more deeply and attempt to make out the main lines of the original. We prefer the latter, and we do so on the basis of what seems the simplest and most reasonable under the circumstances. Acts is not *simply* pure fiction. There is real truth lying behind its substitutions or overwrites and the key often is *the family of Jesus*, in particular James, and how they are treated. Here, it is useful to observe that after the attack on James by Paul in the Pseudoclementine *Recognitions*, James is actually carried to his 'house' in Jerusalem. In the same vein in the Gospel of John, Jesus instructs 'the Disciple he loved' – always unidentified – *from the Cross* no less, to take Mary 'into his own home' (obviously in Jerusalem) and be her '*son*' (19:26–27). This is just following the passage in which Mary is identified as 'the sister of his mother Mary (wife) of Clopas' (19:25). This is precisely how this phrase appears in the Greek.

The reference in Acts 12:17 to 'brothers' is interesting as well. One can take these 'brothers' as brothers in the generic sense, that is, communal brothers, or the like, which is how it is usually taken. Or, since we are following the traces of 'the brothers' in this work, it is possible to take them as 'brothers' in the specific sense, meaning James and the other brothers of Jesus. The first is more likely, but one should always keep in mind the possibility of the second, since Peter has gone to 'Mary the mother of' someone's house to leave a message 'for James and the brothers' – otherwise unexplained.

These kinds of persecutions, too, we can take as authentic. Individuals like Theudas or Judas – Jesus' brother – really did lose their lives. But in Acts' portrayal, the reasons for these persecutions become rather distorted. For instance, in Acts the Jewish crowd is pleased by 'the beheading of James' – that is, in our view, '*Theudas*' – and in the picture of 'Herod' there, being encouraged to take the further step of imprisoning Peter, once again we have the slight lateral movement in the portrayal of these things already signaled in Josephus' critique of the historians of this period.

Of course, the later theology of the Gentile Church is now being retrospectively read back into the history of Palestine as the cause of all the repressions these early members of the Messianic Movement or the 'Jerusalem Community' in Palestine are undergoing. This vituperative theology is fully developed in Eusebius' works by the fourth century, but it is already highly developed in the second and third. But the real reason for these trials has to do with this constant revolutionary and religious strife, which, as Josephus documents, made its appearance with the Movement begun by Judas and *Saddok* at the time of the Census Uprising. These charismatic and religious leaders that punctuate the history of the next 135 years are all in one way or another connected with this Movement for political and religious freedom.

Take, for example, the appearance of another individual a decade or so after the beheading of Theudas, whom Josephus also designates as 'a prophet' and who so resembles 'Jesus' in Scripture. Josephus describes this type of 'Impostor' or 'Deceiver' with amazing perspicuity. As a lead-in to introducing this *prophet*, he says that these '*Impostors* and *Deceivers* called upon the people to follow them into *the wilderness*, there to show them unmistakable wonders and signs, that would be performed in accordance with the providence of God' (*Ant.* 20.168–72). In the Slavonic Josephus, these signs are called the '*signs of their impending freedom*'.

The individual in this episode is designated by no epithet other than 'the Egyptian'. Again he wants to do another 'Joshua'- or 'Jesus'-like miracle, commanding the walls of Jerusalem to fall down and allow his followers to enter the city and presumably liberate it. This *Egyptian* escapes, but 400 of his followers are butchered by the Roman Governor Felix (52–60 CE). For Acts the number grows to 4000 and his followers are specifically called '*Sicarii*'.

In Acts' version of the strife in Jerusalem, repression of theological dissidents of the Pauline kind is substituted for repression of revolutionaries in Josephus, and the consonant pro-Roman and anti-Palestinian theology we know developed. As noted above, Acts' author at this point frames the reference to James as if he had already introduced him. Of course, in Acts in its present form, he did not, but this is not to say that in the source underlying Acts he didn't. I think we will eventually be able to show that he did.

He must have. It is not possible that James suddenly erupts into the text in the same chapter in which the other James is removed and the notice as it now exists assumes that we know who he is. The text as we have it does not say that Peter went to the house of Mary to leave a message for James the Just, Mary's son, called the brother of Jesus. Nor does it, then, go on to delineate who this James was, which would have been normal if he had not previously been mentioned. No, it treats James as *known* – and he *was known*. We will be able to show, when analyzing early Church sources and the Pseudoclementine *Recognitions*, that James was indeed mentioned earlier – probably on several occasions – but the traces have been overwritten with more obscurantist story-telling or mythologizing.

One of the places in Acts James would have been mentioned earlier would have been in the various comings and goings on the Temple Mount, where Peter and John are mentioned, but no James (3:1–11). This is surprising. These lacunae are made good in the Pseudoclementine *Recognitions*, where in the parallel material having to do with these early comings and goings on the Temple Mount, the *real James* – our James – is mentioned extensively.

In addition, James would have been mentioned in the first chapter of Acts, where the most important matter facing the incipient Church would have been regulated – that is, choosing the *successor* to the departed Jesus. Here the choosing of James as Leader of the Jerusalem Community would have been described. Instead, a more folkloric history takes its place, which purports to tell the story of what became of the individual who *betrayed Jesus* named 'Judas' – also the name of *the third brother of Jesus*. It is, rather, Judas' end that is depicted in Acts in the most lurid detail – this and how the matter of *succession to Judas* was regulated.

Then, too, James was probably mentioned a little prior to the material in chapter 12 about Peter and James, which is paralleled by an episode in the Pseudoclementine *Recognitions*, after James is attacked by Paul in the Temple, describing how James sends off Peter from the Jericho area to confront Simon *Magus* in Caesarea. According to Acts' chronology, this would be following the mention of Theudas and Judas the Galilean in chapter 5 and the story of the stoning of Stephen that follows in chapters 6–7 – itself probably replacing this attack on James.

Of course, there is no good reason *to stone* this 'Stephen' and we will show that this episode actually replaces a different one, also preserved in the Pseudoclementine *Recognitions,* about Paul's activities prior to his famous vision on the road to Damascus. This episode will have to do with an actual physical assault by Paul on the Leader of the Community, James. This attack ended in grave injury to James – but not death – and his flight, together with most of the members of his Community, to somewhere in the Jericho area – that is, somewhere in the *neighborhood of Qumran*. The substitution here will follow the same *modus operandi* as some of the other substitutions and overwrites we are noting here, but the main lines of the original materials are still discernible underneath.

Finally, there is the matter of the crucifixion of the two sons of Judas the Galilean, James and Simon, during the Procuratorship of Tiberius Alexander (46–48 CE). This crucifixion, which is a curious one, is also important. In Josephus, it follows the mention of the Famine, the Theudas episode, and the description of the appointment of Tiberius Alexander as procurator.

In an execution resembling both Jesus' and that of John the Baptist, Tiberius Alexander ordered that these two sons of Judas the Galilean be crucified. Here, as we have seen, Josephus mentions Judas the Galilean, who caused the people to revolt at the time of the Census, which forms the basis of the parallel notice in Acts. But why Alexander had these two crucified and what they had done to deserve such punishment, Josephus never explains. In addition, the parallels between the Messianic-style families of Judas the Galilean and that family purportedly stemming from either 'Joseph and Mary' or Cleophas and Mary remain striking. What are the connections between these two clusters of Messianic individuals and in what manner do they overlap? Short of an undoctored presentation of this period we shall undoubtedly never know.

Jewish 66-70 CE Revolutionary Coins showing Amphora and Palm Tree (cf. Vespasian's Judea Capta Coin, p. 5 above)

Chapter 7
The Picture of James in Paul's Letters

James as Leader of the Early Church in Galatians

Paul gives us the most vivid and accurate first-hand account of the preeminence of James in the early Church in Galatians. Paul's antagonism to those in the 'Assembly' in Jerusalem, whom he feels are misguided and persecuting him, is patent. As an admittedly lesser being in a hierarchical organization, he exhibits a certain amount of formal deference to these leaders: 'those reckoned to be something' (Gal. 2:6) or 'recommending themselves, measuring themselves by themselves' (2 Cor. 10:12.), among whom he would include James. In fact, as Paul's tirades in these letters develop, it becomes very clear that, not only is James principal among them, but Paul's respect for the Jerusalem Leadership is only superficial – nothing more.

Actually, he refers to this leadership in the most biting terms. In describing his flight from Judea to Syria and Cilicia in Galatians – locales always important when considering the extent of Herodian family influence in the East – he insists that he will 'not give in or be subjected to those *false brothers* who spy on the freedom we enjoy in Christ Jesus, *so that they might enslave us*' (Gal. 2:4–5). The 'freedom' he is talking about is *freedom from the Law*; the 'slavery', both enslavement to it and the Jerusalem Leadership – the 'we' referring here to his communities. The 'spying' has to do not only with this freedom, but also probably, quite literally, their nakedness (or, as Qumran would have it, 'looking on their privy parts'), that is, to see whether they were circumcised or not.[1]

It is in these passages, which end in an insistence that he 'does not lie' – again important for parallel Qumran aspersions on a person known there as 'the Liar' – that he describes how he first 'made Peter's acquaintance' and 'saw none of the *other Apostles except James the brother of the Lord*' (Gal. 1:18- 20). In doing so, Paul states categorically that he did not 'go up again to Jerusalem for fourteen years' (2:1), which completely contradicts both chronological and factual claims in Acts. The latter describes Paul returning to Jerusalem 'in the time of Claudius' as part of famine-relief activities (11:28–30). This is the one in 46–8 CE that we have just highlighted with regard to the anachronism involving Judas the Galilean's two sons. These famine-relief activities parallel those of another new convert from these Eastern regions, the legendary Queen Helen of Adiabene. For the moment, the reader can take it as a rule of thumb that where there is a conflict between Paul's letters and Acts, the letters are to be preferred.

Paul's Relations with the Jerusalem Leadership and the Pillar Terminology

Paul explains this second visit to Jerusalem extremely defensively as being a result of a private 'revelation' he had, establishing as well that, as he sees it, he had not *been summoned* to give an account of himself, as it might appear to less sympathetic eyes. In doing so, Paul claims a *private* 'revelation'; through it, he would appear to think that he is in direct communication with 'Christ Jesus'. He states this in another way in the very first line of the letter: 'Paul, Apostle, not from *men*, nor through [any] *man*, but rather through Jesus Christ and by God [the] Father, who raised him from [the] dead'. The point here is that he was neither appointed by any 'man', nor the earthly Jesus, whom he never met, nor, for instance, the Elders of the Jerusalem Church. Nor does he carry any letters of appointment from such men (2 Cor. 3:1), but is beyond temporal authority, and not beholden to it.

In particular, he is not beholden to James or the Jerusalem Church Leadership. He is prepared to discuss things with them, but not to defer to them. He makes this clear when he says that he was not called to account by them, but met 'privately', on his own recognizance as it were, to lay before those he speaks of as being 'of repute' (Gal. 2:2) or, sarcastically, as 'considered to be something' (2:6), the Gospel as he proclaimed it 'among the Gentiles', for fear that the course he 'was running or had already run' would be 'in vain'. It is clear that what he means is that he is fearful that the leaders in Jerusalem might disavow the Gospel as he has already started teaching it – obviously without their permission – among the non-Jewish or Gentile 'Peoples'.

At this point he begins to grow extremely agitated about this interview with the Jerusalem Leadership and starts to defend his doctrine that Gentiles coming into the new Movement – whatever one wants to make of it at this point – need not be circumcised. This was evidently part of 'the Gospel' as he taught it among '*the Peoples*' or '*Nations*'. Introducing someone who accompanied him to this interview – now often referred to as 'the Jerusalem Council' – as Titus 'a Greek', Paul insists that on this account Titus was not 'required to be circumcised' (2:2–3).

Much of the rest of the letter has to do with Paul's antagonism to the group he calls 'of the circumcision', even perhaps, 'the circumcisers', a party of people he actually identifies with James (2:12) and an issue he identifies with 'slavery versus freedom' – in this sense, 'slavery to the Law', the sign of which was circumcision, and, conjointly, a slavish adherence to the instructions of the Jerusalem Leadership.

In due course he concludes: '*Stand fast in the freedom with which Christ made us free*, and do not [submit] again to *the yoke of slavery* ... Everyone who accepts circumcision is obliged *to do the whole Law*. Whosoever is justified by the Law *are set aside from the Christ*. You fell from Grace' (Gal. 5:1–4). Here, one has a clear play on the kind of 'setting oneself apart' or 'separation' emphasized in the Dead Sea Scrolls or the 'Naziritism', based on the Hebrew root, *N–Z–R*/'to keep apart from', we shall encounter on the part of those like James. Words with this *N–Z–R* root are widespread in the Damascus Document and there are used to express what one should 'stay away' or 'abstain from', as for instance, 'fornication', 'polluted Evil Riches', and 'unclean' or 'polluted things' generally.[2] 'For in Christ Jesus, neither circumcision nor uncircumcision is in force, but rather Faith working by love. You were *running* well. Who stopped you, that you did not obey the Truth?' (Gal. 5:6–7). One should compare this with the passage in the Letter of James: 'For whoever shall keep the whole Law, but stumbles on one [small point], shall be guilty [of breaking] it all' (Jas. 2:10). Not only does James use all the words Paul is using, like 'love', 'doing', and 'Truth', it is the clear riposte.

For his part, so incensed does Paul become at this point in Galatians that he concludes by making a pun on the act of circumcision itself: 'I even wish that those who are throwing you into confusion would themselves [meaning their own privy parts] *cut off*' (5:12). Paul utters this crudity, not only in the midst of again evoking 'being called to freedom', but the Love Commandment, that is, 'love your neighbor as yourself, which he now describes as being 'the whole Law' (5:12–14). But this is precisely the Commandment cited in the famous passage from James on 'the Royal Law according to the Scripture', also evoking 'doing', but this time in the sense of 'doing' or 'keeping the whole Law', not breaking it (2:8–10). This Commandment is also evoked at a crucial juncture in these passages in the Damascus Document as well.

Paul is having problems with the Jerusalem leadership over circumcision, because as he attests in his own words, 'some *false brothers* stole in secretly to spy on the freedom which we enjoy in Christ Jesus (Paul's name for his Supernatural Savior) so that they might reduce us to slavery' or 'bondage'. The *brothers/pseudo-brothers* parallel may be identical to the play on 'false' or 'pseudo-Apostles' in 2 Cor. 11:13, also in the context of 'bondage' and reiterating that he 'does not lie' (2 Cor. 11:20 and 31). Once again, despite the emotion he displays, Paul's meaning in these passages is unmistakable. When speaking about the Law or James, he uses the language of 'slavery' and 'falseness'.

Something has happened that has put Paul into bad repute with the leadership. That something clearly has to do with circumcision and the fact that some of those accompanying him were not circumcised. For Acts, Paul has such persons circumcised anyhow out of deference to the Church Leadership and in order to continue his missionary activities. We cannot necessarily depend on Acts here, but its gist is the same as Galatians on the issue of whether people like Titus or Timothy need to be circumcised. Galatians appears to be claiming Titus was not. Acts avers Timothy was. It is of little importance – the issue is the same.

Rather what is important is that at this point in Galatians Paul launches into an attack on the Jerusalem Leadership, in which he testifies to the undeniable fact that James was the principal leader and all, even Peter, were subordinate to him and had to defer to him. At the same time, he avows his intention to safeguard 'the Truth of the Gospel' as he teaches it among the Gentiles. As he puts it, 'not even for an hour did we yield in subjection, so that the Truth of the Gospel might continue with you' (2:5), this addressed to those for whom the letter was first intended, his coreligionists in Galatia in Asia Minor, whose situation he claims to be defending.

Paul then moves on to introduce his version of the Central Leadership Trio of the early Church in Jerusalem, and with it, another conundrum, for he does not refer – at least in most versions of this material as it has come down to us – to Peter *per se*, but rather at this point to 'Cephas'. Normally 'Cephas' is taken as identical with Peter, even though Paul resumes the normative reference to 'Peter' two lines later in 2:11. In doing so, he introduces James for the second time and it is crystal clear *this* James is not 'the brother of John' as in the Gospels. 'So James, Cephas, and John, those reckoned to be Pillars, being aware of the Grace which was given to me, shook hands with Barnabas and me in fellowship, that we [should go] to the Gentiles, while they [go] to the circumcision' (2:9).

Here, then, we are not only apprised that James is someone 'reckoned to be something', but one of those in the front rank of the leadership, as it were a 'Pillar' or leader, in fact, as we shall see, the *all-encompassing Leader*. Paul has already belittled these in his aspersion, 'whatever they were makes no difference to me' and 'those reckoned important conferred nothing to me'. In 2 Corinthians 11, Paul will call such persons 'Hebrews' (11:22) and 'the Highest Apostles' – literally 'Apostles of the Highest Degree' or, if one prefers, 'Archapostles' (11:5, repeated in 12:11).

Paul introduces this 'Pillar' terminology here, something we had not heard previously, in confirmation of their importance or status. It is similar to the 'Foundation', 'Rock' and 'Cornerstone' imagery one encounters in the Gospels and Letters with regard to Peter or Jesus himself. These terms can be found in the Dead Sea Scrolls, particularly in the Community Rule and Hymns, including additional ones like 'a firm Foundation which will not shake', 'Wall, and 'Tower' or 'Fortress'.[3] Where the idea of 'Pillar' is concerned, it is also in use in relation to the person of 'the *Zaddik*' in that tradition known as *Kabbalah.*

The allusion 'Pillar' certainly was originally used in Proverbs, which specifically asserts that 'the *Zaddik* is the Pillar of the World' (Prov. 10:25). In turn, this idea is expounded in *Zohar* tradition, where it is associated with Noah, the first '*Zaddik*' mentioned in the Book of Genesis and, in fact, the first archetypal Savior. The exposition is as follows:

> *Noah was a Righteous One.* Assuredly so after the Heavenly pattern, for it is written: '*The Righteous One is the Foundation of the world*' and the Earth is established thereon. For, this is *the Pillar that upholds the world.* So Noah was called *Righteous in this world …*

> and acted so as to be a Perfect copy of the Heavenly ideal ... an embodiment of the world's *Covenant of Peace.* (*Zohar* 1.59b on *Noah*)

There is much more in the *Zohar* on 'the *Zaddik*', including both an allusion to 'protecting the People', an idea just encountered above having to do with James' 'Bulwark' sobriquet and Noah's expiatory suffering.[4] The connection of James with Noah, the first 'Righteous One', is another element that shines through the traditions about James. These include James' vegetarianism, his rainmaking, and his Noahic-like directives to overseas communities as recorded in Acts, to the extent that one can conceive of a *redivivus* tradition associated with the first '*Zaddik*' Noah, not unlike that associated with Elijah and John the Baptist in the New Testament.

In this passage from the *Zohar*, the pre-existence or supernatural nature of 'the *Zaddik*' is stressed, an idea encountered as well in the Prologue of the Gospel of John in terms of '*Logos*' and 'Light' imagery, in the description of Jesus' entrance into the world. But there is another allusion in the recently rediscovered Nag Hammadi Gospel of Thomas – 'the Twin' or 'Judas Thomas' – the putative third brother of Jesus after James and Simon. This bears on the ideal of this pre-existent *Righteous One* or Heavenly *Zaddik* – in more mundane terms, James in his role as *Perfect Righteous One.* In turn this also bears on the appointment of James as Leader of the Jerusalem Church and therefore of all Christianity everywhere as successor to Jesus. It reads as follows: 'The Disciples said to Jesus: "We know that you will depart from us. Who is it that shall be great over us [meaning after he is gone]?" Jesus replied to them: "In the place where you are to go [presumably Jerusalem], go to James the Just, *for whose sake Heaven and Earth came into existence'* (Logion 12).

Aside from being a tradition incorporating the long-lost direct appointment of James by Jesus as Leader of the early Church, it also bears on the idea of 'the *Zaddik*'. Yet it is a thousand years earlier than the above description in the *Zohar*, which was purportedly written in Spain in the 1200s–1300s. Thomas' description of James as 'for whose sake Heaven and Earth came into existence' is related to the one in the *Zohar* about the *Zaddik* being 'the Pillar that upholds the world ... a Perfect copy of the Heavenly ideal'. Not only is it a statement about the pre-existence of the *Zaddik*, it bears on Paul's allusion to 'those reputed to be Pillars' in Galatians 2:9 and later allusions in early Church tradition like the mysterious '*Oblias*' or '*Bulwark*' applied to James. That 'James the Righteous One' is someone for whose sake 'Heaven and Earth came into existence' means that not only are Heaven and Earth predicated on his existence but, as 'the *Zaddik*', he precedes them or is pre-existent.

Noah the First *Zaddik* and Abraham's *Ten Just Men*

There is another tradition associated with the pre-existent *Zaddik* or 'Standing One' in Jewish *Kabbalah*, that is, the legend of 'the Ten Just Men', augmented in later tradition to thirty-six.[5] The tradition is, in fact, a *Noahic*-style one, similar to the one about James as 'Pillar'. Its implications are that the world is supported upon the existence of 'Ten Just Men' – *the Ten primordial Righteous Ones* – and, just as in the *Zohar* tradition about the first *Zaddik* Noah, it is their existence that *upholds the world.*

Actually, in Genesis, there are two 'escape' and 'Salvation' episodes of this kind related to 'Righteous Ones'. The first is the Noah episode where Noah is designated as 'Righteous and Perfect in his generation' (Gen. 6:9). This allusion is also the basis of the 'Perfection' ideal so important, for instance, in the Sermon on the Mount (Matt. 5:48) and for Dead Sea Scroll ideology. It is, no doubt, related to the perception of James' *Perfect Righteousness* and *Piety* as well. Because Noah is so *Perfect* and a *Righteous One*, God is portrayed as saving him and, through this Salvation, allowing him to save the world through his progeny – 'the world below' as the *Zohar* would have it.

The second 'escape' and 'Salvation' episode in Genesis is that of Lot. This is a famous episode, but not everyone realizes it is an episode having to do with the role and nature of 'the *Zaddik*' again. After having encountered three Angels who announce that he and Sarah are going to have a son, Abraham remains with one of these Angels (who later turns out to be God – Gen. 18:22). The other two go down to see how Abraham's nephew Lot is doing in the plain below in Sodom and Gomorrah.

Finding these cities to be full of fornication and illicit sexual behavior – the sexual emphasis in relation to a story about *Zaddikim* (Hebrew plural for *Zaddik*) is important – God determines to destroy these cities. At this point there transpires a bargaining scene between Abraham and God. Abraham asks God to withhold destruction from the city, that is, he intercedes with God on behalf of mankind. God agrees, but only on the basis that there should be found there fifty Just Men, that is, fifty *Righteous Ones*. Abraham asks for forty. God agrees. The bargaining goes on. Finally, it is determined that for the sake of 'Ten Just Men' God will withhold destruction from the city. This number becomes proverbial. In time it also becomes the minimum number required for Jewish communal prayer, the two, no doubt, being seen as connected, that is, the prayer of *Ten Righteous Men* can in some manner provide sustaining power to the world.

Somehow the number here is augmented in Jewish mystical tradition to thirty-six (the numerical value in Judaism of the word *life*). Its bearing, however, on the situation of James and, later, his relationship to the city of Jerusalem, will become clear. James in his role as 'Pillar', 'Wall', or 'Bulwark'/'Shield' will provide the sustaining 'Protection' required to guarantee *Jerusalem's* continued existence – Jerusalem being substituted for Sodom.

The concomitant to this is, of course, that once 'the *Zaddik*' – in this case James – was removed, existence of the city could no longer be sustained and its destruction was assured. Even in the circumscribed materials that have come down to us, the destruction of the Temple and Jerusalem some seven-and-a-half years later by Roman armies was tied by exegetes to his death. In the context of '*Zaddik*' theorizing, the sense of this is not punishment, as per later *Christian* reformulation, but once the requisite 'Shield' or 'Protection', James, had been removed, Jerusalem could no longer remain in existence.

Paul's Picture of the Central Three, James, Cephas, and John

In one of the most meaningful statements in Christian religious history, Paul describes a stay he made in Arabia and his later return to Damascus – whatever might be meant by these geographical notations at this point – and identifies James as follows:

> But when it pleased God, who *chose me from my mother's womb* and called me by His Grace to *reveal His son in me*, that I should announce him as the Gospel among the Nations, I did not immediately confer with *any human being*, nor did I go up to Jerusalem to those who were Apostles before me. Rather *I went away into Arabia* and again *returned to Damascus*. Then after three years I went up to Jerusalem to make the acquaintance of Peter and I remained with him *fifteen days*. Nor did I see any of *the other Apostles except James the brother of the Lord*. Now the things I write you are *true, for before God, I do not lie*. (Gal. 1:15–20)

We have in these sentences some of the most important historical data of early Christianity. First of all, in counter-indicating Acts' presentation, they reveal that document to be defective on these points and a not very artfully concealed rewrite. Secondly, they introduce *the really important James* in no uncertain terms, not only placing him, as someone Paul knows, on a level with Peter, but also *among* the Apostles, another fact that the Gospels and Acts are most anxious to disguise. As we proceed, we shall also be able to show that Jesus' brothers were, indeed, *reckoned as Apostles*. But let us take these points one at a time.

We can say from Paul's testimony that the James he is talking about here – whom he calls 'the brother of the Lord', whether this '*brothership*' is to be taken as real or symbolical – is on the same level as the Peter whose acquaintance he appears to be making *for the first time*. Again, it is not clear whom he means by this 'Peter' as in the next chapter he also speaks about someone he calls 'Cephas' (Gal. 2:19 – 'Cephas' is an Aramaic appellation, usually taken as meaning 'Rock', just as Peter means 'Rock' in Greek). By speaking of 'the other Apostles', it is quite clear that Paul means that *both* James and Peter are to be reckoned among the Apostles, whatever may be meant by the term at this point. This is surprising, as most would not reckon James or the brothers of Jesus generally among the Apostles. Nor, at this point, is Paul speaking of 'Twelve' Apostles as part of a fixed scheme.

As we shall see below, this idea of 'Twelve Apostles', as the Gospels and the Book of Acts would have it, is somewhat formal and even rather childish. As we shall also see, in 1 Corinthians, too, it is pretty clear that not only was James among the original Apostles, this *Twelve Apostle* scheme was one that aided the historiographical and doctrinal approach of books like the Gospels and Acts. Stemming from the ideas of those either unsophisticated in Palestinian history or purposefully trying to archaize or dissemble, it is not at all certain that such a scheme was ever really operative in the Palestine of the time.

In its favor – apart from the rather tendentious Apostle lists in the Gospels and Acts – is the reference in the Community Rule to a central Council made up of 'Twelve Israelites'. This, too, probably archaizes to a certain extent, being based on a no longer extant biblical framework of *twelve* Israelite Tribes. In this reference in the Community Rule, there is allusion as well to 'Three'. But here, too, there are difficulties and it is not possible to tell from the allusion in the text whether we have Twelve plus Three or whether 'the Three' are meant to be included in 'the Twelve', this being the presentation of the Gospels, though not necessarily Galatians. The probability is in favor of the former.[6]

'The Three' being spoken about in the Scrolls are specifically referred to as 'Priests'. The imagery being used here with regard either to 'the Twelve' and 'the Three' is similar to that in the New Testament. In fact, the former are referred to in the Community Rule as 'a House of Holiness for Israel', that is, the Twelve Tribes; the latter, 'a Holy of Holies for Aaron', that is, the Central Priestly Triad.

There can be no doubt that what we have here is what – following Paul's vocabulary in 1 Corinthians 2:13 – should be called 'spiritualized Temple' imagery, both a *spiritualized Temple* and *spiritualized Holy of Holies* within the Temple. In the Community Rule, this is accompanied by *spiritualized sacrifice* and *spiritualized atonement* imagery as well, that is, this Council governing the Community is referred to not only as 'making atonement for the land' and 'atoning for sin by *doing Righteousness*', but 'a sweet fragrance', 'a well-tested Wall, that Precious Cornerstone, whose Foundations shall neither rock nor sway in their place'.[7]

It is when treating these 'Three' that we run into difficulties in the New Testament, because the enumeration of them is not the same in the Gospels as it is in the Letter to the Galatians.[8] We have already heard in Galatians that *the Central Three*, that is, 'those of repute' or 'reputed to be Pillars', are James, Cephas, and John. James and John, here, are not specified as being brothers as they are in the Gospels, and, indeed, whoever this John is, the James reputed to be his brother in Acts and the Gospels had long since disappeared from the scene. However, in the Gospels it is quite clear that the Central Three are supposed to be Peter, James, and *John his brother*, meaning Peter, James, and John 'the two sons of Zebedee' (Matt. 10:2, 17:1, 26:37 and pars.).

It should be apparent that these are slightly different enumerations. In the Gospels, Jesus is pictured as transfiguring himself before the latter Three 'on a high mountain', but, all such recitals in the Gospels must be taken with a degree of skepticism. The rule of thumb we suggested above should apply here. Where there is a conflict between data in these and reliable passages from Paul's letters, the latter are to be preferred. Not only this, but it is the 'brother' theme, when inspected carefully, which will be seen to be causing the difficulties – whether, for instance, with regard to 'Andrew *his brother*' (in this case Peter's 'brother' – Mark 1:18 and pars.), 'John his brother' (Mark 1:19 and pars.), 'James the brother of John' (Acts 12:2), or Jesus' brother, so much so that the movement of this phrase, 'his brother', has all the earmarks of a shell game.

The Post-Resurrection Appearances of Jesus to the Apostles in the Gospels

The reference to Cephas as one of the 'Pillars' in Galatians 2:9 is interesting. In chapter 1, Paul preceded this by referring to someone he calls Peter whose acquaintance he made along with James fourteen years before in Jerusalem (1:18). He follows with his description of the confrontation, when he and Peter meet once again in Antioch and are forced to respond to 'some from James' over the issue of 'table fellowship with Gentiles' (2:11–12). It is not at all certain, as we have suggested, that we are dealing with the same individual in these three separate notices and the problem has been worried over by scholars with little result.

The point is that there may be another individual with this name *Cephas*. Paul refers to him as such in 1 Corinthians on several occasions, particularly regarding disputes in Asia Minor with someone called Apollos (1 Cor. 1:12 and 3:22) – who, according to Acts, 'knew only John's baptism' (Acts 18:25) – or regarding the fact that 'Jesus' brothers travel with women too' (1 Cor. 9:15). But the main reference he makes to 'Cephas' in 1 Corinthians – never Peter – is in the list of post-resurrection appearances by Jesus in chapter 15, where Cephas is listed as the first person to whom Jesus appeared after his death (15:5).

In the way the reference stands at present – Jesus 'appeared to Cephas, then to the Twelve' – Cephas does not appear to be one of the Apostles. All this is very puzzling. The answer again may relate to problems surrounding Jesus' brothers in Scripture. It is possible that the *Cephas* being referred to in Paul's letters is another 'Simon' or 'Simeon' – the Simeon *bar Cleophas* mentioned above as Jesus' *first cousin*. Just as Simon Peter in Scripture is represented as being the successor to Jesus, this Simon or Simeon is represented by early Church tradition as being the successor to James. He is also of the family of Jesus, Cleophas being denoted as the uncle of Jesus.

As we proceed, it will probably transpire that this Cleophas is not the uncle of Jesus, but rather his father, and there are traditions that to some degree represent him as such. In John 19:25, for instance, he is represented as the husband of Mary, and this is probably true. For Origen, when discussing the passage in Josephus ascribing the fall of Jerusalem to the death of James, this Cleophas was actually *the father* of James, Simon, Jude, and Joses – those brothers represented as being the brothers of Jesus in Scripture – but these now by a previous mother, not Mary.[9] Again, the reasons for all these transmutations and circumlocutions should be growing clearer. They are twofold: to protect the divine sonship of Jesus and the emerging doctrine of the perpetual virginity of Mary.

These post-resurrection appearances by Jesus have long been recognized by scholars as being associated with one's place in the hierarchy of the early Church, that is, the earlier he appeared to you, the higher up in the hierarchy you were. Paul sets the stage for this by referring to this appearance to Cephas and others in 1 Corinthians. Unfortunately there is no first appearance to *Peter* recorded in *any* of the Gospels, or anywhere else for that matter. In fact, John 20:6–7 records that when Peter went into the tomb it was empty. For Matthew and Mark, Peter does not even enter the tomb; rather the *two* Mary's do – one specifically called 'Mary the mother of James' (Mark 16:1; cf. Luke 24:10) – where they encounter the Angel who tells them of Jesus' resurrection and his departure for Galilee. For Luke, the two Mary's report to the Apostles, and it is only after this that Peter rushes to the tomb, where, seeing only 'the linen clothes' again, he departs 'wondering at what had happened' (24:10–12).

Matthew also has the two Mary's rushing to tell 'the Disciples' what they had seen. But curiously, at this juncture it is they who actually encounter Jesus, seeing him along the way. For his part, Jesus is presented as uttering words similar to those of Peter at 'the house of Mary the mother of John Mark' in Jerusalem in the crucial introduction of James in Acts 12:17, to wit, 'Go, tell my brothers to go into Galilee and there they will see me' (Matt. 28:10). For most of the Gospels, further appearances then proceed to take place in Galilee, all except the Gospel of Luke.

Luke does record a post-resurrection appearance in the neighborhood of Jerusalem – this, the famous sighting on the Road to Emmaus. Mark 16:12 also refers to this, noting how 'after these things, he [Jesus] appeared in another form to two of them as they walked on their way into the country', but this ending from Mark is considered a later addition.

For Luke, Jesus appeared to someone called '*Cleopas*', obviously identical to the Cleophas considered Jesus' uncle, and *another unnamed person* (24:13–18). The nature of this episode is similar to the 'doubting Thomas' one in John 20:26–29 and an episode in the apocryphal Gospel of the Hebrews, conserved in the writings of Jerome, about a *first appearance to James.* In these, Jesus actually sits down, breaks bread, and apparently eats with the individual(s) involved, to prove the fact of his corporeal resurrection and, therefore, his *bodily* needs.[35] In Luke, however, when report comes to 'the Eleven and those with them' of this appearance on the Road to Emmaus outside Jerusalem to Cleopas and another, they are represented as crying out in unison, 'the Lord is risen indeed and appeared unto *Simon*' (24:33–34).

But, unfortunately, no appearance to a 'Simon' has taken place anywhere – certainly not in this first appearance 'along the way' to Cleopas, unless we are dealing with the traces of an early appearance to *members of Jesus' family.*[36] This would concretize their place in the post-resurrection appearance sequence, given by Paul in 1 Corinthians 15:7, that is, an appearance rather to *James and Simeon bar Cleophas*, the latter, we shall show, all but indistinguishable from 'Simon the Zealot', already being called in writings attributed to Hippolytus and in Syriac sources in the third century, the *second brother of Jesus.*

Paul's *Lying*

Paul's insistence in Galatians 1:16 that he did not discuss the Gospel he taught or the revelation of God's 'son in him' with any *other human being* is interesting. This accords, as we have seen, with the way he introduces himself in Galatians 1:1: 'Paul, Apostle, *not from men nor through man…*'. That is, he did not receive his teaching commission from any man, as, for instance, a leader or 'Pillar' of the Jerusalem Church with the stature or authority of a James, but rather *direct from Jesus himself*, whom, of course, by this time Paul is referring to as 'Christ', to signal his *supernatural* as opposed to his natural persona.

This also recalls the sense one gets from reading 2 Corinthians, confirmed in the Pseudoclementines, that the Apostles required *letters of recommendation from James.* In line with his contempt for such things, Paul insists his appointment is *direct from Jesus Christ* – meaning the *Supernatural Christ*, to whom he has, as it were, a direct line. This is the only certification he needs, which accords with his reasons for not discussing with anyone else the Gospel about *Christ Jesus*, as he taught it among the Gentiles. He didn't need to. He only had to discuss it with the Heavenly Jesus through the medium of the Holy Spirit.

He did not recognize earthly authority, not the Jerusalem Church leaders, nor the decisions of the so-called 'Jerusalem Council' as we shall see – only the visions he was receiving. This was all very well and good for Paul, but one can imagine the kind of problems it might have caused him among his contemporaries. We can get an inkling of these by reading between the lines in his letters and comprehending the doctrines about him in the Pseudoclementines and materials of similar orientation.

Paul was obviously being mocked by some as 'the Man of Dreams', 'Lies', or 'Lying', or what was also characterized in a parallel parlance as 'the Enemy'.[11] This is confirmed tangentially by Paul's defensiveness with regard to such epithets, as evidenced at the end of his testimony in Galatians to his meeting with Peter and James in Jerusalem (Gal. 1:20 and 4:16). It is neither accidental nor incurious that exactly where he comes to speak of 'James the brother of the Lord' and in 2 Corinthians, the Hebrew 'Archapostles', that Paul feels obliged to add: 'Now before God, (in) what I write to you, I do not lie' or, again, 'I do not lie.'

This will not be the only time that Paul will via refraction refer in his defensiveness to 'the Liar' epithet evidently being applied to him by some *within* the Movement. It is connected to the 'Enemy' terminology, known to have been applied to him in later Jewish Christianity or Ebionitism. In the context of referring to Jewish observances and festivals as 'weak and beggarly elements' (Gal. 4:9), his opponents – again *within* the Movement – as 'wishing zealously to exclude' him and his communities (4:18), and the Covenant on Mount Sinai as 'born according to the flesh' of the *Arab bondservant Hagar* and, therefore, 'bringing forth to bondage' (4:24), Paul worries over his '*becoming your Enemy by telling you the Truth*' (4:16). This remark should be viewed over and against one in James 4:4 insisting that 'whoever makes himself into a Friend of the world turns himself into an Enemy of God', which plays, as we shall see, on the original biblical characterization of Abraham as 'the Friend of God'.

There are many other indications of this 'Lying' epithet in the Pauline corpus.[12] That Paul alludes to it here in the midst of this pivotal testimony to the existence of James, while at the same time explaining why he (Paul) was unknown by sight to anyone else in the Movement in Palestine, is extraordinary. It is as if Paul knew some of James' followers were applying this kind of language to him. Why would Paul feel constrained to adjure – and this in the form almost of an oath – that he 'does not lie' with regard to the claims he is putting forth concerning this revelation and his first meeting with James?

Paul uses this 'Lying' terminology at several other crucial junctures in his letters, particularly in Romans 3:4–8 and 9:1, where he speaks about wrongful accusations concerning himself, circumcision, the Law, and how by 'telling the Truth' he has made himself 'a curse from Christ' to his opponents. He also uses it in 2 Corinthians 11:31 to attack his 'Hebrew Archapostle' interlocutors and boast about the escape he made from Aretas' representative in Damascus down its walls 'in a basket' (11:33 – in Acts 9:22-25, typically, this is 'the Jews'). 1 Timothy, the authorship of which is disputed, also pictures Paul as averring he is 'an Apostle' and insisting he 'speaks the Truth of Christ and does not lie' (2:7).

The riposte to these things is, of course, found in the Letter of James at a likewise crucial juncture, following the rebuke of the 'Empty Man' (2:20) and evocation of the Lying 'Tongue', which 'cannot be tamed', 'boasts great things', and is 'a world of Unrighteousness all in itself (3:1–8). It is succinctly put: 'If you have bitter jealousy and contentiousness *in your heart*, do not boast or *lie against the Truth*. This is not the Wisdom that comes down from above, but *earthly*, *man-made*, *devilish*' (3:14–15).

The same context is apparent in the Dead Sea Scrolls: 'Truth' is always juxtaposed with 'Lying', 'Righteousness' with 'Evil', 'Light' with 'Darkness', a fornicating, rebellious, jealous, and spouting 'Tongue' with obedience and good conscience. Not only is the vocabulary in the Scrolls almost interchangeable with these crucial parts of the Pauline or Jamesian corpus, but the same kind of imagery is in use. When one appreciates that James occupies a position in early Christianity equivalent to the one occupied by the Righteous Teacher and the same kinds of allusions are being applied to them and to their enemies, then the points of contact between the two draw ever closer.

Chapter 8
James' Succession and the Election to Fill Judas *Iscariot's Office*

The Succession of James in Paul and Acts

As presented by Paul, James is the Leader of the early Church *par excellence.* Terms like 'Bishop of the Jerusalem Church' or 'the Leader of the Jerusalem Community' are of little actual moment at this point, because when James held sway in Jerusalem, there really were no other centers of any importance. All deferred to the Jerusalem Centre until it was destroyed.

Paul gives more information about the pre-eminence of James in the confrontation in Antioch in Galatians 2:1–10. Of course, Acts 15's presentation of the 'Jerusalem Council' is quite different from Paul's picture in Galatians, and its chronology totally so, to the extent that there is even a question as to whether the events depicted in the two narratives can be considered the same.

Despite problems of this kind, in both accounts James clearly emerges as the Supreme Ruler of the early Church, to whose rulings all must defer or bend. Acts even records James' directives to overseas communities regarding Gentile believers – the upshot of the 'Conference' in Acts – in three slightly varying versions.[1] Something like these directives reported in Acts must have emanated from Jerusalem because several of them turn up in I Corinthians (5–11). There his response is angry and aggressive, whereas in Galatians he blandly remarks that 'those reputed to be Pillars' or 'reckoned as important' had 'nothing to add' to the version of the Gospel that he proclaimed 'among the Gentiles' (Gal. 2:6).

Rather, as Paul states in Galatians 2:10, the 'only' condition that the Pillars, James, Cephas, and John, put on his activities was: that we should remember *the Poor.* The allusion to 'the Poor' at this juncture is another important usage integrally related to James' Jerusalem Community. Though it is possible to take it simply in its adjectival sense of being Poor and nothing more, there can be little doubt that 'the Poor' was the name for James' Community in Jerusalem or that Community descended from it in the East in the next two-three centuries, *the Ebionites.*

These '*Ebionites*' derive their name from the Hebrew '*Ebion*' meaning '*Poor*' (plural *Ebionim*). The term is also used repeatedly at the beginning of the second chapter of the Letter of James, leading up to the citation of 'the Royal Law according to the Scripture' – the Righteousness Commandment, 'you shall love your neighbor as yourself' (2:8). Here James terms 'the Poor' chosen by God as 'the heirs to the Kingdom', to whom the Piety Commandment of 'loving God' is applied (2:2–6).

It is these Ebionites that held the name of James in such reverence, claiming descent from his Movement, whether direct or indirect, in first-century Palestine. For Eusebius in the 300s, this Movement is *too Jewish,* for it insists on circumcision for all converts or participants and, therefore, adherence to Jewish Law.[2] Circumcision is the outward sign of adherence to the Covenant in Judaism, and carries with it, as Paul understands (Gal. 5:3), the implied corollary of observance of the Law.

Eusebius, coming from Palestine, understands the term '*Ebionite*' better than most. For him, these Ebionites have a more primitive understanding of Paul's 'Christ', conceiving of him as 'a plain and ordinary man only', generated by natural means and advanced above other men only in his 'practice of virtue' – that is, his 'Righteousness'. In other words, their Christology is 'poverty-stricken' and Eusebius shows that this is his opinion by making a pun on their name, that is, that *they harbored 'poor and mean' notions about Christ*, primarily, that *he was only a man.*

Peter and Paul Subordinate to James in Antioch

After having made it clear from his perspective what the rulings of the Jerusalem Conference were, Paul now gives his version of events that followed in Antioch. In his confrontation with Peter over *table fellowship with Gentiles* that ensues after 'some from James' come down to 'Antioch', Paul makes it clear that whoever we may think 'Peter' was, he was not *the Head of Christianity in the days of Paul.* Peter emerges as someone in competition to some extent with Paul himself, but not with James. Peter is clearly *under James* and subservient to his rulings, because he must defer to him and follow his instructions when his representatives arrive from Jerusalem (Gal. 2:12).

For Paul, Peter is a figure of respect and authority, but not *too much respect* nor *too much authority*. He is subject to the instructions of James, which makes James' position as the Leader or Bishop of the Jerusalem Church the over-arching one. Peter seems to be functioning – if we can read between the lines – as something of an inspector of overseas communities, a traveling representative of Jerusalem. For these purposes, the Letters from Peter to James and Clement to James, which introduce the Pseudoclementine *Homilies* and are framed in the nature of first-person reports, are edifying.

It is perhaps because of this position that Peter looms so large overseas and that, particularly in Rome, notions of the transmission of the central role or successorship become focused on him ('on this Rock I shall build my Church') and by extension Rome itself. But certainly the overall center at this point is Jerusalem. It is only with the disappearance of the Jerusalem center, an event certainly connected with the 66–70 CE War against Rome (as all our traditions in any case aver),[3] that there was scope for Rome to rise to ascendancy.

Paul writes, 'But when Peter came to Antioch, I opposed him to his face, because he was to be condemned, for before *some came from James*, he used to *eat with the Gentiles'* (2:11–12). This is the 'table fellowship' controversy, that is, *table fellowship with Gentiles.* There is no doubt this James must be the 'James the brother of the Lord' just mentioned by Paul. The problem is simple and has to do with Jewish dietary regulations and the Law, which in turn have to do with circumcision, the outward sign of the Covenant, and therefore, as Paul puts it in Galatians 5:3, being 'a debtor' or one 'obliged *to do the whole Law*'.[4]

Jewish Law encompassed a full set of dietary regulations which made it impossible for Jews observing these regulations to keep normal commerce with non-Jews, who were seen as being in a state of uncleanness, not least because of the foods they ate and the manner in which they prepared them – not just Gentiles, but Jews not keeping these dietary regulations as well, fractiousness that still looms large among modern Jews today.

This is what the question of *table fellowship with Gentiles* is all about – 'keeping' or 'not keeping the Law'. As Paul sees it, the emissaries or representatives of James arrived in Antioch, and when they came, Peter stopped eating with Gentiles 'and *separated himself* being afraid of those of the circumcision. And the rest of the Jews joined him in this hypocritical behavior' (Gal. 2:12–13).

The issues here are much greater than Paul is willing to admit. Clearly all the *Jews* are shunning Paul. James' directives would appear to be all-embracing and everyone must obey him. The only parallel that one can think of is in the Dead Sea Scrolls, particularly the Community Rule and the Damascus Document, where someone who 'overtly or covertly breaks *one word of the Torah of Moses on any point whatsoever* shall be expelled from the Council of the Community', and no one 'shall cooperate with him in work or purse in any way whatsoever', nor shall he 'approach the pure food of the Assembly'.[5]

The parameters of this aforesaid ostracization resemble the rebuke in the Letter of James about the person 'keeping the whole Law, but stumbling over one small point being guilty of breaking it all', which follows the stress on '*doing* the Royal Law according to the Scripture' – the all-Righteousness Commandment (2:8–10).

By 'the rest of the Jews' or '*those of the circumcision*', Paul clearly means *the Jewish Apostles* and others caring about such things and following James' leadership. So, therefore, *all* the Jewish members '*behaved hypocritically*' and appear to have followed James' leadership in the matter of 'eating with the Gentiles' (Gal. 2:13).

Paul puts the issue in terms of 'circumcision' and, throughout much of the rest of the letter, goes on to rail against both the practice of circumcision and Jews generally, so incensed was he at the events he recounts – and so frightened, as he explains at the beginning of the letter, that the Community he planted in Galatia will be likewise turned aside by similar parameters (Gal. 1:6–12). From his presentation it is, not only clear that James is the overarching leader to whom all must defer, but also that Paul's report of 'the Jerusalem Council' and what those in Jerusalem thought they had agreed to is not precisely what Paul says it was or what the author of Acts presents it as being.

It is also clear that in some sense 'circumcision' and 'observing the Law' were considered a *sine qua non* for all full-fledged or bona-fide members of the early Movement or Community – whatever name one chooses to give it. This absolutely accords with the literature we have from Qumran, which in so many ways parallels these materials, that is, first one had to *convert to Judaism*, then one could make some claim to being *heir* to its traditions. Put in another way, before one could claim to be an 'heir to' the promises of the Law (Gal. 3:29) – including the Prophets – one had to take the Law upon oneself. One could not, for instance, participate in the Messianism of the Messianic Movement without first taking upon oneself the traditions of the religion that brought this Messianism into being.

Whether one agrees with this proposition or not, it was, doubtlessly, how the majority of 'those' in Jerusalem saw the situation. Certainly all Jews in 'Antioch' saw the situation like this, at least when they were directed so to behave by those 'from James', who had arrived from Jerusalem and obviously represented his position. So bitter was Paul at this unsettling state of affairs, that he accuses both Peter and Barnabas of hypocrisy, saying, 'and even Barnabas was carried away by their hypocrisy', that is, 'separated and drew back for fear of the party insisting on circumcision' (Gal. 2:12–13).

Being *Separate unto God* or a Nazirite

The use of the word 'separate' or 'separation' with regard to Peter's actions, after he is called to account by the representatives of James, is used in crucial contexts in the two organizational documents from Qumran known as the Community Rule and the Damascus Document. The first uses the term when interpreting the 'Way in the wilderness' Prophecy associated in Christian tradition with the mission of John the Baptist in the wilderness; the second, in interpretation of Ezekiel 44:15, the scriptural basis of the promises about '*the Sons of Zadok*' or '*the Zadokite Priesthood*', and the evocation of what are called 'the Three Nets of Belial'.[6]

While the second 'net' or 'snare' described there has to do with 'Riches', a theme forming the bedrock of the Letter of James' allusions to 'the Poor' and 'the Rich', the first and third 'nets' have to do with 'fornication' and 'pollution of the Temple'. The truly Righteous in 'God's Community' – the *true* '*Sons of Zadok*' – are instructed to '*separate* from the Sons of the Pit' and 'go out from the Land of Judah and live in the Land of Damascus'; in the Community Rule, 'to *separate* from the settlement of Unrighteous men and go out in the wilderness and prepare the Way of God'.[7]

In fact, in the Damascus Document it is improper 'separation' in the Temple that creates the 'pollution' problem – the improper 'separation of clean and unclean', in particular, *improper separation* from people who 'lie with a woman in her period' or, as a matter of course, *marry their nieces or close family cousins*. The Damascus Document adds, 'anyone who approaches them shall not be free of their pollution' (5.6–15).

I have related the 'fornication' and 'pollution' allusions to the practices of the Herodians ('riches' as well). This issue of 'separation' is also of fundamental importance to the 'Two Letters on Works Reckoned as Righteousness' or '*MMT*', which also pay particular attention to the subject of gifts and sacrifices from Gentiles in the Temple and carry some of the points of James' directives to overseas communities as enunciated in Acts.[8] The former, like the theme of 'lying with women in their periods' in the Damascus Document, violates the rules of proper 'separation of clean from unclean. Holy from profane', being raised here.[9]

In Galatians, Peter and other Jews within the Movement are portrayed as being somewhat lax regarding matters such as these. They are being called to account by the evidently more '*zealous*' or '*Zealot*' Jerusalem Community – this is how James and his followers will be described in Acts 21:20 in any event, that is, as '*Zealots for the Law*' – which insists on a more strict legal adherence to these matters. Therefore, James and his representatives are calling those to account in Antioch. Like anyone spending most of his time in *the Diaspora* – except the most rigid or zealous – Peter is presented here as being more easygoing, but still deferential when called to account to James' Leadership. The same is true of Barnabas – whoever he was.

Paul now attacks Peter and *the other Jews* copying him in his behavior in the following manner: 'But when I saw that they did not *walk uprightly* according to the Truth of the Gospel, I said to Peter before everyone: "*If you, being a Jew, live in the Gentile not a Jewish manner, why do you compel Gentiles to Judaize?*"' (Gal. 2:14). Paul does not tell us Peter's response. Rather, he launches into a long diatribe on 'Justification, not by works of the Law, but rather through Faith in Christ Jesus' (Gal. 2:16 and 3:11). This goes on for several chapters and ends up in some of the most important and celebrated formulations of Christian theology, in particular, on circumcision (the issue with which the whole exercise began), the saving death of Christ, and how Christ took the curse of the Law upon himself. These passages will have particular relevance to the kind of curses in both the Community Rule and Damascus Document, most notably in the last column of the latter and the rededication to 'the New Covenant in the Land of Damascus' at Pentecost. Paul closes his attack on Peter in chapter 2 of Galatians with the complaint, '*if Righteousness is through the Law*, then Christ died for nothing' (2:21).

Throughout he mixes symbolic language with rational theology in a way that would confuse even the most hard-headed observer. Paul admits this himself, where he refers to 'allegorizing' and evokes 'the two Covenants', the one of Hagar from 'Mount Sinai in Arabia' (*the Jewish one*) and the new one 'of the Promise' of Sarah, 'the free woman … born according to the Spirit' (4:24–29). Paul's description here in Galatians, therefore – from which he launches into his discussion of Christianity, Christ's death, the value of Grace over the Law – introduces the person of James and his representatives as his interlocutors. As Paul reveals himself – through these verses and by inference – James materializes as well, but in the opposite position. Peter and the other Jewish Apostles become swing figures in this archetypical confrontation between Paul and James; but James is not only identified, the main lines of his positions fleshed out, but also his position in the early Church straightforwardly acknowledged.

The Successor to Jesus

James' position is also developed in various ways in early Church literature, most notably by Clement of Alexandria and Hegesippus as conserved in Eusebius. It is also treated in the Pseudoclementines and to a certain extent in the Gospel of Thomas. By contrast, it is missing from Acts in its present form. In the course of this discussion, how James emerged as the Leader of the early Church will be seen to be present in Acts as well, at least *in the source* the authors of Acts used to reconstruct the material they present.

The first question that should be addressed is how does one choose a leader to head the Community? There are really only two methods. The first is by *direct appointment*, that is, that Jesus personally regulated the situation of succession to him in his life-time. In their own way, this is how the Gospels, and the Gospel of Thomas, present the matter. The second is via an *election* or some kind of *consensus*, either the consensus of the Community as a whole or the consensus of its principal leaders – and this is the procedure presented by Acts where *the succession to Judas Iscariot* is concerned.

Eusebius himself is the best repository of these traditions attesting both to *the direct succession of James* and also his *election* – this to the Office of 'Bishop'. Eusebius puts this as follows: 'James, who was surnamed the Just by the Forefathers on account of his superlative virtue, was the first to have been *elected to the Office of Bishop of the Jerusalem Church'*.[10]

The sequencing Eusebius follows here is important. At the end of Book One, this notice is preceded by an allusion to the execution of John the Baptist, mention of Cephas, Thaddaeus, and James in that order, and the story of the conversion of the King of the Edessenes, 'Thaddaeus' and '(Judas) Thomas' participating.

The references to 'Cephas', 'Thaddaeus', and 'James' occur because he is discussing 'the Seventy' – 'no list of whom is anywhere extant' – as distinct from 'the Apostles'.[11] Eusebius reckons James, not to mention Cephas and Thaddaeus, among these 'Seventy' – clearly the number of 'the Jerusalem Church' or 'Assembly' – and, citing Paul's attestation of Jesus' post-resurrection appearance to him in 1 Corinthians 15:7, for the first time identifies James as 'one of the so-called brothers of the Savior'. Because Cephas is also mentioned in this same context in 1 Corinthians, he puzzles over the fact that Clement of Alexandria in the second century considered Cephas 'one of the Seventy Disciples who had the same name as the Apostle Peter', though he did not consider him the same person.

The mention, too, of 'Thaddaeus' as 'one of the Seventy' leads him directly into the story of the correspondence with 'King Agbarus, the celebrated King of the Peoples beyond the Euphrates', with which he closes Book One and which he places around 29 CE.[12] It is directly following these events that he moves into *the election of James as Bishop of the Jerusalem Church* at the beginning of Book Two – in exactly the place it should have been dealt with – 'at the same time', as he puts it, as the 'election by lot' to replace 'the Traitor Judas'.

His sequencing in the first chapter of Book Two is also important. His reference to choosing the replacement for 'Judas the Traitor', Matthias (Acts 1:26), whom he calls 'one of the Disciples of the Lord' (again presumably one of these 'Seventy'), leads him to mention the appointment of 'the Seven to administer the common fund' by 'the laying on of hands by the Apostles', a procedure specifically applied in the Pseudoclementines to James' appointment of overseas messengers. This, in turn, leads to allusion to Stephen and his martyrdom by stoning '*by the murderers of the Lord*, as if ordained specifically for this purpose' (*EH* 2.1.1).

Curiously, *the election to replace Judas* and *the stoning of Stephen*, like *the laying on of hands*, will have their counterparts in the biography of James and stand-in for critical episodes in it. After detailing the various traditions from Clement of Alexandria about James' election and appointment to the Episcopate of Jerusalem, the very next event he describes is the dispatch of Thaddaeus by Thomas to Edessa and King Agbarus, 'the Great King of the Peoples beyond the Euphrates'. Nor does he mention the beheading of the 'the Apostle James' for another eight chapters (almost a decade later) – and this in a fairly doctrinaire manner right out of the Book of Acts. For him this leads directly into the *beheading of Theudas* and *the Famine* (2.8.1–3).

Election or Casting Lots

The matter of election and/or 'casting lots' needs to be addressed. One first encounters a procedure of this kind in this period in the history of the Maccabean family. It is directly related to the office of the High Priesthood and who should occupy it. From there, it moves into the procedures of what some refer to as 'the Zealot Movement'. When the Jewish religious hero Judas Maccabee purified the Temple after its liberation in the second century BCE, he did so in conjunction with its rededication. This has always been celebrated thereafter by Jews as the Festival of the Rededication or *Hanukkah.*

Judas presided over these activities like some powerful Vicegerent, but Josephus actually represents Judas as being 'elected High Priest'. He repeats this claim three times,[13] though it is nowhere presented in the several Maccabee Books purporting to tell the story of Judas Maccabee, his father Mattathias, and his brothers John, Simon, and Jonathan – popular names that have transferred themselves into the early history of Christianity not without reason.

The Maccabee Books do present an election of sorts, when Judas' second brother Simon is acclaimed High Priest by the priests and people (1 Macc. 14:41). This may be simply pro-Maccabean propaganda, but it was an election of sorts and certainly an acclamation, a procedure also recognized in the Gospels on behalf of Jesus.[14]

But in 'the Zealot Movement' this notion of 'an election' becomes extremely important. Repeatedly, in one uprising after another from 4 BCE to 66–70 CE and beyond, Josephus presents the Revolutionaries as demanding *the election by the people* of a High Priest of *greater purity* and 'Piety' than the Herodian High Priesthood that had been imposed on them. Sometimes this is an outright election; at other times it is represented as 'choosing by lot'.[15] For instance, in his presentation of the revolutionary events of 4 BCE–7 CE after Herod's death, Josephus presents the Revolutionaries – this should mean both religious and political – as demanding *the election of a High Priest.* The demand he describes would seem to have much in common with the procedure called 'choosing by lot'.

When describing 'the last days' – that is, the last days of the Temple in the 66–70 CE events, but particularly as these accelerated after 68 and the elimination of all the Herodian-appointed High Priests – Josephus describes the election by 'the Innovators' of a 'last' High Priest before the Romans invest the city, one 'Phannius' or 'Phineas', a simple *Stone-Cutter.*[16] Josephus constantly refers to 'the Innovators' in this period – the political and religious reformers and/or Revolutionaries who have all been lumped, somewhat imprecisely, under the general heading of 'Zealots', even though it is not clear what the currency of this term actually was or whether it was being used in any consistent way to describe them. Nor does the choice of someone by the name of 'Phannius' seem accidental in view of its symbolic importance to Zealotry in general, making one wonder just how fortuitous or random such a process 'of lots' could have been even in theory.

The archetypical episode in the life of Phineas, evoked in support of Maccabean claims to the High Priesthood, as we saw, was when Phineas, out of 'zeal for God', deflected pollution from the camp of the Israelites *in the wilderness* by killing backsliders marrying Gentiles. As a result, he won 'the Covenant of an Everlasting Priesthood' and the right 'to make atonement on behalf of the Sons of Israel' for himself and 'his seed' in perpetuity

(Num. 25:13). This Covenant is evoked in 1 Maccabees 2:27 on behalf of Judas Maccabee's father, Mattathias or Matthias, the reputed progenitor of the whole family. This is also the name – perhaps not coincidentally – of the winning candidate in Acts' rather fictionalized presentation of the 'election by lot' to fill *Judas Iscariot's* now vacant 'Office'.

Therefore, when Paul, in characterizing his community as 'Abraham's seed', claims they are all now 'Sons of God through faith in Christ Jesus', in whom 'there is neither Jew nor Greek, neither bondman nor free, neither male nor female, but all one in Christ Jesus' (Gal. 3:28–29), it is the direct opposite of the events described above. This more cosmopolitan Pauline Mission 'to the Gentiles' is the mirror reversal, as it were, and the negation of some two hundred and fifty years of Palestinian history spent fighting foreigners, Hellenization, and – rightly or wrongly – perceived pollution incurred by mixing with overseas peoples. That Paul is misunderstood by contemporaries such as these should not be surprising.

That they should wish to kill him, as Acts describes (23:12), should also not be surprising. It all depends on one's point of view, and from the Palestinian point of view, Paul was a cosmopolitanizing '*Traitor*', giving victory to the forces they and their ancestors had fought against incessantly, ever since Matthias had raised the banner of revolt, assuming the purified High Priesthood some two centuries before. Whereas Matthias kills backsliders on the altar at Modein, Phineas deflected pollution from the camp – and God's Wrath consonant upon it – by killing Jews who had *mixed with Gentiles.*

Nothing could illustrate the conflict of these times more vividly, nor the mentality enshrined in the Dead Sea Scrolls. This is *the ethos* of the Qumran documents. In the writer's view, it will also be the ethos of the Movement led by James, the better part of whose followers are distinctly called – even in Acts – '*Zealots for the Law*' (21:20). Paul also uses the term 'zeal' consistently in his letters but, once again, it is clear that he is aware of the use of this term by those opposing him. In every case he reverses their use of the term denoting 'the zeal of the Ancestors', 'zeal for their customs', 'zeal for the traditions and the Law', to indicate rather, *zeal in his mission or zeal for his new-found Faith in Christ Jesus,* by whose 'Grace' Paul had been deputized to preach to the Gentiles. He has also been deputized to found a community based not on the Law, but 'Faith in Christ Jesus', where there are, as Ephesians 2:19 puts it, 'no more aliens or foreign visitors'.

Phineas wins the High Priesthood for his descendants in perpetuity because of the *zealous* behavior he displayed in *killing backsliders* and warding *off pollution from the camp of Israel.* For those of this 'Zealot' persuasion, killing backsliders – including Paul – was no sin at all. It was a virtue. Priests of the Phineas stripe condoned killing as long as this killing was in the interests of Righteousness and purification or, if one prefers, warding off pollution. This is the ethos of 'the Zealot'/'Messianic Movement' – one is not recommending it, simply illustrating it – and this ethos was totally at odds with the Pauline Mission. They are on a collision course. It only remains to insert James into the picture to understand what was taking place from the 40's to the 60s CE, both in Jerusalem and around the Mediterranean in the world at large among those interested in such matters.

Peter's Citation of Psalms 69 and 109 in Acts

The author of the Book of Acts at this point represents this election of Judas' successor as being of such importance that two scriptural passages from Psalms 69 and 109 are applied to it, that is, we are to think the events have either been presaged in Scripture or explained by it. As Acts puts it in a speech attributed to Peter: The Scripture had to be fulfilled in which the Holy Spirit spoke before by the mouth of David concerning Judas, who became a guide to those who took Jesus (1:16).'

The passages from these Psalms are, as usual, taken completely out of context. Neither really fits the situation of Judas in this episode, nor his successor, at all. What has clearly been done was to search Scripture and just so long as a word or phrase fitted or was close to the plotline or event being described, this was seen as sufficient. A similar method is followed in the Dead Sea Scrolls, particularly in the *peshers* – but in the latter not quite so blatantly. The similarity is important here, as it makes one think that these kinds of materials may have been taken from what might have been extant *peshers* of the Qumran type.

Eusebius, quoting Hegesippus, will insist that important cognomens of James, like 'the Just One' or '*Oblias*' ('Protection of the People') could be found just as at Qumran by searching Scripture, most notably Prophets and Psalms. Quoting his second-century source Hegesippus, Eusebius even goes so far as to apply a passage from Scripture to James' fate – this from the Prophets, however, not Psalms – exactly as Acts does the above passages to events connected to its story of Judas' fate. In fact, he develops the circumstances of James' death – just as the Gospels do Jesus' – on the basis of another '*Zaddik*' text, Isaiah 3:10.

The passages quoted in Acts in relation to the election of the Twelfth Apostle come from Psalms 69 and 109. For the Gospels, these are also favorite sources for the biography of Jesus. The quotation from Psalm 69, as given in Acts 1:20, 'let his encampment become desolate and let no one be dwelling in it', in the biblical Hebrew is rather recorded in the *plural* (that is, 'their camp'/'their tents') in what is actually an *extremely Zionistic* psalm, so much so that it even ends on the hope of 'rebuilding the cities of Judah' and 'dwelling in them' (69:36).

The original reads, 'let *their* camp be deserted and their tents be not lived in' (69:25). Psalm 69 is also a '*Zaddik*' text containing references to 'the Poor' and 'the Meek', not to mention the famous passage also found in the Gospels about 'being given vinegar to drink', those bearing on 'being a foreigner to my brothers, a stranger to my mother's sons', and finally the one in the Gospel of John, attributed to Jesus referring to the Temple, 'zeal for My father's house consumes me'; but nothing that could be construed as applying in any sense to *Judas Iscariot* – quite the opposite.

Its commonality with Psalm 109, another 'Suffering Servant'-type recital similar to Isaiah 53, would appear to be the mutual references to 'the Poor' and 'the Meek' (109:16–22), full of meaning with regard to the Community of James, not to mention the Qumran Scrolls. Not only does it use favorite Qumranisms like 'Deceitfulness' and 'a Lying Tongue', but it also has something of the character of an execration text or 'cursing' one also finds in Qumran texts.[17] In fact, its atmosphere is most un-Christian, vengeful, full of wrath, and completely uncharitable – again more like that of Qumran.

The reference to 'let someone else take his Office' (109:8), applied to the election to replace Judas in Acts 1:20, is quoted like most scriptural allusions in the Gospels completely out of context. As in Psalm 69, its atmosphere is once more one of being encompassed by adversaries and the sentiment is being expressed that, just as he ('the Poor One') is being judged by such an *Evil accuser*, that adversary, too, should 'be judged' mercilessly (109:7–20). It really has nothing whatever to do with the situation of Judas *Iscariot's replacement*, though since it does refer to an official capacity of some kind – in this case 'judgeship' – on the face of it, it has more to do with *James' capacity* as '*Bishop*' or '*Overseer of the Jerusalem Church*' than anything involving Judas *Iscariot*. In fact, this is *exactly the sense of the term* Luke uses in Acts 1:20 to translate the usage into Greek – '*Episcopen*', that is, '*Episcopate*' or '*the Office of the Bishop*'!

The Suicide of Judas *Iscariot* and the Succession to his 'Office'

For Acts 1:22, the 'casting of lots' follows these two quotations from Psalms 69 and 109 and the person chosen to fill Judas' 'Episcopate' would then 'become a witness (with the other Apostles) of his Resurrection' – a point we shall encounter in *all traditions about James*. In our view, Acts is overwriting an account that is introducing James at this point and detailing who he was. This would include the two psalms just outlined above, which Acts applies instead to the election of *Judas Iscariot's* successor.

For Acts 1:23 this election is between two candidates, one of whom, *Joseph Barsabas*, 'surnamed Justus', is never heard from in Scripture again. Another 'Barsabas', as we saw, reappears as 'Judas surnamed Barsabas'. We are circling around the names of Jesus' brothers again. Since 'Judas Barsabas' is one of two messengers sent out by the Jerusalem Church with James' rulings following Acts' 'Jerusalem Council', he must be seen at the very least as paralleling those Paul in Galatians 2:12 identifies as 'some from James', whose appearance at *Antioch* provokes Paul's bitter outbursts against 'those of the circumcision'. In our view he (Judas Barsabas) is to be identified with 'Thaddaeus' or 'Judas Thomas' in the Agbarus legend or 'Judas the Zealot' in Syriac sources connected to it.

All such 'Barsabas', 'Barnabas', and 'Barabbas' surnames are important and often connected to the names of Jesus' family members. 'Barabbas', for instance, in the Gospels is something of a stand-in for Jesus himself. He is the man who had been arrested 'in the Uprising' for 'committing treason and murder' (Mark 15:7 and pars.). For John 18:40, this makes him 'a Bandit' (*Lestes*), the word Josephus employs when talking about Revolutionaries and the person the crowd is depicted as preferring to Jesus. In some texts he is even called 'Jesus Barabbas', thereby correctly recognizing *Barabbas* as an Aramaic cognomen with the meaning 'Son of the Father'.

Barsabas has no such ready equivalent in Aramaic, except the '*Saba*'/'*Sabaean*' terminology we shall encounter having to do with daily bathing. Barnabas, if it is a real name and not another circumlocution, would mean something like 'son of the Prophet'. The point is that such names often overlap the members of Jesus' family or Jesus himself. For example, Barnabas is often associated with 'Joseph', the name of either Jesus' father or brother. 'Joseph called Barsabas, who was surnamed Justus', the losing candidate in the 'election' to fill Judas' 'Bishopric' is an obvious write-in *for James the Just himself*. In this regard, the addition of the cognomen 'Justus' to his name and the use of the word '*Episcope*' to describe the 'Office' he is to fill are determinant.

In other words, we have in these passages at the beginning of Acts an election by lot for some leadership position within the early Church, represented here as being because of the treachery and suicide of someone called Judas or 'the *Iscariot*', and the defeated candidate turns out to be someone called *Justus* – the Latin version of James' cognomen transliterated into Greek. The victorious candidate, like Judas *Iscariot* himself, bears the peculiarly Maccabean name of 'Matthias', even though there already is one 'Matthew' listed among the Apostles. Even Matthew is alternatively called 'Levi the son of Alphaeus' in Mark 2:14, 'Alphaeus' being another of those names, such as Lebbaeus, Cleophas, and '*Oblias*', associated with Jesus' family members. Like the Joseph 'called Barsabas surnamed Justus', this Matthias is never heard from in Scripture again except to fill in this somewhat artificial Twelve-man Apostolic scheme.

Mandaean Priest Elders from Southern Iraq, c. 1920

Chapter 9
The Election of James in Early Church Tradition

Eusebius' Account of the Election of James

Eusebius mentions James's election immediately following references to 'Judas the Traitor', the casting of lots to elect Matthias, and the stoning of Stephen. Eusebius' first mention of James, coincident with these events, starts with the clause: '*At the same time also James, called the brother of our Lord, because he is also called the son of Joseph*' (*EH* 2.1.2). Immediately aware that he has a problem, he interrupts his narrative to explain: 'For Joseph was esteemed the father of Christ because the Virgin was betrothed to him when, before they came together, she was found with child by the Holy Spirit, as the sacred writing of the Gospels teaches'. Eusebius' approach here is similar to Origen's a century before, who seems to have first theorized that James was called '*the brother of the Lord*' because he was the son of Joseph by a *different wife*. James is not 'the brother of Jesus'; he is not even his 'cousin'!

Eusebius continues: 'This same James, therefore, whom the ancients on account of the excellence of his virtue surnamed 'the Just', was stated to have been the first to be elected to the Episcopate [*Episcopes*] of the Church at Jerusalem'. Here Eusebius uses the exact same word in Greek, *Episcope* ('Bishopric' or 'Episcopate'), that the narrative of Acts has just used to describe 'the Office' *the successor to Judas Iscariot was elected to* (Acts 1:20).

The hypothesis identifying the tradition about James' election with the election to replace Judas in Acts is virtually proved. Not only is the overlap in vocabulary striking, but Eusebius also uses the word '*Ecclesia*' or 'Assembly' to describe this 'Church' which elects James (again the very same word Josephus uses to describe the 'Assembly' headed by the 'Simon' he knows in the early 40's who wishes to bar Herodians from the Temple as foreigners). Nor is Eusebius in any doubt about the contemporaneity of this event with Acts' picture of the defeat of 'Justus' and the election of Matthias and the martyrdom by stoning of Stephen. He also has no doubt that James' cognomen was this same, 'the Just', and this on account of his *superabundant Righteousness*. Nor does he make any bones about the fact that *an election occurred*. Whether this was similar to 'Zealot'/'*Sicarii*' elections or the one to elect Matthias, which starts the narrative of Acts, is hardly relevant. We have this important missing link in Christian history and tradition, along with a number of other details attested to by Eusebius, just at the place we would expect it to be.

Eusebius now goes on to describe the election of James more fully, as it is evidently of the utmost importance to his sources. In doing so, he changes the substance somewhat of what he has just said. The source he is quoting is Clement of Alexandria (*c.* 150–215) about a century-and-a-half removed from the events in question. The Sixth Book of his now-lost *Hypotyposes* had the following: 'Peter, James, and John after the Ascension of the Savior did not contend for the Glory, even though they had previously been honored by the Savior, *but chose James the Just as Bishop of Jerusalem*'.

But then Eusebius supplies another tradition, this time from the next or Seventh Book of Clement's *Hypotyposes*, now following Paul's presentation of the Central Three in Galatians and 1 Corinthians, where no other Jame*s* is mentioned. This focuses on the post-resurrection appearances of Christ and what Clement calls 'the gift of Knowledge': 'After the Resurrection, the Lord imparted the gift of Knowledge to *James the Just and John and Peter*. These gave it to the other Apostles and the other Apostles gave it to the Seventy, of whom Barnabas was one'. Now the Central Triad has changed. It is no longer Peter, James, and John, but rather James the Just, John, and Peter. Not only does Clement add James' cognomen 'the Just One', missing in Galatians, but he takes the liberty of changing Paul's

'Cephas' to 'Peter', even though one book earlier, as we already saw, he admitted there were 'two by this name', Cephas being 'one of the Seventy'.

Aware that Clement has been sowing not a little confusion, Eusebius attempts a clarification: 'Now there were *two* Jameses, one called *the Righteous One, who was cast down* [*bletheis*] *from the Pinnacle of the Temple* and beaten to death with a laundryman's club, and the other, who was *beheaded*'. This is very interesting indeed, because, firstly, it shows concern for the confusion between the two Jameses, and, secondly, it is the first testimony we have had about two central elements in the descriptions of James' death, *being cast down from the Pinnacle of the Temple* and *being beaten to death with a fuller's or laundryman's club*. Both will loom large as we proceed.

For the moment, it should be remarked that Clement mentions them as separate, if consecutive, events. In doing so, he unwittingly unravels a mystery concerning them that has bedeviled scholarship and puzzled commentators ever since. Josephus presents James as having been stoned to death in 62 CE. However, the relationship between such a stoning and his brains being beaten out with a laundryman's club is unclear. One should remark here, too, the quasi-parallel to the 'headlong fall' Judas *Iscariot* takes in Acts 1:18. As we shall see, both the *stoning* and the *headlong fall* can be shown to have occurred, albeit separately, in James' life. Unfortunately, by the beginning of the third century, Clement no longer knows this and is conflating the two events, and turning them into a single happenstance.

Clement presents the tradition of transmission 'after the Resurrection' as being 'to James the Just and John and Peter' in that order. By insisting that 'these gave it to *the other Apostles*, and *the other Apostles* to the Seventy, of whom Barnabas was one', he implies that James, like John and Peter, was *an Apostle*. Not only this, but the number of Apostles for him at this point appears to be indeterminate (2.1.4). Nor does he mention Stephen at all.

Thaddaeus, Judas Thomas, and the Conversion of the Osrhoeans

Eusebius follows his first mention of Jesus' post-resurrection appearance to James with the conversion of the Edessenes by Judas Thomas and Thaddaeus. This episode, which he claims to have personally 'taken from the public archives of the city of Edessa' and translated from the Syriac himself (1.13.5), is usually referred to as the conversion of King Agbar and associated with a Kingdom Eusebius refers to as 'the Osrhoeans' – meaning 'the Assyrians'.

This episode no doubt represents an attempt to account for the growth of Christianity in Northern Syria and Mesopotamia.[1] For Eusebius, 'Agbarus reigned over the Peoples beyond the Euphrates with great glory' – note the important usage of the word '*Ethne*' for 'Peoples'/'Gentiles' here, which, of course, is the term Paul uses to designate the recipients of *his missionary activities*. The story has probably even moved on to become associated with the *evangelization of India*, still associated in myth and story with Thomas's name, though it is doubtful any real-life Thomas ever went that far – whoever this mysterious 'Thomas' was. It is also probably associated with another conversion in the East, that of Queen Helen of Adiabene. It is difficult to sort out the various borders and kingdoms in this area and a group of petty kings referred to in Roman jurisprudence as 'the Kings of the Peoples'.

The story of the conversion of Queen Helen is told by Josephus just prior to the Theudas episode and the notice about the Famine. It is repeated by Eusebius, sometimes under the title of '*the Queen of the Osrhoeans*'. The extent of this Adiabene – probably equivalent to today's Kurdistan along the Tigris in Northern Iraq – and how far it either encroached upon or overlapped Edessa is not something that can readily be determined.

In Syriac sources, Queen Helen is presented as *Abgarus' wife*.[2] The name '*Agbar*' or '*Abgar*' is somewhat generic, associated with Kings from this area, much the same as 'Herod' was in Palestine and 'Aretas' in Petra and Transjordan. In the same manner, '*Monobazus*' will run through the male members of Helen's family. It should be appreciated that 'Abgar' had *many* wives and marital alliances and that Josephus, also, considers Helen's husband Monobazus, whom he says was *'surnamed Bazeus'*, to be her brother.[3]

Whatever the truth of these assertions, the two conversions – Agbar's and Helen's – are amazingly similar and contemporaneous, and these two buffer areas in Northern Syria and Mesopotamia between Rome and the Parthians in Persia are contiguous. The only difference is that, for Josephus, Helen's conversion is to what he thinks is *Judaism*, not Christianity. The question really is whether at this point there was any perceivable difference.

As Josephus tells the story, two men get in among the women in the harem of a king allied to Queen Helen's husband. One, Ananias, bears the same name as the individual with whom Paul becomes involved in 'Damascus', also in Syria, in the conversion scene in Acts 9:17. He is also the intermediary in the 'Agbar correspondence' in Eusebius' depiction of the conversion of the Edessenes. The second individual is not named, but both appear to teach a doctrine that does not require circumcision for Salvation, because Helen had a horror of circumcision. As Josephus puts the doctrine they are preaching: 'worship of God … counted more than circumcision'.[4] Does this sound familiar? Once again the issue turns on the need or lack of need for it.

These details in Josephus are, of course, much more precise than in the legend of King Agbar as it has come down to us through Eusebius and Syriac sources. That it is a very old legend is clear from Eusebius' personal interest in it and he says he got it from 'the ancients'. We will show that traces of it and the Queen Helen story – which very definitely *is* old – will be discernible in the Book of Acts. Therefore, a version of it that could be parodied in Acts' own inimitable manner was already circulating at the time of Acts' composition. As for Eusebius, he correctly identifies Thomas as 'Judas', which he did not do previously and which not even the Gospels do, except by implication, thus providing additional testimony to the accuracy and antiquity of his source.

As Eusebius recounts the story, 'Judas, who is also Thomas, sent out Thaddaeus [to Agbar] as an Apostle being one of the Seventy'. In the Apostle lists of Matthew and Mark, 'Thaddaeus' comes directly after 'James the son of Alphaeus' and right before 'Simon the Cananaean' ('Simon the Zealot' in Luke). In some manuscripts of Matthew, he is 'Lebbaeus surnamed Thaddaeus'. But in the Gospel of Luke, 'Thaddaeus' suddenly metamorphoses into 'Judas the brother *of James*'![5] The timeframe of the Agbarus affair is 'after the Ascension' and the story itself gives the events it is recounting as 29–30 CE according to the Syriac reckoning, which would then put Jesus' crucifixion somewhat before that.

For his part, Josephus tells his Queen Helen story just prior to his representation of Theudas and relates it to 'the great Famine that then took hold of Judea', which he dates some time before the crucifixion of the two sons of Judas the Galilean in 46-48 CE and regarding which he says both Helen and her son sent up Famine relief.[6] Eusebius does likewise, using the *'Theudas'* narrative from Josephus to trigger his own about Helen and the Famine, to which he adds the detail of her family's marvelous funerary monuments in Jerusalem.[7]

Suffice to say that Acts 11:29–30, in its introduction to the beheading of 'James', claims that Paul returned to Jerusalem the first time with Barnabas in order to bring the collection that had been done in Antioch *because of the Famine*. Eusebius thinks the two accounts about Famine relief are related and no doubt they are, but he also thinks the Famine is related to the beheading of 'James the brother of John' (read 'Judas the brother of James'). Finally, Acts introduces in relation to the Famine, *a purported 'prophet' it calls 'Agabus'*. Like 'Thaddaeus', 'Judas Barsabas', and other presumable messengers *'from James'*, he 'came down from Jerusalem to Antioch' – in this instance, *to predict the Famine* (11:28).

This prophet will reappear again in Acts just before Paul's final trip to Jerusalem to see James. Here, too, he 'comes down from Judea', this time to Caesarea, where he is portrayed as warning Paul against going to Jerusalem and predicting Paul will be sent to Rome in chains (21:10–13). Despite the obfuscation and disinformation going on here, I think we can say that the '*Agbarus*' and Queen Helen legends, however distorted, are making an appearance here in Acts. In the process, we should be able to see that this '*Agabus*' is but a thinly disguised version of Queen Helen's husband 'Agbarus' or 'Abgarus'.

The second prophecy Acts associates with this 'prophet named Agabus' will have its parallels in *two very mysterious oracles* having to do with James in Jerusalem: one the oracle, from Jewish Christian sources, occasioning the flight across Jordan to Pella; the second in Josephus – the mournful prophecy of *Jesus ben Ananias*, who went around Jerusalem for seven-and-a-half years following the death of James predicting its fall before he was finally hit on the head and killed by a Roman projectile.

Be these things as they may, there are some conclusions we can draw from all these overlaps and interplays. Let us assume that the 'Thomas' terminology refers, in addition to 'twinning', to a *brother of Jesus*. Let us also assume that Judas Thomas, Thaddaeus, and Theudas are identical. From other sources like the Pseudoclementine *Homilies* and *Recognitions*, we shall be able to show how James in his role of leader of the Jerusalem Church does send out Apostles and others on overseas missions. Paul confirms this when he discusses the 'some from James' that are sent down to check into affairs in Antioch in Galatians 2:12, but also when he fulminates about his opponents having written recommendations in 2 Corinthians 3:1–8. This is not to mention his parallel reference to '*Cephas and the brothers of the Lord*', who travel with women as he does himself in 1 Corinthians 9:5. These 'brothers of the Lord' cannot include James, since James does not appear to do any traveling, but as far as can be determined remains in Jerusalem.

The question of which 'Antioch' one is referring to also must be kept in mind. Finally, let us also assume our sources are for the most part garbled, and also anxious to cover over the leadership of James, obliterating the traces of his existence. Then we can picture a scenario in which it is rather *James who sends out Judas*, that is, 'Judas of James' or 'Jude the brother of James' (even 'Judas Barsabas' in Acts) *to Edessa*, which ends among other things in the conversion of the Edessenes, an occurrence reverberating throughout our literature, including Acts.

Other Testimonies to James' Election or Direct Appointment as Successor

Eusebius also refers to the direct succession of James in several other contexts in his *Ecclesiastical History*, in the process supplying us with valuable information about his character and person. In book 2, chapter 23, he returns to the matter of James' succession. In his previous discussion, with which Book Two began, it will be recalled that he had put this proposition – in his own words – as follows: 'This same James, to whom men had accorded the surname of the Just One … was recorded to be the First elected to the Throne of the Bishopric of the Church in Jerusalem'. Now, again in his own words, he puts this: 'James the brother of the Lord … was *allotted* the *Episcopate* in Jerusalem *by the Apostles*'. Here his use of the term 'Apostles' is, once again, plural and not limited to the Central Three.

This latest phrasing may be a rephrasing or conflation of what he said on this subject at the beginning of Book Two, either quoting Clement to the effect that the Central Triad chose James as the Leader of the Church or, that James the Just 'was elected' to the Episcopate of the Jerusalem Church – the implication being *by the Assembly*.

In the second version of Clement's testimony about James' succession, the implication was that James received his office *directly from Jesus*, and this *after the Resurrection*. This idea is reinforced towards the end of his *History*, in Book Seven, when Eusebius comes to discuss 'the Throne of James' in Jerusalem.[8] There he varies this position just slightly, saying: 'James, who as the Sacred Scriptures show, was generally called *the brother of Christ*, was *the First to receive the Episcopate of Jerusalem from our Savior himself*'. There is no mention here of 'after the Resurrection', though some texts add 'and [from] the Apostles'. This is the first time we have heard of this *Throne of James*, not Jesus. It was obviously a relic of some kind still extant in Jerusalem in Eusebius' time, for he also notes both that it 'has been preserved to this day' and that 'The Christians there look after it with such loving care, making clear to all the veneration in which saintly men high in the favor of God were regarded in time past and are regarded to this day'. This testimony would appear to reflect what is to be found in the Apostolic Constitutions, a work probably of Syriac origin from the second or third centuries, in which is found the reference about 'Judas the Zealot' taking the Truth to the Edessenes in Northern Syria, *not* Thaddaeus or Judas Thomas.

In the Apostolic Constitutions, the Office of Bishop is much labored over and there is a notice about the *direct appointment* of James almost exactly like the one at the end of Eusebius above. This is given at the beginning of a long speech attributed to James with instructions for future bishops, and reads, with James speaking in the first person: 'I, James, *the brother of Christ according to the flesh*, but his Servant regarding the Only Begotten God and one *appointed Bishop of Jerusalem by the Lord himself* and the Apostles, do ordain....'[9]

Here, of course, we have both the references to 'the brother of Christ' in Eusebius above – and this *in the flesh* – and the appointment 'by the Lord himself', the addition of the words 'and the Apostles' seeming, once again, as an addendum to Eusebius, to be an afterthought in deference to traditional sensibilities. It would also appear to be the source of a similar rendition from Epiphanius, a half-century after Eusebius.

Here we have two further contradictions in the testimonies from Eusebius to the idea of James being appointed by the Inner Three: the one claiming James to have been 'elected' or 'chosen by the Apostles'; and the other, that he received the Office *directly from Jesus*. Admittedly, all this is confusing, but it reflects some of the confusion in the early Church regarding this succession. What is not in question is that James *did succeed* and *did receive the Office*, the only question being, as far as Eusebius or his sources are concerned, *how he received it* and *at what point.*

Eusebius refers to the succession of James one more time, quoting Hegesippus, 'who flourished closest to the days of the Apostles' (*c.* 90–180 CE), to similar effect. In the Fifth Book of his *Commentaries*, he says: 'But James, the brother of the Lord, who, *as there were many of this name, was surnamed the Just by all from the days of our Lord until now*, received the Government of the Church with [or 'from'] the Apostles'.[10]

Jerome (348–420), another scholar who like Origen spent a good deal of his life in Palestine, also picks up material from Hegesippus. For him however, James, 'who is called the brother of the Lord and surnamed the Just', was not 'the son of Joseph by another wife, as some think'. Rather, taking a cue from the Gospel of John, he accepts an even more preposterous solution, that James is 'the son of Mary *sister of the mother of the Lord*'.[11] In other words, Mary has a sister called 'Mary', the wife of '*Clopas*', elsewhere regarded as Joseph's brother and the uncle of James and Jesus and the brothers – all very convenient. For the moment, however, suffice it to remark the lengths to which all commentators will go to rescue the divine sonship and supernatural nature of Jesus Christ even as early as the second century.

Like Eusebius, Jerome gives two versions of James' election or appointment as Bishop of the Jerusalem Church, his own understanding of what he has read and a direct quotation from Hegesippus, both of which more or less parallel Eusebius. According to his understanding, James was either '*ordained*' or '*elected by the Apostles as Bishop of Jerusalem*' *immediately after Jesus' Passion.*

What is significant in this is the time frame, that 'after our Lord's Passion' James was '*immediately elected by the Apostles* Bishop of Jerusalem'.[12] In our view, this is the missing *appointment episode* that should have occurred at the beginning of Acts. This would also have explained James' mysterious emergence in Acts' narrative eleven chapters later, as if we should know who he is.

The next version which he gives, as he says, is a quotation from Hegesippus: 'After the Apostles, James the brother of the Lord, surnamed the Just, was made Head of the Church at Jerusalem'. For Jerome, James received the control of the Church 'after the Apostles', meaning presumably *after their appointment.* For Eusebius it is 'with' or 'from' them.

Another older contemporary of Jerome, Epiphanius, Bishop of Salamis, who lived at the end of the fourth century (367-404), admits to having read Eusebius but, like Jerome, it is not clear either whether he knows Hegesippus first hand or through Eusebius. Epiphanius, too, gives James' various epithets, including 'the Just One' and '*Oblias*', which he translates as 'Wall'. Eusebius translated this as 'Protection' or 'Bulwark'. In doing so, Epiphanius presents exactly what we have already heard from Eusebius about James' succession, that 'he was the First to receive the Office of Bishop' – 'Episcopate' again.[13] Epiphanius' emphasis is on James being 'the First', not on who chose him. Again, there is no doubt that James is the *first* Bishop or Overseer. For Epiphanius, this Office is not just relegated to Jerusalem, but a general title – a more accurate reflection, in our view, of what the situation really was. Epiphanius is obviously not willing to concede necessarily that James was 'chosen by the Apostles', nor the Inner Three, nor even a general election by 'the Jerusalem Assembly'. Rather the implication again is that James received this Office *directly from Jesus.*

This is confirmed in the next bit of information Epiphanius attaches to his testimony: that James was 'The First to whom the Lord entrusted his Throne upon earth'.[14] There isn't a clue as to where Epiphanius got this material or so many of the other interesting details he provides, though it may have come from Hegesippus or the *Ascents of Jacob.* Wherever it came from, once more it shows the tremendous prestige James enjoyed across the whole Eastern Mediterranean up to the 400s, when Epiphanius and Jerome both lived.

Once again, it was Jesus himself who entrusted 'his Throne upon earth' to his brother James, though it is not clear whether he did this *while on earth* or in some other manner. However this may be, the 'Throne' imagery is a central element of it. It also recalls the appointment episode in the Gospel of Thomas: 'In the place where you are to go, *go to James the Just for whose sake Heaven and Earth came into existence'.* Not only is this a direct appointment scenario in Jesus' lifetime, but it contains echoes of Kabbalistic thought about '*the Righteous One*', that is, his pre-existence or the fact that he 'supports the earth'.

There are two more *direct-appointment* scenarios we have not yet treated in any detail. The first is to be found in Book One of *Recognitions* (1.43). There, James is not only repeatedly referred to as 'Bishop', but also 'Bishop of Bishops' or 'Archbishop'. Right before a long excursus by Peter on the identity of the Ebionite 'True Prophet' with 'the Christ', the leadership of James is referred to in a most straightforward manner: 'The Church of the Lord which was constituted in Jerusalem multiplied most plentifully and grew, being governed with the most Righteous ordinances by James, *who was ordained Bishop in it by the Lord'.* Not only is this clearly a 'direct appointment' scenario but, paralleling the Gospel of Thomas and Epiphanius, it seems to have occurred *in Jesus' own lifetime.*

Sleight-of-hand in Acts

We are now in a position to return to Acts' treatment of this missing election or appointment of James as successor. As we have discussed, Acts does not present the election of a successor to Jesus as leader of the Messianic Community in Palestine – by whatever name one calls it, *Christian*, *Zealot*, *Essene*, *Jerusalem Assembly*, or some other – but rather a successor to *Judas*.

As Acts begins, Jesus gives the Apostles 'authority' or 'command' in his resurrected state on earth before the Ascension (1:2). This parallels the notice in Hegesippus and its various reflections about 'the command of the Church being given to James together with the Apostles', not to mention the use of the word 'command' relative to the duties of 'the *Mebakker*' at Qumran.

The author also pictures the Apostles as being instructed 'not to leave Jerusalem', because at some point they were going 'to receive Power via the descent of the Holy Spirit upon' them (1:4–8 – *n.b.*, the use of the word '*Power*' here, which will become more and more pronounced as these notices about James proceed). This will occur at Pentecost with the descent of the Holy Spirit upon the whole Community. After forty days and Jesus' assumption to Heaven, 'they return to Jerusalem' (Acts 1:12–14). At this point Luke names them again, and the names are the familiar ones, including Matthew and Thomas, but Judas *Iscariot* or the son 'of Simon *Iscariot*' is missing. The last three, 'James (the son) of Alphaeus (Cleophas?), Simon the Zealot, and Judas (the brother) of James', are of particular interest, as we saw, because they coincide with the names of three of Jesus' brothers.

Acts 1:14 also notes a house with an 'upper chamber' in connection with the Apostles' return to Jerusalem – presumably the same one as in Gospel portrayals of the Last Supper – where they go or appear to be staying 'together with the women and *Mary the mother of Jesus* and *with his brothers*'. In Matthew a parallel Mary is called Mary 'the mother of James and Joses' (27:56); in Mark, 'Mary the mother of James the Less, Joses, and Salome' (15:40); and in Luke, 'Mary the mother of James' (24:10). Elsewhere, Mark 15:47 simply calls her 'Mary the mother of Joses' and Matthew, totally perplexed, finally ends up calling her simply '*the other Mary*' (27:61). Thus, even in Acts' run-up to its *election by lot* to fill Judas' 'Episcopate' or 'Bishopric', we have *at least* one and probably *two* additional references to the brothers and family of Jesus.

The Book of Acts versus the Pseudoclementines

Chapter 2 of Acts concludes with the following description:

> Every day, steadfastly they went as a body to the Temple and breaking bread in the houses, they partook of food with gladness and simplicity of heart, praising God and finding favor *with the whole of the people* (a clear confirmation of the popularity of this Movement), and the Lord daily added to the Assembly of those being saved. (2:47)

This is just the picture one gets in the Pseudoclementine *Recognitions* as well, of visits to the Temple on a regular basis by James and his Community and their debates or discourses with the Chief Priests either in the Temple or on its steps. As the *Recognitions* puts it (paralleling Acts, Peter narrating) in its run-up to the final debate *on the Temple steps* before Paul's *physical assault on James*:

> The Priests ... often sent to us, asking us to discourse to them concerning Jesus, whether He was the Prophet whom Moses foretold. But while they often made such requests to us, and we sought for a fitting opportunity, the Church in Jerusalem was

most plentifully multiplied and grew (this is followed by the notice about *being governed with the most Righteous ordinances by James, who was ordained Bishop in it by the Lord*). (1.43)

This accords with the various notices which punctuate Acts' narrative of the early days of the Community in Jerusalem and connect each of the separate, if often mythological or fantastic, events together. In Acts 5:12–13, leading to the assault on 'Stephen', the phrasing is: 'They all used to meet by common consent in the Portico of Solomon. No one else ever dared to join them, but *the people were loud in their praise*, and t*he multitudes of men and women who believed in the Lord increased steadily'*. Here the parallel with the Pseudoclementines is almost precise. Only the equally drumbeat picture of James' leadership in the Pseudoclementines is missing in Acts' narrative.

It is interesting, too, that many of the themes at this point in Acts are taken up in the Pseudoclementine *Recognitions* – as for instance the common purse (Acts 4:34–5:10) and the speech by Gamaliel (5:34–40), represented here as a secret supporter of the Community. As in some manuscripts of the Gospel of Matthew, '*Lebbaeus*' is the name of the Apostle called '*Judas of James*' in Luke instead of '*Thaddaeus*'; after he speaks, '*Simon the Canaanite*' takes his turn on the Temple steps and then 'Barnabas who was also surnamed Matthias' and 'substituted in place of Judas as an Apostle' (*thus*), and finally Gamaliel.[15]

In the Syriac rendition of this, 'Barnabas' is now called 'Barabbas who became an Apostle instead of Judas the Traitor'. Even these overlaps and confusions have a certain peculiar logic, and one can perhaps assume that the author of the *Recognitions* was transforming his version of the source underlying Acts in his own likewise tendentious and inimitable fashion.

Following Gamaliel's speech, Acts 5:42 now picks up the theme again of the Apostles being constantly in the Temple: '*They preached every day both in the Temple and in private houses*, and their proclamation of the Gospel of Jesus the Christ was never interrupted'. For its part 6:1, leading into the attack on or the stoning of Stephen and the murmuring of the Hellenists against the Hebrews, picks up the 'multiplication' theme again: 'And in those days, the Disciples were multiplying'.

The language here is almost word for word that of the *Recognitions*, the only thing missing, again, being *the election of James*. The words the Pseudoclementines give us here concerning the requests by the Chief Priests to 'the Archbishop James' for debates with the early Christian Community in the Temple or on its steps are also directly paralleled in chapters 3–5 of the Book of Acts. In turn, these harmonize very well with the requests by the Chief Priests in the long narrative from Hegesippus about James' final days in Eusebius. In this account – to a certain extent also recapitulated in Epiphanius and Jerome – the Chief Priests are shown as coming to James and asking him *to stand* on 'a wing' or 'the Pinnacle of the Temple' and quiet the people.

As Eusebius puts it, quoting Hegesippus verbatim:

From which some believed that *Jesus was the Christ* (this note about Jesus 'being the Christ' is also the point of James' speech at this point in the *Recognitions*). But the aforesaid heresies did not believe either in the Resurrection or that *He was coming to give to every one according to his works*, but as many as did believe, did so *on account of James* (thus far, this more or less parallels the Pseudoclementines) ... There arose a riot among the Jews and Scribes and Pharisees, saying that the whole people was in danger of looking for Jesus as the Christ. So they assembled, and said to James, 'We beseech you to restrain the people, who are going astray after Jesus as though he were the Christ. We beseech you to persuade all who are coming to the feast of the Passover rightly concerning Jesus; for all obey you. For we and all the people testify

> that you are Righteous and *do not respect persons*. Therefore, persuade the people not to be led astray after Jesus, for all the people and ourselves have confidence in you. Therefore stand upon a wing of the Temple that you may be clearly visible from above and your words readily heard by all the people.[16]

There follows the account, again following Hegesippus, of the attack on James and his fall from, not 'the steps' this time, but the wing or Pinnacle of the Temple. This is the sequencing followed in the Pseudoclementines too, though there James only falls from the steps of the Temple and the nature of the attack differs somewhat. Nor does James die because of it. It is our position that this attack, as pictured in the Pseudoclementines, *is a more accurate representation* of the events as they really occurred than those in early Church literature, which are all more or less dependent on each other and will be seen as clearly attempting to cover up *embarrassing* aspects of this attack.

This presentation in Eusebius/Hegesippus is very similar to what we see in the Pseudoclementines and even in Acts. It is also very strong testimony to the authenticity of the Pseudoclementine account at this point anyhow – or at least its underlying source. In this sense, the Pseudoclementine tradition is a *more primitive version* of the episode, which, by the second century and Hegesippus, is already beginning to undergo its various transformations.

Note the great respect the Jerusalem Community leaders enjoy among the crowd. There is really no point to lie in favor of this presentation; on the contrary. James is presented as so popular that the Herodian Establishment feel the people will do whatever he 'commands' them to do. It is even stated that 'all obey you', that is, he is the popular Leader among the people, and they will do whatever he says.

This is exactly the presentation in Josephus of the events surrounding the death of John the Baptist as well. There, Josephus says that Herod Antipas feared that the people would be prepared to do whatever John said and he fears that John will lead an uprising. This is also the approach of the Gospel presentation of Jesus, which constantly emphasizes his wide popularity and the stratagems the High Priests must undertake to incarcerate him. There can be little doubt that this is the truth of the situation.

When discussing James' '*Zaddik*' nature and the 'Righteous One' ideology generally, it is possible to make some sense out of these testimonies. The same where the Righteous Teacher at Qumran is concerned, and his '*Zaddik*' nature, which so parallels James'. In our understanding, James was 'the *Zaddik*' of the Opposition Alliance, meaning that all the people including the Rulers – were obliged to pay him homage, and as such, *obey him*.

Additional Parallels Between Acts and the Pseudoclementines

In the Pseudoclementine *Recognitions,* James' debate with the Priests in the Temple is followed by the attack in which he is thrown down the steps of the Temple and breaks his leg. It comes after the speeches of the other Apostles on the Temple steps and Gamaliel. This is the order in Acts as well. There Gamaliel's speech on the Temple Mount is followed by that of Stephen and the latter's *stoning*, in connection with which Saul or Paul is introduced (Acts 5:34–8:1).

In the Pseudoclementines James 'speaks from a height, so that (he) can be seen by all the people'. This speech has much in common with the one in Eusebius/Hegesippus before *he is stoned* as well. This is particularly true of James' answer to the question, 'what is the Gate to Jesus': 'He is sitting in Heaven *on the right hand of the Great Power* and he is about to come on the clouds of Heaven'.[17] The language here is exactly that accompanying the 'footstool' imagery from Psalm 110:1–3, which Peter uses in the parallel narrative in Acts – also in the general ambience of verbal confrontations on the Temple Mount – to accuse the *Jewish crowd* (not the High Priests) of murdering Jesus (2:30–35).

This imagery, which is based on Daniel 7:13 and contains the 'Great Power' language so important to later sectarian understanding of 'the Christ', is clearly that of the Redeemer Jesus *coming in Power on the clouds of Heaven with the Heavenly Host.* It is paralleled to some degree in James' speech on the Temple steps in the Pseudoclementine *Recognitions* at this point as well. Here James is pictured as giving the scriptural warrants for *two comings*, the first, more humble, having already transpired. But the second 'in Glory' would be more supernatural and mighty – that is, the Messiah coming on the clouds of Heaven with the Heavenly Host – in which he would reign over '*those who believe* in him and *do everything* that He commanded'.

James' proclamation of the Messiah 'coming with Power on the clouds of Heaven with the Heavenly Host' at Passover in the Temple is the crucial one for Jerome as well. The same vision will be attributed to Jesus in what will turn out to be the retrospective presentation of his responses to the Sanhedrin trial for 'blasphemy' in 'the High Priest's House' the night of his execution in the Gospels (Matt. 26:64 and Mark 14:62). But, even more importantly and most tellingly, it is also the vision Acts 7:56 vouchsafes to Stephen immediately preceding its picture of *his stoning* and Paul's appearance on the scene.

It is the author's view that all of these presentations are, in fact, prefigured in the two versions of James' speech in the Temple prior to the attack on him or his stoning in the Pseudoclementine *Recognitions* and early Church accounts.

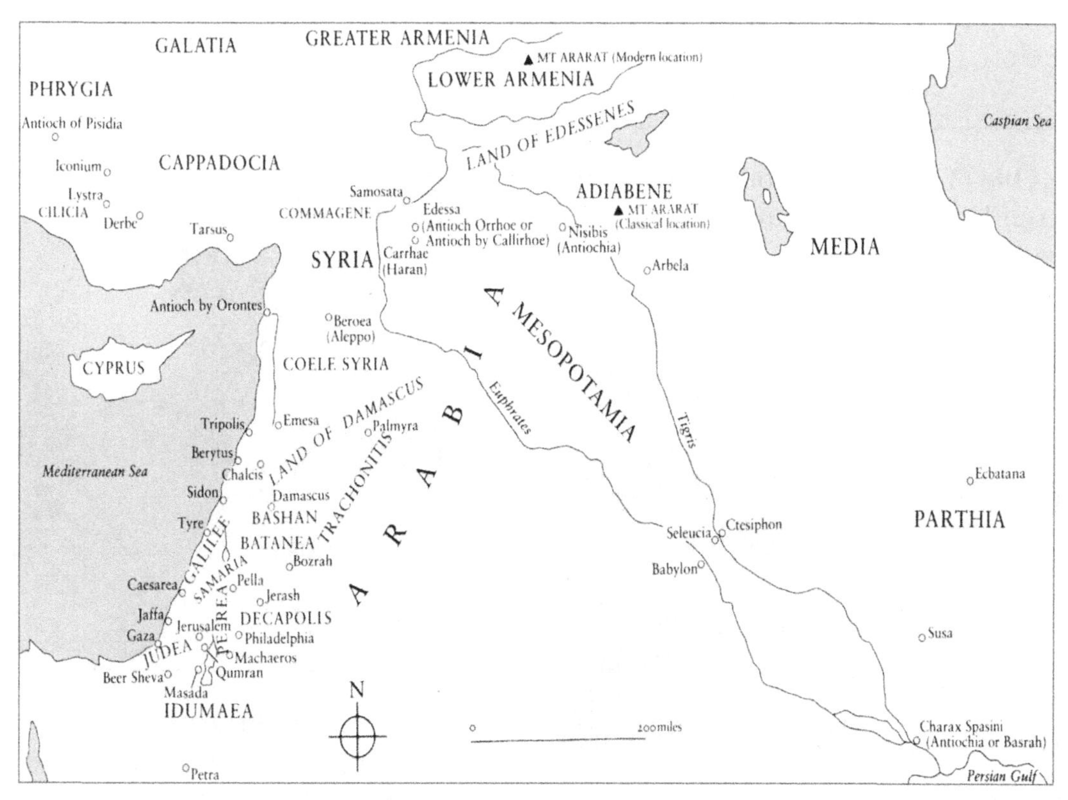

Map of Arabia and Syria

Entrance to man-made water conduit at Qumran that channels run-off water to the pools below.

Run-off of winter rains, flood down the cliffs of the Wadi Qumran, filling the cisterns.

One of the mysterious water storage facilities at Qumran. It was probably used as a ritual immersion pool

View of Qumran's water storage at the bottom of the waterfall, with the Dead Sea in the distance.

Another of the many bathing pools at Qumran, this one still able to hold water.

PART III

JAMES' ROLE IN THE JERUSALEM OF HIS DAY

Chapter 10
James' Rechabitism and Naziritism

The Privy for the High Priests, the Prostitute's Hire, and Judas *Iscariot's 'Price of Blood'*

Having delineated James' election or appointment as leader of the Jerusalem Assembly, we are now in a better position to consider his person and role in the Jerusalem of his day, in particular James as a 'Rechabite' and 'Nazirite'. To do so, it is best to work backwards and begin with the later testimonies in Talmudic and early Church literature and close with the more contemporary literature at Qumran.

The Talmudic references centre on a character called *'Jacob of Sihnin'* or *'Kfar Sechania', a town supposedly in Galilee.* In the most famous of these stories, 'Jacob' (the Hebrew or Greek of 'James') comes to cure a famous rabbi of snakebite.[1] This Rabbi, Eliezer ben Hyrcanus, was supposed to have had heretical tendencies and was actually *excommunicated* at one point by his fellow rabbis on the suspicion of being *a secret Christian.* Jacob tells him a story about *'Jesus the Nazoraean'*, this time relating not to a *'Traitor's hire'* as in the Judas story, but a *'harlot's hire'*.

In support of this, he quotes two scriptural passages: one from Deuteronomy 23:18 about 'bringing a prostitute's hire into the House of God' and the other Micah 1:7: 'from the earnings of a prostitute she (the Temple) gathered them, and to the hire of a prostitute (the High Priesthood) they should return'. Stories about 'prostitutes' or 'harlots' in this period usually have something to do with both condemnations of *'fornication'* and attacks on the Establishment and their sexual mores. Jacob's story, which is rather bawdy and amusing, has to do with how Jesus the Nazoraean saw the issue of contributions to the Temple from *prostitutes.* Not only do Jacob and Jesus exhibit the characteristic hostility towards the High Priests and the Establishment we have come to expect from opposition leaders, but Jesus is presented as being unsympathetic to prostitutes or harlots too, quite different from how the Gospels portray him.

On another level, this story also has to do with the Herodian aristocracy contributing to the Temple, as it would have done regularly and extravagantly. Jacob actually evinces quite a funny sense of humor about this. He provocatively starts the discussion by quoting Deuteronomy 23:18 about *'a prostitute's hire in the House of God'* and, taking advantage of Eliezer's momentary astonishment, rhetorically asks whether or not it would be 'lawful to use such hire to construct an *outhouse for the High Priest'*.

In Deuteronomy 23, this matter about the earnings of sacred prostitutes (17–18) immediately follows curses on *'Balaam the son of Be'or'* and the proscription on admitting Edomites (often designating 'Herodians' in our period) into 'the Lord's Congregation' (23:1–9). This is followed by *'going out to the camps to face the enemy'* and *'God walking with them in the camps'* (allusions found in the War Scroll), and the 'the camps being Holy' (23:19–24). This is the context in which the issue of latrines is discussed and their placement outside the camps.

Picking up this issue of toilets, Jacob answers his own question by citing a quotation he attributes to *'Jesus the Nazoraean'* to the effect that 'since it originated in filth, it can be applied to filth', meaning that it would be a good thing 'to build a privy' or 'outhouse for the High Priest' with such earnings. Not only is the audacity of this question astonishing in its contemptuous sarcasm, but it parallels a saying of Jesus in orthodox Scripture, basically used to widen the permissions regarding forbidden things or, as Mark puts it, to *declare 'all things pure'.* The whole discussion, which begins with 'Jesus' addressing the question of *'eating with unwashed hands'*, ends with the now proverbial *'not that which enters the mouth defiles a man'; this 'is cast into the toilet bowl'*. Rather *'that which goes forth out of the mouth defiles a man'* (Mt 15:17–18 and Mk 7:15–20).

Interestingly, the 'prostitute's wages' of Deuteronomy 23:18 that 'Jesus the Nazoraean' considers to be 'filth' is coupled with 'the hire of a dog', generally thought to carry the sense – clear from the context – of male prostitution.

Mark begins his discussion of 'purifying all food' and 'declaring all things clean' with allusion to 'coming from the marketplace' and not having to wash your hands like 'the Pharisees and *all the Jews* do' (7:2–5). Paul, too, answering James' directives to overseas communities on 'food sacrificed to idols' in I Corinthians 10:23–25, evokes the marketplace in making a parallel point: 'all things are Lawful for me ... Eat everything that is sold in the marketplace. There is no need to raise questions of conscience'. Though Mark, unlike Matthew, does not specifically apply the 'casting out' language to unclean things going out the belly and into the toilet (7:19), he does employ it in the very next episode – his version of Jesus 'casting out the unclean spirit' (*ekballe*) of the Syrophoenician woman's daughter (7:24-26). Like Matthew, however, Mark then does use 'casting down' language in the second half of this episode, the part about 'taking the children's bread and casting (*balein*) (it) to the dogs' (7:27–29). This kind of language and these themes will reappear in John 21's version of Jesus' post-resurrection appearances along the Sea of Galilee and the Disciples – called by Jesus 'little children' – 'casting down' their nets there.

Throughout all of these matters, we will have in the Gospels the typical reversal of themes in favor of the Pauline 'Gentile Mission'. This is also clear in the saying of Jesus Matthew presents about 'things entering the mouth not defiling a man', but 'being cast down the toilet bowl' (Mt 15:11–17), to wit, 'Every plant which my Heavenly Father has not planted shall be uprooted' (15:13). The Jewish legal prohibitions regarding unclean things, including 'washing the hands' and the 'washings of cups and pots and brazen vessels' in Mark 7:4, are just these kinds of 'plants'.

But this position is completely gainsaid in the series of parables – also in Matthew – having to do with 'the Tares of the Field' and 'the Enemy who sowed' the Evil seed (13:24–41). These are just about the only anti–Pauline parables in the Gospels and end with the characteristic condemnation of 'those *doing*' or '*practicing* Lawlessness', who 'shall be *cast* into a furnace of Fire' (*balousin* – 13:41–43). We shall see how this imagery will recur in both the Letter of James and the Habakkuk *Pesher* from Qumran.

Matthew follows this up with another parable comparing the Kingdom of Heaven 'to a net being *cast* into the sea', which like John 21 makes repeated mentions of 'casting down' (*bletheise* – 13:47–50). The unifying allusion in this parable, having to do with fish again – *rotten fish* – with 'the Field of Tares', is 'casting them (*balousin*) into the furnace of Fire' (13:50). Here, the reference is rather to '*separating the Wicked* (the rotten fish) *from the midst of the Righteous*' rather than the Scrolls' *separating the Righteous from the midst of the Wicked.*

Even more startling than any of these is the amazing reversal one finds in Matthew's version of Judas Iscariot's suicide. Like the matter of the prostitute's wages, this also has to do with the High Priests and the Temple Treasury: 'And the High Priests took the pieces of silver and said: "It is not Lawful to put them in the Treasury, since it is *the price of blood*"' (Mt 27:6). Not only does this incorporate a play on the banning of blood in *both* Jewish dietary *and* sexual prohibitions, but also on Paul's contention that 'all things are Lawful for me'. This is the position Matthew basically pictures Jesus as adopting in the 'unwashed hands' episode above that nothing 'entering the mouth defiles a man'. As Paul puts this in 1 Corinthians 6:13, immediately following his first 'all things Lawful' permission and also grouping dietary prohibitions with sexual ones: 'Food is for the belly and the belly for foods, but God will bring both to nothing. However the body is not for fornication, but for the Lord' (1 Cor. 6:13).

The subject of 'blood', central to both of these, will also be integral to 'the Cup of the New Covenant in his blood' ideology, with follows in this section of 1 Corinthians (10:16–11:25). In Luke's version of 'the Last Supper', this will be 'the Cup of the New Covenant in my blood which is poured out for you' (Luke 22:20). This will represent yet another esoteric reformulation into Greek from the Hebrew 'New Covenant in the Land of Damascus', found in both the Damascus Document and the Habbakuk *Pesher* from Qumran – '*Dam*', the Hebrew word for 'blood', being equivalent to the first syllable of the word 'Damascus' as written in Greek; '*Chos*', the Hebrew word for 'Cup', the last.[2]

This proscription on 'blood', part and parcel of the 'First Covenant' with Moses on Mount Sinai and the legendary 'Noahic' one preceding it,[3] is the first and most fundamental element in James' prohibitions to overseas communities, to which Paul seems to be responding in 1 Corinthians 6–11.

The proscription on blood also relates to James' extreme Naziritism and vegetarianism, not to mention his 'life-long virginity'.[4] In turn, all of these will have to do with a group embodying many such 'Nazirite' traits, the 'Rechabites', known as well for their *proscription on wine*, another trait early Church sources will ascribe to James.

In Hebrew, the word 'Nazirite', meaning 'consecrated' or 'separated', is based on a root meaning *set aside* or *keep away from*. One should remark the play on this word represented by the designation 'Nazoraean', applied in Jacob of Kfar Sechania's story to Jesus and, it would appear, to James' followers generally. In Hebrew 'Nazoraean' (sometimes 'Nazarean' in Scripture) has a slightly different root, meaning 'keeping' or 'Keeper'. In Scripture, too, this sometimes – but not always – gets rephrased, particularly in translation, as 'of Nazareth'!

Not only is this 'Nazirite' ideology sometimes expressed as 'Nazoraean', but one should note the play on it represented by the Hebrew term '*Nezer*', 'the Crown' or 'diadem' worn by High Priests, which bore a plate inscribed with the words, 'Holy to God'. Both 'the diadem' and these words will have special import for notices recorded in early Church tradition about James.

In Hebrew, '*Nezer*' also has the secondary meaning of *the unshorn locks of the Nazirite* – his 'Crown', so to speak – which tradition also says was *worn by James*. This symbolism will have particular relevance for Acts' substitution of the stoning of Stephen, a name also bearing the meaning of 'Crown' in Greek, for the attack on or stoning of James.

These references to 'blood' (or 'wine') not only circulate somewhere around Judas Iscariot's attendance at the Last Supper, but Matthew also goes on to describe how the High Priests 'bought the Potter's Field for a cemetery for foreigners' with the money or 'price of blood' that Judas 'cast into' the Temple Treasury (Mt 27:5–6). This episode is transformed in Mark and Luke into Jesus' parable about the 'Poor' widow 'casting' her one or two mites 'into the Temple Treasury'.

It is also echoed somewhat in Jesus' saying about the unclean things of the belly 'being cast into the toilet bowl'. In our view, the presentation of Jesus in Rabbinic tradition, basically supporting extreme purity and cleanliness, is a truer version of what an *Historical* Jesus would have actually said than any of these others, which obviously reflect Paul's perspective of the subject.

One should also note the partial play, in Matthew's reference to 'the Potter's Field' or 'Field of Blood', on his earlier parable about 'the Tares of the Field' (13:36). Even more germane is the *Potter* part of this *Field* allusion. This will allow us to unravel the whole tangle of these materials and connect them to the 'Rechabites', which will ultimately be – along with Ebionites, Nazoraeans, and Essenes – another synonym for James' 'Jerusalem Community'.

The Rechabites, their Abstention from Wine, and the Cup of Blood

In identifying this 'Potter's Field' with 'the Field of Blood' (27:7–8), Matthew says he is going to quote a passage from the Prophet Jeremiah, who first extensively delineated who these 'Rechabites' were. Instead, he quotes a passage from *the Prophet Zechariah*, which he paraphrases as follows:

> Then that which was spoken by *Jeremiah the Prophet* (*thus*) was fulfilled (that is, when the High Priests took the pieces of silver that Judas *Iscariot* had cast into the Treasury and bought with them the Potter's Field, 'called the Field of Blood to this day'), saying 'And I took the thirty pieces of silver, the price of him who was priced, on whom they of the sons of Israel set a price, and gave them for the Potter's Field, as *the Lord had commanded me*'. (27:9-10)

To understand Matthew's confusion about the source of this quotation, one must start with the allusion to 'command' in the last clause, '…the Potter's Field, as the Lord had commanded me'. This nowhere appears in Zechariah, but it is the central focus of *Jeremiah*'s presentation of *Jonadab son of Rechab*'s 'commands' to his descendants not to drink wine, plant no field, nor build any permanent abode (Jer 35:1–19). Likewise, 'the Potter's Field' does not appear in Zechariah 11, but only in Matthew's paraphrase of it above.

Acts 1:18–19 provides a totally different picture, not based on Zechariah 11:12–13, nor mentioning any 'Potters' at all. Nor does Judas *Iscariot* 'hang himself'; rather he 'falls face downwards, his entrails gushing out'. He buys his *own* 'Field' out of his 'Reward for Unrighteousness', the '*Akeldama*, which is, in their own language, Field of Blood'. Judas doesn't 'cast' thirty pieces of silver into the Temple Treasury, nor do the High Priests buy anything 'with them'. In our view, the latter element comes from the story of Jacob of Sihnin above, where *the Priests* buy '*a toilet*' – the 'price of blood' or 'bloody' fornication (Deut. 23:18's 'prostitute's hire') being the key connection.

What *does* appear in Zechariah 11:13 is 'cast them to the Potter in the House of God', and this is what Matthew uses. The passage from Zechariah reads: 'And the Lord said to me, "*Cast it to the Potter* (the reason for the 'casting' language regarding Judas' *casting down the pieces of silver in the Temple* in Matthew 27:5), a goodly price, that I was valued at by them". And I took *the thirty pieces of silver and cast them to the Potter in the House of the Lord'* (11:12–13).

'Casting to the Potter' is normally taken as a euphemism for the Temple Treasury. This is clearly how Matthew understands it too in his version of how *Judas Iscariot cast the pieces of silver into the Temple,* not to mention the variation in Mark and Luke's picture of the *Poor* widow casting her one or two mites *into the Temple Treasury*.

For Matthew 27:6, the High Priests now take the silver and say, 'It is *not Lawful to put them into the Treasury*, because it is *the price of blood*'. The emphasis on 'Lawfulness' here brings us right back to Jacob's anecdote about Jesus' view of the 'Lawfulness' of 'bringing a prostitute's hire into the House of the Lord your God'. It also circles back to the contrapositive of this in Paul's blanket permission, 'all things are Lawful for me'.

The theme of 'joining', connected to both 'a prostitute's members', and 'the House of the Lord' in 1 Corinthians 6:16–17, is also important in the Scrolls and will reappear in the Nahum *Pesher* and Damascus Document in the context of *strangers or foreigners* 'attaching themselves to' or 'joining' the Community.[5] Even more significantly, it follows the Three Nets of Belial prohibitions on 'fornication', 'polluting the Temple', and the charge against the Establishment of 'sleeping with women in their menstrual flow'. In the Damascus Document, this last becomes the bridge between the 'fornication' and 'pollution of the Temple' charges and, in it, all are inextricably connected.[6]

Not only does it directly involve 'blood', it brings us back to Judas' saying, 'I have sinned, delivering up guiltless blood' and the High Priests' refusing to put 'the price of blood' into the Treasury in Matthew 27:4-6, not to mention Pilate 'being guiltless of the blood of this Righteous One' that follows in 27:24. In evoking this refusal on the part of the High Priests to put Judas' silver pieces in the Treasury, Matthew now uses the 'Potter' allusion in the passage from Zechariah that he quoted in support of this to develop his crucial 'Potter's Field' designation (Mt 27:7-9).

Again, none of these elements has survived in Acts, except the allusion to '*Akeldama*' or 'Field of Blood', which appears to be connected as much to *the bloody fall* Judas takes as to 'the price of blood' it is supposedly bought with.

To bring us full circle, in Rabbinic tradition, the 'Potters' as in Matthew's 'Potter's Field' are, in fact, *also Rechabites.* These 'Rechabites', whom we mentioned above with regard to James' Naziritism and *abstention from wine* – not to mention sexual activity – are defined in Rabbinic tradition and in Jeremiah as 'keeping the oath' of their father Jonadab the son of Rechab to 'drink no wine, plant no field, nor build any permanent abode', and are thought to have been 'Potters'. The root used in the Rabbinic tradition to express this 'keeping the oath' is '*linzor*', the root as well of *Nozrim* – 'Christians' in the *Talmud* – and *Nazoraeans*/'Keepers'.[7] Interestingly, Matthew 26:71 now applies this 'Nazoraean' terminology to Jesus – this right after 'the Last Supper' and before his description of 'the Potter's Field' and Pilate 'washing his hands'.

It is this '*Potter*' and '*Field*' imagery that Matthew so deftly capitalizes on to build his version of Zechariah. Now the reason for this incongruous mention of the Prophet Jeremiah should be clear: it is in Jeremiah that 'Jonadab son of Rechab', the proverbial 'father of the Rechabites' and his 'house' are delineated. These are called *Rechabites* because they '*kept the Commandments* their Father *gave them* and *did all he commanded them*' (35:18 – note the 'doing' emphasis here), including 'dwelling in tents' (35:10) and '*living on the ground like Strangers*' (35:7). This is where the allusion to *command* or *commanded* that appears in Matthew's version of Zechariah – which like 'the Potter's Field' nowhere appears in the original – comes from.

In our view, these are the passages that originally appeared in the source underlying our present accounts – which also included the introduction of James missing from Acts in its present form. This source was using part of or the whole of Jeremiah 35:1-19 about 'the Rechabites', just like early Church sources thereafter, to explain the peculiar characteristics of James' being. Matthew also took material from sources like those behind the Rabbinic story about Jacob of Kfar Sechania's story about '*the High Priest's privy*' and overwrote them; Acts, sources behind the early Church accounts of the death of James to develop the story about 'the suicide' or 'fall' of Judas *Iscariot.*

'The Cup of the New Covenant in His Blood' and 'Drinking No Wine'

This refusal on the part of the House of Rechab to '*drink wine*' is exactly the behavior of James in early Church sources. This then is reversed in the Synoptic Gospels with Jesus' *new* Commandment 'to drink' *the wine at the Last Supper* – the wine in this case being *his blood* (Mt 26:27 and pars.).

We have already hinted at the relationship of 'blood' in this context to the terminology 'Damascus' and 'the New Covenant erected in the Land of Damascus' in the Damascus Document. In Matthew's account of the Last Supper, Jesus takes the bread, blesses it, and bids all eat. Then he takes the cup, and bids all drink, words paralleled in 1 Corinthians 10:16 by Paul. Now the 'blood' is 'the blood of the New Covenant'.

Matthew even employs the 'pouring' imagery of the Damascus Document as well but varied somewhat and in the latter applied to 'the Man of Lying' or 'the Lying Spouter'. Now

Matthew applies it, not to 'Spouting' or 'Pouring out Lying', but to 'the blood of the New Covenant being *poured out* for the Many for remission of sins' (26:28). The term 'the Many' is, of course, the Qumran terminology for the rank and file of the Community.[8]

We are now in a world of almost pure allegorization, thematic variation, and repeated wordplay. Judas is the one 'delivering up guiltless blood' (27:4). Not only do we have wordplay here relating to the theme of *consuming blood while eating*, considered 'guiltless' by Paul, but we shall see how this '*delivering up*' is used at one point in the Damascus Document in relation to 'consuming blood'.[9] Judas receives '*the price of Blood*', the '*hire*' the High Priests refuse to put in the Temple Treasury, with which they buy '*the Potter's Field*' ('*the High Priest's privy*' in the story about '*Jesus the Nazoraean*') – now '*the Field of Blood*' – instead.

All this ends up with Pilate averring that he is 'guiltless of the blood of *this Righteous One*' and releasing Barabbas instead, while the Jewish crowd cries out, 'Let his *blood* be on us and our children' (Mt 27:23-25). Note the irony of '*Zaddik*' language and that of 'guiltlessness' and 'blood' put in the mouth of perhaps *the most brutal Roman Governor ever sent to Palestine.*

Here in Matthew, Jesus 'takes the cup' and commands 'all to drink' the wine 'of the New Covenant in (his) blood' (26:28 – 'the Cup (of) the New Covenant in (his) blood' in Luke 22:20). However, in the very next line in Matthew and Mark, Jesus suddenly and inexplicably reverses himself, saying, 'But I say unto you, that I will *not henceforth drink of this fruit of the vine at all* until the day when I drink it with you new *in the Kingdom of my Father*' (Mt 26:29 and Mk 14:25).

There can be very little doubt that this basically repeats the 'Commandment' the sons of the Rechabites receive from 'Jonadab their Father' in Jeremiah 35:6, 8, and 14, to 'drink no wine'. Even the words 'wine', 'vineyard', 'Father', and 'to the day' are to be found in the above passages from Jeremiah. In particular, one should note how: 'Jonadab the son of Rechab, who commanded his sons not to drink wine ... and they did not drink to this day, but rather obeyed the Commandments of their Father' (35:14). We have seen how this 'obeying the command of their Father' reappears in Matthew 27:10's citation of Zechariah 11:13 as 'the Lord commanded me'. This is even more in evidence in the sections of 1 Corinthians 10–13 evoking 'the Cup of ... Communion with the blood of Christ' and 'drinking this Cup'. Here it is stated: 'So that whoever should eat this bread or should *drink the Cup of the Lord unworthily* shall *be guilty* of the body and blood of the Lord ... for *he who eats and drinks unworthily, eats and drinks Judgment to himself...*' (1 Cor. 11:27–29).

Personal pique on Paul's part aside, this is the 'vengeance' imagery we shall find associated with this 'Cup' in the Habakkuk *Pesher* – but, importantly, also in Revelation. It is also Pontius Pilate's disclaimer at the end of this string of references to 'the Cup' and the 'blood' in Matthew – including Pilate now 'washing his hands' (not 'the Jews' as in the Gospels and Paul) – of 'not being guilty of the blood of this Righteous One' and the Jewish crowd, like the descendants of Jonadab the son of Rechab above, taking the 'blood' on themselves and their 'children' (Mt 27:24–25). We shall encounter all of this language in the Habakkuk *Pesher*'s picture of the destruction of the Righteous Teacher – paralleling the death 'of the Lord' above – including *cup/Cup of the Lord* wordplays, allusion to 'the body', the specific command to 'drink', and 'being eaten' or 'swallowed', in this instance by 'the Cup of the Wrath of God'.

This 'drinking the Cup of the Lord' symbolism is now combined by Paul in 1 Corinthians 10–11 with repeated evocation of 'eating everything sold in the marketplace' or 'eating all set before you and not raising questions of conscience' (10:25-27), finally even including what James bans in his directives to overseas communities in Acts, 'things sacrificed to idols' (10:28). But, one should also note, James in these categories is specifically portrayed as also banning 'blood', which must be taken both symbolically and profanely.

All this is another classic case of New Testament reversal – though on a much vaster scale – an absolutely astonishing reversal of the sense of the Prophet Jeremiah's description of the Rechabites, who *keep the command of their Father to drink no wine, own no field, and live only in tents*, so that they 'may live many days on the face of the land on which (they) live'. Just as this bowdlerized or somewhat refurbished description introduces the election to fill the Office of the Overseer or *Mebakker* ('Bishop') in this first chapter of Acts, so too it will serve as a good introduction to James' Naziritism – Naziritism being a basically analogous term to this Rechabitism – this, not to mention the 'priestly' connotations we shall see go along with both.

It also relates to the more distant parallel in the Damascus Document's 'New Covenant in the Land of Damascus', in regard to which the *Mebakker*'s mastery of 'all the Tongues of men' is evoked, and where presumably there was some *living in tents in the wilderness camps*. We shall now encounter all of these traits which Jeremiah ascribes to his 'Rechabites' again in early Church descriptions of James, not to mention a tradition in Eusebius, attributed to Hegesippus and recapitulated by Epiphanius, that identifies the witness to the stoning and death of James – his so-called first 'cousin' (or brother) Simeon bar Cleophas – as '*one of the Priests of the Sons of Rechab, one of the Rechabites*'![10]

James as *Zaddik* – His Righteousness

We shall reproduce Eusebius' famous testimony to James in detail, augmenting it and correcting it, when necessary, with the sometimes more precise materials from Epiphanius and Jerome. We shall also enlarge on it with materials from Origen, the Pseudoclementines, and to some extent the two Apocalypses of James from Nag Hammadi. Origen's source, by his own testimony, is Josephus, a Josephus attested to as well by Eusebius and Jerome, which all may have seen in Caesarea, a version that sadly no longer exists. Jerome may be dependent on the previous two whom, interestingly enough, he seems to view as *heretics*.[11] The source for the Pseudoclementines, particularly the sequence of events in the *Recognitions* – deleted from the *Homilies* – regarding James and the early history of the Church in Jerusalem, is unknown.

The first thing to observe in relation to all these accounts is the coupling of the attribute of pre-eminent Righteousness (*Zedek* in Hebrew; *Dikaios* in Greek) with the person of James and, therefore, the sobriquet 'the Righteous' or 'Just One' attached permanently to his name – sometimes used in place of his name itself. To avoid problems in Greek, Latin, or English, it is often useful to employ the Hebrew original, '*the Zaddik*'.

This attribute is encountered even in the testimony to James which Origen, Eusebius, and Jerome saw in the copy of Josephus available to them. Though nowhere to be found in the extant Josephus, it is quoted by Eusebius – who implies it is from the *War* – in the following manner: 'And these things happened to the Jews to avenge James the Just, who was the brother of Jesus, the so-called Christ, for the Jews put him to death, notwithstanding his pre-eminent Righteousness'.[12] Here it is not immediately clear whether 'the Jews' put James to death, notwithstanding his pre-eminent Righteousness, or Jesus, so close is this last to traditional notions of the import of Jesus' death. But on closer analysis, it is clear Eusebius or the Josephus he saw means James.

Origen reproduces something of the same idea, though he claims Josephus referred to it in the *Antiquities*. Since Josephus' *Antiquities* does not encompass a discussion of the fall of the Temple *per se* as the War does, it is more likely that Eusebius is more correct in this matter. Origen gives the tradition as follows:

> *So great a reputation among the people for Righteousness did this James enjoy*, that Flavius Josephus, who wrote the *Antiquities of the Jews* in Twenty Books, when wishing to

show the cause of what the people suffered, *so great were their misfortunes that even the Temple was razed to the ground, said that these things happened to them* in accordance with the *Wrath of God* in consequence of t*he things which they had dared to do against James the brother of Jesus who is called the Christ.*

Then he adds: '*The wonderful thing is, that though he did not accept Jesus as Christ, he yet gave testimony* that *the Righteousness of James was so great*; and he says that the people thought that they had suffered these things *because of* (*what had been done to*) *James'*.[13] This is extremely interesting testimony and hardly something either Origen or Eusebius would or could have dreamed up entirely by themselves, because it contradicts authoritative Church doctrine, which rather ascribed the fall of Jerusalem, as Origen himself contends, to Jesus' death not James'.

Jerome, too, gives us a version of this tradition about James: 'This same Josephus records the tradition that this James was of *such great Holiness and repute* among the people that the downfall of Jerusalem was believed to be on account of his death'.[14] It is not clear from this, however, whether he has actually seen Josephus for himself or is simply repeating these words of his two predecessors.

Eusebius has also reproduced various early Church traditions relating to the death of James. Two features of these descriptions should be noted. These argue strongly for the authenticity of Hegesippus' very detailed description of James and the existence of a much longer exegetical work on the death of James in the manner of the *pesharim* at Qumran, upon which this was based. The first is the allusion to a key scriptural passage, Isaiah 3:10–11. Not only is this '*Zaddik*' passage exactly parallel to ones like those in the Habakkuk and Psalm 37 *Pesher*s applied to the death of the Righteous Teacher at Qumran but, as we shall see, its vocabulary was actually absorbed into the former of these.

The second feature is the application to James of this important conceptuality of 'the *Zaddik*'. This is also applied to Jesus in the Gospels, which even go so far as to put this precious Palestinian ideology into the mouths of both Pontius Pilate and his wife (Mt 27:14 and 19)! The same concept was also clearly being applied in Qumran exegetical texts to the Righteous Teacher or *Moreh ha-Zedek*, the pre-eminent leader of that Community. Leaving the Teacher of Righteousness at Qumran aside, one might properly say that the ideology applies even more pointedly to James' person than to Jesus' and a certain retrospective appropriation of traditions may have occurred where its application to the highly mythologized figure of Jesus is concerned. Certainly the tradition ascribing the fall of Jerusalem to the death of James is more logical where chronology or ideology are concerned.

Eusebius begins his crucial testimony by describing James as having been: 'universally esteemed to be the most Righteous of men, on account of the elevated Philosophy and Piety (literally 'Devotedness to God') he exhibited during his life'. He no doubt means by these last what we have been calling the Righteousness and Piety dichotomy, consisting of the two virtues that will become very much associated with James' person, as they are in Josephus' presentation of John the Baptist and Jesus, as Scripture presents him. These two attributes are also very much associated by Josephus with Essenes in his descriptions of them and very much in evidence in the documents at Qumran.[15]

In his famous description of Essenes in the *War*, as well as that of John the Baptist in the *Antiquities*, Josephus makes it very clear what was implied by this dichotomy. Righteousness is 'Righteousness towards men', that is, the sum total of one's social obligations in this world towards one's fellow man. This is very often summed up in a single commandment, first alluded to in Lev. 19:18 and often presented as the essence of Jesus' teaching in Scripture, 'love your neighbor as yourself'. This, therefore, can best be termed the *Righteousness Commandment.*

This included an economic dimension as well. One could not *love one's neighbor as oneself* if one made economic distinctions between oneself and one's neighbor or, to put it simply, if one were *Richer than one's neighbor* – therefore, not only the extreme antagonism towards 'the Rich', but the pivotal emphasis on 'the Poor' in all traditions associated with James as well as those associated with the Righteous Teacher.[16]

The second of these virtues, 'Piety' or 'Piety towards God', summed up the totality of one's obligations *towards God.* This was also expressed in terms of 'love', and still is – that is, 'you should love the Lord your God with all your heart and with all your might'. It too is part and parcel of Josephus' descriptions of both Essenes and John the Baptist.

Justin Martyr (*c.* 100–165 CE) designated these two Commandments as the essence of Jesus' teaching.[17] Simply put, they are the basis of all theorizing of those opposing Roman/Herodian hegemony in this period. Both permeate all traditions associated with James and the Letter under his name in the New Testament. They also permeate the documents at Qumran, most notably the Damascus Document. Their use here in Eusebius – at least by implication – is further testimony of the authenticity of these descriptions emanating from the period of such concern to us in the first century, which Eusebius is recapitulating.

This testimony is echoed in the passage from the Fifth Book of Hegesippus' *Commentaries* quoted verbatim by Eusebius: 'He was called *the Just by all men* from the Lord's time to ours', a period of perhaps a hundred years. Hegesippus repeats this attestation to James' 'pre-eminent Righteousness' two more times, even as conserved in Eusebius. There can be little doubt that James' renown in the Palestinian milieu familiar to Hegesippus was widespread or acknowledged '*by all*'.

This 'Righteousness' – and the ideology associated with it – is, not only the basis of the cognomen always attached to his name; it would appear to be a basic element of all traditions associated with James, even more than for his reputed brother 'Jesus'. This 'Righteousness' ideology is also the basic one where 'the Teacher of Righteousness' – the central character in the Qumran documents – is concerned.

If James is not identical with him, then he is certainly a parallel character or one of a series of individuals bearing this title, because James certainly taught a *doctrine of Righteousness.* This doctrine was epitomized by the Commandment to '*love your neighbor as yourself*'.[18] It is epitomized, too, in the notion of 'the Poor', one of the principal forms of self-designation at Qumran and the name either of James' group in Jerusalem *per se* or the group in early Church accounts after this, which took him as its progenitor.

James as 'Holy from his Mother's Womb' and a Nazirite

Hegesippus goes on to distinguish James from others by that name, 'since there were many', by saying, 'He was Holy from his mother's womb.'[19] The word 'Holy' being used here is different from his two other attributes 'Pious' and 'Righteous'. It corresponds to a third Hebrew word, '*Kedosh*', and will bear on the claims for James as High Priest as well. In the plural, it is equivalent to what goes in English by the name 'Saints' – Hebrew, '*Kedoshim*'. Singular or plural, it is a widespread usage in Hebrew prayer and at Qumran.

Jerome repeats a tradition about James' 'Holiness' not present in any other source: 'this same James, who was the first Bishop of Jerusalem and known as Justus, was considered to be so Holy by the People that they earnestly (or 'zealously') sought to touch the hem of his clothing.'[20] The importance of this tradition, relative to James' Holiness, cannot be overestimated. It, too, is retrospectively attributed to Jesus in Scripture, and this repeatedly, including the themes of both 'touching' and 'the hem' or 'fringe of his garment'! The reader should appreciate that the sanctity of the fringes of garments was always a uniquely Jewish concern that would have mystified foreigners. In one important, particularly exaggerated, example of this, a woman, who has had her *menstrual flow for twelve years*, touches 'the hem of his (Jesus') garment' (Luke 8:44–47 repeats the word 'touch' *five* times in four lines; Mark 5:27 –31, *four*). Here Jesus perceives 'the Power' going out of him. In other such examples Jesus cures the sick, who 'earnestly seek to touch the hem of his clothing', so they can 'be made whole' (Mt 14:36 and Mk 6:54).

Eusebius' and Jerome's use of the term 'Holy' for James has a slightly different connotation. Here, one might also use the equivalent 'consecrated' just as in the matter of *Naziritism*, that is, 'consecrated' or 'set aside from his mother's womb', to describe what they are talking about. In fact, the High Priest wore a linen mitre or head-dress, upon which was attached a gold plate with the inscription 'Holy to God' (Exod. 28:36–38) in the sense of being consecrated to God – '*Kedosh*' carrying the sense of *both* 'Holy' and 'consecrated'. This head-dress with the gold plate was also designated as 'the Holy Crown', the '*Nezer ha-Kodesh*' (Exod. 29:6 and Lev. 8:9), as in the case of the unshorn hair or 'Crown' of the Nazirites.

Once again, the use of the word '*Nezer*', combined with the '*Holiness*' or '*Consecratedness*' of the High Priest, will be of significance. Parallel-wise, the notion of '*being consecrated*' or '*separated*' (*'set aside') is the basis of what generally goes by the term 'Nazirite'*, which is based on the same root as '*Nezer*'. In fact, this is the way Epiphanius understands the term as he applies it to James. He even calls James '*a Nazirite*', by which he specifically means *consecrated*, thereby correctly signaling the underlying Hebrew root.[21]

In this sense, the word can be seen as a kind of synonym for 'Holy' and this is what both Hegesippus and Jerome mean when they refer to James as 'Holy'. 'Holy to God', therefore, has both 'priestly' and 'Nazirite' connotations, and the combination of these will have additional significance when both Epiphanius and Jerome come to insist that James wore '*the mitre*' of High Priest – '*Nezer ha-Kodesh*' in Hebrew – and actually *entered* the Holy of Holies in the Temple.

Interestingly, when speaking of James as '*a Nazirite*', Epiphanius gives John the Baptist as another example '*of these persons consecrated to God*'. In doing so, he cites Luke 1:15, in which an Angel predicts that John 'will drink neither wine nor strong drink', so pregnant with meaning regarding so-called '*Rechabites*' and which all sources also predicate of James.

If we also keep in mind the Rabbinic notices that *'the sons' or 'daughters of the Rechabites' married those of the High Priests and did service at the altar*, then again we move closer to the High Priesthood being ascribed to James in early Church sources, even if only esoterically. Luke 1:15 also predicts of John that 'He shall be filled with *the Holy Spirit even from his mother's womb*'. This too simply rephrases what we just heard in Hegesippus about James being 'Holy from his mother's womb'. Once again, additional convergence develops about what the Gospels say or imply either about Jesus or John with known facts about James' life.

Holy from his Mother's Womb* and Jesus the *Nazoraean

The combination of both of the elements of 'womb' and 'the Holy Spirit', now becomes the basis of Luke's account of the birth of Jesus from 1:26–42. These will also include another element from the biography of James, lifelong 'virginity', which Epiphanius considers intrinsic to James' *extreme Naziritism*.[22] This too is now combined with these other two elements in the narratives of Jesus' miraculous birth. For Matthew, Mary is the 'virgin' *not James*, and 'found to be with child of the Holy Spirit' (1:18–23). As Luke enlarges on this, Jesus is 'a Holy Thing' (*Hagion*), which Mary, 'who was a virgin', 'conceived in (her) womb', when 'the Holy Spirit came (down) upon' her (1:27–35). Here again we have the *womb* and *Holy Spirit* elements.

Then, applying 'what has been written in the Law of Moses' to his 'being brought to Jerusalem and presented to the Lord', Luke quotes Exodus 13:2: 'Every male opening a womb shall be called *Holy to the Lord*' (2:22–23 – the variant of the phrase '*Holy to God*' on the High Priest's '*mitre*' or '*nezer*' in Exodus and Leviticus above).[23] Once more terms, known as specifically applying to James, are being applied to somewhat different effect to persons and situations more in keeping with the New Testament or Pauline ethos.

Epiphanius takes the point one step further, tying the whole complex of usages *not to Nazirite, but to Nazareth*, asserting, 'Jesus had been conceived in the womb in Nazareth'.[24] Now we have moved from 'Nazirite' to 'Nazareth', and, as it will transpire, 'Nazarean' or 'Nazoraean'. These last, as we saw, were based on a slightly different root in Hebrew, *N–TZ–R* instead of *N–Z–R*. We encountered this related Hebrew root *linzor* – meaning 'to keep' or 'observe' – with regard to the Rechabites above and how, for instance, the sons '*kept* the Commandments of their Father' Jonadab.

It is this idea which actually underlies the title Luke now applies to Jesus: '*the Nazoraean*' in 24:19. Matthew 26:70 picks up the title '*the Nazoraean*' right after Jesus' evocation of 'the Son of Man sitting on the right hand of Power and coming on the clouds of Heaven' in 26:64 – the exact words of James' 62 CE proclamation in the Temple on Passover in early Church accounts – and the reference to Jesus as 'Jesus the Galilean' (*Galilaios*) in 26:69. After evoking this title, Matthew then goes on to tell us about Judas and 'the Field of Blood'.

It was Matthew who first spread the misconception that the title 'Jesus the *Nazoraean*' should in some manner relate to 'Nazareth', by quoting the prophecy: '*He shall be called a Nazoraean*' which, closing his narrative of Jesus' early years, he associates with 'withdrawing to parts of Galilee and going to live in a city called Nazareth' (2:22–23). This cannot be the derivation of the term, as even in the Greek, the spelling 'Nazareth' and 'Nazoraean' differ substantially.

These scriptural passages also form the basis of Epiphanius' tortuous discussion trying to link the 'Nazoraean' terminology to the town of 'Nazareth', for which he now cites Matthew's story about Jesus growing up in Nazareth. As he tells it, now combining Matthew and Luke, this includes the tell-tale allusion to Jesus being '*conceived in the womb in Nazareth*'. Not only is this simply a variation of the traditions about 'being consecrated' or '*a Nazirite from the womb*', it actually includes the edifying note: 'All Christians were once called Nazoraeans. For a short time they were also given the name Jessaeans, before the Disciples in Antioch began to be called Christians'.[25] The problem is that there is no passage, '*he shall be called a Nazoraean*', in the Old Testament, and the passage on which this was supposed to be based is unclear. One can assume that an Old Testament reference to the idea of being '*a Nazirite*' was probably intended.

Though Matthew says the reference comes from 'the Prophets', examples of individuals of this kind in Old Testament narrative are Samuel and Samson. Again Matthew is probably mistaken. The Bible twice avers about Samson that 'the child shall be a Nazirite unto God' (Judg. 13:5–7) and once – speaking in the first person – that 'I have been a Nazirite unto God *from my mother's womb*' (16:7). Given the references to both 'Nazirite' and 'womb', this last was probably the original behind the refurbishment in Matthew, not to mention these references to 'mother's womb' in early Christian texts about James. Of course, Samson's behavior is *the exact opposite* of what a good Nazirite was conceived of as being, but some of the qualities of a proper Nazirite or a 'Consecrated' or 'Separated One', that is, a razor never coming near his head and not drinking wine, are recapitulated in this parody.

The problem is, as well, that in these two word clusters in Hebrew – Nazirite and Nazoraean – we have two separate consonants, a '*z*' and a '*tz*', which transliterate only into a single consonant '*z*' in Greek. In Hebrew, *Nazoraean*, with a '*tz*', means 'Keeper' as we have seen; 'Nazirite', with a '*z*', *consecrated or separated*. In Christian thought, this often gets confused with what is called by the term 'Nazarene', even though, as Matthew puts it, this really does read 'and he shall be called a Nazoraean'. This is probably due more to Mark's use of 'Nazarene' (1:24, etc.) and confusion of these terms than anything else, but Mark uses 'Nazoraean' in 10:34 as well. All these can be applied to what in Hebrew is meant by the usage 'Nazirite' – a 'Consecrated' or 'Separated One'. But they really cannot mean 'from Nazareth', though all such plays on words were probably purposeful.

In Acts, when Paul encounters James for the famous final showdown during his last trip to Jerusalem, James describes to him how there are quite a few penitents in the Temple who have 'taken an oath upon themselves', meaning not a life-long but a temporary Nazirite oath (Acts 21:18–23). The procedures for these are described in both the Book of Numbers (6:1–21) and, in extended fashion, in the *Talmud*. If this episode is any measure, it would seem James' Community in Jerusalem really *did* value the Nazirite-oath procedures. This would also seem to be true for those *Sicarii*-like assassins, who take an oath or 'with a curse, curse themselves, *not to eat or drink till they have killed Paul*' (Acts 23:12). Since in one form of the notation, the notion of *separation* is closely associated with it, this idea too would have played an important role in the early Community's thinking and religious behavior, as it does Qumran's, which, as the Gospels do John the Baptist, characterized itself as 'separating from the habitation of the Men of Unrighteousness to go out into the wilderness to prepare the Way of the Lord'.[26]

In another episode in Acts, 'Paul had his head shaved' because of a *vow he took* (18:18). 'Shaving the head' occurs upon completion of the oath or vow period, usually seven days, and is a very important aspect of temporary Nazirite-oath procedures, just as letting 'no razor come near one's head' is of life-long Naziritism predicated of James and other 'Rechabite' types. Here in Acts, James has put a penance on Paul to show that he himself still 'walks orderly *keeping the Law* and there is no truth to the rumors circulating' about him (21:24). But, of course, there *is* truth to these rumors concerning Paul's regular observance of the Law – which in Galatians 3:10–13 he describes as 'a curse'.

Be this as it may, Paul pays for the expenses of 'the four who had taken *a vow* upon themselves'. According to James' express instructions, this should have included 'shaving their heads', but it is not clear whether Paul actually does this as these procedures are interrupted by a riot precipitated by Jews from Asia, who see him in the Temple (21:26–27). We can now see that temporary 'Nazirite' activity of this kind clearly also had significance for James' Jerusalem Community or Assembly, at least as portrayed in Acts, and the name often accorded them, 'Nazoraeans', playing on this and no doubt other characteristics, was probably not simply an accidental one.

Where the city 'Nazareth' is concerned, we have already noted that Josephus never mentions it in any of his works, which are *very* detailed. Nor is it listed in any biblical setting previously. In Jesus' case, *Nazoraean* and *Galilean* would both appear to be esotericisms referring to the 'Messianic' or 'Zealot Movement'. 'Nazareth', if it existed at all, may have been a little village not far from Sepphoris. On the other hand, 'Nazareth' may have sprung into life to meet a later need. Where Judas 'the Galilean' is concerned, Sepphoris also has special significance, because Josephus describes how his followers broke into the armory there to arm themselves. Prior to this, Josephus describes the end of a rabbi or teacher (the term he actually uses is '*sophist*'), whom he characterizes as 'expert in the Laws of their country', someone he calls '*Judas the son of Sepphoraeus*'.[27] This clearly relates to the place name '*Sepphoris*' in the same way that 'Nazareth' is supposed to relate to Jesus.

Nazara and Cochaba: the 'Branch' and the 'Star' Prophecies

Likewise, Christians of all ages have generally thought Jesus '*the Nazrene*' denoted a geographical notation, missing the ideological implications of the terminology. Actually, Julius Africanus (170–245 CE) also refers to two villages associated with the members of Jesus' family – the group known as 'the *Desposyni*' in early Christian tradition.[28] These he locates in Judea and calls '*Nazara and Cochaba*'. He says the relatives and descendants of Jesus and his brothers inhabited these cities and came from there. But no such cities can be identified in Judea of this period. Epiphanius places Cochaba in Syria in the region of Damascus. Julius Africanus, however, may have in mind what Matthew 19:1/Mark 10:1 call 'the coasts of Judea on the other side of the Jordan', which dovetails nicely with all these notices about activity across Jordan and in the so-called 'Damascus' region.[29]

Both names have Messianic overtones. '*Nazara*' relates to either 'the Branch' or the '*Nazirite*' terminology; '*Cochaba*' is based on the Hebrew word for star, from which another Messianic Revolutionary in the second century, '*Bar Kochba*', derives his name, even though he seems to have come from another town in these areas, '*Chozeba*'.

We have already mentioned 'the Star Prophecy', quoted three times in very important contexts in the Damascus Document, the War Scroll, and in the collection of Messianic proof -texts known as the Messianic *Testimonia*.[30] It is based on Numbers 24:17: 'a Star will rise from Jacob, a Scepter to rule the world'. For this reason, together with 'the *Shiloh* Prophecy' about 'the Scepter', to whom 'the Peoples would gather', and 'the Staff' (Gen. 49:10), it was called the 'World Ruler Prophecy'.

If any prophecy shows the power of oracles or fortune-telling in human history and on the human mind, it is the Star Prophecy. It is interesting because it is not even associated with a Jewish prophet, but rather a Gentile one, 'Balaam'. Allusions to 'Balaam', seen as one of the archetypal 'Enemies' in the *Talmud*, will occur repeatedly in our texts, as will wordplay related to the archetypal adversary 'Belial' and its underlying meaning in Hebrew, '*balla'-'Am*', '*swallowing*' or '*consuming the People*'.[31]

Josephus understands that the Star Prophecy was the moving force behind the Uprising against Rome in 66–70. This prophecy was pivotal in showing that the Uprising against Rome was not simply a political or anti–colonial one – the manner in which it is normally portrayed – but rather *Messianic* and/or religious. Josephus subverted the revolutionary thrust of this prophecy by applying it to the Roman Emperor-to-be Vespasian. For services rendered Josephus was adopted into the Roman Imperial family itself. The service that Josephus rendered these patrons was to deflect the force of this prophecy from unknown, charismatic insurgent leaders to the events culminating in the rise of the Roman Emperor Vespasian, the progenitor of 'the House of the Flavians'. Rabbinic Judaism, true to its Pharisaic roots, indulges in the same interpretation as Josephus, applying the Prophecy – through the person of its founder Rabbi Yohanan ben Zacchai – also to the Roman Emperor-to-be Vespasian. Paul, of course, applies it to the Supernatural Redeemer figure he calls 'the Christ' or 'Christ Jesus', an individual he never met except through the visionary experiences he claims as his private 'revelations'.

Echoes of this prophecy are found not only in 'the Star' over Bethlehem of the Gospel of Matthew (2:2–10) – where 'seeing the Star, they rejoiced with overwhelming joy' – but also in the name of the Jewish revolutionary hero of the next century, 'Simon *Bar Kochba*'. Correspondence from this legendary hero has been found in caves in the Judean Desert. Here, his name is not Bar Kochba, 'the Son of the Star', but rather Bar Kosiba, demonstrating definitively that the title '*Kochba*' was deliberately adopted and was not a family name. Talmudic writings, playing on the resonance of '*Choziba*' with the Hebrew word for '*Lying*'/'*Chazav*', mock his claims to Messiah–hood, insisting rather that 'a Liar has gone forth out of Israel'.[32] Not only does this last, once again, vividly confirm the anti–Messianic orientation of the Rabbis, it comprises a pointed parallel to the way Qumran is applying this same 'Liar' terminology to an adversary of the Righteous Teacher – one who has so many similarities to Paul.

For Suetonius, Tacitus, and Roman historians thereafter, basing themselves on Josephus, this 'World Ruler Prophecy' is the foundation of the Uprising against Rome, that is, the Jews were led astray by an 'ambiguous oracle' from their ancient literature – capable of manifold interpretation – that 'a World Ruler would come out of Palestine'.[33] They were mistaken in this as Josephus is, also, anxious to point out.

This is the position of Rabbinic Judaism as well following the Pharisaic point-of-view. Of course, the position of Qumran is *directly* the opposite. There is no mistaking this which is why, presumably, these documents ended up abandoned in caves along the Dead Sea shoreline. No one lived to come back and retrieve them. This was the price paid for an alternative interpretation of this Prophecy – the apocalyptic one of the War Scroll recapitulated, too, in James' proclamation of 'the Son of Man sitting on the right hand of the Great Power and about to come on the clouds of Heaven' in the Temple on Passover, 62 CE.

Paul takes the safe side of things applying the 'World Ruler' Prophecy to the other-worldly Redeemer figure he calls 'the Christ'. He was not in too much jeopardy with such an interpretation and, not surprisingly, his is the interpretation that has survived – or at least enjoyed the greatest vogue – for the last nineteen hundred years.

James' Naziritism versus Paul's

This is how important these matters are. Plus, they are intertwined with other complexities. For Eusebius, Epiphanius, and Jerome, James is a lifelong Nazirite. He was also a vegetarian. As Eusebius puts it, quoting Hegesippus: 'He drank no wine or strong drink, nor did he eat meat. No razor came near his head, nor did he anoint himself with oil, and he did not go to the baths'. Whatever one makes of this testimony, it certainly is that of 'a Nazirite', one either 'separated' or 'consecrated', 'Holy from his mother's womb'.

In fact, it is more. The elements of 'not anointing himself with oil', 'not going to the baths', and 'not eating meat', that is, being a vegetarian, are additional to what was normally understood as Naziritism or even, for that matter, Rechabitism. Epiphanius will add the note of *abstention from sexual activity* – 'life-long virginity' as he puts it. All of these writers will add the element of 'not wearing wool, but only linen', which will have much to do with James' role in the Jerusalem of his day and his functioning as a priest, or the 'Opposition High Priest'.

All of these traits would appear to have to do with how James was 'consecrated' or 'Holy from his mother's womb' or his 'very great Holiness'. It is a not incurious parallel that Paul, in airing his differences with James in Galatians 2 or at least representatives 'from James', insists that God 'separated' or rather 'chose' him *from his 'mother's womb'*. The 'some from James' materialize in Acts or Paul's letters, where 'some' come down to 'trouble' Paul's communities, most notably by insisting on circumcision and keeping the regime of extreme purity that would make 'table fellowship' or 'eating with Gentiles' – and thus the whole Gentile Mission – impossible.

Paul speaks about this kind of '*Nazirite from the womb*' or '*consecration*' in the context of speaking about how God 'chose' him and 'revealed His son in (him)', how the Gospel, as he taught it 'among the Gentiles', was the result of a direct 'revelation of Jesus Christ' (Gal. 1:15–16), and how if anyone preached a Gospel contrary to the one he has preached – 'even an Angel in Heaven' – 'he is to be accursed', this in the same breath as affirming his 'zeal for the Traditions of (his) Fathers' (1:6–14).

Paul makes this astonishing claim as well as others about 'not Lying' or 'seeking to please men' amid reference to 'Damascus' and 'Arabia'. One can only assume that Paul knows well the parallel claims circulating around the person of James and chooses to emphasize his own importance by making such claims for himself. Obviously, these were made with much less justification. However, where 'brazen speaking' is concerned, as Paul himself triumphantly avers, he is nothing loath.[34]

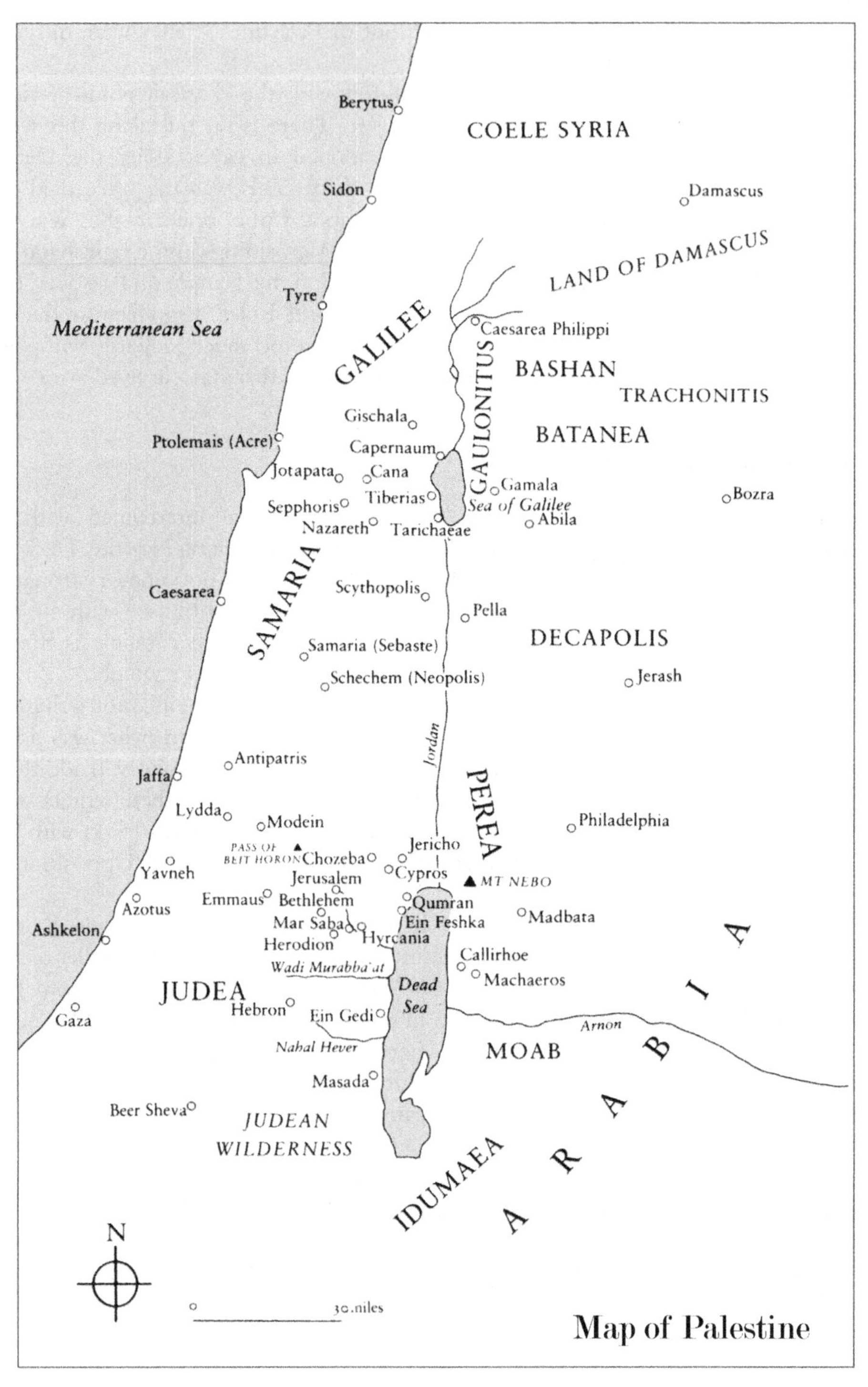

Chapter 11
James' Vegetarianism, Abstention From Blood, and Consuming No Wine

'Loving God', 'Things Sacrificed to Idols', and James' Vegetarianism

James' Naziritism or 'Holiness from his mother's womb' is not the only claim reversed in Paul's discussions. Whereas James clearly is said to abstain from eating meat, Paul emphasizes its consumption as in 1 Corinthians 10:25: 'Eat everything that is sold in the marketplace. There is no need to raise questions of conscience'. Paul expresses this position in chapters 6–10 of 1 Corinthians, where he is discussing one of the categories of James' directives to overseas communities, the prohibition on 'things sacrificed to idols' (1 Cor. 8:1, 8:10, and 10:28). The basic answer Paul gives to *all* James' directives is, 'all things are Lawful for me' (1 Cor. 6:12 and 10:23) even though 'not all things profit' or, as he puts it in 1 Corinthians 8:1, 'build up'.

The 'building' language is fundamental to Paul's view of himself as the 'architect' or 'builder' of a Community (3:9–14). It fixes the context of the contrary kind of aspersion, as for instance, in the Habakkuk *Pesher* on the Adversary of the Righteous Teacher it calls 'the Spouter of Lying, who *led Many astray* by *building a worthless city on blood* and *erecting an Assembly on Lying*'.[1]

So incensed does Paul become with these adversaries, after terming persons who worry over 'reclining in an idol Temple' or 'eating things sacrificed to idols', 'weak' in 1 Corinthians 8:10, that he blurts out: 'So if meat causes offence to a brother, I shall never eat flesh again forever, so as not to offend (literally 'scandalize') my brother' (8:13). This is the same theme he was addressing in 1 Cor. 6:11–13, amid reference to 'being washed', 'justified', and 'made Holy', before he turned to 'fornication' and 'being *joined* to a prostitute's body' in 6:16. It culminated in the allusion to 'meats are for the belly and the belly for meats' and his oblique reference to 'the toilet drain'.

Now, following a discussion of 'loving God' (Piety), 'love building up' and his adversaries' 'weak consciences being polluted', he concludes: 'Food does not commend us to God; neither if we eat do we have any profit, nor if we do not eat do we fall short' (8:8). Here Paul also introduces the language of 'causing to stumble' or 'stumbling block' – 'causing offence' or 'scandalizing' in 8:13 – the same language the Letter of James used to refer to those 'who keep the whole Law, but stumble over one point, being guilty of (breaking) it all' (2:10). Now it is directed against those objecting to 'reclining in an idol Temple' and synonymous with causing 'the weak brother's fall' or even more pointedly, 'wounding their weak consciences' (8:9–12).

But who is Paul's strength a 'stumbling block' to or 'scandalizing' here? Who are these 'weak brothers' with 'their weak consciences' (always a euphemism for those observing the Law), who make issues over table fellowship and consuming unclean foods when these things do not matter – who worry over 'things sacrificed to idols', when they, too, do not matter? 'Then, concerning the eating of things sacrificed to idols, we know that an idol corresponds to nothing in the world and that there is no other God except One … but some with *conscience of the idol*, even now eat as of a *thing sacrificed to an idol*, and *their conscience, being weak, is polluted*' (8:4–7). This has to be seen not only as a discussion of James' directives to overseas communities, enumerated in Acts and refracted here, but also as a *direct attack* on James, even though it is delivered in the most evasive manner conceivable.

Paul's Attack on James' Naziritism and Vegetarianism in Romans

Paul reinforces the 'love' theme and connects it to 'eating' in his Letter to the Romans, again turning both against James. Paul actually quotes the second of the two Love Commandments in 13:9, 'you shall love your neighbor as yourself'. James, on the contrary, discusses it in the context of being 'a *Doer*', not 'a *Breaker*', '*keeping the whole Law*', 'Judgment without mercy' for those who don't, and condemnation of 'making oneself a Friend of the world', not a 'Friend of God'. The Damascus Document, too, evokes this commandment, called in James 'the Royal Law according to the Scripture' and the second part of the Righteousness/Piety dichotomy.

For Paul, however, in another tortured yet clear riposte to James, one should: 'owe nothing to anyone, except to *love one another*, for he who *loves the other has fulfilled the Law* ... Love does not work any ill to one's neighbor, therefore love is the fulfillment of the Law' (Rom. 13:8–10). This too has become part and parcel of Jesus' teaching in Scripture. Continuing in this vein, Paul again raises the issues of eating and foods, turning them around, as per his wont, from the Jamesian position:

> Do not let the one who eats despise the one who does not eat ... do not *put a stumbling block, a cause of offence*, before your brother ... I know and am persuaded in the Lord Jesus that *nothing is unclean in and of itself – except to him who judges things to be unclean.* To him it is unclean. But if, on account of meat, your brother is aggrieved, you are no longer walking according to love. Do not with your meat destroy him ... do not destroy *the work of God for the sake of meat.* (Rom. 14:3–20)

Almost all the themes we have been following can be found in these words.

Discussing the issue of 'consuming meat', Paul inadvertently expresses the opinion, clearly his own basic one: 'One believes he may eat all things; another, *being weak, eats* (*only*) *vegetables'* (13:2). That this is an attack on James seems also almost irrefutable. That its author is cloaking the issue in an attempt to appear accommodating should also be clear. But the basic position here does once again redound to the situation of James' vegetarianism. For Paul, this is just *weakness.* His basic position is that such things do not matter, that *all* the food, as he has told us, in the marketplace *is clean.*

That Paul makes the same claim as James – being 'separated' from his mother's womb – for himself, while all the time adopting the very opposite position to him on the issue of 'separation of clean from unclean', makes all these allusions all the more interesting, and his position regarding them all the more disingenuous.

So, once again, we may see that these traditions about James, preserved via Hegesippus in Eusebius, Jerome, and others, do have substance behind them. These had to do with the manner in which James was seen as 'Holy' or 'consecrated from his mother's womb', or a certain concept of being a life-long Nazirite that seems to have been important to the Jerusalem Assembly and even early Christianity as a whole.

Not only then do we have, in this passage in Paul's Letter to the Romans, collateral verification of James' vegetarianism – insisted on in all the ancient sources – but also something of the reason for it. This, undoubtedly, had to do with following a regime of extreme purity or, as both Paul and the Damascus Document from Qumran put it, of 'Perfect Holiness' or 'Perfection of the Way', and this, in turn, was related to – however obliquely – the issue of accepting or rejecting *polluted gifts and sacrifices in the Temple.*

Pollution in the Wilderness Camps

Similar concerns are in evidence at Qumran, at least where the issue of *gifts* and *sacrifices in the Temple* is concerned. John the Baptist, even in the fragmented and garbled accounts that have come down to us, would seem to have had tendencies in this direction. The problem in John the Baptist's case is the idea that he ate 'locusts' (Matt. 3:4 and Mark 1:6). If he did, he probably would not have survived very long. Luke omits this and there is little about it in other sources about John; it has been suggested that the word 'locusts' is based on a garbled translation.[2] One suggestion is that John ate 'carobs'; there have been others. Epiphanius, in preserving what he calls 'the Ebionite Gospel', rails against the passage there claiming John ate 'wild honey' and 'manna-like vegetarian cakes dipped in oil'.[3]

In any event, John would have been one of these wilderness-dwelling, vegetable-eating persons Josephus regards as either impostors, magicians, or Deceivers, fomenting revolt under the guise of religious 'Innovation'. Josephus says as much in his description of John in the *Antiquities* – though his treatment of John is much gentler than is his normal wont. This is also the inference to be drawn from Luke's testimony, including the note about John's being Holy 'from his mother's womb' (1:15).

As it turns out, one of the first of these vegetarian, insurgent or subversive leaders was Judas Maccabee himself. 2 Maccabees 5:27, describing the founding moment of Judas' revolutionary activities – also in the wilderness – in 167 BCE, has this to say: 'Judas, called Maccabaeus, however, with about nine others, *withdrew into the wilderness* and lived like wild animals in the hills with his companions, *eating nothing but wild plants to avoid contracting defilement'*. This statement just about says everything where these wilderness-dwelling 'Zealots' were concerned, and one has here much of what was behind such behavior in this period, the issue once again being 'contracting defilement' or 'pollution' from unclean persons.

For 2 Maccabees, Judas is the legitimate successor to the previous High Priestly line, which was destroyed by a *foreign power*, in this instance, the Seleucid heirs of Alexander the Great. Judas is a kind of Messianic Priest-King of the kind Jesus is presented as being in later literature. This probably explains Judas' vegetarianism, as it does John the Baptist's, if we see John in succession to Judas as an insurgent, Prophet–like leader demanding a Priesthood of greater purity devoid of pollution by foreigners. For Judas, *the Temple has been polluted.* The sacrifice in the Temple has been polluted, then halted. In the time of John the Baptist, 'the Zealots', James, and Qumran, this will be seen as being because of the acceptance of gifts and sacrifices on behalf of or by Gentiles in the Temple.

Something of this even emerges in the account of Paul's unceremonious ejection from the Temple after James imposes the *Nazirite*-style penance upon him in Acts 21:23–24. This episode connects *Temple pollution* to the *admission of Gentiles in the Temple*: 'He has brought Greeks into the Temple and polluted this Holy Place' (21:28) – a matter very much argued over in this period, as the erection of inscribed stone warning-markers in the Temple barring foreigners from the Temple on pain of death verifies. Two of these have since been found.[4]

In the version of events prompting Judas Maccabee's 'wilderness' sojourn, 'the Abomination of the Desolation' referred to in Daniel has been set up in the Temple by the invading Seleucid King, Antiochus Epiphanes, thereby desecrating it. In this 'Abomination' we probably have a Hebrew play on a Greek name, in this case characterizing the statue of the Olympian Zeus that Antiochus erected in the Temple – or what was left of it. So not only is the Temple in ruins and abandoned, but *polluting idols have been erected in it.* This is the background to Judas' 'wilderness vegetarianism'. He should be seen as not simply a warrior, but a 'Priestly Zealot' of sorts – one probably observing, as well, the extreme purity regulations of the Nazirite regimen or, at least, the one connected to Holy War. The two are not very different in any case.

For elucidation of this, the War Scroll at Qumran is probably one of our best guides. Here the picture is very simple – *extreme purity regulations are in effect in the wilderness camps* because the Heavenly 'Holy Ones', the Angelic Host of Daniel and other prophetic visionaries, were seen to 'be with' the Holy warriors in these camps. As the War Scroll vividly puts it:

> No boy or woman shall enter their camps from the time of their leaving Jerusalem to go to war until their return. And no one who is lame, blind, crippled, or a man who has a lasting bodily sore in his flesh or is afflicted with pollution in his body – all of these shall not go with them to war, but rather, all of them shall be men *voluntarily enlisted for war* and *Perfect in Spirit and body*. And no man who is *sexually impure* on the day of war shall go down with them, *because the Holy Angels are together with their hosts*. (1QM 7.3–6)

The persons barred from these Holy 'camps', for instance, the blind, lame, crippled, or sexually impure, are just the people Jesus is pictured as keeping company with in the Gospels.

Extreme purity regulations associated with temporary or life-long Naziritism, wilderness sojourns, or the kind of wilderness-camp regime described at Qumran are, doubtlessly, also connected to what is implied under the notion of 'the *Zaddik*' or '*Righteous One*' in this period. It also helps to understand the ideology behind this vegetarianism, which is comparatively simple and straightforward.

The First *Zaddik* Noah and Being 'Called by Name'

Both vegetarianism and the *Zaddik* ideal go back to the Noah story in Genesis. In this episode, Noah is described as 'Righteous and Perfect in his generation' and, because of this and for Jewish mystical ideology ever after, he is the first redeemer of mankind. Not only is Noah the first *Zaddik*, but the scriptural warrant for a second ideology is also provided – 'Perfection'. This is very often missing from Rabbinic ideology, but it is a concept Jesus is pictured as teaching in the Sermon on the Mount in Matthew: 'Therefore, be Perfect as your Father in Heaven is Perfect' (5:48).

Earlier Jesus is portrayed as saying this: 'Unless your Righteousness *exceeds* that of the Scribes and Pharisees, you shall in no wise enter the Kingdom of Heaven', coupled with the James-like – and, in this case, anti-Pauline – condemnation: 'Whoever shall break the least one of these Commandments and teach men to do so shall be called *least in the Kingdom of the Heavens*' (5:19–20). Noah saves mankind because of his 'Righteousness' and 'Perfection' and all mankind descends from him – at least in the mythology of Genesis the bibliophiles of the Second Temple Period seem to have been so enamored of.

The Book of Ecclesiasticus too, called '*Ben Sira*' after its author, in its famous enumeration of 'the Pious Men' (*Anshei-Hesed*) presents Noah as 'the (first) *Zaddik*' (44:17). This praise includes Phineas and his '*zeal for the Lord*' and ends, at least in the Hebrew version, with an evocation of 'the Sons of Zadok'.[5] To explain what was meant by '*Perfect*' with regard to Noah, Rabbinic literature contended that he was 'born circumcised'![6] Not only does this show the high regard in which he was held and primitive attempts to wrestle with the 'Perfection' ideology, but not even Christianity went so far as to make such claims for Jesus, a successor among these primordial Righteous Ones who are presented in the literature as Supernatural Redeemer figures.[7]

Noah, of course, is also a very important figure in the Qumran literature as he is in all apocalyptic literature, apocryphal or sectarian. The Damascus Document, in introducing its view of pre-existence, fore-knowledge, and predestination, puts the proposition as follows:

He (God) knew their works before they were created and he hated their generations ... And He knew the years of their *Standing* and the number and the meaning of their Eras for all Eternal being and existences, until that which would come in their Eras for all the years of Eternity. And in all of them He raised for Himself *men called by Name* that a remnant might survive in the Land and fill the face of the earth with their seed. And *He made known to them His Holy Spirit by the hand of His Messiah*, and He (it) is Truth, and *in the correct exposition of His Name, their names (are to be found)*, and those whom He hates, *He leads astray*.

And now, my sons, listen to me and I will uncover your eyes that (you may) see and understand *the works of God* ('he that has eyes let him see' in Gospel formulation) in order to choose that which pleases (Him) and reject that which He hates, in order *to walk Perfectly in all His ways* ... They were caught in them (the 'nets' or sins), because they did not keep the Commandments of God ... All flesh on dry land perished; they were as though they had never been because they *did their own will* and did not *keep the Commandments of their Maker*.[8]

There is so much in these lines that is relevant to a discussion of the differences between Paul and James, but for the purposes of economy, one should note the allusion to the 'Holy Spirit' being revealed 'by the hand of His Messiah' and the strong emphasis on both 'keeping' and 'doing the Commandments'.

This is also strong in the Letter of James as it is in Qumran literature when it comes to defining what is meant by a true '*Son of Zadok*'. The definition of this term – aside from the more eschatological one that follows in the Damascus Document – provided by the Community Rule is: 'the Keepers of the Covenant' (*Shomrei ha–Brit*). This is the synonym for '*Nozrei ha–Brit*' – again 'the Keepers' or 'Observers of the Covenant'. In both contexts, 'the *Nozrim*' or the 'Nazoraeans' are 'Keepers of the Covenant', the exact opposite of what we now after two millennia of Pauline dogma consider 'Nazrenes' or followers of Jesus *the Nazarean* to be.

All of this is very esoteric, but one thing the Damascus Document is doing in these introductory columns is describing just what a true '*Son of Zadok*' is and what he is conceived of as *doing*. Therefore the Document is often referred to as 'The Zadokite Document' which, were it not for another of its esotericisms: '*the New Covenant in the Land of Damascus*', might be a better name for it.

In the *Zohar*, where the passage from Proverbs about '*the Zaddik the Pillar of the World*' is being analyzed, Noah is described as acting as a true copy of the Heavenly Ideal – '*an embodiment of the world's Covenant of Peace*'. Ben Sira vouchsafes this Noahic 'Covenant of Peace' to the archetypal embodiment of the 'Zealot' High Priest, Phineas, as well as to his descendants including the later 'Sons of Zadok'.[9] Whatever one might think of the historical roots of the *Zohar* in thirteenth-century Spain, statements of this kind certainly are instructive and seem to hark back to an earlier time especially in the light of the Dead Sea Scrolls.

The significance of these words is amplified in the section called '*Phineas*', towards the end of the *Zohar*, where its author shows familiarity with the 'suffering *Zaddik*' ideology: 'When God desires to send healing to the Earth, He smites one Righteous One ... with suffering ... to make atonement ... and sometimes all his days are passed in suffering to *Protect the People*'.[10] Statements like this have a peculiar prescience. 'Protection of the People', for instance, appears in the passages Eusebius cites from Hegesippus where James' '*Zaddik*' nature is being delineated.

1 Peter, for instance too, is very much concerned with the idea of 'suffering for Righteousness' sake' (2:19–3:14). It also evokes 'Noah and the Flood' which it identifies with

'being saved by water' – imagery it will then use to propound the new 'Christian' version of the ideal of baptism (3:20–21). But this letter also knows the language of '*being foreknown before the Foundation of the world but manifested at the Last Times*' (1:20), '*the Precious Cornerstone*' (2:7), 'the Name of Christ' (4:19), '*making Perfect*' (5:10), and the living stones being *built up into a spiritual House – a Holy Priesthood to offer spiritual sacrifices pleasing to God* (2:5).

Like the '*suffering Zaddik*' idea in the *Zohar* above, this is paralleled almost word for word in the language of *spiritualized* '*atonement*' and '*Temple*' applied to *the Council of the Community* in the Community Rule at Qumran. Finally, 1 Peter 5:8 talks about '*the Enemy*' in terms of his '*swallowing up*', language absolutely fundamental at Qumran and the description of the destruction of the Righteous Teacher there. Not only does mention of the '*Zaddik*' ideal and Noah being an embodiment of 'the world's Covenant of Peace' link up with 'the Primal Adam' or 'Secret Man' ideology in Ebionite tradition but, as these move West, they become fixed in the more Hellenistic notion of 'the Christ'.

Abstention from Blood

In addition to explaining Noah's 'Perfection' – as is so often the case, *in physical terms not spiritual ones* – Rabbinic Judaism also sets forth a general Covenant in his name, 'the Noahic Covenant'. The ideology behind this Covenant is presented in various places in the *Talmud*, but its main thrust has to do with what is expected by God of all mankind, irrespective of national grouping; since, because of the Flood, Noah not Adam becomes the new father of mankind. Noah is presented, therefore, as setting forth the basic laws that all men are obliged to follow, even if they do not come under the Mosaic Covenant, which applied only to Jews – those born under this covenant.[11]

Paul in his letters is very interested in the ramifications of such thinking, since he has turned to groups theoretically coming under what the Rabbis would refer to as 'the Noahic Covenant'. Paul is anxious to emphasize that his communities should *not* come under the Mosaic Covenant, that, contrary to what seems to have been the position of the Jerusalem Leadership, they should not allow themselves *to be circumcised*; for then they would come under the terms of the Mosaic Covenant, in particular the Law – circumcision being the sign of the Covenant (Gal. 5:1–9). All this, no doubt, strikes the modern reader as somewhat arcane, but these were *real* issues and the real, burning and bitter arguments that were going on at the time.

In the Old Testament presentation, Noah and his family obviously could not have eaten meat, because if they had, there would have been *no* animals left to populate the earth. Again, it should be emphasized, these points may seem silly, but for those people – ancient and modern – who habitually confuse literature or story-telling with reality, these become the terms of the debate. At any rate, Noah concludes a compact of sorts with God. In this, God promises not to destroy the earth again – or as He puts it, 'not to curse the earth again on account of man' (Gen. 8:21). By the end of the second narrative of these events, this has been magnified into a 'Covenant'. This is the 'Covenant' that Rabbis and others at the end of the Second Temple Period are so intent on explaining and giving substance to.

In the course of these matters, Noah makes a sacrifice from the clean animals and birds which propitiates God and he is allowed *to consume flesh* or *meat*. The only caveat that God makes is that mankind was 'not to eat *the blood of flesh with life in it*' (Gen. 9:4). Of course, Jews to this day have taken this as the scriptural warrant for a whole complex of legislation involving the killing, preparation, and eating of animal life, and, in particular, the abstention from *consuming blood* – the life of the slaughtered animal being considered to be in the blood and therefore not consumable. In Islam, the situation is more or less the same. In

Christianity, following the dialectic of Paul in Romans and 1 Corinthians above, this concern has gone by the boards.

But this was *not* the case for early Christianity in Palestine. It was quite the opposite. All of this relates to the issue of 'table fellowship with Gentiles'. The same is true in the Damascus Document concerning why the children of Israel were 'cut off' after the Mosaic period: 'they ate *blood* ... in the wilderness' – 'each man doing what was right in his own eyes'.[12] Whereas Paul will utilize this language of 'cutting off ' to make an obscene pun about cutting off one's sexual parts in circumcision (Gal. 5:12), for the Damascus Document, Abraham and the other 'Keepers of the Covenant' are designated 'Friends' or 'Beloved of God'. This is exactly the language the Letter of James uses, when arguing with its interlocutor – the man teaching that Abraham was rather 'justified by his Faith' not works (Gal. 3:6–29). Speaking to this Adversary, the Letter of James points out:

> *Don't you realize you Empty Man* that *Faith without works* is useless. You surely know that Abraham our father *was justified by works* ... You see that *Faith was working with works* and that *by works Faith was Perfected.* And the Scripture was fulfilled which says, 'Now Abraham believed God and it was reckoned to him as Righteousness, and he was called *Friend of God*'. (Jas. 2:20–23)

This scriptural warrant from Genesis 15:6 is also a cornerstone of Paul's famous discussions in Galatians 3:6 and Romans 4:3, but of course with exactly opposite intent.

This notion of 'blood' and consuming it, is, therefore, one that exercises those responsible for the literature at Qumran to no small degree. In other documents Qumran refers to how '*the Spouter of Lying led Many astray to build a Worthless City upon blood*' and '*a City of Blood*' quite derogatorily.[13] We shall have occasion to connect allusions such as these with Paul's innovative doctrine, '*Communion with the Blood of Christ*' and his reinterpretation of '*the New Covenant*' in 1 Corinthians 10–11. Luke adds, as we saw, the slightly differing twist, '*This is the New Covenant in my blood which was poured out for you*' (22:20).

Certainly '*pouring out*' the blood was a fixture of Jewish ritual practice, as it has become to some extent for Muslims. Even in stories about Abraham's sacrifice of Isaac, which James 2:21 evokes to support its position on Abraham '*being justified by works*' (in Islam this becomes the sacrifice of Ishmael), there is no intimation that the consumption of his blood was permitted even symbolically. In this Noah episode in Genesis, as we saw, it is expressly forbidden: 'You shall not eat the blood of flesh with life in it. I will demand an account of your lifeblood. I will demand an account from every beast and from man. I will demand an account of every man's life from his fellow man' (9:4–5).

When the Damascus Document ascribes the '*cutting off*' of the Children of Israel 'in the wilderness' to the '*consumption of blood*', the reference is to Numbers 11:31–32 and how the Children of Israel ate quail there. While neither the authors of Exodus 16:30 or Psalm 105:40 – which also refer to this episode – regard eating this quail in a negative manner, but rather an illustration of God's solicitude for Israel, Numbers does. For its part, the Damascus Document is so incensed about 'consuming blood' that it deliberately highlights this episode, adding that they '*were led astray in these things*' and '*complained against the Commandments of God*'.

For the Second Temple mind anyhow, it was only after Noah's sacrifice that it was permissible to eat meat again. Once again, to repeat, Noah and those with him clearly did not consume meat during the period of the Flood and their incarceration in the ark. With Noah's atoning sacrifice, they were free to eat meat once again with the caveat *that they abstain from blood.*

Two conclusions emerge from this. The first has to do with James' instructions to overseas communities; the second, Paul's *modus operandi.* James' directives to overseas communities are presented in three different versions in Acts.[14] They are presented there as a result of what is usually called 'the Jerusalem Council'. This episode begins in Acts 15:1 with the laconic note that:

> Some, having come down from Judea, were teaching the brothers: '*Unless you are circumcised according to the custom of Moses, you cannot be saved.*' A commotion, thereupon, ensued and much discussion ... and Paul and Barnabus and certain others were appointed to go up to ... Jerusalem (and inquire) about this question.

James then is clearly presented as making the kind of 'Judgments' predicated of 'the *Mebakker*' in the Damascus Document. He 'rules': 'Therefore I judge, we should not trouble *those Gentiles turning to God*, but write to them *to abstain from the pollutions of idols*, from *fornication, and from what is strangled and from blood*' (15:19–20).

In '*the epistle*' that Acts pictures James as sending to Antioch via 'Judas Barsabas', this is slightly rephrased as '*abstain from things sacrificed to idols and from blood, and from what is strangled and fornication*' (15:29). Six chapters later, Acts 21:25 repeats this second version in James' final confrontation with Paul and the culmination of the speech James makes to Paul, reiterating what Gentile believers are '*to observe*' and '*keep away from*'.

At this point, James sends Paul into the Temple to have himself 'purified' and his 'head shaved' along with the four others evidently under a 'Nazirite' oath of some kind (i.e., a 'temporary' one). Paul was to pay all their expenses. For Acts 21:24, the reason James gives for this penance is simple: so that 'all may know that the things they have been told about you are not so, but that you yourself also walk regularly keeping the Law'. But of course, Paul does no such thing. He does not 'keep the Law' – or, if he does, he does so only as a convenience or to further his mission. Paul's view of the Law is succinctly given in Galatians. It is 'a curse' (3:10–13).

In 1 Corinthians, the letter in which Paul announces himself as the 'architect' or 'builder' and wrestles with James' directives to overseas communities, Paul presents his philosophy such as it is. Some might call it cynical or self-serving. Some would call it pragmatic, but, as we shall see, there can be very little pragmatism in dealing with the Jerusalem Church Leadership or individuals at Qumran like '*the Mebakker*' or '*High Priest Commanding the Many*' and those inhabiting the wilderness camps. They saw things in black and white.

Paul states in 1 Corinthians 9:4, clearly in response to these and other kinds of charges, after having just dealt with the twin issues of 'things sacrificed to idols' and vegetarianism: 'My defense to those who examine me is this: "*Have we not (the) authority to eat and drink?*"' – this directly preceding a reference to '*the brothers of the Lord and Cephas*' (9:5). Here it should, once again, be appreciated that the role of 'the *Mebakker*' at Qumran was *to 'examine' people and make 'Judgments'*.

Then Paul turns again to the issues of authority and freedom:

> *Being free from all, I made myself the slave of all so as to win the most. To the Jews, I became as a Jew to win the Jews. To those under the Law, I who am not a subject of the Law, made myself a subject to the Law, to win those who are subjects of the Law. To those without the Law, I was free of the Law myself – though not free from God's Law being under the Law of Christ – to win those without the Law. For the weak I made myself weak. To all these, I made myself all things to all men that by all means some I might save* (1 Cor. 9:16–22).

No clearer philosophy of '*making oneself a Friend to the world*' has ever been so baldly or unabashedly put on record. In fact, in announcing this philosophy of '*winning*', Paul has perhaps identified himself as *the first modern man.* It only remains for his interlocutor in the Letter of James to turn it around, reversing it into the calumny, '*the Enemy of God*'.

The Issue of Blood and the Ban on Gentile Gifts and Sacrifices in the Temple

One may assume that the proscription on the consumption of blood would also extend to the mystery-religion phenomenon of *Communion with the Cup of the blood of the Christ*, which Paul introduces into his understanding of Messianism and the death of the Messianic Leader in 1 Corinthians 10:14–11:30. The Synoptic Gospels, of course, represent this as being introduced by Jesus himself at 'the Last Supper'.

Therefore James' *proscription on 'blood'* in the directives to overseas communities, as depicted in Acts, would seemingly also extend to the *consumption of the blood of the crucified Messiah*, even if taken in its most extreme sense – this apart from obvious Noahic bans on human sacrifice and consuming human blood generally. This, of course, brings us full circle and back to James' strange evocation of Abraham's willingness *to sacrifice his son Isaac* as evidence of Abraham's '*Faith working with his works*' (2:21–22). This is also echoed in the Gentile Mission claim that God chose 'to sacrifice His only-begotten' son in the world – a comparison expressly drawn in Hebrews 11:17.

The Final Triumph of Hellenization

But this is not the whole story. There is another theme related to it, *the admission of Gentiles into the Temple*, or, if one prefers, *the barring of Gentiles from the Temple.* This also punctuates this period leading up to the Uprising against Rome in 66–70 CE. It is also intrinsic to Paul's activities, both in his own presentation of how God chose him 'from the womb to reveal His Son in' him to 'announce the Gospel among the Gentiles' and how Acts presents the scene in the Temple, in which Paul is mobbed after having been sent in by James to go through the procedures of a temporary Nazirite oath. The cry raised there, aside from '*teaching against the people, the Law, and this place*', is that '*he has brought Greeks into the Temple and polluted this Holy Place*' (21:28 and 24:6).

That this theme was of concern in this period is verified by Josephus' discussion of the stones that were put up in the Temple to warn foreigners on pain of death of inadvertently intruding into the Sacred Precincts. The point made in them about foreigners, that their death would be 'their own responsibility', is exactly the point made in the Gospel of Matthew, where Pilate is depicted as *washing his hands* 'of the blood' of Jesus, but reversed. The crowd, there, is rather pictured as crying out gleefully, 'let his *blood* be upon us and on our children' – a most terrible cry that, it is worth repeating, has haunted the Jews through the ages (27:24).

Paul emphasizes the Community as both spiritualized Temple and body of Christ. As Paul reiterates, he is 'building' a Community where both Greeks and Jews can live in harmony (Gal. 3:28).[15] Using the language of the Community Rule at Qumran and Paul elsewhere in 1 Corinthians, Ephesians 2:19–22 insists that Jesus Christ is the Precious 'Cornerstone'; the Prophets and Apostles, 'the Foundation'; and the members 'the building', all growing into 'the Holy Temple in the Lord'.

Those who wish to bar Paul from the Temple are reflecting their awareness that he *wishes to bring foreigners into it* – whether actually or spiritually. There is no doubt he does spiritually. As he puts it in 1 Corinthians 2:10–15, he teaches 'spiritual things spiritually'. All these matters were comprehensible to the Hellenistic spirit and mind. *The consumption of blood* was part and parcel of the ceremonies of a welter of Hellenistic mystery cults that had as their goal the conquest of death – the same goal Paul announces in his letters (1 Cor. 15:54–57), the end being, as he puts it, to enter the tomb with Jesus or 'being crucified with Christ' (Gal. 2:20). They are certainly *not* comprehensible in a Palestinian Jewish milieu.

One should correct this slightly – at Qumran, there was the imagery of spiritualized Community, spiritualized Temple, spiritualized sacrifice, and spiritualized atonement, as in the Community Rule. But Paul's imagery is a little more circuitous; the Community *is* Jesus, Jesus is the Temple, therefore, the Community *is* the Temple. The end is the same. There is even the imagery in the Community Rule of the 'three Priests' of the Community Council as the 'Holy of Holies' or 'Inner Sanctum of the Temple'. But further than this, those of a Palestinian perspective were generally unable to go. Nor did anyone see the Law as metaphor, except someone like Philo in Alexandria – but his arguments were already highly Hellenized and, in any event, not in Palestine, which is an important difference.

For those *in* Palestine, Paul was, indeed, trying to introduce Gentiles into the Temple, spiritualized or real. Therefore there were plots to kill Paul – again seemingly among some who had taken a kind of *Nazirite* oath as described in Acts 23:12. But it is doubtful whether Jesus could have held a doctrine such as *introducing foreigners into the Temple or consuming blood* even if only symbolically, and still have been the popular leader he is presented as being. Such an anomaly could only have existed in the always-mischievous imagination of those responsible for the dissimulation in the Gospels and the Book of Acts. This was certainly aimed at pulling the teeth of 'the Messianic Movement' in Palestine, reversing it, and turning it against itself and into its mirror opposite.

Seen from this vantage point, Paul represented the final triumph of that Hellenization the Jews began struggling against in the generation of Judas Maccabee, two centuries before, and had been combating ever since. From Paul's point of view, it was normal to reconcile the claims of Judaism with those of Hellenism, and profitable to do so. From the Jewish perspective in Palestine, particularly the 'Zealot' one, it was anathema to do so. Therefore, the clash – the very real 'plots' against Paul become transmogrified in these accounts into *Jewish plots* against Jesus or the Messiah.

There were also very real plots against James, but these were on the part of the Herodian quasi-Jewish Establishment, *not the Jewish mass.* The majority of James' *Jerusalem Church* followers are described, by no less an authority than Acts itself, as '*Zealots for the Law*' (21:20). These are the actual words used. They are, also, the horns of the dilemma. The only escape from this dilemma is to the Dead Sea Scrolls, which lead us in the proper direction where Jewish life and thought in Palestine from the first century BCE–CE is concerned.

The Simon who Wishes to Bar Herodians from the Temple as Foreigners

Initially, then, we have these 'Zealot'-like groups that wish to kill Paul for introducing Gentiles into the Temple even if only spiritually or allegorically or as '*heirs according to the Promise*', as he puts it in Galatians 3:29. But there are also Zealots who wish to bar Herodians from the Temple.

Josephus will introduce us to one such Zealot leader, one 'Simon' who called an '*Assembly*' *of his own* in Jerusalem.[16] The time is the early 40's. The very word Josephus uses here in the Greek is the same word used throughout our sources for the '*Church*' or '*Assembly in Jerusalem*' – that is, this Simon, whom Josephus refers to as a '*somebody*' again and '*very scrupulous in the Knowledge of the Law*', is the head of his own 'Church' in Jerusalem, contemporaneous with Simon Peter depicted in Acts.

And what does this Simon wish to do? He does not wish to *admit Gentiles into the Community*, as Acts pictures Peter being instructed to do after receiving his vision of the Heavenly tablecloth on the rooftop in Jaffa (10:1–11:18). Rather the Simon in Josephus wishes to *bar Herodians from the Temple* ('*which belonged only to native Jews*') as non–Jews and 'unclean'. It is the position of this book that the Simon in Josephus is *the demythologized Simon* in the New Testament, just as Josephus' John the Baptist is *the demythologized John*. Furthermore, in the next generation, not only do these same 'Zealots' wish to bar Agrippa I's son Agrippa II from the Temple, but his sister Bernice too.

Josephus, true to his penchant for sexual innuendo, notes that Bernice was rumored to have had an incestuous relationship with Agrippa II, her brother.[17] This is very much the picture that emerges too in Acts, where Bernice appears together with Agrippa II – seemingly as his consort – in amiable interviews with Paul (25:13–26:30). So does her sister Drusilla, whom Acts 24:24 has the temerity to identify only as 'a Jewess', even though by this time, after a number of sexual indiscretions, she had *deserted the Jewish religion altogether* – this Josephus specifically notes – and married Nero's freedman, the infamous Governor Felix (52 –60 CE).

Of course, all this will bear on the second theme in the 'Three Nets of Belial' in the Damascus Document and the Letter of James, 'fornication', which Paul, too, is anxious to paper over, despite his pro forma protestations to the contrary, since he himself has relations with clear fornicators – most notably these same Bernice, Agrippa II, Drusilla, and Felix. One could hardly imagine John the Baptist, who had but two decades before lost his head because of such confrontations, conversing so congenially with such persons, or James, for that matter, from what we know of his uncompromisingly continent life-style. As it is, Paul converses with them – there is no reason to contradict Acts' picture at this point – with his usual congeniality or deference, even obsequiousness.

It is here Acts 24:6 acknowledges for the second time that the *actual charge* of 'pollution of the Temple' was being directed against Paul, then calling Drusilla 'a Jewess' without further explanation. But what kind of a Jewess could Drusilla have been? It was only her father's grandmother Mariamme who was 'native-born', as Josephus puts it in the episode about Simon wishing to bar her father Agrippa I from the Temple, the rest of her ancestors being either Idumaean Arab or Greek. Acts does not explain how she merits the appellation, nor, what is even more important, that she was *an Herodian*.

As Luke presents it in Acts: after *often* conversing with the blood–thirsty Felix about 'Righteousness' and the coming 'Judgment' (24:22–26), Paul obsequiously asks Agrippa II and Bernice of all people, 'King Agrippa, do you believe the Prophets? I know that you believe' (26:27) and discoursing with them in detail about his vision on the road to Damascus and the Gentile Mission. Then Agrippa II responds: 'In a little while you would persuade me to become a Christian.' And Paul: 'Not only in a little, but I would wish to God you and all those hearing me this day would very much become as I also am except for these bonds' (26:28–29). At this point according to Acts, Agrippa II and Bernice turn aside to Festus (60–62 CE) and say more or less what Pontius Pilate and other Roman Governors are depicted as saying in the literature: 'This man has done nothing deserving of death or chains' (26:31).

Festus was Felix's successor and it is upon his death that King Agrippa II and his High Priest Ananus get together *to destroy James*. As if to emphasize the parallel with what happened to Jesus, Acts has Agrippa add, 'This man might have been let go if he had not appealed to Caesar' (26:32). The scenario here of an intervening interview with high Herodians, combined with hearings before the Roman Governor, is exactly the same as the Gospel of Luke, who *also authored Acts*. As Acts develops the story, it is a good thing Paul was not let go, as '*the Jews* ... were preparing an ambush to put him to death' (25:2–3). Earlier, similar partisans or '*Sicarii*'/'Zealots' are pictured as having 'made a plot, putting themselves *under a curse* and *vowing neither to eat or drink until they killed Paul*' (23:12).

At this time Paul's 'sister's son', a person of some influence – though Acts interestingly declines to name either *him* or *his mother* – intervenes and informs the Roman Captain commanding the Citadel of these things.[18] The latter, thereupon, provides Paul with a huge escort: 200 soldiers, 200 auxiliaries, and 70 cavalry, and conducts him to Caesarea on the coast (23:23). The gist of this Captain's letter to Felix is revealing: 'This man had been seized by the Jews and would have been put to death by them, but having come upon the scene with troops and learned that he was a Roman citizen, I rescued him' (23:27–28).

In the run-up to the Uprising against Rome in the 60s, King Agrippa II and Bernice are finally barred from the Temple and for that matter *all* Jerusalem, even though his great-grandfather Herod and father King Agrippa I had been involved in rebuilding the Temple. In fact, this building had just been completed in time for its destruction by the Romans in 70 CE. Just prior to James' death at the beginning of the decade, the same sort of 'Zealots' responsible for this had already *erected a wall to block Agrippa II's view of the sacrifices in the Inner Court of the Temple.* It had been Agrippa's habit to eat while reclining with his guests on a veranda of his palace which had a fine perspective of the sacrifices in the Temple.[19] *It would have been interesting to know what kind of food he was eating and who his guests were on these occasions.*

These were the things – not to mention that 'Zealot' groups like the one led by Simon (the head of an 'Assembly of his own' in Jerusalem) would not even have considered him Jewish in the first place,[20] to say nothing of the rumor of his incest with his sister Bernice – that led to their both being banned from Jerusalem by '*the Innovators*' or '*Revolutionaries*' and the burning of their palaces during the War.

Belial, Balaam, and Polluting the Temple

The extreme purity demanded by such Temple 'Zealots' throughout the Century is vividly presented in the Temple Scroll. Some call this document 'a Second Law', because it deals with much more than just 'the Temple' and was delivered in the first person as if God were speaking – presumably to Moses and the whole people. In the column about *the exclusion of certain classes of unclean persons from the Temple* (just preceding the one about the *inadmissibility of bringing 'skins sacrificed to idols' into the Temple*), a barrier of the kind erected against Agrippa II and his dining companions around 61 CE above is called for. This was to protect the Temple from *even being 'seen' by such persons*; and the reference is coupled with *the use of the terminology 'Bela°* or '*balla°*/'*to swallow*'.

Of course, this relates to the '*Belial*' terminology at Qumran and the *B–L–'* ('*swallow*'/'*consume*') circle-of-language which, more or less, functions in opposition to language with the *Z–D–K* root meaning of '*Righteousness*'. 1 Peter 5:9 knows this language, and uses the 'Enemy' terminology in speaking of the '*Diabolos*' ('*Belial*' at Qumran), then connecting it with an allusion to 'being swallowed up'. It is also connected to allusions in the New Testament like '*Balaam*'. Not only is '*Balaam the son of Be'or*' referred to in 2 Peter 2:15 and Jude 1:11; but Revelation 2:14, in the context of referring to '*the Diabolos*' (2:10) and 'Satan' (2:13), describes how '*Balaam taught Balak to cast* (*balein*) *a net before the sons of Israel to eat things sacrificed to idols and commit fornication*'. This is the '*Three Nets of Belial*' language of the Damascus Document.

When the 'Zealots' or '*Sicarii*' finally did seize control of the Temple Mount in the aftermath of all these demands as the Uprising turned more extremist and moved into its 'Jacobin' phase, the first thing they did was to burn the debt records 'to cause a rising of the Poor against the Rich'.[20] They also burned the Herodian palaces, including both Bernice's and that of her brother Agrippa II, presumably the one in which he had reclined and viewed the Temple sacrifices while eating. Later, they also burned all the palaces of the High Priests appointed by Herodians, all of whom appear finally to have been slaughtered, including James' nemesis Ananus.

In fact, the issue we have been discussing here was the crux of the issue chosen by the lower priests when they stopped sacrifice on behalf of foreigners, including the Emperor, and rejected their gifts in the Temple. This rejection was contrary to the practice and point of view of the reigning Herodian High Priests responsible for the death of people like James. The rejection of these gifts and sacrifices was the issue on which the lower priests (called by some 'Levites') chose to take their stand *three and a half years after the death of James.*

The carnage that ensued – including the butchering of most or almost all of the High Priests and the burning of their palaces and those of the Herodians – culminated in the election, as we have mentioned, of the simple 'Stone-cutter' Phineas. As opposed to this, the highly Paulinized 1 Peter, however retrospectively, presents the following recommendation:

> For the sake of the Lord, accept the authority of every social institution, *the Emperor as the Supreme Authority* and *the Governors as commissioned by him to punish criminals*, and praise good behavior. God wants you to behave well, so ... *fear God* (here is the *'God-fearing'* terminology) and *honor the Emperor* (2:13; cf. Paul in Romans 13:1–8 which uses the 'all Righteousness' Commandment of James' 'Royal Law according to the Scripture' to the same effect).

At this time, right before the Uprising, the lower priests or Levites won the right to wear *the white linen of the High Priests.*[21] Acts is very interested in 'the number of priests' who are joining the new Movement. As it avers in the preamble to the stoning of Stephen: 'And the word of God increased. And the number of the Disciples in Jerusalem multiplied exceedingly, and *a great multitude of the Priests* were obedient to the Faith' (6:7). In the same vein, later on, Acts 21:20 characterizes the majority of James' followers as *'Zealots for the Law'*, a priestly notation, as we have seen, going back both to Maccabean High Priestly claims and the zeal of Phineas by virtue of which they were said to have won their High Priestly office in perpetuity. To put this into a proper context, these same early Church descriptions of James that we are considering here, as we have as well, not only insist that he wore the mitre of the High Priest, but also that he wore *white linen.* It is difficult to escape the impression that all these matters are connected in some manner, and that the Qumran documents, however one chooses to date them, are the key to unlocking these connections.

Noah's and James' Vegetarianism Re-evaluated

We now have the wherewithal to explain both the vegetarianism ascribed to Judas Maccabee in 2 Maccabees and to James in these various early Church accounts and its sophisticated reversal in Paul. Judas *goes out into the wilderness with nine other men and eats nothing but 'wild plants to avoid contracting defilement'.* John the Baptist – also designated *'a Righteous One'* in both Josephus and the Gospels – does so as well. James, too, because he was *'Holy'* or *'consecrated from his mother's womb'* – and also presumably because he was *'a Zaddik'*, is pictured as *abstaining from animal food as well.*

Where eating only vegetable fare is concerned, one can conceive of a scenario based on this Noahic ideology, where because the sacrifice in the Temple was interrupted or performed improperly by impure men having no claim to Righteousness and, as a consequence, 'polluted', the 'Noahic' permission to eat meat was considered to be withdrawn or no longer in effect by these desert sojourners mindful of the *extreme purity demands of Perfect Righteousness.* This goes back to the salvationary experience of the first *Zaddik*, Noah. He was not permitted to eat meat all the days of the Flood until he gained dry land and made a proper sacrifice. But he was to pour away the blood and not eat the flesh with blood in it, because 'the life' of the animal was in the blood. Only then was he permitted to resume eating animal life. To some, however, this permission might have appeared dependent on a proper sacrifice made by *Righteous Priests in the Temple.* Judas Maccabee was probably not a vegetarian while the Temple was properly functioning, but became one when it was considered defiled or the sacrifice was interrupted.

Often James' vegetarianism and the peculiar dietary habits of many of these charismatic 'Revolutionaries' or 'Innovators' is taken for some kind of asceticism. From what we are seeing here, this is not the case. It has to do with the demands of *all Righteousness and Perfect Holiness.* Just as those following *the regime of 'Righteousness towards one's fellow man' and 'Perfecting the Way'* developed an extreme poverty regime, because to make economic distinctions between oneself and one's neighbor would not be *Righteous*; so too, those following the extreme purity commandments had some question about the permissibility of eating meat.

The last category of James' directives to overseas communities, as pictured in the Book of Acts, is '*abstain from strangled things*'. This prohibition of James probably had to do with what in English goes by the name of '*carrion*', again probably based on the Noahic Covenant. Therefore it would have been seen as applicable to all Noah's human descendants and, as in Jewish Law generally, probably included some sense of beasts or fowl that died of themselves or as a result of disease.

Pseudoclementine *Homilies* 7.8, not only presents Peter as a daily bather and vegetarian (like James), but teaching '*to abstain from the table of demons (cf. Paul in 1 Cor. 10:21), that is, food sacrificed to idols, dead carcasses from animals which have been strangled or caught by beasts*, and from blood'.

From here one may go to the Koran again, the heir to many of these traditions and formulations. As Muhammad succinctly puts it: '*Abstain from swine-flesh, blood, things immolated to an idol, and carrion*' (2:172, 5:3, 16:115, etc.). The '*swine-flesh*' prohibition, of course, is normative in Jewish dietary law. It was, no doubt, also understood in James' instructions to overseas communities and probably so self-evident that it was not even thought worthy of mention. But the interesting things in Muhammad's presentation are *that which is 'immolated to an idol', 'blood', and 'carrion'.*

The Noahic Covenant, the 'Balaam' Circumlocution, and the 'Joiners' at Qumran

All the themes of these directives are connected in some way, as we have suggested, with *the Noahic Covenant.* Preserved in Rabbinic literature, this Covenant is usually presented as comprising a variety of moral and behavioral qualities, chief among which are the three commandments against: (1) idolatry, (2) fornication, and (3) man-slaughter or murder. All of these are implied in one way or another, too, in the directives given by James to overseas communities, even in Acts' admittedly tendentious picture.

We have been insisting all along that the one on 'food' or 'things sacrificed to idols' is just a variation of the one on idolatry generally. This is verified for us in Paul's correspondence as well, tendentious as it may be. This is also certainly the thrust of the '*Three Nets of Belial*' allusion in the Damascus Document, backed up in the presentation in Revelation of what *'Balaam taught Balak' by way of 'deceiving Israel'.* That these so-called 'prophets' are Gentiles from areas on the other side of the Jordan in Syria, Perea (Moab), and Idumaea is also interesting when it comes to considering Paul's claims, as reported in Acts, of being a 'teacher or prophet' of some kind (13:1).

In fact, Paul's claim to be of '*the Tribe of Benjamin*' is also interesting on this account, 'Benjamin' sometimes functioning as a variation of the '*Belial*'/'*Balaam*' terminology. '*Bela'* in Old Testament genealogies – reliable or otherwise – is not only an Edomite King but '*the Son of Be'or*', the *same* parentage ascribed to *Balaam.* He is also presented as *Benjamin's firstborn son* (Gen. 46:21 and 1 Chron. 7:6)! Not only have we already noted a word or name identical to it in the Temple Scroll *connected with classes of persons debarred from the Temple*, on at least four different occasions the epithet '*Sons of Belial*' is applied in the Old Testament specifically to *Benjaminites* (Judg. 19:22, 20:13, etc.).

It is for reasons such as these that we believe the Belial/Balaam/Bela' circle-of-language was being applied in some manner to Paul by those hostile to him – *as it was to all Herodians.* Of course, because of their Edomite or Idumaean origins or connections, the Herodians may already have been making such claims themselves to consolidate the dubious proposition of their Judaic or Hebraic origins – both Edom's progenitor Esau and Ishmael *being descendants of Abraham.* Paul is also making this a claim on his own behalf in the context of reference to Abraham in Romans 11:1 and Philippians 3:5 above. He never calls himself '*a Jew*', simply an '*Israelite*' or '*Hebrew*' – in Philippians 3:5 'a Hebrew of the Hebrews' – to which of course his '*Benjaminite*' origins, real or symbolical, would have entitled him (even in 1 Cor. 9:19 above, when he reveals his dissimulationist approach, he only says: '*To the Jews, I became as a Jew, so Jews I might gain*' – how's that for cynicism?)

In Romans 11:1, he adds, not insignificantly nor unlike Muhammad thereafter, '*of the seed of Abraham*'. At this time there were no longer any real tribal affiliations among Jews of the kind Paul is signaling, except where Priests and Levites were concerned. Significantly, no such claims really ever occur at Qumran where the term 'Jew' is already in use – these having *largely disappeared some 700 years earlier.* There also is some indication in Rabbinic literature and certainly in the War Scroll at Qumran that '*Benjamin*' was a terminology applied to all *overseas persons* or *Diaspora* Jews. That Paul was of '*the Tribe of Benjamin*' would in these contexts appear to be more obfuscation and reverse polemics, converting what may have been his opponents' pejoratives into their mirror opposite again and to positive effect.

In addition, where the Arab connections of Herodians are concerned, Herod's mother *was an Arab from Petra* and his sister was *originally married to Costobarus the Idumaean, whose progeny were systematically mixed into the Herodian line.* In respect to their 'Arabness', Herodians too take on the appearance of precursors of Muhammad. Where Paul – originally 'Saul' – is concerned, there is another reason '*Benjamin*' specifically is evoked in this literature directed at relatively naïve overseas ears. Conveniently, the archetypical Saul, David's predecessor as king, was of the Tribe of Benjamin (Acts 13:21) – *ipso facto*, so too was his latter-day namesake Paul.

The applicability of James' ban on 'fornication' – like that of Qumran – to this state of affairs is also self-evident. It goes far beyond the rather pro-forma and superficial references to it in Paul's letters, though there is this more or less straightforward overt sense too. For instance, as we saw, when Jesus is presented 'si*tting with tax collectors and Sinners*' or speaking positively about '*prostitutes*', this is meant to counter-indicate just the kinds of injunctions one gets in James' directives and at Qumran – to show that Jesus, the loving and forgiving Messiah, did not judge persons of this genre but even *kept 'table fellowship'* and *ate with them*, always an important theme.

This is the upshot, too, of 'the tablecloth vision' vouchsafed to Peter in Acts, in which he learns not to make distinctions between 'Holy and profane' just in time to inspect the household of the Roman Centurion Cornelius from Caesarea. Here, Cornelius is described as '*a Righteous One*' and '*a God–Fearer*, one *borne witness to by the whole nation of the Jews*' (Acts 10:22; cf. 1 Pet. 2:13), much as Felix, merciless butcher of innumerable resistance leaders, is described later in Acts as 'having very accurate knowledge about *the things of the Way*' (24:22). Both assertions are, quite simply, preposterous. The visit Peter makes to Cornelius' household in Caesarea, where he again explains, '*God has taught me not to call any man profane or unclean*', while the '*pious*' Roman Centurion is '*fasting and praying*' (Acts 10:30 – cynicism worthy of Paul above), will be equivalent to the one his namesake, the 'Simon' in Josephus, pays to the household of Agrippa I – again in Caesarea. In Acts' version of these occurrences, not only does Peter assert '*that it is unlawful for a Jewish man to keep company with or come near one of another race*', but he concludes that '*in every Nation, he who fears Him or works Righteousness is acceptable to Him*' (10:28 and 35).

Unlike Acts' 'Peter', the 'Simon' in Josephus *who inspects the household of Agrippa I in Caesarea*, wants to *bar Herodians from the Temple as unclean*, not accept them. Agrippa – whose beneficence and reputation among the Jews Josephus, as we have already remarked, extols – showered this Simon with gifts and then dismissed him. For his part, the 'Simon' in Acts learns to make no distinctions between men nor '*call any man unclean*'!

But these 'table fellowship' scenes in the Gospels are such favorites for precisely the same reason that more obsessive, purity-minded Jews have never comprehended how much foreigners in general instinctively wished to see them discomfited. The man-on-the-street in the world at large – if not in Palestine – wishes for the most part to feel that 'prostitutes', 'tax collectors', and 'Sinners', like himself, are acceptable and rub the faces of the Holier-than-thou, more piously-pretentious types into the mud of everyday existence. The presumably Hellenistic authors of these Gospel scenes seem to have understood this very well and played on it – as Paul obviously did.

What fun it must have been to portray *the Messiah in Palestine* as *keeping company* with such persons, knowing full well the opposite was true and how much types like those at Qumran abhorred them. This is not to mention the latter-day satisfaction they would have derived from having people *actually believe it for nearly two thousand years* had they but been around to enjoy it.

But these scenes have a political edge as well. The Herodians in this period were the Roman tax collectors in Palestine. Their usefulness to Rome in part rested on their effective collection and transmission of revenues. If some spilled off into their own pockets, so much the better. But of course the Herodian Princesses we have thus far encountered were also 'harlots', none more so than Bernice, whose 'Riches' even Josephus admits were prodigious. There is little doubt that her sister Drusilla – Felix's 'Jewish' wife in these scenes in Acts – was Rich too. Otherwise, apart from her royalty, what would Felix's interest in her have been?

When Jesus is portrayed as '*eating and drinking* ... a glutton and a wine-bibber, *a friend of tax collectors and Sinners*' (Mt 11:19 and Lk 7:34) – this right after John the Baptist is portrayed as '*neither eating bread, nor drinking wine*'; Scripture is saying that the 'Jesus' it is portraying *approved of such persons*. Nor does it picture 'Jesus' as fussing over purity regulations – particularly where food is concerned, nor making distinctions between people or nations on such a basis regarding '*table fellowship*' – meaning, Jesus was a '*Paulinist*' or *Paul knew Jesus better than any of his closest associates*!

In fact, as we have remarked, one can almost make a rule of thumb regarding such polemics. Where there is a statement in Paul – who according to his own testimony never met the 'Jesus' he is speaking about and had no first–hand knowledge of his teaching – that is echoed in the Gospels; one can assume the progression is from Paul and then into Gospel redaction and not *vice versa*. The unschooled person, innocent of such stratagems and the power of literary or retrospective recreation, normally reverses this.

We have already seen one important such speech above, where Jesus is portrayed as saying: '*Not that which enters the mouth makes a man polluted; but that which goes forth out of the mouth, this pollutes a man*' (Mt 15:11; Mk 7:15). In response to questioning, 'Jesus' is portrayed as becoming so agitated that he lists most of the Noahic prohibitions, that is: Evil inclination, murder, adultery, fornication, theft, Lying, blasphemy, covetousness, etc. (Mt 15:19 and Mk 7:22) and, then, adding how '*that which goes into the mouth, goes into the belly, and is cast out the toilet bowl*'!

The Gospel redactor, however, grows so effusive on this score that he ends up having Jesus conclude: '*These are the things which pollute a man, but eating with unwashed hands does not make a man unclean*' (Mt 15:20 and pars.). Because of an ancient artificer's antinomian bias, poor 'Jesus' is pictured as gainsaying what has become for modern hygiene a fundamental rule. Setting aside for the moment the issue of whether the Law is relevant or not, to consider material of this kind either 'the Word of God' or 'a revelation of the Holy Spirit' is simply absurd. Rather, it is more edifying to regard it as the mischievousness of malevolent polemical interchange.

Since the meaning of the Greek term 'strangled things' can also be looked upon as having to do with homicide and since the priestly author of this aspect of the Noah narrative does consider the taking of animal life to be a form of homicide, then we have in James' directives to overseas Communities, even as refracted in Acts, a reflection of three of the principal Noahic proscriptions: idolatry, manslaughter, and fornication. If the episode as Acts records it, or something somewhat approximating it, is true, then it should not be surprising that 'the *Zaddik*' James applied the terms of the Noahic Covenant to the salvationary status of persons who had not yet come into the Mosaic Covenant. Often such persons are referred to as 'God -Fearers'. A 'God-Fearer' would appear to be someone who has attached himself to the Jewish Community or 'Synagogue', but has not yet come in completely or taken the whole of the Mosaic Law upon himself.

We can detect such a status in the usage '*ger-nilveh*', resident alien, or the allied terminology, '*Nilvim*' or 'Joiners', evoked in the Damascus Document's eschatological exposition of the 'Zadokite Covenant' from Ezekiel. In the Book of Esther, the term 'Joiner' specifically denotes non-Jews 'attaching themselves to' the Jewish Community in some kind of associated status (9:27). In important contexts in the Damascus Document, for instance, the one referring to '*seeing Salvation*' and the Temple Scroll on *barring classes of unclean persons from the Temple* noted above, there is conspicuous reference to this idea of 'fearing God' as well.[22] That in these directives, depicted in Acts, James would apply the categories of the Noahic Covenant to the salvationary state of such God-Fearers, '*ger-nilveh*'s, or '*Nilvim*' is, not only not surprising, but eminently reasonable.

The Rechabites as ***Keepers, Doers*** and Potters Once Again

This wilderness life-style based on '*separation from the Sons of the Pit*' so as not to *incur their pollution* or *mix with* them or those having contact with them,[23] either parallels or to some extent is actually based on the *Rechabite* life-style. It is difficult to know whether there were any actual '*Rechabites*' as such left in the Second Temple Period, but, as we shall see, Eusebius' source Hegesippus is certainly using this expression in the Second Century to apply to successors or supporters of James.

The expression is curious – one shrouded in mystery. The fullest presentation of Rechabites, as we have seen, comes in Jeremiah 35 where Jonadab the son of Rechab is pictured as giving instructions to his descendants that *they would neither 'drink wine ... plant vineyards, build houses, sow seed, nor own property', but rather live only in tents 'so that you enjoy long life on the land which you sojourn upon'.* This takes us back to the 800s BCE, when Jonadab is pictured as an associate of the Israelite King Jehu, a king chosen by the Prophet Elisha.

Jeremiah emphasized in his panegyric to Jonadab's descendants both the themes 'keeping' and 'doing', that is, they '*kept* the Commandment their ancestor gave them' or 'observed all his rules and *did* all that he commanded'. The '*Rechabites*', therefore, are one of the first groups of so-called '*Keepers*', the basis of the definition of '*the Sons of Zadok*' in the Community Rule at Qumran. The behavior of these Rechabites – to whom the Prophet Jeremiah himself seems to have been connected – is contrasted sharply with the other Israelites in Jeremiah's own time (*c.* 605 BCE), who are about to be destroyed by God for just the opposite kind of behavior, i.e., '*lack of Faithfulness*'.

In 2 Kings 10, Jonadab is presented as a colleague of Jehu. His 'heart' and Jehu's are 'True' to each other. Together they destroy the family of Ahab and Jezebel and wipe out the remnants of 'Baal' worship or idolatry. Importantly, aside from the episode in Numbers about Phineas' '*zeal*' and Elijah's '*burning zeal*' in 2 Kings, this is the only other episode in the Old Testament where '*zeal for the Lord*' is specifically evoked (2 Kings 10:16). Therefore Jonadab son of Rechab is also 'zealous for God' or a prototypical 'Zealot'. In addition, like James and other Nazirites, *he does not drink wine or strong drink*. Whether or not Rechabites as such still existed some 700–800 years later can be debated, but the connection of this picture with the life-style attributed to James should be patent.

The life-style of the Rechabites, as we have implied, also has something in common with that of 'Nazirites', the classical account of whom occurs in Numbers 6:1–21. There the two characteristics that are emphasized are: '*separation from wine and strong drink, and neither drinking the juice of grapes, nor eating grapes, fresh or dried … no razor shall touch his head until the time of his consecration (or 'separation') to the Lord is complete*' (6:3–5). Obviously both of these themes bear on the description of James via Hegesippus in all early Church sources: '*He was Holy from his mother's womb; he drank no wine or strong drink, nor did he eat meat; no razor touched his head, nor did he anoint himself with oil …*'.[24] Epiphanius adds, *he 'died a virgin at the age of ninety–six'*, which relates to the Rechabite '*long life on the land*' in Jeremiah above.

But the strong emphasis on 'abstention from wine' or 'strong drink' and neither 'drinking the juice of nor eating grapes fresh or dried' in Numbers' description of the Nazirites also bears on the life-style of Jonadab's descendants, who seem to have made this the very basis of their unsettled or sojourning life-style embodying non-attachment to material or settled produce.

Where James is concerned, both the themes of *abstention from wine and 'a razor not touching his head'* reappear in connection with the idea of his either being '*consecrated*' or '*separated*'. This is also a *priestly* theme, even evoked in Ezekiel's 'Zadokite Statement' (44:20–21). For the Rechabites, the '*abstention from wine*' theme, if not the 'long hair' one, is central – though the themes of 'the unpruned vine' and 'unshorn hair' (not to mention that of 'the *Nezer*' or '*Crown*' of the High Priests as we shave seen) are related in Hebrew.

Eusebius is well aware of the connection of the '*Rechabite*' theme to James and/or the members of his immediate family. In the account of the death of James, which follows the account of his life-style and epithets in Hegesippus, the Rechabite ideal very prominently comes into play. Hegesippus also knows that these are the '*Rechabites spoken of by Jeremiah the Prophet*'. In this account, 'one of the Priests of the sons of Rechab' calls out to those who are stoning James, to cease what they are doing, saying 'the Just One is praying for you'. Now it is James 'on his knees' who repeats the cry attributed to Jesus in Luke 23:34: 'Father, forgive them, for they know not what they do'.

In Epiphanius' parallel account, where he actually says that James '*was a Nazirite and therefore connected to the Priesthood*', this '*Rechabite Priest*' is named and now becomes Simeon bar Cleophas.[25] That is, in Epiphanius' view, the cousin of and successor to James as Head of the Jerusalem Community, was 'a Rechabite Priest'. In the writer's view, much can be made of this, particularly when one reviews the evidence and data from the Scrolls in conjunction with these early Church accounts of the Jewish Christians or so-called '*Ebionites*'. If we take full note of the contexts in which the term emerges, which ancient exegetes also did, then both '*keeping*' and '*zeal*' are associated in some manner with either the Rechabites or their progenitor.

In the letter ascribed to James, too, the '*keeping*' terminology is prominent throughout, not to mention the '*doing*'. It is also the essence of the definition of '*the Sons of Zadok*' at Qumran, that is, '*the Keepers of the Covenant*'. In the first adumbration of this in the Community Rule, the Priests are associated with this as well, not to mention the command 'to separate from all the men of Unrighteousness, who walk in the Way of Evil'.[26] Therefore, one can conceive of all of these terminologies, '*Nazoraeans*', '*Sons of Zadok*', '*Rechabites*', and the like, as being in a sense parallel or variations on a theme.

For the Letter of James and the Scrolls, there is an additional one, that is, the 'doing' or 'Doers' just referred to. This finds repeated use in James and it and variations of it are found throughout the literature at Qumran – as it is in all literature from the works–Righteousness perspective – as, for instance, the Koran. '*Doers of the Torah*' is a key terminology in the Habakkuk *Pesher*. This is particularly the case in exegesis of Habakkuk 2:3, the scriptural warrant in the *pesher* for what goes by the name of '*the Delay of the Parousia*' in Christianity, that is, the delay of the Last Days and the coming of Christ in Glory. It is also a precondition to the exegesis in this *Pesher* of Habakkuk 2:4, '*the Righteous shall live by his Faith*' – the basis of Paul's theological approach in Galatians and Romans – making it clear that we have to do with an approach opposite to him on just about all these things.[27]

We are in the rarefied air of high theological debate here, one side marshalling its scriptural passages against the other, one side turning the scriptural passages evoked by the other back against it. For the Letter of James, these 'Doers' '*keeping the Royal Law according to the Scripture*' are ranged against 'the Breakers of the Law' in exactly parallel fashion as at Qumran (2:8–9).

This term, '*Osei ha-Torah* (*Torah*-Doers), has been identified as one of the possible bases of the nomenclature 'Essenes'. Another possible derivation of 'Essenes' is via the Aramaic for '*Pious Ones*' (*Hassidim* in Hebrew), but this cannot be proved. Epiphanius thinks that the word actually denotes 'Jesus' or his father 'Jesse', that is, 'Jesusians' or 'Jessaeans'.[28] But this, too, is labored. ''*Osei ha-Torah*' or ''*Osaeans*' (in Epiphanius, 'Ossaeans' or 'Ossenes') works best, and has the additional benefit of not only being Hebrew, but an actual term used in the Qumran documents. If this is true and the basis of 'Essenes' is the word 'Doers' in Hebrew, then we have another additional parallel here not only to Nazirites, but Nazoraeans, Rechabites, and Sons of Zadok as well.

Another notice about Rechabites in 1 Chronicles 2:55 identifies them as 'Kenites'. Their genealogy is traced back to Caleb the son of Hur from Ephratah (2:50). This last has significance regarding the location of Jesus' birth, 'Ephratah' in Scripture being designated as equivalent to Bethlehem. Now 'the Kenites' were considered to be Jethro's people from Sinai, with whom Moses resided, a daughter of whom he married – that is, Moses' descendants were to some degree to be identified with 'Kenites'. Subsequently, tradition pictures them as living among the Tribe of Judah.

Though these relationships are somewhat abstruse, what is most important in all this is that these 'Kenites' were considered to be metal-workers or smiths, that is, 'Potters' – the words are interchangeable in Hebrew, '*Yozrim*', a term moving directly into the usage '*Nozrim*' for Christians, itself underlying the 'Nazoraean'/'Nazarean' terminology.

This brings us full circle. If we now return to the Rabbinic tradition about '*Potters being Rechabites who kept the oath of their father*', a gloss on 1 Chronicles 4:23, we can see that these 'Tinkers' or 'Potters' are considered to be descendants of the Tribe of Judah as well. They are described as 'sojourning in plantations and enclosures' and employed 'in the workshop of the King', with whom they are said to have 'dwelled' as well. This brings us back to the workshop of 'the Potter in the House of the Lord' in Zechariah 11:13, alluded to in connection with Judas *Iscariot*'s suicide in Matthew 27:9.

It also follows a garbled note in 1 Chronicles 4:22 about a previous involvement of some kind with Moab across the Jordan – the 'Perea' of John the Baptist's area of activity – and perhaps 'Bethlehem'. The Catholic Vulgate has them, like David's ancestor, taking wives from 'Moab before returning to Bethlehem long ago'. These accounts also associate them with an area or town in this region known as 'Chozeba' (4:22). This may have been the original behind Bar Kochba's name, the Jewish Messianic leader and revolutionary of the next generation.

Whatever the significance of these aspects of the *Rechabite/Potter* problem, those called 'Rechabites' had no fixed abode, lived in tents, and, in particular, were not attached to material things. Not only did Jonadab give them commandments and ordinances, which '*they kept*' (*linzor*), he was also a '*Zealot for the Lord*' involved in Jehu's final destruction of idolatry. The reason, clearly, that his descendants were pictured as '*living in no fixed abode nor cultivating the grape*' was to emphasize their nonattachment to material things and, therefore, their 'zeal for God'.

Whether they still existed in James' time is beside the point. James too, is pictured by Eusebius, Epiphanius, and Jerome as '*abstaining from wine and strong drink, no razor ever touching his head*', and '*a Nazirite*', in his case – since 'he was consecrated from his mother's womb' – *a life-long Nazirite.* Further, as the term 'Holy' or 'consecrated' sometimes implies, a 'Priest'. If we combine the accounts of Eusebius and Epiphanius, both obviously based on Hegesippus before them, then James also had a brother who was a 'Rechabite' priest.

What does this mean? All three, Eusebius, Epiphanius, and Jerome, will now go on to proclaim not only James' claims to priestliness, but, also, the even more astonishing claim that he actually wore the mitre of a *High Priest.* This will be associated with another claim, that James '*wore no woolen garments and only wore linen*', that is, *the linen the priests in the Temple wore.*

The Sons or Daughters of the Rechabites as High Priests

In the Qumran literature there are the '*Sons of Zadok*' claims associated with 'the Priests who were the Keepers of the Covenant'; there is the priestly behavior of the 'Essenes'; there is the note in Acts about a 'multitude' of Priests joining the Movement connected to James' leadership in Jerusalem; there is 'the Zealot Movement' itself and its allied claim of 'the zeal of Phineas' first raised by Maccabeans to legitimatize their new Priesthood and reflected in the one notice we have about Jonadab son of Rechab; and finally, there are the High Priestly claims made on behalf of Jesus in the Letter to the Hebrews, that he was a 'Priest after the order of Melchizedek' (5.6, etc.), which even the unschooled will be able to recognize as a variation, when taken esoterically not literally, of '*the Sons of Zadok*' claim.

There is also an earlier notice about a Rechab – the first one we have – that may or may not have something to do with our subject, namely, that '*Rechab*' in the period of David and Saul was a Benjaminite, connected in some manner to '*Be'orite*'s (2 Sam. 4:2). Though this is a negative notice, again we are cutting into familiar themes here. There is a hint in this notice, too, of being '*sojourners*' or '*resident aliens*' (4:3). This theme of 'resident aliens' is important *vis-à -vis* the '*God-Fearer*' ideology we have been encountering and the language of 'joining' or 'Joiners' connected to it denoting Gentiles associating themselves in some fashion with the Jewish Community, but not necessarily taking the Law upon themselves in a permanent or thoroughgoing manner.

This theme of 'resident alien' (*ger-nilveh*) is very strong, too, in another Qumran Document, the Nahum *Pesher*. This is an important Qumran document, almost rivaling in significance the *Pesher* on Habakkuk. As usual, it is a '*Zaddik*' text, that is, in the underlying biblical text, there is a reference to the Hebrew word 'Zaddik' or 'Righteous One', James' cognomen. In this *Pesher* 'the resident aliens' (*ger-nilvim*) are associated with two further esoteric usages. Firstly, the 'City of Blood' which, as we have already suggested, connects in some manner to Paul's 'erecting a Community' – even if only symbolically – based 'on blood', that is to say, *drinking 'the Cup of the blood of Christ*'. Symbolic or real, it would not matter to the purist at Qumran or 'the Zealot'. The second is a usage which plays off another found in the Habakkuk *Pesher*, 'the Simple of Judah *doing Torah*'. This allusion to 'Simple' not only is the parallel of 'these Little Ones' in the Gospels, but of 'the Poor' or 'the Meek'. The last notice about Rechabites we have in the Old Testament is that one of their descendants, Malchijah son of Rechab, returned with the émigrés in the time of Ezra and Nehemiah (Neh. 3:14 – *c.* 450 BCE). To him was given the responsibility of repairing one of the Jerusalem gates known as 'the Dung Gate', hardly distinguishable from 'the Gate of the Essenes'. Malchijah is one of the twenty-four priestly courses listed in 1 Chronicles 24:9. If this is the same group as that of 'Malchijah the son of Rechab', then we have another notice of a further genealogical link of the Rechabites to the Priesthood functioning in Jesus' and James' day.

But in this idea of their ability '*to repair gates*', one also has a hint of their craftsman-like skills, and we are back to our Potters, smiths, or tinkers again. This is not to mention the note of 'carpentry' associated with either Jesus in Mark 6:3 or his father in Matthew 13:55. In Nehemiah 3:31, this Malchijah is actually also called '*the metalsmith's son*'!

This brings us back to Rabbinic literature once again and not only reinforces these notices about the *Rechabite* life-style, but once again connects them, however tenuously, to the High Priesthood and *doing service at the altar*. Let us assume that these wilderness 'sojourners' or 'Potters' – people, who with an eye towards extreme purity regulations and avoiding human entanglements, purposefully pursued a life-style with no permanent abode and abstained from wine or even cultivating vineyards – did somehow become involved in a genealogical manner with the High Priesthood, as these Rabbinic notices attest. Then these notices give the impression not only that this did occur, but how it happened.

In these Talmudic notices we hear in a *midrash* – a folkloric expansion – on Jeremiah 35, that '*the sons of Rechab were married to the daughters of the High Priests*' and '*did service in the Temple*' at least in the period just preceding the compilation of the materials in question. Another Talmudic tradition reverses this claiming '*the daughters of the Rechabites married the sons of the High Priests*'. This last brings us very close to the picture in the Gospel of Luke of John the Baptist's origins, who 'drank no wine' and wore a kind of clothing typical of the wilderness-dwelling descendants of these 'Potters'.[29] However these things may be, we have in these Rabbinic notices extremely important testimony to the fact of wilderness-dwelling types like such 'Rechabites' – whom in other descriptions might be called '*life-long Nazirites*' or even possibly '*Nazoraeans*' – *doing service in the Temple.*

In fact, around 1165 CE, the Spanish traveler Benjamin of Tudela claims to have encountered large numbers of just such *Jewish 'Rechabites'* in Arabia north of Yemen – *who 'ate no meat, abstained from wine', 'lived in caves', and continually fasted, being 'mourners for Jerusalem' and 'Zion'.*[30]

An aerial view of Caesarea, the center of Roman administration in Palestine from the Herodian Period onwards

Chapter 12
James' Bathing and Clothing Habits

James Wearing Only Linen and His *Yom Kippur* Atonement

The next point in early Church testimonies, that James wore only linen and was in the habit of entering the Temple *alone*, now becomes more important than ever and is connected with Temple service and priestliness. The text from Hegesippus (quoted by Eusebius) reads:

> He did not anoint himself with oil, nor did he go to the baths. He alone was allowed to enter into the Place of Holiness, for he did not wear wool, but linen, and he used to enter the Temple alone, and was often found upon his bended knees, interceding for the forgiveness of the people, so that his knees became as callused as a camel's, because of the constant importuning he did and kneeling before God and asking forgiveness for the people.[1]

The handling of this pivotal notice by our three principal sources illustrates how their minds were working and what they saw in the sources before them. Jerome echoes Eusebius' version of Hegesippus in connecting James' 'wearing only linen and not wool' with his 'entering the Temple'. But, whereas Eusebius speaks of James entering 'the Sanctuary' or 'Holy Place', Jerome actually calls this '*the Holy of Holies*', meaning the Inner Sanctum of the Temple.

Given the fact that the two usages, 'Temple' and 'Holy Place', which occur separately in Eusebius' quotation, are different in Greek, I think we can be persuaded that Jerome, who knew Hebrew, is more accurate on this point. In addition, it is equally clear, when taking into consideration Jerome's rendering, that what is being spoken of here is the atonement that the High Priest was permitted to make once a year in the Holy of Holies, supplicating God for forgiveness on behalf of the sins of the whole people.

The sins can be thought of either as communal or of omission, that is, sins that you were not conscious of or had no power over in their commission. Sins that you were aware of or had power over obviously could be expiated in the normal manner. This is the basis of the annual Jewish Day of Atonement or Festival of *Yom Kippur* to this day. That is, it is quite clear that what is being pictured here in these somewhat garbled accounts is a *Yom Kippur* atonement of some kind which James was reported to have made.

The Day of Atonement was commemorated on the Tenth Day of the Seventh Month (Exod. 12:3 and Lev. 27:32), the people already having been prepared for it by festivities at the beginning of this the Jewish holy month. These rose to a climax in the pilgrimage festivities at Tabernacles or the Feast of Booths in the Temple, thought to commemorate not only 'wilderness' sojourning, but also in some manner dedication to or receiving the *Torah*.

The purity arrangements regarding this atonement were stricter than normal and definitely involved 'bathing' (Lev. 16:4). Normally the High Priest wore eight garments of fine linen and wool. But on the Day of Atonement, he wore only four: linen coat, linen breeches, linen girdle, and linen head-dress or mitre. These were to be white and of coarse, not refined linen, in pursuance of Leviticus 16:4's prescription that these also be 'Holy'. These are clearly the clothes James is pictured as wearing on an ordinary basis in consequence of his extreme Holiness.

As Jerome puts it: 'He alone had the privilege of entering the Holy of Holies, since indeed he *did not wear woolen garments only linen*, and he went alone into the Temple and prayed on behalf of the people, so much so that his knees were reputed to have acquired the hardness of camels' knees'. Here Jerome reproduces all Eusebius' points, but in a more convincing rendition, since he makes plain what was meant by 'Holy Place'. Epiphanius reproduces these things somewhat differently again and, fanciful or not, he does have the merit of understanding their significance *vis-à-vis* the matter of a *Yom Kippur atonement.* As he puts it, having just noted that James was 'a Nazirite' and, therefore, 'consecrated' – once again Epiphanius, aside from his numerous *faux-pas*, shows himself adept at grasping the true thrust of many of these matters: 'But we find further that he also exercised *the Priesthood according to the Ancient Priesthood.* For this reason he was permitted to enter the Holy of Holies once a year, as Scripture says the Law ordered the High Priests'. He rephrases this in his second version of these things as follows: 'To James alone it was permitted to enter the Holy of Holies once a year, *because he was a Nazirite and connected to the priesthood* ... James was a distinguished member of the priesthood ... James also wore a diadem (the '*Nezer*' or sacerdotal plate) on his head'.[2] In the first version, he reiterates this, saying: 'Many before me have reported this of him – Eusebius, Clement and others. He was, also, allowed to wear the mitre on his head as the aforementioned trustworthy persons have testified in the same historical writings'.

Epiphanius has substituted 'mitre' for 'linen' here, but in all Old Testament accounts 'the mitre' or High Priestly head-dress was made of linen anyhow (Exod. 28:39 and pars.). Since both Jerome and Epiphanius associate it with his entering the *Inner Sanctum* of the Temple, I think we can assume that James did wear linen, always keeping in mind that the claim of wearing the mitre of the High Priest – with the words 'Holy to God' emblazoned on its plate – was always possible as well.

James' 'asking forgiveness on his knees on behalf of the whole people' is noted in all accounts of James' death – accounts in which Epiphanius substitutes the name of Simeon bar Cleophas ('Clopas') for 'one of the Priests of the sons of Rechab, a son of Rechabites' found in Eusebius. Though it is possible Epiphanius confused 'linen' and 'headplate', both characteristic of what High Priests wore, it is difficult to believe that he made up 'Simeon bar Cleophas' as the witness to James' death all by himself. For this reason and others, Epiphanius would appear to be operating from sources additional to Eusebius where these matters are concerned. That all accounts connect James' 'praying on behalf of the people' with both his atonement in the Temple and his stoning will have interesting consequences when it comes to connecting his stoning with the atonement in the Inner Sanctum. In Epiphanius Simeon bar Cleophas cries out with regard to James' stoning, 'Stop, he is uttering the most marvelous prayers for you'; in Eusebius simply, 'the Just One is praying for you'.

James' 'knees growing as hard as the nodules' of the knees of a camel, because of all the 'supplicating God' or the 'praying' in the Holy of Holies or in the Temple he did, is so original that it is difficult to imagine that Hegesippus simply made it up. It is eye-catching bits or snippets of information like this that often add to the credibility of the whole testimony. It is easy to imagine that at one point James did go into the Holy of Holies to make atonement on behalf of the whole people and that he was so 'Holy' and 'Pious' that he stayed there 'on his knees' the whole day in supplication to God. In other words, this was the Righteous prayer of a Priest/*Zaddik*.

This is one way of looking at it. There may be others. Much scorn has been heaped upon this testimony, particularly in Christian scholarship, but this was before the discovery of the Dead Sea Scrolls. Since that time, not only do we have the ideology to support such a picture of an 'Opposition' Righteous (or 'Zadokite') High Priesthood, but in the Habakkuk *Pesher*, there is a tantalizingly obscure notice about seemingly mortal difficulties between the Righteous Teacher's followers – referred to as 'the 'Poor'/'*Ebionim*' – and the Wicked Priest.[2] The details of this scenario recommend themselves as a prelude to the events of James' execution.

The Background to James' Atonement in the Temple

James' 'wearing only linen' also bears on the notice in Josephus about the lower priesthood winning the right to wear 'linen' at the end of the period James held sway in Jerusalem. Josephus does not date this event precisely, but he obviously considers it an '*innovation*' and one more nail in the Temple's coffin, for, as he puts it, '*all this was contrary to ancestral Laws, and such Law-breaking was bound to make us liable for punishment*'.[3] He means, of course, Divine retribution and Divine punishment and the coming destruction of the Temple.

He uses the same language to describe another '*innovation*', the stopping of sacrifice on behalf of Romans and other foreigners in the Temple by these same lower priests in this same period, which started the Uprising against Rome. As he describes the run-up to this in the 50's, he refers to the '*bands of brigands and impostors who deceived the masses. Not a day passed, however, but that Felix captured and put to death many of these Deceivers and Brigands.*'[4] For Josephus, it will be recalled, '*Those who would deceive the people and the religious frauds, under the pretence of Divine inspiration fostering Innovation* and *change in Government*, persuaded the masses to act like madmen and *led them out into the desert* promising them that there God would give them *the tokens of freedom*'.[5]

Having just described the attack 'the Egyptian' launches on the Temple, Josephus sums up the situation as follows: '*The Deceivers and the Brigands, banding together, incited Many to revolt, exhorting them to assert their freedom and threatening to kill any who submitted to Roman Dominion and forcibly to put down any who voluntarily accepted slavery*'. In the process, Josephus notes that these people went through Judea '*plundering the houses of the Rich and murdering their owners*'.[6] When the Revolt finally broke out, those Josephus describes as '*Innovators*' or '*desirous for social or revolutionary change*' burned the debt records in an attempt '*to turn the Poor against the Rich*'. Later, they not only burn the palaces of the Herodians and High Priests – the Herodians by this time had already departed into the Roman camp outside the city – most of whom, they killed, the High Priests that is. For his part, perspicacious reader must pay careful attention to the vocabulary of this period and all overlaps in the sources, no matter the context, while at the same time attempting to part the mist of purposeful obfuscation.

In the *Antiquities*, when describing the '*pollution* with which *the works* of the *Brigands infected the city*', Josephus describes the situation that developed under Felix, during whose Procuratorship similar problems broke out in Caesarea between the Greeks there – who had the support of the legionnaires – and the Jews.[7] After the assassination of Ananus' brother Jonathan by the most extreme group of Revolutionaries, he calls '*Sicarii*'; Josephus notes how:

> They committed these murders not only in other parts of the city but even in some cases in the Temple; for … they did not regard even this as a *desecration*. This is the reason why, in my opinion, *even God himself, loathing their Impiety*, turned away from our city, and because He *deemed the Temple to no longer be a clean dwelling place for Him, brought the Romans upon us and purification by fire upon the city, while He inflicted slavery upon us together with our wives and children*; for He wished to *chasten us by these calamities*.

Not only is the charge of 'blasphemy' we shall see leveled against James and, in the Gospels against 'Jesus', now turned against the extremists; but the woes of the Jews are now *the fault of the Sicarii*. This is the way, with hindsight, that Josephus describes the events in the 50s. He is, of course, turning the language of the pursuers of such '*Innovations*' in upon themselves. One should remark how self-serving or facile his view of history is – not to mention, how closely it and he parallel the way the Gospels portray the death of Christ.

We shall see the same language used in the Damascus Document, but there applied to '*the Seekers after Smooth Things*' and other collaborators *who attacked 'the Righteous One' and 'all the*

Walkers in Perfection with the sword'. As a result of this, '*the Wrath of God was kindled against their Congregation, devastating all their multitude, for their works were as unclean before Him' and 'He delivered them up to the avenging sword of vengeance of the Covenant'* – a favorite theme throughout the Damascus Document.[12]

Josephus speaks the same way when the Roman garrison in the Citadel is slaughtered in the early days of the Uprising, all save one, its captain, who agreed to have himself circumcised: 'And the city polluted by such a stain of guilt as could not but arouse a dread of some *Visitation from Heaven*, if not of vengeance from Rome'.[9] Josephus is, of course, writing with the advantage of hindsight, as did Eusebius much later:

> *The Divine Justice for their crimes against Christ and his Apostles finally overtook them, totally destroying the whole generation of these Evil-Doers from the earth. But the number of calamities which then overwhelmed the whole nation* ... the vast numbers of men, women and children that fell by the sword and famine, and innumerable other forms of death ... *and the final destruction by fire*, all this I say, any one that wishes may see accurately stated *in the History written by Josephus* ... *Such then was the vengeance that followed the guilt* and *Impiety of the Jews against the Christ of God*.[10]

Eusebius has no pity here, not even for the suffering of women and children, nor the starvation of thousands upon thousands; in fact, so intoxicated is he by theology that he revels in it.

But the real truth of the time undoubtedly lies embedded in these descriptions in Josephus and their obvious reversal of the real philosophy of 'the Innovators'. This last, as repeatedly signaled in this book, can now be said to be manifestly revealed in the documents known as the Dead Sea Scrolls and a *real* understanding of the Community led by James the Just. Writing of the end of the governorship of Felix, Josephus states:

> There was now enkindled *mutual enmity and class warfare* between *the High Priests on the one hand and the Priests and Leaders of the masses of Jerusalem on the other*. Each of the factions formed and collected for itself *a band of the most reckless Innovators, who acted as their leaders*. And when they clashed, they used abusive language and *pelted each other with stones*. And there was *not even one person to rebuke them*.[11]

Here we have a moment of candor rare in Josephus. Seen in a different light, one can see in this description the debates in the Temple between the two factions, pictured in both the Pseudoclementines and Acts, however tendentiously – including even the rioting – and events like the stoning of James. Even the note of there being 'no one to rebuke them' is reversed in the picture in early Church sources of the words of James' successor Simeon bar Cleophas, the 'Rechabite Priest' who *rebukes* those stoning James the Just.

Not only do we have in this picture both the themes of the High Priests being opposed by the lower priests – who, in turn, were 'the leaders of the masses' – but Josephus follows up this description with his picture of how *the High Priests shamelessly sent their servants to the threshing floors* '*to steal the tithes of the Poorer*' Priests, who consequently '*starved to death. Thus did the violence of the contending factions overwhelm all Justice*.'[12] One can picture this description being applied to and even seen in terms of the death of James 'the Just One', who was the Leader of the faction calling itself – both at Qumran and in early Christianity – '*the Poor*'.

Josephus portrays the fact of the lower priests winning the right to wear linen in the context of these events and this kind of rioting. Though these facts all need further elucidation, for the moment it should suffice to state that James' role as a priest among the masses in the midst of all this revolutionary strife is emerging. Nowhere is it better explained than in the Scrolls, the literature of that group we can now see as part of those seeking just these kinds of 'Innovations'. We certainly do have in those texts the theme of *the Rich High*

Priests 'stealing' the tithes of the Poor Ones.[13] Moreover its authors saw the Temple as *'polluted'*, but not for the reasons Josephus attempts to disseminate or, from a slightly different perspective, Paul and early Christian theologians following his lead do. *The Temple is polluted because of the acceptance of polluted gifts in the Treasury*, because of the acceptance of fornicators in the Temple, because of improper 'separation of Holy Things', and relations with foreigners and those to whom Paul's very mission is addressed – Gentiles.

In such a context, one can see Paul's final entry into the Temple to show that *'there is no truth to the rumors' that he does not 'regularly follow the Law'* as something of a stalking horse for Herodian family interests in the Temple. The charge raised among the mob in the riot Acts pictures as ensuing there is that Paul is *introducing foreigners in the Temple*. One way or another he is. The same cry is no doubt on the lips of these extreme '*Zealots*' or '*Sicarii*', who are behind the troubles in Jerusalem being described by Josephus. As Acts would have it, James' followers are a mixture of 'priests' – obviously lower priests – and others who are *'zealous for the Law'* (21:20). This is the same picture Josephus has just given us regarding confrontations and stone–throwing on the Temple Mount in the early 60s.

James and *Banus*

To go back to this reference to James *'wearing only linen'*. Not only does it resonate with Qumran, but it also has interesting overtones with someone Josephus calls only '*Banus*', clearly another of these individuals *dwelling in the wilderness showing the signs of 'impending freedom'* or '*Deliverance*'. John the Baptist and others are of the same mould. Never explaining what he means by *Banus*' name, Josephus describes him as 'living in the wilderness' and *'eating only what grew of its own accord', meaning, he was a vegetarian*!

Even *Banus*' name is probably really a title. Never definitively deciphered by scholars, it is probably a loan word via Latin having something to do with his most characteristic activity, '*bathing*'. If not, then like James' other title, '*Oblias*' or '*Protection of the People*', it is probably a code.

There is a 'Rechabite' aspect to Josephus' description of *Banus*, since he does not *cultivate*. Like Judas Maccabee earlier he eats *only wild plants*. Once again, many of the themes we have been pursuing come together. *Banus* has to have been functioning 'in the wilderness' in the mid–50s, the period Josephus – who was born in 37 CE – states he spent three years with him. If Josephus did spend three years with him, it would account for his sympathetic treatment, even though he is normally opposed to such religious *'impostors and Deceivers' who lead the people out 'into the wilderness'*.

Three years, too, is the time frame Paul describes in Galatians of his having been '*to Arabia and then returned to Damascus*' (1:17–18). It is also the approximate novitiate period for the Movement described in Qumran documents, another of these Communities 'in the wilderness' or 'at Damascus'. However one takes this allusion by Paul to 'Arabia', 'wilderness' areas of this kind in Judea and Transjordan were not highly populated. Certainly Josephus' knowledge of the 'Essenes' must have come from this period, as in the *Vita* he describes having made a trial of the three sects: Pharisees, Sadducees, and Essenes, undergoing great hardship in the process.

Josephus also describes '*Banus*' as a daily bather and utterly chaste. This is exactly the same language Epiphanius uses to describe James, that '*he died a virgin at the age of ninety-six*'. Again, this links up with notices in both Josephus and Hippolytus about how incredibly 'long -lived' those they call 'Essenes' were because of their continent life-style: '*They are long-lived – most over a century – in consequence of the simplicity of their diet and the regularity of the mode of life they observe*'.[14] We can forgive exaggerations over the age of these 'elderly and honorable' men who followed the 'Nazirite' life-style. In a similar vein, following Hegesippus, Eusebius contends

'*Simon* son of *Clopas*' (*sic*) was crucified under Trajan at the age of a hundred and twenty'. This would have been in approximately the year 106–7.[15] These exaggerations should not be too disconcerting.

Epiphanius, quoting a book he calls '*The Travels of Peter*' – meaning the Pseudoclementines – says that the Ebionites thought Peter was *celibate* too – in addition claiming that he was a *daily baptizer* and *vegetarian.* The reason, he says, the Ebionites give for this last is important: *because animal fare was 'the product of sexual intercourse'* too.[16] For Epiphanius – and he does not give his source for this, but most likely it is Hegesippus – all '*Joseph*'s *sons revered virginity and the Nazirite lifestyle*'.[17] In associating the 'virginity' of these life-long Nazirites with the doctrine of 'the Holy Virgin', Epiphanius once again points the way towards comprehending another reversal. But what makes sense with regard to James and individuals like '*Banus*' *following the regime of extreme purity in the wilderness* makes little, if any, sense when it comes to '*honoring the vessel in which the Salvation of the human race dwelt*' – words, Epiphanius uses in explaining why the '*Holy Virgin*' was also revered, aimed at and clearly originating in a Greco-Roman/Egyptian milieu; but, words, in a Palestinian one, *more aptly descriptive of James*!

As Epiphanius, again so incisively, expresses this: 'She would not have sexual relations *with a man*.'[18] But, of course, this claim, except theologically speaking, is absurd, and James' *chasteness* has simply been transferred in tradition to Mary and the '*Virgin birth*' – comprehensible, as we have said, to Greco-Roman Society. It is almost certain, despite facile attempts to disclaim it, that whoever Mary was, she had *at least four sons and two daughters.* Rather, it is James, who had *no sexual relations with women*, another example of retrospective theological inversion of, in our view, *real* detail from the life of James. James' and *Banus*' 'chaste' life-style was, no doubt, connected to the extreme purity regime and that abhorrence of 'fornication', we have already seen integrally associated with James' name, not to mention the ethos of the Scrolls.

Banus' eating things growing only of themselves is best explained by the notice about Judas Maccabee, who, when the sacrifice in the Temple was interrupted, retreated into the wilderness, lived in caves, and ate nothing but '*wild plants to avoid contracting defilement*'. Here, too, we have the extension of the 'vegetarian' theme to the Rechabite life-style of individuals, who, to avoid earthly attachments and corruptions would cultivate nothing and would not even construct a permanent dwelling. Doubtlessly they, too, lived in caves, tents, or lean-tos of the kind probably preferred in the wilderness 'camp' ideology of the Scrolls. All these matters are connected and, depending on the observer, a given nomenclature is employed to describe them – thus, the plethora of titles we see associated with them.

In any event, all these nomenclatures are not all separate reckonings. Where the descriptions overlap, however tenuously, they must be seen as the same or allied movements. The same for these various groups. They are connected with the Maccabean ideal of eating non-cultivated plants. They are connected with living in caves. They are connected with the extreme purity regime. They are connected with attempts to bring on 'the Last Days'. They are connected with the description of the wilderness 'camps' in the Qumran literature. They are connected with Josephus' numerous and fulsome condemnations of such groups – meant, of course, to impress his Roman overlords – even though as a young man he spent time among them. Paul too, no doubt, did the same. Hence his in-depth knowledge of them also.

A final note about *Banus*' clothing, which now connects with our 'linen' theme where James is concerned, as it does the general one of noncultivation about Rechabites and that of not wearing *woolen* garments reported of James. When speaking of *Banus*' clothing, Josephus tells us he wore nothing but '*clothing that grew on trees*'. He means 'plant'- or 'vegetable'-based not *woolen* clothes, that is, that '*Banus*' and other 'Priests' *would only wear clothing of natural fiber* or *linen.*

Not only are '*Banus*' and James contemporaries, but the connections between them grow stronger, as do Josephus' connections to and reticence about them both. We have already seen that by the time of writing the *Antiquities* in the 90s, Josephus felt more secure than he had directly after the Uprising. He could afford to be less circumspect regarding his own activities with such 'wilderness'-dwelling types. In light of the execution of his patron Epaphroditus, and one or two other reputed Christians in the then-Emperor Domitian's household, including Flavius Clemens (possibly the Clement of literary fame) and possibly his wife, Flavia Domitilla, and new accusations surfacing against Josephus himself; this sense of security might have been ill-founded.

Banus', John the Baptist's, and James' Bathing, Food, and Clothing

The 'bathing' ideology goes back, at least in Western Christian tradition, to John the Baptist. The kind of clothing John wore and the food he ate are matters of intense interest in all extant descriptions of his activities. He is described in the famous passages in Matthew and Mark as wearing '*camel's hair clothing* and a leather girdle *about his loins*' and eating 'locusts and wild honey' (Mt 3:4/Mk 1:6). It is phrases like 'about his loins' and 'wild' that are the link to descriptions of our other *vegetarian* types and daily bathers like James and/or the 'Essenes', Masbuthaeans, etc. The *clothing* part of this description goes back to that of Elijah as 'hairy and gird with a leather girdle about his loins' (1 Kings 1:8).

In the second part of this description of John, if not the first, one must make allowances for inaccuracies arising out of translations of little understood terms from Hebrew or Aramaic into Greek. In both Josephus' and Hippolytus' descriptions of the 'Essenes', we observed that the idea of wearing 'linen about their loins', *even when they bathed* because of their modesty and sexual chastity, is a persistent one. In turn, this moves through descriptions of *Masbuthaean* Bathers in Northern Syria, like the '*Elchasaites*', down to the *Mandaeans* in Southern Iraq – '*the Subba' of the marshes*' down to the present day. Hippolytus in his extended presentation of '*the Essenes*', when speaking of their '*ablutions in cold water*', actually uses the words '*linen girdles' to describe how they clothed themselves 'for the purpose of concealing their private parts*'. Josephus speaks of 'the linen cloths' with which the Essenes 'girded their loins' before 'bathing their bodies in cold water'.[20] The only difference is that New Testament accounts, in portraying John as an Elijah *redivivus*, have substituted the 'leather girdle' for 'linen girdles'. It is impossible to tell what the actual truth is here, but since what is at issue where John and the Essenes are concerned is 'bathing' – not an issue in the biblical accounts of Elijah's archetypical, 'exceeding great zeal' – in the writer's view this is what the New Testament accounts are really trying to say and are really aiming at.

In any event, where John's food is concerned, it is doubtful such fare could have sustained him, nor was insect fare of this kind really considered fit consumption for strict constructionists of the Law, which these *wilderness 'Keepers'* normally clearly were. Epiphanius' lost '*Gospel of the Ebionites*' maintained that John ate 'wild honey' and vegetarian 'cakes baked in oil', reflecting the picture of Lucian of Samosata's daily baptizers in Northern Syria who ate 'wild fruits and drank milk and honey' and slept out 'under the open sky'.[59] This description, coupled with the 'eating nothing but wild plants' in 2 Maccabees' description of Judas' wilderness regime, is a more convincing picture of the diet of these wilderness–dwellers than the highly improbable and even perhaps, quasi-illegal, 'locusts and wild honey'.

In fact, Josephus' description of '*Banus*'' food consumption and the type of dress he wore would probably be a more accurate reflection of what John would have eaten or worn than these more popular New Testament retrospections. As will be recalled, Josephus contends that '*Banus lived in the wilderness and wore no other clothing but that which grew on trees (linen) and had no other food than that which grew of its own accord, and bathed in cold water persistently, night and day, in order to preserve his chastity*'[22] – the last paralleling Epiphanius on James' sexual continence.

Where the rest of the New Testament presentation of John is concerned, it must be treated with the same extreme caution. At every point, Josephus is superior. For instance, for him, 'John was a good man and exhorted the Jews to live virtuously, both as to *Righteousness towards one another* and *Piety towards God.* And so to come to baptism, for that *washing* would be acceptable to Him if they made use of it, not in order *to remit whatever sins they committed,* but for *the purification of the body* only, provided that the soul had been thoroughly *cleansed beforehand by practicing Righteousness'*.[23] Not only do we have here the Righteousness/Piety dichotomy, but this description of John's baptism is exactly *the reverse* of New Testament ones and undoubtedly *more reliable.* It also accords with that in the Community Rule.[24]

Herod Antipas, seeing '*the great influence John had over the masses*' and the enthusiasm with which they received him, 'feared he would lead them to rise up' and revolt and, therefore, took him to Machaeros bordering his domain on the other side of the Dead Sea and the domain of the Arab King Aretas' in Petra. There he had him put to death. No mention is made of Herodias, nor her daughter Salome's tantalizing dance, though references to these characters abound in the surrounding materials in Josephus. Nor is there any mention of the hallowed and, shall we say, rather sensational picture – missing, in any case, from Luke and John –of John's *head upon a platter sent to Salome and Herodias.* One should also add that it is to Josephus we actually owe the name of Herodias' famous daughter '*Salome*' at all – the Gospel writers being, seemingly, ignorant of the name of this fabled temptress!

In Josephus, this note about '*sending someone's head to someone*' is also *part of the story of the execution of John*; but there it is, rather, the *Roman Emperor Tiberius who wants the head of the Arab King Aretas of Petra* '*sent to him*' *for what he had done to Herod Antipas* – that is, defeated him militarily after Antipas had divorced Aretas' daughter in order to marry Herodias. This, Josephus says, '*the Jews considered vengeance on him for what he had done to John the Baptist*' – another example of Gospel *lateral transference* and *inversion* and probably the truth of the matter.

It should be clear that Josephus' presentation is the *demythologized* John, although highly mythologized portraits in the New Testament incorporating the kind of 'birthday parties' Romans loved so much (even today attractive to a wide popular audience) and flattering portrayals of the Herodian family certainly made better story-telling. The baptism in Josephus' description of John was simply a water cleansing or immersion, and, no doubt – as in the accounts of '*Banus*' and '*the Essenes*' – a *cold water one* at that, 'provided the soul had already been *purified* beforehand by *the practice of Righteousness*'. This is the Qumran view as well, just as it is the presentation we are developing of *the demythologized James.*

To show the tendentiousness of these various New Testament accounts, the Gospel of Mark, which has the fullest presentation of these materials, states that 'Herod feared John, *knowing him to be a Righteous One* and *Holy*' (6:20). In other words, Herod recognizes John as *a Zaddik* and Holy One. This replicates parallel materials in Josephus noting that Herod '*feared John*', but *not* because he considered '*him a Zaddik and Holy*'. For Josephus, rather, Herod '*fears John*' because of his influence over the crowd, '*who were greatly inflamed by his words' and 'seemed as if they were of a mind to be guided by John in everything they did*'. Therefore, the execution is with malice aforethought. As Josephus puts it, '*Herod thought it best, fearing an Uprising, to strike first* and *put him to death, lest he should later repent of his mistake when it was too late*'. It is a preventative execution, and here we have the typical New Testament reversal of themes, particularly the one of political revolution.

Essenes, Zealots, and Nazoraeans

To go back, now, to 'the Essenes' too, Josephus describes the them, both in the *War* and in the *Antiquities.* Both descriptions begin with the discussion of *Judas the Galilean's activities at the time of the Census of Cyrenius/Quirinius* – coincident in Luke's Gospel with 'Jesus'' birth moment. The discussion in the *War* ends up dwelling on so-called 'Essenes', while making short shrift of Sadducees and Pharisees, and ignoring Judas' revolutionary 'sect' altogether. In the later *Antiquities*, Josephus drastically curtails his treatment of '*the Essenes*'. In fact, he cuts a section from his discussion of '*the Essenes*' in the *War* and adds it to his presentation of Judas the Galilean's '*Fourth Philosophy*' in the *Antiquities*. This is the section about their willingness to undergo '*deaths of the most horrific torture*', which Hippolytus connects to their refusal '*to eat things sacrificed to an idol*'. Josephus simply presents this last as 'to eat the things forbidden them'.

The one thing Josephus makes quite clear about Judas' sectarians is that '*they have an inviolable attachment to freedom*, insisting that *God alone is their only Ruler and Lord*', and '*having had God for their Lord, refuse to pay taxes to the Romans and submit to any mortal masters*'. For lack of a better term, many call these 'Fourth Philosophy' Innovators 'Zealots', even though Josephus never uses the term until the Uprising against Rome and this only after he has begun referring to the 'pollutions' in both the city and the Temple of those he designates '*Sicarii*'. When he does use the term 'Zealots', he really applies it only to one of several contending subversive groups – specifically the one *opposing the High Priest Ananus, James' executioner* who seem, significantly, to be occupying the Temple.

Ultimately these let the unruly '*Idumaeans*' into the city, who proceed to slaughter all the High Priests, ending up in possession of the Temple. For Josephus, these '*Idumaeans*' along with '*the Zealots*' are more blood-thirsty even than '*the Sicarii*', who end up in the fortress on Masada.[25] But, the common point between his first description of the '*Essenes*' and his later description of Judas' Galilean '*Innovators*' is that: 'They also think little of dying any kind of deaths, nor do they heed deaths of their relatives or friends, nor can any such fear make them *call any man Lord*'. But this is exactly what Hippolytus adds to his description of those '*Essenes*' who 'will *not slander the Law* or *eat things sacrificed to an idol*'. Immediately one recognizes this last as the characteristic of James' followers at almost precisely this point in history.

In Hippolytus' version of Josephus, the more extreme group of '*Essenes*' – those who even kill persons '*refusing to undergo the rite of circumcision*' – '*are called Zealots or Sicarii*'.

> Some have declined to such an extent in discipline, that as far as those are concerned who follow *the ancient customs*, they refuse even *to touch them*, and if they come in contact with them by chance, they *immediately resort to washing*, as if they had touched some one belonging to an alien tribe.[26]

Like Josephus' '*Zealots*' above, these, too, 'refuse to call *any man Lord*, except the Deity, even though someone tries to torture or even kill them'.

At one point Josephus described these '*Essenes*' as recommending to the young Herod '*to love Righteousness and practice Piety towards God*'. He repeats this, in describing the final initiation of the novice into '*the Pure Food*' of their Community after a three-year probation – in addition to '*swearing not to reveal any of their secrets to others even if compelled under mortal torture to do so*' and '*to expose Liars*', 'he is made to take the most *tremendous oaths* that, in the first place, *he will practice Piety towards God* and then, that *he will observe Righteousness towards men*'.[27]

This is, of course, exactly what he pictures John the Baptist as teaching in the *Antiquities*. This is also the essence of 'Jesus'' teaching, according to the Gospels, and is central to James' position as the letter transmitted in his name makes abundantly clear (James 2:5–8). We can now identify these '*Commandments*' as the basic ideology of '*the Opposition Alliance*', '*Piety*' being the sum total of *all one's obligations towards God – one's ceremonial obligations* – and '*Righteousness*', *one's obligations to one's fellow man – one's social obligations*. This is exactly how Josephus portrays them in his description of '*the Essenes*' too.

Chapter 13
James as Opposition High Priest and *Oblias*

James as *Oblias* or Protection-of-the-People

Both Eusebius and Epiphanius, again basing themselves on Hegesippus, tell us that James was known by two important cognomens, 'the Righteous' or 'Just One', and '*Oblias*'. Both are a consequence of James' '*Holiness from his mother's womb*' and his having entered the Holy of Holies to make a *Yom Kippur*-style atonement on behalf of the whole people.

Neither writer is able properly to transliterate '*Oblias*', providing only an approximate transliteration in the Greek. Nor has anyone ever discovered exactly what the Hebrew it was originally based on was, though Eusebius and Epiphanius *think* they know what the word meant. To be sure, there is always the possibility that the term was just another variation in the *B–L–*' language circle in Hebrew and Greek. There is something of this root in the mysterious '*Lebbaeus*' name found in some versions of the Gospel of Matthew and attached to the Apostle '*Thaddaeus*', an individual we shall also show to be part of James' and Jesus' family circle. '*Oblias*' and '*Lebbaeus*' probably represent something of the same thing, their relationship having to do with the curious recurrences of the letters *B* and *L* making up their names whether in Hebrew or Greek.

The first syllable, '*Ob*', would seem to be based on some Hebrew description involving 'Protection', 'Bulwark', or 'Strength' (in Hebrew, '*'Oz*' or '*Ma'oz*'). Both Eusebius and Epiphanius, though in the dark as to its precise derivation, think '*Oblias*' means this. Eusebius tells us: 'Because of his superlative Righteousness, he was called the Righteous One (*Dikaios*) and Oblias, which translates out in Greek, 'Protection-of-the-People' and 'Righteousness'' (*Dikaiosune*). He then adds, '*as the Prophets declare concerning him*'.[1] This is a very pregnant addition, for it means that James' two cognomens, '*Zaddik*' and '*Oblias*', were to be found by searching Hebrew Scripture, particularly the Prophets, and Psalms.

For Epiphanius, James was surnamed 'the *Zaddik*' and called '*Oblias*', which for him means either '*Fortress*' or 'wall'.[2] It should be remarked that he leaves out '*of the People*', as in Eusebius' *Oblias* as 'Protection-of-the-People', but otherwise he is in substantial agreement with Eusebius on this mysterious term's meaning. In a later description of James, Eusebius provides a variation on the term – '*Bulwark*', which still retains the general sense of Wall, Fortress or Protection. Whatever it means, it results from James' superabundant Righteousness and his functioning in the Temple as a Priest or *Opposition* High Priest. Both Eusebius and Epiphanius present the epithet in this context.

But what is the meaning of this '*Wall*' or '*Fortification*' language connected with James' second cognomen '*Oblias*'? How is it to '*be found in Scripture*' as Eusebius reports? This is an intriguing question.

There are several possibilities. First, it should be appreciated that this *Protection*, *Fortress*, or *Bulwark* language is of the same genre and sense as the *Pillar* language Paul has already applied to James, Cephas, and John (Galatians 2:9). But there are other words in Hebrew, also synonyms, which come close to the sense of this usage. These, found in Psalms and Prophets and reflected to some extent in the New Testament, are also in use in both the Community Rule and the Qumran Hymns.

Fortress, *Rock*, *Bulwark*, and *Cornerstone* Imagery at Qumran

In the Hymns Scroll found at Qumran, we find much of the imagery that we have already encountered in these passages describing James in early Church Literature. These should, perhaps, not be called 'Hymns', which is a little misleading. It implies a parallel with the Psalms in the Bible, but this document, found in the first cave discovered at Qumran in 1947, also tells something of a story. Written in the first person, it relates some of the experiences of its narrator, who appears to be a real person.

He repeatedly refers to himself as '*the Poor One*' or '*Ebion*' – familiar terminology where James' followers are in question – as well as what he repeatedly calls '*the soul of the Poor One*', apparently meaning, as in the biblical Psalms, his quick or 'life'.[3] In a key allusion in the Damascus Document, for instance, we hear of an attack or '*pursuit with the sword*', apparently led by the Liar, on '*the soul of the Righteous One (Zaddik) and all the Walkers in Perfection*', which parallels the sense of 'the Soul of the Poor One' here in Hymns.[4]

In addition, Hymns repeatedly refers to 'Righteous works', 'Perfection', 'the Way', 'Piety' – even 'the Poor Ones of Piety' (*Ebionei-Hesed*) – 'zeal for Righteousness', 'zeal' against 'the Seekers after Smooth Things', and 'zeal' against all 'Lying interpretations'.[5] There is also a distinct note of predetermination and foreknowledge not very different from Paul in Romans 8:28–9:11, also discussing '*loving God*' (*Piety*), '*separating*', and '*telling the Truth*' and '*not Lying*', or the famous prologue to the Gospel of John – not to mention the same intense interest in 'Light' one finds there. The author of the Hymns writes: '*You alone created the Righteous One, establishing him from the womb*'. Nothing could better give the sense of early Church testimonies to James being '*consecrated*' or '*a Nazirite from his mother's womb*' than these passages.

But our text goes further, using the language of '*Strength*', '*Fortress*', and '*Protection*' we have been encountering with regard to James and 'Peter'. We are even treated to '*Rock*' imagery so familiar in Peter's very name, which is, indeed, parallel to the kinds of allusions we are encountering regarding James and now in these Hymns relating to their author. As these Hymns from Qumran put it in two succeeding sections (and, in one way or another, throughout):

> But I will be as one who comes to a Fortified City and strengthened behind a Strong Wall until rescued, and … I will depend on You, my God, for You put (the) *Foundation on Rock* and … build *a Bulwark of Strength*, which shall not sway, and … its *Gates shall be Doors of Protection*, barring entrance with bars of Strength which cannot be broken.[6]

> For You have upheld me by Your Strength, You have *poured your Holy Spirit upon me* … and Strengthened me before the wars of Evil … You have made me like *a Fortress of Strength, like a Strong Wall, and established my Building upon Rock* and my Foundations are like Eternal Foundations … and all my Ramparts are like Fortified Walls, which do not sway on their Foundations.[7]

One immediately sees that this imagery is the same as that being applied to James in early Church sources. In these Hymns we have the essence of what lies behind the peculiar epithet '*Oblias*', which apparently carried the sense of 'Protection', 'Shield', or 'Strong Wall'.

As we saw, the Hebrew *'Oz* ('Protection', 'Shield') is closest to the '*Ob*' of '*Oblias*'. This word '*'Oz*' is often coupled in the Biblical Psalms with the phrase 'to the people'. In Psalm 29, it is used on two occasions amid imagery important to Qumran. In the first instance, 'give unto the Lord … Strength' (29:1), it introduces allusion to the 'voice of the Lord breaking the cedars of Lebanon' (29:5) and 'the voice of the Lord shaking the wilderness' (29:8). Allusion to 'Lebanon' and 'the cedars of Lebanon' is important in many Qumran *pesharim*,[8] while 'a reed shaking in the wilderness' is just the allusion the New Testament uses in describing John the Baptist (Mt 11:7 and Lk 7:24). Finally the psalm concludes with the assurance that 'the Lord will give *Strength to His people*' (29:10–11).

In Psalm 61 the actual words from the Hymns Scroll are used, 'a Fortress of Strength', together with 'Rock' imagery (61:2–3), which fairly permeates the next Psalm. Psalm 62 not only includes three references to 'Salvation' – '*Yesha°*' or '*Yeshu'a*' (62:1–7) – but also allusion to 'Piety' (*Hesed*) and 'paying a man according to his works' (62:12). '*Strength*' or '*'Oz*' is also used repeatedly in Psalm 68, preceding the thoroughly Messianic Psalm 69, in which two allusions familiar from Gospel presentations of Jesus are used, 'zeal for (my Father's) House consumes me' (69:9) and 'for my thirst, they gave me vinegar to drink' (69:21), and over and over again the language of 'the Righteous', 'swallowing', 'the Poor', 'the Meek', and 'Salvation' occurs (69:15–33).

In Psalm 68, the phrases 'Strength', '*Strength to the People*', and even 'His Strength is in the clouds' (68:28 and 34) – again together with references to 'Salvation' (68:19) and 'the Righteous Ones' (68:3) – are actually used, finally in terms of 'rain' and 'the coming of the Heavenly Host *in Power* upon the clouds' (68:35). This last allusion, again incorporating the imagery of 'Power' and applied to the imminent return of Jesus in Scripture, will not only be at the heart of James' Messianic proclamation in the Temple – which all these early Church sources will integrally tie to his demise – but the like-minded proclamation in the Qumran War Scroll as well, where, incorporating the imagery of Daniel too, the 'Messiah' is presented as coming with the Heavenly Horsemen or Heavenly Host upon the clouds, that is, 'the clouds of Heaven', and bringing Judgment 'like rain'.[9]

There is also one other important occurrence of this 'Fortress' imagery at Qumran, that of 'the Precious Cornerstone', meaning *the Cornerstone of the Temple*. This is found in a crucial passage in the Community Rule, where it is connected to the spiritual Temple. The last is described as an 'Eternal Plantation', language Paul reproduces in discussing how Apollos does the watering and himself as the architect who lays the Foundations of 'God's building' (1 Cor. 3:6–12). This kind of 'Foundations' and 'Cornerstone' imagery is also present in Ephesians 2:19–22's characterization of the Community as 'the Holy Temple' and 'Household of God'. As Acts 4:11 puts this in Peter's mouth, referring to Jesus (echoed in 1 Peter 2:7): 'This is the Stone, which you the builders have set at naught, which has become the Head of the Corner' (Psalm 118:22).

Amid allusion to '*being set apart as Holy*' – our '*Nazirite*' language again – and spiritualized 'atonement' imagery, the members of this Council are described as 'a sweet fragrance', 'an odor of Righteousness', 'a House of Perfection and Truth for Israel', and finally again, 'a Fortified Wall, a Precious Cornerstone, whose Foundations will neither rock nor sway in their place'. All this is delivered within the context of the commandment, used in the New Testament to describe the mission of John the Baptist: 'separate from the midst of the habitation of the Men of Unrighteousness and go into the wilderness, to prepare the Way of the Lord, as it is written, "Prepare in the wilderness the Way of (the Lord), make straight in the desert a Pathway for our God"' (Isa. 40:3).[10]

How could one get closer to the imagery of the first 'Christians' than this? It should be clear that this imagery in the Community Rule parallels what is being applied in these early Church testimonies to James, not only regarding the mysterious *Oblias* cognomen connected in some manner with his '*Zaddik*' nature, but also the references to James providing '*Protection to the People*' or being a '*Strong Bulwark*' or '*Fortified Wall*'.

Onias the Righteous and Honi the Circle-Drawer

James has a relationship to an individual referred to in Talmudic literature as 'Honi *the Circle-Drawer*', another name for 'Onias *the Righteous*', that is, Onias the *Zaddik*. This '*Righteous One*' terminology in this period is interesting. The first person referred to in this manner is an individual called Simeon *the Righteous* around 200 BCE or before. This individual turns out to be the hero, not only of Talmudic transmission scenarios, but an apocryphal biblical book, Ecclesiasticus – in Hebrew, *Ben Sira*, after the name of its putative author, Jesus ben Sira.

Ben Sira was previously known only in Greek and allied recensions, though it was always suspected that a Hebrew original had existed. Such an original finally came to light in a huge cache of medieval Hebrew manuscripts found in a synagogue *Genizah* in old Cairo in 1896. Fragments of this Hebrew version of Ben Sira were then found not only among the Dead Sea Scrolls, but in the debris at Masada, *where the Jewish 'Sicarii' committed suicide* in the year 73 CE rather than submit to Rome.

What the relationship of *Ben Sira* is to Qumran is difficult to say, but it very likely centers about the '*Zaddik*' cognomen attached to Simeon's person in his capacity of High Priest in the era just prior to the Hellenizing 'pollutions' that led to the Maccabean Uprising. Not only does this prefigure the similar title attached to James' name, but several other individuals, particularly someone in the next century known as '*Honi the Circle-Drawer*' after *the circles he* drew to *bring rain*.

Ben Sira is the only biblical work signed with a date. It was written, presumably in Egypt, in 132 BCE by a grandson of the individual whose name it bears. Not only is 'Simeon' or 'Simon', with whom the famous panegyric to 'Famous Men' concludes, surnamed 'the Righteous One', he is pictured in his glorious High Priestly vestments, which 'shone like the sun shining on the Temple' (50:7), making a *Yom Kippur* atonement. The Hebrew version of this paean makes it clear we are dealing with '*Men of Piety*' or *Hassidim*, not the '*Famous Men*' of Greek translation.

Ben Sira applies both the '*Sons of Zadok*' terminology and '*the Covenant of Phineas*' co-equally to the High Priesthood of Simeon the *Zaddik* and his descendants in perpetuity.[11] This paean to the '*Men of Piety*' of preceding generations not only includes the Noahic 'Covenant of Peace', but begins in the Hebrew version with a reference to Noah also as 'the Righteous', 'Perfect and Righteous in his generation', with whom 'Everlasting Covenants were made' (44:17–19). It ends with a quotation from Psalm 148:14, again on behalf of Simeon the *Zaddik*: 'He lifted up the horn for His people, the praise for all His Pious Ones' (*Hassidim* – 51:15).

Not surprisingly, considerable attention is paid to both Phineas and Elijah as priests. The latter is praised for his 'word', called 'a flaming torch', and his 'zeal'. Phineas, described as 'third in Glory' (after Aaron and Eleazar), is likewise praised for 'his zeal' and 'being steadfast when the people rebelled' – words reminiscent of the Damascus Document.[12] He is also extolled for the atonement he made on behalf of Israel, as a result of which the Noahic '*Covenant of Peace*' was sealed with him and his descendants securing for them 'the Command of both Temple and the people … and the High Priesthood in perpetuity' (45:23–24).

Not only was Simeon the *Zaddik* descended from an Onias, but he was the father of an Onias, the names 'Simon' and 'Onias' seeming to alternate in his genealogical line. Simeon's son Onias is an important character in 2 Maccabees, and he would appear to have been the High Priest just prior to the outbreak of the Maccabean Uprising. His 'Piety and Perfect observance of the Law' are specifically remarked and 2 Maccabees goes on to describe him as 'the Protector of his countrymen' and 'this Zealot for the Laws' (3:1 and 4:2). The parallel at this point with James could not be more precise.

Onias' martyrdom under Antiochus Epiphanes (175–163 BCE), the Eleventh Horn 'with a mouth full of boasts' of Daniel 7:8, triggers the Uprising led by Judas. Together with the Prophet Jeremiah, this Onias makes a post-mortem return at the end of the narrative to give the Messianic sword of vengeance to Judas, presumably in confirmation of both his High Priestly and avenging activities (15:26). There is, therefore, in the view of 2 Maccabees, no interruption between the High Priesthood of Onias and that of Judas Maccabee. Nor does Judas' father, Mattathias, play any role as he does in 1 Maccabees – Judas is simply the *direct* heir to the saintly Onias. Not only does Onias appear to be surnamed, like his father, 'the *Zaddik*', but the description, 'Protector of his fellow countrymen', applied to him in connection with evocation of his 'zeal for the Law' – not to mention his martyrdom – prefigures the application of this '*Oblias*' terminology to James two centuries later in these early Church accounts, the resonance of this epithet with the name 'Onias' also being curious.

Another 'Onias the *Zaddik*' in the next century, 'Honi *the Circle-Drawer*', also prefigures James in at least two respects – in the application of the cognomen 'the Righteous One' to his name, and that he is described as being able *to bring rain*. And like James, he suffers martyrdom and this by stoning.[13] Though possibly casual, these connections seem too real to be simple coincidence.

In Talmudic tradition, Honi is the father of another individual called 'Righteous' with a curious sobriquet, 'Hanan *the Hidden*'. Not only does he also appear to have been *a rainmaker*, but identical with John the Baptist, the name 'Hanan' in Hebrew coming from Johanan (John), 'God comforts'. The *Talmud* calls Hanan (sometimes 'Hanin') the son of a daughter of Honi and, in its own picaresque style, says he was called 'Hidden because he liked to *hide himself in the toilet*', reminiscent of its 'toilet' traditions regarding 'Jesus the Nazoraean', James, and 'the Essenes'.[14]

Actually this 'Hidden' tradition is probably to be associated with the 'Hidden' or 'Secret Adam' tradition, which ultimately goes into what Shi'ite Islam is calling to this day 'the Hidden *Imam*'. As such, it carries a *redivivus* aspect. In the *Zohar*, the first *Zaddik* Noah, who 'sought Righteousness', is twice referred to as '*hiding* himself' or '*being hidden* in the Ark on the Day of the Lord's Wrath to escape the Enemy'.[15] The allusion to 'the Enemy' in this context, applied in Jewish Christian/Ebionite tradition to James' assailant, *Paul*, is always interesting.

In the *Talmud*, there is also a 'Rip van Winkle' tradition associated with this Honi, which carries with it the implication of a *redivivus* tradition like the one associated with Elijah and John in the Synoptics. Honi is said to have fallen asleep under *a carob tree*, only to awake seventy years later, when his grandson was still alive and the tree bore fruit! We have already seen how in some traditions 'carobs' were said to have been the true composition of *John's* food.[16]

Finally, the *Talmud* knows another rainmaking grandson of Honi it calls 'Abba Hilkiah', contemporary with James. The rainmaking tradition adhering to all these priestly *Zaddik*s was obviously an important one, and not unconnected with the '*Oblias*' or 'Bulwark' tradition adhering to James' person.

This 'rain' often carried with it the connotation of eschatological Judgment. In the War Scroll, this 'Judgment' is associated with the coming of the Messianic 'King of Glory' and Heavenly Host ('*upon the clouds*') and it '*falls like rain on all that grows on Earth*', meaning, as in Matthew 5:45 in 'the Sermon on the Mount', '*sending rain on the Just and Unjust*' alike. This is the sense, too, of 'the Flood' associated with the *saving* actions of the first *Zaddik* Noah. This association of the 'coming of the Son of Man' with 'the days of Noah' and 'entering the ark' is expressly drawn later in Matthew's Little Apocalypse (24:37–39; also Lk 17:26–27); and, in *Ben Sira*'s praise of former 'Men of Piety', even Ezekiel's '*Vision of the Glory of the Chariot*' is linked to '*torrential rain*' and apocalyptic Judgment (*Ben Sira* 49:8–10 based on Ezekiel 13:11–

13 – '*the Lying Spouter*' section as found in Ezekiel and so important to Qumran – and 38:22).[17]

Phineas too, the archetypal progenitor of '*priestly zeal*', was considered one of these rain-makers. Since this was a *redivivus* tradition as well, it seems to be a part of the '*Primal Adam*' tradition too – a conceptuality hinted at in Ben Sira 49:19 introducing Simon the *Zaddik* – that '*above every living creature is Adam*'.

Elijah's miraculous rain-making, hinted at in *Ben Sira* 48:3, is also signaled in the last Chapter of the Letter of James in the context of apocalyptic Judgment, '*rain*', and '*the coming of the Lord*'/ '*the Lord of Hosts … with Power*', as it is in '*the prayer of a Righteous One*' which brings the '*rain*' (5:4–18). This evocation of Elijah's prayer and rain-making, in fact, directly connects to the picture of James' rain-making in the extant account of Epiphanius.

Epiphanius makes this claim in the aftermath of his description of James' '*Naziritism*' and how he never cut his hair, wore only linen, and was connected to the Priesthood, entering the Holy of Holies once a year to '*ask forgiveness before God out of his super-abundant Piety*'. He then informs us: '*And once during a drought* (c. 45 CE?), *he lifted his hands to Heaven and prayed, and at once Heaven sent rain … Thus, they no longer called him by his name, but his name was, rather, "the Just One"*'.[18] This association of '*the Just One*' with rain-making is extremely important. For the Letter of James, so efficacious was this 'prayer of the Just One' that Elijah, who in 1 Kings 20:10–14 is not simply '*zealous*', but '*exceedingly zealous* for the Lord', could both '*pray a prayer*' *for the rain to come, but also for it to cease* (Jas. 5:18).

Honi, whom Josephus calls '*Onias the Just One*', received his other sobriquet, '*the Circle-Drawer*', on account of the *circles he drew to bring the rain*, out of which he would not step until it came. We hear about similar circles being drawn by Josephus' and Hippolytus' 'Essenes', who in their observation of the Sabbath would not step out of a certain radius even to relieve themselves – this, of course, the parody in the Rabbinic tradition about Hanan *the Hidden* '*hiding himself in the toilet*'! Not only is Qumran concerned with such scrupulous purity, specifying the exact location of the latrines from 'the camp',[19] but we have also seen the caricature of such concerns in the somewhat ribald Rabbinic tradition about Jacob of Kfar Sechania (or Sihnin) and Jesus the Nazoraean's recommendation to the High Priests about their toilets and 'a prostitute's hire'.

But the connections go deeper than this. If Honi is the father of Hanan the Hidden, and Hanan equivalent to John the Baptist, then James is probably a descendant of Honi. Again, the Rabbinic notices about '*the sons' or 'daughters of the Rechabites' marrying 'the sons' or 'daughters of the High Priests'* give us additional basis for understanding relationships such as these. In particular, the Gospel of Luke portrays Jesus as related to John the Baptist and, specifically, that their mothers, who were '*the daughters of Priests*', were cousins (1:36). Setting aside theological concerns about the bona fides of James' relationship to Jesus – or, for that matter, the historicity of 'Jesus' himself – if we accept the materials before us at face value, this would place James the Righteous and Josephus' 'Onias the Righteous' (the *Talmud*'s 'Honi the Circle -Drawer') in a direct genealogical – to say nothing of an ideological – line.

Epiphanius, charming as ever, but also sometimes incisive, puts this proposition as follows. Following his points about 'no razor ever touching' James' head, etc., he insists that James

> wore *no second tunic*, but used only a linen cloak, as it says in the Gospel, 'The young man fled, leaving behind the linen cloth which he had around him' (Mark 14:51 – this the 'bathing' clothing of the 'Essenes'). For it was John and James and James, these three, who practiced this way of life: the two sons of Zebedee and James the son of Joseph and brother of the Lord … *But to James alone, it was allowed to enter once a year into the Holy of Holies, because he was a Nazirite* and *connected to the Priesthood.* Hence

> Mary was related in two ways to Elizabeth and James was a distinguished member of the Priesthood, because the two tribes alone were linked to one another, the royal tribe to the priestly and the priestly to the royal, just as earlier in the time of the Exodus, Nahshon, the scion from the tribe of Judah, took to wife a previous Elizabeth daughter of Aaron (Ex 6:23).[20]

Aside from the overlapping between the two Jameses and a certain amount of garbling, this is extremely incisive testimony and parallels the Talmudic traditions about 'the sons of the Rechabites marrying the daughters of the High Priests' or vice versa. Not only do we have a certain resonance of the name '*Nahshon*' with Hippolytus' '*Naassenes*', but Exodus has Elizabeth as *Aaron's wife* and *Nahshon's sister*, not *Nahshon's wife* and *Aaron's daughter*, reflecting these reversals concerning 'sons' or 'daughters' of the High Priests in Talmudic traditions about these Rechabites.

Elsewhere Epiphanius sets forth the proposition that Alexander Jannaeus – the most powerful of the previous Maccabean Priest-Kings – prefigured the combination of priestly and royal lineages one finds in James and Jesus.[21] The same combination of lineage in the Damascus Document (a 'Messiah from Aaron and Israel') has always puzzled commentators, but we see in these references about James' lineage in Epiphanius a parallel ideology in formation.

The story of John's birth in Luke, and the consanguinity of Elizabeth and Jesus' mother Mary signaled there, also bears the seeds of this kind of dual royal and priestly genealogy. That the zealous Maccabean Priest-Kings, the forerunners of these kinds of heroes, incorporate the same combination of priestly and royal offices points to the closeness of these kinds of conceptions.

From the early Christian perspective, the whole presentation of Jesus as 'a (High) Priest forever after the order of Melchizedek' – a concept also seemingly in vogue among the Maccabeans – is set forth in a letter addressed, interestingly enough, 'to the Hebrews' in Rome (Heb 7:16–26). Though the authorship of this letter is disputed, there can be no disputing the concept that Epiphanius is drawing on to arrive at his conclusions. The same ideology is to be found in the Qumran materials, even the ideological interest in Melchizedek. This, in turn, supports the interpretation of the Qumran documents we have been attempting to delineate, that the Maccabean and early Christian approaches flow into each other, and the Qumran documents do not differ appreciably from either.

Far from being anti-Maccabean, the view propagated by the scholarly cartel controlling them for decades, the Scrolls – being opposed to any hint of compromise or accommodation – have everything in common with the ethos of the Maccabeans and nothing whatsoever with those opposing them. What the Scrolls are is *anti-Herodian*, Herod being perceived both as a '*foreigner*', *whom the Romans appointed King*, and a '*Covenant-Breaker*'. By extension, the Scrolls are also opposed to that Priesthood owing its appointment to him and therefore perceived of as '*polluted*', his heirs, and the Roman Governors *in collusion with all of them*, i.e., basically the whole Pharisaic/Sadducean Establishment as pictured in the Gospels and by Josephus.

The Zadokite Covenant and the *Zaddik*-Idea

This brings us back directly to Honi's death, his rain-making, and the reason for the '*Zaddik*' appellation applied to him. Honi, who would not tolerate *accommodation with foreigners* or *collaboration of any kind,* drew circles to bring rain – whether eschatological or material 'rain' is beside the point – during one particularly severe drought, according to Talmudic sources. This is the context as well of James' rain-making in Epiphanius' testimony. Here one has good insight into the newly emerging terminology of 'the *Zaddik*' or '*Righteous One*' in this period; because Honi was '*a Righteous One*', he presumably – like Elijah – had influence in both the earthly and Heavenly spheres.

This concept seems to have first emerged in Ezekiel. Not only is Ezekiel responsible for 'the Zadokite Covenant' found in an addendum to his other ecstatic and apocalyptic prophecies – an addendum about the ideal or the new reconstructed Temple (Ezek. 40–48) – this is the material seized upon in the Scrolls to develop an ideology of a 'Priesthood', referred to, as we have seen, in terms of 'the Sons of Zadok'.

Some might consider 'the Sons of Zadok' to be simply genealogical descendants of the first Zadok in David's and Solomon's time, the first High Priest of the First Temple. This would appear to be the normative definition of those called 'Sadducees' in the Herodian Period. In Ezekiel, however, the Sons of Zadok are represented as *opposed to* a previously reigning Establishment in the Temple which, on a strictly genealogical basis, might also be construed as being descendants of the original Zadok of David's time and therefore legitimate (44:6–15).

However, the new 'Sons of Zadok' in Ezekiel have a qualitative component as well. They are '*the Holy*' or '*consecrated ones*' – note the variation of the '*Nazirite*' terminology – who '*kept* what they were *charged to keep*'. In other words, they were 'Keepers of the Covenant' (Ezek. 44:15 and 48:11). But in addition – and perhaps more importantly – they *object to Gentiles in the Temple*. Despite Josephus' rather disingenuous protestations to the contrary, Ezekiel is quite specific about this, repeating it twice:

> Say to those that have *rebelled against God* of the House of Israel ...: 'May your hearts be full with *all your Abominations*, in that you have *admitted foreigners, uncircumcised in heart* and *uncircumcised in body into My Temple to pollute it* ... *breaking My Covenant* and ... *not keeping what you were charged to keep regarding My Holy Things* ... *No foreigner, uncircumcised in heart* and *uncircumcised in body shall enter My Temple*, nor any foreigner among the Children of Israel (that is, 'resident alien'). (44:6–9)

Not only should one remark the note about 'rebelling against God' with regard to the praise of Phineas in *Ben Sira*, also a staple in the Dead Sea Scrolls, Ezekiel goes on to remark the idolatry of the previous Establishment (44:12) and how the new 'Keepers' or 'Sons of Zadok ... *are not to wear wool', but only 'linen diadems ... linen girdles about their loins, so as not to be moist (meaning 'to perspire') nor shave their heads ... nor drink wine ... but to teach My people (the difference) between Holy and profane, polluted and clean ...*' (44:15–23). Ezekiel even includes in these instructions the ban on carrion found in James' directives to overseas communities (as well as in the Koran): '*The priests should not eat of any thing that is dead of itself, nor torn, whether it be fowl or beast*' (44:31).[40]

This ban on 'admitting foreigners into the Temple to pollute it' is exactly the objection that Josephus ascribes to Simon, the Head of his own 'Assembly' (*Ecclesia*) in Jerusalem. He is against *admitting Herodians* into the Temple. Two principal characteristics of Ezekiel's description are picked up in Qumran representations of its *new* 'Sons of Zadok': firstly, they are defined as '*the Keepers of the Covenant' par excellence*; and, secondly, it is quite clear that they disapprove of Gentile gifts and Gentile sacrifices in the Temple.

This last is, of course, the behavior of so-called 'Zealots' or '*Sicarii*' among the lower priesthood in 66 CE, who stop sacrifice on behalf of Romans and other foreigners in the Temple, thereby triggering the War against Rome. Remembering that the prototypical ancestor of Zadok, Aaron's grandson Phineas, warded off pollution from the camp by killing backsliders – specifically designated as those marrying Gentiles; the Herodians, regardless of gender, would have been seen by persons of this persuasion as being involved in approximately the same behavior.

The Damascus Document adds an additional, 'eschatological' dimension to the qualitative ones being expressed here. In its delineation of 'the Zadokite Covenant' of Ezekiel 44:15, it describes '*the Sons of Zadok*' as 'those who would *stand*' or '*stand up at the End of Days*'. These would both '*justify the Righteous* and *condemn the Wicked*'. Not only do we have here the essence of '*Justification*' theology as Paul is developing it, the emphasis on '*Last Times*'/'*Last Days*' turns the whole exegesis eschatological. When linked to the notion of '*standing*' or '*standing up*' – so much a part of the '*Standing One*' vocabulary – then one begins to have a statement close to what is being developed in New Testament Redeemer scenarios, such as Jesus participating in '*the Last Judgment*'.

For Qumran, there are two streams of people entering 'the Kingdom' or, if one prefers, the Heavenly Domain of the Righteous: firstly, the Righteous *living*, and, secondly, the Righteous *dead*. Where the first category is concerned, since in theory they go into the Kingdom living, presumably *they would not have to be resurrected.* Paul wrestles with this '*Mystery*' in 1 Corinthians 15:51–57 after evoking both the '*First*' and '*Second Adam*' and the '*Primal Adam*' and '*Last Man*' ideologies. It is for such persons that the notion of '*standing*', in the sense of '*going on' functioning at 'the End of Time*' in the Damascus Document, might be appropriate. The Righteous dead would have to be resurrected first. Though nowhere explicitly stated in the materials before us, this ideology is implied.

The '*Sons of Zadok*', therefore, according to the Damascus Document's exegesis of Ezekiel 44:15, would appear to refer to a supernatural class of quasi-Redeemer figures. At Nag Hammadi, something of this role and theme is certainly being accorded James in the Apocalypses ascribed to his name, which are full of many of the motifs we are analyzing here.[22] We say 'supernatural', because anyone who has gone through a dying and a resurrection process, must to a certain extent be, as Paul implies in 1 Corinthians 15:52–54, taken as being beyond the natural. For Christianity, 'Jesus' is obviously such a figure, though, for the authors of the New Testament, he not only enjoys a supernatural resurrection and ascension, but a supernatural birth as well. This is beyond the ideology of Qumran, as we have it, which runs more towards the 'adoptionist sonship' schemes one finds among more 'Jewish Christian' groups.[23]

This brings us to the etymological links of the words '*Zadok*' and '*Zaddik*'. Even the uninitiated in the complexities of Semitic languages will be able to see that these two words are based on the same three-letter root, *Z–D–K*. 'Zadok' is a proper name; while '*Zaddik*' is a verbal noun based on a concept. The double '*D*' in the second does not appear in Hebrew orthography and is a matter of grammatical convention – and, to a certain extent, transliteration into Greek – only. Also, in Qumran Hebrew, the letters '*o*' and '*i*', again matters of convention, are indistinguishable. So, in very real terms, '*Zadok*' and '*Zaddik*' are, at least, in written Hebrew of the period *the very same word.* This fact was, surely, not lost on our biblical exegetes of the time, who enjoyed both wordplay and stretching the conventions of the language before them, wherever it could serve an exegetical end.

This point is reflected in the transliteration into Greek of the familiar word 'Sadducees'. This term is based on the same Hebrew root *Z–D–K*, in this case, '*Zadok*' or even '*Zadduk*'. Once again, we are clearly in the realm of conventions or confusions relating to transliterations into a second tongue. 'Sadducee' can just as easily be based on the Hebrew word '*Zaddik*' as '*Zadok*', the vowels *i*, *u*, and o being virtually indistinguishable where Qumran epigraphy is concerned.

In fact, in our interpretation of the 'Sadducee' problem – Qumran *Sadducees* following a Righteousness–oriented interpretation, as we have seen, of '*the Zadokite Covenant*' of Ezekiel, and Establishment *Sadducees* of the Herodian Period and perhaps earlier, only insisting on a genealogical link with the '*Zadok*' of ancient times – we come down very heavily on the point about one group following a more esoteric understanding of 'the Zadokite Covenant' and insisting on a qualitative dimension involving '*Righteousness*', even going so far as to introduce an additional eschatological dimension to this. Even the Book of Acts, Josephus, and the Pseudoclementines insist that '*the Sadducees' were 'stricter in Judgment' than other groups*, whatever might be meant by '*Judgment*' in this context.[24] The 'Priesthood forever after the order of Melchizedek' as developed in the Letter to the Hebrews, again incorporating the *Z–D–K* root, is but a further eschatological adumbration of this ideology.

Josephus introduces the character he is calling '*Sadduk*' or '*Saddok*' at the beginning of the First Century. Along with Judas the Galilean, he leads the agitation against Roman taxation in Palestine. This accompanies the Census of Cyrenius/Quirinius in 6–7 CE, that Luke, anyhow, identifies with the circumstances surrounding the birth of *Jesus Christ*. Though Luke's may or may not be a historical account, it does relate the circumstances of Jesus' birth to the Tax Revolt in Palestine coincident with the birth of the Movement associated with Judas and *Saddok*. Is this an individual with the actual name of '*Zadok*' or a teacher with the title of '*the Zaddik*' – much as the Righteous Teacher seems to be in Qumran tradition and, of course, James in early Church tradition? It is impossible to say, only that confusion over the derivation of the term 'Sadducee' is apparent in these materials as well.

This same confusion, also, exists in James' title 'the Just' or 'Just One', which Epiphanius tells us was so identified with his person as to replace his very name itself. This is the implication of Hegesippus' account as well. Are we dealing simply with the descriptive epithet '*the Just One*' or does this imply the use of the Hebrew name '*Zadok*' itself as applied to James, since the two are interchangeable? It is impossible to say, but, as explained, '*Justus*' in Latin is equivalent to '*Zadok*' in Hebrew. Once again, we have come full circle.

The Stoning of Honi the Circle-Drawer

Josephus recounts the episode of the stoning of Onias the Righteous, which prefigures the stoning of James, at a key juncture in the story of the loss of Jewish independence. It would perhaps be well to summarize to some extent events leading up to this.

After the Maccabean Uprising, from the 160s to the 140s BCE, the mantle of successor in the Jewish independence movement fell to Judas' brother Simon's heirs – Judas himself seemingly having no children. The first of these was John Hyrcanus (134–104 BCE), Judas' nephew, who, Josephus claims, wore three mantles: 'King, High Priest, and Prophet' – giving examples of each.[25]

The next was Alexander Jannaeus (103–76 BCE) – also called 'Jonathan' – John's third son, who married his brother's wife, Salome Alexandra, after his brother was killed. Like John, he was having difficulties with the Parties, which seem to have been developing at this time, particularly the Pharisees. This is the first mention of 'Pharisees' who, for the most part, *opposed the Maccabees*. Despite their pretence of legal and religious scrupulousness, they always appeared to be willing to accommodate themselves to foreigners and accept foreign rule in Palestine, most notably High Priests receiving their appointment from foreigners just so long as these priests could come up with a satisfactory genealogy and the Pharisees were accorded the proper respect and kept their hands on true power. This is certainly the situation as it develops into the Herodian Period.

This Salome Alexandra and the elder of her two sons, Hyrcanus II (76–31 BCE) – who appear to be mentioned negatively in a calendrical Scroll from Qumran[26] – were the sole Maccabeans that can safely be said to have been 'Pharisees'. Indeed her uncle, one Simeon ben Shetach, was one of the conservators of Pharisaic tradition and an heir, according to Rabbinic tradition, of Simeon the *Zaddik*, leading some decades thereafter to the famous Pharisee pair Hillel and Shammai.[27]

Her younger son, Aristobulus II (67–49 BCE), was more impulsive and of a different stripe altogether, resembling more his revolutionary great-uncle Judas, at least where the issues of national independence and zeal were concerned. When the crisis arrived, the people ultimately show what side they are on. This crisis arrives in the midst of the events recorded about Honi the Circle-Drawer, his rain-making, and his stoning by the Pharisaic partisans of Hyrcanus II. In Josephus the 'rain-making' as such is really accorded to the partisans of Aristobulus II.[28]

For lack of a better term, we have termed Aristobulus' Party, '*Purist Sadducees*', as opposed to a more compromising Sadducean strain in the Herodian Period. Thus, there are really *two* groups of '*Sadducees*', one along with Pharisees and Herodians forming the Establishment in New Testament presentations. These are best termed '*Herodian Sadducees*'. Like the Pharisees, by whom Josephus says they were dominated, they are accommodating in the extreme. However, unlike the Pharisees, when the Temple is destroyed in 70 CE, they cease to exist, having completely lost their *raison d'être*.

The other '*Sadducees*' – epitomized by Judas Maccabee, his father Mattathias, Alexander Jannaeus, and this Aristobulus II – are consistently more resistance-minded, xenophobic, non -accommodating, and '*zealous for the Law*', no doubt following a more Phineas–minded approach to Ezekiel's 'Zadokite Covenant'.

'*Purist*' Sadducees in the Maccabean Period, they become the '*Messianic*' Sadducees in the Herodian Period. They develop in the First Century into so-called '*Zealots', 'Essenes*', or '*Sicarii'*, and '*Palestinian Christians*' or the '*Jerusalem Church*' followers of James the Just, and follow a more esoteric understanding of the Zadokite Covenant based on '*Righteousness*' and/ or '*zeal*' – the two attributes we most often hear about in early 'Christian' reports about James.

Their orientation was consistent: they would never compromise with foreign power, would not accept foreign gifts or sacrifices in the Temple (considered a form of '*pollution*' or '*idolatry*' by James and at Qumran), and reckoned Herodians both foreigners and fornicators whose authority in Palestine could and should never be acquiesced to. In the run-up to the War against Rome, as we shall see, they would not even allow Herodians to enter the Temple, they themselves had built, nor could High Priests appointed by the Herodians or the Romans be considered legitimate by them. With the destruction and almost total obliteration of the Maccabees by Herod (what remained were absorbed into the Herodian family), a new principle of authority emerged – *the Messianic one*. *Uncompromising* and *inflexible*, this Movement also tended towards an apocalypticism of the 'Last Times'/ 'Last Days'.

Which brings us to the direct circumstances surrounding Honi's death. Alexander Jannaeus' son Aristobulus, impatient of his mother's Pharisee policies and involvement with foreigners like Antipater and Aretas in Petra, overthrew his Phariseeizing brother Hyrcanus II after their mother Alexandra's death. Backed by the same popular support and representing the same ideological perspective as his father Alexander Jannaeus, he defeated his brother in battle *near Jericho*, forcing him to make over his Kingly and High-Priestly offices to him and ended the Pharisee depredations on their father's supporters.

Herod's father, Antipater, an extremely able operative with contacts both in 'Arabia' and along the Palestinian Coast, found sanctuary for Hyrcanus II with King Aretas in Petra; and finally enlisted Pompey and his adjutant, Aemilius Scaurus (referred to at Qumran as a 'murderer') – who were making their way down from war with the Persians in Anatolia and Armenia into Syria – to his cause.

In the meantime Aristobulus, now king, and his proto-'*Zealot*', '*Purist Sadducee*' supporters – who, as it turns out, seem to have been mostly priests – take sanctuary, importantly, *in the Temple*. Antipater then returns with an army comprised of King Aretas' '*Arab*' forces and the few collaborationist supporters of Hyrcanus, besieges Jerusalem, and prepares to assault the

Temple. It is at this point that Josephus interrupts his narrative to tell us *about* the miracles of Honi or Onias whom he now, not only calls '*a Righteous Man*', but '*the Beloved*' or '*Friend of God*'.

For a change, Josephus' story more or less accords with what the *Talmud* has to say about Honi, which also applies the '*the Righteous*' cognomen to Honi. But, it is Josephus' application of '*the Beloved*' or '*Friend of God*' description to Honi that *absolutely* accords with the way 'Zadokite' history is presented in the Damascus Document, as well as the description of Abraham as 'a Friend of God' in the Letter of James 2:23 and 4:2 – to say nothing of the Koran.

Josephus describes Honi as follows: '*At the time of a certain drought, he (Onias the Righteous) had prayed to God to put an end to the searing heat, and God heard his prayers and sent them rain. This man had hidden himself, seeing that this sedition would last a long time*'.[29] Not only do we have here '*the prayer of the Zaddik ... bringing rain*' of the Letter of James 5:16–18, but also the '*Hidden*' ideology already noted with reference to Noah and the Flood above. The *Talmud*'s 'Honi' was *hidden* for 'seventy years' because it took that long for the fruit of the carob (or possibly even a palm tree), under which he slept, to ripen. At the end of this period, he awoke and *ate its fruit.*

The '*Hidden*' terminology is also applied to Honi's putative heir, John the Baptist, whose mother Elizabeth is described as '*hiding herself*' in the infancy narrative of Luke 1:24, as it is in the *Talmud* to Honi's grandson '*Hanan the Hidden*', who, it will be recalled, was supposedly accorded this name because '*he hid himself in the latrine*'. Even more telling, in the parallel Koranic presentation, the *Talmud*'s '*carob tree*', associated with Honi's seventy-year sleep, now enters Muhammad's description of John's relationship to Jesus as well, only it is now *Mary* instead of Honi, who *sits down under the carob* tree and *eats* the '*ripe fruit*' *that falls from it.*[30]

Nothing could better demonstrate the interrelatedness of all these traditions than this. In some manner they are all part of an identifiable whole and the story of Honi and his progeny is somehow connected to these traditions about John, Jesus, and James. It should also be clear that all these motifs then move into the Islamic Shi'ite doctrine of the '*Hidden Imam*' or '*Standing One*' as well.

The Stopping of Sacrifice on Behalf of Romans and Other Foreigners in the Temple

With Aristobulus and his priestly partisans in the Temple and Hyrcanus' besieging them outside, Hyrcanus' supporters now trot out Honi. Here Josephus specifically notes that they are aware of and wish to make use of the intercessionary power he previously displayed in praying for rain. Hyrcanus' supporters rather want him *to curse 'Aristobulus and those of his faction' in the Temple.* When Honi refuses, *they stone him* – the first paradigmatic stoning. It also demonstrates the configuration of parties and forces that then develop.

The time is Passover, 65 BCE, two years before Pompey's Roman army – with *Pharisee* support – storms the Temple, putting an end to the nationalism of Maccabean rule and ushering in the *Herodian Period.* It is the *only* Sanhedrin-style stoning, Josephus records, before the stoning of Honi's putative descendant James, another of these probably *Rechabite*-style 'Priests'.

In Honi's case, the *Talmud* had already recorded the threat of excommunication leveled against Honi by Simeon ben Shetach – the archetypal progenitor of the Pharisees and brother of Salome Alexandra. In the course of these confrontations, the *Talmud* compares Honi – not John as in the New Testament – to *Elijah*, observing, in words attributed to Simeon ben Shetach, that he *alone possessed 'the keys to rain' and was allowed, therefore, to take 'the Name of Heaven' in vain.*[31] From this, one is permitted to conclude that the stoning of Honi by

Hyrcanus' Pharisee supporters was based on their perception of his '*blasphemy*' related to possessing just such '*powers*' and such '*keys*'.

For Josephus, the 'zealous' priests, making up the majority of Aristobulus II's supporters, had been cheated by those outside the walls of the animals they had purchased for the purpose of making Passover sacrifices. Therefore, *they took vengeance for this 'Impiety towards God' and, by implication, the stoning of Honi, by themselves, now, praying for rain* – in this case, Divine '*rain*' as eschatological vengeance. In other words, Aristobulus' supporters, as pious priests, are also '*rain-making*' *intercessors.* At this point, according to Josephus, God sends down '*a terrible hurricane*' which devastates the whole country – in his words, 'taking vengeance on them for the murder of Onias'.[32] All of these points, most particularly the Divine vengeance following Onias' stoning, prefigure events both before and after the stoning of James.

Herod's father now brings Pompey, the Roman Commander, into this configuration of forces, to finish what had been interrupted by Honi's stoning. As he describes it, both brothers, Hyrcanus the older and Aristobulus the younger, rushed to Pompey as he made his way down from Damascus, attempting to conciliate him with gifts. However, Aristobulus soon '*turned sick of servility and could not bear to abase himself any further*' to the Romans.

This is a turning point of Jewish history and, once again, Aristobulus' actions are paradigmatic of the 'Purist Sadducee' or 'Zealot' orientation. Antipater now transferred his allegiance from the Arab King Aretas of Petra to Pompey.[33] Herod's father is adept at exploiting the connections he developed with Pompey, his adjutants, and their successors, like Gabinius and Mark Anthony, who develops a special fondness for Herodians (no doubt because of the lucrativeness of their bribes). Aristobulus is put under arrest and ultimately sent to Rome in chains, while his supporters, once more, take refuge in the Temple for a last stand.

The year is 63 BCE. Pompey's forces now besiege the Temple, and, as Josephus portrays it, Pompey is *amazed at the steadfastness of those Jews who resisted and could not help but admire it.* In the midst of the bombardment by catapult, Aristobulus' priestly supporters went about their religious duties in the Temple, as if there were no siege at all. They performed the daily sacrifices and purified themselves with the utmost scrupulousness, not interrupting these even when the Roman troops finally stormed the Temple:

> Even when they saw their enemies overwhelming them with swords in their hands, *the priests* (Aristobulus' supporters) with complete equanimity went on with their Divine worship and were *butchered while they were offering their drink–offerings and burning their incense, preferring their duties in worship of God before self-preservation.*[34]

These are obviously exceedingly zealous and Pious '*Zadokite*' priests. Josephus adds, almost as an afterthought, that '*the greatest part of them were slain by their own countrymen of the opposing faction*' – that is, *the Pharisees supporting the turncoat Hyrcanus, who with the help of Herod's father Antipater, brought the Romans into the country in the first place.* The inevitability of the process is stunning. This pattern is consistent and will be re-enacted in the events of 37 BCE, where Herod himself, now backed by Roman troops provided him by Mark Anthony – his father's friend – storms Jerusalem, thereby putting an end to insurgency and Maccabean hopes. Once again, it is the Pharisees, *Pollio and Sameas* – probably the Rabbinic 'Pair' *Hillel and Shammai* – *who counsel the people to 'open the gates to Herod' and the Romans.* For this, they are duly rewarded and *Herod, not surprisingly, 'prefers them above all others'.*[35] Typically, the people, however, ignore this advice in favor of resistance, again showing that *the Pharisee position on accommodation to foreign power was not the popular one.*

The same is true in the period of the New Testament during the run-up to the War in 66 CE. It will be recalled that, in another crucial insight in his work, Josephus reveals that it is '*the Chief Priests (the Herodian Sadducees), the principal Pharisees, and the men of power (the Herodians themselves)', and, as he puts it, 'all those desirous of peace', who send for the Roman Commander, Cestius, outside the city to enter Jerusalem with his troops and put down the Uprising.* Likewise, the Uprising was triggered by *the same 'zealous' lower priesthood, who stopped sacrifice on behalf of Romans and other foreigners in the Temple and rejected their gifts.*

This picture of a 'zealous' lower priesthood stopping sacrifice on behalf of Romans and other foreigners not long after the stoning of James replicates to some extent that following the stoning of Honi, '*Onias the Righteous*' – '*the Friend of God*'; and Honi's refusal to condemn those of similar zeal in the Temple in the previous Century. *These priestly supporters of the more nationalist, last real Maccabean Priest-King, Aristobulus, go on with their 'Pious' sacrifices in honor of God, to the amazement of the Romans, as we saw, even while they are being cut down by those of the opposite faction in the Temple precincts.*

They are the epitome of later 'Zealots', the same class of priests who supported Judas Maccabee's activities a century before and those pictured in the Book of Acts as joining the Movement led by another latter-day 'Pious *Zaddik*' and '*Righteous*' High Priest James (in this instance, directly *preceding the stoning of Stephen*), the greater part of whose supporters even Acts calls '*Zealots for the Law*' (Acts 6:7 and 21:20). Not only are they responsible for the War against Rome, they are epitomized by the documents we find at Qumran, and the mindset they represent is that of an absolutely unbending insistence on purity and uncompromising militancy, best expressed in terms of the word 'zeal'.

By the time of the First Century, there is a 'Messianic' strain to their mindset and ideology. This can be seen, not only from the general tenor of most of the documents at Qumran and those sources underlying the New Testament approach – transformed to bring them in line with a more spiritualized and Hellenized 'Messianism' overseas, but also from *the identification of 'the Messianic Prophecy' by Josephus as the driving force behind the Uprising against Rome.*

The moment we have before us here is a pivotal one. It is pivotal not only in illustrating this unbending, uncompromising attitude of priestly and apocalyptic 'zeal', but also in defining the situation that would characterize Jewish existence from that time forward. Josephus describes this very well. *From the time of the stoning of Honi and the massacre of the 'Zealot' priests in the Temple following it, the fact of Roman power has to be reckoned with and how parties respond or adjust to it. All parties opposing it will ultimately be eliminate*d.

Josephus' Testimony Connecting James' Death to the Fall of Jerusalem

There is one further point that must be considered with regard to the '*Oblias*' epithet, and it was already noted, as remarked at the beginning of this book, as early as the Third Century by the Alexandrian theologian Origen. In two works, *Contra Celsus* and his *Commentary on Matthew*, he claims to have found in his copy of the *Antiquities* of Josephus a passage *attributing the fall of Jerusalem to the death of James not Jesus.*[36] Eusebius seems to have seen a similar passage in his copy of Josephus' works – in his case, he claims it was in the *Jewish War*. Jerome in the next century – like these other two, someone with access to Palestinian documents – claims to have seen the same passage, though it is not clear whether he actually saw it or heard about it through the works of these others. As he puts it: '*This same Josephus records the tradition that this James was of such great Holiness* and enjoyed so great a reputation among the people (for Righteousness) that *the downfall of Jerusalem was believed to be on account of his death*'.[37]

In normative Christian usage, 'Jesus' is considered to have predicted both the downfall of Jerusalem and the destruction of the Temple, and Origen's outrage at having come upon these passages in the copy of Josephus available to him – presumably in the library at Caesarea on the Palestine coast, where Eusebius, too, had later been Bishop – and Eusebius' own concern over this discrepancy, might be not a little connected to its disappearance in all extant copies of Josephus' works. It should be recalled that in 'the Little Apocalypses' of the

Gospels, where Jesus is presented as both predicting Jerusalem's encirclement by armies and the destruction of the Temple, Jesus is normally considered to have predicted the destruction of Jerusalem as well.[38]

As Origen puts the proposition in *Contra Celsus*:

> But at that time there were no armies besieging Jerusalem … for the siege began in the reign of Nero and lasted till the government of Vespasian, *whose son Titus destroyed Jerusalem on account, as Josephus says, of James the Just, the brother of Jesus, who was called Christ; but, in reality, as the truth makes clear, on account of Jesus Christ the son of God.*[39]

Origen puts this proposition even more vehemently earlier in the same work, attacking his interlocutor Celsus as *'a Jew' who is willing to accept that 'John baptized in the wilderness', but not 'the descent of the Holy Spirit on Jesus in the form of a dove'.* Directing Celsus, therefore, to Josephus' description of John's baptism in the *Antiquities*, Origen now uses this reference to Josephus to raise the question of 'seeking the cause of the fall of Jerusalem and the destruction of the Temple'. He contends that in the *Antiquities*, Josephus said that *these disasters happened to the Jews as a punishment for the death of James the Just, who was the brother of Jesus called the Christ, the Jews having put him to death, although he was a man of pre-eminent Righteousness.* He grants that *Josephus, 'though not a believer in Jesus as the Christ … in spite of himself, was not far from the truth … since he ought to have said that the conspiracy against Jesus was the cause of these calamities befalling the people, since they put to death Christ, who was a Prophet'.*[40]

But, not satisfied with this, Origen demonstrates how much the issue exercises him by repeating the position in a somewhat different form. Starting with the point that Paul – '*a genuine disciple of Jesus*' – admitted that '*this James was the brother of the Lord*', he adds a new caveat not found in Paul's writings or, for that matter, the Gospels, that this was '*not so much on account of their blood relationship or having been brought up together, as because of his virtues and doctrine*'. This is a new understanding of the issue, that James and the other brothers were not '*blood*' brothers, but rather symbolic or adoptionist brothers. He now proceeds, once more, to interpret the statement about James in Josephus:

> If then, he (Josephus) says that *it was on account of James that Jerusalem's destruction overtook the Jews, how much more in accordance with reason would it be to say that it happened on account of Jesus Christ,* of whose Divinity so many churches, converted from a flood of sins, bear witness, having *joined themselves* to the Creator.[41]

Origen's expressions of outrage surely had much to do with this passage or passages being omitted from versions of Josephus' works thereafter. It is interesting how developed this theological approach had already become by Origen's and Eusebius' time.

As in the case of God's '*vengeance*' for the death of a previous 'Righteous One' Honi and the defeat Herod Antipas suffered in his war with Aretas of Petra and which Josephus says the *people attributed to what Antipas had done to John the Baptist – this attribution to James' death followed by the fall of Jerusalem is the kind of sequentiality that would make most sense to the general population.* To have attributed the fall of Jerusalem and the destruction of the Temple to Jesus' death, except retrospectively, would be something like people today attributing the Second World War to the assassination of President McKinley or the election of Theodore Roosevelt to the assassination of Abraham Lincoln.

Furthermore, such an attribution has the additional factor in its favor of *being surprising and running counter to received tradition or orthodoxy.* In historical research, it is often traditions of this kind, bearing the most surprising content, that carry a kernel of actual historical truth. In his *Commentary on Matthew*, Origen puts the proposition of Jerusalem being destroyed on account of the death of James with greater equanimity, also focusing on James in a sharper manner:

> And so great a reputation for Righteousness did this James have, that Flavius Josephus, who wrote the *Antiquities of the Jews* in twenty volumes, when wishing to exhibit the cause why the people suffered so great misfortunes that even the Temple was razed to the ground, said, *that these things happened to them (the Jews), because of the Wrath of God in consequence of the things which they had dared to do against James the brother of Jesus*, who is called the Christ.

This he repeats, for perhaps the fifth time: 'And the wonderful thing is that, though he did not accept Jesus as Christ, *he yet gave testimony that the Righteousness of James was so great, saying that, the people thought they had suffered these things on account of James*'.[42]

For his part, Eusebius puts the same proposition as follows. Whether he is dependent on Origen is not clear:

> *So admirable a man, indeed, was James, and so celebrated among all for his Righteousness, that even the wiser part of the Jews were of the opinion that this was the cause of the immediate siege of Jerusalem, which happened to them for no other reason than the crimes against him. Josephus, also, has not hesitated to super-add this testimony (elsewhere) in his works: 'These things', he says, 'happened to the Jews to avenge James the Just, who was the brother of him that is called Christ, and whom the Jews had slain, notwithstanding his pre-eminent Righteousness.*'[43]

Even in the 400s, though emphasizing James' '*Holiness*' – *that is, his Naziritism – rather than his Righteousness*, Jerome, as we saw, puts the proposition much in the way Eusebius and Origen did, which makes it seem as if *these various commentators were seeing something like these words somewhere in Josephus' works*. Still, Eusebius does not hesitate throughout his *Ecclesiastical History* to reinterpret the words he himself reports seeing and *castigate the Jews for what they did to Jesus, repeatedly asserting that the loss of their Temple and country was the result.*

But the attribution of the destruction of the Temple and the fall of Jerusalem to the death of James, of course, makes more sense not only because of the proximity of these several events; *but also the constant insistence on the theme of James' Righteousness and the Oblias/ Bulwark/ Protection-imagery associated with it.* In ending his quotation from Hegesippus' testimony to the circumstances and events surrounding the death of James, Eusebius collapses the time interval between these events even further, with the words: '*Immediately after this (that is, James being thrown down from the Pinnacle of the Temple and stoned) Vespasian invaded and took Judea.*'

Ananus' Death and the Death of James

In the extant *Jewish War*, Josephus does relate someone's death to the fall of Jerusalem; however, interestingly enough, it is *not James*, but his opposite number and nemesis, *the High Priest Ananus*. Responsible along with Agrippa II for the death of James, this Ananus, as we saw, was the son of the Ananus mentioned in the Gospels as having a role in the trial and condemnation of Jesus. Since Josephus is such an uneven observer, in the *War* he is at his obsequious best where Ananus is concerned; but in his *Vita* – appended two decades later to his *Antiquities* – he castigates this Ananus so vehemently that it makes one wonder whether he could be talking about the same person.

Since Josephus had business and other dealings with Ananus during his tenure as military commissar of Galilee, responsible – or so he claims – for its fortification; he had been in personal touch with the latter, who was then in control of affairs in Jerusalem – most notably, it would appear, perhaps profiteering or skimming the profits along with Josephus from the corn and olive-oil price-fixing schemes of another of Josephus' enemies, John of Gischala.[44]

Since Ananus does turn out to be the *bête noire* of our study, and the man primarily responsible for *the 'conspiracy' to remove James* and since these discrepancies are so glaring, it might be worth subjecting them to a little more scrutiny. Because of the animus he has developed against Ananus, who was involved in attempts to remove him from command in Galilee; Josephus characterizes such attempts as basically being '*bribes*' and Ananus, consequently, as '*corrupted by bribes*'. He even implies that Ananus 'was conspiring' to have him killed, a theme bearing comparison to the characterization of the Establishment in its dealings with Pontius Pilate in the presentation of the execution of 'Jesus' of the Gospels.

In the *War*, however, Josephus describes Ananus quite differently. He describes him as '*venerable and a very Just Man*', the very words that all sources use to describe James and our '*Zaddik*' terminology again, now applied to James' nemesis Ananus. Nothing loath, Josephus goes on to extol him, saying:

> Besides *the grandeur of that nobility and dignity, and honor*, of which he possessed, *he had been a lover of equality (thus!). Even with the Poorest of the people, he was a great lover of liberty and an admirer of democracy in government, and did ever prefer the public welfare before his own advantage.*[45]

Not only is it hard to suppress a guffaw here, but these are almost exactly the kinds of things one hears in sources about James. *Particularly the note about Ananus being 'a lover of equality' replicates the descriptions of James as 'not deferring to persons' we have already heard about* and will hear about further in descriptions of James' death, not to mention their additional refurbishment in Paul above. Again, there would appear to be reversals going on in our literature here – now regarding James' executioner Ananus,

Ananus is in control of Jerusalem after the initial rebellion in the period from 66–68 CE with another of Josephus' very close 'friends' among the Chief Priests, Jesus ben Gamala. Josephus reproduces long speeches by both, demonstrating that they were *'friends' of Rome*, attempting only to reign in the extremist lunacy of those who had got control of the Temple and whom, for the first time, *he has started calling 'Zealots'*. Though claiming, as he puts it, like the followers of James in Acts, to be 'Zealots for good works'; in Josephus' view, they were rather 'Zealots for Evil and Zealots for Pollution' – exactly the kind of thing we hear from Paul in Chapter 4 of his Letter to the Galatians.

Note here, too, how Josephus has started using the language of the Qumran charges against the Establishment but, once again, reversed. This is the moment that those he is now calling 'Zealots' depose the High Priests. Preferring a venerable procedure of their own, the '*casting of lots*' also employed in the election of James as 'Bishop' or the election to replace Judas *Iscariot* in Eusebius via Hegesippus, not to mention Qumran; they elect an individual of the meanest blood and circumstances, choosing one '*Phannius*', that is, *Phineas, a simple 'Stone-Cutter'*.

These '*Zealots*' now invite another group of unruly and extremely violent individuals into the city, with whom, probably through their mutual Trans-Jordanian connections, they appear to be allied. Josephus calls *these unruly or 'violent Gentiles', 'Idumaeans'*, and they are at this point, most certainly, pro-revolutionary and anti-Roman. Later, when the revolutionary cause goes badly, Titus himself personally conciliates them.[46] Let into the city by '*the Zealots*', they rush crazily through its narrow streets, relieving the siege of the Zealots in the Temple by the orthodox High Priests. They then proceed to slaughter all the High Priests, in particular, Josephus' two friends Ananus and Jesus ben Gamala. *Upbraiding and desecrating their naked bodies* – possibly even urinating on them or cutting off their sexual parts – *they then 'cast' (ballousin) their corpses outside the walls of the city without burial 'to be devoured by dogs and gnawed on by wild beasts'*.[47]

It is at this juncture that Josephus takes the opportunity to make his accusation against the whole of the Jewish people, now attributing the destruction of Jerusalem and the Temple to the 'impious' death of James' opponent Ananus, not James' (or even 'Jesus'' as per the contentions in Christian sources). He opines that:

> I cannot but think *it was because God had doomed this city to destruction as a polluted city and was resolved to purge his Temple by fire*, that he cut off these *its greatest defenders and Protectors*, who had but a little time before worn the sacred vestments … and been esteemed venerable by those dwelling in the whole habitable earth …. [48]

Not only do we have here again the Qumran language of '*pollutions*', but also of '*Protection*' applied to James in early Church sources, both, as usual, turned into their mirror reversals.

At this point, too, Josephus compares *the 'Impiety' involved in the treatment of Ananus' corpse by the Zealots and Idumaeans to not taking down those crucified from the crosses before sundown* or, as he puts it:

> *They proceeded to such a degree of Impiety, that they cast out their corpses without burial, even though the Jews would take so much care for the burial of men, that they even took down malefactors, condemned to crucifixion, and buried them before the setting of the sun.*

It is difficult to escape the impression that this is the point being made in the parallel description in the Gospel of John about the crucifixion of Jesus (19:31–37), and, of course, the implied accusation of the 'Impiety' involved in *his* crucifixion. Points from this description also emerge in descriptions of the death of James, in particular, the motif of 'breaking his legs', but with slightly varying connotation, and further ones like breaking his skull with a laundryman's club, and constant reiteration of the 'casting' language.

This is certainly bizarre and there is something peculiar here, particularly in view of the fact that in his later *Vita*, Josephus denounces Ananus as 'corrupted by bribes'. *That all these early Church fathers, Origen, Eusebius, Jerome, etc., feel that they saw a copy of Josephus attributing the fall of Jerusalem to James' death – not Jesus' and probably not Ananus' either – averring that the greater part of the Jewish people held this view as well, just compounds the conundrum.*

Josephus completes this panegyric by insisting that Ananus too knew 'the Romans were not to be conquered' and, like 'Jesus' in the Gospels, foresaw '*the Jews would be destroyed*', then going on to attribute the destruction of Jerusalem and the purging of the Temple by fire to the impious things done to Ananus' corpse by 'the Zealots' and 'the Idumaeans'.

Not only do these points dovetail perfectly with the descriptions in the Dead Sea Scrolls, *relating the destruction of the Wicked Priest to 'the Violent Ones of the Gentiles' – paralleling 'the Idumaeans' – who took vengeance 'upon the flesh of his corpse' for what he had done to the Teacher of Righteousness*; they parallel almost perfectly the kinds of things being said about James the Just, *including the attribution of the fall of the city to his death in all these sources.*

In his description of Ananus' trumped-up charges against James in the *Antiquities* and about how '*those of the citizens who cared most for equity were most uneasy at the breach of the Law involved*', we have already seen that Josephus calls Ananus '*rash in temperament and very insolent*' and as a 'Sadducee' – meaning, an *Establishment Sadducee* – '*more savage than any of the other Jews in judging malefactors*'. If we add to these reversals the parallel embodied by the care displayed by the Jews to take those crucified down before sundown in order to afford them a proper burial – a key component in the story of the crucifixion of Jesus in the Gospels, it should be clear that one is treading in these accounts on very delicate ground indeed.

The solution to these numerous contradictions and overlaps will never be accepted by everyone, but certainly in the version of Josephus' works that was circulating among Hebrew or Aramaic-speaking people in the East – most notably probably in Edessa and Adiabene in

Northern Syria and Iraq – which Josephus says he wrote before the Greek which was produced for a more Roman-oriented audience in the West, one can imagine Josephus saying something of what he is recorded as saying about the High Priest responsible for James' murder about James himself. This is particularly true if the '*Banus*' referred to above, an individual Josephus seems to have viewed with more than ordinary affection, has any relationship to James. We have already expressed the view that he does.

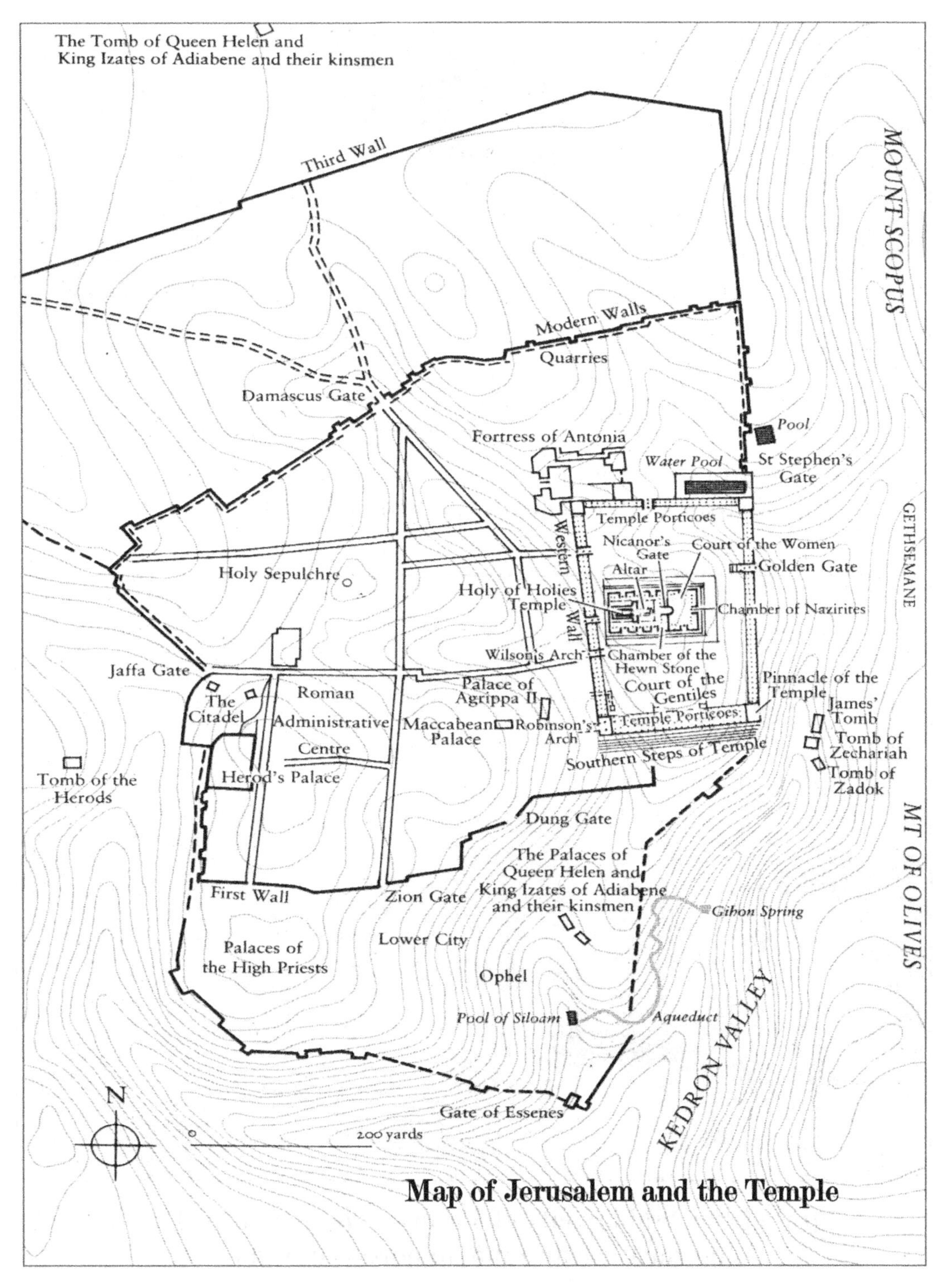

Map of Jerusalem and the Temple

Tomb believed in Christian pilgrimage tradition to belong to James, in the Kedron Valley beneath the Pinnacle of the Temple.

Ruins of the Arabian city of Palmyra in the Syrian Desert, on the caravan route to northern Syria.

PART IV

THE DEATH OF JAMES

Chapter 14
The Stoning of James and the Stoning of Stephen

The Traditions about the Death of James

We are now in a position to discuss the several versions of the death of James and relate these not only to the religio-political circumstances of the Jerusalem of the day, but to the death of the High Priest Ananus, the death of the Righteous Teacher in the Dead Sea Scrolls, and, curiously as it may seem, the stoning of 'Stephen' in Acts. The best place to begin is, once again, early Church sources and Josephus.

Eusebius gives us three separate notices about the death of James: the first from Clement, the second from Hegesippus, and the third from Josephus. The first two, though patently distorted, are less corrupted by the retrospective imposition of a later religio-historical consensus than parallel materials in the Book of Acts. There are complementary materials in Epiphanius, Jerome, and in the Pseudoclementine *Recognitions*.

This raises the question of why the Book of Acts didn't include such a pivotal event as the destruction of James, 'the Bishop of Jerusalem'. Didn't it know what happened to James? In turn, we are reminded of the puzzling fact that Acts didn't include the equally important election or appointment of James as successor to his famous kinsman 'Jesus'. It is these defects in Acts that make the material from extra-biblical sources about James, as persistent and numerous as these are, so impressive.

One does not usually get this sort of historical data about any other character in the New Testament from sources outside the New Testament. For instance, even a character as substantial as Paul all but vanishes when one considers reliable sources *outside* the New Testament. Jesus' story, more highly mythologized and retrospectively fleshed out than Paul's, is, again, virtually non-existent when one considers extra-biblical sources. Aside from Josephus' picture of John the Baptist, only James emerges as a really tangible and historical character when one considers the length and breadth of these sources.

James' *Broken Legs* and Proclamation in the Temple at Passover

Eusebius recounts the death of James in two places. The first draws upon Clement of Alexandria's lost work *Hypotyposes* (*Institutions*). This he gives right after Clement's description of how Peter, James, and John, though they were preferred by Jesus, did not contend for the honor, but rather '*chose James the Just as Bishop of Jerusalem*'. Here Clement, aware of the difficulties inherent in both his account and that of the Book of Acts, adds: '*There were however, two Jameses, one called 'the Just One', who was thrown (bletheis) from the Pinnacle (or 'Wing') of the Temple and beaten to death with a fuller's (laundryman's) club, and the other who was beheaded.*'[1]

Picking up this account again some chapters later in his discussion of the '*plots and crimes of the Jews*' against Paul, and for that matter James, Eusebius states:

> Unable to endure any longer the testimony of the man, who on account of his elevated philosophy and religion was deemed *by all men to be the most Righteous*, they slew him, using anarchy as an opportunity for power, since at that time Festus (Procurator 60–62) had died in Judea, leaving the province without governor or procurator.

The lack of a governor following Festus' death in 62 CE is a detail from Josephus' account of the death of James. He continues: 'But as to the manner of James' death, it has already been stated in the words of Clement, that "*he was thrown (beblesthai) from a wing of the Temple and beaten to death with a club*".'[2]

Jerome avers that this is the bare bones of what existed in early Church testimony from Hegesippus (now lost) and Clement, but he adds an important new element not found in previous accounts. Combining the material, as he himself states, from the Twentieth Book of Josephus' *Antiquities* with that of the Seventh Book of Clement's *Institutions*, he writes:

> *Cast down* from a Pinnacle of the Temple, *his legs broken*, but still half alive, raising his hands to Heaven, he said, 'Lord, forgive them for they know not what they do.' *Then struck on the head by the club of a fuller*, such a club as fullers are accustomed *to wring out wet garments with*, he died.[3]

The point about James' prayer is from Hegesippus, though it also appears in Acts' account about Stephen and may have appeared in Clement as well. But there are several new points, including the more detailed description of the fuller's club, and *the element of James' broken legs*.

This is extremely important material and one does not know from where Jerome got it, but likely from Hegesippus. In any event, this phrase will provide one of the final keys to unraveling what really happened in these times of such importance to the ethos and self-image of Western historical understanding. It will be possible, even without this notice, by using other elements in these overlapping traditions about the death of James – not to mention Jesus' – to determine what really took place, but, with it, we will be able to reach what amounts to confirmation of the scenario we are proposing.

Clearly we are in the tangle regarding the death of James' nemesis, the High Priest Ananus, and the mix-up between what Josephus seems to have said about Ananus and what, according to other traditions, he said about James. For instance, Jerome knows the tradition attributing the downfall of Jerusalem to James' death, saying, 'This same Josephus records the tradition that this James was of such great Holiness and reputation among the people that the fall of Jerusalem was attributed to his death'; yet, in Josephus' extant *Jewish War*, the same seemingly irrelevant note about *the Jews' 'breaking the legs' of the victims of Roman crucifixion to ensure they received a proper burial before the sun went down*, follows the description of *what was done to Ananus' corpse*. Both precede Josephus' eulogization of *Ananus*' '*Righteousness and Piety*' and claim that *the removal of this 'benefactor of his countrymen' made Jerusalem's destruction a certainty*. This claim, as remarked, even included *Ananus' prediction of this destruction*. Once again, this tangle of themes exposes the overlap and revision of materials we are encountering in these sometimes conflicting or diametrically opposed reports.

To return to the most detailed report about James, Eusebius notes, '*but Hegesippus, who belongs to the first generation after the Apostles, gives the most accurate account of him*'. Now quoting verbatim from the Fifth and final Book of Hegesippus' *Commentaries*: 'Some of the seven sects, therefore, of the people, which have been mentioned by me in my *Commentaries*, asked him (James), "What is the Gate (or 'Way') of Jesus?"' Eusebius retains Hegesippus' internal references, even though at this point he does not enumerate what these sects were. He does in a later passage, where his note about the election of Simeon bar Cleophas to succeed James, for some reason, triggers a discussion of Hegesippus' life.

Eusebius, not only notes here that Hegesippus knew Hebrew, but that he was '*a convert from the Hebrews*'. There can be little doubt, therefore, that Hegesippus knew the traditions of Palestine quite well, but came out of a group we should call, for lack of a better term, '*Jewish Christian*'. Hegesippus describes these '*sects*' as *denying 'the Resurrection' and that 'he was coming to give everyone according to his works' (obviously meaning the Messiah)*. For some reason, then, describing them as '*being against the Tribe of Judah and the Messiah*', Hegesippus insists that '*as many as did believe, did so on account of James*'.[4] Not only is this vivid testimony to the power of

James' presence in the Jerusalem of his time and, by consequence, his status as '*the Zaddik*', it is an unequivocal assertion of the clearest doctrine associated with James, *works Righteousness*, the denial of which Hegesippus sees as heretical.

This idea of someone '*coming to give everyone according to his works*' is also part and parcel of his account that follows of James' apocalyptic proclamation in the Temple at Passover – presumably 62 CE but possibly earlier – of *the imminent coming of the Messiah and the Heavenly Host with Power on the clouds of Heaven.* This proclamation in Hegesippus' account is the crucial one, lea*ding directly to James' death.*

That Hegesippus portrays James as making it in the Temple at Passover (the Jewish National Liberation Festival) is significant. James is asked by the Pharisaic/Sadducean Establishment to pacify these assembled crowds in Jerusalem. He then delivers his oration. It is equivalent to lighting an incendiary and crying 'fire' in a crowded room.

James' Popularity in Eusebius

James' oration directly links him to the perspective of the War Scroll found near Qumran – the famous '*War of the Sons of Light against the Sons of Darkness*' – which mounts to a climax in its interpretation of the key 'Star Prophecy' with the *same Messianic proclamation*, including even '*the coming of the Heavenly Host on the clouds of Heaven*' in two columns – in the middle and at the end.

The proclamation of final Messianic Judgment that James makes – where the Messiah, Daniel-like, 'on the clouds of Heaven' leads the Heavenly Host – with the kind of apocalyptic 'Judgment' that in the War Scroll from Qumran '*is poured out like torrential rain on all that grows*', would appear to be *an authentic piece of data from the biography of James.*

Hegesippus via Eusebius now proceeds to picture the consternation in the Pharisaic/Sadducean Establishment, and the 'tumult' related to James' proclamation in the Temple. The Jewish Establishment is concerned that 'there was danger that the whole people would now expect Jesus as the Christ' (read 'Messiah', the 'Christ' concept in Greek probably having no currency in Palestine yet). Therefore, they send to James and say, 'We beseech you, restrain the people, since they are being led astray regarding Jesus as if he were the Christ.' Here, again, we have vivid testimony to James' influence among 'the people' in the Jerusalem of his day.

This request to James, consistent in all sources, forms the backdrop of the Pseudoclementine *Recognitions'* account of the debates on the Temple steps between the Temple Establishment and the Apostles led by James. It forms the backdrop, as well, of accounts of how James' putative forebear in the previous century, Honi the Circle-Drawer, is sent for by a similar configuration of parties, either to make rain or to quiet the assembled crowds opposing foreign rule in Pompey's time, as it does the way another of Honi's putative descendants in James' time, one 'Abba Hilkiah', is sent for.

The *Talmud* portrays the representatives of this same Establishment, because they are afraid of Abba Hilkiah, as sending 'two students' to him *while he is working in the fields to ask him to make rain* (in a related incident, it sends *'little children to get hold of the hem of the clothes' of Hanan the Hidden – Honi's daughter's son*).[5] It is useful to remark in this episode, which forms part of the accounts of rain-making in Tractate *Ta'anith* in the *Talmud*, how gruffly Abba Hilkiah treats the Establishment Rabbis, further bringing into focus *the picture of Opposition Zaddiks with power and influence among the people as opposing Establishment Pharisees and Herodians.*

In Hegesippus' account, the Scribes and Pharisees are constrained not only to recognize James' following 'among the people' as a popular charismatic leader, but also to utilize it in damping down the rampant Messianic agitation and expectation. This picture of rampant energized Messianism is borne out, not only by Josephus' ascription of the final cause of the

Uprising against Rome to *the effect of the Messianic 'Star Prophecy' on the young men 'who were zealous for it'*, but also in the wide-ranging Messianism of the Dead Sea Scrolls.[6] Regardless of the tenor of his Messianism – whether pacifistic and Romanizing, like the picture of Jesus in the Gospels and Paul; or more aggressive and eschatological, the sense in Josephus and the Scrolls – one cannot escape the impression that James' popularity *as 'Zaddik' of the 'Opposition Alliance'* was of such magnitude that even the Establishment had to reckon with his pre-eminent standing among the people and defer to it, even while attempting to exploit it.

The same picture emerges in the *Anabathmoi Jacobou*, which, like the Pseudoclementines, focuses on James' pre-eminent position in the Temple and Jerusalem twenty years earlier in the mid-40's. As in the *Recognitions*, to which it is probably related, James is pictured as a powerful force among the masses. For its part, the scene in the *Recognitions* culminates in a debate on the Temple stairs. Even the Book of Acts, regardless of how overwritten, contains vestiges of these debates in its picture of early Christian comings and goings on the Temple Mount and the extreme interest generated by this among the people over the Messianic issues being discussed and disseminated.

These chapters from Acts 3–6 clearly provide a retrospective and highly-Paulinized, anti-Semitic picture of these debates in the Temple or on its steps. Though these are framed in terms of arguments about the doctrine of the supernatural 'Christ' and Jews as 'Christ-killers' and, from which, James as a central figure is entirely deleted; still, shining through the whole is the true situation of the time and *the extreme 'Messianic' agitation of the period from the 40's to the 60's CE*.

For his part, Hegesippus puts the gist of this request by the Scribes and Pharisees as follows:

> We beseech you, persuade all the people who are coming for the Passover Festival concerning Jesus, for we all have confidence in you. For *we and all the people testify to you that you are the Just One and not a respecter of persons*. Therefore, persuade the people not *to be led astray* concerning Jesus, for *we and all the people must obey you.*

Again, this is extremely revealing testimony, for it shows James' influence and position among the general populace. However, yet again, it mirrors what Josephus has just finished telling us about James' opposite number, namely that Ananus 'delighted in treating the humblest persons as equals'. To repeat, it is difficult at this point not to break out laughing at such blatant dissimulation by pro-Roman and Establishment writers of this kind.

The traditions Eusebius has preserved about James' popularity among the people and being a '*Zaddik* and not respecting persons' – *most particularly, where 'Riches' or 'Poverty' are concerned* – do not aid Roman Church claims for the pre-eminence and proper traditional line of Peter, which Eusebius also presents. Rather, Eusebius *reproduces these claims on behalf of James in spite of himself, because they were in his sources*. When taken seriously, this testimony about James' popularity and his influence – and that of the '*Zaddik*'-idea generally – over the mass is of the utmost importance for understanding the true state of affairs in Jerusalem in the run-up to the War, as it is for understanding some curious and thoroughly unexpected positions in the Scrolls.

If one allows for the retrospective understanding of Second- and Third-Century Church theologians, who are already convinced about the antiquity of 'the Christ' terminology, one imagines that what James was called upon to discourse on in the Temple to quiet the Passover crowds hungering after the Messiah was the nature and understanding of 'the Messianic idea'. This is the basic issue in the debates on the Temple steps, as recorded in the Pseudoclementine *Recognitions*, leading to the attack on James by the 'Enemy' Paul. Epiphanius' *Anabathmoi Jacobou* adds the two issues of *the legitimacy of the Herodian Priesthood and the rejection of the sacrifices.* Whatever the conclusion about these things may be, these issues set the stage for the final destruction of James.

James' Proclamation in the Temple and Jesus' Temptation by the Devil

Eusebius, quoting from Hegesippus, now continues his description of these tumultuous events:

> 'Stand, therefore, upon the Pinnacle of the Temple that you may be clearly visible on high and your words readily heard by all the people, for because of the Passover all the tribes have gathered together and numbers of Gentiles too.' So the aforesaid Scribes and the Pharisees made James stand on the Pinnacle of the Temple, and shouting to him, cried out, '*O Just One, whose word we all ought to obey, since the people are led astray after Jesus, who was crucified, tell us what is the Gate to Jesus?*' And he answered shouting out loudly, '*Why do you ask me concerning the Son of Man? He is now sitting in Heaven at the right hand of the Great Power and is about to come on the clouds of Heaven.*'

The word 'Pinnacle' (*Pterugion*) here may also be translated 'wing' or 'parapet' and it is twice repeated in the narrative. This links it indisputably with the famous story about 'Jesus'' 'Temptation in the Wilderness' after his baptism by John where exactly the same phraseology is used: '*He (the Devil (Diabolos)) set him upon the Pinnacle of the Temple*' (Mt 4:5, Lk 4:8). In this episode, Jesus '*is led by the Holy Spirit out into the wilderness', where he is 'tempted by the Devil' for forty days.* Rather than '*Diabolos*', Mark 1:13 uses '*Satan*' and portrays Jesus, not as '*led out*' as in Matthew and Luke, but '*cast out*' (*ekballei*).

This 'Temptation' episode in the Synoptics is nothing but a negative parody of Josephus' '*Deceivers and false prophets, who lead the people out in the wilderness, there to show them the signs and wonders of their impending freedom*'. In Matthew 4:3 and Luke 4:3, 'the Devil' even tells Jesus that, if he is 'the Son of God', he should 'command these stones to become bread', *precisely the kind of miraculous 'signs or wonders' Josephus condemned.* In later Gospel episodes, Jesus does do such miracles – even this very 'multiplication of loaves' in the wilderness, this 'Temptation by the Devil' episode, *denies he is willing to do* (Mt 15:33 and Mk 8:34)!

But to come to the point about 'the Pinnacle of the Temple', as the episode continues, the Devil now 'sets him (Jesus) upon the Pinnacle of the Temple' and challenges him to 'cast (himself) down'. This is precisely the scenario in the James story, including almost the exact same language. The only difference is that in Clement and Hegesippus, as we saw, *James actually is 'cast down' from the Pinnacle of the Temple* – in the Pseudoclementines, as we shall see later, *'headlong' and from its 'steps'.*

The implication in these Gospel scenarios – which in this sense must be *late* – is that what happened to James was '*Evil*' or a 'temptation by the Devil'. Jesus wouldn't do such things! In the Gospel rewriting, Jesus is only *challenged* by the Devil to 'cast himself down'. Though the Devil ('*Diabolos*') offers him 'all the Kingdoms of the world and their Glory', Jesus refuses, answering in words now proverbial, 'Get thee behind me Satan' (Mt 4:10, Lk 4:8).

Since these Gospel Temptation narratives are, at once, so polemical and symbolic and so clearly directed against those going out into the wilderness to do miracles or, as Josephus explains, '*to show the people the signs of their impending freedom there*'; there can be little doubt – regardless of how astonishing this might at first appear – that *the original tradition about 'being set upon the Pinnacle of the Temple' first appeared in these traditions about James being placed upon 'the Pinnacle of the Temple' to quiet the Passover crowds hungering for the Messiah,* conserved by Hegesippus in the middle of the Second Century.

The Gospel refurbishments of these various materials are, once again, clearly directed *against* those looking to build earthly 'Kingdoms' and to challenge Caesar's Dominion in this world. But this is exactly the point about the polemic over the tax issue accompanying the description of Jesus (not James) as '*not deferring to anyone nor regarding the person of men*' in the series of questions put to Jesus (again not James) by the Establishment Parties, directly followed in Matthew and Mark (Luke puts this elsewhere) by the citation of *the Righteousness/ Piety dichotomy*, in particular, '*you should love your neighbor as yourself*'. This is exactly the order followed by Paul in Romans 13:6-9, citing *the Righteousness Commandment* as a reason for '*paying taxes' to Rome and 'giving all their due'*.

In these Gospel renditions of Jesus' responses to the Establishment, Jesus is portrayed as recommending, at least on the surface, 'to give tribute unto *Caesar*', which all these Zadokite-style Revolutionaries were quite unwilling to do. In fact, the 'Galilean' or '*Sicarii* Movement', founded by Judas and *Saddok*, is pictured in Josephus as beginning on just this note of *opposition to paying the tax to Rome.* By the same light, for Luke 23:2, '*misguiding the people, forbidding (them) to pay tribute to Caesar, claiming that he himself, "Christ", was a King', is just the charge leveled against Jesus.*

In addition to all these retrospective and polemical reversals; it should now be growing clear that the tradition about the Devil 'setting Jesus upon the Pinnacle of the Temple' and Jesus' refusal to 'be tempted' and 'cast himself down' (*kataballō*) was first probably an element in these traditions about James, to whom – like the related matter of Jerusalem's fall – they more properly appertained. In addition to this, it should be clear that the extent of the absorption of materials about James into the biblical narrative about 'Jesus' is also increasing.

The phrase about 'the Door' or 'Gate to Jesus', too, is also a possible synonym for the 'Way of Jesus'. In fact, in John 10:9, 'Jesus' calls himself 'the Door', by which he appears to mean '*the Gate of Salvation*'. In Hegesippus' version of these matters, James ostensibly declines to answer the question about 'the Gate of Jesus' in favor of the more apocalyptic and biblical proclamation of '*the Son of Man', 'sitting in Heaven on the right hand of the Great Power about, to come on the clouds of Heaven.'* For him, anyhow, '*the Son of Man*' is literally '*the Gate of Jesus*' or '*the Second*' or '*Primal Adam*'.

Before proceeding, however, it is important to grasp that in Hebrew 'Son of Man' literally is 'Son of Adam' and, therefore, the reference to the imminent '*coming of the Son of Man on the clouds of Heaven*' is basically a more incendiary version of the 'Primal' or 'Perfect Adam' ideology. As Paul puts it in his own inimitable way in 1 Corinthians 15:45–47: '*Also it is written, "the First Man Adam became a living soul", so the Last Adam became a life-giving Spirit ... The First Man is made of dust out of the earth. The Second Man is the Lord out of Heaven.*'

The quotation attributed by Hegesippus to James, which we compared to throwing a lighted match into an excited mix of pilgrims, is both immediate and intense. When one grasps its aggressively-apocalyptic Messianic character, it becomes the central proclamation of one of the most amazing episodes ever recorded in religious history. Not only are the words attributed to James paralleled almost word-for-word in the War Scroll from Qumran, they come precisely at the point where the Messianic 'Star Prophecy' is being elucidated in that Document.

James' Proclamation of the Son of Man Coming on the Clouds of Heaven and the Dead Sea Scrolls

The sequence in Church accounts of the destruction of James followed by the appearance of the foreign armies and their devastation and destruction of the country is, for all intents and purposes, replicated in the Habbakuk *Pesher*. That Commentary expounds the first two chapters of the Prophet Habakkuk in an eschatological and apocalyptic manner, including both James' and Paul's key proof text 'the Righteous shall live by his Faith' which it elucidates in terms of a final apocalyptic Judgment.

The subjects treated – though not exactly in order – are: *the destruction of the Righteous Teacher by the Wicked Priest for which 'the Cup of the Lord's Vengeance would come around to him'* (the Wicked Priest); the devastation of the country by foreign armies, called 'the *Kittim*' or 'the Additional Ones of the Peoples'; and how the booty and Riches *'of the Last Priests of Jerusalem, who gathered Riches and profiteered from the spoils of the Peoples'*, would *'in the Last Days be delivered up to the hand of the Army of the Kittim'*.[7] In the last Column, all of these will ultimately be condemned and *'destroyed from off the earth'*, as would all backsliders and idolaters generally – including *'all Gentiles serving stone and wood' which 'would not save them on the Day of Judgment'* (apostate Jews would be included under the idea of *'backsliders'*).[8]

Anyone conversant with Scripture will recognize that James' response to the Scribes and Pharisees alludes to Daniel 7:13: 'And I gazed into the visions of the night and I saw, coming on the clouds of Heaven, one like a Son of Man.' This title, 'the Son of Man', is one of the most precious of those applied to 'Jesus' in Scripture, but what is not normally recognized is that 'Son of Man' means exactly what it says – someone with the image of a 'man' but not exactly one. As for 'the Messiah' and 'the clouds of Heaven', one should realize that the War Scroll is operating in exactly the same ideological and scriptural framework.

In Column XI, where 'the Star Prophecy' is finally expounded, first the actual Prophecy: 'a Star will rise from Jacob, a Scepter to rule the world' from Numbers 24:17, is quoted in its entirety. Then it is analyzed in detail. But in the three columns preceding this (VIII), *the situation in 'the camps', where 'the Holy Angels are with our Hosts' and those 'Perfect in Spirit and body prepared for the Day of Vengeance' is delineated.*[9] *God 'strengthens' and 'fortifies all the mighty Warriors', 'making war through the Holy Ones of His People' (the last equivalent to Daniel 7:21's 'Kedoshim' or 'Saints').* For this reason, *'all indecent lewdness is to be kept from the camps', 'since the Holy Angels are together with their Hosts'*. Furthermore, the 'linen' battle raiment of the Priests is described in great detail. This is not to be worn 'in the Temple' thereafter, nor are these Priests 'to profane themselves with the blood of the Nations of Vanity'.[10]

Over and over again it is reiterated that *military victories are accomplished by the human 'Holy Ones of the Covenant' with the help of 'the Holy Angels' and 'the Host of the Heavenly Holy Ones' on the clouds.* This is expressed as follows: 'The Power is from You not us. Our Strength and the Power of our hands accomplish no *mighty works*, except by Your Power and the Power of Your mighty bravery.'[11] Aside from this tell-tale 'Power' vocabulary, one should also note the belligerence of this expression, important for fixing the ethos of the literature at Qumran.

In the War Scroll, David's victory over Goliath sets the *Davidic* ambience of what follows, including the interpretation of 'the Star Prophecy'. This is a crucial moment for Qumran exegesis, and it is no overstatement to say, for that matter, the world generally. Not only is this interpretation specifically framed in terms of the Messiah-like 'no mere Adam', showing, as nothing else can, that *this 'Star Prophecy' was being interpreted Messianically at Qumran*;[12] but it will now develop into the language of Daniel's *'Son of Man coming on the clouds' with the Heavenly Host* or, as Matthew puts it, *'the Son of Man coming with Power and great Glory' or 'sitting on the right hand of Power and coming on the clouds of Heaven'* (24:30, 26:64, and pars.).[13]

Quoting Isaiah 31:8's *'by the sword of no Man, the sword of no mere Adam'*, the War Scroll now goes on to evoke the 'Primal Adam', thus tying all these themes – the Davidic, 'the Star', 'the Son of Man', 'the Perfect Adam', and the 'Messiah' – together in one extended proclamation, ultimately combining 'clouds' and 'rain' imagery and expressing this Judgment in terms of 'coming on the clouds' and the 'shedding of rain on all on earth'. That all of these motifs come together here in exegesis of 'the Star Prophecy' in the War Scroll is about as much proof as one could ask that the approach we have been following produces results. Nothing less would have prepared us for this and, without it, we could not have appreciated the presence of all these motifs here. This exegesis is directly followed by an extended description of the Heavenly Host coming on the clouds, richer than in any other source and repeated a second time at the end of the Scroll as we have signaled.

For it, the Messiah-like Leader *'joins the Poor'* ('*Ebionim*' repeated twice) and '*those bent in the dust' to rise up 'against the Kittim'*.[14] It reads:

> By the hand of Your Messiah ... so that You may glorify Yourself in front of Your Enemies and overthrow Belial's Legions, the Seven Nations of Vanity, and *by the hand of the Poor Ones of Your Redemption, with the fullness of Your Marvelous Power, You have (opened) a Gate of Hope to the cowering heart ... for You will kindle the Downcast in Spirit, who shall be as a flaming torch in the chaff to ceaselessly consume Evil until Wickedness is destroyed.*

In the Damascus Document too, 'the Scepter' is the Messianic 'Leader', also referred to in another Messianic fragment seemingly connected to these matters, 'The Messianic Leader (*Nasi*)'.[15] In that Document, he 'will utterly destroy the Sons of Seth' – synonymous with 'the Seven Nations of Vanity' and mentioned in Numbers 24:17 as well.

One should compare the 'torch in the chaff' simile at this point in the War Scroll to the words of John the Baptist, quoted in Matthew 3:11–12 and applied to '*one coming more Powerful than' he: 'He shall baptize you with the Holy Spirit and Fire, whose winnowing fan is in His hand to purify His threshing floor, and He will gather His wheat into his storehouse, but He will burn up the chaff with unquenchable fire'*. The references to 'harvesting wheat', 'burning', and 'Fire' will, to be sure, recur in the sequence of parables following the evocation of 'the Enemy' in 'the Parable of the Tares' in Matthew 13:24–50, the only real Jewish Christian parable in Scripture. The allusions to 'burning' and 'Fire' are also very strong in eschatological contexts elsewhere at Qumran – as they will be later throughout the Koran – particularly in evocation of 'the Last Judgement'.[16]

At this point, the passage from Isaiah 31:8, referred to above, is introduced into the exegesis *implying the Messiah to be 'more than a Man, more than a mere Adam'*. At the same time, it links him to *vanquishing the Kittim – here clearly the Romans – with 'the sword'*. It reads as we also saw: '*And from that time, You announced the Power of Your hand over the Kittim with the words, "And Assyria shall fall by the sword of no Man, but by the sword of no mere Adam You shall consume him (Hebrew: 'eat him')."*'

The idea of 'consuming' or 'eating' here plays off the 'flaming torch consuming the chaff' descriptive of 'the Poor in Spirit' above, now applied directly to the Star/Messiah and his constituency, the Poor (*Ebionim*) and 'those Bent in the Dust'.

> Because, *by the hand of the Poor Ones and the hand of those Bent in the Dust* (i.e., *'the Poor in Spirit'*) *will the Enemies from all the lands and the Mighty Ones of the Peoples be humbled, so that they will be paid the Reward on Evil Ones ... to justify the Judgment of Your Truth on all the sons of man in order to make for Yourself an Eternal Name among the People.*[17]

Therefore, in the War Scroll, *the Messiah will render Judgment with the help of 'the Poor' and 'those Bent in the Dust' on 'the Mighty Ones of the Peoples'*.

Not only do we have in these climactic portions of the War Scroll 'the Star Prophecy' interpreted in terms of Daniel 7's 'Son of Man' – the basis as well of James' proclamation in the Temple on Passover, 62 CE – but this is accompanied by inclusion of the scriptural warrant for someone 'more than Man' or 'the sword of a Higher Adam' to accomplish this victory over all foreign armies and bring the final eschatological Judgment. Again we have the coupling of nationalist and 'Zealot' Messianic war-likeness with what superficially, anyhow, would appear to be the more spiritual 'Primal Adam' ideology of daily-bathing Ebionite/ Essene groups.

This is a crucial melding and defines the religio-historical situation in 62 CE almost perfectly. For its part, the War Scroll moves directly into an extensive description of '*the coming of the Heavenly Host on the clouds of Heaven*' of such ecstatic beauty and brilliant creativity as to be overwhelming:

> For You will fight with them from Heaven … because the majority of these Holy Ones are in Heaven along with the Host of Your Angels in Your Holy Abode praising Your Name together with *the Elect of the Holy People, whom You have set aside for Yourself … for whom You have recorded … the Covenant of Your Peace and over whom You will reign for all Eternal Ages.*[18]

The text then turns completely war-like, having the nature of an exhortative for battle or, as it now must be termed (using the language of Islam), 'Holy War':

> For You have commanded the Hosts of Your Elect in their thousands and their Myriads, together with your Holy Ones and the Army of Your Angels, who are mighty in battle, together with the Elect of Heaven and Your blessings, to smite the Enemies of the land with the Greatness of Your Judgments … because you are a Terrible God in the Glory of Your Kingdom and the Assembly of your Holy Ones is among us to give us Eternal aid.

Its imagery is now purely confrontational, militaristic, and eschatological, including the rationale for the Qumran '*camp*'-style communities:

> We shall despise kings and mock and scorn the Mighty, because our Lord is Holy and our Glorious King ('His Messiah') is with us, together with the Holy Ones, the Mighty Host of Angels are under His command[19] and the Valiant Warrior is among our Assembly, and the Hosts of His Spirits (Islam: '*Jinn*') are with our foot soldiers and our horsemen.

This finally gives way to a key simile comparing 'the coming of the Heavenly Host' to 'clouds', making it clear we are completely in the realm of Daniel, the New Testament's '*Son of Man coming on the clouds of Heaven with Power and Great Glory*', and the totality of 'rain' and 'Judgment' imagery we have been following: '*They are like clouds, clouds of dew (covering) the earth, as torrential rain, shedding Judgment on all that grows on earth.*'

Here, of course, is the 'rain' imagery that we have been signaling in our presentation of the *Zaddik* as rain-maker and one begins to appreciate that one is in a much more sophisticated universe of poetic imagery and symbolism than one might have previously suspected. Of course, Paul is working in the same poetic universe of allegory and metaphor – but to opposite effect. The allusion to '*shedding Judgment on all that grows on earth*' parallels Matthew 5:45's God '*sending rain on the Righteous and the Unrighteous*' alike, as well as *allusions comparing the coming of the Son of Man to 'the Days of Noah*' (Mt 24:37–38, Mk 13:26–27, Lk 21:27).

Just for good measure this 'rain' simile is repeated again, almost word-for-word, at the end of the War Scroll. Here, referring now to *God 'keeping his Covenant with us and opening the Gates of Salvation for us numerous times*', the text proclaims again:

> *For Yours is the Might and in Your hands, the battle … for our Ruler is Holy and the Glorious King is with us. The Host of His Spirits is with our foot soldiers and horsemen. They are as clouds, clouds of de)w covering the earth and as torrential rain shedding Judgment on (all that grows there. Arise hero) … smite the nations, your enemies, and consume guilty flesh with your sword* (this last clearly being a Messianic allusion).[20]

Not only do we have here the 'God our Ruler' ideology of Josephus' 'Zealots' or '*Sicarii*', there can be little doubt of the 'Messianic' thrust of all this, not to mention its blood-curdling war-likeness – perhaps a necessity in the circumstances. The fresh and original imagery here, once again, recapitulates the Messianic '*sword*' of the '*no mere Adam*' passage from Isaiah 31:8 above, including even the allusion to '*consuming*'/'*eating*'.

The Imagery of the Heavenly Host and Coming Apocalyptic Judgment in James

This is almost precisely the picture one gets in early Church accounts of James' proclamation in the Temple on Passover of *the Son of Man coming on the clouds of Heaven.* That such a proclamation is attributed to James, to whom the 'rain-making' tradition also adhered, at this pivotal moment in his activity is astonishing – but the parallels in materials relating to James go further than that.

The Letter of James is also steeped in the language of '*doing*' and '*Doer*', the same root as the word, '*works*' (*ma'asim*), so much a part of the vocabulary at Qumran. In it, '*Salvation*' is not simply '*a free gift of Faith*' as in Paul; rather there will be '*Jud*gment without mercy on those who do not do mercy' (2:13). In the last chapter, its author – James or another – launches into a thoroughgoing and completely uncompromising apocalyptic. This begins with condemnation of *the Rich*: 'And now you Rich, weep, start crying for the miseries that are coming to you' (5:1).

This condemnation of 'the Rich' is also a set piece of Qumran ideology, expressed most vividly perhaps in the 'Three Nets of Belial' section of the Damascus Document. But the condemnation of 'the Rich' is also a principal theme associated with those holding the tradition associated with James' name most dear, 'the *Ebionim*' or 'the Poor'. The same was no doubt true for those following the Righteous Teacher of the Scrolls, where the terminology 'the Poor' and several of its parallels permeate the corpus.

The tirade against 'the Rich' in the Letter of James, including the assertion that *the Rich 'put the Righteous One to death*' (5:6), rises to its climax with the apocalyptic proclamation of 'the *coming of the Lord*' (5:8). That this involves 'the Lord of Hosts' is made clear as well four lines before (5:4). It is this same 'Lord of Hosts' implicit in the War Scroll. This is also the implication of the episode from early Church literature about the proclamation by James of 'the Son of Man sitting on the right hand of the Great Power', to say nothing of its New Testament parallels.

As in these other contexts, in James we even have an allusion to the telltale Messianic 'Gate' or 'Door' usage again: '*Behold, the Judge is standing before the Door*' (5:9). This also incorporates the 'standing' imagery again, amid that of the final apocalyptic Judgment, and even ends with the evocation of the coming of 'spring' and 'autumn rain' – the implication being that this is the equivalent of eschatological Judgment. Its spirit is vengeful, uncompromising, and completely parallel to the spirit one finds in the War Scroll. It reads as follows: '*Your gold and silver are corroding away, and the same corrosion will be like a testimony against you, and shall eat your flesh like Fire. It was a burning Fire that you stored up as treasure in the Last Days*'.

Not only do we have here the language, attributed to Jesus by Matthew 6:19–20's 'Sermon on the Mount', of 'moth and rust' corroding stored-up earthly treasure, but also that of 'eating' or 'devouring flesh with a sword', used in the War Scroll and in Isaiah 31:8's 'no mere Adam' Prophecy above. Linguistic parallels such as these should not be dismissed lightly. One should also note the language here of 'the Last Days' and 'a burning Fire', which fairly permeates the literature at Qumran, particularly the Habakkuk *Pesher* – as it does the Koran in Islam. These allusions pinpoint the Letter of James as being thoroughly apocalyptic and eschatological; and, as in the interpretation of Habakkuk 2:4 in the Habakkuk *Pesher* and the interpretation of 'the Zadokite Covenant' in the Damascus Document, once again we are in the world of 'the Last Generation' or 'the End Time'.

It is here the letter ascribed to James evokes 'the Lord of Hosts': *'Look, the hire of the workers who mowed your fields, which you kept back, cries out, and the cries of the reapers have reached the ears of the Lord of Hosts'* (5:4). Interestingly, the Hebrew word for 'Hosts', '*Sabaoth*', is transliterated in this passage *directly into the Greek*. James continues:

> It was you who condemned and put the Righteous One to death. He offered you no resistance. Therefore, be patient, brothers, until the coming of the Lord, just as the farmer waits for the precious fruit of the earth, having patience until it receives the rain (either) earlier or later, you also must *be patient, fortifying your hearts*, because *the coming of the Lord* has drawn near. Do not *grumble against each other*, so that you will not be condemned. *See, the Judge stands before the Door* (James 5:4–10).

This is the whole scheme of the climactic end of the Habakkuk *Pesher*, which also deals with eschatological Judgment and counsels patience, presenting the scriptural warrant for what goes in Christian eschatological theory as 'the Delay of the Parousia'. This exegesis is delivered in interpretation of Habakkuk 2:3, *'if it tarries, wait for it', and it asserts that 'the Last Days' would be 'extended beyond anything the Prophets have foretold'.*[21]

In the section evoking the Righteousness Commandment, 'loving one's neighbor', and the Piety Commandment, 'loving God'; James asserts that it is the Rich who oppress the Poor by 'dragging them before tribunals' (2:6). Again in the Damascus Document at Qumran, the penalty for having people condemned to death in the Courts of the Gentiles – which has not a little relevance to the portrait of the death of Jesus in the Gospels – is death.[22]

This allusion to the coming of the Lord of Hosts in eventual final Judgment and the consonant condemnation of the Rich 'for murdering the Righteous One' in James also concludes with the efficacious 'working prayer of the Just One' citing, as we saw, Elijah as a man with the power to pray for it not to rain and, praying again, causing the 'Heaven to send forth rain' (5:16–18).

The Stoning of Stephen in Acts

We saw how James, placed upon 'the Pinnacle' or 'steps of the Temple' by the Jerusalem Leadership to quiet the Messianic expectation rampant among the people, instead proclaimed *the standing of the Messiah 'on the right hand of Power' and his imminent coming 'with the Heavenly Host on the clouds of Heaven'*. There is one final point relating to this episode which again helps point the way to Acts' historical method – in particular, helping to unravel the mystery of the attack upon someone Acts presents as being called 'Stephen'.

In a significant parallel to the attack on James described in the first Book of the Pseudoclementine *Recognitions*, it is at this point also that Paul is introduced. To draw the parallel closer, 'Stephen' undergoes the same ultimate fate as James – stoning. In addition, just as the character in Acts who is the witness to this stoning afterwards emerges as *Paul*; in Eusebius' version of the stoning of James, the witness turns out to be 'one of the Priests of the Sons of Rechab, the *Rechabim*' (Eusebius actually preserves the Hebrew plural here, transliterated into the Greek). In Epiphanius it is Simeon bar Cleophas, James' close relative and direct successor in the Leadership of the Jerusalem Church. But whereas both Epiphanius' Simeon and Eusebius' 'Rechabite Priest' disapprove of the stoning and call upon those perpetrating it to stop, Paul 'entirely approves'. As Acts puts this: '*And the witnesses laid their clothes at the feet of a young man called Saul ... and Saul entirely approved of putting him to death*' (7:58–8:1). 'Saul', of course, will metamorphose into 'Paul'.

As presented in Acts, this speech, seemingly lifted almost bodily from Joshua's farewell address (Josh. 24:2–24), makes a mistake in the location of Abraham's burial site traceable to the speech attributed to Joshua in 24:32. Stephen is presented – however bizarre this may appear to be from the mouth of a seemingly Gentile convert – as *telling the Jews (now his tormentors) their own history*. The speech ends with a Pauline-style attack on all Jews, including presumably the Jerusalem Church Leadership, as '*always resisting the Holy Spirit*' (7:51). Then, alluding to the Prophecy of '*the coming of the Just One*' (language we have already seen tied to attacks on the Rich in the Letter of James), Stephen, too, accuses the Jews of killing the Prophets and of being Christ-killers. He says: '*Which one of the Prophets did your fathers not persecute, and they killed the ones who prophesied the coming of the Just One, of whom now, too, you have become betrayers and murderers*' (7:52).

The importance of this passage from Acts, however, doesn't end here: 'Filled with the Holy Spirit and gazing intently up to Heaven, Stephen, James-like, now *sees the Glory of God and 'Jesus' standing at the right hand of God*, and cries out, "*Behold, I see the Heavens opened, and the Son of Man standing at the right hand of God*"' (7:55–56). Here, of course, are almost the exact words and the same proclamation attributed to James at this critical juncture in early Church sources, including even the words, '*at the right hand of God*' and '*the Son of Man*' (this last, though missing from the War Scroll at Qumran, implied there as well) – not to mention these two reiterations of the '*standing*' terminology.

But the resemblance does not stop there. The next words are also simply variations of those we encounter in the story of James' death, including the note of being '*thrown*' or '*cast*' (*ballo*) *down* – here '*cast out*' (*ekballo*) – and '*crying out*', virtually the exact words attributed to James in these early Church accounts and Jesus, too, in Gospel accounts of his last words on the cross.

The episode closes as follows: 'And crying out *with a loud voice*, they stopped their ears with their hands and rushed at him with one mind, and having *cast him* (*ekballo*) *out of the city*, they stoned ... Stephen *as he prayed* ... and *falling to his knees*, he cried out *in a loud voice*, "Lord lay not this sin on them"' (Acts 7:57–60). Again, these are almost precisely the words attributed to James in Hegesippus' account reproduced by Eusebius and, of course, those attributed to Jesus on the Cross in the Gospels. The parallels and overlaps between the various accounts of the stoning of James and the Book of Acts' account of the stoning of the elusive and quite puzzling character known as 'Stephen' are unmistakable.

The constant themes of James' '*praying*' and his '*falling*' reiterated here, but so are those of James *crying out with a 'loud voice'*, twice repeated in dramatic style in the account in Hegesippus, not to mention the ever-present motif of '*his knees*'. Not only does '*Stephen*' mean '*Crown*' in Greek, it parallels the word in Hebrew used to designate the mitre worn by the High Priest – also a colloquialism, as we saw, for the *hair of the Nazirites* – both themes again connected with James.

Why these resemblances? What is behind these overlaps and reversals? We identified the election of 'Judas *Iscariot*' (not to mention the suspicious '*fall*' he takes) as a substitute for James' election – one meant to write James out of scripture; 'James the brother of John' may be a similar sort of stand-in, and quite a few others – including 'Agabus', the 'eunuch' of the Ethiopian Queen, 'Cornelius', and Peter – may be of the same species. Thus, this episode involving 'Stephen' takes the place of an extremely embarrassing, actual physical assault by Paul on James, which is now recorded only in the Pseudoclementine *Recognitions*.

We are now in a position to reassess the received narrative in light of some of these other curious survivals in early Church history and thus reconstruct the actual history of the Jerusalem Community of James the Just.

The Wicked 'Encompassing' or 'Swallowing' the Righteous in both Eusebius and at Qumran

After James' proclamation of 'the Son of Man coming on the clouds of Heaven', the account preserved by Eusebius presents the masses as 'glorying' in this testimony and crying out – as in Gospel accounts of Jesus' entry into Jerusalem – 'Hosanna to the son of David', meaning '*Save us, son of David*' (Mt 21:9–15 and pars.). Understandably, 'the same Scribes and Pharisees' are pictured as having thought better of their action in giving James such a prominent forum at such a Feast Day, and conspiring with one another:

> They said to each other, 'We made a mistake in providing Jesus with such testimony, but let us go up and *cast him* (James) *down* (here '*kataballo*'), so they – the people – will be frightened and not believe in him.' And they *cried out*, saying 'Oh! Oh! Even the Just One has erred' (or 'is deceived').

Not only do we have here the use of James' title '*the Zaddik*' in place of his very name and the language of '*casting*', Acts is applying to the attack on Stephen; but also the words, 'crying out' (used twice in Hegesippus), to describe the manner in which Scribes and Pharisees addressed James. Acts also uses *these very words*, '*they cried out with a loud voice*', to describe the manner in which 'the Elders and the Scribes' of the Sanhedrin 'stopped their ears with their hands and rushed on Stephen with one mind, *casting him out* of the city' (7:57).

In Hegesippus, the stoning of the Just One James fulfilled the Prophecy written in Isaiah, '*Let us take away the Just One, for he is abhorrent to us, wherefore they shall eat the fruit of their doings.*' This version of Isaiah 3:10 differs from the received version which reads: '*Say to the Righteous, all is well, for they (the Evil) shall eat the fruit of their doings.*' The important thing is that the vocabulary that so appealed to the sectaries at Qumran and early Christianity is present. In this case, it is the contrast of the Wicked doing something Evil to the Righteous – even including the additional tell-tale play on '*eating*' – here implying punishment or vengeance.

Similar passages are present in other documents from Qumran, for instance, at the beginning of the Habakkuk *Pesher*, where the words '*the Wicked encompasses the Righteous*' basically begin the exegesis (Hab. 1:4 but also note Habakkuk 1:13 where the usage '*swallowing*' occurs as well). Passages such as these at Qumran are usually interpreted in terms of something terrible happening to the Righteous Teacher. The same is true in this parallel early Church account relating to James. This is persuasive evidence that this kind of scriptural exegesis involving the same vocabulary was in use at Qumran regarding the Righteous Teacher as in early Christianity regarding James. Hegesippus himself says as much in elucidating James' cognomens with the comment, '*as the Prophets declare concerning him*'.

For the Habakkuk *Pesher*, '*the Zaddik is the Moreh ha-Zedek*' (that is, '*the Righteous Teacher*'). In the *Pesher* on Psalm 37 – another '*Zaddik*' text – passages like '*the Wicked plots against the Righteous*' (Ps. 37:12) or '*the Wicked watches out for the Righteous and tries to put him to death*' (37:32) are subjected to this same kind of exegesis. Therefore, the usage '*Zaddik*' in any underlying text from Scripture is almost without exception exploited in Qumran exegesis to mean '*the Righteous Teacher*'. This is parallel to the way Isaiah 3:10 is being interpreted in early Church accounts having to do with James – not to mention others being applied to 'Jesus' in the New Testament. Again, this is what Hegesippus seems to have meant by asserting '*as the Prophets declare concerning him*'.

However, if one looks at the other usages contained in these key passages about these deaths, one can go further than this. 'Righteous' and 'Evil' in any biblical text are almost always interpreted in the Scrolls to mean 'the Righteous Teacher' and 'the Wicked Priest' respectively. Where the biography of James is concerned, these would be James and his nemesis *the High Priest Ananus*. On one occasion, '*Evil*' in the underlying text (Hab. 1:13) is applied to another adversary of the Righteous Teacher, '*the Liar*'; and others of his persuasion seemingly '*the Traitors*' – terminology also not unknown in the Gospels. The former is described as '*rejecting the Torah in the midst of their whole Congregation*'. In James' biography, such an individual would be equivalent to his ideological adversary Paul.

The actual usage in Habakkuk 1:13 is, '*the Wicked swallows up one more Righteous than he*' ('*balla°* – used in the sense of 'destroying' and paralleling our 'eating'/'consuming' allusions).[23] As we have been remarking, these letters, *B-L-'*, also at the root of the Hebrew names 'Belial' and 'Balaam', strangely as it may seem, appear to go into parallel accounts of the death of James in the Greek. To say nothing of the usage we have been highlighting with regard to these, '*ballo*' ('*casting*' or '*throwing down*') as well as the Greek parallel embodied in the peculiar nominative, 'the *Diabolos*' or '*Devil*'. These parallel usages fairly permeate Gospel narratives and the New Testament generally.

At Qumran, important usages like these are legion and seem to provide the *modus operandi* the sectaries used to choose the texts they wished to interpret. These include '*the Poor*' (*Ebion*), '*the Meek*' ('*Ani*, a synonym for '*the Poor*' in Psalm 37:15), '*Lebanon*' (Hab. 2:17), '*plotting*', '*booty*', '*Riches*', '*Anger*'/'*Wrath*', '*Perfection*', etc. Psalm 37, for instance, contains allusions to: '*though he falls, he shall not be cast down*' (24) and '*the Salvation of the Righteous Ones is from the Lord. He is their Protection*' (39). A not unsimilar phrase, '*Protection on the day of trouble*', occurs in Nahum 1:7 in passages also subjected to exegesis at Qumran.[24]

If one looks at Isaiah 3:10, a passage applied to the death of James, one finds similar vocabulary – for instance, '*Lebanon*' (Isa. 2:13) – another favorite at Qumran particularly where *the fall of the Temple and the Priesthood is concerned.* In fact, almost every occurrence of '*Lebanon*' in the Bible is subjected to exegesis at Qumran even in the extant corpus. These occur mostly in Isaiah and Habakkuk, but also in a particularly pregnant context of apocalyptic final 'Judgment', 'whirlwind', and 'Flood' from Nahum 1:4. In Rabbinic literature, '*the fall of the cedars of Lebanon*' is a metaphor for the fall of the Temple, specifically the one in 70 CE, the '*whiteness*' inherent in the Hebrew word, *playing on the white linen the Priests wore in the Temple*, not to mention the fact that *the Temple had originally been constructed out of cedar wood.*

There is also reference to causing the people 'to go astray and swallowing the Way of Your Paths' (3:12), 'Tongue' imagery (3:8), 'grinding the face of the Poor' and 'robbing the spoils of the Poor' (3:14–15), 'the Lord of Hosts taking away from Jerusalem and Judah the stay and the staff' (3:1), 'foreigners devouring' the country (1:7 – '*eating it*', again the exact sense of the Habakkuk *Pesher* and Isaiah 31:8 in the War Scroll), 'washing clean' (1:16 and 4:4), and 'idolatry' (2:18). There is even the tell-tale allusion to the favorite usage at Qumran, *B-L-'* or '*swallowing*', in Isaiah 3:12. This occurs *directly following* the verses applied to James' death in Hegesippus and, following this, '*leading the people astray*' – an allusion also found at both the beginning of and in the Last Column of the Damascus Document where the teaching of '*the Liar*' is being described.

It is hard to believe that such a fortuitous conjunction of images would not have appealed to our sectaries. This crucial *B-L-'* language circle, as we have been implying, is pregnant with meaning when discussing the destruction of 'the Righteous Teacher' at Qumran, as it will be when discussing James. At Qumran, it will not only be applied to what the Wicked Priest did to the Righteous Teacher, but also *the Vengeance God, in turn, would take on him for 'swallowing the Righteous Teacher'*.

As the Habakkuk *Pesher* pointedly puts it, just as the Wicked Priest 'swallowed him' or 'swallowed them' (the followers of the Righteous Teacher, called 'the *Ebionim*', even though '*Ebionim*' nowhere appears as such in the underlying text at this point); so too 'would he be paid the reward which he paid the Poor', always combined with the reiteration of the idea of God's Vengeance – 'God would condemn him to destruction' – for what he had done to the

Righteous Teacher[25] This is also expressed in terms of another important genre of imagery – 'Cup' imagery, symbolizing God's retribution and which we shall elucidate further as we proceed – or '*the Cup of the Wrath of God would come around to*' or '*swallow him*' as well.

This notion of retribution is also the context of these lines applied by early Church exegetes to the death of James, 'Let us remove the Just One, for he is abhorrent to us.' Taken according to the received version, the line following this reads: 'Woe unto the Wicked. It shall be ill with him, for the Reward (*Gamul*) of his hands will be done to him' (3:11). The very same word, '*Gamul*' or '*Reward*', used in exactly the same way, is brought into the crucial description of the destruction of the Righteous Teacher in the Habakkuk *Pesher* and how the Wicked Priest, who '*plotted to destroy the Poor*', '*swallowed*' *the Righteous Teacher*.

As this is then put, '*the Reward which he paid the Poor would be paid to him*'. Here the word '*Gamul*' again comes into play, as in Isaiah 3:11 and as we saw it above in the War Scroll on '*the Poor*'. That we are, in these lines surrounding Isaiah 3:10 applied in early Church literature to the death of James, in a similar exegetical framework to that of Qumran should be patent.

The conclusion is, therefore, simple. Since this material about the Wicked '*being paid the Reward he paid*' *others* from Isaiah 3:10–11 nowhere appears in the materials from Habakkuk under consideration, it is clear that the writers at Qumran knew this material from Isaiah 3:10–11 and were incorporating it into their presentation of *the death of their 'Righteous Teacher'*. In other words, the Community of James in Jerusalem and the Community at Qumran were using *the exact same passage in exactly the same way and applying it to the destruction respectively of two leaders, James the Just and the Righteous Teacher*. One could not ask for more powerful proof of their identity than this.

James' Death in the Account of Hegesippus

As the Eusebius extract from Hegesippus finishes the account of the stoning of James the Just: 'So they went up and *cast down the Just One*, saying to one another, "Let us *stone* James the Just," and they began to stone him, since *the fall* had not killed him.'

This parallels almost completely the account in Acts of Stephen's stoning, including the very same repetitions of the words '*stoning*' and '*casting*', not to mention the tell-tale allusion to the '*fall*' James took, which reappears in both Stephen's '*falling* to his knees' and the bloody '*fall*' Judas *Iscariot* takes at the beginning of Acts.

It will be recalled that Acts' account is preceded by Stephen's verbal attack on the Jews as 'receiving the Law and not keeping it' (7:52–53) – this as part and parcel of his charge that *they 'killed all the Prophets' and were 'Traitors' because they put 'the Just One' to death*. It is interesting that just as Stephen hurls the charge of being 'uncircumcised in heart' against the Jews generally (7:51), in the Habakkuk *Pesher* this is hurled against the Wicked Priest (in the Damascus Document on Ezekiel 44:15, its root, its reversal is the basis of who '*the Sons of Zadok*' are).[26]

In looking at the description of Stephen's death again, it would be well to repeat the echo one finds there of James' words to the assembled Passover crowds about the Son of Man coming on the clouds of Heaven. The account of Stephen's last words in Acts reads:

> Looking up to Heaven, he (Stephen) saw the Glory of God and Jesus standing at the right hand of God. He *cried out*, 'Look, I see the Heavens opening and the Son of Man standing on the right hand of God. And *crying out in a loud voice*, they … rushed on him with one accord, and *casting him out* of the city, they *stoned him* … And they stoned Stephen *as he prayed* … and *falling down on his knees, he cried out in a loud voice, 'Lord, do not account this sin to them.'* (Acts 7:55–60)

For its part, Hegesippus' account of James' stoning continues as follows: 'But he turned and *fell to his knees*, saying, "I beseech You, O Lord God and Father, *forgive them, for they know not what they do*."' There are so many important overlaps in these brief descriptions of the two stonings that it is difficult to know which ones to stress more.

Where the '*casting down*' or '*falling*' goes, we shall have occasion to inspect such language further to determine whether at some point James 'was cast down' or 'fell', or both. In fact, this element probably first appears in the story of the attack by Paul on James in the Pseudoclementine *Recognitions*. The attack on James by Paul that it presents – *in the 40's not the 60's – takes the place of the attack on Stephen in the Book of Acts*, after which, even in Acts Paul is pictured as going berserk in a frenzy of riotous behavior. As the *Recognitions* vividly pictures it, this attack is a physical one too and results in the tell-tale 'fall' James takes, but this time *not his death*. The 'fall' in the allusion to James' and Stephen's death in Hegesippus and in Acts really paves the way to connecting the two attacks and sorting out some of the conflicting elements.

The 'fall' James takes 'down the Temple steps' in the 40's does not result in his death, merely injury. He is taken down to Jericho (in the region of Qumran) by his followers since he is injured and lives to fight another day. It is this that becomes confused and for various linguistic reasons, which we shall come to understand, is played upon in all the early Church accounts of James' death as they have come down to us. Even, as we have them, these accounts appreciate that James was not killed in this 'fall' – it took a stoning to do this – and even Acts' replacement account seems to conserve some of the sense of these variations by having Stephen '*fall to his knees*'. Whatever one finally makes of this, at least it preserves the curious motif of the matter of James' '*knees being as hard as a camel's hide on account of all the praying he did*'.

As the *Recognitions* puts this attack on James by *the Enemy* Paul:

> Our James began to show … that the two advents of him (Jesus) are foretold: one in humiliation, which he has accomplished; the other *in Glory* (cf. Acts 7:55's Stephen 'seeing *the Glory of God*') … And when matters were at that point … *an Enemy* (a marginal note in one of the manuscripts identifies this 'Enemy' as Paul) entered the Temple with a few others and began to *cry out* … to excite the people and raise a tumult …. Therefore he began to drive all into confusion with shouting … and like a madman, excite everyone to murder (cf. Acts 8:3). Then ensued a tumult on either side of beating and the beaten. Much blood was shed and there was a confused flight, in the midst of which *the Enemy attacked James* and *threw him headlong from the top of the steps*, and supposing him to be dead (the Syriac adds, 'since he fell'), did not care to inflict further violence upon him. But our friends lifted him up, for they were more numerous … and we returned to the house of James (the house in Jerusalem to which Peter goes to leave a message for 'James and the brothers' in Acts 12:20) and spent the night there in prayer. Then before daylight we went down to Jericho to the number of five thousand men.[27]

This is then followed by the information that *'the Enemy' received letters from the Chief Priests to go to Damascus 'to arrest all who believed in Jesus* and, with the help of Unbelievers, *throw the Faithful into confusion*' (compare with Acts 9:22's account of how Paul '*confounded the Jews who dwelt in Damascus*'), which makes it *unmistakable that it is Paul we have to do with in this account.*

This is the attack that is replaced by the stoning of Stephen in the orthodox story in Acts. In the writer's view, the 'Stephen' in Acts is a fictitious stand-in, as are quite a few other characters we have already called attention to in Acts (there will be more). It is a stand-in for the attack by Paul on James in the early 40's, which was evidently considered so embarrassing by early

Church writers that it was unmentionable – but not forgotten. *It is reconstituted with elements taken from the stoning of James*, which early Church tradition considers to have occurred in the 60's. This account in Acts, as to some extent the presentation of Jesus in the Gospels, was manufactured with an anti-Semitic patina which, over the millennia, has not failed to have its effect.

One should finish the description of James' stoning in the 60's as Eusebius has conserved it. This is found in one form or another in a variety of sources, including Manichaean ones and now Nag Hammadi. It concludes in the following manner:

> Thus they were stoning him, when *one of the Priests of the sons of Rechab, the son of those Rechabites, spoken of by Jeremiah the Prophet*, cried out, saying, 'Stop what you are doing, the Just One is praying for you.' And one among them, who was a fuller, took the club with which he beat out clothes and struck the Just One on the head .... Thus, he suffered martyrdom, and *they buried him on the spot by the Temple and his monument is still there by the Temple.... And immediately Vespasian began to besiege them.*

This then is the account of the martyrdom of James given by Eusebius, purportedly a word-for-word translation of Hegesippus. Except for mix-ups between whether James was in the Temple or Holy of Holies and regarding his bathing habits, this seems likely.

Eusebius adds the pious words, whether his own or Hegesippus': 'He became a true witness both to Jews and to Greeks that Jesus is the Christ', and then moves on, giving the relevant materials from Josephus *connecting the siege of Jerusalem and the destruction of the Temple to James' death.*

James' Burial Marker, Judas *Iscariot's Fall*, and *the Field of Blood* Again

The reference Eusebius preserves to a grave-marker or monument to James at the place 'where he fell' is interesting and not without relevance. Eusebius or his source – it is impossible to tell which – certainly considers it was still there at the time of writing. This would mean either the Second or the Fourth Century. Had Eusebius, who like Hegesippus came from Palestine, not seen it, one imagines he would have said so. Jerome does in his seemingly more precise variation on the tradition: '*His tombstone with its inscription was well known until the siege of Titus and the end of Hadrian's reign (meaning Jerome did not see it).*'[28]

Regardless of chronology, there can be little doubt that *someone saw* James' grave-marker or monument outside the Temple in the Kedron Valley at some point. This is directly beneath the Temple compound walls as one looks down from what is being called in these traditions 'the Pinnacle of the Temple'. Somehow the tradition developed that James was pushed down from here – a place too from which 'Jesus' was purportedly tempted 'by the Devil' to jump in Gospel traditions.

Today there are still funerary monuments there from the Second Temple period – one identified as 'the Tomb of St James'. The tradition identifying James' tomb with this monument at the bottom of the Mount of Olives in the Kedron Valley beneath 'the Pinnacle of the Temple' is very old and Jerome seems to know something of it by his words, 'Some of our writers think he was buried on the Mount of Olives, but they are mistaken.' The significance of this monument for the stories that developed about James' death is important. Even today, if one stands on the south-east corner of the Temple wall facing the Mount of Olives and the Kedron below, one readily sees the this monumental tomb.

From the still-legible Hebrew inscription carved on the stone within, it can be identified as the sepulcher of 'the Priestly Course of the *Bnei-Hezir*' – one of the priestly clans returning with either Ezra or Nehemiah from the Babylonian Captivity (Neh. 10:20). This in no way invalidates it as related to James' family, since the relationship of James' priestly ancestors to one priestly clan or another is impossible to determine.

Interestingly enough, the names listed in the dedicatory inscription, as it now stands, appear to be from the family known as '*the Boethusians*', so either they were of 'the *Bnei-Hezir*' or they, too, appropriated it. This is the priestly clan Herod brought in from Egypt after he executed his Maccabean wife to marry their daughter – also called Mariamme.[29] In the next generation, one Joezer b. Boethus becomes the direct opponent of Josephus' Judas and *Saddok* in the matter of the non-payment of the newly-imposed Roman tax at the time of '*the Census of Quirinius*'.

In fact, the takeover of this tomb, implied by its association with James' burial, might be the root of another highly-prized but almost certainly mythological tradition about 'Joseph of Arimathaea' donating his richly-appointed tomb *for the burial of Jesus* (Mt 27:57 and pars.). 'Joseph of Arimathaea' is another name without historical substance and the location 'Arimathaea' has never been identified.

However this may be, one can certainly envision a set of circumstances where someone conversant with the tradition about James' '*fall*', looking down on the Kedron Valley monumental tomb from the walls of the compound of the Temple, might have imagined the tomb – so clearly visible below – implied that James took this fabulous '*fall*' from '*the Pinnacle of the Temple*', when in reality he only '*fell headlong down the Temple steps*' *during the attack by 'the Enemy' Paul.* A '*fall*' from the Pinnacle, of course, few could have survived, which is the thrust of its transmogrification into the story of 'Jesus'' Temptation by the Devil in Matthew and Luke.

The element about James' '*headlong fall*' also reappears, as already remarked, in the story about the '*headlong fall*' that Judas *Iscariot* – another largely mythological character with a curious surname – supposedly takes in the Book of Acts, accompanied by its own suitably bloodthirsty details. This, too, was connected with some kind of burial ground. Called 'the Field of Blood' in Acts and Matthew, the latter also identifies it as 'the Potter's Field', a field supposedly 'for the burial of strangers' or possibly even 'the Poor'. Interestingly enough, as we saw, it is connected to 'Rechabite' priestly traditions, and by extrapolation, 'the Essenes'.

It will be recalled that the story was told at the beginning of Acts as part of the 'election' scenario to explain why it was necessary to fill the 'Episcopate' of Judas and the defeated candidate was called 'Justus' even in Greek (1:23). Having 'bought a field out of the reward for Unrighteousness, he *fell headlong* and *bursting open, all his bowels gushed out.*' Not only is the parallel with the '*head-long fall*, *James took, down the Temple steps* when attacked *by 'the Enemy' Paul* in the Pseudoclementines clear, but the one he took *from the Pinnacle of the Temple*, where his head *burst open* from the blow of the fuller's club, should be too.

Once again, we are in the area of fictional refurbishment. Even though these are some of our most cherished cultural heirlooms, the overwritten original elements do, on careful inspection, shine through. What originally was in the underlying material is impossible to say with precision, only *something about the election of James as successor in the Leadership of the Community combined with intimations of what was later to befall him.* As already stressed, all materials having a bearing on the family of Jesus, the brothers, or namesakes of anyone connected family-wise to the Messianic Leader, must be treated with the utmost circumspection.

For instance, in this tradition, instead of the curious material about 'a fuller' with his club, we now have an interesting parallel allusion to 'Potters', even though 'the Potter's Field', as such, nowhere appears in the original Prophecy being cited in Matthew – whether from Jeremiah or Zechariah. Both this 'fuller' and this 'Field' are connected in some manner either to death or a burial place. This is not to mention the whole matter of 'the Rechabites', to whom both traditions in some sense also relate.

Then there is the notice, also supposed to relate to this 'Prophecy', about coins both being 'thrown' into the Temple Treasury and rejected from it. The last is one of the principal themes of this period, and something we shall have occasion to identify with James' name as well, that is, *the rejection of gifts and sacrifices on behalf of foreigners in the Temple*, the issue that finally started the *War against Rome.*

Those who reject moneys and gifts such as this are the more '*Zealot' lower priesthood*, the same individuals who want to *ban Gentiles – including Herodians – from the Temple as polluting it.* Not only does this become a principal theme leading up to the Uprising, but we have identified it as being at the root of one of the 'Three Nets of Belial' accusations in the Fifth Column of the Damascus Document. Even the specific charge of 'polluting the Temple Treasury' occurs in the exposition of this 'pollution of the Temple' charge in the Sixth Column. Parallels of this kind, if not finally decisive, are none the less extremely persuasive.

Furthermore, if James can be identified as more than simply parallel to 'the Teacher of Righteousness' at Qumran, but *actually identical with him*, then the 'Three Nets' of 'Riches', 'fornication' – both paralleled in known materials about James – and 'pollution of the Temple' become prototypically his. In fact, his prohibition of 'things sacrificed to idols' or 'the pollutions of the idols' in Acts 15:20–29's formulation of the results of 'the Jerusalem Council' – which we shall also show to be at the root of the *MMT* correspondence – can be seen as being but one important aspect of the more over-arching '*pollution of the Temple*' charge.

In explaining this '*pollution*' charge, the Damascus Document invokes the issue of '*blood*', in this instance *menstrual blood* and the consonant charge of *sleeping with women in their periods.*[30] It uses this, not only to link the 'fornication' with the '*pollution of the Temple*' charge, but in doing so, to imply that it is contact with Gentiles, in this case, their gifts and sacrifices in the Temple, that has occasioned the problem of 'pollution of the Temple' in the first place. As the Damascus Document so graphically expresses it in Columns Five and Eight, enlarging on the issues of 'fornication' and 'pollution of the Temple Treasury', '*whoever approaches them cannot be cleansed ... unless he was forced*' – in our view, in this case implying approaching Herodians and other foreigners.[31] But Matthew identifies his '*Field of Blood*'/'*Potter's Field*' in some manner with Gentiles or foreigners too.

The common element in Matthew's and Luke's accounts, this 'Field of Blood' has interesting parallels in the literature of Qumran as well – that is, the 'City of Blood' or 'Assembly built upon Blood' allusions encountered in two separate contexts in the Nahum *Pesher* and the Habakkuk *Pesher*. In the former it involves the sending of emissaries or '*Apostles to the Peoples*'; while in the latter, the '*City of Blood*' is accompanied by 'building' metaphors and is interpreted, in turn, in terms of *'leading Many astray' and 'performing a Worthless Service' and 'raising a Congregation upon Lying' – identified with 'the Lying Spouter''s doctrine.*[32]

In perhaps our boldest attempt at achieving a synthesis between the Community of James and the Community at Qumran, we have identified these kinds of allusions in the Habakkuk *Pesher* with Paul's '*building a Church' upon 'Communion' or the 'consumption of the Blood of Christ*'. As Luke puts it in his version of the Last Supper, '*This Cup is the New Covenant in my Blood, even that which is poured out for you*' (22:20).

Not only is the idea of '*pouring out*' integrally connected with the Pauline idea of '*the Holy Spirit*' in the Book of Acts, but where connections involving plays on language and doctrines at Qumran are concerned, '*the New Covenant*' is an important aspect of what is going on in the wilderness at '*Damascus*' in the Document by that name and '*pouring out' is the root of the way Qumran is referring to 'the Spouter of Lying*' – which quite literally means, '*the Pourer-out of Lying*'. We shall take one final step more in this regard when we show that even the word 'Damascus' in Greek (of '*the New Covenant in the Land of Damascus*' at Qumran) is being utilized by Paul or these Gospel artificers in some esoteric manner to produce the new formulation, *'the Cup of the New Covenant in my Blood' – 'Blood'* and *'Cup'* being in Hebrew, as we shall see, *'Dam'* and *'Chos'*.

It is in this same Letter to the Corinthians that Paul not only ranges himself against James' 'Jerusalem Council' directives prohibiting the consumption of 'blood' and 'things sacrificed to idols', but first develops this idea of 'Communion with the Blood of Christ', however repugnant such a notion might have seemed to such 'Zealot'-minded groups as those at Qumran, not to mention James *who specifically forbids it.* It is this doctrine that is retrospectively attributed to Jesus in these highly prized scriptural accounts of the 'Last Supper'. If anything proves the dictum, referred to in the Introduction, *'Poetry is truer than History'*, then this does.

Paul also develops this idea of *'Communion with the Blood of Christ'* by using *'building'* imagery – at one point, as we have seen, even calling himself *'the architect'* (1 Cor. 3:10). In the Nahum *Pesher*, a variation of this *'City of Blood'* notation is developed in terms of a *'City of Ephraim'* and 'those Seeking Smooth Things at the End of Days, who walk in Lying and Unrighteousness'.[33] The imagery is complex, but none the less not undecipherable. Once again, we have come full circle – *'the City built upon Blood' relating to Paul's understanding of the death of Christ and the 'Fellowship' or 'Communion' (he stresses) engendered by the Blood of Christ.*

Here too, then, this 'Field of Blood' allusion has its overtones, not all completely straightforward and some esoteric, but none-the-less part and parcel of the overlaps, plays on words, and doctrinal reversals in the interests of the ongoing Gentile Christian and anti-Semitic (in the national, not necessarily the ethnic sense) polemic.

The Trials of Jesus and James for Blasphemy or Political Conspiracy

In these kinds of parallels to the *'headlong fall'* Judas *Iscariot* takes, one should remark the parody his suicide embodies of *that carried out by the 'Sicarii' followers of Judas the Galilean on Masada three years after the fall of Jerusalem* – not to mention, *the implied condemnation of this earlier 'Judas'.* Contrariwise, in the Letter of James, *Abraham's willingness to sacrifice his son Isaac* – not unlike what these extreme *'Sicarii'* did on Masada and 'Zealot' practice generally – might have been seen as *the ideological license for such a 'suicide' or 'Sanctification of the Name'(Kiddush ha-Shem)/ martyrdom.*

In James, it is taken as the supreme testing of the *'Faith'* of this archetypal *'Friend of God'* and the epitome of the most elevated sort of *'works Righteousness'* (2:21). *Par contra*, in the more Pauline-like Hebrews, it is taken as the most elevated example of Abraham's *'Faith'* (11:17).

The conspiratorial note, also part and parcel of this account of Judas' *'Treachery'* and that of *'blasphemy'*, repeatedly reiterated in the Gospels' scenario for Jesus' trial, are also present in the James scenario. In the case of James, the cast of characters is slightly different – the 'conspiracy' being between Ananus and the King Herod Agrippa II. This same sense of 'the Wicked Priest conspiring to destroy the Poor' is also present in the Habakkuk *Pesher*, that is, between the Herodian King and the High Priest appointed by him, not between 'the Chief Priests' and the largely mythological 'Judas *Iscariot*' – whose name has now become proverbial for 'Treachery' – of Gospel narration.

John 18:1 even brings the Kedron Valley, in which the tomb beneath the Pinnacle of the Temple assigned by 'Christian' tradition to James is located, into this arrest scene. Where Acts 1:12 is concerned, the Mount of Olives is 'a Sabbath's distance' from Jerusalem which was probably meant to show that 'Jesus' did not go beyond 'the Sabbath limit'. Since the Mount of Olives is about a fifteen-minute walk from the East-facing Gate of the Temple or 'the Steps' leading up to the Gate on the South side of the compound; this vividly illustrates the derivative nature of the narrative, showing familiarity with the dictum, known in both Rabbinic literature and at Qumran, that 'the Sabbath limit' was about half a mile.

One should note that in the material prefacing Matthew's picture of Judas' suicide, now it is the High Priest who tries to *identify 'the Christ' with 'the Son of God'* (26:63 and pars.). It is at this point that Jesus, like James in Hegesippus, announces to him and the rest of the Sanhedrin that *'You shall see the Son of Man sitting at the right hand of Power and coming on the clouds of Heaven'* (26:64). For Luke, the question is, *'are you then the Son of God'* and Jesus' reply is: *'the Son of Man'* (regardless of the difficulties, we have already signaled regarding this expression) *is simply 'seated at the right hand of the Power of God'* (22:69–70).

It is at this point that the High Priest 'rends his clothes' and accuses Jesus of '*blasphemy*'. Consulting the Chief Priests and the members of the Sanhedrin *assembled at 'his House' in the middle of the night*, together these *pronounce him 'worthy of death'* (Mt 26:65–66/Mk 14:64). But this is the same sequence of the scenario of James' proclamation in the Temple of '*the Son of Man standing on the right hand of the Great Power*' and his condemnation for '*blasphemy*' by the Sanhedrin convened by the High Priest. On these points there would appear to be overlaps between the two narratives and elements of the 'Jesus' narrative are being absorbed into that of James or *vice versa* – probably *vice versa.*

If James really did go into the Holy of Holies of the Temple to pronounce the Holy Name of God in a kind of *Yom Kippur* atonement – the basis of the charge of '*blasphemy*' in the *Talmud*– such a charge more suits the circumstances of James' stoning, the punishment for blasphemy, than it does the crucifixion of Jesus. For Roman juridical practice, crucifixion is one of the punishments for insurrection and has little, if anything, to do with blasphemy. Typically, in the Synoptics anyhow, 'Jesus' is pictured as remaining silent and refusing to answer – except for small, annoying responses – any questions about the basically parallel 'Son of Man'/'Christ'/'Son of God' notations.

The parallels do not end here. Matthew continues: *'They spat in his face, beat on him, and some struck him with the palm of the hand'* (instead of '*with the laundryman's club*' – Matt. 26:67 and pars.). This is immediately followed by materials about Jesus being '*a Galilean*' and '*a Nazoraean*' (Mt 26:69–71 – in Mk 14:70/Lk 22:69 it is *Peter*, rather, who is *mistaken for* '*a Galilean*'), Judas' suicide and the High Priests buying 'the Potter's Field', and the interview with Pilate.

Appropriately, in line with the punishment of crucifixion for '*sedition*' not stoning for '*blasphemy*', after the intervening episode of what to purchase with Judas *Iscariot*'s '*hire*' in Matthew; the twin issues of Jesus' Kingship and whether it is Lawful to pay the tribute money to Caesar are raised. In Luke, who adds this second part of the charge sheet, this reads: 'We found this man perverting our nation, *forbidding* (*the nation*) *to give tribute to Caesar* and *claiming himself to be Christ, a King'* (23:2). This charge about *'forbidding to pay the tax to Caesar'* – aside from the related one about '*claiming to be a King*' – is completely surprising as the Gospels go to such lengths to portray 'Jesus' as recommending just the opposite (Luke 20:22–25 and pars.). In our view, *forbidding the people to pay the tax* in this charge sheet in Luke was the *authentic* position of '*the Messianic Movement in Palestine*' and all its *bona-fide* representatives, there being *no Messianism in Palestine that recognized the Roman Emperor.*

Pilate is now pictured asking whether Jesus was 'King of the Jews' (Mt 27:11 and pars.), a question appropriate to the crucifixion penalty for '*sedition*' that ensues. If Jesus was or did claim to be 'a King', in particular without Roman authorization, the implication is that this was a treasonable offence. For Luke, Herod even asks if Jesus is 'a Galilean' (23:6), clearly meaning – since we have just been talking about *the tax issue* – someone of the stripe of Judas the *Galilean.* Pilate interprets this to mean Jesus *comes from Galilee* – a point Luke now uses to move over to an intervening interview with 'Herod', missing from the other Gospels, because the administrative jurisdiction of this 'Herod' included Galilee!

Theoretically, the 'Herod' who interviews Jesus is the same *Herod the Tetrarch* (Herod Antipas) who condemned John the Baptist in a similar scenario because he, also, had administrative jurisdiction across Jordan in Perea on the Eastern side of the Dead Sea. There now follows the material in Matthew 27:19–24 about Pilate wishing 'nothing to do with' or being 'guiltless of the blood of this Righteous One', which, again, has more to do with the nomenclature of the James story than that of 'Jesus'. This episode culminates in that terrible cry in Matthew 27:25 that has haunted Western Civilization ever since: '*His blood* be upon us *and on our children*'.

But the ultimate reason behind all these feints and sleights-of-hand is simple. Josephus straightforwardly presents it when he states in his Preface to the *Jewish War* (to repeat):

> The War of the Jews against the Romans was the greatest of our time, greater too, perhaps than any recorded struggle whether between cities or nations. Yet persons with *no first-hand knowledge*, accepting baseless and inconsistent stories on hearsay, have written garbled accounts of it; while those of *eyewitnesses have been falsified either to flatter the Romans* or *to vilify the Jews* – eulogy or abuse being substituted for accurate historical record.

One could not wish for a more prescient comment historically-speaking and it essentially sums up the situation regarding historical writing in this period – this in a Preface, in which Josephus otherwise claims that: 'The Romans *unwillingly set fire to the Temple* ... as Titus Caesar, *the Temple's destroyer* has testified. For throughout the war, he (Titus) *pitied the common people*, *who were helpless against the Revolutionaries* ... *And for our misfortunes we have only ourselves to blame*.'

Josephus' picture of the Romans '*unwillingly setting fire to the Temple*' matches the Gospel picture of Roman Governors and their Herodian minions *unwillingly condemning Christian Leaders to death*. To make the parallel even more immediate, one has only to remember that, in the Gospels, '*Jesus*' *is the Temple*![34]

These are the kinds of insights that can emerge from looking at the parallels in a seemingly inconsequential story like that of the '*headlong fall*' Judas *Iscariot* supposedly takes and how his stomach '*burst open*' and comparing it with that of the story of the '*headlong fall*' James takes in early Church sources either from the Pinnacle of the Temple or its steps.

The reason we opt for the historicity of the James materials (with reservations) over the Gospels is that they are more consistent and *make more sense in their historical context*. It is that simple – *historical sense can be made out of them*, which is more than can be said for the story of 'Judas *Iscariot*'s stomach bursting open' or, for that matter, the story of Jesus being condemned by the High Priest for 'blasphemy' and taken for 'a Righteous One' – first by Pontius Pilate's wife and then by Pilate himself.

This is the same Pilate, whom Philo of Alexandria records in his Mission to Gaius (37 CE), was the most blood-thirsty among the Governors in Palestine. This is quite bizarre since Pilate was removed on this account in disgrace by – of all people – the equally blood-thirsty and insane Caligula. The testimony about the attack on James in the Temple and James' '*fall*' is extremely important and *makes sense*, that is, elements from it can be fitted into the historical background of Palestine and what we know from other sources from this period and they mesh. Before going on to resolve those elements which do not make sense and which are either overwrites, garbled tradition, or out-and-out fraud, it is important to remark that these stories about 'Judas *Iscariot*', 'Stephen', 'Mary the mother of John Mark', 'John the brother of James' – often even 'Jesus' himself – make the material relating to James' death, his being buried on the spot where he 'fell' (connecting with 'the Potters Field'/'Field of Blood' above story about 'Judas'), very old indeed.

If we accept the basic core of historicity in them – and there is a lot to accept in Hegesippus' materials paralleled by those in the Pseudoclementine *Recognitions* and what remains of the lost *Anabathmoi Jacobou* from Epiphanius' excerpts, regardless of how these have been transmogrified or garbled in the accounts by Clement of Alexandria, Origen,

Eusebius, Jerome, and the two Apocalypses of James from Nag Hammadi – then we have to accept a central core of material about James, together with its tell-tale notices about a *'fall'* of some kind, his proclamation of *'the Son of Man coming on the clouds of Heaven'* in the Temple at Passover, the charge of *'blasphemy'*, his *'stoning'*, and the various allusions to *'the Righteous One'*, *'his knees'*, the *'efficaciousness of his prayer'*, and his *'falling to his knees and praying'*, at least as old as the earliest redactions of Gospel accounts and the Book of Acts. These latter contain the same or parallel materials about their heroes or, sometimes, their enemies.

The traditions about James, therefore, were known and had already begun to be overwritten at least by the time of the *earliest appearance of parallel materials* now in the New Testament documents we are so familiar with and which have become cornerstones of Western culture. When was this? Dare we say probably before 100 CE? Justin Martyr, for instance, who was born in Samaria but afterwards lived in Asia Minor, by the 130's appears to know many Gospel traditions and stories, particularly those of Matthew and Luke – which he calls 'the Memoirs of the Apostles', but not exactly in the form we have them. However, he shows little, if any, knowledge of the Book of Acts. Nor does he mention Paul's name at all, though he does have a quasi-parallel theology. Justin, for instance, knows Isaiah 3:10 in the *Septuagint* version above, *'Let us bind the Just One, for he is abhorrent to us'*; but, interestingly enough, he is already applying it to *'Jesus''* death not *James'*.[35]

Left: Steps at the Southern Wall of the Temple, where James perhaps debated with the Temple Authorities, and where Paul, aided by the Roman Chief Captain, addressed the crowd.

Right: The pinnacle of the Temple, from which James is said to have been 'cast down'.

Chapter 15
The Death of James in Its Historical Setting

The Stoning of James in Other Early Church Sources

Eusebius goes on to present the passages from Josephus relating to James' trial and execution, as well as those which connect the fate of Jerusalem to his execution. These materials for the most part do exist in the Josephus we have and, if authentic – which they appear to be – really do give proof of the impact James was having in the Jerusalem of his day and, it seems, thereafter, till the time of Josephus' writing at the beginning of the 90s.

Before going on to examine additional material Eusebius provides, we should compare the Hegesippus passages in Eusebius to parallel notices in Clement, Epiphanius, the two Apocalypses of James from Nag Hammadi, and Jerome. Eusebius more or less sums up what Clement of Alexandria in the latter part of the Second Century knows about the traditions regarding James' death as follows: 'But as to the manner of James' death … in the words of Clement, "He was cast (*beblesthai*) from the Pinnacle and beaten to death with a club."' This doesn't differ from Hegesippus, who wrote some twenty or more years earlier.

Epiphanius does not add much more. He corrects Eusebius' version of James' activities in the Temple, making it clear he went into 'the Holy of Holies', as he puts it, 'once a year', where he prayed on his knees till they became 'hard as camel's hide from his continued kneeling before God out of his excessive Piety' – an obvious description of a '*Yom Kippur*' atonement. Epiphanius is obsessed with James' age: 'he also died a virgin at the age of ninety-six',[1] which, as in the case of the age of Simeon Bar Cleophas succeeding him – 'one hundred and twenty years', according to Hegesippus – can be viewed as simply recapitulating Josephus' contention about how 'long-lived' those he is calling 'Essenes' were. For Epiphanius, James reigned in Jerusalem for 'twenty-four years after the Assumption of Jesus', which, if Josephus' dating of James' death is correct, would place 'Jesus'' crucifixion in 38 CE, approximately the year Josephus assigns to the execution of *John the Baptist*.

When it comes to James' death, Epiphanius basically repeats Eusebius' presentation, though the language is even more that of the attack on James by Paul in the 40's, as per the Pseudoclementine *Recognitions*:

> A certain fuller beat his head in with a club, *after he had been thrown headlong from the Pinnacle of the Temple* and *cast down*. But having done no wrong at all, *he fell to his knees* and *prayed for those who had thrown him down*, entreating God with the words, 'Forgive them, for they know not what they do.'

Not only do we have the 'casting down' language again here (repeated three times), but the reiteration of the 'being thrown headlong', seemingly from the Pseudoclementine *Recognitions*' account of Paul's attack on James on 'the steps of the Temple' in the 40's. The '*falling to his knees and praying*' is, of course, part and parcel of Acts' presentation of Stephen and his prayer.

But Epiphanius adds new material: 'Thus, even Simeon bar Cleophas, his cousin, who was *standing* not far away, said, "Stop, why are you stoning the Just One? Behold, he is praying the most wonderful prayers for you."'[2]

Aside from another of these tell-tale allusions to '*standing*', again one has here '*the Just One*' epithet used in place of James' name and the crucial emphasis on 'praying'. But now, in place of Eusebius' '*one of the Priests of the Sons of Rechab*', one has the startling reference to James' '*cousin*', Simeon bar Cleophas.

Should we credit this tradition? It is extremely original and there is nothing to counter-indicate it. Nor does it create a wrench in the historical processes as we have been documenting them. But where did such a tradition come from and why isn't it in Eusebius? There is no way of knowing, except that Epiphanius' information in general is richer and fuller than Eusebius', even though he is not quite so meticulous in quotation and/or citing of his sources.

Like his contemporary Jerome who, not surprisingly, dislikes him personally, Epiphanius is prepared to conflate various sources. But he does give more accurate information than Eusebius about James *actually entering the Holy of Holies to make an atonement* and a wealth of additional material about James' 'Naziritism', vegetarianism, sexual abstinence, and the like. He also has vastly superior material about the sectarian situation in Palestine generally and the '*Primal Adam*' ideology, in particular. For instance, under his description of the Ebionites, he says:

> For some of them say *Christ is Adam, the First created* ... *a Spirit higher than the Angels and Lord of all* ... He comes here when he chooses, *as when he came in Adam* ... *He came also in the Last Days, put on Adam's body, appeared to men, was crucified, resurrected, and ascended* ... but also, they say ... *the Spirit which is Christ came into him and* put on the Man who is called 'Jesus'.[3]

This doctrine seems more and more accurately to describe the incarnations of this period.

Suppose we were to say that, by 'Rechabite', Eusebius was trying to say something similar to 'Essene', 'Nazirite', or 'Ebionite'; then out of this band of 'Essene' or 'Ebionite Priests', one, James' 'cousin' and successor, Simeon bar Cleophas, emerged as the next '*Bishop of the Jerusalem Community*' (only, after the fall of the Temple and Jerusalem, there clearly was no longer any '*Jerusalem Community*' to speak of in Palestine).

Suppose too that, instead of any of these vocabularies, we were to use one more familiar to modern ears – especially since the discoveries of the Dead Sea Scrolls – the Qumran 'Priests' or '*Sons of Zadok*'. For Epiphanius, James is a '*Nazirite*' Priest with an obviously even greater concern for purity matters than usual. Now our sources begin to *mesh absolutely*. We shall have more to say about Simeon bar Cleophas when we treat the subject of 'Jesus' Brothers as Apostles' below, but for the time being it might be well to entertain the implications of both accounts, that the witness to this stoning was *both 'a Rechabite Priest' and James' 'cousin'* without attempting to determine where the material came from (probably Hegesippus).

In the story of the stoning of Stephen from Acts 7:58–8:1, the 'witness' becomes James' (and presumably Simeon's) ideological adversary *Paul*. As Acts puts it, after describing how 'having cast him out of the city, they stoned him': 'And *the witnesses* put down *their clothes at the feet of a young man Saul.* And *they stoned Stephen as he was praying* (repeated a second time) ... And Saul consented to putting him to death'.

The '*clothes*' theme is an important one, as in the traditions about James we have the reiteration of the type of '*clothes*' he wears, but there is also the play on the special linen bath-clothing the Essenes wore generally and now the additional implied play on the '*laundryman beating out clothes*' in the picture of James' death. What are we to make of these curious usages and overlaps? How else can sense be made of such senseless survivals from earlier traditions? Why would the witnesses lay 'their clothes' anywhere when, according to Talmudic tradition, it is the condemned individual who was to undress?

However this may be, once again, in line with the mirror reversals we find in this literature, Paul takes the place of his opposite number, James' successor in Palestine, Simeon bar Cleophas – the only difference being that, while one approves of what was done, the other disapproves. We shall have more to say about interesting juxtapositions such as this presently, but before attempting to resolve some of the contradictions and *non sequiturs* in this account, we should take a look at two other sources: the two Apocalypses of James and Jerome's account.

The Stoning of James at Nag Hammadi

In the First Apocalypse of James from Nag Hammadi, an oracle to 'leave Jerusalem' is attributed to Jesus. In early Christian usage, the 'Pella Flight Tradition' is attributed to James or occurs either consonant with or as a consequence of his death.[4] Throughout this First Apocalypse, not only do we have repeated reference to the 'seizing' found in these early Church accounts of the death of James, but also the omnipresent use of the language of 'casting down' or 'casting out', which also occurs in the Second Apocalypse.

The Second Apocalypse of James is more straightforward, containing many of the details of James' death with which we have already become familiar in these early Church accounts. In its picture, James is standing not '*on the Pinnacle*' but, as in the Pseudoclementines, '*on the steps of the Temple*' – in this instance '*the fifth flight*' – whether to deliver his 'discourses', or the speech in Hegesippus, or as part of '*Ascents*' of some other kind, is not completely clear (45:24).

By far the most interesting material in the Second Apocalypse comes in the first place, at the beginning with the reference to '*Theuda* ('*Theudas*'?), *the relative of the Just One*', who basically takes the place of the individual referred to as '*Addai*' ('*Thaddaeus*'?) in the First Apocalypse and, at the end of the Apocalypse, with the narrative of *the stoning of 'the Just One'*. It contains many colorful new details which are, certainly, not all reliable, but they show how vibrant and alive this tradition about James' stoning was in the East in the Second and Third Centuries.

After a reference to the coming destruction of the Temple and to 'the judges taking counsel' (60:20–25), it reads as follows: 'On that day, the whole people and the crowd were getting stirred up and appeared to be disagreeing with each other; and he arose, after speaking in this way and departed. But he entered again the same day and spoke for a few hours (this appears to parallel the debates on the Temple steps, as recounted in the Pseudoclementine *Recognitions*, which has James' departing after his first speech only to return again the next day). And I was with the Priests, but I did not reveal our kinship.'

It is difficult to understand who this narrator can be other than Simeon bar Cleophas, the witness to the stoning of James in Epiphanius' version of Hegesippus – either him or a reference of some kind to the '*kinship*' of James and Jesus. The mention of 'Priests' is interesting in view of the reference to James' Disciple 'Mareim' (which so parallels the female names of 'Mariamme' or 'Mary' elsewhere) at the beginning of the Apocalypse as being 'one of the Priests' and the whole issue of the relationship of Rechabite/Nazirite/Essene Priests to those in the Temple generally. It also links up with the peculiar notice in the Book of Acts of *a large number of Priests having made their conversion*. The '*kinship*', then, is either between James and Jesus or Simeon bar Cleophas and James – even perhaps Jude and James – it is difficult to decide which.

The Second Apocalypse continues: 'For all of them were crying out in unison, "*Come, let us stone the Just One.*" And they arose, saying, "Yes, let us put this man to death, that he will be taken from out of our midst, *for he is abhorrent to us*."' But, of course, this is almost a word-for-word quotation from the account of Hegesippus, including even the citation from Isaiah 3:10, '*Let us remove the Just One, for he is abhorrent to us*' (according to the Septuagint version) now molded into the very narrative itself, 'and when they came out, they found him *standing on the Pinnacle of the Temple beside the firm Cornerstone.*'

The '*Cornerstone*' allusion attached to this episode about James' death is a new element, but not a completely surprising one. The imagery of '*Stone*' and '*Cornerstone*' is part and parcel of that applied to the Disciples in early Christianity and omnipresent in the Dead Sea Scrolls as we have seen. It is interesting, too, that in the Epistle of Barnabas the imagery of the '*firm Cornerstone*' is linked to the quotation of this same Isaiah 3:10 passage above.[5] There can be little doubt that what we now have here in this Apocalypse is the picture of *James standing on the Temple Pinnacle* or *possibly the Temple balustrade*, common to all these early Church accounts.

The text then reads: 'And they were bent upon *throwing him down* from that height. And *they cast him down*.' As in Epiphanius' and Eusebius' version of Hegesippus, the '*casting down*' language is repeated *twice*. Unfortunately, there now follows a short lacuna in the text and, though one would like to know what is missing, the narrative then resumes with a completely new twist: 'And they ... seized him (this clearly after his '*fall*') and (struck) him as they dragged him on the ground. They stretched him apart and *placed a stone on his stomach* (this '*placing a stone on his stomach*' reflects Talmudic parameters for stoning), *which they all kicked with their feet*, saying, "*You have gone astray*."'

Not only do we have here the allusion to 'being misled' or 'erring' that one has in Hegesippus, but one assumes that what was meant here was the accusation of '*blasphemy*' regarding James, lost somewhat in translation, though the sense of theological error is present. Our writer now, of course, fairly runs away with himself in blood-thirsty enthusiasm:

> Again, they raised him up since he was still alive. They made him dig a hole. Then they made him stand in it. After they covered him up to his stomach, they stoned him in this way (all this is truly original, but, except in so far as it reproduces Talmudic parameters for stoning, one can assume, more or less apocryphal). But he stretched forth his hands, *saying the following prayer*, which he was accustomed to saying.

We are now in familiar terrain again, including the element of '*praying*'. We shall treat this gruesome account of their making him dig a pit and placing a stone on James' stomach further below. Once again, these last have to do with refracted Talmudic accounts of such procedures.

The prayer that is given is not the 'Forgive them Father, for they know not what they do', but rather an entirely original, more Gnosticizing, one. One can imagine that this prayer was recited in the Community that produced this account in commemoration of what it thought James said when he was stoned. It is a totally original 'discourse' and may be one of the '*discourses*' he was said to have '*given Mareim*' at the beginning of the Apocalypse or something from Epiphanius' *Anabathmoi Jacobou*. In kind, though not in subject, it is not so different from the discourse attributed to James in the debates on the Temple steps in the Pseudoclementine *Recognitions* before he was '*cast down headlong*' by '*the Enemy*' Paul.

Its main emphasis is on asking for 'Grace', 'Salvation', and 'resurrection'. Interestingly enough, it uses the language of 'Strength', so associated with James in the other sources, and of 'Light', 'Power', and 'being saved' – the last phraseology prominent in the description of the destruction of the Righteous Teacher in the Habakkuk *Pesher* at Qumran.[6] Even more interestingly, there is the tell-tale reference to the 'Enemy', that appears in the Pseudoclementine account of the attack on James by Paul.[7]

The Importance of James in Jerome

The material about the stoning of James in Jerome, though derivative and clearly abbreviated, is equally interesting. This is not only because of the prominence Jerome accords both James *and* Jude, but because of the way Jerome combines sources and finally introduces new – and in fact crucial – material that will eventually show the way towards a synthesis of *all our sources.*

We have already seen how in his Commentary on Paul's famous testimony to James in Galatians, Jerome supplies the additional piece of information that '*so Holy was James that the People tried to touch the fringes of his garment' as he passed by*. For Jerome, James is second in importance only to Simon Peter; and Jude, whom he identifies (as in the Letter attributed to his name) as '*the brother of James*', he places fourth after Matthew – even before Paul, whom he places fifth. Jerome is writing about 'famous' or 'illustrious writers' in the history of the Church up to his time, among whom he includes – notably – the non-Christians Philo, Seneca, and Josephus as eleventh to thirteenth respectively. In this work, *Lives of Illustrious Men*, treating one hundred and thirty-five persons from Simon Peter onwards, *the section on James is the longest except for Origen.*

Beginning once again with James' cognomen, '*the Just One*', Jerome allows Joseph as his father. However, like his sometime acquaintance Epiphanius, he continues the theme of *a second mother*, only adding the preposterous *Mary 'the sister of' her own sister Mary* of the Gospel of John as his candidate.[8] He goes on to give most of the details regarding James' person and life, we have already encountered in other sources, most notably his view that James '*was immediately appointed Bishop of Jerusalem by the Apostles after our Lord's Passion*'. 'Immediately' is the operative word here, which echoes the position of the Pseudoclementine *Recognitions* on this point, only for him James '*ruled the Church at Jerusalem for thirty years*', while for Epiphanius above it was only '*twenty-four*'.

He quotes Hegesippus on James' Naziritism (he 'was Holy from his mother's womb'), i.e., his abstention from strong drink, meat, anointment with oil, shaving, etc. He insists he wore *only linen, not 'woolen clothes'*. Here is the omnipresent theme of '*clothing*' again. In addition, there is the one of his being 'on his knees' and 'praying' and how 'his knees were reputed to be of the hardness of camels' knees' because of all the praying he did, i.e., '*He alone enjoyed the privilege of entering the Holy of Holies … and went into the Temple alone and prayed on behalf of the people, to such a degree that his knees were reputed to have acquired the calluses of a camel's knees.*' But in this he agrees with Epiphanius, whom he considered 'an old fool', not Eusebius. To arrive at the picture of a perfect *Yom Kippur* '*atonement*', one has only to substitute the phraseology: '*he went into the Holy of Holies alone*' – not the Temple.

Jerome presents a version of the stoning and death of James which is obviously derived from what he saw in both the no longer extant Sixth Book of Clement of Alexandria's *Institutions* and in the Fifth Book of Hegesippus' *Commentaries*. What is new in his account is that he combines this with the testimony from the Twentieth Book of Josephus' *Antiquities* – as Eusebius also tried to do – which Jerome claims was also present in the Seventh Book of Clement's *Institutions*. This is a new claim, the veracity of which it is impossible to measure. To do so, it would be useful to quote at length what Josephus actually said in his famous testimony to James with which he, more or less, brings his *Antiquities* to a close.

Before doing so, however, one should recall that Jerome claimed that: '*This same Josephus records the tradition that this James was of so great Holiness and reputation among the people that the destruction of Jerusalem was believed to have occurred on account of his death*' – this, in addition to his claim, we have already quoted above, that 'so great a reputation did James have for Holiness' among the people of Jerusalem that, like the Rabbinic tradition about Honi's 'grandson', *they used to try to 'touch the fringes of his clothing' as he walked by.*

It is interesting that Jerome also emphasizes the claim that James was an 'Apostle' in his note about Josephus as a writer. He phrases this as follows: 'In the Eight(eenth) Book of his *Antiquities*, he (Josephus) most openly acknowledges *that Christ was put to death by the Pharisees on account of his great miracles, that John the Baptist was truly a Prophet, and that Jerusalem was destroyed because of the murder of James the Apostle.*' It should now be becoming clear that, very early on, even serious-minded Churchmen were reckoning 'Jesus'' brother James as an 'Apostle.' What is also interesting here is that Jerome finally actually reveals just where, in his view, this testimony about *Jerusalem falling because of the death of James* came from in Josephus' works – *Book Eighteen* of his *Antiquities*, two books earlier than the normative description of *the death of James.*

Of course, the testimonies about John and Jesus are in Book Eighteen, but not as Jerome presents them. For instance, it is not specifically stated 'that Christ was slain by the Pharisees on account of his great miracles', nor that Josephus considered John 'a Prophet', at least not in the testimony to John as it presently stands in Josephus' *Antiquities.* But Jerome is a careful scholar. One must assume that he saw something of what he says. Perhaps the nonsense 'Paulina and Fulvia' episodes that follow the suspicious-sounding account of the crucifixion of Christ in Book Eighteen replaced some more extensive commentary of the kind Jerome says he saw there, an account which included the material about *Jerusalem falling 'because of the death of James the Apostle' not 'Jesus'*.

In his biographical note about James, Jerome also mentions Paul's testimony to seeing James in Jerusalem in Galatians 1:19, which, he claims, 'even the Acts of the Apostles bear witness to'. However, he does not note that the two accounts are in almost total contradiction. He also presents material about James from a no-longer-extant apocryphal Gospel – not Thomas but one he calls *'the Gospel according to the Hebrews'*. Not only does Jerome claim that 'Origen, too, often made use' of this Gospel but, like Eusebius in matters of import, he quotes the relevant passage relating to a first post-Resurrection appearance by Jesus to James. This, he personally claims to have 'translated into Greek and Latin' from the Hebrew.[9]

This tradition from the Gospel of the Hebrews relates to the missing tradition of *a first appearance by 'Jesus' after his resurrection* – itself alluded to by Paul in 1 Corinthians – *to James the Just.* In it, we have Jesus *'giving his grave clothes to the Servant of the Priest'* – in the Dead Sea Scrolls, this almost always means *'the High Priest'* – which makes altogether more sense than anything we have so far encountered about *'clothes'* or *'the High Priest's Servant'* in the Gospels or Acts.

In it, too, is a reference to *'the Cup of the Lord'* which James is supposed to have drunk – perhaps at 'the Last Supper', perhaps symbolically. We have been describing how this imagery functioned in the Gospels, Revelation, and the Scrolls regarding both *'the Righteous Teacher'* and *'the Wicked Priest'*, but it has not previously been clear that this could be related *directly to James.* This theme of *'the Cup'* is also related in Gospel tradition to 'the two sons of Zebedee', that they would *'drink the Cup'* Jesus was going to drink – meaning martyrdom (Mt 20:20–28 and Mk 10:35–45), even though no martyrdom tradition has come down to us for *'John the brother of James'* as it has Acts' *'James the brother of John.'*

Still, heretofore, we never had such *'Cup'* imagery directly applied to James. The next step is a comparatively simple one, but here is a hint of it. In the Habakkuk *Pesher*, when it comes to presenting what *'the Wicked Priest'* – i.e., *the Establishment High Priest* – did to 'the Righteous Teacher', *'Cup'* imagery is employed in the following manner – just as *he* ('the Wicked Priest') *tendered the 'Cup' to the Righteous Teacher, so too would 'the Cup of the Lord's Wrath' come around to him 'and he would drink his fill'*. This is generally interpreted by Dead Sea Scrolls researchers – often incapable of relating to literary metaphor – to mean that *the Wicked Priest was 'a drunkard'* (*sic*), meaning, 'he drank too much wine'! The proper understanding, as will become clear, has to do with *'drinking the Cup of Divine Vengeance'* as we shall see in due course – *not drunkenness.*

Unlike Epiphanius, Jerome also thinks, as we also saw, that James *'ruled the Church of Jerusalem for thirty years'* until, as he presents it with his customary precision, *'the Seventh Year of Nero and was buried near the Temple, from which he had been cast down'*. Here is the now-familiar theme of *'casting down'*, once again associated with James' death. As we saw as well, like

Eusebius, he too notes that '*his tombstone, with its inscription, was well-known until the siege of Titus and the end of Hadrian's reign*', i.e., *c.* 138 CE actually – the end of the Bar Kochba Revolt too.

James' Death in Josephus: Opposition and Establishment Sadducees

In order to see how Jerome incorporates the testimony of Josephus into his account of James' fall from the Temple Pinnacle and his stoning, it would be well to present the testimony of Josephus about James' death in its entirety. It is, not only the most accurate material we have relating to James' death, but also fixes the chronology of these events which, thereafter, lead up with some inexorable fatality to the outbreak of the War against Rome.

Eusebius himself also makes this clear in the finale of his account of the death of James after relating this death to the coming destruction of the Temple and the fall of Jerusalem and gives Josephus' actual testimony itself. His version is, for all intents and purposes, equivalent to that in Josephus' Antiquities, the received text of which reads as follows:

> Upon learning of the death of Festus, Caesar (Nero) sent Albinus to Judea as Procurator, but the King (Agrippa II) removed Joseph from the High Priesthood and bestowed the dignity of that office on the son of Ananus, who was himself also called Ananus. It is said that this elder Ananus was extremely fortunate for *he had five sons, all of whom became High Priests of God* – after he had himself enjoyed the office for a very long time previously – *which had never happened to any of our other High Priests.*[10]

This additional information in the present text about the High Priest Ananus' family – whose son by the same name is *our candidate for 'the Wicked Priest' in the Dead Sea Scrolls* – is missing from Eusebius; but it is interesting because firstly, Josephus elsewhere says that the destruction of Jerusalem was the result of James' nemesis, this latter Ananus' grisly death, and, secondly, the elder Ananus – who was High Priest either just prior to or in the period of Pontius Pilate – is pictured in the Gospels as having played a significant role in the death of their 'Jesus' (Lk 3:2/Jn 18:3).

Even as a young man, Agrippa II (49–93), by virtue of the dignity bestowed on his father Agrippa I (37–44) by Caligula and Claudius, enjoyed the privilege of appointing Jewish High Priests – a practice that, after Herod's death, had devolved upon the Roman Governors or Procurators. In the Maccabean Period, this privilege was not an issue since the Maccabees themselves functioned in the manner of hereditary High Priests and Kings. Only with Herod's ascendancy and the absorption or destruction of the Maccabean family did this become an issue. Herod's father, *the first Roman Procurator in Palestine*, carved out a Kingdom with the help of the Pharisees, but it was Herod who first insisted on controlling the vestments of the High Priest – a powerful lever of control in Judeo-Palestine in this period. In fact, at the beginning of Book Twenty of the *Antiquities*, Josephus provides Claudius' 45 CE letter '*to the whole Nation of the Jews' granting to Agrippa II and his uncle, Herod of Chalcis and his son Aristobulus, control over the High Priest's vestments.*[11]

The testimony of Josephus continues as follows:

> The younger (Ananus) who, as we have said, obtained the High Priesthood (from Agrippa II), was *rash in his temperament and very insolent.* He was also of the sect of the Sadducees, who were the most uncompromising of all the Jews, as we have already observed, in execution of Judgment (one sometimes wonders which '*Judgment*' Josephus has in mind, human or eschatological).

His manner of describing 'Sadducees', here, is interesting because elsewhere he tells us that the Sadducees in the Herodian Period *were dominated in all things by the Pharisees*. This is the impression that emerges in the Gospels and Acts too. The Pseudoclementine *Recognitions*, cognizant of *the derivation of 'the Sadducees' from the root 'Righteousness'*, rather has it that the Sadducees considered themselves '*more Righteous than the others – separating from the Assembly of the People*'. For it, the division of '*the People into many Parties began in the days of John the Baptist*'. As this is put in the Syriac version: '*The Sadducees arose in the days of John and, because they were Righteous Ones, separated from the People*'.[12]

Obviously these are not 'the Sadducees' presented in Josephus or the New Testament which is one of the reasons I have argued for *two groups of Sadducees*: the first made no such claim to *being 'more Righteous' than anyone else* and only had *a tenuous genealogical link to the 'Zadok' of David's time* a thousand years before; the second was *an 'Opposition' group emphasizing 'Righteousness' as the key component in Salvation*.[13] Their literature, as it is found at Qumran, advocates '*separation from the People*' – *the basis of the 'pollution of the Temple' charge as found, for instance, in the Damascus Document.*

As mentioned previously, after Herod stormed Jerusalem in 37 BC with troops Mark Anthony had given him, he had all the previous Sanhedrin executed except Pollio and Sameas, the two *Pharisees* who predicted his rise to power and recommended to the people 'to open the gates' to him – these, the new-style 'prophets' of the Herodian Period that Paul and the Book of Acts seem never to tire of referring to.[14] For Josephus, *while he 'never left off taking vengeance upon his enemies', these two were 'honored by Herod above all the rest'.*

Herod's 'enemies' must be seen as the previous Sadducee-dominated Sanhedrin and the supporters of Aristobulus II and his two sons. *Herod 'had spies placed everywhere', even sometimes joining them surreptitiously himself, 'and many there were who were brought to the Citadel Hyrcania both openly and in secret, and there put to death'.* This is exactly the treatment meted out a generation later by Herod Antipas – '*Herod the Tetrarch*' in the Gospels and Acts – to John the Baptist *at the Fortress of Machaeros across the Dead Sea.*[15]

Though these '*Maccabean*' or '*Purist Sadducees*' might have been '*stricter in Judgment*' and more thoroughly uncompromising than others; they were *certainly never collaborators, nor did they have anything in common with 'the Sadducees' of the Herodian Period except the name*. The latter were rather a motley assortment of '*Rich*' families vying with each other – often through bribes and contributions to Herodians rulers or Roman officials – to occupy the High Priesthood, obviously making no insistence other than *a genealogical one for the High Priesthood* – and, according to Josephus, *sometimes not even this*. Certainly they made no claim for '*Piety' or 'higher purity' as so-called 'Galilean' Zealots or 'Sicarii' did.*

The Dead Sea Scrolls evince a similar uncompromising insistence on 'Righteousness' and absolute, unrelenting 'Judgment'. They do not compromise, nor is there any ethos of accommodation – particularly with foreigners – but always exhibit *a thoroughgoing and unbending 'zeal' that even considers the Temple polluted because of the accommodating behavior of the Establishment High Priests there* – it is hard to conceive that this should in any way relate to Maccabeans or the Maccabean Period!

Our presentation of *two* groups of Sadducees is borne out in Rabbinic tradition as well. Here, *two* groups of 'Sadducees' are noted, those following 'Boethus' and those following '*Saddok*'.[16] But this allusion to the name 'Boethus' makes it crystal clear, even in this Rabbinic tradition garbled as it may be, that we are in the Herodian Period and the rise of the Zealot Movement – the Movement *founded by Judas the Galilean and his mysterious colleague Saddok*. It was in this period that the Sadducees *split* into sycophant and resistance wings – the latter better understood perhaps as '*Messianic* Sadducees'. This was also the time consonant with 'the birth of Christ' in Christian tradition.

To crown his destruction (or co-option) of the Maccabean line, Herod brought a High Priest in from Egypt, Simeon b. Boethus, whose daughter, Mariamme II, he married after putting the last Maccabean Princess – his previous wife – Mariamme I to death. It was this Priest's son, Joezer ben Boethus, whom Josephus portrays as *opposing 'Judas and Saddok' over the issue of paying taxes to Rome*, that is, Roman rule in Palestine.

Where James, who is one of the heirs of this 'Opposition Sadducee' tradition as we are describing it, is concerned; Josephus' account now, perhaps more comprehensibly, continues:

> Ananus, therefore, being of this character, and supposing that he now had a favorable opportunity – Festus being dead and Albinus still on the road – called a Sanhedrin (Assembly) of the judges and brought before them *the brother of Jesus, who was called 'the Christ', whose name was James, along with certain others*; and, when he had presented a charge against them of *breaking the Law, delivered them to be stoned.* But those citizens who seemed *the most equitable and the most careful in observation of the Law* were offended by this and sent to the King secretly asking him to send to Ananus requesting him to desist from doing such things, saying that he had not acted legally even before.
>
> Some of them also went out to meet Albinus, who was on the way from Alexandria, informing him that *it was not lawful for Ananus to convene a Sanhedrin without his consent. Induced on account of what they had said, Albinus wrote to Ananus in a rage threatening to bring him to punishment because of what he had done. As a result, King Agrippa took the High Priesthood from him after he had ruled only three months and replaced him …*

This is an extremely detailed testimony and it certainly has – except perhaps for the point about '*Jesus being called the Christ*' which has the sense of a copyist's addition – the straightforward ring of truth. It is matter of fact, down to earth, and unembellished. There is, in the manner of Josephus' often rather flat prosody, nothing fantastic in it – no exaggeration. In particular, the note about Albinus being on the way from Alexandria, when he received the information about Ananus' illicit condemnation of James, has the kind of detail and immediacy that carries the sense of historical reality.

Since Josephus immediately goes on to present Albinus as being no better than previous governors and corrupted by the gifts and bribes from these same 'Rich' Sadducean High Priests, he is no apologist for Albinus' behavior and seems willing to give a fair appreciation of his flaws, as well as his one seeming virtue – *his objection to the flouting of his authority in the matter of the execution of James.* Whereas before he arrived in the country he seems to have resented the affront to his authority represented by Ananus' behavior; afterwards, he gave a free hand to the Richest High Priests and made common cause with them against those Josephus has now started calling '*Sicarii*'.

As Josephus describes it, these 'Rich' Sadducean High Priests, allying themselves with '*the boldest sort of men', went to the threshing floors and violently appropriated the tithes due to 'Priests of the Poorer sort*'. He repeats this notice twice, first under Felix around 59–60 CE, and again, under Albinus, 62–64 CE, directly after the illegal stoning of James.

In both instances, these predatory activities of the High Priests give way to violent clashes, stone-throwing, 'and class hatred between the High Priests on the one hand and the Leaders of the Multitudes of Jerusalem on the other'. These are exactly the sort of 'Leaders', the early Christians are portrayed as being in Jerusalem – especially in the Temple, in Acts. These last Josephus again now calls 'Innovators' – a term in Greek, as we have seen, also meaning 'Revolutionaries'.[17]

The first description of this kind of behavior in 59–60 CE is followed by the '*Temple Wall Affair', directed against Agrippa II's viewing of the Temple sacrifices while reclining on his balcony and eating.* This is sometime after 60 CE, around the time he and his sister, Bernice, appear in Acts

25:13–26:32, interviewing Paul. The second such description is followed by rioting led by one 'Saulus', his brother 'Costobarus', and their 'kinsman Antipas', whom Josephus describes as '*using violence with the People*', in the aftermath too of James' stoning, around the year 64 CE. In 64, this same Albinus, hearing the next Governor Florus (64–66) was coming to replace him, emptied the prisons, arbitrarily putting many to death while letting others go with '*the payment of bribes*'; so that Josephus ruefully observed, '*the country was filled with Robbers*'.[18] This seems to be something of the backdrop the New Testament uses to portray Pontius Pilate's behavior three decades before.

In fact, Josephus would have been in a good position to know about many of these things, because, as he tells us in his *Autobiography* – written around the year 93 CE – after the War, he struck up a very close friendship in Rome with this same King Agrippa, who therefore wrote sixty-two letters to him and appears to have vouchsafed him much information he did not previously know. Two of these letters, addressed 'my dear Josephus', he appends to his book.[19]

The theme in Josephus' notice about James' death of Ananus' 'ruling' agrees with the manner in which the Habakkuk *Pesher* presents 'the Wicked Priest', who at one point is referred to as '*ruling Israel*'. This comment has much disturbed commentators, making them think they had to do with Maccabean Priest-Kings not Herodian High Priests. As can be seen from this allusion to Ananus ben Ananus in Josephus, *all High Priests can be said to have 'ruled Israel'*. This is again emphasized at the end of the *Antiquities* when Josephus enumerates all the High Priests starting in David's time, saying: 'Some of these (the High Priests) *ruled during the reign of Herod and his son Archelaus* although, after their deaths, *the Government became an aristocracy and the High Priests were entrusted with ruling the Nation*.'[20]

The idea that James was stoned with 'several colleagues' also agrees with the way the various attacks on the Righteous Teacher and his colleagues is delineated at Qumran. These last, too, are often presented in the plural.[21] In our view, James was the Leader of these '*Poorer sort of Priests*'. As we have seen, this is supported by Acts 6:7's notice of 'a great multitude of Priests being *obedient* to the Faith' – the word 'obedient' here linking up with the repeated allusions to '*obeying the Just One*' in Hegesippus' account. These might be termed '*Nazirite*' or '*Essene Priests*'. In any event they were, in the words of Acts 21:20, '*all Zealots for the Law*'. As such, James was '*the Zaddik of the Opposition Alliance*' – the centre, about whom all these disturbances and/or confrontations in the Temple turned, whose removal in 62 CE made 'the Messianic Uprising' that followed inevitable.

The Conspiracy to Remove James

Josephus' account definitely points to a conspiracy between Ananus and Agrippa II to take advantage of the anarchy, consequent upon the interregnum in Roman Governors, to remove James. Their friendship was solidified in Rome in the early 50s during the course of previous disturbances of this kind and appeals to Caesar, which resulted in Felix, the Emperor's freedman, being sent out to Palestine as Governor.[22] Felix's brother, Pallas, was Nero's lover, and Nero took power almost directly after this event, after having his kinsman Claudius assassinated, which may have contributed to the downward spiral of events in Palestine.

'Conspiracy' is definitely the language the Dead Sea Scrolls use, too, with regard to the destruction of the Righteous Teacher by the Wicked Priest – the word in Hebrew there is *zemam/zammu*, '*he conspired*' and '*they conspired*'.[23] But why was this and what could this 'conspiracy' have been? Josephus complains bitterly about Agrippa II's role in saving his enemy, Justus of Tiberius, who, following recent Messianic disturbances in Libya or 'Cyrene', came forward with new accusations of sedition against Josephus, which may ultimately have led to Josephus' demise.[24]

Agrippa had almost as much cause to seek James' removal as the High Priest Ananus did. If we place James at the centre of agitation over whether to allow Herodian Kings into the Temple, to accept their gifts or appointment of High Priests, and the acceptance of gifts and sacrifices from foreigners generally – including on behalf of the Roman Emperor – then these individuals had ample reason to blame James for a good many things, not least of which, his continued attacks on their 'Riches'. In fact, the way the James episode is interposed between several other important bits of information at the very end of the *Antiquities* – most of which are missing from the *War* – makes it clear that more emphasis should be placed on it than might otherwise be the case. Again, it is important to look at the sequencing of the events covered in the all-important, last book of the *Antiquities* (Book Twenty).

Immediately following James' death, Albinus co-operated with the High Priests in launching a campaign to rid the country of the *Sicarii* – whom Josephus also calls '*Robbers*'.[25] In fact, Josephus uses the term '*Sicarii*' to designate those following the Fourth Philosophy even before he uses the term '*Zealots*' at a later point in the *Jewish War*, and, in the *Antiquities*, the designation '*Zealot*' doesn't even occur. Rather, Josephus first uses the term '*Zealots*' to describe (in the War) those who slaughter the Establishment High Priests responsible for the death of James, burning all their palaces as the Uprising moves into its more virulent or 'Jacobite' phase. In our view, this is vengeance for what these Establishment 'Sadducees' did to James.

As for 'the *Sicarii*' – those allegedly carrying curved, Arab-style daggers under their garments – they are first introduced in 55 CE, when they are responsible for the assassination of Ananus' brother Jonathan, the then High Priest.[26] No doubt they did not call themselves by this appellation, but Josephus makes it clear that, extreme 'Zealots' as they were, they were the heirs to the Movement founded by Judas the Galilean and *Saddok*. They finally end with their families at Masada where they commit mass suicide rather than surrender to the Romans even after the fall of the Temple. In this sequence, the judicial murder of James in the early 60's by Ananus is retribution for the murder of his brother in the 50s by 'the *Sicarii*'.

In discussing this assassination of Ananus' brother, Jonathan, by 'the *Sicarii*' in the 50s in the *Antiquities*, Josephus makes the same accusation against extremist groups he does in discussing the butchering of Ananus in the *War* in the 60's. In the latter, it will be recalled, he stated: 'I cannot but think it was because God had condemned this city to destruction as a *polluted* city that He *cut off* these its greatest defenders and benefactors (meaning Ananus ben Ananus and Josephus' own friend, Jesus ben Gamala).'[27] In the former, he goes further, falling back on the *mea culpa* admission of guilt, which so punctuates his assessment of the lawlessness of the Zealots. This is certainly one of the prototypes for the more famous cry, 'his blood be upon us and our children', in Christian Scripture and theology thereafter. In both instances, these accusations have been enlarged from an accusation against a particular extremist group to one against *a whole people*. Regarding Jonathan, this reads as follows:

> And this seems to me to have been the reason why God, out of his hatred for these men's Wickedness (the *Sicarii*'s), rejected our city. As for the Temple, He no longer considered it sufficiently pure for Him to inhabit therein, but brought the Romans upon us and threw fire upon the city to cleanse it, and brought upon us, our wives and children, slavery, that he might teach us wisdom.[28]

This is, of course, exactly the accusation in Christian Scripture and Christian theology, slightly transmuted and transferred, as it has come down to us. But Josephus is saying that it is because of terrorist murders of Establishment High Priests like Jonathan and Ananus, not because of the Jews' murder of Christ, that the Jews suffered. Still, the common thread of the motif of the '*Sicarii*' – if '*Iscariot*' and '*Sicarios*' are related usages – occurs in both. Of course, Josephus is displaying the groveling sycophantism and subservience of the typical captive, but even the theme of 'pollution of the Temple', so fundamental to the Qumran position remarkably is present in the above extract and reversed. For Josephus, it is now the fanatical, purity-minded extremists who are *polluting the Temple*, not the *collaborating High Priests*.

One can, however, take a further step and state with some certainty that it was because the Jews *were so Messianic* that they lost everything, not *vice versa* as in the New Testament and Phariseeizing Rabbinic Orthodoxy too, the mirror reversal of Christian Orthodoxy. The last step in this is simple. One need only identify these 'lawless' bands of '*Sicarii*' and 'Zealots' as enthusiasts for 'the Star Prophecy' and part and parcel, therefore, of the Messianic Movement. And Josephus does just this, as we have seen, in a much overlooked key section at the end of the *War* dealing with omens and oracles of the destruction of the Temple.

He concludes these by saying that 'what most encouraged' the Jews to revolt against Rome 'was an ambiguous oracle found in their Sacred Writings, that at that time, one from their country would become Ruler of the whole inhabited world', 'ambiguous' because Josephus, as Rabbinic Judaism thereafter, then goes on to apply it to *Vespasian their conqueror*. In the parallel to the New Testament 'Little Apocalypse's above, he had observed in the *Antiquities* that the spread of the Movement he calls 'a disease', started by 'Judas and *Saddok*' '*among our young men, who were zealous for it, brought our country to destruction*'.[29] In other words, it was *because the Jews were so 'zealous'* for the World-Ruler Prophecy, and that Messianism consequent upon it, that they lost everything – not the opposite way round.

The New Testament has by implication rather reversed this, making it seem as if – because of the accusation of *killing Christ* – the Jews as a whole were *anti-Messianic*. But this is patently untrue as we can see. The Establishment Classes were, including the Pharisee progenitors of Rabbinic Judaism. But, by making it seem as if *the Jews as a whole* killed or collaborated with the Romans in the killing of Christ – the point of the Gospels and the Pauline corpus – they make it appear as if the mass of the Jews were not Messianic and opposed Messianism, when, in fact, just the opposite was true. It was because the mass of the Jews *were* so Messianic, as Josephus amply illustrates, not because they supported the Establishment and/or the *Pax Romana*, however one interprets this, as the Gospels would have us believe – that God brought these calamities and political disasters upon them. Thus Josephus.

In his description of the significance of the World-Ruler Prophecy at the end of the *Jewish War*, Josephus also describes the signs and portents connected to how God, disgusted with the Temple, departed from it – things that, no doubt, much impressed the superstitious Romans. These included the appearance of '*armed chariots and armies marching across the clouds at sunset*', certainly a play on the coming of the Heavenly Host on the clouds in James' proclamation and the War Scroll. There is also '*a Star, which stood like a great dagger*', not over the birthplace of 'Jesus' in Bethlehem *portending the Salvation of Mankind*, as in the Gospel of Matthew but, now rather, *over Jerusalem portending its doom*.[30]

In these descriptions, Josephus repeatedly reverses the charges of '*Impiety towards God*' and '*pollution of the Temple*' on the part of the Authorities into '*Impiety towards God*' and '*pollution of the Temple*' because of the blood shed by these *Sicarii* and Zealot bands. So intent is Josephus on these charges against the *Sicarii* that he even follows them down into Egypt and Libya after the War is over with the same charges.[31]

In the Damascus Document and to some extent in the document called *MMT*, the charge of '*pollution of the Temple*' is directed against the Establishment Parties and probably included this matter of accepting gifts and sacrifices on behalf of foreigners. But, according to

Josephus, it is 'the Chief Priests and principal Pharisees' – the same groups the New Testament blames for the condemnation of 'Jesus Christ' – who try to dissuade the people from rejecting such 'gifts and sacrifices', claiming it would lay the city open 'to the charge of Impiety'.

As Josephus avers, the last-named claim is 'an innovation in their religion', since their forefathers had always accepted gifts from foreigners and forbidden no one from offering sacrifices, even adorning the Temple with them and raising dedicatory plaques to them.[32] But by saying this, Josephus neglects to mention the view of Ezekiel 44:1–15 above, so dear to the Damascus Document and the prophet perhaps held in highest repute by such extremist partisans and these 'zealous' Lower Priests who wish to reject such sacrifices.

This is the problem with Josephus, who rarely gives the entire picture where insurgent groups are at issue. His account shifts according to what his sources say and what seems most expedient. Like Paul, who follows a similar *modus operandi* regarding doctrinal matters, Josephus is an apologist, who is completely unaware of his own disingenuousness.

Revolutionary Disturbances in Josephus and Acts

In this period, it is useful to group parties together according to who their common enemies were. On this basis, the 'Christians' in Jerusalem (whatever one might wish to say about their ideology or whatever name to apply), the 'Zealots', '*Sicarii*', and the 'Messianists' responsible for the literature at Qumran, can all be said to have the *same* enemies, namely the Pharisees, 'Establishment Sadducees' or the High Priests, and the Herodians. In addition to this, when one examines the sequence of events before and after James' judicial murder in the *Antiquities*, one first encounters the disturbances of the late 40's and early 50s involving hostilities between Samaritans and Jews as well and their apparent respective Messianic expectations.

However distorted, this is echoed in Acts in the confrontation in Samaria between Peter and Simon *Magus* (8:18–25). It is as a result of these disturbances that Ananus is sent to Rome with another High Priest called Ananias, on one of these by now familiar 'appeals to Caesar'. There he cements his relationship with Agrippa II in the days just before Claudius' assassination (*c.* 53 CE). Ananus was only Captain of the Temple at this point, while Ananias was the 'Richest' of the High Priests. It is clearly on account of his 'Riches' that Albinus, following James' stoning, co-operates with him in mopping up 'the *Sicarii*'.[33]

In Acts, Peter follows up this visit to Samaria by 'going down to the Saints that lived in Lydda'. In the above episode in Josephus, Lydda is the scene of the Messianic disturbances between Samaritans and Jews. Acts pictures Peter as curing a paralytic 'named Aeneas' and raising a sick widow 'called Tabitha', which Acts reinterprets as 'being called Dorcas', in Lydda (9:32–43).[34] All this without comment, as if it were perfectly normal.

We must compare this to Josephus' collateral account of *Messianic disturbances* and *rapine* between Samaritans and Jews *in Lydda*. Josephus calls the Jewish leader of the 'Innovators' or 'Revolutionaries' there, '*Dortus*'! This individual, who he says was reported by 'a certain Samaritan' to have had *four assistants*, was executed – presumably by crucifixion. What malevolent fun the authors of Acts would appear to be having, transmuting history into meaningless dross.

Josephus then interrupts his narrative to discuss the intricate tangle of marriages and divorces and the personal and political consequences of these relating to the family of Agrippa II and his three sisters, Bernice, Drusilla, and Mariamme III, all relevant to the 'fornication' charge at Qumran and its seeming reflection in the Letter ascribed to James and James' directives to overseas communities in Acts. This is followed in Chapter Eight by Josephus' picture of how the *Sicarii* '*went up to the city* (Jerusalem), *as if they were going to worship*

God, while they had daggers under their garments, and by mingling in this manner among the crowds, they slew Jonathan'.

Then commenting how 'the Robbers (*Lestai*) infected the city with all sorts of pollution' and 'Impiety', terms he basically uses to designate all 'Messianists', 'Zealots', or '*Sicarii*', Josephus now reiterates the familiar: 'The impostors and Deceivers persuaded the Multitudes to follow them out into the wilderness under the pretence that there they would perform marvelous wonders and signs made possible by God's Providence.'

In the *War*, it will be recalled, he varies this slightly, saying: 'Wishing to foster revolutionary change, they exhort the masses to assert their liberty' and, feigning Divine inspiration, 'lead the people out into the wilderness in the belief that there God would show them the signs of their approaching freedom'. Adding, '*they also threaten to kill all those willing to submit to Roman Rule*', he goes on to describe in both, how they rob and burn the houses of the Rich, killing their owners.[35]

At this point, too, in both books, Josephus describes Felix's brutality in dealing with one of these 'impostors' or 'Messianic Leaders', the unnamed Egyptian, for whom Paul is mistaken, again by a Roman Centurion, in Acts 21:38 – the chronology of both is the same, *c.* 59–60 CE. Not only does Josephus call this 'Egyptian' 'a Prophet', he describes the Joshua-like miracles he wishes to do, such as commanding *the walls of Jerusalem to fall down.* For the *War*, '*He wished to establish himself as a Tyrant there, with his companions as his bodyguard* (*sic*!)'.[36]

Some would identify this 'Egyptian', who in both accounts escapes in the subsequent confusion, with Simon *Magus*, who was also said to have come from '*Gitta*' in Samaria. The Redeemer figure of the Samaritans, called 'the *Taheb*', also seems to have been a Joshua-like figure or a 'Joshua *redivivus*' ('*Joshua come-back-to-life*'). Some twenty-five years before – again under Pontius Pilate and coinciding with our 'Jesus' episode in the Gospels – Josephus records another disturbance or uprising led by such a Messiah-like individual in Samaria. Looking suspiciously like the 'Jesus' episode in the Gospels, this Uprising was also brutally repressed by Pilate, including, it would appear, a number of crucifixions – only the locale was not the Mount of Olives, but Mount Gerizim, the *Samaritan Holy Place*.[37] In fact, early Church writers often mix up Samaritan sects, including ones supposedly originated by Simon *Magus* and a colleague of his, 'Dositheus' – probably our '*Dorcas*' or '*Dortus*' above – with sects involving Daily Bathers like John, James, and other 'Essenes'/'Ebionites'.[38]

Confusion between the activities of Paul and Simon *Magus* also bedevils Pseudoclementine literature. For whatever the reason, both Paul and Simon would seem to have been in the service of the Herodian family – Simon *Magus* conniving at the marriage between Felix and Agrippa II's sister Drusilla. This marriage is also mentioned by Josephus, where characteristically Simon is called '*a Cypriot*' – a mix-up probably having to do with Simon's place of origin, '*Gitta*', or the general Jewish name for Samaritans, '*Cuthaeans*' ('*Kittim*'?). Where Paul is concerned, we shall in due course suggest that he is probably an actual member of the Herodian family. Again, all of these episodes and issues would appear to bear a relationship – however remote – to James' position of authority over the masses in Jerusalem and on the reason for his ultimate removal.

Arguments in the Temple and Increasing Violence

As Chapter Eight of Book Twenty continues, Josephus documents the warfare that broke out, following this violence between Samaritans and Jews, between the Jewish residents of Caesarea and the Greco-Syrian ones. The last he describes as 'being proud of the fact they supplied the greater part of the Roman soldiers there'! In Josephus, this strife in Caesarea is part of the background to the stoning of James. In Acts, similar strife is part of the background to the stoning of Stephen, which is occasioned by 'the murmuring' of so-called

'Hellenists' (that is, 'Greeks') against 'Hebrews' over 'the daily (food) distribution', in which *widows were somehow overlooked* (6:1 – thus). In Josephus, it is the equal citizenship and privileges the Jews of Caesarea claimed with the '*Hellenists*' or '*Greeks*' there.[39]

In Josephus, this strife is so important that 'it provided the basis for the misfortunes that subsequently befell our nation', something he has also said concerning various incidents surrounding the stoning of James. Not only will the Greek residents in Caesarea bribe Nero's Secretary for Greek Letters 'with a large sum of money' to write a letter 'annulling the grant of equal privileges *to the Jews*'[40] (*n.b.,* how this theme of '*equal rights*' is reversed in Acts' portrayal of problems between '*Hebrews and Hellenists*'), but Felix, the Roman Procurator, finally crushes these disorders by slaughtering a good many of the Jews. In doing so, '*he allows his soldiers to plunder many of their houses which were full of money*', until 'the more responsible Jews (that is, the more accommodating ones) alarmed for themselves, begged for mercy' and 'to be allowed *to repent for what had been done*'.[41]

In pursuance of this theme of violence in Caesarea, Josephus will go on to describe the brutality of these same Caesarean Legionnaires in the next decade (the 60's), leading up to the War against Rome, as being the foremost cause goading the Jews to revolt. It is, almost incredibly, a Centurion from these same brutal Caesarean Legionnaires that Acts 10:2 portrays as 'Pious and God-fearing, doing many good works for the people, and (James-like) *supplicating God continually*'. In Acts 10:22, continuing this indecent parallel with James, it calls him 'a *Zaddik* ('Righteous Man') and God-fearing, confirmed by the whole nation of the Jews' (*thus*)!

It is worth remembering that this Centurion called Cornelius is said to come from the '*Italica Contingent*', Italica being a town in Roman Spain near present-day Seville, whence both Trajan and Hadrian in the next century came (Acts 10:1). For his part, Trajan's father had been a decorated soldier in Palestine with Vespasian's and Titus' victorious legions. It is interesting that in *Antiquities*, one 'Cornelius' is a messenger from this same Caesarean milieu sent to Rome to request that the High Priestly vestments be given over to the control of the Herodians, Herod of Chalcis, Aristobulus his son and husband of the infamous Salome, and Agrippa II, still a minor. This is to say nothing of resonance with the '*Lex Cornelia de Sicarius*'.[42]

According to Acts, it is in anticipation of visiting Cornelius that Peter receives his tablecloth vision on the rooftop in Jaffa, where he learns that there are no forbidden foods; that he was wrong to think he should not keep table fellowship with Gentiles; and, that it is 'wrong to make distinctions between clean and unclean', 'Holy and profane'. Since God '*is not a respecter of persons*', all being equal in Christ Jesus, the conclusion is that 'the repentance unto life having been given to Gentiles too' (Acts 10:1–11:18).

Not only do we have here the expression, 'not respecting of persons', found in descriptions of James, but the actual use of the word 'repentance' found in Josephus' narrative above, but used there to characterize how the more 'accommodating' Jews in Caesarea begged forgiveness from Felix for their countrymen's behavior.

In the *War*, Josephus characterizes 'the number of Robbers he (Felix) caused to be crucified, and the common people caught and punished with them were a multitude not to be enumerated'.[43] This is the same Felix with whom Paul converses so felicitously along with Drusilla, Felix's wife, whom Acts somewhat disingenuously only identifies as 'a Jewess' (24:24). Actually, she is a Herodian Princess, the sister of King Agrippa II. For Acts, Felix 'knew a lot about *the Way*', a designation it uses throughout when speaking about early Christianity in Palestine (24:22). He should, since he put to death a good many of its representatives, a point wholly lacking in Acts' portrayal.

Ultimately complaints made by the Jews of Caesarea against Felix reach as far as Rome and he is removed by Nero – though not otherwise punished because of the high connections he enjoys – and replaced as procurator by Festus (60–62). According to Acts, Paul converses rather congenially with Festus too – along with Agrippa II and Bernice – over a variety of Jewish subjects and Messianic expectations. This, for some two chapters (25:1–26:32). Bernice, it will be recalled, is Agrippa II's sister too, about whom Josephus preserves a charge of illicit sexual connection with her brother.

The High Priest, earlier identified as 'Ananias', is presented as preferring charges against Paul (25:2). Earlier, too, the Pharisees and the Sadducees were presented as arguing with each other in a Sanhedrin setting over the issue of the Resurrection of the dead and Paul, as cleverly exploiting this to get the better of both of them (23:6–10). In Acts 24:15 he gives *Felix* a lecture on the same subject!

Nor is there any hint in Acts' presentation of Paul's arrest and transport under protective escort to Caesarea (where Acts 23:35 actually allows that he stayed in *King Agrippa II's palace*) of the strife between Hellenes and Jews at this time in Caesarea documented by Josephus. Rather the issue is presented as being complaints against Paul to Felix by the Jews, specifically including Ananias and one 'Tertullus' (24:1), and the strife is either between different parties of Jews arguing with each other or with Paul over issues like 'the Resurrection of the dead' (in 24:15, of 'the Just and Unjust alike').

In the earlier episode, Ananias is actually pictured as ordering Paul to be 'hit in the mouth' (23:2) – in the succeeding interview before Felix, he only calls Paul '*a Leader of the Nazoraean Heresy*' and '*a disease-bearer, moving insurrection among all the Jews in the habitable world*' (24:5). This is hardly Paul, though the accusation is certainly true of some others. In any event, Ananias probably wasn't even High Priest at this time (60 CE) and the picture of him participating in complaints before the Governor probably has more to do with those, a decade before, when he did hold that office and the above Messianic disturbances broke out between Samaritans and Jews under the Procurator Cumanus (48–52 CE). This brought on the military intervention of Quadratus, the Governor of Syria, who thereupon sent all parties, including Cumanus, to plead their case before Claudius not Nero.

This is the first appearance of the Younger Ananus on the scene, who was then only Captain of the Temple, and it was as a result of these appeals to Caesar that he and Agrippa II became close friends in Rome – the time approximately 54 CE just before Claudius' death.[44] Still, for once Acts has the issue right, 'pollution of the Temple' (24:6), because Paul is perceived as having introduced Gentiles and, no doubt consequently, their gifts as well into the Temple – which he most certainly did, if not physically, then certainly spiritually. In fact, Caesarea is a favorite centre for Pauline activities, as will become clear in the run-up to Paul's last confrontation with James in Jerusalem, before the mêlée in the Temple, which occasions Paul's arrest in Acts and confinement in Agrippa II's palace in Caesarea.

But, in our view, the real cause of James' death and the real arguments between the Jews are documented in the very next episodes in *Antiquities*, leading directly to the stoning of James and its aftermath. None of those things is properly documented in Acts. Here, 'the High Priests and the principal men of the multitude of Jerusalem, each gathering about them *a company of the boldest men and those that loved Innovation* ... and when they fought each other, they hurled reproachful words at each other, *throwing stones as well*.'

This is, of course, the situation in Jerusalem showing serious argument and stone-throwing between two factions, the High Priests and those described as being of the People. It is also the prototype for the situation in the Temple, as described in early Church sources centering around the stoning of James. Not only would these disputes appear to be the immediate historical context of James' death, but the events that follow them lead directly to the outbreak of the War against Rome – itself provoked by the Caesarean Legionnaires under Fadus (64–66 CE) who succeeds Albinus (62–64) – and the destruction of the Temple. All that is left to do is to place James at the centre of the faction representing the People.

But there is more. It is at this point in the *Antiquities* that Josephus first gives us his description of 'the impudence and boldness of the High Priests, who actually dared to send their assistants to the threshing floors, to take away those tithes that were due the Priests, with the result that *the Poor among the Priests starved to death*'.[45] It will be recalled that Josephus repeats this description a second time directly after the stoning of James during Albinus' regime. Josephus ties this 'robbing sustenance' or 'robbing the Poor', which we shall also see reflected in descriptions of 'the Last Priests of Jerusalem' in the Habakkuk *Pesher*, not only to Ananias, but also the other priests, saying, '*they took away the tithes that belonged to the Priests and did not refrain from beating such as would not give these tithes to them, so that these Priests, whom of old were supported by these tithes, died for want of food*.'[46]

Josephus clearly has mixed emotions here. Sometimes he sympathizes with *the Lower Priests dying for want of sustenance* whom he actually designates as '*the Poor*'. He must have understood this situation very well, for this would be the class he came from – therefore his criticism of 'the Chief Priests'. But, at other times, he catches himself and continues his criticism of 'the Robbers' or '*Lestai*', whom, he now says, caused the Uprising against Rome. Sometimes he treats Agrippa II – later his confidant – and Bernice, Agrippa II's sister, sympathetically, while at other times he is critical.

As a young Priest, Josephus studied with the '*Banus*' described previously, that is, he followed the regime of daily bathing in the wilderness, telling us that '*Banus bathed both night and day in cold water* to (like James) *preserve his virginity*', and that for three years he, Josephus, '*imitated him in this activity*'. We have suggested that these activities, centering about this contemporary of and 'double' for James, comprised something of a training ground for young priests, at least '*Rechabite*'-style ones. Josephus has, therefore, conflicting emotional allegiances, mixed with a strong desire to survive. Both are evident in the various contradictory statements he makes.

The next episode he describes exhibits these personal conflicts as well. Here, too, Josephus notes how Festus (60–62 CE), like Felix before him and Albinus to follow, was active in putting down such wilderness 'sojourners' or 'Deceivers'. Acts, too, talks about Festus' regime in Judea regarding the unjust imprisonment of Paul, who was mistaken for such a 'Deceiver'.

Here, Josephus tells us that 'Festus, too, sent armed forces, horsemen and foot soldiers, to fall upon those seduced by a certain Impostor, who had promised them *Salvation* ('*Yeshu'a*' or '*Yesha*°' in Hebrew) and *freedom* from the troubles they suffered if they would follow him into the wilderness.'[47] Josephus refrains from naming this '*Impostor*', simply stating that the forces Festus dispatched destroyed 'both the Deceiver himself and those following him', information even more scanty than that concerning 'the Egyptian' preceding it. There can be little doubt that this event is a repeat of the previous one, the only difference being that 'the Egyptian' escaped. As in the stone-throwing on the Temple Mount and the 'Rich' Priests plundering the Poorer ones, events framed in Josephus by the murder of James, there does seem to be some repetition or telescoping of events, perhaps due to faulty redaction or Josephus' own dissimulation.

But not a murmur about these sorts of difficulties is ever uttered in Acts' narrative of parallel events, only that 'the Jews' – *all of them*, including what appear to be Nazirite-style '*Assassins*' or '*Sicarii*' – are trying *to kill Paul*, because he has tried, even by Acts' own rather one-sided presentation of their complaints, to *introduce Gentiles into the Temple*. 'The Jews' also make an endless series of complaints against Paul both to Felix and Festus, and Paul himself is finally saved by the sympathetic intervention of these governors, not to mention that of Agrippa II and his two wayward sisters. It is even possible that Felix, with his intimate connections to Nero's household, actually paves the way for Paul's trip to Rome a year or two after his own return. In any event, the reader will now come to appreciate that Acts' account is quite obviously skewed or, at the very least, flawed.

The Temple Wall Affair in 62 CE

This brings us to a closer look at 'the Temple Wall Affair'. It took place almost simultaneously with Paul's 'appeal to Caesar' in Acts (25:21–25). So important was this confrontation between Temple purists and those supporting the admission of Herodians into the Temple that its upshot involved appeals to Caesar on the part of numerous individuals, two of no less importance than the High Priest appointed by Agrippa II and specifically identified by Josephus as Ishmael b. Phiabi – not 'Ananias' as in Acts above – and one 'Helcias', the Keeper of the Temple Treasure! In fact, Paul and even Josephus himself may have been involved in the appeals surrounding this incident, which led inexorably to the death of James.

Helcias' father or grandfather – the genealogical lines are unclear – had been a close associate of Herod. Herod had specifically chosen him to marry his sister Salome after forcing her to divorce an earlier husband, the Idumaean 'Costobarus', whom Herod suspected of plotting against him; and ever after, the genealogies of all these lines are very closely intertwined.[48] That the Herodians generally kept a tight grip on money matters through this side of the family is clear. If our contention that Paul was a 'Herodian' can be proved, it is this line going back to Costobarus and Herod's sister Salome to which he belonged.

The second or third 'Helcias' in this line, he was a close associate of Herod of Chalcis. His son, Julius Archelaus, whom Josephus also knew in Rome and compliments in the dedication to his *Antiquities* as an avid reader of his works, was married for a time to the Herodian Princess Mariamme III, Agrippa II's third sister, before she divorced him in favor of, probably, the even 'Richer' Alabarch of Alexandria, Demetrius.

It will be recalled that Philo, the Alexandrian Jewish philosopher, and his nephew, Tiberius Alexander, the son of the previous Alabarch, Philo's brother Alexander, were members of this fabulously wealthy Egyptian Jewish family. Tiberius Alexander, Titus' military commander at the siege of Jerusalem, presided over the destruction of the Temple, while the family itself seems to have had control of commerce down the Red Sea as far as India and the Malabar coast. It is from this it derived its wealth – 'Riches' that, no doubt, played a role in some of the dynastic and political maneuvering going on here.

Ten other unnamed participants in '*the Temple Wall Affair*' were sent to Caesar as well. Since their appeals occur at *exactly the same time* as Paul's in Acts, it is hard to conceive the situations involved are not connected in some manner. In fact, all do relate in one way or another to *barring Gentiles* or *their gifts from the Temple – the issue that starts the War against Rome.* Herodians had been perceived of as foreigners ever since the visit of Simon to Caesarea in the 40's. 'The Temple Wall Affair' is the same genre of episode as this and relates to the wish on the part of this mysterious 'Simon' to *bar Agrippa II's* (even more 'Pious') *father from the Temple as a Gentile.*

Here, Josephus again shows why he is in such a quandary, for he is clearly on the side of the 'Zealot Priests' in the Temple who build the wall to block Agrippa II's view of the sacrifices being conducted there. As he describes this affair, which *immediately* precedes the stoning of James, Agrippa II built himself a very large dining room in the royal palace at Jerusalem. This palace appears to have been first erected by the Maccabees, just overlooking the Western Portico of the Temple. Since it was situated on higher ground, it provided an excellent prospect of the sacrifices there. As Josephus describes the scene:

> The King was enamored of this view, and could observe, as he reclined and ate, everything that was done in the Temple. This very much displeased the Chief Men of Jerusalem (whoever these were), for it was contrary to tradition and Law that proceedings in the Temple, particularly the sacrifices, be observed. They, therefore, erected a high wall upon the uppermost portico which belonged to the Inner Court of the Temple towards the West (that is, directly over our present-day 'Wailing' or 'Western Wall').[49]

But though his behavior was certainly in poor taste, particularly if he was entertaining Gentiles and eating forbidden foods as he reclined and ate, which one imagines he was, it is not specifically against the Laws of the country, at least not as these are preserved in the Pharisaic tradition represented by the *Talmud. Mishnah Yoma* 2:8, for instance, notes how on the Day of Atonement the people stood in the Court of the Temple, from where they presumably viewed the sacrifices. There is only a prohibition of being in the Temple when the priestly functions *per se* were being performed.

But the problem here is more complicated than this and has to do with the attempt by Simon to have Agrippa I barred from the Temple as a foreigner. By the time that gifts and sacrifices from Gentiles are banned altogether by the 'Zealot' Lower Priesthood in 66 CE, Agrippa II himself, together with his sister, the arch-fornicator Bernice, will have been barred from Jerusalem altogether, not to mention that their palaces will be burned in the immediate euphoria of the early days of the Uprising.[50]

In fact, this is the position of one document from Qumran, the Temple Scroll. This document as we saw, not only devotes a whole section to this and related issues but, in doing so, uses the language of 'Bela'' or '*balla'*'/'swallowing'. We have already discussed how this usage has something to do with Herodians, 'Bela'' in the Bible having been not only a 'Benjaminite', but also the first *Edomite King*.

In the Temple Scroll, it is explicitly set forth that a high wall or a wide escarpment of some kind be built around the Temple, so that what goes on inside would neither be interrupted nor, it would appear, even 'seen' by Gentiles and other classes of unclean persons. The relevant passage reads: 'And you shall make a great wall measuring a hundred cubits wide in order to *separate* the Holy Temple from the city, and (they?) shall not come (plural, but unspecified) *Bela'* (or *balla'*) and *pollute it*, but make My Temple Holy and fear My Temple.'

This directive can be seen as directly relating to both the issue of Agrippa II's dining habits and Simon's attempt to bar his father from the Temple as a foreigner.

Herodians in the Temple and Appeals to Caesar

Despite Josephus' somewhat ambiguous attitude towards Agrippa II, there is no hesitation on the part of the Zealot/Messianic extremists as to what they think of him: he is charged with incest with his sister Bernice and both are barred, not only from the Temple, but all Jerusalem by these same Zealot 'Innovators' after the Temple Wall Affair, this in spite of the fact that his great-grandfather, Herod, started the reconstruction of the Temple and it was finished owing to his own and his father's 'philanthropy'.[51]

It is this Temple Wall Affair that immediately preceded the stoning of James. Alongside the consolidation of relations between Agrippa II and Ananus in Rome and the attempt by Simon to have Agrippa I barred from the Temple as a foreigner in the 40's, it provides something of the backdrop to the devastating and catastrophic events that are to follow.

The sequencing in Book Twenty of the *Antiquities* is interesting. Just after he describes the beheading of Theudas (ca. 45 CE), we have the preventative crucifixion of Judas the Galilean's two sons James and Simon at the time of the Famine by the Jewish Alabarch of

Alexandria's son Tiberius Alexander (46–48 CE). Then he describes an attack just outside Jerusalem on someone he identifies as the Emperor's servant 'Stephen', followed by the Messianic disturbances between Jews and Samaritans in the environs of Lydda and leading to the appointment of Felix as Governor. At this point, Josephus describes how *at Passover*, one of the soldiers guarding the Temple and standing on the top of the Portico, 'lifted up his skirt and exposed his privy parts to the crowd'. In the *War*, he is described as turning around, lifting up his clothing, and *farting* at the assembled multitudes, which strikes one as being even more realistic. In either case, the soldier expressed his sentiments in an extremely graphic and unambiguous manner.[52]

One should note the quasi-parallel sequence in Acts of reference to 'Judas the Galilean' in chapter 5, the stoning of Stephen (in 6–7), and Peter's problems with Simon *Magus* in *Samaria* and Peter's subsequent visit to Lydda (in 8–9). Tiberius Alexander, whom Josephus also describes as a backslider from 'the religion of his country', appears in Acts in the context of disturbances on the Temple Mount as well (4:6); and the circle of Jewish turncoats and Herodians he is involved with will grow in importance as events mount towards their climax.

In the matter of the soldier exposing his privy parts to the crowd, his lewd gesture provokes a huge stampede in which thousands (in the *War*, Josephus speaks of 'ten thousand'; in the *Antiquities*, 'twenty') are supposedly trampled, and this at Passover. Again Josephus explains that it was 'the customary practice of previous governors of Judea', fearing revolutionary activity – literally 'Innovation' – on the part of the crowds at Festivals, to station 'a company of soldiers at armed alert to stand guard on the Porticoes of the Temple to quell any attempts at Revolution that might occur'.[53]

At this point, too, in its narrative of how Paul was mobbed at Pentecost, because the crowd thought he had introduced foreigners into the Temple, Acts also introduces the reference to 'the Egyptian'. For his part, Josephus places the affair of this 'Egyptian, claiming to be a Prophet' right after he described 'the Robbers' who concealed 'daggers under their cloaks' and assassinated Ananus' brother, the High Priest Jonathan, and right before his description of the bloody battles between Greeks and Jews in Caesarea – which would put us some time in the mid-50s.

In Acts' picture, the 'Chief Captain', responding to Paul's question about whether he knew Greek, concludes Paul is 'not the Egyptian who before these days caused a disturbance leading some four thousand of the *Sicarii* out into the wilderness' (21:38). The reference here to '*Sicarii*' again corresponds to Josephus' introduction of the term just prior to the Temple Wall Affair, itself followed in the *Antiquities* by the exodus of *a second*, unknown 'certain Impostor' into the wilderness under Festus (60–62 CE). In the *War*, Josephus introduced the terminology '*Sicarii*' five years earlier at the time of the murder of Jonathan.[54]

At the conclusion to the construction of the Temple wall during Festus' Procuratorship, Josephus describes both Festus and King Agrippa as extremely angry. When Festus instructs the Jews to tear it down, they, in turn, send ten principal men together with Ishmael and Helcias the Temple Treasurer mentioned above – *twelve in all* – to Nero. In Rome, Nero's wife Poppea, whom Josephus describes as a 'Worshipper of God' (a term paralleling that of 'God-Fearer' usually applied to Gentiles attaching themselves to the Jewish Community in some manner, but not yet taking all the requirements of the Law upon themselves),[55] intercedes on behalf of *the builders of the wall.*

These she allows to go free – all except Ishmael the High Priest and Helcias, whom she, with Nero's seeming connivance, keeps back, obviously expecting to get some financial consideration from them, which, no doubt, they eventually provided. One can imagine that there was some financial remuneration that went along with such decisions. Special attention should be paid to these contacts in the household or entourage of Nero. Later, in Domitian's time, there are actually said to be *Christians* in the Imperial household, Flavius Clemens and

Flavia Domitilla. The reader should note that, as in Josephus' case, the forenames here associate them with the Flavian family. As will become clear, Paul, too, has his own high-level contacts in the household of Nero.[56]

For his part Agrippa II, hearing the news of his discomfiture in the matter of the Temple Wall Affair, changes the High Priest. This sets the stage for what he does shortly thereafter, when Festus dies suddenly (62 CE) – he immediately changes the High Priest, this time, seemingly, *to pave the way to dispose of James.* In such a scenario, one must conclude that Agrippa II sees James as the real focal point behind the various difficulties he is experiencing in the Temple and appoints a High Priest more willing to deal with this irritant. It would also appear that by this time Nero is becoming quite fed up with all these various representations on the part of Jews – among which one should include Paul's – for his future behavior towards them not only becomes more extreme, but the last Governor before the War, Florus (64–66), would appear to be purposefully attempting to goad the Jews to revolt.[57]

Where such appeals to Caesar go, we have had appeals to Caesar on the part of 'the High Priest' Ananias and Ananus in the previous decade over the matter of Messianic disturbances and problems between Jews and Samaritans at Lydda and on the part of Paul, but also Josephus himself records in his *Autobiography* that *he made his first trip to Rome at the age of twenty-six – a year or so after the stoning of James – in relation to another such appeal.* This one, as he tells us, was on behalf of *'certain Priests of (his) acquaintance', who were arrested 'on a small and trifling charge ... put in bonds and sent to Rome to plead their case before Caesar when Felix was Procurator of Judea'.*[58] This was around the time of Paul's original arrest in the Temple, protective custody in Agrippa II's palace, and his discussions with the Roman Governor Felix and his wife Drusilla. It is on behalf of these unnamed 'Priests' that Josephus now goes directly in Rome to this same *Empress Poppea*, Nero's wife who, in addition to taking an interest in religion and interceding in cases connected with it, seems to have had a propensity for young men. In fact, it is not long after this that Nero, in 65 CE, in a fit of rage, kicked her to death in the stomach, presumably because she was pregnant.

Unfortunately, Josephus does not tell us what the 'trifling charge' was for which these 'certain Priests' were being held for so long – by his reckoning, some five years or more – but his silence perhaps speaks reams. However, he does tell us that, like James, they were 'very excellent men' and vegetarians on account of 'their Piety towards God' (the first element in our 'Piety'/'Righteousness' dichotomy).

The 'Priests', therefore, on whose behalf Josephus undertook his journey to Rome, must have been 'Essene'-type or 'Rechabite Priests' of the 'Jamesian' stripe, eating nothing but nuts and dates in their incarceration. This they did, it seems clear, both to preserve their purity, but also because, like James and *Banus, they were observing the absolute purity regulations of extreme 'Naziritism'.* One can be sure, too, that they did not eat 'things sacrificed to idols' either in Palestine or Rome. For his part, it should be remarked, *it was during this trip that Josephus laid the groundwork for his own eventual betrayal of the Jewish People.*

Though, atypically, Josephus declines to reveal the reason why these Pious Priests, on whose behalf he first went to Rome, were detained, it is hard to believe it did not relate in some way either to the Temple Wall Affair, or, at least, the plundering of tithes of 'the Poor Priests' by the 'Rich' High Priests, and even James' death. We have already expressed the view that the Temple Wall Affair provides the actual backdrop for the removal of James. Read discerningly, it not only provides insight into what the issues really were and what was going on behind all these events, but the reason why Josephus was of such two minds about them, and this despite his later friendship with Agrippa, who died in 93 CE around the time he came to publish the *Antiquities* and *Autobiography*.[59]

This then becomes the backdrop for the removal of James after Festus dies and Albinus is on the way, at which point Agrippa appoints Ananus High Priest. But none of these matters are covered in the parallel account at the end of the Book of Acts. Rather, disturbances in the Temple – such as they are – are represented as being occasioned by reactions to *Paul's* person, teaching, and activities. Not only is the Roman Chief Captain pictured as allowing Paul to deliver a proselytizing speech to the Jewish mob 'wishing to kill him', but after discovering Paul to be a Roman citizen, he forces 'the Chief Priests' and the entire Jewish Sanhedrin to hear him. Here the High Priest, now called 'Ananias' – this is very definitely an anachronism – hits Paul in the mouth and Paul responds (presumably because of the white linen he wears) by calling him 'a white-washed wall' (23:3). Paul proclaims that he is a Pharisee and being judged because of his hope for 'the Resurrection of the dead' and the Jews now fall to fighting among themselves over this doctrine (23:6–10).

The same scenes are more or less re-enacted under Felix and Festus in Caesarea in the next few chapters over the next two years, where Paul is in what appears to be a kind of protective custody. But there is nothing about these other disturbances, nothing about warfare between Jews and Samaritans, nothing about debates, riots, and fights between the High Priests and the Jewish mob, between King Agrippa and the Jews in the Temple, between the people of Caesarea and the Jews – none of these things – only Paul's difficulties with the Jewish people, itself presented as a unified whole.

This situation is clearly not credible, especially in view of the fact that *James apparently goes on functioning in Jerusalem during the next two years while Paul is supposedly imprisoned in Caesarea with little serious difficulty from these groups until Agrippa II* – taking advantage of the interregnum in Roman Governors caused by the death of Festus, *after his discomfiture in 'the Temple Wall Affair' – uses the occasion of his appointment of Ananus as High Priest to definitively remove that individual whom he has clearly identified as the source of his various problems, James the Just.* Nor do James or the other members of the Jerusalem Community appear to visit Paul at all during his two-year incarceration, at least not by Acts' testimony, which is rather intent on calling attention to Paul's cordial relations with Roman Governors and Herodian Princesses and Kings – *hardly the social companions of James.*

If we place James at the centre of these various disturbances in the Temple and identify him as the popular *Zaddik* – '*the Zaddik of the Opposition Alliance*' – and Paul, rather than his confederate, as his opponent in this same Movement, *we arrive at a more credible picture of the true situation in Jerusalem in these times.* Then *the removal of James becomes crucial* and necessitated by his position *representing the 'Zealous' forces among the more purity-minded Lower Priest classes within the Temple.*

The Dead Sea Scrolls delineate just such a 'Zealot Priestly' or 'purist' strain within an 'Opposition' framework and the ideological and literary framework upon which it might be constructed – particularly their idea of an '*Opposition High Priesthood' based on the Righteousness ideology*, that is, 'the Sons of Zadok' were not simply genealogical High Priests, but *High Priests of 'the Last Times' basing their qualifications on Higher Righteousness and Perfect Holiness.* In this context, one might also wish to identify James as *the author of MMT, since it fits perfectly into the range of issues and circumstances we have been delineating here.* This, in fact, would make '*MMT*', which is definitely framed in terms of a '*letter*' – however alien it might superficially appear – *the actual 'letter' sent down by James to Antioch with 'Judas Barsabas' at the conclusion of the so-called 'Jerusalem Council' in Acts.*

Adding selected materials from the Book of Acts just lends further credence to this picture. For instance, just prior to the *stoning of Stephen*, Acts describes a large number of Priests coming over to so-called 'Christianity' in Judea. Furthermore, as already remarked, it describes the larger part of James' 'Jerusalem Assembly' followers – in the midst of James' final verbal encounter with Paul and just prior to Paul's subsequent mobbing in the Temple – as 'zealous' or 'Zealots for the Law' (21:20).

In the follow-up to this book, *James the Brother of Jesus and the Dead Sea Scrolls* II: *The Cup of the Lord, the Damascus Covenant, and the Blood of Christ,* I will treat in more detail Paul's final confrontation with James over the issues of '*teaching all the Jews among the Gentiles to break away (literally, 'apostatize') from Moses and not to circumcise their children, nor walk in the customs (of the Forefathers* – 21:21)'. To this, the Jewish mob then adds the charges of '*teaching everywhere against the People, against the Law, and against this Place*', *meaning the Temple*, which it claims he (Paul) has '*polluted*' *by introducing foreigners into it* – that is, 'Greeks' (Acts 21:28).

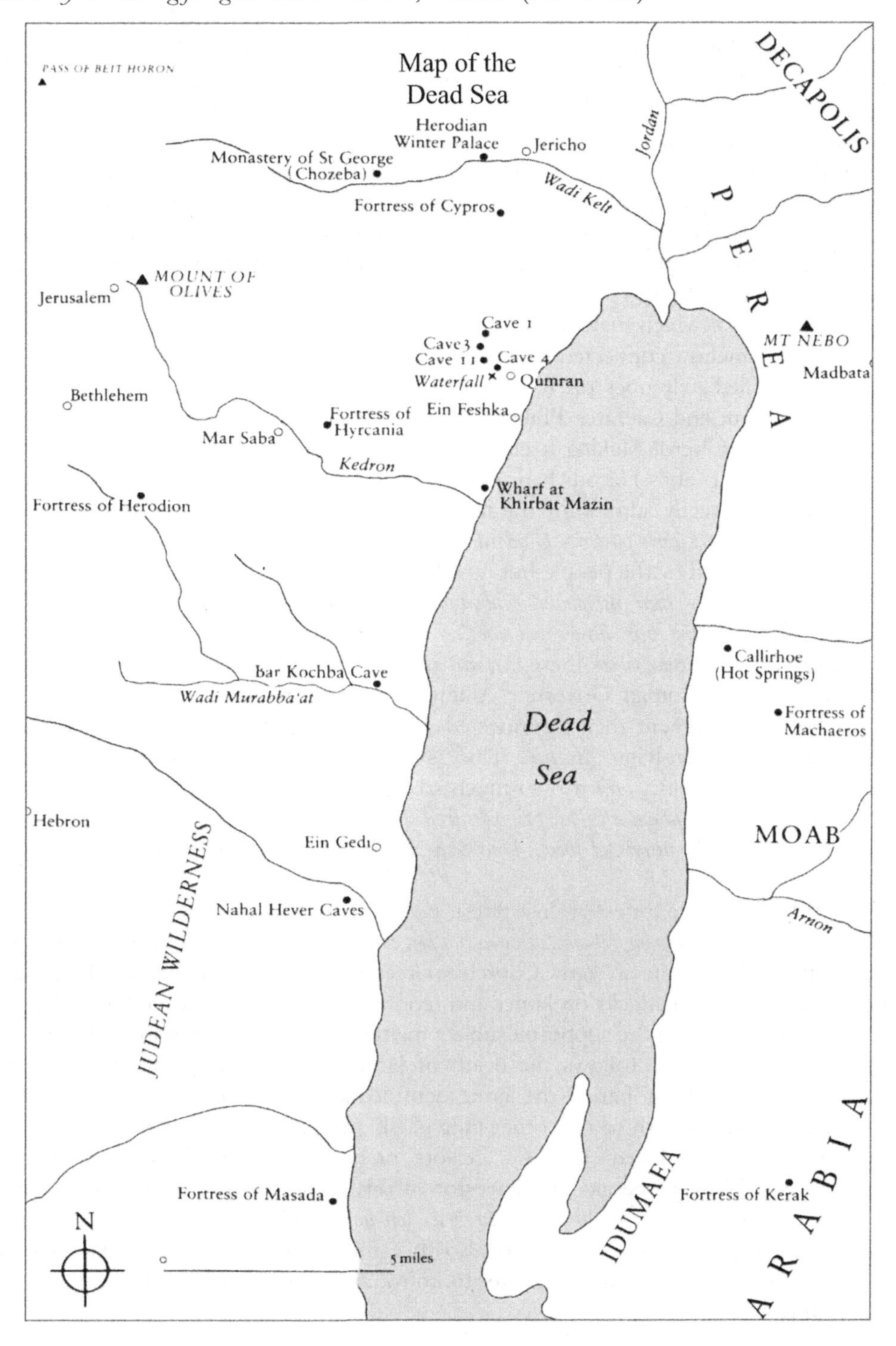

Chapter 16
The Attack by Paul on James and the Attack on Stephen

The Violence in Jerusalem and the Riot Led by Saul in Josephus

Following the stoning of James, Josephus describes how Ananias and the other High Priests, who 'joined themselves to the most brutal kind of people', sent their servants to the threshing floors to steal the tithes of 'the Priests of the Poorer sort', beating those who resisted, so that 'those of old' – possibly our purist Nazirite-style 'Priests' – who used to be maintained by tithes, died of want.

Reference to this brutality is made twice in the *Antiquities* approximately four years apart – once at the end of Felix's tenure just before the Temple Wall Affair and James' death that followed and once in Albinus' just after it. This is interspersed with notices about how the '*Sicarii*' now struggle daily with the 'Rich' High Priests (particularly Ananias), kidnapping each other's partisans and the attempts by the latter in conjunction with the new Roman Governor Albinus to suppress them. Though this same Ananias is pictured as making complaints against Paul in Acts – which may or may not have substance – it is impossible to think these matters are not somehow connected with the death of James.[1]

Josephus immediately goes on to describe how Agrippa II now beautifies two largely Gentile cities, Beirut and Caesarea Philippi, which he renames – temporarily one assumes – 'Neronias' to honor Nero! Making it clear that this included erecting pagan statues, as his ancestors Agrippa I and Herod had done before him, Josephus, in another of his turnarounds, now directly admits for the first time that: '*The hatred of his subjects for him increased accordingly, because he took their posterity to adorn a foreign city*.' This is as we would expect, that these Rulers were hated by the people but now Josephus, not only admits it, but provides one of the reasons for it – *their cosmopolitan involvement with foreign powers and interaction with foreigners generally including beautifying their shrines and cities*.[2]

Josephus, not only describes these '*Sicarii*' as per usual as '*Robbers*' (*Lestai*), but also how they try to force the Roman Governor Albinus through Ananias '*to release prisoners*'! Here, again, we have a prominent theme connected with the presentation of Jesus' death in the Gospels, only now involving '*Sicarii*'. This is coupled with the reiteration of another omnipresent Gospel theme, *bribery* – so much so that when Albinus finally leaves Jerusalem two years later '*he brought out all those prisoners who seemed to him most plainly worthy of death and … took money from them and dismissed them. Thus were the prisons emptied but the countryside filled with Robbers* (*Lestai*).'

The level of violence, priest against priest, now increases: '*They got together bodies of the people and frequently went, from throwing reproaches at each other, to throwing stones*.' Again, this atmosphere is familiar from the picture in early Church sources of confrontations and debates in the Temple centering around attacks on James and reports of riots that finally end up in his death – the only difference being the supposed subject matter behind these riots and debates.

In particular, Josephus follows the death of James with an extremely interesting note about one 'Saulus and Costobarus', the latter identified as Saulus' brother in the *War*. In the same work he connects both to two other individuals Antipas, another of their '*kinsmen*' and Temple Treasurer-to-be, killed either by 'Zealots' or by '*Sicarii*', and Philip, the Captain of Agrippa II's guard. The namesake and ancestor of this 'Costobarus' was married to Herod's sister Salome I. He was *the real 'Idumaean' in these Herodian genealogies*, the forebear too probably of this just-mentioned 'Antipas'. He was also the grandfather or great-grandfather of one 'Julius Archelaus' whom Josephus was later to know, as he tells us in his *Autobiography*, fairly intimately in Rome.

In Josephus' words, Saulus and Costobarus now 'collected a band of thugs', doubtlessly not unlike the violent bands of ruffians collected by the High Priests, he had just been describing two sentences earlier. In this regard, one should bear in mind Acts' picture of the authorizations the young 'Saul'/'Paul' obtains – also *from the High Priests – to pursue so-called 'Christians' to Damascus* (9:2). As Josephus describes them: 'They were of the Royal Family and, *because of their kinship to Agrippa, found favor* – obviously with the Establishment – *but they used violence with the People and were ready to plunder anyone weaker than themselves.*' Josephus adds as usual, but significantly in view of the context: '*And from that moment, particularly, great suffering fell upon our city and all things grew steadily worse and worse.*'[3]

This theme of '*Violence' done to People or land* is very strong in the Dead Sea Scrolls, where it is linked to the expression '*the Violent Ones*'. This violence is described in great detail, including extended reference to '*the Poor*' (*Ebionim*), the situation of how '*the Last Priests of Jerusalem' and the Wicked Priest 'gather Riches' and 'spoils' in the run-up to the destruction of the Temple and the fall of Jerusalem.*

In the course of these presentations, we hear about '*the Violent Ones*', not only in the Habakkuk *Pesher*, but also in the Psalm 37 *Pesher*, where they are called, significantly, '*the Violent Ones of the Gentiles*'. In the Habakkuk *Pesher*, the expression occurs in particularly crucial sections relating to the destruction of 'the Righteous Teacher' and a number of individuals with him, referred to as '*the Poor*'. The text runs:

> The Wicked Priest … became proud and he deserted God and betrayed the Laws *because of Riches. He plundered and collected the Riches of the Men of Violence* – themselves rebels against God – and *took (in the sense of, 'profiteered from') the Riches of the Peoples* (in our view, Herodians who, it should be appreciated, were at this time Roman tax collectors or, even more accurately, tax-farmers in Palestine) *multiplying upon himself sinful guilt.*[4]

This is broken by the reference in the next column to '*the Last Priests of Jerusalem*' – this plural usage, too, would seem to place this firmly in the Herodian Period, *not the Maccabean.* Our writers certainly knew whereof they spoke, when they further described these '*Last Priests' as 'profiteering from the spoils of the Peoples. But in the Last Days their Riches together with their booty would be given over to the hand of the Army of the Kittim'.*

Moving back to the subject of 'the Wicked Priest', our text now goes into the passages, we have treated above, about the 'Vengeance' God would visit on him '*because he conspired to destroy the Poor*' (the name, of course, of James' Community):

> And as to what is written, 'Because of the blood of the township and the Violence of the land,' its interpretation is (*peshero*): 'the township' is Jerusalem *where the Wicked Priest committed his works of Abominations* (to be contrasted with the Righteous Teacher's '*works of Righteousness*') *polluting the Temple of God*; and 'the Violence of the land' relates to the cities of Judah *where he plundered the sustenance* ('*Riches*') *of the Poor* (*Ebionim*).[5]

Josephus' Saulus and Paul's Herodian Connections

The notice in Josephus about Saulus '*using violence with the People*' has a bearing, not only on *the attack by the Enemy Paul on James* as described in the Pseudoclementines, but also the real events lying behind the '*Stephen*' episode in Acts. Paul himself writes in his Letter to the Romans in a passage not generally disputed that the bearer should send his regards to someone, he calls, *his 'kinsman Herodion'* (i.e., '*the littlest Herod*' – 16:11). In the same breath, he sends regards, as well, to those he refers to as '*of Aristobulus*', i.e., either '*relatives of*' or '*of the household of Aristobulus*' (16:10).

Agrippa I's brother and successor Herod of Chalcis (44–49 CE), originally married to Agrippa I's daughter Bernice, had a son by the name of '*Aristobulus*' who was married to *the Salome connected in the Gospels to the death of John the Baptist.* No doubt, they spent much of their time in Rome, but when Nero enlarged Agrippa II's Kingdom at the expense of Herod of Chalcis's domains, he compensated Aristobulus and Salome by giving them the Kingdom of Lower Armenia in Northern Syria and Asia Minor not far from Paul's own base of operations there.

But Paul, as did 'Herodians' generally, also held Roman Citizenship – a rarity in Palestine at this time. Acts makes much of this, for instance, in the jovial banter between Paul and the Roman Chief Captain on the Temple steps following Paul's ejection from the Temple by the crowd (Acts 22:26–29). Josephus, too, acquired Roman Citizenship – obviously going through much to obtain it – and was *adopted into the Roman Imperial family itself.*

However Roman Citizenship had already been bestowed in the previous century upon all the offspring of Antipater and his son Herod *for conspicuous service to Rome* – in fact, the Roman takeover of Palestine itself was due in no small part to their efforts. Where Paul is concerned, his citizenship clearly enabled him to wield inordinate importance in Jerusalem at a comparatively young age in the employ of the High Priests. Moreover, it repeatedly saved him, by Acts' own reckoning, from imminent punishment and even death. It is hard to picture 'Jesus' in similar circumstances pulling out a Roman Citizenship to escape the same kind of punishment or death.

Be this as it may, one of the most curious and, as it turns out revealing, examples of such an escape comes when a nephew of Paul, whom Acts declines to name – but living in Jerusalem with an entrée into Roman official circles – discovers 'a conspiracy' on the part of the Jews 'to kill Paul' (23:16). This is on the part of those who have all the characteristics of '*Sicarii*', except for taking a suspiciously-familiar *Nazirite*-style oath – '*cursing themselves not to drink or eat till they had killed Paul*'. This 'oath'-taking is *repeated three times in this episode*, the language varying to '*with a curse, we have cursed ourselves to taste nothing until we have killed Paul*' (Acts 23:14; in 23:21, this is '*not to eat or drink*').

Paul's nephew (still unnamed), then, informs the Roman Chief Captain of the Temple Guard in 'the Fortress' (probably Antonia) of same who, *with 'seventy horsemen, two hundred soldiers, and two hundred spearmen*', *sends Paul to Felix in Caesarea to be 'kept in Herod's Palace'.* One should note the apparently historically precise detail at this point in Acts which even includes the contents of the letter, the Captain sends to Felix. This contrasts markedly with the general mythologizing of Acts in earlier chapters.

It would be interesting to know who the mother was – also unnamed but living in Jerusalem – of this young man who himself had such cordial relations with the Romans that he could enter their fortresses and produce such an astonishing results. Six years later, at the time of the outbreak of the War with Rome, Josephus' '*Saulus*' seems to enjoy a similar relationship with the Roman Chief Captain in either the Fortress called Antonia or the Citadel.

The mother of this '*young man*' – '*Paul's nephew*' – is possibly to be identified with Cypros IV, the wife of 'Helcias the Temple Treasurer' (preceding the 'Saulus' in Josephus' comrade and '*kinsman*' Antipas above).[6] In Herodian genealogies, this would make her not only *the sister of both Saulus and Costobarus,* but also the mother of that 'Julius Archelaus', just mentioned above also, who like Josephus also *ended up in Rome obviously living in some comfort and an avid reader of the latter's works*!

If this is so, then Paul comes from a very important line indeed and it is not surprising that his nephew – whom we might tentatively identify as 'Julius Archelaus' – had such ready access to the Temple Guard. As we have noted, this line goes back through *a daughter of Herod and his Maccabean wife Mariamme I to the Idumaean Costobarus,* the husband of Herod's sister Salome I. The endogamy here, so roundly condemned at Qumran, is dizzying.

This is consistent as well with the picture of the 'Herodian' Paul in the Pseudoclementine *Recognitions*, leading the attack on James in the 40's. The only problem is the time frame – approximately twenty years' difference. The 'Saul' in Josephus reappears in 66 CE as the intermediary between '*the Peace Party' in Jerusalem* and Herod Agrippa II's army and that of the Romans outside it. Again, this Saul has either just escaped from Agrippa II's palace or the Citadel where the whole Guard has just been slaughtered in the initial moments of the Uprising – all, that is, but the Captain who was *forcibly circumcised* thereby saving himself.[7]

This linking of Saulus with the names of Costobarus and Antipas is certainly genealogical. This younger Antipas was also for a time Temple Treasurer as we signaled; however was killed by '*the Robbers*' (the *Sicarii* – specifically, one '*John the son of Dorcas*'), prior to *the irruption into the city of 'the Zealots' with their 'Idumaean' partisans* and *their consonant slaughter of the High Priests, including James' murderer Ananus.*[8]

In the meantime, Saulus fled with his brother Costobarus and Philip to the Roman Commander Cestius' camp, and, from there, to Nero who was, at that time, *residing in Corinth.* There, Saulus reported on the situation in Palestine and blamed the then-Governor Florus (64–66 CE), rather than the Roman commander Cestius, for the catastrophe that had occurred. It is at this point and location that the future Roman Emperor Vespasian is given his commission to repress the Jewish Uprising in Palestine. Since this also seems to have been part of Saulus' recommendation to Nero, Saulus may have accompanied him – but Josephus trails off here and we do not hear of his ultimate fate.

If Paul is related to the original '*Costobarus*' and, in addition, *Herod Antipas*, that is, '*Herod the Tetrarch*' – as the name '*Antipas*' above would also seem to imply – whose '*foster brother*' was referred to in Acts 13:11 as one of the founders of Paul's curious 'Community' in Antioch *where 'Christians were first called Christians'*; it would explain what Paul was doing on his mysterious visit to Damascus when he ran afoul of the Arabian King Aretas (2 Cor. 11:32). This is the same 'Aretas' who was, then, at war with Saulus' putative kinsman 'Herod Antipas', who executed John the Baptist not long before or at about this time. For Acts 9:22, it will be recalled, Paul rather *ran afoul of 'the Jews, who dwelt in Damascus*'.

However these things may be, Acts' presentation of Paul's last days is fuzzy in the extreme. Acts appears to know nothing about Paul's death or, if it does, is unwilling to tell us about it because, presumably, it was too embarrassing. It is to early Church sources we must turn for the information *that Paul was beheaded*, probably by Nero, and a somewhat preposterous version of Peter's death as well.[9] Acts ends in 62 CE, the year of James' death, with Paul under loose house arrest – if even this – in Rome (28:30–31).

In Romans 15:24–28, the same letter that includes these pointed greetings to Paul's '*kinsman the Littlest*' or '*youngest Herod*' – more than likely the son of Salome and Aristobulus whose household in Rome, as we saw, has also possibly just been greeted in the preceding line (Rom. 16:10) – Paul also expressed *his intention to visit Spain from where Gallio and his brother Seneca came.* Galba, who succeeded Nero in 68 CE, had been Governor there too, and it was the place of origin of the future Emperors Trajan (98–117) and Hadrian (117–138).

Not only did Gallio, whose presence in Corinth in the early 50's as Governor has been archaeologically verified, intervene to save Paul – even going so far as to have the Jewish leader of the synagogue there beaten in his presence because, as Acts 18:17 so charmingly puts it, '*none of these things* (that is, Jewish legal quibbles) *mattered to Gallio*' – but a lively apocryphal correspondence has been preserved between his brother Seneca and Paul.[10] Here, Acts is involved in another of those stupefying reversals, mistaking Paul's acolyte 'Sosthenes' in 1 Corinthians 1:1 for 'the ruler of the synagogue' there, whom Gallio had driven from the Judgment Seat in Corinth and beaten.

Seneca was the young Nero's tutor and the real power, at first, behind Nero's Emperorship before Nero forced him to commit suicide in 65 CE. There is no reason to suppose this correspondence between Seneca and Paul to be totally groundless but, whether it was or not, Paul's contacts went very high up in the Emperor Nero's household. At the very least these involved his own intimate associate 'Epaphroditus', by whom he sends greetings '*especially to those in Caesar's household*' (Phil. 2:25 and 4:18). It would be difficult to conceive that this Epaphroditus could be *anyone other than Nero's own* secretary *by the same name*, later blamed by Domitian for killing or, at least, helping Nero to kill himself.

This same Epaphroditus also seems to have been Josephus' publisher and Josephus even notes, in a brief dedication to him, how he had been involved in '*great events*'. Eventually Domitian had Epaphroditus – who had been his secretary as well – executed in 95 CE, a year or two after the appearance of the *Antiquities* and about the time Domitian executed his own uncle Flavius Clemens for being 'a secret Christian'! For his part, Josephus may have also run afoul of Domitian.

Whether or not everyone can agree with all these points, there is no reason to believe that Paul could *not* have returned to Palestine, *after his 'appeal to Caesar' and his initial trip to Rome to see Nero around 60 CE.* Of course, if he did so, this had to have been with and by Nero's accord, that is, *he would have entered Roman service.* Perhaps this is why Acts is so silent as to Paul's ultimate fate.

As noted, Paul is reputed to have planned or made at least one additional trip to Spain following his appeal to Caesar in Rome and, with the contacts he had in Corinth and Rome, this too would not have been surprising or difficult. If he did return to Palestine, thereafter, he could have done so around the time that the 'Saulus' in Josephus led the riot in Jerusalem in the run-up to the Uprising against Rome.

Early Church texts put Paul's death some time after the outbreak of the War against Rome, around the years 68–69 CE. Here we do begin to approach convergence with Josephus' 'Saulus' who disappears at approximately the same time from Josephus' reporting, though not before he provided Nero with a final briefing in Corinth on events in Palestine, as we saw, where he was possibly also involved in the appointment of the Roman General Vespasian as Commander of the troops in Palestine. There are too many coincidences here for them simply to be casual.

The Attack on James and the Attack on Stephen

These matters, true or otherwise, are not completely un-germane to the presentation in the Pseudoclementine *Recognitions* of Paul's attack on James in the Temple in the 40's, which itself bears on the tangle of data relating to the stoning of Stephen in the 40's and the stoning of James in the 60's. In Jerome's presentation of James' death, one or two interesting points emerge relating to how the *Recognitions* presents the attack on James in the Temple by '*the Enemy*' *Paul in the 40's*, if not *the 60's*.

There is something very peculiar about the sequencing of events relating to these two 'stonings' as we have them in Acts and Josephus. Of course there is the twenty-year gap in the chronology between them but we have this concerning the two riots too, the one in Acts led by Paul after the attack on Stephen in the 40's and the other in Josephus led by 'Saulus' after the attack on James in the 60's. It is almost as if these two documents are totally remaking each other's chronology. Then, too, though Acts places the riot led by Saulus in the 40's – when, according to the *Recognitions,* it most likely occurred – it *transposes the stoning of*

James in the 60's with that of Stephen in the 40's. Josephus does the same with the riot led by Paul in the 40's seemingly transposing it with the one led by Saulus in the 60's.

What is the explanation? There is none that will satisfy everyone. Not only does *the riot led by 'Saulus' in Josephus follow the stoning of James in the same manner that the riot led by 'Saul' in Acts follows the stoning of Stephen*, we also have the various repetitions in Josephus of the theme of *the 'Rich' Priests robbing those of the 'Poorer' kind*, which ties these matters directly to the picture in the Habakkuk *Pesher* at Qumran of *the death of the Righteous Teacher.* This is not to mention the picture of *the Rich High Priests and their violent minions arguing with the 'representatives of the People' in the Temple* – which, in these various documents, always goes *from harsh debate to riot and stoning* – and the picture in both Josephus and the New Testament of *the violence such 'Violent Ones' are willing to use with the People* – terminology actually appearing and used at Qumran.

Again, the reader must always keep in mind that the Gospels and Acts have more the *character of literature*; while Josephus, *that of history*. Can we think that, for some reason, Josephus has transposed these two riots? It would be difficult to imagine why, and there is also the matter of the alleged crucifixion of Judas the Galilean's two sons, James and Simon, in the 40's in the *Antiquities* – all three of these, incidentally, being the names of Jesus' three brothers – missing from the *War*, but seemingly foreshadowing the crucifixion of Simeon bar Cleophas and possibly the grandchildren of Jesus' brother Judas under Domitian or Trajan.

On the other hand, the question about the authenticity of the picture in Acts is simpler – either one accepts Acts' presentation as it is, full of fantastic history, repetitions, and rewriting and/or overwriting, or admits there are huge holes in it, mistaken historical information, bodily liftings from other sources, and over-simplification verging on disinformation and/or outright fallaciousness. Unfortunately, some of this last occurs in precisely the area having to do with final confrontation in Jerusalem between Paul and James, the arrest of Paul, his incarceration under protective custody in Caesarea, and his appeal to Caesar.

This last includes the picture of the Chief Priests wanting – *Sicarii*-style – *to kill Paul and making grandiose 'plo–ts' against him*, a totally unconvincing picture when we know that earlier in Acts they were *in league with him* and, in Josephus, that at that time they were, in fact, rather *involved in intense internecine strife with the Leaders of the insurgent mob in Jerusalem.*

Then, too, there are Paul's various theological speeches – one like James' 'on the steps' of the Temple in front of a Jewish mob thirsting for his blood (Acts 21:40); another, before the Chief Priests and the Sanhedrin. There is also the charge against Paul by the High Priest Ananias, the 'Elders' (*Presbyteros*), and someone called 'Tertullus' – hardly a Hebrew name – in Caesarea before Felix of 'being a ring-leader of the Nazoraean Heresy' and 'a trouble-maker, moving insurrection among all the Jews in the habitable world' (24:5) – a charge that, while certainly true for some others, hardly describes Paul.

There is also Paul's own obsequious remark to Felix, the butcher of so many Jewish Revolutionaries in Palestine and himself promoting or exacerbating the strife between Greeks and Jews in Caesarea: 'Knowing, as I do, that for many years you have been the Judge of this Nation, the more cheerfully do I make my defense as to things concerning myself' (Acts 24:10). This sycophancy compares favorably with Tertullus', ostensibly speaking in condemnation of Paul: 'We are enjoying great peace through you (Felix) and by your forethought very worthy things are being done for this Nation' (24:1). Perhaps Tertullus is speaking for the Greeks of Caesarea; he can hardly be speaking on behalf of the Jews. But if this is true, then why this alleged attack on Paul?

This is paralleled by the complete confusion Acts shows about Hellenists and Jews in the early Community in Jerusalem, in which Stephen, perhaps the archetypal *Gentile* convert, with a typically Greek name meaning 'Crown' (interpreted in early Church literature to mean the martyr's 'Crown', not unrelated to the 'Crown' of James' Nazirite hair), is presented as a 'Hebrew', while his antagonists within the Community are presented as 'Hellenists'. Not only is Paul's reference to the number of years Felix had been in the country a little exaggerated, but the obsequiousness Paul displays, if Acts is to be believed, fairly takes one's breath away. Of course, this is quite normal for Paul when dealing with powerful people from whom he wanted something.

The note about finding Paul 'attempting to pollute the Temple' in Acts 24:6 and earlier in 21:28 does, however, ring true. At least, this charge was in the air in this period, both where the relevant documents from the Dead Sea Scrolls are concerned and Josephus' description of events leading up to the stopping of sacrifice on behalf of foreigners in the Temple in the *War*. We even hear of it by refraction in Paul's letters. But Tertullus' accusation of being a 'Nazoraean' and 'fomenting world revolution' would be more appropriately directed against James and his mass of 'Priestly' followers, 'all Zealots for the Law' – and, in fact, probably was.

Then there is the picture of Felix and Drusilla listening to Paul declaim about Faith in Christ Jesus, 'Righteousness', and the Last 'Judgment', and Felix talking with Paul *often*, hoping, in Acts' words, 'Riches would be given him by Paul' (*thus*). This finally ends with Felix, in order 'to find favor with the Jews, leaving Paul in bonds' for Festus the next Governor to deal with (Acts 24:26–27).

But Felix is not interested in finding favor with 'the Jews', as by Josephus' account it is 'the principal Jewish inhabitants of Caesarea who went to Rome to accuse Felix' before Nero and, of course, ultimately fail. In fact, the outcome of these complaints is disastrous for the Jews and the equal privileges they previously enjoyed with the Greeks of Caesarea are annulled. This, not because of bribery *by the Jews*, but rather because the Hellenizing inhabitants of Caesarea *bribe* Nero's Secretary for Greek Correspondence! Josephus calls this individual 'Beryllus', but Epaphroditus too probably occupied a similar post. According to Josephus, this and the brutality of Caesarean Legionnaires generally – individuals such as 'Cornelius' – is the direct cause of future Jewish misfortune, because the Jews of Caesarea became 'more unruly than ever' because of this, until War with Rome was kindled.

This chaos between Greeks and Jews in Caesarea also finds an echo, however remote, in the background to the stoning of Stephen in Acts, just as that between Samaritans and Jews, following the beating of 'the Emperor's Servant Stephen' by 'Revolutionaries' does in the unlikely stories about confrontations between Philip, Peter, and Simon *Magus* in Samaria and Lydda. So, too, the various appeals to Caesar relating to these matters find their echo in the various appeals to the Roman Governor in Caesarea in Acts, all of this supposedly *on account of Paul*, and, of course, Paul's own appeal to Nero Augustus Caesar in Rome.

Acts throws Paul into this mix in Caesarea on several occasions without one word about the inflammable social and political situation there between Greeks and Jews. Rather, in its view, it is Paul's own 'Hellenist' or 'Greek' associates from Caesarea and further afield, some of whom accompany him on his last trip to Jerusalem to see James, that provoke the attack on him in Jerusalem because the crowd thinks that 'he has brought Greeks into the Temple' (21:28).

The Two Simons in Josephus and Acts and their Confrontations in Caesarea

Another picture in Acts which is both cynical in the extreme and clearly deceptive – even dissimulating – is the designation of Agrippa II's second sister Drusilla where she is pictured as talking with Paul with her third husband, the Roman Governor Felix (the third Mariamme also went through similar marital travails, even being married at one time to Julius Archelaus above before finally ending up the wife of Philo's nephew, *the Alabarch of Alexandria himself!* – see Appendix on Herodian Family Genealogies) – simply as '*a Jewess*' and not either a '*princess*' or an '*Herodian*' (24:24).

This is dissimulating because Josephus specifically tells us *she left 'the Jewish Religion' to marry Felix* – whom he also identifies *inter alia* as the most brutal Roman Governor – and also because *whether 'Herodians' like her were 'Jewish' or not was the burning issue of the day*. In addition to this, the 'circumcision' issue looms large in Drusilla's marital difficulties, as Josephus reports them. Agrippa I, her father – the single 'Herodian' who made the greatest efforts to mollify his subjects in this regard – first demanded from Antiochus the King of Commagene (near Cilicia and Lower Armenia) *that he circumcise his son Epiphanes* – later Leader of the Roman '*Macedonian Legion*' in the 66-70 Jewish War – before he could marry her. When Antiochus bridled at this, Drusilla was then given by her brother Agrippa II after her father's death to Azizus the King of Emesa (present-day Homs near Damascus – still a hotbed of revolt) who *did 'consent to be circumcised*'.

The next point provided by Josephus is *very interesting*. At the conniving of one '*Simon a Magician*' – contemporary with the famous '*Simon*' in Acts and the Pseudoclementines – whom Josephus calls '*a friend' of Felix* in Caesarea, she was finally persuaded '*to forsake her current husband and marry*' *Felix*.[11] Also conniving at this marriage was her sister Bernice, whose marital practices like her sisters as we have seen (she, too, had once been married to the son of the Alabarch of Alexandria, the famous '*Tiberius Alexander*''s – mentioned in Acts and Titus' second-in-command at the siege of Jerusalem – brother), were a catalogue of actions railed against in *the 'Three Nets of Belial' section of the Damascus Document*. Their behavior is '*fornication*' at its highest. Bernice is characterized along with 'Simon' as helping 'to *prevail upon her (Drusilla) to break the Laws of her Ancestors and marry Felix*' (as she finally did with Titus)![12]

Though in some manuscripts of Josephus, this 'Simon' is sometimes called '*Atomus*' – probably a garbled allusion to '*the Primal Adam*' idea, attributed to '*Simon*' particularly in the Pseudoclementines; this *Simon* can be none other than the proverbial 'Simon *Magus*' of Acts and early Church literature, and, should we say it, *the demythologized Simon*. Though Josephus also calls him '*a Cypriot*', this would appear to be another of those confusions based on the notation '*Kittim*' in Hebrew – in the Bible originally, the islands Crete or Cyprus but generalized in Daniel, 1 Maccabees, and the Scrolls to include Western Nations generally – particularly those across the sea. Nevertheless, the Pseudoclementines and most early Church works correctly identify Simon's place of origin, as we have seen, as '*Gitta*' in Samaria.

Acts has quite a few of such '*Cypriots*' involved with Paul and his teaching, including even Barnabas whom it also calls '*Joses a Cypriot*' (4:36). For it, Paul, as part of his first missionary journey with Barnabas – supposedly also *to* Cyprus – even has a Peter-like confrontation with one 'Elymus *Magus*' (13:8). Not only is this individual called '*a Jewish false prophet whose name was Bar-Jesus*' and associated with a certain '*Roman Proconsul in Cyprus*' named '*Sergius Paulus*'; Paul's confrontation with him, as a '*Son of the Devil*' (*Diabolos*) and the '*Enemy of all Righteousness*' – here, not a little reversal, is clearly mythological and smacks of the confrontations between Peter and Simon *Magus* in Acts and parallel materials.[13]

If we now identify '*Peter*' with another of these '*Simon*'s in the same period – the one whom Josephus identifies as '*the Head of an Assembly of his own in Jerusalem*', who wants to *bar Drusilla and Bernice's father Agrippa I from the Temple as a foreigner and comes to Caesarea to inspect the latter's household*; then we get an almost *perfect match* – only we must, as above, *remember to reverse everything*.

According to Josephus, Agrippa I invited this third '*Simon from Jerusalem*' *to come down to Caesarea and inspect his household to see 'what was being done there contrary to Law*' – dismissing him afterwards with a trifling gift.[14] Of course, the reader will immediately recognize this to be *a perfect example of the kind of reversal and dissimulation that was going on* and the original behind *the visit of 'Simon Peter' to the household of the Roman Centurion Cornelius in Caesarea, where he learns not to make distinctions between Jews and foreigners* and *not 'to call any man profane'*.

We are now in a position, as well, to identify correctly the true nature of the confrontation between the two '*Simon*'s *in Caesarea – not in Samaria* as in Acts, which relate to other confrontations described by Josephus there: first, between '*Galileans*' and '*Samaritans*' and next between '*Jews*' and '*Samaritans*', in the course of this last someone called '*Doetus*' or '*Dorcas*' was ultimately crucified.

That Paul is seemingly sometimes mistaken in both Acts and the Pseudoclementines for Simon *Magus*, both of whom probably ultimately went to Rome in Felix's wake, is another interesting aspect to this complex of data. That Felix, according to Acts 24:26, *left Paul 'in bonds'* when he went back to Rome because he worried about Jewish public opinion, is however also quite far-fetched. What is far more likely is that Felix – with his close contacts in Nero's own household in Rome – *paved the way for Paul's appeal to Caesar.* This would be particularly so if, as we have suggested, Paul was a Herodian with links to Felix's wife Drusilla and if the numerous sessions they had – 'over two years' according to Acts – were more in the nature of intelligence briefings which on the face of them also seems more likely.

Notwithstanding, once in Rome Paul finds himself relatively free. He '*stayed two whole years in a house he rented himself ... proclaiming the Kingdom of God and teaching the things about the Lord Jesus Christ without hindrance and with all freedom*' (28:31). This is the note upon which Acts ends with not a word about Paul's fate; nor for that matter about James', which seems an incredible lacuna. Nor did his supposed 'house arrest' seem to limit his activities in any way.

The reason why it has been suggested that '*the Egyptian*', for whom Paul is mistaken at the time of his arrest by the Roman Chief Captain (Acts 21:33-40), is a representation of 'Simon *Magus*' is that the latter was reputed to have *learned his magical arts in Egypt.* That 'Simon' was also responsible, together with '*Dositheus*' ('*Doetus*' above?) – *according to the Pseudoclementines, both allegedly Disciples of John the Baptist* – for many of the disturbances in Samaria, just increases these points of contact. One can still dimly perceive through all the dissimulation the real nature of the conflict, refracted in the Book of Acts, between Simon and the Simon *Magus* in Josephus. These confrontations *in Caesarea on the Palestine coast, not in Samaria as in Acts*, also form a main focus of the Pseudoclementine literature.

The real course of events in Caesarea up to the time of Felix's marriage to Drusilla, despite all this fantasy and romance, shines through pretty clearly in Josephus and can be fairly reliably reconstructed. Acts' version of the protests against Paul in Caesarea by the High Priests to the Roman Governors, Felix and Festus are more like the protests these various groups – including these same 'High Priests' – were making in Rome over how Roman Governors were behaving in Palestine, most notably relating to problems in Lydda, Samaria, Caesarea, and '*the Temple Wall Affair*'.

There is no historical basis to Acts' '*visit by Peter to the household of the Roman Centurion Cornelius* in Caesarea'. What there is, is this visit of the *Zealot* 'Simon', *who wanted to bar Agrippa I from the Temple*, to the latter's household in Caesarea in the early 40's '*to see what was done there contrary to Law*'. We never hear of this 'Simon' in Josephus again – nor really, for that matter, 'Peter' in Acts.

The confrontation between Simon Peter and Simon *Magus* in Acts has to do with '*the laying on of hands*', '*the Holy Spirit*', and *Simon offering to buy this 'Power' with money.* These encounters take place in '*Samaria*', following which everyone seems to make up and *together 'they preached the Gospel to many villages of the Samaritans*' (8:25). For the Pseudoclementines, they occur more accurately in Caesarea and have to do with debates over various subjects like '*the Primal Adam*', '*the True Prophet*', and *the nature of 'the Christ'*.

But having regard for the anti-'*fornication*' theme in both the Letter of James and the materials at Qumran – not to mention the confrontations between John the Baptist and these same Herodians over the same issue in the previous decade – I think we can safely assert that the confrontations in Caesarea between *the two Simons* had principally to do with Simon *Magus* conniving at the divorce by Drusilla, whom Acts identifies only as '*a Jewess*' and not as an '*Herodian Princess*', of King Azizus of Emesa (something also expressly forbidden at Qumran and falling under the definition of '*fornication*') *who had expressly had himself circumcised for this purpose*, and *convincing her to marry Felix instead.*

So this 'Simon *Magus*' was a henchman – perhaps not unlike Paul – of Felix whereas Peter, in the manner of Qumran and like John the Baptist in the previous decade, who lost his head in the same kind of confrontation, *opposed this kind of 'fornication' among Herodians.* Even Josephus is forced to remark that '*divorce on the part of the woman was against the Laws of her country*' and that, by doing so, Drusilla had both '*transgressed the Laws of her Forefathers*' and *left the Jewish Religion* (i.e., she was no longer '*a Jewess*').

I think it is safe to say that the '*Simon, the Head of an Assembly of his own in Jerusalem*,' who agitated against allowing Agrippa I into the Temple – despite the fact that his ancestors built it – and went so far as to '*inspect his household in Caesarea*', would ultimately have been arrested, notwithstanding Josephus' silence on this point – if not by Agrippa I, then certainly by Herod of Chalcis (44–49 CE), his less tolerant brother (who may also have '*beheaded James the brother of John with the sword*' – *sic*!) who succeeded him.

Acts' Paulinization of Peter in Jaffa and Caesarea

Acts' portrayal of Peter's visit to Cornelius' household is just the opposite of the account in Josephus upon which it is based – *the visit by Simon to Agrippa's household in Caesarea.* Acts describes Cornelius, it will be recalled, as *'a Righteous One', 'Pious and God-Fearing', 'doing many Righteous works to the people and praying to God continually', and finally 'borne witness to by the whole Nation of the Jews'* (10:2 and 10:22). Not only do we have here *almost all the elements from early Church portraits of James*, but the cynicism of applying these characteristics to a *Roman Legionnaire from Caesarea*, the brutality of and incessant goading of the Jews by whom to revolt against Rome is described by Josephus, is extreme. Were it not that these matters were so serious and have been repeated as pious truisms for almost two millennia, it would be difficult to suppress a fulsome guffaw.

In this episode, Peter learns '*not to make profane what God has made clean*', nor '*to call any man profane or unclean*' as we saw (Acts 10:15 and 28), that is, *not to make problems over dietary regulations and make distinctions between men on the basis of race* – noble sentiments, but just the opposite of what the 'Simon' in Josephus is envisioning regarding Agrippa I – to say nothing of the portrayal of Peter's teachings in the Peudoclementine *Homilies.*

In Acts, Peter goes on to characterize God as '*not being a respecter of persons*' (10:34), basically a variation of the words Paul uses in Galatians 2:6, '*God does not accept the person of man*', to attack the '*Pillar*' Apostles John, Peter, and James. We already saw, as well, how this also represented an inversion of the description of James as '*not respecting persons*' in Hegesippus' account of his proclamation in the Temple on Passover – reversed, yet again, in Josephus' fawning description of James' murderer and arch-nemesis, the High Priest Ananus above, as 'treating even the humblest as equals'.[15] Once again, it is difficult to repress a guffaw.

Paul's attack in Galatians on the 'Pillar' Apostles then moves on to excoriate 'Cephas' and '*those of the circumcision party*' generally on just the points about *keeping dietary regulations and separating from Gentiles*, we have in Acts' account of Peter's reaction to and understanding his vision of the descent of 'a tablecloth' on the rooftop in Jaffa. The only problem is that, according to Acts' chronology, his 'vision' precedes this encounter in Antioch, so if Peter or *Cephas* had ever really experienced such a 'vision', why would Paul have to be attacking him – even going to the extent of calling him '*a hypocrite*' – on these issues here in the first place?

Nor is this to mention the fact that they are totally gainsaid in the Pseudoclementines anyhow.

In any event, the upshot of this episode in Acts is that Peter is now represented in a speech to Cornelius' '*kinsmen and closest friends*' (*thus*!) as extending the applicability of James' '*Righteousness of works*' ideology to all Gentiles and, in the process of course once again, making a '*blood accusation*' *against* '*the Jews*' – to wit:

> In every Nation he, who *fears* (*God*, i.e., is '*a God-Fearer*') and *works Righteousness*, is acceptable to Him .... Jesus, who was *from Nazareth* ... went around *doing good* (*works*) and healing all those who were oppressed by the Devil (*Diabolou*) ... *in the country of the Jews and in Jerusalem, whom they put to death by hanging on a tree* (Acts 10:35–39 – this last patently echoing Paul in Galatians 3:13 as well)

The issue of '*circumcision*' crops up at this point in Galatians too, as it does Acts' picture of those supposedly accusing Peter when he went back 'up to Jerusalem' to report what had happened in Jaffa and Caesarea following this: '*Those of the circumcision* (this, word-for-word from Galatians 2:12 describing James' followers) *contended with him*, "You went in to men uncircumcised and ate with them"' (11:2–3 – clearly a caricature). This portrait of what are obviously supposed to represent James' '*Jerusalem Community*'/ '*Church*' supporters as 'Peter's interlocutors verges on derogation. Still, in the real world, Acts' alleged '*Jewess*' Drusilla (and her sisters) did much worse.

Not only does this episode anticipate Peter's behavior as portrayed in Galatians, but the very words it uses more or less echo Paul's rebuke of Peter there – itself turning on the matter of James' leadership: 'For before *some from James* came down, (Peter) used to eat with the Gentiles, but after they came, he *drew back and separated himself* being afraid of *those of the circumcision*' (Gal. 2:12, as Acts 11:2). Here again we have '*separation*', so important to the charge sheet of '*the Three Nets of Belial*' in the Damascus Document and the Qumran orientation generally.

The reference to '*circumcision*' too, not only links it to the episode we are exploring in Acts above having to do with 'Peter' on a rooftop in Jaffa and visiting the Roman Centurion '*Cornelius*' in Caesarea (the '*Lex Cornelia de Sicarius*'?) and its aftermath in Jerusalem, but further unequivocally identifies those in Jerusalem '*insisting on circumcision*' with James' 'Jerusalem Church' Community (and possibly even, as already signaled, '*forced circumcision*' and '*the Sicarii*').

Knowing the history of Caesarea in this period, which more or less paralleled that of another hotbed of Greek anti-Semitism Alexandria, the authors of Acts must have been in a really mischievous mood when composing these scenes about '*Peter*' *on a rooftop in Jaffa* and *visiting a Roman Centurion in Caesarea*! Something approaching one million Jews were wiped out (that is, just about the whole Egyptian Community – the numbers have never been accurately counted) during the course of apparently 'Messianic' disturbances in Alexandria and its environs during Trajan's reign (98–117 CE).

There can be little doubt that Acts' 'Cornelius' episode, just as the 'Stephen' episode preceding it to like effect, *never actually happened*. In fact, regardless of what 'Peter' is depicted as learning or unlearning here, the episode in its present form definitively proves that 'Jesus' (however we might speak of him) did not *definitively regulate the twin issues of* '*forbidden foods*' or '*table fellowship with Gentiles*' in his lifetime and *never taught anything* on these issues *remotely resembling what is attributed to him in the Gospels*.

The over-zealous artificers in the Book of Acts have, at least, established this, though it was not their goal. The reason is quite simple – had Jesus done so, Peter, his purportedly closest living associate, *would have known of it* and, therefore, not needed this Paulinizing '*tablecloth*' vision to so conveniently regulate these issues *on the eve of his visit to the Roman*

Centurion's household in Caesarea. On the contrary, since 'Peter' is portrayed as *not knowing such things*, 'Jesus' did not teach them either; and this episode in Acts or the picture of 'Jesus' teaching things like '*nothing which enters the mouth defiles a man, but that which goes forth out of the mouth defiles a man*' in Matthew 15:6's '*toilet bowl*' episode or eating with classes of unclean persons like '*tax collectors*', '*Sinners*' (a catchword for 'Gentiles' in Galatians 2:15), and '*being a glutton*' (i.e., *eating all foods* without distinction), preferring 'prostitutes', etc., is false.

In any event, the episode is really included only to counteract the one, pictured by Paul in Galatians, where Peter is portrayed as withdrawing from '*table fellowship*' with Gentiles when '*some from James*' and '*the Party of the circumcision*' come down to Antioch. It *Paulinizes* Peter, putting the basic elements of the Pauline approach – '*food is for the belly and the belly for food*' and '*circumcision is nothing and uncircumcision nothing*' (1 Cor. 6:13 and 7:19) – into his mouth.

Of course, official history and orthodox doctrine, as presented in the Gospels and the Book of Acts, have a ready response to this. Peter, who denied Jesus three times on his death night (Mt. 26:75 and pars.), simply *misunderstood* the teaching of the Master. In this episode in Acts, the Heavenly Voice that accompanies the descent of the Heavenly tablecloth with its forbidden foods – similar to the Voice Paul is always hearing – *cries out to him three times* before Peter understands the gist of its teaching (Acts 10:16). In the Gospels, Peter sinks into the Sea of Galilee for *lack of Faith* – the quintessentially Pauline position – when trying to replicate Jesus' miracle of 'walking on the waters' (Mt 14:31 and pars.).

In fact, the real Peter shines through, even in the tablecloth episode as it presently stands, in his insistence that '*I have never eaten anything profane or unclean*' (Acts 10:15, repeated with slight rephrasing in 11:8). In effect, this visionary episode puts the overall issue very eloquently when it has Peter explaining to Cornelius and entourage, '*You know, it is not Lawful for a Jewish man to have conversation with or come near one of another race*' (10:28) – thus directly relating it, whether by design or accidentally, to the impetus behind the visit of the '*Simon*' in Josephus, *also to Caesarea*, who rather wants to *exclude Agrippa I from the Temple as a foreigner.*

Confrontations over Circumcision and the End in Acts

'Circumcision', too, was the issue complicating both Drusilla's and Bernice's marriages to royal personages in Syria and Asia Minor and to Felix – whose brother Pallas stood at the hub of power in Rome. It is also at the heart of Paul's confrontations in Galatians with those 'from James', who came down to press the 'table fellowship' issue in Antioch, and Peter's riposte to '*those of the circumcision*' following his 'tablecloth' vision in Acts, which permits him not only to eat with Gentiles, but even to visit the household of a Roman Centurion in Caesarea.

As a result of these interventions, clearly by James, those formerly keeping company with Paul in Antioch, including Peter and Barnabas, '*drew back and separated' themselves 'for fear of those of the circumcision*' – this within the Church not outside it. This kind of ban or excommunication by Paul's Jewish associates – shunning might be more to the point – is a typical Qumran procedure, familiar from the literature there.[16]

It should be noted that in the aftermath of this 'tablecloth' vision, too, Barnabas is pictured as being sent by 'the Assembly in Jerusalem' to Antioch, where Acts observes '*the Disciples were first called Christians*' (Acts 11:26). A series of passages ensues with representatives repeatedly coming down *from Jerusalem to Antioch*, beginning with this one involving 'Paul and Barnabas' in 11:22, but also one immediately following having to do with '*prophets coming down from Jerusalem to Antioch*', one of whom has the most peculiar name of 'Agabus' – about whom we shall hear more in due course.

The chapter ends with Paul and Barnabas returning again to Jerusalem supposedly on 'Famine-relief' operations consonant upon the 'Prophecy', by this so-called '*Agabus*', of the

Famine (46–48 CE – 11:29). This is totally gainsaid by Paul's own testimony in Galatians, which has Paul, as we have seen, not returning to Jerusalem – after his initial flight – 'for another fourteen years' or approximately 51–52 CE. This is continued into chapter 12 with the totally extraneous information about the elimination of the other '*James the brother of John*', Peter's miraculous escape from prison and subsequent flight, the completely off-hand introduction of the principal James ('the brother of Jesus'), and how 'Herod' – no further identification given – '*being eaten by worms expired*' (Acts 12:23). But, as usual, nothing about what Barnabas and Paul did in Jerusalem is mentioned during the whole of the chapter – only the laconic observation at its end that, 'having completed their mission', they returned to Antioch 'taking John Mark with them' (12:25).

Chapter 13 returns to the enumeration of these so-called '*prophets and teachers of the Assembly at Antioch*', including Niger, Paul, and the curious individual called '*Herod the Tetrarch's foster brother*'. Then ensues the confrontation with 'the Son of Devil' ('*Diabolos*', that is, 'Belial') and 'Enemy of all Righteousness', Elymus *Magus*, followed by the laconic aside about how 'John left them and returned to Jerusalem' (13:13). Finally, in chapter 15, '*Certain ones, having come down from Judea, were teaching the brothers that unless you are circumcised according to the Law of Moses, you cannot be saved*' (15:1). This will be the exact point that will emerge in both Josephus' and Talmudic descriptions of the conversion of Queen Helen of Adiabene's son somewhere in the region of Haran in Northern Syria by a teacher who finds him reading the Law of Moses.

In Acts' reckoning, it provokes the so-called 'Jerusalem Council', resulting in *the directives James sends in the letter to overseas communities*. Two individuals, identified as Judas Barsabas and Silas – '*themselves also prophets*' – are sent with Paul and Barnabas to convey James' letter *to 'the Many' in 'Antioch'* (15:30). These matters would appear to be *the real reason behind the break between Paul and Barnabas* who are rather presented as *parting company here because of a rift over 'John Mark' – 'the man'*, in Paul's view, '*who withdrew from them in Pamphylia and would not share in their work*' (15:38–39).

Just about everything from Chapters 11-15 in Acts deals with the repetitious theme of *representatives coming down from Jerusalem to Antioch* – mostly spurious and retrospective – *to cover over the rift that occurred in Antioch after Paul's return from Jerusalem* as told by Paul in Galatians. As is made clear in that Letter and intermittently in Acts, *for the most part these come directly 'from James'*, dogging Paul's footsteps over circumcision, table fellowship with Gentiles, and dietary regulations generally.

Paul's easy-going view of circumcision, no doubt, would have been very convenient for Herodians wishing to marry local kings in Northern Syria and Asia Minor and also well in line with his – and what would appear to be *Herodian* – aims generally in the East: *to build a community where Greeks and Jews could live in harmony* (cf. Gal. 3:2.8, 1 Cor. 3:24, etc.). Chapters 16 –21, however, are really simply about one extended journey in Asia Minor and mainland Greece, at the end of which Paul *hurries back to Jerusalem to be in time for the Festival of Pentecost* – apparently the time of reunion of the Community as it is of '*the wilderness camps*' in the Damascus Document of the Dead Sea Scrolls – and runs into the well-known difficulties with James and the Jerusalem mob in the Temple we have been describing.

Where the rest of Acts is concerned, we would contest the picture of 'the Jews' from Jerusalem bringing 'many and weighty charges against Paul' and Paul's defense, that '*neither against the Law of the Jews, nor against the Temple, nor against Caesar, did I commit any infraction*' (Acts 25:8). We would also contest Festus' desire, repeated twice, '*to acquire favour(s) with the Jews*' (25:7–9). Before this, as already observed, Acts has Felix '*hoping Paul would give him Riches*' (24:26). In fact, the situation was just the opposite, and a Jewish delegation went to Rome to complain about Festus as well and, because Festus was less well placed than Felix, they were more successful.[17]

Nor is the picture of Paul discoursing in detail about his career and other doctrinal concerns with Agrippa and Bernice, asking the former obsequiously, '*King Agrippa, do you believe in the Prophets? I know you believe*' (26:27) completely without exaggeration. As will be recalled, Agrippa II replies, '*A little more, and you would persuade me to become a Christian' and, nothing loath, Paul responds, 'I wish to God in no small measure that both of you soon … should become such as I also am*' (26:28–29). The scene, while no doubt essentially true, is a good example of how far New Testament authors were willing to go in refashioning the fundamentals of '*the Messianic Movement*' in Palestine and retouching the image of the ruling élite. This is the point, at which Bernice and Agrippa stand up and say, speaking aside to one another, '*This man has done nothing deserving of death or chains*' and, then to Festus, '*If he had not appealed to Caesar, this man could have been set free*' (26:31–32).

The picture of Paul trying to convert Agrippa II would, no doubt, have sent 'Messianists' of the time into paroxysms of derision – just the attitude one finds in the *Pesharim* at Qumran concerning 'the Lying Spouter' or 'Man of Lies' there. Not only was Agrippa, along with the High Priest he appointed, *responsible for the death of James, but the licentious Bernice* – who also appears in this scene – *was the future mistress of Titus.* Both were connected to people like Philo's nephew, Tiberius Alexander, the Roman Commander at the siege of Jerusalem and, to whose brother, she had previously been married. All, no doubt, were involved in the decision by the Romans *to destroy the Temple.* In fact, Agrippa II had already been involved in the decision to call Cestius' Roman troops into the city to put down the Uprising four years before. In the end, Agrippa retires along with 'Traitors' like Josephus to spend his last days comfortably in Rome.

Not only did the Zealot 'Innovators', in the aftermath of this revealing scene in Acts, ban both Agrippa and Bernice from Jerusalem altogether; but, to show their real attitude towards them – and that of 'Messianic Revolutionaries' generally – *their palaces were burned in the first days of the Uprising when Josephus tell us these same 'Innovators' 'turned the Poor against the Rich'.* No doubt Paul did confer with Agrippa II, Bernice, and Festus at some length, as he did Felix and Drusilla earlier; but it is doubtful that the picture in Acts is accurate as to the subjects discussed. As we have already suggested, the numerous sessions Paul had with Felix over the 'two-year' period detailed in Acts (24:26–27) were doubtlessly *more in the nature of intelligence debriefings than theological or religious discussions,* as Acts attempts to portray them. It was likely during the course of these exchanges that James' pivotal role among the Jewish mass and at the centre of Messianic agitation in the Temple and in Jerusalem was made plain by Paul to his Roman and Herodian overlords.

If this is so, then Paul also has a hand in the '*conspiracy*' to destroy and bring about the death of James, which would not be surprising in view of Paul's manifold differences with him, the manner of his frequent discomfiture by James, and his admitted previous destruction of such Messianic Leaders (1 Cor. 15:9 and Gal. 1:13). Paul would, then, have identified James as the pivotal figure behind the unrest in Jerusalem – certainly among so-called 'Zealots' and probably *Sicarii* as well. If James is a parallel figure to and has anything in common with the individual known as 'the Righteous Teacher' at Qumran, then this certainly would be the case. In our view, this is the ultimate reason behind James' demise and why, at one point in the Qumran Habakkuk *Pesher*, the same '*swallowing*' metaphor that is applied to the Wicked Priest's 'conspiracy' to destroy the Righteous Teacher is also applied to '*the Liar*''s activities.[18] Of course, Acts, as usual, reverses this into *a conspiracy* by the Zealots and the High Priests *to destroy Paul*!

One should also remark, when Festus is explaining to Bernice and Agrippa II Paul's appeal 'to be examined by Augustus', how he '*found him to have done nothing deserving of death but, because he had appealed to Augustus*', he decided to send him to Rome (Acts 25:21–25:25).

There is surely more lurking beneath these events than appears on the surface. The fact of these sessions in Caesarea and the space Acts devotes to them in its apologetics is impressive – almost a quarter of the narrative. Certainly they took place, but more was probably discussed during the 'two years' of these sessions than this. But why is Acts so silent as to whether anyone from James' Jerusalem Community ever came down to visit Paul during his entire 'imprisonment'? Rather Acts only emphasizes these contacts with Roman Officials and their protégés. This is not the only thing Acts is silent about.

Left: Trajan (98–117 CE), who was reportedly responsible for the deaths of 'Jesus cousin' Simeon bar Cleophas and those of the descendants of Jesus' third brother, Judas.

Above: The Emperor Hadrian (117–138 CE) – like Trajan from Italica in Spain – who crushed the last Messianic Uprising, the Bar Kochba Revolt.

Right: Statue of Titus, the destroyer of Jerusalem and the Temple.

Left: Statue of Josephus' publisher Epaphroditus, who helped Nero commit suicide and was, seemingly, Paul's colleague by the same name in Phil. 2:25 and 4:18.

Chapter 17
The Truth About the Death of James

The Blasphemy Charge Against James

We now turn to the Fourth-Century theologian Jerome, who in a few allusions finally gives us the key to sort out all these overlaps, transpositions, and *non sequiturs* in the various stories about the attack on and death of James. Though Jerome presents the data about James' death in just a few sentences, several points emerge from his version which overlap the presentation of the attack on James in the Temple by 'the Enemy' Paul in the 40's not the 60's in the Pseudoclementine *Recognitions*. Can it be possible that Paul did this – can *Recognitions* be true? Not only is it possible and it did probably happen, but there is more – much more.

When one reads Jerome carefully, one can see he knows many of the things we know today about biblical research. For instance, he is aware that *not all the letters of Paul may have been written by Paul, that Hebrews might have been written by Barnabas, that Jude is the brother of James, and that there is a question about the authenticity of the Letter attributed to James because of its excellent Greek* – all points still discussed by biblical scholars today. Nevertheless one must approach his work with caution, for in it there is still an orthodox theological orientation, coupled with a desire to protect the Church at all costs which must be reckoned with.

When Jerome comes to present the death of James, he prefaces this with the usual – probably direct – quotation from Hegesippus, describing James' Naziritism, which is worth repeating: '*He alone enjoyed the privilege of entering the Holy of Holies since, indeed, he did not wear woolen, but only linen clothes, and went into the Temple alone and prayed on behalf of the People, so that his knees were reputed to have acquired the calluses of a camel's knees.*' This could be nothing other than an account of a *Yom Kippur* atonement.

Like Eusebius, Jerome also claims to be quoting Hegesippus directly but makes no bones about the fact that *it was the Holy of Holies into which James went.* For Jerome, this atonement was a function of James' 'Priestly' activities and, therefore, his functioning as a kind of '*Opposition High Priest'* – not so much of his 'bathing' ones or the other aspects of his 'Piety' or life-long Nazitism or 'Holiness', which were more in the manner of those Josephus is calling 'Essenes' or parallel 'Sabaean', 'Elchasaite', or 'Mandaean' practices of Northern Syria and Southern Iraq.

Then Jerome, combining what he claims to be the accounts of both Clement and Josephus, provides the following description:

> On the death of Festus who governed Judea, Albinus was sent by Nero as his successor. Before he had reached his province, Ananias the High Priest (*thus*), the youngest son of Ananus of the class of Priests, taking advantage of the state of anarchy, assembled a Sanhedrin and publicly tried to force James to recant that *Christ was the Son of God.*[1]

Here Jerome replaces the usual chronology of James' death, being immediately followed by the fall of Jerusalem of the other early Church accounts, with Josephus' chronology.

By 'Ananias' he clearly means Ananus, but his confusion is interesting, since the distinction between Ananias and Ananus is not always clear even in Acts, which knows no 'Ananus' – nor clearly drawn in Josephus. Both were extremely 'Rich' and we have already noted the pivotal role Ananias played in collusion with Governors like Albinus in 'robbing the tithes of the Poorer Priests' in Josephus' accounts of the violence High Priests were willing to use with the People.

In combining Josephus and the early Church accounts, which Jerome generally credits to Clement of Alexandria, the charge against James in the Sanhedrin trial that he extracts from Josephus becomes one of refusing to deny that Jesus was 'the Son of God'. This charge, along with *the Sanhedrin trial*, is missing from the accounts we have excerpted from Eusebius, Epiphanius, and Hegesippus; however, the charge brings us right back into the Gospel accounts of *the death of Jesus*.

As in the Gospels, it is James' insistence that in Jerome's account leads directly to the '*blasphemy*' charge, for which stoning was the punishment in the classical Jewish sources. This point may have been in Clement's no longer extant account. The charge itself is certainly not in Josephus, though the trial, of course, is.

It will be recalled that in Eusebius, in response to the question 'the Scribes and Pharisees' demanded of James when he 'stood on the Pinnacle of the Temple', 'What is the door to Jesus the Crucified One', James simply moves on to his proclamation of how Jesus – specifically identified as 'the Son of Man' – is 'sitting on the right hand of the Great Power and will come on the clouds of Heaven' (presumably meaning, 'with the Heavenly Host'). This is a scenario of final apocalyptic Judgment which, as we saw, has much in common with the extended exposition of 'the Star Prophecy' in the War Scroll.

In most early Church accounts of the debates on the Temple steps, such as those in the *Recognitions* – refracted to some degree also in Acts – the writers are mainly intent on showing James to be demonstrating how Jesus could be 'the Christ'. That is to say, a Supernatural Being, a Redeemer Figure seated 'on the right hand of Power', but with distinctly Greco-Hellenistic overtones. As in the case of the 'Son of Man' notation, one might legitimately call this too a Greco-Hellenistic variation of the '*Primal Adam*' ideology of the various Ebionite/Nazirite/Elchasaite groups dressed up in new attire.

It is Paul who is wedded to the idea of a Supernatural Figure, with whom he is in contact – at least he claims that he is – and whom he calls '*Christ Jesus*'. This may or may not be the same individual Jerome is referring to in this single reference to 'the Son of God'. Obviously normative Christian theology would say it is. It is only a fine point, but it is important for determining just what early Church accounts thought the charge against James for 'blasphemy' really was.

Finally one must always keep in mind the confluence of all these terminologies in Paul's 'Second Adam' or the Ebionite 'Primal Adam' terminologies, which certainly have a Supernatural aspect or – put in another way – a component involving 'Divine Sonship'.

The Parallel Blasphemy Charge in Pictures of the Trial of Jesus

'Blasphemy' really is a specific charge in Judaism. It is outlined in some detail in the *Talmud*, which is claiming to present materials going back to the period in question or even before. Whether it does or not or how accurately it might do so is a matter of opinion. In the *Talmud*, the punishment for blasphemy is stoning, though this is less clear in the Old Testament.[2]

Jesus, therefore, does not die a blasphemer's death. Jesus may have been condemned for blasphemy, which the New Testament appears sometimes to be claiming (Mt 26:65 and pars.), but the charge sheet against him is unclear and varies from Gospel to Gospel. The Gospel of John, for instance, puts this charge into the mouths of the Jewish crowd, who purportedly cry out that 'he made himself the Son of God' (19:7). For Matthew 26:63 and Mark 14:61, it is the High Priest who identifies 'the Christ' with 'the Son of God', but both charges appear simply to be a retrospective emendation. The second, in any case, more properly relates to the James story as Jerome recounts it.

According to the Gospels, Pilate, quite properly, shows himself interested only in the charge of '*making himself a King*' when examining Jesus. In the Gospel of John, Pilate is corrected by the Jewish mob, which once more tells him his job: '*Everyone that makes himself a King, speaks against Caesar*' – whereupon Pilate condemns Jesus. John even depicts the crowd as warning Pilate that, if he releases Jesus, he is not 'a Friend of Caesar' (19:12) – terminology used on Herodian coins such as those of Agrippa I and Herod of Chalcis.

The answer Jesus gives to Pilate's question, 'Are you the King of the Jews?': 'My Kingdom is not of this world' (John 18:33–38), identifies John, anyhow, as late – demonstrably later, for instance, than the early Second Century and the correspondence between Pliny the Younger and Trajan. The latter, at least according to Eusebius, when instructed by Trajan as Governor of Bithynia in Asia Minor to investigate Christians (112 CE), '*found no fault in them*' – a response equivalent to Pilate's in John, '*I find no fault in him*' (19:4–6, paralleled in Luke 23:4–15).[3]

In any event, it is as late or later than similar inquiries – also described by Eusebius, this time following Hegesippus again – in Domitian's time (81–96 CE) of *the sons (or grandsons) of* Jesus' *third brother Judas.* Depicted as simple country menials, these respond to questions 'concerning the Christ and His Kingdom' almost exactly as Jesus is depicted as doing here in John: 'That it was not of this world nor earthly, *but Heavenly and Angelic, when He would come in Glory to judge the quick and the dead and give every man according to his works.* At this, Domitian *found no fault with them*, but having contempt for them as simpletons, dismissed them.'[4] The reader will note the repetition here of James' proclamation of the Son of Man coming in Glory in the Temple at Passover, again precisely as depicted in Hegesippus – including the note about '*giving every man according to his works*'.

For Luke, the charge sheet to Pilate is quite specific: 'We found this man leading the people astray and forbidding them to pay tribute to Caesar, saying that he himself, Christ, is a King' (23:1). Here Luke combines Jesus' 'being a King' – which Pilate alludes to in his 'Are you the King of the Jews' question – with the 'Christ' ideology. Going on to emphasize the issue of 'insurrection and murder' concerning Jesus' alter ego Barabbas (23:19), Luke also twice plays on the point concerning whether Jesus and his followers – Peter in this case – were 'Galileans'. In the process, he shows an understanding of the confusion between taking this terminology literally or in the more symbolical sectarian or subversive sense (22:59 and 23:6).

In his picture, the Jewish crowd is now doing the 'blaspheming' (22:65: 'they said many other blaspheming things to him'). When 'the Chief Priests and Scribes gather' in his Sanhedrin scene, the two questions, 'are you the Christ' and 'are you the Son of God', follow one after the other (22:67–71). These then lead into the only real answer Jesus makes as far as Luke is concerned: 'Henceforth shall the Son of Man be seated at the right hand of the Power of God' – which is again, of course, the proclamation attributed to James in the Temple on Passover by Eusebius and Hegesippus, as well as by Jerome – before all three move on to the stoning material.

But Luke is quite consistent in the manner in which he separates the thrust of these 'blasphemy' materials – which hardly concern Pilate at all, or for that matter the Romans – from social agitation or insurrectionary activities, for which in Roman Law (*not Jewish*) the punishment was *crucifixion.* Matthew and Mark, on the other hand, rather combine the two queries into a single question: 'Are you the Christ, the Son of God' (26:63 and 14:61), showing that they think the two expressions, 'the Christ' and 'the Son of God' are basically either two aspects of the same thing or identical.

Mark, however, like John above, is the only Synoptic to have Jesus actually answer in the affirmative – Jesus' words, 'I am', taking the place of 'henceforth you shall see, etc.' in Matthew and Luke. But this being said, Matthew and Mark also go on to attach their version of the two notations combined into a single phrase to *Jesus'* proclamation (not *James'*): 'Henceforth you shall see the Son of Man sitting at the right hand of Power and coming on the clouds of Heaven' (Mt 26:64 and Mk 14:62). It is at this point that Matthew and Mark depict the High Priest as 'rending his clothes', specifically giving the verdict, 'You have spoken *blasphemy*', and 'all of them condemning him to be worthy of death'.

But this is just what one would expect, because the claim of being either 'the Christ' or 'the Son of God', or both, is a theological one and the crux of issues between Christians and Jews even today. Since the claim is not on the surface, anyhow, a political one, *this is the claim* that gives rise to the 'blasphemy' charge – just as in Jerome's account of the events leading to *James'* stoning.

For his part, not only does Luke avoid any overt mention of the blasphemy charge against Jesus – picturing it rather as what the men taking Jesus to the 'High Priest's House' do to him (22:65: 'and they said many things to him, blaspheming him') – he also uses the issue of Jesus 'being a Galilean' to interrupt the more political scene with Pilate with an intervening interview with 'Herod' (namely Herod Antipas, Tetrarch of Galilee and Perea). This interview and this scene are unique to Luke's Gospel and are followed directly by the final climactic condemnation before Pilate.

However, in all three Synoptic Gospels, *the Sanhedrin trial of Jesus* for blasphemy at 'the High Priest's House' ends on the note of their 'spitting in his face and striking him with blows'. This is not only similar to how 'the High Priest Ananias' has people hit Paul 'in the mouth' in Acts 23:2, but, as we have already remarked, also the James martyrdom scene in all the various presentations. Matthew adds 'with the palms of their hands' (26:67). For Luke, the men conveying Jesus 'beat' him, 'striking his face' (22:63–64).

Mark and Luke even include the curious element of their 'covering' Jesus' face, which parallels the bizarre picture in the Second Apocalypse of James of James' stoning, where after having James dig a hole, they 'cover him' up to his abdomen before they stone him.[5] In fact, the sequence and scenario here in the Gospels is exactly the same as that of James' martyrdom scene in all sources above. Of course, this may have been common to all the puppet trials and executions of the period, but in the James scenario the blasphemy charge with more sense does move directly on to a stoning, and this, without the patent attempts – in spite of the fact that crucifixion in this period was pre-eminently *the Roman punishment for insurrectionary* and *subversive activities* – to rescue Roman officials or their underlings from any taint of collusion or responsibility.

Jesus Before Herod and Paul Before Agrippa II and Bernice

Luke takes these whitewashing attempts or the power of creative writing to even greater heights. As in the case of 'Jesus the Nazoraean' or 'Nazirite', supposedly coming from 'Nazareth' elsewhere in the Gospels, Luke either misunderstands or purposefully obscures the 'Galilean' accusation, making it appear as if it involves only geographical and not socio-revolutionary aspects (23:4–6). Using his superior knowledge of Josephus, Luke exploits Pilate's question about whether Jesus was 'a Galilean' to intersperse a quick intervening interview with 'Herod' (that is, Herod Antipas), since this was his 'Jurisdiction' (23:7).

The Herod in question, Herod 'the Tetrarch', is the one who carried out the execution of John the Baptist across the Jordan, also in 'his Jurisdiction'. It is his 'foster brother' supposedly who is a *founding member* of the Pauline 'Antioch' Community. The picture of Jesus' execution even outdoes this in the way it dissimulates on the question of Roman and/

or Herodian involvement. In the Gospel of Matthew, Pilate's wife sends him a message, warning him to 'have nothing to do with *that Righteous One*' (in other words, now *she* is using the '*Zaddik*' terminology), because just that day she had a dream, where she 'suffered many things because of him' (27:19). Once again, we are in the Roman world of superstitious fantasy and 'birthday parties'. Luke adds the colorful detail that Herod and Pilate, supposedly 'previously at odds, both became friends with each other on *that very day*' (23:12)!

At a later period consonant with the stoning of James, Agrippa II and Ananus the High Priest do seem to have become friends in Rome, during the latter's 'appeal to Rome' following the beating of 'the Emperor's Servant Stephen' and the crucifixions at Lydda, as do the Roman Governor Albinus and the 'Rich' High Priest Ananias thereafter in Judea. Of course, Felix is such a friend of the Herods that he even married one of their daughters, the 'Jewess' Drusilla. In Luke, however, the note about this alliance between Romans and Herodians just serves to exculpate them both from any complicity in the murder of 'Christ', which is the real point of the episode. Therefore, at its conclusion, Pilate is made to say to the 'Chief Priests and the Rulers and the people': 'You brought this man to me as one who perverts ('misleads') the people, but behold, having examined him before you, *I found no fault in this man touching on those things you charge him with. No, nor yet Herod … nothing deserving of death has been done by him.* I will, therefore, punish and release him' (Luke 23:13–16). But, of course, this is just the conclusion we would have expected if Christianity were to circulate and survive in the Roman Empire at this time. If it had not been, we would have had to invent it – as it, no doubt, was in the first place. In any event, it agrees perfectly with the scenes in Acts between Agrippa II (who really was a 'King', unlike the Herod the Tetrarch who interviews Jesus and, in Mark 6:14 below, destroyed John the Baptist) and the Roman Governor Festus, who really do examine Paul and conclude with even more verisimilitude: '*This man might have been released* if he had not appealed to Caesar' (Acts 26:32).

Of course, the intervening interview with 'Herod' in Luke is nothing but a refurbishment of this more substantial one in Acts. The dramatis personae, Agrippa II and Bernice are, therefore, correctly identified, because, although undergoing a certain amount of enhancement, the episode is not a *complete* historical rewrite or completely counterfeit. The real fate of people who incurred the displeasure of Herodian Rulers or Roman Governors is described in Josephus' presentation of the followers of 'the Egyptian', whom Felix mercilessly butchers, or the two sons of Judas the Galilean, reportedly crucified during the Governorship of Tiberius Alexander, and others.

Folkloric presentations, as in the case of the Gospels on John the Baptist's being considered by 'King Herod' a 'Holy and Righteous Man' (Mk 6:14 and 20), or Pilate's wife considering Jesus a 'Righteous One', or here, 'Herod, rejoicing greatly when he saw Jesus because for a long time he had *desired to see him do some miracle*' (Lk 23:8), are simply the stuff of bedtime stories. But here, even worse, they have the additional intent of 'flattering the Romans and vilifying the Jews' (as Josephus himself put it). For Luke 23:47, to add insult to injury, it is another of these ubiquitous Roman Centurions, who, upon viewing Jesus' death on the cross, after which 'darkness came over the land' for three hours, concludes 'surely this was a *Righteous One*'!

Time and time again, elements integral to the story of James, such as his being called '*by all* a Righteous One' or being brought before the Sanhedrin on a charge of blasphemy, appear to be retrospectively assimilated into the details of Jesus' end.

The *Blasphemy* Charge and James' *Yom Kippur* Atonement

So one is left with the conundrum, what was the basis of the blasphemy charge against James. There are two principal death penalties in Jewish practice of this period, as reflected and sometimes even refracted in the *Talmud*. The first is for subversive or insurrectionary behavior – beheading, and the list of the various beheadings in this period is worth cataloguing.

Beheading was also known to the Romans, but their preferred means of exemplary punishment for low-caste malefactors was crucifixion, at least this was so since the Spartacus Uprising in the early First Century BCE, in the aftermath of which the road from Rome to Naples was filled with crosses.[6] This was not the case for patrician malefactors and other *citizens*, who were usually banished or offered the choice of committing suicide.

The second Jewish death penalty is stoning. The examples of these are straightforward: Honi the Circle-Drawer (Onias the Just), Stephen, and James the Just. Though there are a few other, even more lurid, punishments described in *Talmud Sanhedrin* (one, for instance, paralleling the picture of dropping a stone on someone's heart in the Apocalypse of James' depiction of James' death),[7] blasphemy, for which stoning was clearly the prescribed punishment, is quite specifically related to taking the Lord's Name in vain, in particular, pronouncing the forbidden Name of God.[8]

This does not seem to have specifically included claiming to be 'the Son of God'. In any event, there is no evidence of it in any source, that is, outside the New Testament. In Jewish literature from this period, all 'the Righteous Ones' were considered to be 'Sons of God', as several texts attest.[9] That this idea was an issue, either in the execution of Jesus or the execution of James, is most likely a retrospective imposition of later differences between Christians and Jews. This is because the specific doctrine of Jesus' Divinity itself had probably not even developed by this time. In any event, 'Divine Sonship', at least in its esoteric sense, was not really an issue in this period.

The other concern in these texts, the idea that *Jesus was the Christ*, again seems to have been an ideology with more meaning overseas in the Hellenistic world than Jewish Palestine, since the term does not seem to have any currency in this period in Palestine as far as one can tell. Even the author of Acts admits that 'Christians' were first so called in Antioch in Syria – if indeed it is this 'Antioch' Acts has in mind – some time around the 50s.

There is no evidence of such a concept in the Scrolls, though there is evidence of the 'Primal Adam' ideology related in some manner to it. In addition, there is the idea of a Supernatural 'Messiah' in the War Scroll, related to notions of Divine Sonship, 'the Christ', and 'the Primal' or 'Second Adam' ideology, who comes on the clouds of Heaven with the Heavenly Host to 'shed Judgment like rain on all that grows on earth'. In it, too, the Archangel Michael is in some manner associated with this process, but this is about as 'supernatural' as the Dead Sea Scrolls and probably James ever get.

Nor do either of these two concepts form part of any blasphemy proceedings against James or Jesus, despite New Testament and early Church claims to the contrary, though Jerome does include it as one of the charges against James. But, aside from assuming that one or another of these ideas did upset the Jerusalem Authorities in some undocumented way, one can make sense of the blasphemy charge, where James is concerned, in a way one cannot with Jesus. James' stoning certainly implies such a blasphemy charge was made against him, anyhow, if not against Jesus. The solution, therefore, has to do with James' 'Nazirite' Priestly activities – in particular, his wearing the High Priestly diadem with the words 'Holy to God' emblazoned on it and entering the Holy of Holies at least once. It involves all the supplicating before God for 'forgiveness for the People', presumably as part of an atonement he did there in the manner of an 'Opposition High Priest' of some kind, so that his 'knees became as callused as a camel's'.

These activities are *actually* documented on the part of James and render the blasphemy charge sensible where he is concerned, in a way that it is not regarding Jesus. True, the Gospels do show Jesus at one point taking over the Temple and interrupting commerce, as well as exhibiting other intemperate forms of behavior there,[10] but nothing in the picture of Jesus, as we have it, suggests 'blasphemy'. Insurrection and subversion yes; blasphemy no – unless, of course, he too *went into the Holy of Holies*. But James did. All the sources are unanimous on this point, and, astonishing or otherwise, we must consider it sensible. It was the practice of the Jewish High Priest to go into the Holy of Holies to seek forgiveness on behalf of the people for communal sins and/or sins of omission, if not commission, once a year on *Yom Kippur*, the Jewish Festival of Atonement. The point is that it was forbidden to pronounce the sacred Hebrew Name for God represented by the four letters *YHWH*, except in this way by the High Priest on *Yom Kippur*, God's Divine Name being considered so Holy it was not to be uttered. According to tradition, only Moses and a few Patriarchs before him had been taught it and uttered it.[11]

This is why the details that these early Christian sources describe regarding James most certainly do seem like a *Yom Kippur* atonement. For, if James went into the Holy of Holies once a year alone, by himself, praying 'on his knees for forgiveness of the people' so that they grew 'callused like a camel's' and if he did wear the mitre and linen of the High Priest as they attest; then this was what he was doing. However intriguing, it is useless to ask how or why he did this or had this right. This is what our sources are telling us, even perhaps without realizing it.

For this reason, James has been described by more contemporary, hostile 'Christian' reactions as '*the Pope of Ebionite fantasy*'.[12] This is a matter of opinion. Surely what he is pictured as doing here is less fantastic than some of the things we are asked to believe about Jesus in the Gospels and many of the Apostles in the Book of Acts, things these same critics hardly blanch to credit.

How James as Opposition High Priest Could Have Made Such an Atonement

But, regardless of such ideas, there are two ways of understanding this testimony. The first is from the 'Zealot' perspective. From the beginning of this 'Movement' – actually as far back as the days of Judas Maccabee and his father Mattathias – the 'Zealots' did not fail to *make the claim for a High Priest of greater purity and higher Piety*.[13]

This finally plays out in the butchering of all the High Priests appointed by the Romans and Herodians and the burning of their palaces by 'Zealots' as the Uprising became more extremist from 68 CE onwards. These Zealots or extreme *Sicarii* elect as High Priest a Poor 'Stone-Cutter' by the name of 'Phannius' (Phineas), against whom Josephus rails as if he was 'no Priest' at all (note the 'Rechabite' theme of being *an artisan* again here).

The second concerns the Dead Sea Scrolls. These postulate a new Priesthood, '*the Sons of Zadok*'. Though the latter may have a genealogical dimension, this is nowhere stated as such. Rather it has a qualitative or eschatological one, that is, these 'Priests' are primarily described as '*keeping the Covenant*'. In addition, there is definitely an esoteric play in this terminology on the idea of 'Righteousness' ('*Zedek*' in Hebrew) as we have seen and, in the only other real definition we have of these in the Dead Sea Scrolls, 'the Sons of Zadok' are definitely spoken of in terms of '*Justifying the Righteous (that is, 'making the Righteous Righteous') and condemning the Wicked*'.[14]

It is also said that *the period of their rule is preordained* and *they are 'the Elect of Israel who will stand at the End of Days'*. None of these appositives is genealogical; *all are qualitative and even eschatological*, meaning they have to do with the 'Last Things' or 'the Last Times' – things like, 'the Day of Judgment', expressly evoked as well in the Habakkuk *Pesher*. In fact in the Habakkuk *Pesher*, 'the Elect of Israel' are described in just this manner, that is, like Jesus' favorite Apostles in the New Testament they participate in the Last Judgment or, as it is expressed there, '*God's Judgment before many Peoples*'.[15] Therefore, it is fair to say, there is even *a 'Supernatural' component to these definitions of 'the Sons of Zadok' at Qumran.*

In the 'Three Nets of Belial' section of the Damascus Document, these new 'Zadokite' Priests are clearly opposed to the reigning Establishment or Priestly Hierarchy of the day. Therefore we have described them as an 'Opposition High Priesthood'. In it, 'Priests' are matter-of-factly defined as '*the Penitents of Israel who departed from the Land of Judah to dwell*' or '*sojourn in the Land of Damascus*' and, aside from the numerous esoteric implications of this, note the play on the 'Rechabite' ideal of 'sojourning'.[16]

There is even an individual described in the literature at Qumran as 'the *Mebakker*' or '*Overseer' of the wilderness camps.* He would definitely appear to be paralleled by someone called 'the High Priest commanding the camps', and he acts in all things like a 'Bishop' (Gr. *episkopos* – lit. 'Overseer') in early Christianity.[17]

If we put James – whose followers in Acts are identified as 'Zealots for the Law' – into either of these scenarios, we are close to achieving a perfect match. At the very least, we have the wherewithal for understanding not only how this presentation of James as a kind of 'Opposition High Priest' arose, but also how at least once, in or before 62 CE, he could have been allowed into the Holy of Holies of the Temple and stayed there 'on his knees' importuning God to forgive them – themes that are constant in all the traditions relating to him.

The Habakkuk *Pesher* delineates the argument between 'the *Zaddik*' or 'Teacher of Righteousness' – also called 'the High Priest' there and in parallel materials in the Psalm 37 *Pesher* – and 'the Man of Lying', *who 'rejected the Law in the midst of their whole Assembly'*. It also delineates a dispute with 'the Wicked Priest', clearly the Establishment High Priest eventually responsible for the death of or destruction of 'the Righteous Teacher'. It even tells us in its somewhat obscure manner of those events leading up to the destruction of the Teacher of Righteousness and difficulties on *Yom Kippur* between this Priest and the Teacher's followers, known as 'the Poor'.

The signification of these events is not easily clarified because of the obscurity of some of the language being used, but we unravel it further in the follow-up to this book (Volume II), mentioned above. At the very least, these events *involving the Teacher and 'the Poor'* do tell us about *confrontations between them and the Establishment High Priest – 'the Wicked Priest' – on Yom Kippur*, which seems to have been celebrated on different days because of calendrical differences between those depicted in the Qumran texts and the Establishment.

These bitter confrontations lead to tragic consequences – also treated in the Psalm 37 *Pesher* – in the course of which, the Hebrew word '*causing to stumble*' or '*casting down*', used both in the Letter of James and corresponding Pauline and early Christian language, is also employed.[18]

If, as such an 'Opposition High Priest', James did go into the Holy of Holies on *Yom Kippur*, whether on the date celebrated by the Establishment High Priests or as determined in the Scrolls, then *he certainly would have pronounced the Divine Name of God in the course of it.* Retrospective attempts to impose later theological consenses on these materials notwithstanding, *this certainly could – and probably did – lead to the Sanhedrin trial and the charge of blasphemy, for which James would have been stoned.* Those described in Josephus as 'the most equitable of the People' would, no doubt, also have sent representatives to Albinus who was then on the road, pointing out to him his prerogatives as Governor, just as Josephus describes they did.

The picture of such complaints to the Roman Governor on the part of the Jewish mob is paralleled in our Gospel accounts of the death of Jesus but again with inverted and, as it were, hostile effect. However preposterous it may be, the High Priest, 'the whole Jewish Sanhedrin', and the crowd never tire of pointing out to Pilate that *he is obliged to put*

Revolutionaries and insurrectionists (like 'Jesus') *to death.* Otherwise, he 'is no Friend of Caesar' (John 19:12).

This is hardly the sense of the representations of those Josephus calls 'the most equitable' of the Jews, who 'were most rigorous in observation of the Law and disliked what was done' to James. These, rather, explain to Albinus that the High Priest *had not the power to convene the Sanhedrin* and *impose the death penalty without the consent of the Roman Governor*[19] – totally different advice – and, therefore, even according to Roman administrative practice, he had acted illegally. Again, another of these multitudinous contradictions between the *real* facts of this period and how they are portrayed in the Gospels.

In fact, the *Talmud* contends that *the Jewish Sanhedrin did not apply the death penalty during this period because for 'forty years' prior to the fall of the Temple it 'was exiled'* – these are its very words – *from its previous location in 'the Stone Chamber' on the Temple Mount to a new place of sitting outside it called 'Hanut'.* This language is played on in this sensitive passage of the Habakkuk *Pesher* about how the Wicked Priest

> pursued after the Righteous Teacher to *swallow him with his venomous anger in his House of Exile.* And at the completion of the Festival of Rest of the Day of Atonements (*thus*), he appeared to them to *swallow them*, causing them to stumble (literally, '*cast them down*') on the Fast Day, *the Sabbath of their Rest* –

'them' being 'the Poor' and/or 'the Simple of Judah doing *Torah*' upon whom the Wicked Priest committed 'Violence' and whose 'sustenance he stole'.[20] In Josephus' account, paralleling this, 'certain others' – in these accounts, always the ubiquitous followers of James – were also 'accused of being Law-Breakers and delivered over to be stoned'.

Since the three successive 'his'es or 'him's in this passage are indefinite in Hebrew, we will be able to show in due course how they have been misinterpreted by a majority of commentators and how the allusion to this mysterious '*his House of Exile' or 'Exiled House' will actually reflect these Talmudic references about 'the Exile of the Sanhedrin' in the period* of the stoning of James (not to mention Jesus' crucifixion) *from its normal place of sitting on the Temple Mount.* Not only this, but they will also reflect the peculiar reference to *the 'Sanhedrin' trial of Jesus in 'the High Priest's House' in most Gospel accounts*, not to mention the play, encompassed by the various allusions to '*anger*' or '*cha'as*' one encounters here, on *'the Cup' or 'Chos' of Divine Vengeance.*[21]

Unlike the picture of the complaints by the Jews to Pilate of the opposite kind in the Gospels, *the complaints to Albinus over this infraction were probably true* – but to little avail. After an initial show of pique and some play-acting, Albinus soon followed the ways of previous governors and *made alliances with these same High Priests*, exerting himself with them to destroy 'the *Sicarii*' and leaving the country, in Josephus' words, *in worse condition than it was before.* In fact, almost in a shambles.

The Crucial Elements in Jerome's Testimony about James' Fall

As Jerome's testimony, conflating Josephus with early Church sources, continues: '*When he (James) refused to deny that Christ is the Son of God, Ananius (thus) ordered him to be stoned.*' Jerome now proceeds to portray this stoning exclusively on the basis of early Church sources (except for the information from his now-lost version of Josephus, on the basis of which he concludes that *Jerusalem fell because of the 'great Holiness and reputation of James among the People'*). This reads:

> *Cast down* from the Pinnacle of the Temple (we have just encountered this 'casting down' or 'causing to stumble' language in the Habakkuk *Pesher* above), *his legs broken*, but still half alive, and raising his hands to Heaven, he said, 'Lord, forgive them for

they know not what they do.' Then struck on the head by the club of a laundryman, such a club as laundrymen are accustomed to beat out *clothes* with, he died.

In the rest of his biographical description of James, Jerome provides the new traditions he knows from a document he calls '*the Gospel of the Hebrews*' which, he explains, he '*recently translated into Greek and Latin and which Origen, too, often made use of*'. This, he vouchsafes, not only includes a note about how Jesus *gave his 'grave clothes to the Servant of the High Priest*', but also the description of how *James was the first to see Jesus after the Resurrection*, which we shall treat further later. Here, the point about 'clothes' or 'grave clothes' is a little further clarified.

Jerome ends this biographical note about James with the tradition we have noted above of how James was '*buried near the Temple from which he had been cast down* (again *kataballo*)'. Here we have once again the repetition of the '*B–L–°*' language circle, now expressed, not in the Hebrew where it relates to the idea of '*swallowing*' and '*destruction*', but in Greek where it is *always* associated with *James' being 'cast* down' *from the Temple.* As should be becoming clear, the repetition of this linguistic usage in all traditions in Greek relating to attacks on or the death of James is the exact parallel to its use in the traditions relating to the death of the Righteous Teacher at Qumran.

We shall also find this linguistic usage reappearing in the various mythological descriptions of how Jesus' Apostles, as 'fishermen', 'cast down their nets', not to mention allusions connected to the '*Diabolos*' ('*Belial*' in Hebrew*) being 'cast into a furnace of the Fire*' (Mt 13:42–50). There is even a possibility, as we saw, that the usage relates to the '*Oblias*' terminology, so significant where James' role of '*protecting the People' from precisely the kind of 'Devilishness*' implied by this linguistic configuration is concerned.

Jerome ends this testimony with the note that '*His tombstone with its inscription was well-known until the siege of Titus and the end of Hadrian's reign. Some of our writers think he was buried on the Mount of Olives but they are mistaken.*' This presumably relates to a locale in the Kedron Valley below the Pinnacle of the Temple where the present-day tomb, ascribed by pilgrims over the centuries to James' name, now stands. Again, tomb traditions, familiar from the story of Jesus, seem to be impeding into the details about James or *vice versa.*

There are other thematic repetitions in this testimony from Jerome which, short as it is, is packed with data. Most important of these are the 'blows to the head' we have already encountered with regard to 'Jesus', 'Stephen', and, in Acts, even Paul. Where James is concerned, they are tied to an allusion to 'a fuller's' or 'laundryman's club', one used to 'beat out clothes'. The theme of this 'striking' again, joined to the motif of how James 'raised his *hands* to Heaven', is not un-reminiscent of the phrase, 'some struck' Jesus 'with the hand' in Matthew 26:67.

This prayer, attributed to James, is also recapitulated in the New Testament in both the last words ascribed to Jesus and Stephen's last prayer – also significantly 'on his knees'. The 'clothing' theme is this time associated with the double reference to the 'laundryman's club', not to mention the reference in Jerome's 'Gospel of the Hebrews' above to Jesus' 'grave clothes'. Here it is combined with the new one of James 'breaking his legs' in the fall – in Jerome, from 'the Pinnacle of the Temple'; but in Clement's *Recognitions*, from 'the top of the Temple steps'. It also recurs in the Gospels in connection with 'Jesus'' crucifixion and how the soldiers *'broke the legs' of those on the crosses who had not yet expired.*

We shall presently encounter this same allusion to the 'laundryman's club' in Mark, in crucial scenes about Jesus' 'Transfiguration' before his core Apostles; however here in Jerome, the idea of this 'club' or 'clubbing' definitely relates to the Rabbinic material from *Talmud Sanhedrin* about how stoning procedures were carried out. In Rabbinic tradition, this will also relate to information about *falling from the Temple wall.* An interesting example of such a 'fall' or 'push' in the *Talmud* relates to an individual who, though condemned by the

Sanhedrin to death – in this case, *by stoning* – but, because of *whose popularity* the punishment could not be effected, *the priests were to gather around jostling him and cause him to fall off the Temple wall (thus)*.[22]

In *Mishnah Sanhedrin*, which deals with things like trials for 'blasphemy', as well as these sorts of punishments before the Sanhedrin, it is specifically stated that 'If a priest (other versions add the words: 'even a High Priest') served in a state of uncleanness … *the young men among the priests were to take him outside the Temple and split open his brain with clubs*.'[23] It should be noted that in Hebrew the word being used here for 'clubs' is actually *faggots*, the precise word that will reappear in the scene in the Pseudoclementines of Paul's attack on James in the Temple where '*the Enemy*', as we saw, *picks up 'a faggot' or 'stake' from those by the Temple altar*. It should be appreciated that it was the custom to stack such 'faggots' near the altar for firewood.[24]

When coupled with these Talmudic notices, the implication is that James was *serving in a state of uncleanness or he had no right to be there in the first place*. The reference here to 'splitting open his brain', as well, is exactly parallel to all our accounts of James. It should be patent that aspects from both of these traditions have been absorbed into the James story as it has come down to us in early Church tradition or *vice versa*. But the important note here is that the priest was '*serving in a state of uncleanness*', which turns around the charges being made in Scroll texts (echoed with inverted signification even in the Pauline corpus) of '*polluting the Temple*'. That charges of this kind were being hurled back and forth in the Temple between opposing groups of 'priests' and their more violent-minded partisans – particularly in the time James held sway in Jerusalem – is particularly clear from Josephus' accounts, again tendentiously refracted in the parallel narrative of Acts.

Here once again, then, is evidence relating to *a priest, accidentally on purpose either being 'thrown down' from the Temple wall or taken outside the Temple and having his brains beaten out with a club on charges having something to do with improper Temple service or serving in a state of uncleanness*. This links up very strongly with the idea that James *went into the Holy of Holies and there rendered atonement on behalf of the people on the most sacred day of the Jewish year*. For those of the opposing party, no doubt, he would not even have been considered a proper priest at all; for those of his own party, if not genealogical, he was 'consecrated to God' or 'Holy to God' and, therefore, *the High Priest by virtue of the 'Perfection of his Holiness'*. The calendrical differences, of the kind signaled in the Qumran literature and known to have existed between the Establishment Priest class and these opposition groups, would only have exacerbated these differences and the feeling that – at least from the Establishment perspective – these 'blasphemy' or 'uncleanness' charges were legitimate.

I think we can safely say that this is where the idea of people *beating James' brains out with a club* in early Church literature comes from – not to mention the whole scene of James being put into a hole in the Second Apocalypse of James, which echoes Talmudic parameters for such alternative stoning methods in Tractate *Sanhedrin* almost precisely – this, plus the very real likelihood that this was the *coup de grâce after being stoned for blasphemy* as the *Talmud* attests. That James, under such circumstances and in the course of a *Yom Kippur* atonement, would have *pronounced the forbidden Name of God* – and this in the *Inner Sanctum* of the Temple – would only have increased the determination of his opponents to destroy him in this manner.

James *Broke His Legs* in a Fall

It is now possible to turn to the new data Jerome has provided us regarding James' 'being cast down' from the wall or Pinnacle of the Temple and 'still half alive', his legs only having been broken in the fall. That Jerome combines this point with the picture from early Church sources about the final attack on James in 62 CE and the convening of a full Sanhedrin to try him has to do with Jerome's understanding or, perhaps, misunderstanding of the sources before him. In providing us with this note about his '*legs being broken' in the fall*, he took, *prior to his stoning*, Jerome – no doubt unwittingly – supplies us with the key datum to sort out all these traditions and overlaps.

As already remarked, this theme has been absorbed in a most macabre manner and combined with similar material in Josephus in accounts of Jesus' crucifixion and death. The Gospel of John, for instance, shows an intense interest in whether Jesus' '*legs were broken' or 'not broken*', repeating the point three times in as many lines (19:31–33). For John, *because 'bodies might not remain on the cross on the Sabbath, for the Festival Day was a Sabbath', the soldiers went and broke the legs of the 'two Robbers' (Lestai again), with whom he was crucified, but Jesus' legs didn't need breaking because 'he had already expired*' (19:32).

Curiously enough, this follows a note about Jesus' '*clothes*' again. To focus momentarily on this '*clothes*' issue – first, as vividly described in Scripture, the Roman soldiers '*divided*' these among themselves and then '*cast lots for' his cloak*. For the Gospel of John, however, because Jesus' cloak was '*seamless, woven from the top throughout', they could not divide it* (19:23)!

Not only was *the division of these clothes and the casting of lots for his cloak* supposedly the fulfillment of a prophecy from Psalm 22:18: 'they divided my garments among them and cast lots for my clothes'; for John 19:28, the point that follows about Jesus crying out concerning his thirst is based on Psalm 22:15 as well.

However, Psalm 22 – which also begins with the famous words attributed to Jesus on the cross as well, '*My God, my God, why have you forsaken me*' – actually contains the key passage, we have been following throughout, about the 'adoptionist' or 'Divine Sonship of the Righteous Ones' and about James' life-long Naziritism: namely, 'You drew me *out of the womb*. You entrusted me to my mother's breasts. Cast out upon Your lap from my birth, *You have been my God from my mother's womb*' (22:9–10). Clearly a wellspring of scriptural proof-texts, this Psalm also focuses throughout on the terminology '*the Meek*', synonymous at Qumran with '*the Poor*', both so important to that form of Christianity called therefore 'Ebionitism'.

But John also uses this point about their 'breaking Jesus' legs' or, rather, their 'not breaking' them, to proceed to give some extremely gruesome details about Jesus' death *in order that several additional scriptural passages could 'be fulfilled'*. In the first of these, to fulfill Zechariah 12:10 referring to '*being pierced*', the Roman soldiers now pierce Jesus' side in the famous passage about 'blood and water coming out' (19:34). Next, both of these occurrences – not pictured in any of the Synoptic Gospels – are presented as fulfilling another scriptural passage, '*not a bone of him shall be broken*' (19:36), combining materials from Psalm 34:20 and Exodus 12:46.

Interestingly, the first-named is another of these Psalms centering around the fate of 'the *Zaddik*', to whom three references are made in some six lines (34:15–21). Like Psalm 22, it makes repeated reference to '*the Meek*' as well as to his '*soul*' and '*the soul of His Servants*' (34:3 and 23) – language also permeating the Qumran Hymns. Even more importantly, in the First Column of the Damascus Document, the 'Liar' and his confederates are described as attacking '*the soul of the Zaddik' and some of his colleagues*. For Psalm 34, 'the Angel of the Lord encamps round about' these 'Meek' and 'Righteous', saving them and delivering the Righteous One – 'not one of whose bones, therefore, was broken'.

It is also interesting to note that in the Talmudic passages dealing with executions, such as stoning for blasphemy and the like, the rationale given for such alterations in the execution scheme – as, for instance, pushing a man off a precipice above – was the dictum that *it was preferable that the outward appearance of the accused's body should look, for all intents and purposes, undamaged*! It is interesting to remark, as well, the Talmudic insistence that *an individual be stoned naked* – having to do with the 'clothes' issue again, an issue that then looms large in subsequent discussion about what to do in the case of the stoning of a lewd woman, whose body her executioners might find attractive![25]

But John neglects to tell us that the context of the second of these two passages about 'no bones being broken' – the one from Exodus 12:46 – has to do with the *barring of foreigners and those 'who are not circumcised' from taking part in the Passover meal!* Not only does this passage, then, have to do with the eating of the Passover meal; but the implication of quoting it is that 'Jesus' is now he new Passover meal – that is, Paul's 'Communion' with the body and blood of Christ Jesus again.

Here in Exodus, it is laid down that *the meat thereof 'shall not be carried out of the house, nor shall a bone of it be broken*', which is about verbatim the quotation from John above, although here meaning the Paschal lamb. But the context in Exodus is, quite specifically, that *no 'foreigner* or hired servant shall eat thereof' – only 'the sojourner' or 'resident alien', on the condition that he *be circumcised* (12:45–48). Exodus continues in this vein in the following manner: 'No *uncircumcised person* may take part. *This same law applies to the native and the resident alien among you … All the males of his household must be circumcised. He may then be admitted to the celebration, because he becomes, as it were, a native-born*' (12:48–49).

Nothing could be further from the spirit of Christianity, as we now know it, than this – in fact, it is *the very opposite of it.* Why, then, does John feel free to take it out of context from a passage with the exact opposite sense of the one he is giving it? No doubt, he considered himself to be following the same allegorical approach to Scripture which Paul employed in his Letters to similar effect.

Materials of this kind were undoubtedly part of a compilation of Messianic proof-texts of some kind. One of these is still known today and called 'Pseudo–Epiphanius'. Shorter such compilations have also been found at Qumran, whose exegetes would have reveled in the above materials. The same is true for those teachers, Paul so fulminates against – in Galatians 2:12 '*some from James*'; in Acts 15:1 '*some who came down from Judea*' – who, in particular, are *teaching circumcision* to his Communities (Gal. 5:11–12). John, however, is not particularly interested in the true import of the materials he is employing – and, typically, reversing – which, in their original context, have nothing whatever to do with the point he is making – only that they can be used to propel his narrative forward and make his choice of key words or turn-of-phrases seem either legitimate or portentous.

The same is true for the other Gospel writers. Nevertheless nothing could be more disingenuous than the manner in which they feel free to take material out of an original scriptural context that *has just the opposite sense of what they now intend it to have*, relying on the relative ignorance of their audience and *that it, satisfied by their analyses, would not normally go or be able to go to the original.* This is clear in the manner in which John pretends he has proved the point about *Jesus' legs not 'being broken' on the cross* because he had *already died* and, in any event, *it was improper that the Paschal lamb should be so defiled.*

Josephus, too, raises this issue when comparing how the Idumaeans treated *the corpse* of the High Priest Ananus by throwing it naked (perhaps this very *nakedness*, retribution for the stoning of James) outside the city without burial as food for jackals. In doing so, he remarked the scrupulousness with which Jews usually took care of the dead, *observing how they even 'broke the legs' of those being crucified so they would not remain on the cross past nightfall.*[26] In the Talmudic passages we remarked above about crucifixion and stoning from *Tractate Sanhedrin*, the same point is made quoting Deuteronomy 21:23: 'His body shall not *remain all night upon the tree*, but you shall surely bury him the same day, for he that *is hanged is a curse of God*.'

Even this, John garbles, making it seem as if the point had something to do with '*the Sabbath*' (not the '*night*') – probably because he has heard or knows that the Jews begin the Sabbath at nightfall – that is, that '*the bodies should not remain on the* cross *on the Sabbath*' (19:31). This he then links to '*preparing for the Passover*', calling it '*the Sabbath*'. This in itself has sent biblical scholars throughout the centuries to calendrical sources to determine when the Passover fell on a Sabbath, so they could then determine the true date of the crucifixion of Jesus.

Though, as just observed, this does recall the material in the Habakkuk *Pesher* about the Wicked Priest's attack on '*the Poor*' partisans of the Righteous Teacher, '*causing them to stumble*' or '*casting them down' on 'the Sabbath of their rest*'; the issue of breaking the bones in crucifixion probably has little or nothing to do with any 'Sabbath' or 'Feast Day' but is probably a garbling by John of the above comment Josephus makes about how '*the Zealots*' along with their '*Idumaean*' allies treated the corpse of James' nemesis Ananus ben Ananus.

The same is true for the point in the Synoptics about *the sun growing dark for three hours 'until the ninth hour*' (Mt 27:46 and pars.) – again more fantasy, but this time again probably based on another note Josephus makes at the end of the *Jewish War* saying more or less *just the opposite*. In giving the portents for the fall of the Temple, Josephus lists: *a cow 'giving birth to a lamb in the midst of the Temple' at Passover time (thus), 'a star which resembled a sword and a comet standing over the city for a whole year', 'chariots and armored battalions running through the clouds and surrounding cities*', and one of the Temple gates, which was fixed in iron and bolted firmly to the ground, notwithstanding *opening by itself in the middle of the night*.

Among other such inanities, he also includes how, yet again, at Passover:

> *At the ninth hour* of the night (the repetition of the *actual* hour in the Synpotics just about proves literary interdependence on this point or, more accurately, literary *gamesmanship*), *so great a light shone around the altar and the Temple, that it appeared to be the brightness of midday*. This light continued for half an hour … and was interpreted by the sacred scribes *as a portent of events that immediately followed upon it* (meaning, God leaving the Temple and its destruction).[27]

Strictly speaking, John is correct in one sense, since a 'Feast Day' was treated in Jewish Law systematically with '*the Sabbath*', even if it did not fall on the Sabbath. But the point he is exploiting here – '*breaking the bones*' of those crucified – has nothing whatever to do with either the 'Sabbath' or any 'Feast Day', but simply the scrupulousness the Jews showed in their care for the dead. That the point about a '*hanged one being a curse of God*' occupied the attention of Christian exegetes to no small degree is made clear in both the presentation of Peter's attacks on 'the Jews' before the Sanhedrin and before Cornelius' household in Acts 5:30 and 10:39 and Paul's theological exploitation of it in Galatians 3:12–13.

What is even more striking is that it can be seen that even here we have an echo of the kinds of vocabulary being used in the Habakkuk *Pesher* from Qumran in its presentation of the death of the Righteous Teacher and several of his followers whom it calls '*the Poor*'. It will be recalled that in referring to difficulties over *Yom Kippur*, the very point being made here in John about a Feast Day being a Sabbath is also found there, when it speaks about '*Yom Kippur*' being a '*Fast Day, the Sabbath of their rest*' (Lev. 16:31) – and this in regard to such crucial materials regarding both the destruction of 'the Righteous Teacher' and 'the Poor' as well. Again, the parallels are startling.

It is to the account of the attack on James by 'the Enemy' (Paul) in the Pseudoclementine *Recognitions* that we now must turn in order to make final sense of this welter of data. Even without this tell-tale note of '*his legs broken*' in Jerome's account of James' fall and his subsequent beating and stoning, it would have been possible to sort out the various traditions which have been conflated to form a single unified story; but this note from Jerome simply clinches the matter.

What early Church accounts are confusing – and this as early as Clement and Hegesippus in the mid-Second Century – is that *there were two attacks on James*, one in the mid-40's, for which Acts substitutes the attack on Stephen. The other attack on James, which results in his death, is the one in the 60's having to do with his *Sanhedrin* trial, which ends with his stoning.

These two attacks have been conflated in early Church accounts like Jerome's *into one single attack* occurring in the 60's and resulting in his death. All of these accounts contain the elements of James being '*cast down*' or the '*fall*' he takes, his stoning, and his brains being beaten out with a laundryman's club. To the fall from the Pinnacle of the Temple, which James supposedly took according to all these accounts, Jerome – meticulous to a fault – adds the specific element of '*his legs being broken*'.

We have already noted how this 'fall' or being 'cast down' or 'cast out' is incorporated into the accounts of Stephen's stoning and Judas *Iscariot*'s suicide, where it is Judas' stomach, not his brain, that 'bursts open'. The *real fall* James takes, however, is the one down the Temple stairs in the 40's, after the attack on him by Paul, in which it is made crystal clear, James *broke either one or both of his legs*.[28] Otherwise, all the elements of *both* attacks on James are present in conflated form in these accounts – the 'headlong fall', the beating or clubbing, the bizarre stoning, and, finally in Jerome, 'his broken legs'.

If we now turn to this Pseudoclementine account of Paul's attack on James in the Temple, resulting in his fall from '*the Temple steps*', *not* '*the Temple Pinnacle*' and not in his death, we are finally in a position to solve all these puzzles. It is this that Luke's Acts, embarrassed as ever, is at such pains to cover up – turning it into its very opposite, namely, *an attack by the Jews against the archetypal Gentile believer Stephen*. All the same, Acts uses it as the springboard to introduce the 'Enemy' Paul who, then, becomes the hero of its whole ensuing narrative!

Paul's Physical Assault on James in the Temple

In the *Recognitions*, Peter, in Caesarea to engage in his own debates with Simon *Magus*, tells Clement the story of the debates on the Temple steps between James and the High Priests or Temple Establishment, ending in the riot led by Paul – in which Paul picked up the 'faggot' – that resulted in James being injured and left for dead. The fact of such interesting material delivered in such precise detail is not easily gainsaid, nor does it suffer from the often miraculous signs and wonders that mar parallel accounts in the New Testament.

Peter tells Clement that the High Priest sent priests to ask the leaders of the Assembly in Jerusalem, led by James, whether they would enter into debates on the Temple steps with the Orthodox Priesthood. They accept and preliminary debates between the Apostles, on the one hand, and Caiaphas and the other High Priests, on the other, ensue (1.65–1.67). As in parallel material in Acts 5:34–39, the Pharisee Gamaliel speaks in support of the early Christians.

In the midst of this, James '*the Bishop* – '*Bishop of Bishops*' in 1.68 – *went up to the Temple … with the whole Church*' (1:66). Though the subject of these speeches is not particularly enlightening and, like the Book of Acts, largely retrospective – including discourses on 'the True Prophet' and the nature of 'the Christ', both identified with each other and then with 'the Primal Adam', John the Baptist's differences with Simon *Magus* (along with Dositheus, formerly among his Disciples), and the like – some of the historical detail is compelling. In fact, in the author's view, we have a truer picture of these clashes in the Temple than Acts presents.

For instance, when 'James the Bishop' went up to the Temple, there was 'a great multitude who had been waiting *since the middle of the night*' to see him. This kind of non-fantastic detail is impressive. 'Therefore, standing on an elevation so that he might be seen by all the People' – this can be nothing other than the picture of James standing on the Pinnacle of the Temple in early Church accounts – James takes his stand, as the other Apostles had done before him, 'on the steps of the Temple'. From this location, James begins his discourse which supposedly lasts over seven days – shades of the *Anabathmoi Jacobou*.

One immediately recognizes that one is in the same milieu as that reflected in Hegesippus via Eusebius, of James placed by the 'Scribes and Pharisees' on 'the Pinnacle of the Temple', so that he could be seen by all the People. However the physical setting in the *Recognitions* is more convincing. Just as in the mix-ups in Jerome over James' 'legs being broken', the *Recognitions*' account is in the 40's while the early Church ones are in the 60's. We are also in the world of Josephus' narrative of arguments between rival groups of Priests, the Establishment and those supported by 'the Poor', once again, even ending in rioting or stone-throwing as the accounts begin to converge.

At the point when James is about to win over 'all the People' including the Priests (compare this, with Acts 6:7's notice about a large group of 'Priests' making their conversion), an 'Enemy' entered the Temple with a few other men and started arguing with him (1:70). A marginal note in one manuscript states that this 'Enemy' was Saul. This is confirmed in the next section, as we have seen, since after getting letters from the Chief Priests , as in Acts, 'the Enemy' pursues the Community – which has fled to Jericho – *all the way to Damascus.*

By his loud shouts, abuse, and vilification, this 'Enemy' raised such a clamor in the Temple that the people could no longer hear what James was saying. Behaving '*like one insane, he excited everyone to murder*' and '*setting an example himself, he seized a strong stick from the altar*', at which point there '*ensued a riot of beating and beaten on either side*'.

One should note the intimate and precise detail here – often a sign of authenticity. According to the *Recognitions*, 'much blood was shed', followed by 'a confused flight, in the midst of which the Enemy attacked James, and threw him *headlong from the top of the steps*'. This, of course, is James' '*headlong*' fall from the Temple Pinnacle in Jerome, *etc.*

The version we have before us is from Rufinus' Latin. There is no Greek version, which is not surprising, but there is a Syriac one – again, not surprisingly. In it, this passage reads as follows: 'A certain man, who was an Enemy, with a few others came into the Temple near the altar. He cried out, saying: "What are you doing, O Children of Israel? Are you so easily carried away by these miserable men, who stray after a magician (this, of course, a reference to Jesus)?"'[29] Argumentation then followed, and just at the point, when he was about to

> be overcome (in debate) by James the Bishop, he began to create a great commotion, so that matters that were being correctly and calmly explained could not be either properly examined, nor understood and believed. At that point, he raised an outcry over the weakness and foolishness of the Priests, reproaching them and crying out, 'Why do you delay? Why do you not immediately seize all those who are with him?' Then he rose and was first to seize a firebrand from the altar (that is, 'the faggot' in the Talmudic accounts of the young men among the Priests seizing clubs and beating someone – even a High Priest – serving at the altar in a state of uncleanness) and began beating (people) with it. The rest of the Priests, when they saw him, then followed his example. In the panic-stricken flight that ensued, some fell over others and others were beaten.

Here, then, is the parallel to the young men of 'the bolder sort' allied to the High Priests, beating the Poorer Priests on the threshing floors that immediately precedes Josephus' introduction of the Herodian he is calling 'Saulus' and the picture in Book Twenty of the *Antiquities* of the various brawls on the Temple Mount between 'Zealots' and the High Priests.

One should also note in these Pseudoclementine accounts the allusion to an escape or 'flight'. In both Latin and Syriac recensions, this 'flight' continues down to Jericho. This idea of a flight is in turn picked up in Flight traditions of the early Church, specifically related to the Jerusalem Church of James the Just. This later 'Flight', which is supposed to have occurred some time prior to the fall of the Temple, is known as the 'Pella Flight' tradition. The one in *Recognitions* occurs in the early 40's. It is directly paralleled by the notice in the Book of Acts of a similar 'flight' after the stoning of Stephen and the riot Paul leads after that (8:1). In Acts' rather telescoped and somewhat inverted historical chronology, this 'flight' purportedly included everyone in the Church 'except the Apostles' and leads directly to the confrontation between Peter and Simon *Magus* in 'Samaria' (8:9–25).

The reason 'the Apostles' were not included in this flight is obvious. Immediately thereafter, according to the logic of Acts' rather topsy-turvy or collapsed narrative, they are, once again, in Jerusalem as if nothing had happened. The flight in the Pseudoclementines is also on the part of the whole Community, now estimated at some 'five thousand' souls, but this is to *the Jericho area.* This number for the members of the Community is paralleled in Acts 4:4 ('and the number of the men became about five thousand'), also amid confrontations between the Apostles and the rulers of the people in the Temple and probably on the Temple stairs!

To continue in the language of the Syriac: 'Much blood poured from those that had been killed. Now the Enemy *cast James down from the top of the stairs* (both Latin and Syriac use the word 'top' here), but since he fell as if he were dead, he did not (venture) to hit him a second time.' Not only does 'the top of the stairs' metamorphose, as these accounts are conflated with James' stoning, into 'the Pinnacle of the Temple', but the telltale allusion to 'casting down' is central to both groups of sources.

The Latin version of Rufinus expressed this as follows: 'The Enemy *attacked James* and *threw him headlong from the top of the stairs* and, thinking him dead, cared not to inflict further violence on him.'

The account of this bloody mêlée is then followed by the Disciples going to '*James' house*' in Jerusalem with his seemingly 'lifeless body'. Here they 'spent the night *in prayer*'. This is, of course, paralleled by the notice in Acts about Peter going to 'Mary the mother of *John Mark's house*' to leave a message for 'James and the brothers', where in Acts' picture too, 'many are gathered *and praying*' (12:12–17). Anyone should be able to appreciate not only that both accounts are integrally related, but the kind of purposeful obfuscation that is going on in Acts.

> The Enemy, then, in front of the Priests, promised the High Priest Caiaphas that he would kill (the Latin uses the word 'arrest' here, as does Acts) all those believing in Jesus. He set out for Damascus to go as one carrying letters from them, so that wherever he went, those who did not believe would help him destroy those who did. He wanted to go there first, because he thought that Peter had gone there.

Where this application of the 'Enemy' terminology to Paul is concerned, one should remark that in his prefatory Letter to James, Peter describes how: 'Some from among the Gentiles have rejected my legal preaching and rather attached themselves to the lawless and trifling preaching of the man who is my Enemy.'[30]

The note in the *Recognitions* above about James either being 'taken for dead' or being 'half dead' is picked up in Jerome's later account of the attack on James in the 60's, culminating in his *stoning.* As we have seen, it combines Josephus and other early Church sources, but also includes the important notice about 'his legs being broken' based on the point in the *Recognitions* that follows – Peter speaking to Zacchaeus about a month later in Caesarea – that James was 'still lame on one foot' (1.73). That is, Jerome, obviously operating off additional interesting data, has conflated all three sources into a single whole.

This brings us back to the account in the Gospel of John above about how, after giving Jesus vinegar to drink, the soldiers 'when they saw he was already dead ... did not *break his legs*'. Rather they '*broke the legs*' of the two that were crucified with him, after 'the Jews asked Pilate that *their legs might be broken*' (19:31–34). Not only is this repetition of the 'legs being broken' theme too insistent to believe that John does not know something more, but immediately preceding this, directly after the notice of the soldiers who crucify Jesus supposedly 'dividing up his clothes' to 'fulfill' Psalm 22:18 (19:24), John also refers to a 'house'. But this 'house' turns out to be the 'house' of 'the Disciple Jesus loved', in connection with which John now evokes Jesus' mother as well and, in another total absurdity which we shall address further below, '*his mother's sister* Mary the wife of Clopas' (19:25).

In Matthew 27:56, this woman is called 'Mary the mother of James and Joses and the mother of the sons of Zebedee'; in Mark 15:40, 'Mary the Mother of James the Less and Joses, and Salome'. As John 19:25–27 pictures the exchange at this point, Jesus in some of his last words upon the cross, seeing 'the Disciple whom he loved standing by', says to his *mother*, '(This is) your son', and to the Disciple, in words almost proverbial, '"(This is) your mother", and from that hour the Disciple took her into *his own home*'. This 'house' is clearly none other than 'the house of James', just encountered in the Pseudoclementine *Recognitions* account of the flight of those carrying James to his house above – refracted too in Acts 12:12's account of *Peter's flight* and going to leave a message for 'James and the brothers' at 'the house of Mary *the mother of John Mark*'!

Not only do we have the key motif in the first two of these notices of taking someone 'to' or 'into' a 'home' in Jerusalem, connected in some manner to personages belonging to *the family of Jesus*, but the Mary involved in the last of these has a son called 'John Mark'. In the first, she is instructed by 'the Disciple Jesus loved', usually taken to be another 'John', the so-called '*brother of James*', 'the son of Zebedee'. But most telling of all, in addition to the motif about a *house* he owns in Jerusalem, this Disciple is now *adopted as Mary's own son* and by extension, therefore, James' and Jesus' brother! All of this is just too incredible to be believed. Nor, we can be sure, are all these coincidences and overlaps accidental. The Pseudoclementine account of a house owned by James in Jerusalem is the authentic or more straightforward one. All the others, including 'the upper room' where 'Mary the mother of Jesus and his brothers' 'steadfastly continued in one accord with prayer and supplication' and to which all the Apostles – including 'Judas (the brother) of James' – retreat in Acts 1:13–14, are either variations on this or obfuscations of it.

The Flight of James' Community to Jericho

To return to the language of Rufinus' Latin version of the Pseudoclementine *Recognitions*, not only is James not dead, but *only injured*, his associates carry him 'after evening came and the Priests shut up the Temple ... to *the house of James*'. *Then 'before daylight', with some five thousand others* – the number of the early Community in Acts and those called 'Essenes' in Josephus – *they 'went down to Jericho'*. There, *three days later*, they receive word '*that the Enemy had received a commission from Caiaphas, the Chief Priest, that he should arrest all who believed in Jesus, and should go to Damascus with his letters and that there also, employing the help of the unbelievers, he should raise havoc among the Faithful*' (1:71).

For the Book of Acts, Paul, 'having come to bring those bound to the Chief Priests, ever increasing in power, threw the Jews who were dwelling in Damascus into confusion (by the manner in which) he proved this is the Christ' (9:21–22). *As usual then, 'the Jews plotted to kill him'*.

However, for its part in the *Recognitions*, when James is 'thrown down headlong' from the 'top of the Temple stairs' by the Enemy Paul and 'left for dead', he only broke one or both his legs (that is, rather than be killed). This is made clear in what subsequently follows in both recensions – Rufinus' Latin and the Syriac – because 'thirty days' later, when the Enemy Paul 'passed through Jericho on the way to Damascus'; James, '*still limping on one foot*' from his fall, sends out Peter from somewhere outside Jericho – where the Community had gone – *on his first missionary journey with orders to confront Simon Magus in Caesarea.*

Not only do we have the incredible detail of his '*still limping on one foot*' here, but also that of the entire Community having fled to a location somewhere outside of Jericho echoes. This, not only resonates with the site where the Dead Sea Scrolls were found, but also the references in the Community's own 'flights' or exoduses to 'the Land of Damascus'. Again the precision in geographical detail of the *Recognitions* in such matters is far superior to Acts. In the Clementines, we only have to wrestle with whether James fell from the top of the Temple steps or the Pinnacle of the Temple; whereas in Acts we have to do with *disembodied spirits, tablecloths from Heaven, individuals supposed to be on their way to Gaza but ending up in Caesarea instead, 'Ethiopian' eunuchs, 'a prophet called Agabus'*, and similar flights-of-fancy.

In Acts' portrait of parallel events: after 'Saul agreed to Stephen's death', 'a great persecution broke out that day against the Assembly which was in Jerusalem and all were scattered throughout the countries of Judea and Samaria *except the Apostles*' (8:1). First then 'Philip went down to a city in Samaria (unnamed) and proclaimed the Christ to them' (8:5). There, he cast out evil spirits, healed the blind and the lame, and encountered Simon *Magus*, who, 'amazed at the signs and great works of Power (our Ebionite/Elchasaite '*Power*' language again) being done', was baptized (8:13). 'And when the Apostles in Jerusalem heard that Samaria had received the word of God, they sent Peter and John to them' (8:14). There follow confrontations over 'the laying on of the hands', pictured in the Letter of Clement to James, at the beginning of the Pseudoclementine *Homilies*, as the ceremony Peter used to make Clement his successor as Bishop of Rome. Following this in *Homilies* 1:6, Jesus is pictured as 'receiving *Power from God* ... to make the deaf hear, the blind see ... and to cast out every demon'.

Here in Acts, this '*laying on of the hands*' is connected with the receipt of the Pauline 'Holy Spirit', for which Simon *Magus*, pictured as full of 'the gall of bitterness and the chains of Unrighteousness', first wishes – as we saw – to offer the Apostles 'Riches' (8:19–23). Then he 'repents' and the episode closes with the three of them together '*preaching the Gospel in many villages of the Samaritans*' (8:18 and 8:25 – nothing about 'Caesarea' at this point, soon however).

Of the utmost importance in Acts, before Paul, '*still breathing out threats and manslaughter against the Lord's Disciples*', gets his letters from the High Priest on his way to Damascus (9:1–30), there interposes the curious episode about Philip and the Treasurer of the Ethiopian Queen Kandakes, whom Acts also designates, equally importantly, as a 'eunuch' and who agrees to '*go into the water' and be baptized* (8:26–39). We shall see below how this episode relates to the conversion, described in Josephus, of Queen Helen of Adiabene in Northern Mesopotamia. A favorite character in the *Talmud* too, she sends her purchase agents – possibly including Paul – to Palestine and further afield, *to buy grain because of the Famine.* It is, in connection with this, that Acts' method of historical transformation and retrospective obliteration and will be totally revealed.[31]

Paralleling these events for the *Recognitions* James, '*still limping on one foot' from the injury he received in his 'headlong' fall down the Temple steps* – it is important to note, once again, this incredible but down-to-earth and not fantastic detail, having missed Paul when he passed through Jericho on his way 'to Damascus', received word from someone called 'Zacchaeus' in Caesarea '*that one Simon, a Samaritan magician was leading many of our people astray and creating factional strife*'. Again, it is worth repeating the description of him in the *Recognitions*: 'He claimed to be *the Standing One*, or in other words, *the Christ* and *the Great Power* (literally the meaning given the denotation '*Elchasai*' in Epiphanius) *in Heaven, which is superior to the Creator of the world*, while at the same time working many miracles' (1.72 – the Syriac adds 'by magic').

James then sends out Peter on what amounts to the first missionary journey, adjuring him to '*send me in writing every year an account of your sayings and doings, and especially at the end of every seven years*'. Not only does this first missionary journey by Peter seem to arise somewhere in the neighborhood of Jericho, that is, not far as just noted from present-day Qumran; but the Pseudoclementine *Recognitions*, yet again, evinces by this commission no doubt that James is the Supreme Ruler of the early Church even above Peter. At this point in Acts, the same character 'James' *hasn't even put in an appearance* – only the other 'James'.

Peter then goes to Caesarea and '*Zacchaeus' house*', where he is to stay. It is at this point, when Zacchaeus asks after James that Peter tells him he was '*still limping on one foot*', because when he '*was called by the Priests and Caiaphas the High Priest to the Temple, James, the Archbishop, stood on the top of the steps*', when '*an Enemy did everything I have already mentioned and need not repeat*' (1.73).

Curiously, so deeply has the author of the Pseudoclementines imbibed the fact and so deeply is it embedded in his narrative that James broke either one or both his legs in his fall, that he does not even say it *per se*, rather only giving us the effects of this fall thirty days later, when according to Peter James is 'still limping on one foot'. It is Jerome, also the heir of Palestinian tradition, who first tells us two or more centuries later that *James' 'legs were broken'* in the fall, now assimilated into the narrative of James' stoning and final demise. Nothing could better show us the authenticity and intimate detail of this First Book of the *Recognitions* – deleted from the *Homilies* – than this.

Curiously, too, this episode has its counterpart in the Gospels in chapters 18–19 of the Gospel of Luke – the author also credited with Acts. In this episode (18:35), not James nor even Peter, but now rather Jesus '*drew near to Jericho*' just as Paul in Acts (9:3) on his way to his fateful vision 'drew near to Damascus' (Acts 9:3 – unrecorded in the *Recognitions*). Still, like Paul in the Pseudoclementines, Jesus, '*having entered, passed through Jericho*' – only the itinerary is just the reverse. 'Jesus' is not on his way to Damascus or Caesarea, but to his fateful demise in Jerusalem (Luke 19:1).

In Luke, 'Jesus' has just spoken in favor of *the Righteousness of Roman 'tax collectors' over those 'trusting themselves to be Righteous', who observe the letter of the Law but 'despise others' who don't* (18:9–14). How cynical could its author be? He couldn't sound more like Paul here. From the language of the episode, Zacchaeus also seems to be a Gentile – at least, being a '*tax collector*', he is classified as a '*Sinner*' (19:7 – cf. Paul in Gal. 2:15 above on '*Gentiles*' as '*Sinners*').[32]

As with the identification of James' followers at the famous Jerusalem Conference in Acts 15:5 as 'Pharisees', all legal hair-splitters in the language of Jesus' preaching in this episode in Luke are referred to under the blanket heading of 'Pharisees'. To these, 'Jesus', speaking on behalf of *the 'Unrighteous', 'rapacious', 'fornicators', and 'tax collectors'*, applies the favorite scriptural aphorism, '*everyone who exalts himself shall be humbled and he that humbles himself shall be exalted*' (18:11–14). *He has also just praised the 'Rich' Ruler, who 'keeps' all the Commandments and 'gives to the Poor'* – clearly intending the Herodians. Of course this is more like Queen Helen of Adiabene and her son Izates than any 'Herodian' Palestinian Ruler. Here, too, 'Jesus' applies one more, beloved aphorism, that about 'the Rich Man entering the Kingdom of Heaven' and the camel, 'the eye of a needle' (18:18–25).[33]

This serves to introduce 'Zacchaeus' who is also – unlike, patently, in the *Recognitions* – one of these, '*a Chief Tax Collector*' and '*Rich*' (19:2). As the logic of the Gospel narrative continues, '*because he was small in height* (is this serious?), *he climbed a sycamore tree in order to see (Jesus), for he was about to pass*' (19:3–4); but 'Jesus', rather, calls him down, suddenly informing him – in the manner he does Paulinizing doctrine in general – '*Today I must stay in your house*' (19:5). But of course, this is nothing but '*the house*' that Peter with more justification goes to in Caesarea in the *Recognitions*' narrative – 'Zacchaeus', as we just saw, being the *leader of the nascent Messianic Community in Caesarea* (Jewish or otherwise, it is impossible to say).

This is the same kind of 'house' manipulation one gets regarding 'James' house' in the *Recognitions*, 'the house of Mary *the mother of John Mark*', where James also is to be found, in Acts, and 'the house of the Disciple Jesus loved', whom Mary – 'his mother's sister' – adopts as a son and where she is about to go to live in the Gospel of John. Could anything be clearer than what is going on here and where the authentic tradition lies?

When the Jewish mob, which perhaps here and certainly elsewhere includes the Apostles (and echoes Acts' portrayal of the reaction in Jerusalem of James followers to 'Peter' visiting the Roman Centurion Cornelius 'house'), 'murmurs exclaiming, "*He has gone in to stay with a Sinner,"' Zacchaeus responds that he has given half of what he owns 'to the Poor' and returned anything he 'has taken by fraud ... four times'* (19:8) – this from a 'Rich' Chief Tax Collector, in Roman practice in Palestine usually the Herodian King!

Just as 'Peter', too, in Acts' picture of his visit to the Roman Centurion's house in Caesarea (we already saw the relationship of this to Agrippa I), 'Jesus' then spouts Pauline doctrine, observing, '*Salvation has come to this house today, because he is also a Son of Abraham*'(so, then 'Zacchaeus' is not a 'Gentile' but, then, 'Herodians' could make the same claim being considered partly 'Idumaean'). In due course, we shall show the special significance this phrase '*Son of Abraham*' held for those in Northern Syria, Edessa, and Adiabene – the area of Abraham's reputed birthplace.

Here for some reason Zacchaeus, making this speech, is suddenly described as 'standing' (before he was 'up in a sycamore tree' or 'hurrying' home), paralleling the reference to 'the Standing One' in James' instructions outside Jericho in the *Recognitions* to Peter, before the latter goes off to confront Simon *Magus* in Caesarea. Again, the relationship between this episode and 'Peter' going to stay in 'Zacchaeus' house' in Caesarea, transformed and packed now with 'Gentile Christian' motifs, should be unmistakable. Only now it should be clear – the same kind of retrospective absorption of materials, we have already demonstrated to be transpiring in Acts, is also occurring in the Gospels.

Fortress of Machaeros, where John the Baptist was executed, across the Dead Sea in Transjordan and Perea.

Chapter 18
Peter's Visit to Cornelius and Simon's Visit to Agrippa

Paul's Letters from the High Priest and the Way to Damascus

It would now be well to look at how Acts introduces Paul and presents his behavior after Stephen is 'cast out' of Jerusalem and 'stoned', and 'the witnesses laid *their clothes* at the feet of a young man called Saulus' – when it should have been *vice versa* (7:58). The Book of Acts follows the same sequence of events as the Pseudoclementines, up to the point in the latter when Paul '*stopped on his way while passing through Jericho going to Damascus*' (1.71) – almost word-for-word the language of the 'Zacchaeus' episode in Luke in the opposite direction.

At this point the Pseudoclementines branch off, depicting James ('still limping on one foot') sending off Peter to confront Simon *Magus* in Caesarea on his first missionary journey. In the meantime, James' Community has gone outside Jericho to visit the graves of some brethren which *miraculously 'whitened of themselves every year'* thereby restraining the fury of their enemies because *they 'were held in remembrance before God'* (1.71 – these words too are paralleled in the Damascus Document). For Acts Paul, like Jesus 'drawing near Jericho', was 'drawing near Damascus' when suddenly he gets a vision and '*a light from Heaven shone all about him*'.

The rest of Paul's 'Damascus-road' vision-drama ensues. The parallel between the '*light from Heaven that shone all around him*' in Acts and *the tombs of the two brothers that miraculously 'whitened of themselves every year'* in *Recognitions* should not be missed as well, not to mention the additional possible parallel provided by the 'whitewashed wall' vocabulary Acts 23:3 later depicts Paul as applying to the High Priest Ananias. Nor is Paul's Damascus-road vision paralleled in Galatians, which has Paul '*going directly away into Arabia'* – whatever Paul means by this – and '*returning again to Damascus*' only after this (1:18), and doesn't agree with Acts any more than the Pseudoclementines do in the sequence of events or their substance. For Acts, after '*Pious Men buried Stephen and made great lamentations over him … Saul was ravaging the Assembly, entering house after house and dragging men and women (out), delivered (them) up to prison*' (8:3).

Here are interposed in Acts the two chapters we have described on Peter, Philip, and Simon *Magus* in Samaria, ending with Philip baptizing the Ethiopian Queen Kandakes' '*eunuch*', *who had power 'over all her Treasure*' (8:27), after which '*the Spirit of the Lord took Philip away so the eunuch never saw him again*' (*thus* –9:39).

Then Philip, '*passed through all the cities, evangelizing them till he came to Caesarea. But Saul, still fuming threats and murder towards the Disciples of the Lord, went to the High Priest, asking for letters from him to the synagogues at Damascus*' (8:40-9:2). For the Damascus Document, 'Damascus' was the area outside 'the Land of Judah', where the wilderness 'camps' were located, which the priestly 'Penitents' and others went out to and to which the Messianic 'Star' – also called 'the Interpreter of the *Torah*' – came. It is here that 'the Faith', 'Pact', or 'Covenant', called '*the New Covenant in the Land of Damascus*', was raised – the New Covenant *which 'the Liar together with the Men of War' deserted.*[1]

Acts continues: 'So that if he found any there (in Damascus) *of the Way*, whether men or women, he might bring them bound to Jerusalem' (9:1). After 'the light shone about him' and the voice cried out from Heaven to him, Paul is greeted at 'the house of Judas' on 'Straight' street in Damascus by one Ananias (9:11). Here, Ananias '*lays hands on' Paul*, just as in the Pseudoclementines' Letter of Clement to James, Peter '*lays hands on' Clement* making him his successor as 'Bishop' (that is, 'of Rome').

Whatever one might think of these events at Acts' '*Damascus*', those residing there repeat the same accusation we have already heard in Galatians 1:23: '*Is this not he who in Jerusalem destroyed those who called on his Name? He has come here for this, to bring those bound to the Chief*

Priests' (9:21). It should be noted that in whichever version, *Paul's relationship to the Chief Priests is never gainsaid.* Acts uses this designation, '*of the Way*', as a name for early Christianity in Palestine. It repeats this in several other contexts, once in describing why the Roman Governor Felix was so interested in Paul's teaching (24:12). This usage, directly related to the characterization of John the Baptist's activities in the wilderness – described in the Gospels as 'making a straight Way in the wilderness', *itself reiterated in two places in the Community Rule* – is common in the Scrolls generally.

It is also instructive to contrast this theme of Paul getting letters from the High Priest to that of James, giving letters to and requiring reports from emissaries. In addition, the Letter of Peter to James and James' response in the Pseudoclementine *Homilies* are particularly firm on the point of *not communicating doctrines to those found unworthy*, in particular, *not to Gentiles.*

James even sets down a probationary period of *six years before the postulant is allowed to enter the 'water where the regeneration of the Righteous takes place*' (Ps. *Hom.* 4:1). As opposed to this, the Gospels are fond of presenting 'Jesus' as saying '*nothing is hidden which shall not be made manifest, nothing secret that shall not be known and come to light*' (Luke 8:17) or, as Matthew puts this, '*I will utter things Hidden from the Foundation of the world*' (13:35).

Of course, in James' response to Peter, prefixing the *Homilies* – which has all the hallmarks of authenticity – circumcision is a *sine qua non* for membership and, as Paul puts it in Galatians 3:29, for becoming 'heirs according to the Promise'. For James in this response to Peter, '*keeping the Covenant*' – the definition of '*the Sons of Zadok*' at Qumran – entitles one to be '*a part with the Holy Ones' as does 'living Piously*'. But, pointing up this issue of secrecy and reversing Paul's 'cursing' language again, 'the Enemy' or 'Liar', who broke this oath of secrecy, '*shall be accursed living and dying and punished with Everlasting Perdition*'.[2] At this, 'the Elders' are pictured to be 'in an agony of terror' – as well they might.

Acts and the Pseudoclementines: Common Elements and a Common Source

The conclusions, we can now draw, should be obvious. Whenever Acts comes to issues relating to James or Jesus' brothers and family members generally, it equivocates and dissimulates, trailing off finally into disinformation – sometimes even in the form of childish fantasy. Though sometimes humorous, especially when one is aware of what the disputes in this period *really* were, this is almost always with uncharitable intent.

For instance, where the election of James as successor should have occurred, we are met only with stony silence and are not introduced to the 'Historical James' until chapter 12 *after the removal of the other 'James'*. Instead, we are presented with an obviously skewed election involving someone called 'Joseph Barsabas Justus' to replace 'Judas *Iscariot*'.

When James *is* finally introduced in Acts, it is only after a whole series of events like the stoning of Stephen, Peter's encounter with Simon *Magus* in Samaria, Paul's vision on the road to Damascus, Peter's 'tablecloth' vision preceding his visit to the home of the 'Pious and God -Fearing' Roman Centurion Cornelius, 'Herod the King's' well-timed beheading of the other 'James', and Peter's arrest, seemingly by this same 'Herod'. After miraculously escaping from prison, Peter then goes to the house of '*Mary the mother of John Mark*' (not previously introduced – more dissimulation?) to leave a message for the *real* James – though why he should go here to leave such a message is never explained.

Then 'Peter' flees, never to be heard from again – except as '*Simeon*' to make a rather improbable appearance at the so-called 'Jerusalem Council' in chapter 15. With no explanation of why the death sentence on him has suddenly evaporated, there he is pictured as making a short speech *supporting Paul and the Gentile Mission* (15:7–11).

When Acts does finally introduce James, it is as if we had already met him. There is no introduction of him, no explanation of who he might be, no attempt to distinguish him from

'James the brother of John'. In fact, if it weren't for other early Church sources and Josephus we wouldn't even know he was Jesus' brother and Leader of the early Church in Palestine.

But, of course, in the manuscript available to the final redactor(s) of Acts, *James had* already *been introduced* and, as already signaled, *the traces of this are still present.* In the preface to his Gospel, Luke admits that he was compiling his data on the basis of previous accounts. The author(s) of Acts – Luke or whoever – are, however, at great pains to disguise this fact but they are unable to do so absolutely, because by Chapter 12 *James must come into the text* since he must be involved in the 'Jerusalem Council' that follows three chapters later, because *the directives emanating from it are ascribed to his name* and *were undoubtedly well-known.*

In addition, by Paul's own testimony in Galatians 2:12, *it is James who has sent the messengers down to Antioch* (Acts 15:1). Acts has many names for these representatives, referring to this episode often since it is so important and one of the only really certain bits of information it can rely on until the *'We Document'* begins in the next chapter. Moreover, James must be present for the climactic final confrontation with Paul in Chapter 21 as well.

It is the position of this book that the authors of Acts and the authors of the Pseudoclementines are, in fact, *working off the same source.* Both are Hellenistic romances, but where points of contact can undisputedly be shown between the two narratives – as, for instance, in the First Book of the *Recognitions* – the Pseudoclementines are more faithful to the original source than Acts. Not only is there less fantasy, there is less obfuscation and out-and-out fabrication. This is particularly the case in the matter of the key attack on James in the *Recognitions*, where the 'Enemy'/Paul is introduced and we can see it paralleled in Acts by the attack on Stephen which introduces Paul ('Saulus') as well. By the same token, it is also true of the picture of Peter's conduct and teachings – *the direct opposite of Acts.*

This is not the normal scholarly view, which holds the Pseudoclementines to be late. But on this point, scholars – many governed as in the field of the Dead Sea Scrolls by preconceptions or orientations they, themselves, may often be unaware of – are simply mistaken. There is no other response one can make. It is patent that the Pseudoclementines are superior, at least as narrative – and, no doubt, ideology and history as well – except where the *'We Document'* intrudes into the second part of Acts. Perhaps this was why Jerome was so angry at his erstwhile colleague Rufinus, who published the Pseudoclementines in the West at the end of the Fourth Century – probably based on a Syriac original.

Granted, speeches in the Pseudoclementines cannot be relied on any more than those in Acts (there are exceptions), but neither can they in Josephus – to say nothing of the Gospels. But where historical sequencing and actual physical actions go, the First Book of the *Recognitions* is very reliable indeed, as is Acts from Chapter 16 onwards where the 'We Document' first makes its appearance – thus, giving Acts too the character of a travel narrative written by someone who actually accompanied its principal character Paul on his journeys. This is similar to the *modus operandi* of the Pseudoclementines (where Clement begins his travels with Peter), though, unlike these, Acts inexplicably shifts back and forth between first person plural and the third person even in some of these later chapters.

In Chapter 15, for instance, after the so-called 'Jerusalem Conference' and just prior to the irruption of the 'We Document', Acts asserts that 'the Apostles and Elders with the whole Assembly decided to choose representatives to send down to Antioch with Paul and Barnabas' to deliver a letter containing James' directives to overseas communities. 'Judas surnamed Barsabas and Silas' were chosen (here our amazing 'Barsabas' again, previously encountered in the 'election' to succeed Judas *Iscariot* as *'Joseph Barsabas surnamed Justus'* – 15:22.

Just to confuse things further, *Recognitions* 1.60 says Barnabas was also *'called Matthias'*, the name of the victorious candidate in this election to fill Judas' 'Office' above. Complementary as ever, Acts 4:36, introducing 'Barnabas', calls him – like the *'Joseph Barsabas Justus'* above –

'Joses' and identifies him as *'a Levite of Cypriot origins'*. But 'Joses' is also the name of Jesus' *fourth* brother in Scripture.

In 15:32 these representatives of James are called *'prophets'* (like 'Agabus' and the others who came down from Jerusalem earlier and supposedly predicted the Famine in Acts 11:27 – not to mention the original 'prophets and teachers' of Paul's original 'Antioch Church' in Acts 13:1) and, immediately after the delivery of this letter, Paul and Barnabas part company because they have 'a violent quarrel' over John Mark, *'the man who separated from (them) in Pamphylia'* (15:38–39)! To be sure, that these mysterious representatives *insisting on 'circumcision'* were sent down from Jerusalem by James is covered quite emotionally by Paul in his attack on James and Peter as 'hypocrites' in Galatians 2:11–21, as is the real nature of the quarrel that broke out between Paul and Barnabas.

Interestingly enough, this first person plural voice makes itself felt in Acts' narrative just at the point *Paul crosses over with his new companions* – the curious 'Silas' and a new individual called 'Timothy' (probably identical with 'Titus' in Galatians 2:1–3) – *into Europe or mainland Greece*, where Paul presumably encounters 'Stephanos', his first convert in Achaia (1 Cor. 16:15). Paul has this Timothy, 'whose mother was a believing Jewess but whose father was a Greek' – just the Herodian mix – *circumcised* expressly for the purpose of these travels and, again, of course, *'because of the Jews who were in these places'* (16:1–4)!

This is most revealing testimony and is paralleled by Paul's protestations in Galatians about *'those who come in to spy on the freedom we enjoy in Christ Jesus, so that they can reduce us to slavery'*, that is, *'slavery' to the Law*, and how Titus who was with him, *'being a Greek, was* – according to him – *not obliged to be circumcised'* (Gal. 2:3–4).

Here, one should take note of additional overlaps and mix-ups, not only between Titus and Timothy, but also Silas and Silvanus, who are – despite attempts to portray them otherwise – probably the same person. The point is that they are Greeks or, in Silas' case, Hellenized Palestinians or Herodians, and join Paul after the row in Antioch as the only people now willing to travel with him *'after the rest of the Jews', including Barnabas, 'jointly dissembled following' Peter in his 'hypocrisy'* (Gal. 2:13). Paul is clearly talking here about Jews *within* the Movement, not outside it.

The Source of the Blunder about Abraham's Tomb in Stephen's Speech

In Acts', Stephen is arrested on charges of *'blasphemy'*, literally 'because he *blasphemes this Holy Place and the Law'* (6:12–13). To be sure, the picture of such *'blasphemy'* charges is very important where James' death is concerned but, even more to the point regarding Stephen, they echo almost verbatim the charges against Paul when, a decade or so later, he is mobbed on the Temple Mount. As Acts expresses this: *'This is the man who teaches everyone everywhere, against the people and the Law and this place, and further he has brought Greeks into the Temple and defiled this Holy Place'* (21:28). This is almost word-for-word the charge against 'Stephen' and, just as 'Stephen' in the earlier episode in Acts, Paul too is presented as *giving a long speech at this point to the angry Jewish mob.*

At Stephen's trial for 'blasphemy', the 'false witnesses' further contend that *'we have heard him saying that Jesus the Nazoraean would destroy this place and change the customs given to us by Moses'* (6:14). But, of course, what we have here is nothing but the reverse and a reflection of James' arrest and trial for blasphemy two decades later, which, unlike the episode before us, *really did happen* and *for exactly opposite reasons.* Of course, here too, only Stephen is arrested, not Peter, nor John, not even James, still the *éminence grise* unmentioned in the narrative.

As the narrative continues, Stephen, with the 'face of an Angel', then goes on to give his long speech – Acts' longest – and, like Paul's, purportedly in response to the High Priest and the *whole Jewish Sanhedrin* (6:12–15), though why a presumable *Greek* should be brought before a Jewish Sanhedrin is never explained. Rather, Stephen tells them their entire history – on the face of it, a Gentile to Jews, patently absurd – typically ending with the most crucial of Gentile Christian accusations, and, needless to say, completely untrue: 'Which one of the Prophets did your fathers not persecute? And they killed the ones who announced the coming of the Just One, whose betrayers (the accusation against Judas *Iscariot*) and murderers you have now become' (Acts 7:52).

But a glaring error in the speech Stephen makes as reproduced here by Luke actually allows one *to pinpoint the source of this speech*, as a result of which the entire episode unravels and its improvisation made plain. It is *Joshua's farewell speech* to the assembled tribes in Joshua 24:1–24, not unremarkably, at *Shechem in Samaria*. The play on the name 'Jesus' ('Yeshua' equaling 'Joshua') represented by this, too, would have pleased the author of Acts. The error occurs in line 7:14, when Stephen comes to telling how Joseph brought back the bodies of '*our ancestors … to Shechem and buried them in the tomb that Abraham had bought and paid for from the sons of Hamor the father of Shechem*'.

Unfortunately, as anyone versed in the Hebrew Bible would know, the ancestors were buried in a tomb called *Machpelah in Hebron which Abraham bought from Ephron the Hittite* (Gen. 23)! It is Joseph, who is buried in the tomb mentioned by Stephen and it is *Jacob who buys it from Hamor the father of Schechem* (Gen. 34). This mistake, made in a speech supposedly delivered by a Gentile or archetypical Gentile convert to the whole Jewish Sanhedrin, would have given rise to the most incredible derision, as anyone familiar with the mindset of such an audience might attest.

Even if one granted that Stephen (whoever he was) never made such a foolish error, but only the authors of the Book of Acts did because of careless transcription, this will not do, because, first of all, the speech is lifted almost bodily from Joshua's speech. But, second of all, at the end of Joshua's speech, after he cautions against foreign gods, 'making a Covenant with the People … and wrote these things in the Book of the Law of God', the text concludes: '*The bones of Joseph*, which the sons of Israel had brought from Egypt, *were buried at Shechem* in the portion of ground that *Jacob had bought for a hundred pieces of silver from the sons of Hamor the father of Shechem*' (Josh. 24:32), and we have almost word-for-word the source of Stephen's startling blunder, showing that this was where the author went to retrieve it, not to mention, its being practically the source of his whole speech in Acts! It becomes abundantly clear that someone was transcribing this information from Joshua either too quickly or too superficially – even perhaps from memory, though this is doubtful.

Since we can now just about dismiss the whole 'Stephen' episode, which one would have done on ideological and historical grounds anyhow – starting with the anachronism introducing it regarding 'Theudas' and 'Judas the Galilean' drawn from a too-superficial reproduction of Josephus' works – one can more or less present the background to this episode and, to a certain extent, material that will throw further light on the true circumstances surrounding the death of James. Once again, we are in the world of Josephus' *Antiquities* where Theudas and his kind – people like James and Simon, the two sons of Judas the Galilean, '*who drew away the people to revolt when Cyrenius came to take a census in Judea*' – are mentioned.[3]

Parallel Sequencing in Acts and Josephus: the Conflation Unravels

In Josephus too, as in Acts and the Pseudoclementines, it is always the sequence of the events – not necessarily the precise substance – that is important. Josephus moves from the 'Impostor' or 'Magician' Theudas (Acts 5:36) to Tiberius Alexander (Acts 4:6), his crucifixion of James and Simon 'the two sons of Judas the Galilean' (Acts 5:37), to the riot after the Roman soldier exposed himself on the wing of the Temple at Passover, to the beating and robbing of 'Stephanos, Caesar's retainer', just outside Jerusalem by seditious 'Innovators' or 'Revolutionaries' (Acts 6–7).

This is followed by the problems between the Samaritans and Jews because of confrontations with 'the Galileans', who were traveling through their country (paralleled in Acts 8:1–25 by the confrontations of Philip and Peter with Simon *Magus* in 'Samaria'), and the crucifixion of the Jewish Messianic pretender 'Doetus' or 'Dortus' – 'Dorcas' in Acts and probably 'Dositheus' in the Pseudoclementines and other heresiologies – and four of his colleagues at Lydda (paralleled in Acts 9:31–42). It is at this point that the High Priest Ananias and his Temple Captain, Ananus ben Ananus, are sent to Rome in bonds to give an account to Claudius of what they had done, and there make the acquaintance of Agrippa II.

An additional, but shorter, set of sequencing, with much in common with this one, goes from the stoning of James ('Stephen' in Acts), to the plundering of the tithes of the Poor Priests by the Richer ones (the theme of squabbling over the improper food distribution to the 'widows' in the background to the 'Stephen' episode in Acts 6:1–3), to the riot led by Saulus, 'a kinsman of Agrippa', who with a bunch of thugs 'used Violence with the people', 'plundering those weaker than themselves', so that the 'city (Jerusalem) became greatly disordered and all things grew worse and worse among us'.[4] The riot led by Saulus in Acts (and the Pseudoclementines) is about as graphic.

There are three other matters overlapping material in Acts which are worth mentioning. The first is the visit by Simon the Head of 'an Assembly (*Ecclesia*) in Jerusalem' to Caesarea to inspect the household of Agrippa I in the early 40's to 'see what was being done there contrary to Law'. This is inverted in Acts' presentation of Peter visiting the Roman Centurion Cornelius' household in Caesarea (preceded by his vision of the Heavenly tablecloth giving him the Divine dispensation to do this).

The second is the conflict between the Jewish and Greco-Syrian inhabitants of Caesarea. The latter, though inferior to the former in wealth, in Josephus' words, end up plundering them. This is paralleled, again in the background to the Stephen affair in Acts, by the squabbling between 'Hebrews and Hellenists' (6:1–15) – to say nothing of how, later in Acts, this same 'High Priest Ananias' goes down with 'the whole Sanhedrin' to Caesarea supposedly to complain about Paul (but apparently about no other 'Christians') for *introducing foreigners into the Temple* (Acts 24:1–25:12).

Finally, there is Acts 11:27–30's note of how one Agabus, 'a prophet', 'rose up' and 'via the Spirit' predicted the Famine, in relation to which Paul and Barnabas, commissioned by the Community in Antioch, visit Jerusalem to bring Famine-relief funds. This visit is not paralleled by Paul in Galatians. Rather he specifically denies any such visit there – this on the strength of an oath 'before God' that he 'does not lie' (Gal. 1:17–2:1). But it is paralleled by the note in Josephus about Queen Helen of Adiabene's grain-buying operations, in which she 'spent vast sums of money *in Egypt*', distributing it in Judea. This last is sandwiched in between Josephus' two notices about Theudas' beheading and the crucifixion of the two sons of Judas the Galilean, James and Simon, by Tiberius Alexander, who in Acts 4:6 actually does appear (somewhat anachronistically) as the enemy of *John* and *Peter*.

It is this grain-buying mission to Egypt on the part of Helen's Treasury agents, as we shall see, that will serve as the underpinning for Philip's encounter with the Treasurer of 'the Ethiopian Queen' Kandakes 'on the way ... *to Gaza*' in Acts (8:26–38).[5] We have already alluded to the conversion of this Helen, Queen of Adiabene – East of Edessa, though perhaps connected to its domains – in connection with Paul and the mysterious 'Ananias' he meets, according to Acts, at Damascus (Acts 9:12–20). We shall have more to say about this Ananias and Helen in due course, when it comes to discussing the so-called 'prophet called Agabus', who, as Acts would have it, supposedly predicts the 'Great Famine' (11:28).

In Syriac sources, Helen is always associated – as she is in Eusebius, drawing on these – with 'Abgarus' or 'Agbarus' (even contemporary commentators acknowledge the difficulty translating or transliterating names such as this), '*the King of Edessa*' or '*of the Edessenes*' or '*Osrhoeans*' (Assyrians). Indeed, the legend concerning Abgarus/Agbarus' conversion is very old and widely disseminated. Even Eusebius, who refers to him as '*the Great King of the Peoples beyond the Euphrates*', reproduces it and there is a lively apocryphal tradition surrounding it.[6]

It is curious that whereas Josephus appears to misplace the riot led by Saulus in the 40's, placing it after the stoning of James in the 60's, for its part Acts misplaces the stoning of James, replacing it with the stoning of Stephen in the 40's, following which, it too places a riot led by Saulus. There is very little one can do to explain these parallel inconsistencies, except remark them.

It is also clear from the *Antiquities*' sequencing of the assassination of Ananus' brother, the High Priest Jonathan, by 'Robbers' or '*Sicarii*' around 55 CE, leading to the Temple Wall Affair and the conspiracy by Ananus and Agrippa II to remove James in 62 CE, that James is seen as being at the centre of these disturbances, at least in the eyes of the Establishment High Priest and the Herodian King. If the relationship of Saulus – 'a kinsman of Agrippa' – with Paul can be confirmed, it is legitimate to ask just what Paul's repeated conversations during two years of protective custody in Caesarea with Agrippa II's brother-in-law, the Roman Governor Felix and with Festus and Agrippa II himself, were really about (Acts 24:24 –26:32).

If one places the *first* attack on James led by Paul in the 40's, and the stoning of James, described in Josephus and in all early Church sources, in the 60's – then it is clear that there was *not one but two attacks on James.* The first was roughly as the *Recognitions* describes it. It was actually perpetrated by 'the Enemy' Paul. It is this Acts 9:1 tantalizingly refers to as Paul's '*threats and murders against the Disciples of the Lord*' and, in 22:4, even quotes Paul as admitting, 'I persecuted this Way *unto death*'. But this attack did not result in James' death, only his 'headlong fall' from 'the top of the Temple steps' (as we have seen, not 'the Temple Pinnacle' as in chronologically-later early Church conflations).

The second attack is as described in Josephus and it, too, is refracted with additional fabulous accretions in the early Church accounts delineated above. This attack correctly came in the early 60's and really did involve a trial by a Sanhedrin for blasphemy. Unlike, however, Acts' descriptions of Stephen and Gospel representations of what took place at 'Jesus'' trial; where James is concerned, *a full Sanhedrin trial really did take place and really did involve blasphemy.* Both of these attacks have been compressed in early Church accounts, as we have seen as well, into the single account of James' death in the early 60's. This process began with Hegesippus and Clement of Alexandria in the Second Century, ending with Jerome in the early Fifth – the final result containing elements from both attacks: *falling headlong down, being clubbed, praying on his knees, and being stoned.*

For its part Acts doesn't directly mention either attack, telling us only about *the attack on Stephen* (also conflated), while the *Recognitions* tells us only about *the attack on James in the 40's* which Acts replaces with the stoning of Stephen. Neither deigns to tell us about the stoning of James in the 60's – which is where an undoctored Acts probably should have ended. If one keeps one's eyes on the *two elements of the fall from the Temple stairs* and *the stoning,* one can sort these out. The keys to the conflation are the words '*throwing*' or 'casting down' (*kataballo* in Greek) and the '*headlong* fall' James takes at least in the first attack – in the New Testament, *'Judas Iscariot' and 'Stephen' along with him.*

In the final early Church accounts, whether at Nag Hammadi or in the Church Fathers – even reflected in later Manichaean texts – these are also conflated with Rabbinic notices either about: *'Zealot' priests in the Temple pushing someone down from a wall, accidentally on purpose,* or *making someone, who is supposed to be stoned for infractions like blasphemy, accidentally fall into a hole* or *actually having his head split open.*

This language of '*casting down*', expressing this in Greek in all these accounts of the attack on or death of James in early Church sources, not to mention that of Stephen in Acts, is but another reflection of the mysterious language circle at Qumran having to do in its Hebrew variation with *B–L–'*, '*swallowing*' or '*consuming*', and the associated nomenclature of '*Devilishness*' connected to it in both languages – which, in turn, is always applied in Qumran texts to *the destruction of the Righteous Teacher by a Wicked Establishment.*[7]

Parallels with the Gospels: James and Jesus on the Pinnacle – Neither Ever Happened

To sum up: in the tradition known to the Pseudoclementines, but suppressed in Acts (though echoed three centuries later in Jerome's allusion to James' 'broken legs'), the attack by Paul on James in the 40's ends up with James only injuring one or both of his *legs*. It does not kill him. Both attacks, the one ending in the fall from the Temple stairs and the other, stoning – with the curious addition (probably from Talmudic sources) about James' head being beaten in by a fuller's club, not to mention the note about his being 'cast down' – are conflated in early Church accounts into a single whole involving *both* a 'headlong fall' or 'being cast down' and a stoning resulting in James' death in the 60's.

This last is also possibly reflected in notices in the Dead Sea Scrolls – depending on chronological problems in these – about the attack on or death of 'the Righteous One' or 'Righteous Teacher'. In fact, both attacks on James, the first by 'the Liar' Paul and the second by 'the Wicked Priest' Ananus, are reflected in the Scrolls, if the dating problems regarding these can be resolved to everyone's satisfaction – an unlikely prospect.

They are, however, very definitely reflected in other New Testament stories, like the ones about Judas *Iscariot* and Stephen, but also even Jesus himself. In the Gospels, Jesus like John the Baptist is also 'led out into the wilderness by the Spirit, where he is tempted by the Devil' and, as we saw, in another one of those typical reversals based on motifs in the James story, to 'cast himself (*bale*) down from the Pinnacle of the Temple' (Matt. 4:1 and pars.). The key to the textual dependency here, of course, comes in the tell-tale use of the expression, 'the Pinnacle of the Temple', not to mention the allusion to 'casting down' accompanying it, which is the language of all the presentations of James' fall.

Actually, as one might have suspected from the beginning, there was no 'fall from the Pinnacle of the Temple' by James in the 60's, only the Sanhedrin trial for 'blasphemy' and the stoning – correctly recorded in Josephus. That this, too, in turn relates to the proclamation James made and the other activities he was involved in the Temple, is confirmed in a rather bizarre manner in the Gospels themselves, where materials more appropriately relating to James are retrospectively absorbed into stories about Jesus.

In Matthew 9:2–8, Luke 5:17–26, and Mark 2:1–12, Jesus, who is portrayed as curing a man with palsy, 'forgives his sins'. The Scribes and/or Pharisees then cry out, 'blasphemy', and insist only God 'has the power to forgive sins'. Carefully considered, what is actually concretized in this exchange is the point in all the early Church accounts about James, that he *really did* go into the Holy of Holies on *Yom Kippur* to *ask forgiveness for the sins of the whole people* and *make atonement for them.*

Even in this obscure episode about 'Jesus'' 'blasphemy' and his 'forgiving sins' in the Synoptics, the tell-tale allusions to 'the Son of Man', 'the Power' and 'glorying', present in all the above accounts of James' proclamation in the Temple, are incorporated, however tendentiously, into the context of Jesus curing this paralytic. Here Jesus is now made to say '*the Son of Man* has *Power* on earth to *forgive sins*', upon which the crowd then '*glorifies God*' – thus linking all these accounts together.

This is followed in all Synoptics by an episode where Jesus purposefully eats with 'Sinners' (in Gospel code, 'Gentiles') and 'tax collectors' (Herodians) – as opposed, for instance, to the barring of such classes from the Temple in the Temple Scroll alluding to the catchword '*balla*' or '*Bela*'. Jesus even goes so far as to call one of his Apostles in Mark, 'Levi the son of Alphaeus' – this is supposed to be 'Matthew' – out of '*the tax office*' (Mk 2:14 and pars.)! The Scribes and Pharisees, echoing precisely the 'Zacchaeus' episode we just examined in Luke above, now 'murmur at his Disciples, saying, "Why do you *eat and drink with tax collectors and Sinners*?"' (Lk 5:30 and pars.). Jesus is then made to answer, rather pointedly, the now proverbial, '*I did not come to call the Righteous to repentance, but Sinners*.'

To show that in all this symbolic and polemical repartee, we are still in the world of James' 'Righteous' *Yom Kippur* atonement, this is immediately followed in all Synoptic Gospels with an aspersion on, of all people, the Disciples of John the Baptist. To compound this particular circle of *non sequiturs*, it is these *very classes* of 'Scribes and Pharisees' – just presented as 'murmuring against' Jesus and his Disciples 'eating and drinking with tax collectors and Sinners' – that John *fulminates against* and rejects, characterizing them as '*offspring of vipers*' (Mt 3:7)!

Not only is this '*eating and drinking*' theme basic to differences between Paul and James, but here in the follow-up to these reverse 'blasphemy' and 'eating and drinking' charges in the Synpotics, 'John's Disciples', linked with 'the Pharisees', supposedly now complain: 'Why do we and the Pharisees *fast often*, but your Disciples *do not fast at all*?' (Mt 9:14 and pars.). Luke 5:33 actually changes the '*fasting*' here to '*eating and drinking*', showing that in his mind all these matters are the same. But, of course, Jews 'fast' on *Yom Kippur*, and the direct evocation of the theme of 'fasting', immediately following the portrait of 'Jesus' being accused of 'blasphemy' following his *forgiving men their sins* in the matter of *the curing of a paralytic*, ties this whole set of episodes and allusions to James' *Yom Kippur atonement in the Temple*. In addition, it is conveniently linked to an attack on '*the Disciples of John*' – who, like '*Nazirite*' *daily-bathers* generally, followed the Law in the most extreme manner conceivable – whom it *compares to the Pharisees*!

This linking of John's followers with 'the Pharisees' bears on the linking of James' representatives with 'the Pharisees' in Acts 15:5 (even though it was Paul who specifically claimed to be 'a Pharisee' in Phil. 3:5). These Pharisees, it will be recalled, complained at the 'Jerusalem Conference' over the issue of circumcision, and, according to the view of modern scholarship, represent the 'Judaization' of early Christianity at this point – a Judaization that never occurred. The opposite is the more likely scenario, that is, *a progressively more all-encompassing Gentilization*!

But this portraiture is patently tendentious and what we really have here in this language in these Gospel episodes is *symbolic skirmishing* between opposing polemical groups – 'Pharisee', at this point anyhow (if not elsewhere), representing a catchphrase for those *following the Jamesian orientation on things like circumcision*, *table fellowship* (that is, '*eating and drinking*' *or keeping dietary regulations*), and the like.

Beelzebul, Belial, and *Satan Casting out Demons*

The set of themes now recurs in another very significant episode that follows in Mark – some time later in Matthew and Luke – in regard to '*blasphemy*', '*forgiveness for sins*', *allusion to 'the Son of Man', and Jesus' healing, this time of 'a blind and dumb man'*. Again 'the Pharisees' object, this time to the all-important formulation, '*casting out demons*' (*ekballo*), supposedly being done with the help of '*Beelzebul*, Prince of Demons' – also now identified with 'Satan' (Mk 3:22–30, Mt

12:22–37, and Lk 11:14–18 – *n.b.,* in the Greek, this is not the more well-known '*Beelzebub*' which is *an incorrect modern transliteration*).

The lengthy speech that ensues, which is 'Jesus'' response to the Pharisees and basically gibberish, turns on the confusion of the two terms, '*Beelzebul*', that is, '*Belial*', and 'Satan'. Not surprisingly, the formulation '*casting out*' (*ekballo*) is repeated approximately six times in just this one speech – a usage we have already encountered in Acts' picture of Stephen '*being cast out of the city and stoned*' and which Josephus uses to describe what Essenes do to backsliders![8]

For his part, Mark places this episode immediately following Jesus' appointment of the 'Twelve who would be with him', to whom he gives the authority on earth '*to cast out demons*' (*ekballein*). By contrast, in Luke 5:1–11, this appointment episode is preceded by Jesus' calling of Simon Peter and 'James and John the sons of Zebedee', Simon's fishing 'partners', all now presented as *fishermen on the Sea of Galilee.* Another long discussion ensues, this time rather about their 'nets', which is simply another play on and adumbration of the Dead Sea Scrolls' '*Three Nets of Belial'* theme. Whereas in the Markan scenario, it is Beelzebul 'casting our demons', in Luke Jesus' principal Apostles are 'washing' and 'letting down' their 'nets' (5:2–4). But later this will actually involve these being 'cast out' as well.[9]

In Mark this episode about Jesus appointing his Apostles follows an account of the crowds trying 'to touch' Jesus (3:10), paralleling Jerome about *the people in Jerusalem trying to touch James because of his superabundant Holiness.* Also, these episodes about John the Baptist fasting, and Beelzebul casting out demons are followed by the twin issues of Jesus '*forgiving sins' and blaspheming* – this time directed to '*the Sons of Men*'. This is expressed in terms of '*whatsoever blasphemies they blasphemed' being forgiven, 'except the one who blasphemes against the Holy Spirit, who shall not be forgiven*' (Mk 3:28–29 and Mt 12:31–32).

In both Mark and Matthew, this leads directly into *a key attack by Jesus on his mother and his brothers* (Mk 3:31–35 and Mt 12:46–50). In Luke this does not come until 8:19–21, right before Jesus goes out on the boat, once again, with his Disciples to 'command' the wind and the raging sea, but *immediately after 'the Parable of the Tares*'. Not insignificantly, in the light of this telltale context, the mother and brothers of Jesus are described in all the Synoptics as '*standing outside*' (again, allusion to the '*standing*' ideology should be remarked), but unable to get into him 'because of the crowd'.

Jesus then responds, 'Who is my mother and who are my brothers?' Looking at his new Apostles sitting around him in a circle, he pointedly adds, 'Behold, my mother and my brothers.' All three Gospels now have him attach to this pronouncement a reference to that '*doing*', so much connected to the name of James and, as it turns out, '*the Righteous Teacher*' at Qumran – for Matthew and Mark, '*doing the will* of my Father'; for Luke, '*doing the word* of God'.

A related episode in John now presents this 'blasphemy' as involving Jesus making the twin claims of being 'the Christ' and 'the Son of God' (also here in Mk 3:11 and as in the Synoptic trial scenes before '*the Sanhedrin' at the 'High Priest's house*'), for which 'the Jews' in this picture now actually '*take up stones in order that they should stone him*' (Jn 10:24–36). These are, of course, the two themes – together with the third, the 'Son of Man' related to them – which we have already encountered with regard to the two attacks on James in the Pseudoclementines and early Church sources.

This conflation of the stoning of James for 'blasphemy' in the 60's, as recorded in Josephus, with the account of the attack by Paul and James' resultant 'headlong fall' from the Temple stairs in the 40's, gives some idea of the lateness of these Gospel scenarios, late enough for these kinds of conflations to have occurred and then been retrospectively absorbed into the story of Jesus. Conversely, this also means that the traditions about these attacks on James and the transformations they underwent are as early as these first Gospel portraits incorporating aspects of them into the story of their 'Jesus'.

These notices about Jesus' blasphemy in the Gospels, not to mention the charge against Stephen in Acts of 'speaking blasphemy' against Moses, God, the Law, and the Temple, provide the best proof, however tendentious, that James was *tried for 'blasphemy' as a result of the atonement he made on behalf of the whole people in the Holy of Holies on Yom Kippur.* Once again, they show, however indirectly, the *modus operandi* of the Gospel artificers. If one collates them, one finds that the significant ones are almost always connected to the motif of *the 'Son of Man having Power' to 'forgive sins on earth'*. This, as already noted, was not blasphemous in itself – only the *pronouncing of the Divine Name of God in conjunction with an atonement of this kind.* This is exactly what James would have done in the Holy of Holies if these early Church reports have any substance.

Outside Palestine, the significance of this, together with James' proclamation of '*the Son of Man coming on the clouds of Heaven with Power*', would easily have become garbled and confused with something relating to his being able to, or in this instance the Messiah being able to, 'forgive men's sins' or 'forgive sins on earth', which in Palestine, of course, no one ever claimed, imagined, or thought to be an issue. What was thought in Palestine was that the atonement performed by the High Priest in the Temple on *Yom Kippur*, whether the Establishment one or the Opposition, was for *forgiveness of sins.* The association of words like 'the Son of Man', 'Power', or 'glorified' with many of these passages in the Gospels just further increases the points of contact with the proclamation James is reported to have made in the Temple according to all accounts.

The motif of being 'in the wilderness', found in the Temptation of 'Jesus' by '*Satan*' or '*Belial*', also just tightens the connections with the similar allusions at Qumran about '*making a Way in the wilderness*' or '*going out from the Land of Judah and dwelling in the Land of Damascus*'. This last is connected to the definition of '*the Sons of Zadok*' at Qumran or *flights to the wilderness camps*, again assimilated into all traditions about John the Baptist as well. The idea of a 'fall' or 'casting oneself down' in these materials, in any event, fits more logically and more realistically into the story of James' lectures on the Temple stairs, reflected in another, no longer extant work reported by Epiphanius, the *Ascents of James.*

But the themes of James 'falling' or 'being cast down' from the 'top' of something – in the first instance, only injuring himself; in the second, being murdered – clings to James in all the traditions. There is, doubtlessly, an element of truth in them. It is also more credible than any parallel stories like those of Jesus' 'Temptation by the *Devil*' or Stephen's improbable execution. In the 60's, anyhow, if not the 40's, there was only a stoning not a fall. This stoning probably took place outside the city, as all sources and Acts' narrative about 'Stephen' suggest. Here James was buried on the spot, as both Eusebius' source and Jerome attest. Curiously enough, the story of James' Tomb together with its marker leaves off with the testimony of Jerome in the fourth-fifth centuries.

Three-four centuries later, the thread reappears, at least according to tradition, in the stories about bringing the bones or ossuary of someone also identified as 'James' – allegedly the *other* James – to a village outside Santiago de Compostela in Northern Spain, the pilgrimage to which continues to the present day. Since there probably really was no '*James the brother of John*' and we know such a burial marker regarding James really *did exist*, wouldn't it be ironic, if, after all these years, what was being revered in this peculiar survival in Northern Spain were, in fact, the bones of 'James the brother of Jesus' not his fictional counterpart – not only ironic, but extremely fitting.

This idea of a fall may have also developed via the over-active imagination of early pilgrims who, as Jerome – nay even Hegesippus – suggest, were already visiting the place associated with his interment, *popularly called 'the Tomb of St James' ever since*, which from its location in the Kedron Valley looks directly up at 'the Pinnacle of the Temple' some hundred meters above. As we have suggested, the idea could have developed that James died from either being pushed or falling that distance.

The note in these traditions about a laundryman beating in James' brains with a club, however colorful, no doubt comes from all the various beatings we have reviewed above, in particular, Paul taking a faggot from the wood piled at the altar and calling on others to do the same, swinging it around wildly to begin the riot that ends in James being beaten, his fall, and his broken leg(s)! Vivid and realistic detail such as this is not to be dismissed lightly.

Nor is the vivid detail about a flight of the whole Community to the Jericho area thereafter, whence Peter is sent out by James on his first missionary journey to encounter Simon *Magus* in Caesarea. Nor that of James still 'limping' from his fall thirty days later. All these matters have been purposefully refashioned and systematically overwritten in the traditions that have gone into the Book of Acts in the manner we have seen – thus revealing the *modus operandi* behind these overwrites in a most patent manner.

The Talmudic material about the young priests taking a fellow priest outside the Temple and beating out his brains with clubs if he served in a state of uncleanness – note how in the Pseudoclementine tradition, the 'Enemy', Paul *calls to the young priests to help him* – relates to these traditions as well. So does the equally colorful one in the Second Apocalypse of James about James being forced to dig a pit and a heavy stone being placed upon his stomach, which comes directly from the *Mishnah Sanhedrin*'s descriptions of such stoning procedures.

What is even more interesting about this one in Nag Hammadi lore is that it includes all the additional motifs of 'casting down', 'being thrown down from a great height', 'taking away the *Zaddik*', and James now 'standing' down in the hole! But in addition, the Pinnacle of the Temple is replaced by 'the great Cornerstone', thus linking it to traditions about 'Peter' generally and allusions in the Scrolls to the Community Council being the Cornerstone – to say nothing of those in Scripture about '*Jesus' being 'the Stone which the builders rejected*'.

Paul's Contacts in the Household of Nero

Paul, of course, knows the '*Belial*' terminology, because he refers to it, however defectively, in 2 Corinthians 6:15. Not only is the 'Belial' terminology relevant to Herodians, but the 'balla''/'Bela''/'Balaam' circle of language, relating to this root in Hebrew, has to do with what the leaders of this Establishment did to those objecting to their behavior, that is, '*swallowed*' or '*consumed them*' – '*Belial*' in the Damascus Document becoming '*Balaam*' in Revelation, 2 Peter, and Jude.

It is even possible that the circle relates to the '*Benjamin*' appellation as well, a terminology that Paul applies to himself in Romans 11:1 (echoed in Acts 13:21). It is extremely unlikely that Jews were evoking their tribal affiliations by this time in their history – except for 'Priests' or 'Levites' – most other tribes having long since been absorbed into the principal group, 'Judah' – *the source of the appellation 'Jew' or 'Yehud'.* But in Paul's case, when he describes himself in Philippians 3:5 as 'of the race of Israel', 'a Hebrew of the Hebrews', he conspicuously avoids any reference to the appellative '*Jew*'.

There is some indication that overseas Jews may have been using this '*Benjamin*' appellation to apply to themselves too, though Paul might simply have been evoking his biblical namesake, the Benjaminite King Saul, a thousand years before. Even more germane, as we have also suggested, it is possible that Herodians and others, because of their peculiar quasi-Jewish status, used the terminology – as Muhammad does '*Ishmael*' in a later generation – to show that they too were originally '*heirs to the Promise and Children of Abraham*', or, as Paul puts it, '*Israelites*' and '*Hebrews*' – but not '*Jews*'.

Edomites, too, were children of Abraham, but, in view of these very interesting overlaps between Edomites and Benjaminites in the matter of their eponymous ancestor, *Bela' the son of*

Be'or (in Biblical writ, both *the first Edomite King and one of the principal Benjaminite clans* – not to mention that Benjaminites in Judges 19–20 being referred to as '*Sons of Belial*'), the Herodians may have been turning the insults of their detractors around into testimony to their own legitimacy. If the Herodians were using this terminology and applying it to themselves, it would be further verification that Qumran's use of this cluster to imply everything negative – in fact, *the epitome of Evil incarnate* – and our identification of it as *a leitmotif for Herodians* is correct.

In Philippians also, Paul makes use of another allusion right out of the Community Rule from Qumran and applies it to Epaphroditus, whom he calls his '*brother and fellow worker*', '*an odor, a sweet fragrance, an acceptable sacrifice, well pleasing to God*' (2:25 and 4:18). At Qumran, this latter allusion is the kind of simile actually applied to the Community Council, whose members are described as '*a sweet fragrance*', '*an acceptable sacrifice atoning for the land*', *and* '*a tested Wall and Precious Corner-Stone ... establishing the Holy Spirit according to Truth forever*'. In this regard, for the Community Rule too, *prayer rightly-offered is described as* '*a pleasing odor of Righteousness and Perfection of the Way, an acceptable free-will offering*' – again, the same kind of language Paul is applying to his '*brother and fellow-worker*' (even his '*Apostle*') Epaphroditus above.[10]

For his part in Philippians, after then referring to having '*Riches in the Glory of Christ*', Paul sends his greetings 'to *every Holy One ... especially those of the household of Caesar*' (4:19–22.). This Epaphroditus would appear to be an interesting person. 'Epaphroditus'' name, also, appears as the name of Josephus' editor and patron. Josephus refers to 'Epaphroditus' as the 'most excellent of men' and 'a lover of all kinds of learning ... *principally the knowledge of History*', who 'himself *had a part in great events* and *many turns of fortune ... showing the wonderful vigor of an excellent constitution and an immovable virtuous resolution in them all*' – flattery on a par with Paul above.[11]

Like Felix, a freedman of Nero, Epaphroditus was also involved in Nero's death, helping him commit suicide – though this may actually have been an assassination. As a reward, he would also appear afterwards to have become Domitian's secretary, until the latter turned on him and put him to death supposedly for *daring to kill an Emperor*. This was around 95 CE and the same time that Domitian was reputed to have put to death or banished two other 'Christians' in his household, Flavius Clemens (possibly Clement) and his wife or niece, Flavia Domitilla (and possibly even Josephus).

Paul also refers to Epaphroditus in Philippians 2:27 as at one point having been sick and near death. The reference to him connected to '*the household of Caesar*' in Philippians 4:22 makes it virtually certain we are speaking about the same person as the 'Epaphroditus' just described above. One should note the parallel reference to '*those of (the household) of Aristobulus*' in Romans 16:11 and '*the littlest Herod*', his and the infamous Salome's putative son, in 16:13. Herod of Chalcis' son Aristobulus was certainly very close to Claudius since the latter, not only conferred upon him the Kingdom of Lower Armenia, but also the title of 'Friend'. Doubtlessly, this same 'Aristobulus' was on equally friendly terms with persons in Nero's household as well and the Flavians after that – if he lived that long. His son seems to have.

It is a not incurious footnote to all these relationships that *the offspring of the marriage of Drusilla and Felix perished in the* '*conflagration of the mountain Vesuvius in the days of Titus Caesar*' – a matter Josephus promises to relate further but never does.[12] Josephus, also, promises to tell us *more about the family of Philo and the Alabarch of Alexandria* but, likewise, never does.

Final Conclusions about Peter and Josephus' Simon

To go back to John the Baptist's Qumranic-type complaints against the Herodians – clearly, what he objected to on the part of Herodias and Herod Antipas was their '*fornication*' to say nothing of their '*Riches*'. The New Testament presentation of an arcane problem over levirate marriage may or may not have played a part. The issue of whether 'Philip' (actually

'Herod' the younger) did or did not have children is, in any event, moot. *Herodias divorced 'Philip'*, which even Josephus notes was illegal. Nor did this 'Herod', who was the son of Herod's second wife called 'Mariamme' as well, die at this point.

As the Gospel of Luke graphically expresses it, '*but Herod the Tetrarch was reproved by (John) concerning Herodias, the wife of his brother Philip*' (3:19). The issue as Josephus graphically delineates it *vis-à-vis* Herodias was her marriage with, *not one* but *two uncles* and *her illegal divorce from the first of them*, all things roundly condemned at Qumran and, no doubt, in John's complaints against her too – for which he loses his life.

Likewise, the confrontation between Peter and Simon *Magus*, so creatively enhanced in our several sources, had little probably to do with theological problems *per se*, though these may have played a part as, for instance, *ideologies surrounding 'the True Prophet', 'the Primal Adam', and 'the Christ'*. It is impossible to tell, but Josephus does unequivocally state that there was *a 'magician' called 'Simon' in Felix's employ*.

As we saw, Felix used this individual to convince Drusilla, not only to '*break the Laws of her Ancestors*' ('*the First*' in the parlance of the Damascus Document), but *to divorce a previous husband and marry another* – all roundly condemned at Qumran. Moreover, while the previous one had *circumcised himself expressly to marry her*, Felix, quite obviously, *did not*. Furthermore, in the Pseudoclementine *Recognitions* – which makes so much of Peter's confrontations with Simon *Magus* up and down the Palestine coast – we have it that James sent out Peter from somewhere outside of Jericho around this time *to confront Simon Magus in Caesarea*.

In all the materials about James, condemning '*fornication*' is a most insistent theme as it is in the literature centering around '*the Righteous Teacher*' at Qumran. I think we can safely say that the same 'Simon', *who wanted to bar Agrippa I from the Temple as a foreigner* despite the latter's obvious attempts at 'Piety' and *inspected his household to see what was being done there contrary to Law*, confronted Simon *Magus* in Caesarea as well and the issue between them was '*fornication*' – *the 'fornication of the Herodian family*'!

That the Felix, who employed a namesake of this 'Simon' in the next decade was a foreigner, to say nothing of his repression of Opposition leaders and self-evident brutality, just compounds this same issue. Finally, one can take it as a given that Felix was *neither circumcised*, nor scrupled *to sleep with women during 'the blood' of their periods* (as Qumran would put it) – not issues, one can assume, of *very great moment in the Hellenistic world he functioned in*.

The key allusion in the Damascus Document to this last practice relates to *how foreigners were perceived in Palestine*. That is not to say that all foreigners did these things, only that this is *how they would have been perceived in Palestine*. These are the kinds of aspersions that would have circulated in everyday conversation – and everyone would have known what they meant. The calumny as it is present in the Damascus Document, *relating to* '*the Priestly Establishment*', did not mean that all such persons *slept with women 'during the blood of their menstrual flow'*. They most certainly did not.

However, what it did mean was that *they had commerce with persons who did* and, in the Damascus Document's own words, they incurred their '*pollution*' thereby – meaning primarily Herodians. In the case of the High Priests, *they accepted their appointment from such Herodians*, considered by extremist 'Zealot' types irretrievably '*polluted*'; and, worse still, *from Roman Governors – sometimes even for bribes*. This is why 'the Zealots' and probably those represented by the literature at Qumran and proto-'Christians' in Palestine were so intent on '*electing a High Priest of greater purity and Righteousness*' (Heb. 4:14 and 7:26).

This allusion to '*sleeping with women in their periods*', which is directly connected in the Damascus Document to the one about '*each one (of them) marrying his brother's daughter*' (*obviously having to do with Herodians whose marital practice this was*) – in the former instance, *specifically has to do, therefore, with foreigners, and those perceived of as having commerce or intercourse with foreigners*. This would include Herodian Kings and Princesses, all reckoned by extremists of the stripe of *the*

'Simon' in Josephus above and those at Qumran, as *'foreigners'*. Additionally, such aspersion would *include Paul and his so-called 'Gentile Mission' too.* Peter, no doubt, confronted Simon *Magus* on issues such as these as well. Certainly the 'Peter' pictured in the Pseudoclementine *Homilies* would have. This is why Acts is at such pains to counter-indicate and reverse all such issues absolutely.

These are the parameters of 'Palestinian Christian' activity – these are the parameters of Qumran, not retrospective historical re-creation. These become transformed in what is perhaps one of the most cynical examples of overseas dissimulation or inversion into 'Peter' *learning that he should not make distinctions between 'foreigners' or 'uncircumcised men' and their opposites* (Acts 10:28 and 11:3). In effect, *Peter is Paulinized*, the recipient of a Paul-style 'Heavenly vision' to confirm it, and *on a rooftop in Jaffa no less* – this, when Galatians 2:12 *specifically testifies that he 'separated' himself from Paul concerning it* despite being, perhaps, a little less stringent regarding this issue than James. This too is emphatically confirmed in the Pseudoclementine *Homilies*.

To add insult to injury, Peter is then portrayed as greeting a Roman Centurion from Caesarea as we saw and *returning with him to visit his household there* – a Roman Legionnaire whom Acts describes *as caring intensely about Judaism and all things Jewish* (should one suppress another guffaw here?). This, in spite of the fact that over and over again Josephus makes it clear it was *these same legionnaires from Caesarea who exacerbated the problems in the country* – no Governor ever feeling confident enough over a twenty-year period to exercise control over them – and finally goaded the Jews to revolt!

That someone, overwriting this episode about the Jerusalem 'Simon's visit to Agrippa I's household in Caesarea and presenting it, rather, in terms of *Peter's visit to the house of the Roman Centurion Cornelius in Caesarea* – from *'the Italica Contingent'* no less – may or may not have intended to *gain the attention of either Trajan or Hadrian, to convince them of what a positive attitude their predecessors in 'the Italica Regiment'* (Trajan's father anyhow having served in the Palestinian War) *had had to Christian leaders*, has to be considered. In this regard, not only did both Trajan and Hadrian come from the Roman garrison town of 'Italica' in Spain, but both were very active in putting down Messianic uprisings in Palestine and around the Mediterranean at the end of the First and beginning of the Second Centuries.[13]

In fact, Trajan's correspondence with the younger Pliny, who unlike the descendants of Drusilla and Felix survived the eruption of Vesuvius, raised issues not unrelated to these. It will be recalled that Trajan had requested Pliny in his capacity as Governor of Bithynia in Asia Minor to investigate 'Christians' there – obviously 'Gentile' ones. Eusebius, who preserves this from Tertullian (160–221 CE), has Pliny concluding: *'They did nothing evil or contrary to the Laws (Roman Law)* ... beyond their *unwillingness to sacrifice to idols, he found nothing criminal in them.*'

One should remark here – contrary to Paul – the observance of James' prohibition on *'eating things sacrificed to idols'*. In addition, this is the verdict that basically reappears in the Roman Governor's mouth in Judea – if not Pliny's certainly Pilate's – who in Luke 23:4, anyhow, after examining Jesus, concludes, *'I find no fault in this man'*. John even more precisely echoes the words imputed to Pliny above, again quoting Pilate as saying, *'I find no crime in him'* (19:4). At this, Eusebius' version of Tertullian's testimony has Trajan *ruling that 'Christians should not be inquired after further'*. This is not precisely the outcome of the actual correspondence which *has survived and records something of a less sanguine upshot.*

Eusebius also records a similar episode that happened not long before – at least according to his understanding. This one, under Domitian (81–96), ends up in the arrest of *'the offspring of one of those considered the brothers of the Lord, whose name was Judas'*. This is about the same time as the executions of Epaphroditus and Flavius Clemens and the exile of the latter's wife or niece, Flavia Domitilla. It is interesting that *it is this Domitilla's servant* – again curiously named '*Stephanos*' – *who assassinates Domitian the same year.*[14]

A third episode of this kind under Trajan (98–117), at the time seemingly of Messianic disturbances in Egypt and Cyrene (Libya), ends up in the torture and crucifixion of Simeon bar Cleophas – either Jesus' 'cousin' or second brother – around 105–6 CE whom, Eusebius or his source Hegisippus avers, '*terminated his life with sufferings like those of our Lord*'.[15] To confuse the matter still further, Eusebius, again following Hegesippus, supplies us with yet another note about *a third such round-up under Vespasian even earlier.* He explains: '*Vespasian gave an order that a search be made for all descendants of David, and this resulted in the infliction of another widespread persecution on the Jews.*'[16] In all these notices, Eusebius basically uses the same words, '*A search was made for the Jews that were of the descendants of David.*'[17]

One should note here again – if the notice is true – that the Roman administrative practice at the time treated so-called 'Christians', 'Messianists', and Jews virtually indistinguishably. '*Domitian had issued orders that the descendants of David should be slain*', again showing, if true, that he knew the disturbances in Palestine in this period – which were apparently still going on – to be *Messianic.* Whereupon '*the descendants of Judas, as the brother of our Savior according to the flesh, because they were of the family of David, and as such, also related to Christ ... were brought to Domitian*'.[18] Following Hegesippus, now verbatim, Eusebius identifies these as '*the grandchildren of Judas, called the brother of our Lord according to the flesh.*'

Domitian examines them and Eusebius proceeds with the notice that '*the hardness of their bodies was evidence of their labor and the calluses of their hands from their incessant work was evidence of their own labor*' which, ever so slightly, evokes how hard *the calluses were on James' knees from all the 'incessant praying' he did in the Holy of Holies* (*n.b.,* too, the repeat of the word '*incessant*' here as well). Also like James, they are portrayed as answering the charges against them in terms of Jesus' 'coming in Glory to judge ... every man according to his works'. This is almost word-for-word a combination of the Letter of James and the account of James' proclamation in the Temple before the assembled Jewish crowds on Passover. Whereupon '*Domitian despising them ... as simpletons, (supposedly) commanded them to be dismissed and by Imperial order commanded that the persecution cease*'.

Domitian clearly treats them as simpletons because politically-speaking they are no threat, *their Kingdom being only other-worldly.* Still, all of these descendants would appear to have been, once again, rounded up and executed under Trajan a decade later at the time Hegesippus describes the martyrdom of Simeon bar Cleophas because, as he writes (paralleling Eusebius' earlier description of 'Stephen'), these were the persons '*who took the lead of the whole Church as martyrs – in particular, the family of our Lord*'.[19]

The Saleb of Syria, Beduin wanderers and tinkers, possibly descendants of the Judeo-Christian Rechabites.

Left: Wall painting from early Christian catacombs in Rome, with Balaam pointing at the star – by implication, evoking 'the Star Prophecy'.

Below: Columns 11–12 of the Habakkuk Pesher from Qumran, referring to 'the Cup of the Wrath of God' and 'the Day of Judgment'.

PART V

THE BROTHERS OF JESUS AS APOSTLES

Chapter 19
The Apostleship of James, *Cephas*, and John

The Letters of Introduction from James

We should now look at the way the Gospels, Paul's Letters, and other materials present Jesus' brothers and family members generally. In early Church accounts, it is traditionally understood that the James, called '*the brother of the Lord*' is a 'Bishop' rather than an 'Apostle' – as if 'Apostle' were, in some sense, greater than 'Bishop'. It is '*the first James*' – '*James the brother of John*' – who, following the Gospels, is presented as an 'Apostle' and there is rarely any perception about who 'the second James' was (except by Paul, who realizes he is both an 'Apostle' and a 'Pillar'), nor is he ever spoken about to any extent.

In the first sixteen chapters of Acts before the 'We Document' is introduced, we have seen how the traces of real events lie just beneath the surface, glittering like bright pebbles beneath the surface of a stream. Often these involve those who are called 'the Central Three' or 'the Twelve' – meaning 'the Twelve Apostles' – even 'the Seventy', meaning 'the Seventy Disciples'. Problems where these are concerned often have to do with the different enumerations of the Apostles both in and outside of Scripture which, in turn, are connected with problems regarding Jesus' brothers and family generally – and attempts either to diminish or to obliterate them. These, in their turn, are connected to the order of post-resurrection appearances by Jesus, which have been recognized as confirming one's status or place in the hierarchy of the early Church.

In the Pseudoclementines, it becomes very clear that proper Apostles had to carry appointment letters of some kind from the 'Bishop of Bishops' James. At one point, this is expressed in words attributed to Peter (instructing Clement) as follows:

> Observe the greatest caution, that you *believe no teacher unless he brings the testimonial of James the Lord's brother from Jerusalem*, or whomever comes after him. *Under no circumstances receive anyone or consider him a worthy and faithful teacher for preaching the word of Christ unless he has gone up there, been approved, and, as I say, brings a testimonial from there.* (Ps. *Rec.* 4.25)

The negation of this proposition is to be found in the Letters of Paul, who often shows his sensitivity to the issue of appointment letters or proper credentials, thereby indirectly verifying their existence.

This illustrates a point we have been emphasizing about reading between the lines in our sources in order to discern what the accusations were that were circulating around different individuals or what the procedures were such individuals were reacting against or attempting to countermand. For instance, at the beginning of Galatians, Paul insists he is '*an Apostle, not from men nor through man, but through Jesus Christ and God the Father, who raised him from the dead*' (Gal. 1:1). Paul is claiming here that he has *a direct appointment from 'Jesus' himself* – better still '*the Christ*' – an individual whom in bodily form on earth he never seems to have encountered and the followers of whom he admits to 'persecuting' – *some even 'unto death'* (Gal. 1:23).

This seemingly innocuous formulation of his Apostolic qualifications is, of course, *a direct riposte to those who claim to have their appointment either directly from Jesus himself in his human form* or *who carry 'written' credentials from James* – or both. These are the same genre of persons who, as Paul expresses it again in the context of alluding to now to '*the brothers of the Lord*' (plural) in 1 Corinthians, would presume '*to examine*' him (9:3). This should not be surprising since, what

Paul is calling his work or mission depends on a direct 'revelation', as it were, via the mechanism of the Holy Spirit from the Supernatural Being, now residing in Heaven, he denotes as 'Christ Jesus' or 'Jesus Christ' (Gal. 2:2).

In 2 Corinthians 3:1, again employing the imagery of spiritualized Temple and sacrifice and the allegorizing approach, he so loves, Paul pointedly picks up this issue of '*written* credentials' – these obviously, as per Pseudoclementine tradition, from James. Paul asks rhetorically, though none-the-less bitingly:

> Do we start again to recommend ourselves? *Unlike some who need either letters to you or from you to recommend themselves* (here his use of '*some*' again, usually reserved for contemptuous reference to those of the 'Jamesian' orientation), *you are our letter, having been inscribed in our hearts*, being known and read by all men, showing that *you are Christ's Letter served by us*, not being written with ink, not on *tablets of stone*, but with the Spirit of the Living God *on the fleshly tablets of the heart.*

In his riposte here, Paul achieves several things. Not only do we have incredible figurative language here, but he makes it clear that the people with whom he is arguing *care about written things, particularly 'stone tablets', by which he clearly means the Ten Commandments.* Moreover, these persons *are inside not outside the Church*; and, *heaping scorn on those who require 'written appointments' and documentary 'recommendations' to serve as Apostles*, he uses his favorite rhetorical device of '*teaching spiritual things by the Spirit*' to do so (1 Cor. 2:13 and Rom. 2:29).

He goes on in 2 Corinthians 3:6 to use this kind of *spiritualized imagery* or *allegorization* to attack *the written letter of the Law*: '*for the letter kills, but the Spirit gives life*'. Here is the '*Holy Spirit*' language, upon which his own legitimacy and ministry so rest; but, as in the Letter to the Romans, now tied to the '*spiritualizing*' process generally. The chasm here is that Paul is using *poetic* rhetorical devices to reply to interlocutors who are basically using *legal* concepts. It is an unbridgeable one.

Warming to this imagery, Paul now attacks both 'the Law' and 'Moses', the foundation pieces of the people opposing him, obviously meant to include James and the rest of the *Jewish* Apostles and 'Jerusalem Church' Leadership – and the standpoint of the Qumran literature as well – referring to all of these in one of the most biting aspersions conceivable, as '*the Service of death cut in letters into stone*' (2 Cor. 3:7). At the same time and always mindful of this issue of 'letters of recommendation', he evokes his idea of 'the New Covenant', which will now be 'not of the letter but of Spirit' (2 Cor. 3:6). Here the 'New Covenant' in the body and blood of Jesus Christ is presented as being opposed to *physical* letters – whether those sent out to certify its Apostles or those on stone – and totally allegorized.

Picking up, then, the imagery of 'Glory' and 'splendor' – in this instance, 'the splendor on Moses' face', which he says 'was bound to cease' – Paul now contrasts it with his own 'Service' or 'the Ministry of the Spirit in Glory' (2 Cor. 3:8). Not only are we playing once again on 'the Son of Man coming in Glory', already encountered with regard to James' proclamation in the Temple above; but one should compare the use here of this word 'serve' or 'Service', namely 'the Service of the Spirit', with how the 'Service' of the Spouter of Lying is characterized in the Habakkuk *Pesher*: as the 'Service of Vanity' or 'a Worthless Service'.[1]

Paul's use in this context too of phrases like 'the Servants of the New Covenant' and 'the Service of Righteousness in Glory' (2 Cor. 3:9) will be played on later in 2 Corinthians by the use of the phrase 'the Servants of Righteousness' to attack those he will call 'Super Apostles' and even 'Pseudo-Apostles' (2 Cor. 11:13 and 11:15).

At this point, carried away by his enthusiasm for the spiritualizing imagery he is employing, Paul makes one of the most outrageous accusations ever made by one religion against another. He evokes an episode from Exodus in the Old Testament. When emerging from the Tent of Meeting, after speaking with God face to face, Moses veils himself so that the Children of Israel will not be irradiated from his brilliance or 'splendor' at having been in the Presence of God (Exod. 34:33). Paul rather asserts that Moses 'put a veil over his face, so that the Children of Israel would not notice the end of what had to fade' (3:13)! In other words, Moses was a deceiver and a charlatan, who veiled himself because he did not want the Children of Israel to see there was no 'splendor' associated with his relationship with God and the revelation of the Law consonant upon it. Regardless of the thrust of the various imageries being used or the rightness or wrongness of the polemics involved, no more scurrilous accusation has ever been recorded by the founder of one major world religion against that of another.

The relationship of these imageries to Jewish Mysticism of the Middle Ages makes it fair to ask whether this kind of thinking was actually already functioning in Paul's time. The very 'splendor' used to describe the brilliance on Moses' face as a result of his encounter with God becomes the title of the most representative and well-known document of this underground Jewish mystical religious tradition, popularly known as *Kabbalah*, 'The *Zohar*' or '*Book of Splendor*'.

Paul's Attacks on the 'Apostles of the Highest Degree'

At the end of 2 Corinthians, Paul responds to the charge that, though he writes strong and powerful letters at a distance, in person his body is feeble, his speech even feebler. He does so by attacking 'some' who 'write their own recommendations, who, measuring themselves by themselves and comparing themselves to themselves, lack all understanding' (10:10–12).

Unctuous and self-deprecating, yet biting in the extreme, Paul refers now to the 'Authority which *the Lord* gave' him – meaning *not* that which the Apostles or James gave him. He does so in terms of 'building up and not tearing down' (2 Cor. 10:8), while at the same time starting to employ his language of 'boasting', which for him will serve as a substitute for *written credentials*. In 1 Corinthians 8:1–13, attacking those with 'weak consciences', who make 'stumbling blocks' over 'things sacrificed to idols', and evoking the Piety Commandment of 'loving God' – evoked to exactly opposite effect in the Letter of James 2:5–14 – it is rather 'Love' that 'builds up', as opposed to 'Knowledge' which 'puffs up'.

In fact, this same 'puffing up' language will be used in the Habakkuk *Pesher*, in the prelude to its interpretation of the all-important Habakkuk 2:4 – 'the Righteous shall live by his Faith', to attack those disagreeing with its interpretation (as well as that of Habakkuk 2:3 on 'the Delay of the *Parousia*' preceding it), who 'will not be pleased with their Judgment'. Not only is this 'puffed up' allusion based on the language of Habakkuk 2:4, but the *Pesher* actually refers to the Righteous Teacher as the person 'in whose heart God put *the Knowledge* to interpret all of the words of His Servants the Prophets'.[2]

In both these passages, Paul is using the same 'building' metaphor with which he began 1 Corinthians, where he referred to himself as the 'architect' of God's Community and the 'building' which was Christ (1 Cor. 3:9–14). This is important for determining the historical provenance of Qumran aspersions on '*the Spouter of Lying*' in the Habakkuk *Pesher*, which as part of its attack on his *'Vain' or 'Worthless Service', refers to 'the Liar' as 'misleading Many to build' a Congregation ('Church') on 'Lying' and 'blood' 'for the sake of his Glory'.*

Again, warming to his subject and the motifs of '*boasting*' and his own '*foolishness*', Paul protests that he '*does not lie*' and turns his opponents' accusations against them, *attacking 'those people' he bitterly describes as 'Pseudo-Apostles, Lying workmen disguising themselves as Apostles of Christ'* (2 Cor. 11:13). The assurance that he is '*not Lying*' encountered here is repeated not only in Galatians, but throughout Romans. In vituperative language such as '*Lying workmen disguising themselves as Apostles of Christ' and 'Pseudo' or 'Counterfeit Apostles'*, one sees again the typical inversions of key themes in the Scrolls which by now are becoming so familiar.

Paul asks rhetorically: 'And no wonder, for *even Satan disguises himself as an Angel of Light*; it is no great thing that his servants disguise themselves as *Servants of Righteousness*, whose *End shall be according to their works*' (2 Cor. 11:14–15). Of course, not only does Paul identify the individuals he has in mind by the linguistic inversions he uses and the pun he makes on their principal doctrine – *their 'End shall be according to' the 'works' they so extolled* – but the allusion to '*the Servants of Righteousness*' exactly parallels the kind of emphases one encounters at Qumran and in all traditions relating to James – including the Letter in his name.

Losing control of his '*Tongue*' almost completely now – as even he acknowledges – Paul makes it unmistakably clear that his opponents in the Church actually are '*Hebrews*' not others. In passing, one should also note the relation of this loss of control to *the aspersion on 'the Tongue' being 'an uncontrollable Evil, full of death-bringing poison'* in the Letter of James (3:5–12) and the derogations on '*the Pourer out of Lying*'/ '*Spouter of Lying*' or '*Comedian*' at Qumran.

> But if anyone wants brazenness – *I am still talking as fool* – then I can be just as brazen. *Hebrews are they?* So am I. *Israelites are they?* So am I. *Of the seed of Abraham are they?* So am I. *Servants of Christ are they?* I must be insane to have to say this, but *so am I*, and *more than they, more because I have worked harder.* (2 Cor. 11:21–23)

It is also significant that when speaking of himself, as in Philippians, Paul never calls himself '*a Jew*' – a term that even the Dead Sea Scrolls attest was current in this period – only *a 'Hebrew', an 'Israelite', and 'of the seed of Abraham'*. Whether Paul means by these allusions simply his affiliation to '*Benjamin*' – '*Benjamin' not being 'Jewish' per se* (meaning, *of 'the Tribe' or 'House of Judah'*) only *Israelite* – or a further manipulation through the common ancestor, '*Bela°*' or '*Belah*', shared in the Bible by Benjaminites and Edomites (or Idumaeans) which would then include Herodians as well, is impossible to say.

Given his emphasis on being of '*the seed of Abraham*' and his theological concentration on the same individual – a claim, which will have particular relevance for those in the area of Edessa (or Haran in Northern Syria, Abraham's city of origin) and probably Adiabene (and presaging the later one on behalf of all 'Arabs' by Muhammad in Islam and which Herodians as 'Edomites' also probably claimed) – I would be disposed to respond in the affirmative – that Paul was alluding to wider, so-called '*Benjaminite*' affiliations, whatever he meant by these.

Again Paul goes on to make it very clear with whom he is arguing and who his opponents are in the matter of Apostleship and the necessary letters of recommendation accompanying it – high-minded and poetic assaults on the superfluousness of such 'unspiritual' letters notwithstanding – when he goes on to refer to 'danger from *pseudo-brothers*' (2 Cor. 11:26), which parallels the reference to '*Pseudo-Apostles as Lying workmen disguising themselves as Apostles of Christ*' preceding it (2 Cor. 11:13). It is, therefore, 'brothers' of some kind, to whom he is replying.

Ending his response to his lack of credentials, he contends that he has been forced to 'become a fool' because, instead of 'commending' him – again the play on letters of recommendation here – his communities have forced him to boast of his achievements and, as the Letter of James and even the Dead Sea Scrolls would put it, *lose control over his Tongue*.

With this, he cannot refrain from making one final defiant, if obsequious, boast: '*For in nothing was I behind these Apostles of the Highest Degree* as well, if *nothing I am*' (12:11). In referring once more to these '*Highest Apostles*' in this manner he makes it unmistakably clear that they are the very same '*Hebrews*', to whom he referred so venomously as being '*Pseudo-Apostles*' and '*Servants of Satan'* – not to mention his aspersion on '*those reckoned as important*' or *the 'Pillars' whose 'importance nothing conferred*' in Galatians 2:6–9. In regard to this last, one should note the repetition of the word '*nothing*' here in 2 Corinthians too, now applied to '*the Apostles of the Highest Degree*'.

Where Paul's use of this non-specific title '*Apostle*' is concerned, it is noteworthy that he, not only applies it 'to those who were Apostles before me' (including James) in Jerusalem in Galatians 1:17, but also to Gentiles he is intimate friends with in Asia, Greece, and Rome. We already saw how in Philippians he calls Epaphroditus (*'his brother, fellow worker, and comrade in arms'*) an '*Apostle*' as well (2:25). This allusion to Epaphroditus is directly followed by the greeting 'to every Holy One ('Saint') in Christ Jesus' and '*especially those in the household of Caesar*' (4:18–22), a reference that would have made the inhabitants at Qumran blanch. As we saw, Epaphroditus was in all likelihood identical with Nero's secretary by the same name, ultimately involved in some peculiar way in the latter's murder or, at least, helping him commit suicide.

It will be recalled that Paul also uses this 'household' language in similar and related salutations at the end of Romans. In one of these, he refers to such persons as 'noted among the Apostles, who were in Christ before me' (16:7). Among these is one '*Junias*', to whom Paul refers as well as his '*kinsman*' – symbolic or real. This may well have been the 'nephew' Acts 23:16 refers to, *the son of Paul's sister with a house in Jerusalem* whom, we have identified as '*Julius Archelaus*'. There is no doubt that this individual whose father was 'Helcias', the Temple Treasurer, *ended up living in Rome too, where Josephus alludes to him as an avid reader of his works.*[3]

There is also a greeting at the end of Romans to one 'Rufus', whom Paul also describes as 'the chosen of the Lord', and whose mother, in some kind of adoptionist manner – like 'Jesus' on the cross to 'the beloved Disciple' – Paul calls his own (16:13). This recalls the individual the Gospel of Mark calls 'Simon of Cyrene', 'the father of Alexander and Rufus', who, 'coming from a field, carried the cross of Jesus' (15:21). The way Mark refers to 'Alexander and Rufus', they are known in some Gentile Christian Community – presumably Rome, where Mark is thought to have been written.

In Josephus, coincidental or otherwise, there is another 'Rufus', a Roman soldier again, who at the end of the *War* does somewhat parallel things. What he does is *make a daring foray, again across Jordan near Machaeros, where John the Baptist met his end, and 'carry off' one of the local Jewish partisans.* This man is then crucified before his own town and, because of his pitiful cries, many surrendered. Those who did not were butchered and the women and children enslaved – this, the '*carrying off*' and '*cross*' themes associated with the '*Rufus*' in Josephus.[4]

A second '*Rufus*', Josephus speaks of, is *the Roman Commander, left in control of Jerusalem after Titus went to Rome for his victory celebrations* who, as Josephus himself opines, *turned Jerusalem into a ploughfield.* One hopes this was not what, using the phraseology of Paul's greeting here in Romans, he was 'chosen *by God*' to do. All these parallels may simply be coincidental, but they are nevertheless illustrative of the atmosphere of the times and what intercourse with individuals called 'Rufus' *in Rome* might really have meant.

Coincidentally, this last-named 'Rufus' is also associated with one 'Simon'. But this Simon is now 'Simon Bar Giora', a leader of the Revolutionaries. Josephus dwells on his capture in detail, reveling in telling us how through Rufus' determination, 'God brought this man to be punished'. As with Niger previously, after Jerusalem fell, Simon was apparently at first taken for dead by his partisans. But, like Niger too, staying 'three days' underground, to their amazement, he suddenly reappeared to his followers, who then 'took him for an apparition'. Again, all these common themes might be sheer coincidence, but Josephus concludes this episode with the pronouncement: 'His wicked actions did not escape the Divine Anger, nor is Justice too weak to punish offenders, but in time overtakes those who break its Laws and inflicts its punishments upon the Evil in a manner even much more severe, inasmuch as they expected to escape it on account of their not being punished immediately.'[5] This Simon was kept by Titus to be featured in his victory parade in Rome, at the end of which he was beheaded.

Again for his part, Josephus follows his account of Simon's capture by Rufus with his descriptions of Titus celebrating his brother Domitian's 'birthday party' in Caesarea on his way to Rome, in which some *twenty-five hundred prisoners* were killed by burning, being eaten alive by animals, and in gladiatorial contests. These were followed by similar festivities in continuation of these 'birthday celebrations' in Beirut, where like numbers of prisoners were killed in even more impressive ceremonies.

The Testimony in Paul to James as Apostle and Brother of the Lord

Aside from referring to himself repeatedly as 'Apostle', Paul also makes it clear that James was an Apostle. All the other early Church accounts we have been considering present James as an Apostle as well. For example, to use the words Eusebius conserves from Hegesippus: '*this Apostle was Holy from his mother's womb*'. It will be recalled that analogously, Paul also makes the same claim for himself, that God *chose him from his 'mother's womb*' and called him '*by His Grace to reveal his son in' him* (Gal. 1:15–16).

Paul confirms James' Apostleship in his first reference to him in Galatians 1:19: '*Of the other Apostles*, I saw none, except *James the brother of the Lord*.' This statement is in itself significant. Not only does he not even mention any other Apostle called 'James' at this point (who would have still been alive at this time), but Paul evinces no embarrassment whatsoever about James being '*the brother of the Lord*'. He does not qualify it, as later theologians do sometimes tortuously, nor try to explain it away by making excuses about it – for instance, that he was the son of a different mother or the son of a different father or the like. Nor does he treat it symbolically, which given his tendency to allegorize he might have done. He just states it as a known fact.

In the second place, as we saw, it contradicts Acts' presentation of events and their sequence. In Galatians, Paul is answering the accusation that he 'seeks to please men' not God (1:10). This accusation echoes the charge found in the Letter of James, whoever makes himself a 'friend of the world, turns himself into an Enemy of God' (Jas. 4:3). This last is the key epithet applied to Paul in all Judeo-Christian sources.

In Galatians, too, in describing how he 'ravaged the Assembly of God', Paul tells of how 'zealous for the Traditions of his Fathers', beyond many of his contemporaries of his 'own race', he was – thereby effectively calling himself 'a Zealot' (1:14). In the process, he assures everyone he 'does not lie' (1:20). This 'not Lying' contention is particularly relevant not only to the claim of having private 'revelations', but also to how, in undertaking to teach his version of the Good News 'among the Gentiles', he did not stop to discuss it with 'any flesh and blood, nor go up to Jerusalem (to consult) with those that *were Apostles before me*' (1:16). Notice here, again, he does not precisely specify the number of these 'Apostles'.

The import of this is obvious. One should also note his emphasis here on his idea of 'flesh-and-blood' Apostles, which emphasis for him is, of course, inferior to 'spiritual' ones. This accords with the fact that his appointment was 'not from men' and he was not interested in *written credentials* – neither letters written in ink nor upon stone – from such persons either, which bring, as he so graphically puts it, only 'death' (2 Cor. 3:6–7).

This also relates to the accusation reflected here of '*trying to please men*', thereby turning himself '*into the Enemy of God*' – this, because he was not properly *credentialed by men*, either the Jerusalem Assembly, the Twelve, or the Inner Three. James, on the other hand, as per the Letter attributed to his name and in the manner of Abraham, because *he (like Abraham) was perfectly 'Righteous', was the true 'Friend' or 'Beloved of God'*, as presumably all the '*Righteous Ones*' were.

It is at this point in Galatians that Paul claims he '*went away into Arabia and again returned to Damascus*' – whatever might be meant by '*Arabia*' and '*Damascus*' here – and did not go up to Jerusalem for *another three years* (1:17–18). It is legitimate to inquire, in regard to this '*return to Damascus*', whether it had anything to do with a first visit there at the time of the confrontation between Aretas and Herod Antipas, reflected in 2 Corinthians 11:32 also in conjunction with the affirmation of '*not Lying*'.

The Letter of James at this point is attacking the 'Empty Man', who is teaching that Abraham '*was not justified by works' but Faith*, which is, of course, what Paul is doing in Romans 4:2–5 and Galatians 3:5–10. Paul, on the other hand, likes to turn the epithet '*Empty*' or '*Vain*' – notations also found in the key Habakkuk *Pesher* passages describing *the 'Mission'* or *'Service' of 'the Liar'* – against his adversaries by claiming that their endless nit-picking and debates over the Law of Moses are 'Empty' or 'Vain'.

For Acts 9:22–23, after Paul '*confounded the Jews who dwelt in Damascus' by the way he proved that Jesus was 'the Christ*' (the same thing James is supposed to have been proving in early Church accounts of the events leading to the riot on the Temple Mount), 'the Jews plotted to kill him'. Paul then escapes in the 'basket' episode – not from Aretas but from 'the Jews', who were '*watching the gates night and day in order to kill him*' (Acts 9:24). However preposterous, it should be recalled that this 2 Corinthians notice comes in the midst of Paul's attack on the 'Apostles of Surpassing Degree' as 'Pseudo-Apostles' and 'Servants of Satan' amid his bragging about his endless 'toil and service' and protestations about 'not Lying'.

When Paul gets to Jerusalem, he tries to '*join himself to the Disciples*' who are, not surprisingly, all afraid of him and '*don't believe he is a Disciple*' (Acts 9:26). Barnabas then brings him 'to the Apostles', where he explains how Paul *'saw the Lord in the Way, speaking to him, and he had spoken boldly in Damascus in the Name of Jesus*' (Acts 9:27). Barnabas' description 'to the Apostles' of Paul's vision of the resurrected Jesus, which differs markedly from the way in which Acts earlier described it, is similar to the way Jesus appeared to one 'Cleopas' (Cleophas) and another unnamed person 'along the Way' in the Gospel of Luke and to James in the Gospel of the Hebrews.

Be this as it may, Acts now records that Paul was with the Apostles 'in their comings and goings in Jerusalem, speaking boldly in the Name of the Lord Jesus'. This is paralleled in Galatians – or rather not paralleled – as follows (Paul speaking in the first person):

> Afterwards I came into the regions of Syria and Cilicia, but *I was not known by face to the Churches (Assemblies) in Christ in Judea,* who had only heard that *he, who had formerly persecuted them, was now announcing the Gospel (and) the Faith he had once ravaged,* and they were *glorifying God in me* (now, *'God' in him,* not '*his Son in' him* as earlier – Gal. 1:21–24)

It is leading into this that he asserts: '*After three years I went up to Jerusalem to make Peter's acquaintance,* and I remained with him for fifteen days, *but I did not see any of the other Apostles,* except James the brother of the Lord' (1:18–20). Of course, the two accounts, Galatians and Acts, contradict each other here. Being earlier and on the surface anyhow not overwritten, Galatians is always to be preferred.

Acts finishes its version of this episode by having Paul now arguing with '*the Hellenists*', *blaming them* – whoever they were and however illogical – *for the problems he was having.* It will be remembered that it was arguments between this same group and '*the Hebrews*' that supposedly triggered Stephen's stoning two chapters before. It will also be recalled that in 2 Corinthians, Paul's opponents, the 'Apostles of the Highest Rank' were described as 'Hebrews'. Now Acts recounts this as follows: 'And he spoke and reasoned with *the Hellenists, but they took it in mind to put him to death*, but hearing of it, the brothers (whether symbolical or real) *brought him down to Caesarea and sent him away to Tarsus*' (9:29–30). None of this, of course, makes any sense whatsoever and all is dissimulation or a garbled overwrite of more embarrassing material, of which the underlying lines should be clear.

Paul also refers to both *James and 'the brothers of the Lord*' in 1 Corinthians, the latter in the context of a reference to 'those who would examine' him as we saw (9:5). It should immediately be clear that this usage 'brothers of the Lord' is a variation of the way Paul described James as 'the brother of the Lord' in Galatians 1:19. In this 1 Corinthians material, Paul has just finished giving his answer to one of the key strictures of James' prohibitions to overseas communities, as Acts presents them, 'things sacrificed to idols' – accusing those who made an issue over such matters of being '*weak*' (1 Cor. 8:7–12).

This mention of '*weakness*' is the same way he expressed himself with regard to those who '*eat nothing but vegetables'* in Romans 14:2. There he used it, not only to apply to people who were vegetarians, but also in the more general sense to apply to those who *made issues regarding dietary matters.* In Romans, he had just evoked *the Righteousness Commandment of 'loving your neighbor as yourself*' (13:8–11), called in the Letter of James '*the Royal Law according to the Scripture*' (Jas. 2:8), and directed his followers 'to *obey the governing Authorities' and pay their taxes, since all governing officials are 'Servants of God*' (*sic* – Rom. 13:1–7).

Before going on to claim *in the name of 'the Lord Jesus that nothing is unclean in itself*' (Rom. 14:15) – this obviously meant to include unclean food as well as other things – Paul calls persons who eat only vegetables 'weak'. In the same vein in a grandiloquent flourish at the end of the 1 Corinthians' polemic against the 'weak consciences' of his opponents, who will not 'recline in an idol temple', nor 'eat things sacrificed to idols'; Paul states: 'Since *meat causes my brother to stumble* (lit. 'scandalize my brother', but Paul actually uses the language of 'stumbling' preceding this in 1 Cor. 8:9), *I will never eat flesh again for ever*, in order not to *cause my brother to stumble*' (8:13). This crucial language of '*scandalizing*' or '*stumbling*' is reiterated, following the citation of 'the all-Righteousness Commandment', in the Letter of James in the famous allusion to '*stumbling* over one small point of the Law'.

At the conclusion to this Romans passage condemning vegetarianism and judging a brother's eating habits, Paul speaks, in a play on the whole Jewish Christian notion of 'adoptionist sonship', in terms of being 'received by' or 'adopted by God'. In the process, he repeatedly evokes the word '*standing*' – again implying he knows the '*Standing One'* ideology as well: '*Do not let the one ... who does not eat judge the one who eats*, for God has *adopted him for Himself. Can you judge another's servant* (this is classic)? He *stands or falls* to his own master and he shall be *made to stand*, for God is able to *make him stand*' (Rom. 14:3–4). This recapitulates almost precisely the language introducing the 'Three Nets of Belial' in the Damascus Document, that: '*at the completion of the end of these years*, there will be *no more joining to the House of Judah*, but each man *will stand on his own watchtower* (the Cairo version, which is probably wrong, has this as '*net*')'.[6]

Going back now to 1 Corinthians and continuing in this vein, Paul concludes preparatory to launching into his monologue on '*Communion with the blood of Christ*': '*All things are Lawful for me ... eat everything that is sold in the marketplace. There is no need to raise questions of conscience*' (always a euphemism in Paul for '*the Law*' – 1 Cor. 10:23–27). At this point in 1 Corinthians, directly following his first reference to 'Communion with the blood of Christ' and imprecations to 'flee the worship of idols'; to show that he is still talking about James' directives to overseas communities, Paul again raises the issue of 'things sacrificed to an idol', which he now discusses – somewhat disingenuously – in terms of his '*freedom being judged by another's conscience*' (1 Cor. 10:28).

His meaning is, however, once again clear. Earlier, in raising this issue in terms of '*weakness*', he had already used that same '*building*' imagery so dear to the description of '*the Spouter of Lying*' at Qumran (1 Cor. 8:1–12).[7] He had also, it will be recalled, even repeated the very assertion, '*all things are Lawful to me*' of 1 Corinthians 10:23 – earlier in 1 Corinthians 6:12 in the midst of his '*food for the belly*' and '*being joined to the flesh of a harlot*' remarks introducing the subject of '*fornication*' in 6:9–6:20.

Now in chapter 9 of 1 Corinthians, before mentioning '*the brothers of Jesus' traveling around with women* – and before his excursus on '*being all things to all men' and 'running the race to win*' – he asks defiantly, '*am I not free?*' (1 Cor. 9:1). He asks this, starting with a direct reference to his own '*Apostleship in the Lord*', as a prelude too to his cynically opportunist remarks about '*making himself weak to gain those who were weak*' or '*outside the Law to gain those outside the Law*' (1 Cor. 9:20–22).

At the same time he reveals a defensiveness against charges of profiteering from his 'work' or 'mission' and using, as he puts it, 'the Authority' of his office to enjoy its fruits (by which he clearly means monetary ones) or even 'to stop working'. In particular, he enjoys the opportunity to indulge in a little additional word-play concerning his insistence on '*freedom from the Law*' while, at the same time, *teaching the Gospel for 'free'* (9:18–19). All this, he puts somewhat rhetorically as follows: 'Am I not an Apostle? Am I not free (meaning '*free from the Law*' and, by extension, *free of Authority*)? *Have I not seen Jesus Christ our Lord?* Are you not *my work in the Lord*?' (1 Cor. 9:1).

Here, playing on the most well-known doctrine associated with James, 'Justification by works', he characterizes his Community as his '*works*'. In referring to '*seeing Jesus*' too here, Paul is not only comparing himself to the other principal Apostles, but seems to mean that whatever visionary experience this involved was in the course of things sufficient to make him an 'Apostle'. We shall see as we proceed that 'seeing Jesus' and the order in which this occurred were very important aspects to Apostleship generally (it is also a phraseology directly replicated towards the end of the Damascus Document from Qumran).

Paul now continues in this vein, thus proceeding to make his remark about 'the brothers of the Lord': 'Even if to others I am *not an Apostle* (here Paul certainly recognizes that there are those who do not accept his Apostolic credentials), without doubt I am to you. *For you are the seal of my Apostleship in the Lord*' (1 Cor. 9:2). The reference to 'Apostleship in the Lord' parallels James as 'the brother of the Lord'.

As Paul continues, 'My answer to those who would examine me is this. Do we not have authority to eat and drink?' (1 Cor. 9:3). Here the dietary matter again, now expressed in terms of Apostolic rewards. 'Do we not have authority to take a sister (or) wife around with us, as also the *other Apostles and the brothers of the Lord and Cephas do*? Or is it only Barnabas and I who do not have the authority not to work? *Who serves as a soldier at any time at his own expense?*' (again his cynicism shines through – 1 Cor. 9:4–6). He also raises here the Biblical injunction: 'You shall not muzzle an ox treading out corn' (Deut. 25:4) which 1 Timothy 5:18 repeats in almost exactly parallel context. Paul does this to again raise the issue of 'wages' or 'toil', as usual taking the opportunity to play yet again with his allegorizing language on 'sowing spiritual things' (1 Cor. 9:9–11).

His reference here to 'the brothers of the Lord' then repeats the ascription in Galatians 1:19, only now it is in the plural. That these are grouped systematically with and on the same level as 'Apostles' is clear from the context. In Galatians, this was even clearer, as James was actually considered part and parcel of what was meant by 'the other Apostles'.

There can be little doubt that Paul is dealing with the question of 'Authority' here – as he himself avers – his own and others' over him. He puts this in terms of '*the authority to eat and drink*', a key component of his rupture with James, but a euphemism, too, in the Gospels and in Paul used to attack a variety of individuals of the 'Jamesian' mindset generally – the point being that James and his followers *do not freely eat* and certainly *did not drink*.

The traveling around with women, as wife or in some other arrangement, would appear to relate to that brother of Jesus known as 'Judas' or 'Jude' – in other sources, sometimes referred to as 'Barnabas' and even, perhaps, 'Judas Barsabas'. But it clearly did not relate to either James or his and Jesus' alleged 'cousin', Simeon bar Cleophas, whom all our sources seem unanimous in identifying as *life-long* Nazirites (and, likewise, the *Homilies*, Peter).

No doubt James, anyhow, would have remained in Jerusalem and was never 'on the road', as it were, but if Hegesippus, Epiphanius, and Jerome are to be believed, *he probably was a 'life-long virgin'*. Epiphanius, it will be recalled, even puts forth a claim to the High Priesthood on his behalf based on his Naziritism and purity, which as far as he, anyhow, was concerned – and probably Jesus and Simeon as well – included absolute sexual continence. We have already seen the relationship of such claims both for the later 'Christian' doctrine of the 'Virgin' Mary, but also for Josephus' picture of the bathing '*Banus*' constantly did 'in cold water'.

This would not necessarily be the case for the other brothers, such as Judas who, as we have seen, according to the several notices in Hegesippus and Eusebius, had children or grandchildren. In this context, too, one must always keep 'Joseph' or 'Joses Barnabas' in mind. If he were one of these siblings, this would answer a lot of questions about the confusions regarding his forename and eponym, how suddenly he materialized out of nowhere, and how Paul got into the Movement in the first place – still, this is only a query.

The Central Three, the Poor, and Circumcision Again in Galatians

Where sequencing is concerned, Acts moves from 'Agabus'' prediction of the Famine (46 –48 CE) to Saul's and Barnabas' Famine-relief mission to Judea – about which it tells us nothing – on to the death of 'James the brother of John' (12:2), Peter's arrest and subsequent flight, and the introduction of James (12:17). As we have seen, its notice at this point about '*prophets coming down from Jerusalem to Antioch*' parallels that in Galatians about the '*some coming from James*', who were also '*of the circumcision*'. These come down 'from Jerusalem to Antioch', triggering the confrontation there over *the issue of table fellowship with Gentiles*, which for Acts also involves '*circumcision*' and culminates in its presentation of the 'Jerusalem Conference'.

In Josephus the sequence is rather different. It goes from his lengthy description of the conversion of Queen Helen of Adiabene and her sons, Izates and Monobazus – the key issue again here being '*circumcision*' – by one '*Ananias*' (the name of the individual who met Paul in Damascus in Acts after his Damascus-Road vision) and an *unnamed other*. This '*unnamed other*' – who, in our view, is Paul – teaches that '*circumcision' is unnecessary for 'Salvation' (yesha'/yeshu'a* in Hebrew).

This is immediately followed by Queen Helen's dispatch of her representatives *to buy grain in Egypt and Cyprus* – in our view this is, in part, the root of all these 'Cypriot' and 'Cyrenian' denotations in Acts – *to relieve the Famine*, followed by *the beheading of Theudas* and *the crucifixion of James and Simon, the two sons of Judas the Galilean*. In fact, in another variation of these denotations – all part and parcel of Acts' basic dissembling – even Josephus' note at this point in his narrative about 'the Census of Cyrenius' here is precisely recapitulated in Luke's spelling of 'Cyrenians' in these various notices.

For Paul, too, the key issue in Galatians, to some extent paralleling these things, is 'circumcision' – along with that of 'table fellowship' connected to it. In turn, 'circumcision' is very much tied to the matter of Apostleship, for directly after averring the Jamesian 'God does not accept the person of men' (Gal. 2:6), Paul sets forth his understanding of Peter's '*Apostleship of the circumcision*' in contrast to his own '*of the uncircumcision*' or '*to the Gentiles*'. Curiously, in the several references at this point in Galatians, Paul uses only the appellative 'Peter' not 'Cephas' (2:7–8); but immediately following these, he makes the reference to '*the Central Three*' or '*those reputed to be Pillars*' as '*James and Cephas and John*' in that order and by that nomenclature – for the first and only time in this letter, introducing the name '*Cephas*' (Gal. 2:9).

Whatever one might wish to make of this, Paul now goes on to aver that he shook hands with '*these Pillars*' in agreement that he and Barnabas were to go 'to the Gentiles' while 'they to the circumcision' (2:9). It is for this reason that all these references to 'circumcision' in Acts, and their contrapositive in the matter of so-called 'Hellenists' – like 'Cananaeans' or 'Canaanites' elsewhere (probably a substitute for '*Zealots*' and/or '*Sicarii*') – are so important; for they camouflage or confuse the situation surrounding Apostleship generally – in particular the Apostleship of these 'Three' and Paul's own – and the central issue seemingly impinging on these things, '*circumcision*'.

For Paul, the only qualification he thinks he must observe with regard to his 'Mission' or 'Apostleship' is 'to be sure to remember *the Poor*', which, as he observes, was the very thing he 'was most intent on *doing*' (2:10). However, it is not clear here whether this was the point of view of the Central Three as well – it probably wasn't. The meaning of 'the Poor' here has been variously debated, but there can be little doubt that in some sense it refers to the pseudonym for James' Community in Jerusalem, from which the term 'Ebionites' has been derived. However, as we have seen, this term also comprises one of the principal terms of self-designation in the literature at Qumran, particularly in the Habakkuk and Psalm 37 *Peshers*, where it is specifically applied to the followers of 'the Righteous Teacher' *in Jerusalem.*

The allusion to '*the Poor*' aside, in his testimony to James the Just being one of the Central Three – for this is obviously what he is saying – Paul again shows no embarrassment or reticence about James' exalted stature in the early Church, other than he is not impressed by it except when he finds it useful to be. Nor can there be any doubt that this is James the Leader of the early Church, '*the Bishop of Bishops*' or, as Qumran would put it, '*the Mebakker*' or '*Overseer*'. Nor does Paul mention any other James. There is only James 'the brother of the Lord' or, if one prefers, 'the brother of Jesus'; despite the fact that Gospels, downplaying him, refer to him rather derogatorily as '*James the Less*' (Mark 15:40) or '*James the son of Alphaeus*' (Mark 3:18 and pars.).

Paul does not mention any '*James* the *brother of John*' in other letters either – nor do the other New Testament letters; so apart from these testimonies in the Gospels and Acts we can have no idea who this other James was, if indeed he existed, which is questionable. In the letters in the New Testament the only James ever mentioned is *James 'the Just'*. In Gospel lists and in the description of the witnesses to the crucifixion, there is a 'James the Less' or 'the Littler James' – a designation clearly aimed at belittling him and contrasting him with 'the Great James' – variously called 'James the brother of John', 'the son of Zebedee' (also known as '*Boanerges*' in the Gospel of Mark, 'the sons of Thunder' – 3:17). This 'James the Less' is, also, to be identified with another James in Apostle lists called 'James the son of Alphaeus' (Mt 10:3 and pars.), whom we shall show is identical to the James before us here. As should be clear, the *real Great James* is the one before us, the one Mark calls in an obvious attempt to reduce his status, *James the Less.*

But is '*Cephas*', too, to be reckoned among the Apostles and is he the same as the individual usually called 'Peter'? All other references in Galatians, as we have seen, are to 'Peter' not 'Cephas', but here Paul lists 'James, *Cephas*, and John' as the Central Triad of Pillar Apostles. The question cannot be answered on the basis of the data available to us, any more than the question of who Peter was, Gospel fantasizing about 'fishermen' on the Sea of Galilee notwithstanding. As we have seen, some early Church accounts definitely assume the two are separate or that there are two Cephas', listing 'Cephas' also among 'the Seventy'. But given what we have before us here in Galatians and the reference in the Gospel of John indicating that Simon was to be called '*Cephas*' – even interpreted there to mean 'Stone' in Greek, thus, '*Peter*' (1:42) – one can assume that for the purposes of discussion he is.

It is perhaps also proper to point out that, except for what we shall see to be the interpolation of 'the Twelve' in 1 Corinthians 15:5 (there were only 'Eleven' at the time), Paul *never does number the Apostles*. In fact, neither he nor anyone else at this juncture seems to have any idea of *a limitation in the number of Apostles to a fixed number 'Twelve'*. Acts, though, is very interested in this scenario in attempting, as we have seen, to explain the problem of the election of a successor in early Church history.

So are the Gospels except for John. Though mentioning 'the Twelve', again in the context of negative allusion to Judas *Iscariot* – now called (*'the son'* or *'brother'*) *'of Simon Iscariot ... one of the Twelve'* (6:67–71) – and *'Didymus Thomas one of the Twelve'* (that is, *'Judas Thomas'* – 20:24), John never actually enumerates them – probably because of problems over 'Jesus'' brothers and family as well; nor does he ever call these individuals *'Apostles'* – only *'Disciples'*. For their part, the Synoptic Gospels both describe and enumerate 'the Twelve', enumerations we shall presently consider in attempting to develop more information about the person of James and the other 'brothers'.

James, *Cephas*, and John and Jesus' Transfiguration before the Central Three in the Gospels

Nor does Galatians speak about a core of 'Twelve' Central Apostles; rather only 'Apostles' in general. But it does, as we have seen, enumerate 'a Central Three of James and *Cephas* and John', all persons Paul seems to know in some way or with whom he has had dealings. These are real people, not inventions or, as elsewhere, fantastic overlays.

For Acts, it will be recalled, someone called 'Apollos' (18:24 – also mentioned by Paul in 1 Cor. 1:12–4:6) is identified as *preaching 'John's baptism' in Asia Minor.* This, it implies, was *a 'water baptism' only* (cf. Paul in 1 Corinthians 3:6: *'I planted, Apollos watered, but God caused to grow'*), the Ephesians never even having heard *'that there was such a thing as the Holy Spirit'* (Acts 19:2).

The 'John' being referred to here is normally taken as 'John of Ephesus'(not 'John the Baptist') and the 'John' in these various enumerations of 'the Central Three' – whether 'the brother of James', 'the son of Zebedee', or some other. But, as we have argued, 'the baptism of repentance' attributed to Apollos here (Acts 19:4), as opposed to Paul's new 'Holy Spirit Baptism', would make more sense as a 'water baptism' if it had to do with the original John *the Baptist*, not another 'John'.

For his part, 'Cephas' – though not 'Peter' – is also mentioned twice more at the end of 1 Corinthians, both in connection in some way with James or 'the brothers of the Lord' (9:5 and 15:5). He is mentioned two additional times in the context of these references to Paul and Apollos at the beginning of 1 Corinthians as well, where baptism, 'the Holy Spirit', and 'building up' the 'building' are being discussed (1:12 and 3:22).

Further to the background of choosing the Central Three in the Synoptic Gospels, their 'appointment' is introduced by the presentation of 'Simon Peter' as answering 'Jesus'' question: 'Who do men say the Son of Man is?' with the conveniently familiar riposte, *'the Christ'* or *'the Christ of God'*. Matthew adds the tell-tale *'Son of the living God'* we encountered in Jesus' trial scenarios above (16:13–16 and pars.).

But when 'Peter' then objects to Jesus' prediction of his own coming death and resurrection, Jesus rebukes him. This rebuke Jesus frames in terms of worrying about 'the *things of men*, not the *things of God*', uttering the now famous 'Get thee behind me Satan' (Mt 16:21–23 and pars.) – after he has just finished, in Matthew anyhow, designating Peter as 'the Rock' of his Church and giving him 'the keys to the Kingdom' (16:17–20)!

Jesus' rebuke of Peter calls to mind the one in the Letter to James to its interlocutor Paul about the *'Friend of men* turning himself into *the Enemy of God'* and Paul's apparent response at the beginning of Galatians, that *anyone preaching a Gospel different from his own should 'be cursed'* (Gal 1:8–9). Paul repeats this twice and, seemingly satisfied with his own intolerant rhetoric, then asks: 'So now, *whom am I trying to please, man or God*? Would you say it is *men's approval I am looking for*? If I still wanted that I should not be what I am, *a Servant of Christ*' (Gal. 1:10).

Then bearing on his Apostleship and lack of either direct appointment or letters of recommendation from James, he concludes: 'The fact is, brothers, and I want you to realize this, the Good News I preached is not a human message that I was *given by men*' (Gal. 1:11). We had already suspected this, but here Paul makes it incontestably clear: 'It is something I learned only through *a revelation of Jesus Christ*' (1:12).

So, for Paul, *the Gospel he teaches is a direct revelation from the figure he calls 'Christ' or 'Christ Jesus'*, his Supernatural Redeemer figure or Guardian Angel, with whom, as it were, he is *in direct communication in Heaven.* This is a perfectly valid visionary experience for Paul, which should not be discounted; but it has nothing whatever to do with 'Jesus' or his brother James, or any doctrines that can be attributed to either of them – and this, we submit, was also the attitude of Paul's detractors then.

In Matthew, Jesus' rebuke of Peter also includes calling him 'a stumbling block' (16:23), language we have already seen to be charged with significance in the mutual polemics of the Letters of Paul and James. At this point too, leading directly into the introduction of 'the Central Three', the Synoptics hark back to Matthew's earlier allusion to 'the Son of Man', all then specifically evoking the vision attributed to James in all early Church sources of: 'The Son of Man coming in the Glory of his Father with his Angels, and he shall then render unto every man according to his works' (Mt 16:27 and pars.), but now rather attributing it to Jesus.

Over and over again we have encountered this vision, the essence of James' proclamation in the Temple when he was asked what was 'the Door to Jesus' or, in effect, who 'Jesus' was. We have also seen how this proclamation corresponds with the exegesis of the War Scroll at Qumran of the Messianic 'Star Prophecy' and its evocation of *the Messiah coming with the Heavenly Host on the clouds 'to rain Judgment on all that grows' on earth* – but here the correspondence is even closer, as 'the Holy Angels' of the War Scroll are being specifically evoked.

In 2 Corinthians 12:1–7, Paul describes knowing a man 'fourteen years before' who had also been 'caught away to Paradise' – and known 'the magnificence of (Heavenly) revelations' and 'visions', 'hearing unutterable words'. Curiously the time frame here agrees with that in Galatians between his *two* visits to see James. In some sense, then, if this individual was James, it is possible to conceive that his visionary experience, which probably really did occur, made it more possible for Paul's more extended concept to find an even wider acceptance.

Of course, the '*Righteousness of works*', Jesus is now pictured as speaking about in the Synoptics, runs directly counter to Pauline '*Faith*' and '*Grace*' doctrines; however it does *precisely reflect* the position of the Dead Sea Scrolls on these matters, as it does the 'Jamesian' one generally (as it will Islam's in succession to these in the future).

The next statement Jesus is pictured as making in the Synoptics: 'Verily, I say unto you, there are some of those *standing* here, who shall in no wise *taste of death* until they have *seen the Son of Man coming in his Kingdom*' (Mt 16:28; for Mk 9:1, which adds the words '*with Power*', this usage is '*standing by*') is, once again, clearly emphasizing the '*Standing One*' ideology of the early Christian Ebionites and Elchasaites – Mark even encompassing the idea of '*Power*', that is, '*the Hidden*' or '*Great Power*' (also the meaning of '*Elchasai*'). It precisely parallels, too, the key definition of '*the Sons of Zadok*' in the Damascus Document. It will be recalled that '*the Sons of Zadok*' were defined as those 'who would *stand at the End of Time*' and '*justify the Righteous and condemn the Wicked*'.

Both 'the Son of Man coming with Power' above and 'the Sons of Zadok' here (not to mention the 'Standing One' ideology) are, of course, eschatological definitions involving 'the Last Times'/'Days'/'Things'. The idea, too, of *'seeing the Son of Man'*, namely *'Jesus'*, also parallels that of *'seeing His Salvation' (Yeshu'ato)* at the end of the expository section of the Damascus Document we have noted above. Here in the Synoptics the allusion to such *'seeing'* serves to introduce the appointment of 'Peter and James and John, *his brother*'. It will also include the imagery of miraculous *'whitening'* encountered in the *Recognitions*, in the account of how James' Community *visited the tombs of two brothers outside Jericho which miraculously 'whitened of themselves every year'*. As this miraculous *'whitening'* imagery develops now in the Synoptics, it encompasses a usage that will tie it to both this same *Recognitions* and early Church accounts of the death of James in the most forceful manner conceivable.

In this episode about the appointment of 'The Central Three' in the Synoptics, Jesus takes 'Peter (not *Cephas*) and James and John his brother' (Jesus' or James'?) and, like Moses before him, *'went up on a high mountain to pray'*. There, he *'was transfigured'* before the Three *'and his face shone as the sun and his garments became effulgent white'* (Mt 17:1–3 and pars.). The Central Three see him conversing with Moses and Elijah. For Luke, Jesus is *'in Glory'* as are Moses and Elijah (9:31–32). But aside from this emphasis on the *'splendid effulgence'* or *'miraculous whitening of the tombs'* (not to mention the *'clothes'* theme once again); the main thrust of this episode is the revelation by another of these *'Heavenly voices'* as in Acts – this time, not insignificantly, *'out of a cloud'* – that *Jesus was God's Son* (*thus*).

The familiar words of this revelation, as quoted here in Matthew, *'This is my beloved son. In him I am well pleased'* (17:5 – Mark and Luke vary this to *'listen to him'*), are the same as those used at the beginning of the Synoptic Gospels to describe Jesus' baptism by John, when *'the Heavens were rent asunder and he saw the Spirit descending on him in the form of a dove'* (Mk 1:10 and pars.).[8] In this picture of John baptizing Jesus, *'the voice out of Heaven'* again is said to cry out, *'This is my beloved Son. In him I am well pleased'* (Mt 3:17 and pars.).

Whatever the significance of the repetition of these words, John the Baptist plays a role, however indirect, in the 'Transfiguration' scene too; since, in *all the Synoptics*, he *is identified with Elijah* – a point 'Jesus' himself is pictured as making to the Three immediately thereafter on their way down the mountain (Mt 17:13 and Mk 9:13).[9] In this conversation with them too, 'Jesus' picks up the motif of *'the Son of Man'* again and, by means of it, *identifies himself as the Divine 'Son'* – *'Man'*, it will be appreciated, being identified with *'the First Man'* or *'Primal Adam'*, not to mention in Aramaic sources that *'Enosh'* or *'Man'* was *'John'* – Jesus, even in Paul, being *'the Last Adam'* or *'the Second Man, the Lord out of Heaven'* (1 Cor. 15:45–47).

It should be clear that all these themes are being recapitulated here. If we now slightly transpose the way the Central Three are being described in this episode to, not *'Peter and James and John his brother'*, but *'Peter and James his brother and John'*, recorded by Paul in Galatians, we would achieve an even more perfect fit with James *'the brother of Jesus'*, not John being *'the brother of James'*. Transpositions of this type, as already described, occur elsewhere in Acts or the Gospels, particularly in the presentation of James and John *'the two sons of Zebedee'* as here – whoever such a *'Zebedee'* might have been.

Discrepancies of this kind with how Paul enumerates 'The Central Three' in Galatians, if taken at face value, become irreconcilable. But in cases such as this, as already emphasized, Paul is to be taken as primary and the Gospels secondary. This would be the proper way out of the present conundrum as well, i.e., to take the Central Three as *'James the brother of Jesus, Cephas, and John'* and either to ignore or to discard Gospel representations as the refurbishments they are.

The Brightness of Jesus' Clothes at the Transfiguration and Hegesippus' Reference to the 'Fuller's Club'

Crucial to connecting the presentation of Jesus' Transfiguration to the attack on James in the Temple, his proclamation there of 'the Son of Man coming on the clouds of Heaven', and his flight to Jericho, is the 'resplendence' with which he is portrayed. By using '*his face shone as the sun*', Matthew 17:2 is drawing the correspondence with *Moses talking to God on Mount Sinai*, where there and later in the Tent of Meeting, *his face also glowed after his encounter with God*. In 2 Corinthians 3:7–18, Paul scoffingly dismisses this imagery, *in* asserting that *Moses veiled himself because he didn't wish the Children of Israel to know the light* – which he also repeatedly refers to as '*the Glory*' – *of the Law had expired*.

Though this note about Jesus' '*shining face*' is missing from Mark and Luke, all three insist that '*his clothing' became 'white as the light*' (Mt 17:2), '*white and effulgent*' (Lk 9:29), or, as Mark, which is most complete, characterizes it, '*His clothes* became *glistening*, exceedingly *white as snow*, whiter than *any fuller on earth could have whitened them*' (9:3). In this last, once again, we have the all-important theme of the '*fuller*' or '*laundryman*' that goes back at least as far as Clement's and Hegesippus' accounts of the death of James – now in an entirely new form where we would never have expected to find it.

The occurrence of this allusion here is, to say the least, hardly less than astonishing. This is the only instance of '*laundryman*' in the whole New Testament. Indirectly, it ties all these threads together – namely, the '*laundryman*' or '*fuller*' motif in all early Church accounts of the death of James, along with the effulgence of Jesus' '*garments*' or '*clothes*', and the Pseudoclementines' miraculous '*whitening*' of the tomb of the two brothers.

This motif of the '*clothes*' or '*garments*' will become even more insistent as we proceed. We have already seen it in the aftermath of *Stephen's stoning*, when *those stoning him, for some unfathomable reason, 'deposit their clothes at the feet of a young man called 'Saul'* (as already remarked, these should have been *Stephen's clothes*), or, in Jerome's 'Hebrew Gospel', when Jesus '*hands his clothes to the Servant of the High Priest*'. This is not to mention the '*linen clothes*' James wore, as did all Essene or 'Masbuthaean' Daily Bathers in these accounts of the special linen '*girdles*' or bathing clothes they wore, which made such a big impression on all observers. Now we come upon it here in the matter of Jesus' '*white and effulgent*' clothing upon his Transfiguration. Presently, we shall see it anew in the '*empty tomb*' scenarios on the matter of his '*grave-clothes*'. 'White clothing' would also have had a specific meaning to the audience of these accounts, i.e., that of being a member of *the Community of all 'the Righteous' washed 'white' of their sins*.

But these passages about Jesus' 'clothing' becoming 'white as light' and 'effulgent' are seemingly also incorporating the vocabulary of the 'miraculous whitening' of the tomb of the two brothers (to say nothing of the matter of the 'tomb' in the related stories of the faces 'like lightning' and 'the clothing as white as snow' of the 'Angel' or 'Angels' in Jesus' empty tomb), found in *Recognitions'* account of the flight by the injured James to the Jericho area.

In the Scrolls, not only is this 'whitening' imagery, playing off the word '*Lebanon*' in underlying Biblical texts ('Lebanon' meaning 'white' in Hebrew) tied to the '*white clothes*' worn by the Community Council and/or the Priests in the Temple; but this word '*fury*' is the very one the Habakkuk *Pesher* used to describe the '*hot anger*', with which, '*the Wicked Priest pursued the Righteous Teacher*'. This language of '*Wrath*' and '*Fury*' is then played upon to produce various combinations and metaphorical reversals having to do with 'the Cup', 'the Anger of God', Divine 'Vengeance', and even the 'venom' of the Establishment and 'the wine' of its ways.

That the blessed dead should be '*remembered before God*', as alluded to in connection with this '*miraculous whitening*' of the brothers' tombs in the *Recognitions*, is, in addition, also a fixture of Jewish *Yom Kippur* observances to this day. So too is the color white – and, for instance, not wearing leather shoes – symbolizing such atoning purity. Problems surrounding such observances are alluded to in the passages surrounding the death of the Righteous Teacher in the Habakkuk *Pesher* and are intrinsic in traditions about James' death as well, as they are in the accounts of his High Priestly atonement activities in the Holy of Holies on the Temple Mount – also probably on *Yom Kippur*.

But these two episodes – firstly, the flight of James in *Recognitions*, culminating with '*miraculous whitening*' of these tombs, the visit to which saves James and his followers from the Enemy Paul, and secondly, the story of the 'laundryman' or '*fuller beating in James' brains with a laundryman's club*' – are now, not only connected, but seemingly combined in these rather more fantastic Gospel presentations of Jesus transfiguring himself before the core Apostles (Peter, James, and John '*his brother*').

Such combinations, or variations on a theme, will be no more surprising than those we shall presently encounter surrounding Belial's '*nets*' and the various adumbrations of the '*casting down*' allusions related to it. In Mark, these 'whitening' and 'fuller' themes, surrounding James' death, appear to become the single allusion about how '*his clothes turned white as snow, whiter than any fuller on earth could have whitened them*'. But, in addition, these have been both preceded and followed by or even compounded with evocation of 'the Son of Man' and/or his 'coming' – the essence basically of James' proclamation in the Temple.

The result, then, of looking into these parallel testimonies about the Central Three in both Galatians and the Synoptics leads us to a surprising result, which, if true, could not have been anticipated. If accurate, it ties our sources together and confirms, in the most roundabout way, that our hypothesis about the method of composition of these well-informed – if tendentious – Hellenistic romances we call 'Gospels' is correct.

Pursuing the themes of the proclamation by James of the coming of the Son of Man, the attack on James in the Temple, and his death, has led us to results that we would not otherwise have imagined. In addition, however, as with the Gospel stories about Jesus being 'tempted by the Devil in the wilderness' or to 'throw himself down from the Pinnacle of the Temple', these stories about the flight of James, the 'miraculous whitening' of the 'brothers'' tombs, and the beating in of James' skull with a laundryman's club, must be older than or have preceded, at least, Mark's account of Jesus' 'Transfiguration' in its present form.

The reason we say 'must' here is that these traditions about James and even their conflation must have preceded their reflection in the Gospels. This is, admittedly, a surprising conclusion, but the fair observer, upon reflection, will be forced to acknowledge its logic. This means that either the Gospels are fairly late or the traditions about James, even in the conflated form in which we sometimes see them reflected in the Gospels, were actually circulating quite early.

The 'white as snow' simile involved in these portraits of the Transfiguration of Jesus' '*clothes*' brings us around too, however circuitously, to Daniel's original vision of '*the Ancient of Days, sitting upon the Throne, whose raiment was white as snow*' (Dan. 7:9), not to mention the proclamation directly following this of '*one like a Son of Man coming on the clouds of Heaven*'. For Daniel 7:13–14, it was upon him that '*Sovereignty, Glory, and Kingship' would be conferred* and '*his Sovereignty would be an Eternal Sovereignty which would never pass away*'. Again, the range and imagination of these ancient amalgamators and artificers are, as breath-taking, as they are impressive.

Chapter 20
James the First to See Jesus

The Reversal of 'Hating the Men of the Pit' into 'Hating One's Family'

The reference to James at the end of 1 Corinthians involves the twin topics of Apostleship and post-resurrection sightings of Jesus. Here we come directly to the matter of the existence or non-existence of 'the Twelve'– at least from a Pauline perspective.

Before pursuing these issues, it should be pointed out that Paul, in the background to his first reference to the Central Three – the Historical Three of 'James the brother of the Lord, *Cephas*, and John' not the artificially surreal one – even calls them 'the Apostleship of the circumcision'. Claiming that 'these Pillars' gave them (himself and Barnabas) 'their hand in agreement'; he interprets this to mean that, just as he and Barnabas would go 'to the Gentiles', they (the Central Three and others) would *go 'to the Circumcision'* (Gal. 2:7–8). The historical understanding of this was that there were or at least had been 'Twelve Tribes' of Israel and, therefore, *the symbolical thrust of the idea of there being 'Twelve Apostles' in the first place* was that, theoretically, they should go to *the Twelve Tribes of Israel.*

This is the thrust, too, of similar numerology in the Community Rule, where the Community Council is distinctly enumerated as being composed of '*Twelve Men and Three Priests*'.[1] The question of whether these '*Three Priests*' – symbolical or real – were to be *from among the 'Twelve'* or *in addition to them* has never been fully resolved, though the implication of other documents leans towards the latter. For our purposes, however, it doesn't particularly matter since most of these kinds of conceptions are esoteric.

This same Community Rule, in what can be only understood as its climax in Column Eight, where the 'Inner Twelve' and 'Inner Three' are set forth at its start, also contains the first elucidation of the '*making a Straight Way in the wilderness*' Prophecy from Isaiah 40:3, applied to John the Baptist's activities in the Gospels and, for that matter, the whole world. In addition to interpreting this Prophecy in terms of '*separating from the habitation of the Men of Unrighteousness and going into the wilderness*', this Column also expresses such Christian notions as *making atonement by 'doing Righteousness* (note the 'Jamesian' emphasis here) *and suffering the sorrows of affliction*' and '*Precious Cornerstone*' imagery.

Using the kind of esoteric language that in Paul borders on allegorization, it describes 'the Community Council' , where this Inner Twelve and Inner Three are mentioned – as we have to some extent already seen – as '*a Holy Temple of Israel*' and '*an Assembly' or 'Church of the Holy of Holies for Aaron*'; and the '*Perfection of the Way*', it thereby embodies, as '*a pleasing odor of Righteousness and an agreeable sacrifice', upon which 'to establish the Holy Spirit according to Eternal Truth*'.[2]

There are so many parallels of this kind in the Qumran corpus to 'early Christian' notions, particularly in the Pauline corpus, that it would be difficult to catalogue them all; still, it is perhaps important to remark from the start that the Qumran documents *are less cosmopolitan and not antinomian at all*, but rather always *nationalist or xenophobic.* They are also less prolix and more terse, but the themes and vocabulary are recognizably the same – albeit for the most part usually *inverted or reversed.*

Aside from these parallel imageries of *spiritualized Temple, sacrifice, and atonement* in these important Columns Eight–Nine of the Community Rule, the orientation is always the opposite of 'Christianity' as we know it, that is, 'Pauline' or 'Overseas Christianity'. For the former, '*the Way*', in the '*prepare in the wilderness the Way of the Lord*' citation, *is 'the study of the Law as commanded by the hand of Moses*', not the 'Pauline' *descent of the Holy Spirit upon Jesus.* According to the Qumran interpretation, *'the Penitents' in the wilderness are 'to separate from the Men of the Pit'* – our *'Nazirite'* terminology again – for whom *'Everlasting hatred* (not love!) *in a spirit of secrecy'* is reserved.

They are instructed to *'do all* that is required' as we just saw – again note the 'Jamesian' emphasis – to be as *'one zealous for the Law, whose time will be the Day of Vengeance'*! This is the second interpretation of the 'Preparation of the *Way*' proof-text from Isaiah 40:3 in the Community Rule at Qumran *and it is hardly very peaceful*! One can't get much more militant. That this is *'Zealot'* needs no further elucidation; but it is also combined with this spiritualized esoteric imagery where 'the Community council' is concerned.

For instance, one can even detect a basis for the 'atonement', James is said to have made in early Church sources, in the above description at the start of this Column of the Community Council as *'atoning for the guilt of sin and rebellious transgression and be a pleasing sacrifice for the land without the flesh of holocausts and the fat of sacrifice'*.[3]

The members of this 'Council' also participate in some manner in an eschatological 'Judgment on Evil' or a type of 'Last Judgment' just as 'Peter' and, to some extent, 'John and James the sons of Zebedee' do in the Gospels.[4] In Matthew, after 'Peter' recognizes Jesus as 'the Christ' and is designated, in turn, by him as 'the Rock' upon which 'his' Community will be built (imagery extant in this section of the Community Rule as we just saw); he is given *the keys to the Kingdom* – obviously esoterically – to *'bind on earth what will be bound in Heaven'* and *vice versa* (Mt 16:16–20) and people still speak in terms of 'St. Peter at the Gate' even today.

This notion of *'going to the Circumcision'*, as described by Paul, is incorporated in Matthew as 'Jesus' sending out *'his Twelve Disciples'* with instructions *not to go the 'way of the Gentiles, nor enter the cities of the Samaritans', but to go rather only to 'the House of Israel'* (Mt 10:1–5).[5] Mark and Luke abjure the use of *'Disciples'* – terminology also preferred in John – referring only to *'the Twelve'* (Mk 6:7 and Lk 9:1). For his part, Matthew then lists *'the Twelve Apostles'* (10:2–4). Jesus' instructions to the 'Apostles' here includes the *'casting out'* language (*ekballo*), in this case, 'unclean spirits' or 'demons', and this variation on the 'Belial'/'Balaam' language circle will even be used to characterize the activities of the Apostles in other ways.

These passages even contain veiled attacks, as we have seen, on someone as important as 'Peter'. In addition to details like those in the previous chapter in Matthew, that *'many tax collectors and Sinners came and dined with Jesus and his Disciples'* (9:10 – again, our by-this-time customary guffaw); statements like *'Whosoever denies me before men, him also will I deny before my Father in Heaven'* (10:33) have direct relevance to 'Peter' pictured, in the Gospels, as having *denied Jesus three times* on his death night (Mt 26:69–75)! This, of course, is part and parcel of the retrospective polemics of these Paulinized and Hellenized, Gentile Christian Gospels (to say nothing of *their drama*) as we have them.

They even contain explicit attacks on the *'secrecy'* of groups, such as those at Qumran and baptizing groups generally. We have just heard the stricture, *'Everlasting hatred for the Men of the Pit in a Spirit of secrecy'* in the Community Rule's interpretation of the 'making a straight Way in the wilderness' citation – applied to John the Baptist in Christian Scripture. This is also the picture in the Pseudoclementine *Homilies*, in which James requires the Elders to swear *'not to communicate in any way, either by writing' or 'by giving them to a writer', to any unworthy person anything that they have learned or will be teaching*.[6]

For Matthew, both this *'hatred for the Men of the Pit'* and this *'secrecy'* are inverted in 'Jesus'' proclamations that *'You shall be hated by all on account of my Name'* and *'there is nothing secret that shall not be revealed, nothing hidden that shall not be made known'* (10:22 and 26). This last even goes on to parody the 'Light' versus 'Dark' imagery so prevalent in the Scrolls – proclaiming *'What I tell you in the Dark, speak in the Light* and *what is whispered in your ear, proclaim it on the rooftops'* (10:27). In the *Homilies*, the Epistle of Peter to James, giving rise to this response by

James, even uses the Qumran language of '*the Pit*', declaring how *false teaching can drag people down 'into the Pit of Destruction*' (1.3).

As we saw, Peter uses the following language to characterize this in this 'Letter' prefacing the *Homilies*: '*Some among the Gentiles have rejected my preaching about the Law, attaching themselves to a certain Lawless and trifling preaching of the Man who is my Enemy*'(1.2 – Paul or Simon *Magus*). In Matthew's charges by Jesus to *his Apostles*, however, this now becomes – instead of '*the man who is my Enemy*' – '*a man's Enemies shall be those of his own household*' (10:36).

Once again, the polemical reversal here is patent. That this is an attack *on the brothers and family of Jesus* needs no further elucidation. The parallel to this in Luke 14:26 now adds the Qumran language of '*a spirit of hatred against the Men of the Pit*' turning it, too, *against the family of 'Jesus' instead,* reading: 'If a man comes to me and *does not hate his own father and mother and wife and children and brothers and sisters … he cannot be my Disciple*' (*thus*!). This attack in Luke comes after the picture of 'Jesus' having just attacked '*dining with brothers, kinsmen, and the Rich*' rather than '*the Poor, blind, and the lame*' (14:12–21) – the last two, anyhow, comprising a part of the classes of persons *forbidden to enter the Temple* according to the Temple Scroll from Qumran.

In turn in Luke rather, it is preceded by evocation of '*the Last being First and the First being Last*' and aspersions on *Jerusalem for* '*killing the Prophets and stoning them that are sent to her*' – the import of which should be clear – followed by allusion to '*the resurrection of the Righteous*' (13:30 –14:14). Nothing could better illustrate the manner in which the Gospels reverse themes found, for instance, in the Pseudoclementines and in the Scrolls, turning them into thinly disguised attacks on the *family of Jesus, the Jews, and even 'the Jerusalem Church' Leadership*!

In Matthew, these attack rather come directly after 'Jesus' begins his charges to 'the Apostles', paralleling the opposite genre of imprecations James makes to 'the Elders of the Community' after receiving Peter's letter in the *Homilies.* So awe-inspiring was James in the sight of these '*Elders'* that they are pictured, as we have seen, as '*being in an agony of terror*', calming down only after James speaks about how those '*keeping this Covenant' and 'living Piously' have 'a part with the Holy Ones*' (1.4–5)!

That versions of this material, along with documents with the vehemence of those at Qumran, were circulating in some manner among 'Opposition' Groups *before* the present documents we call '*the Gospels*' achieved their final form begins to emerge as the inescapable conclusion. Only the additional '*Truly you shall not have gone through the cities of Israel till the Son of Man be come*' in Matthew's version of 'Jesus'' admonitions to his Apostles has an authentic 'Jamesian' ring to it.

In another reversal and in regard to how 'Simon' and 'Simeon' are slightly different names in Hebrew, one should note Luke's presentation of the 'Jerusalem Council' in Acts – ending in James sending out his rulings about '*Gentiles … keeping themselves from the pollutions of idols, fornication, strangled things, and blood*' in the form of an 'epistle' again (15:20) – how, just before *sending his emissaries with this letter* '*down to Antioch*' and *right after Paul and Barnabas report about the 'miracles and wonders God had done by them among the Gentiles*', James is portrayed as referring to how Peter, like himself, *opposes those who believed 'it was necessary to circumcise themselves and to keep the Law*' (Acts 15:5). This is, not only just about totally at odds with the picture in the Pseudoclementines, but also that Paul's Letters – in particular, Galatians.

Post-Resurrection Appearances to *Cephas* or Peter in 1 Corinthians or the Gospels

Having covered all these things including '*Communion with the blood of Christ*'; as Paul now explains it, leading up to his last mention of James, '*the Gospel*' which he announced to his communities was what he himself '*received, that Christ died for our sins according to the Scriptures and that he was buried, and that he was raised on the third day according to the Scriptures*' (1 Cor. 15:4). In connection with his 'announcement of this Gospel', he uses the words, '*in which you also stand*' *and 'are being saved', ending with the phrase, 'unless you believed in vain*'.

Paul put this as follows: '*But, brothers, I reveal to you the Gospel which I preached, which you also received, in which you also stand (and) by which also you are being saved – if you hold fast to the Word which I preached to you, unless you believed in vain – for I delivered to you in the first place what I also received …* ' (1 Cor. 15:1–3). All of these expressions just about exactly parallel, as we have seen, vocabulary in use at Qumran – the '*standing*', in particular, directly preceding the '*Three Nets of Belial*' condemnations in the Damascus Document.

Relating to the elaboration of '*the Sons of Zadok*', the last was expressed in terms of there being '*no more joining to the House of Judah* (i.e., no more '*Jews*' *per se*), *but each man standing on his own net*' or '*watchtower*'. Either of these would be equivalent to what Paul is intending by '*Word*' or '*Gospel*' here. This is not to mention the relationship of this word 'standing' generally to the '*Standing One*' doctrine of the Ebionites and other Jamesian groups, we have already been calling attention to above, and elaborations of the doctrine of Resurrection generally.

Paul's allusion to '*believing in vain*', which he goes on to use repeatedly in this Chapter particularly as regards this same Resurrection, that is, *Christ having been 'raised from the dead'* (15:14–17). Both this and mention of '*saved*' parallels materials in the Habakkuk *Pesher* as well, in particular, the doctrines of the individual it designates as '*the Spouter of Lying*'.[7] In describing these last, the Habakkuk *Pesher* uses the same set of words, 'Empty' and 'Vain' or 'Worthless', to describe what 'the Man of Lying' is 'building' and the 'vainglory' of his 'mission' or 'service'.

One should also appreciate that in the course of these references to 'speaking in Tongues', 'building up the Assembly', 'being zealous (*zelotai*) of Spirits', and 'being zealous to prophesy'; Paul twice parodies the 'Zealot' terminology, reversing normal Palestinian usage of this term and connecting it instead now to his idea of '*prophesying*' and '*speaking in Tongues*'. As he puts it, one should not forbid such things, as most *'Zealots for the Law' like James* would undoubtedly have done, *but 'be zealous' for them* (1 Cor. 14:11 and 39).

In mentioning Christ 'being resurrected and dying for our sins', Paul is clearly signaling something of what must have been extremely early doctrine in Palestine. The '*Resurrection*' part of this is from Hosea 6:1–2, but there it occurs in the plural – in the sense of a *plural* restoration: '*After two days He will restore us to life, the third day will He raise us up to live before Him*' (*thus*)! The interesting allusions that follow in Hosea 6:3–5, to both 'Ephraim' and 'Judah' – widespread in the Scrolls, the 'coming of rain', and *the Prophets 'slaying them by the words' of their mouth*, are noteworthy as well. This last, for instance, as it becomes transformed in Gospel usage and transmitted – as it turns out – into the Koran, appears to develop into, *the Jews 'killed all the Prophets'*![8]

The notion of 'dying for our sins' harks back to Isaiah 53:10–12, a typical scriptural '*Zaddik*' passage. There, it is applied to '*justifying the Many*' or '*making them Righteous*' and '*Justification*' generally. Not only are these the basis of the presentation of the Jesus' crucifixion in Christianity, they are also typical Qumran doctrines and very likely provide the basis for the organizational framework found there of the rank and file of the Community – called '*the Many*' – being '*made Righteous*' or '*Justified*' by '*the Sons of Zadok*' or '*the Righteous Teacher*'.[9]

To this, Paul now attaches his list of post-Resurrection appearances by 'Jesus'. In modern times, this has always been thought of as containing an interpolation.[10] It probably does since it is composed of *two distinct parts*. The only real question has been which part contains the fabrication and which does not – the first, having to do with '*Cephas and the Twelve*', or the second, referring to '*James then all the Apostles*'. These are clearly parallel denotations and cannot really be seen as separate, but they do contradict one another.

The second, of course, is less doctrinaire and more general, but those of an orthodox and unquestioning mindset have always assumed the first to be authentic and more accurate; and the second, the interpolation, representing a sinister attempt by the 'Jewish Christian' supporters of James not only to insinuate him into Apostle lists, *but to gain equal status for him with the Apostles.* It was impossible for persons of this outlook even to conceive of another scenario. We, of course, favor the second as the authentic history and consider the more orthodox to be the interpolation since, however one parses it, there were only '*Eleven*' at the time – 'Judas *Iscariot*' purportedly having self-destructed or removed himself.

The passage in its interpolated form is already known at the end of the Fourth Century to Jerome who is not embarrassed and, in his usual meticulousness, is anxious to cite materials from Jewish Christian sources giving support to this testimony of an appearance by 'Jesus' – *even a 'first' appearance* – to James, although not perhaps completely grasping the import of what he was reporting. The passage from 1 Corinthians 15:5–9, in which Paul seems to be claiming he was taught this in addition to the two doctrines mentioned above, reads as follows:

> and that *he appeared to Cephas*, *then to the Twelve* (the orthodox part, only there were supposedly only '*Eleven*' at the time). *Then he appeared to over five hundred brothers at once*, most of whom now still remain, but *some have also fallen asleep. Then he appeared to James*, then to all the Apostles (indeterminate – the unorthodox part), and *last of all, as if to one born out of term* (literally, '*an abortion*') he appeared also to me. *For I am the least of the Apostles, who is not fit to be called an Apostle*, because I persecuted the Assembly of God.[11] But by the Grace of God, I am what I am, and *His Grace towards me has not been Empty* (gainsaying the '*Empty Man*' attacks in the Letter of James and at Qumran?)

Not only do we have here terminology, '*the Last*' or '*least of the Apostles*', important for determining the historical provenance of polemical statements in the Gospels attributed to 'Jesus' like '*the First shall be Last and the Last shall be First*' – also reflecting Qumran '*Last*' versus '*First*' parameters – but also the '*Empty*' or '*vain*' language, which the Habakkuk *Pesher*, as just suggested, uses when discussing *the 'Worthless Service' of the Liar.* Here, too, the number of 'Apostles' is indeterminate and simply plural again.

Paul goes on in this vein. Not only has he referred to this 'vanity' in connection with 'the Gospel he announces' above, but he repeats it a few lines later, saying, 'If Christ has not been raised, then our preaching *is worthless* (or 'void') and your Faith, too, *also worthless*' (1 Cor. 15:14). Note, too, the use of the word 'preaching' here, the very word Peter is pictured as using in his Letter to James, prefacing the Pseudoclementine *Homilies*, to describe '*the* preaching of the Man who is my Enemy'.[12]

First, one can say outright that the reference to '*Cephas and the Twelve*' is just a superficial statement of what was perceived as orthodoxy by the time the interpolation was made, that is, if '*Cephas*' and 'Peter' are taken to be identical – which we should grant for the sake of the argument – then it is more likely that a statement of this sort is an interpolation than something that is patently schismatic and against the current of this orthodoxy.

The reference, too, to '*the Twelve*' is the only reference of this kind in the Letters section of the New Testament but, as we have been noting, there were supposedly only 'Eleven' Apostles at the time. Mark 16:14, though itself considered interpolated, nevertheless draws the correct inference from the data, and specifically states this: '*he appeared to the Eleven*' – so for that matter, do Acts 1:26, Matthew 28:16, and Luke 24:9 and 33.

For Luke, it is 'Cleopas' (*thus*) and another of these mysterious unnamed others, to whom Jesus first appears outside Jerusalem '*along the way*' to Emmaus, even '*breaking bread*' with them. These then return and report this – *also to 'the Eleven assembled' in Jerusalem* (Luke 24:1–35). Where the ending of Mark is concerned – in any event probably based on this material in Luke – after 'Jesus' *appeared 'to two of them as they walked on their way in the country'*, he simply '*appeared to the Eleven as they ate meat*' (Mark 16:12–14). In Luke, too, Jesus also then '*stood among them*', that is, '*the Eleven*' gathered together in Jerusalem (*n.b*, our '*Standing*' imagery again), and '*ate before them*' (24:36–46).

Though Luke confines himself to appearances in and around Jerusalem only and does not move on to the Sea of Galilee, he more or less repeats Paul's statement in I Corinthians 15:1 above, too, about the Gospel he '*received*' and on which his Disciples '*also should stand*'. As Luke puts this, 'Jesus', like 'the Righteous Teacher' in his scriptural exegesis sessions in the Habakkuk *Pesher*, '*opened their understanding to understand the Scriptures*, saying to them, "*Thus, it has been written, that the Christ should suffer and rise again from among the dead the third day and that repentance and remission of sins should be proclaimed in his Name to all the Nations, beginning at Jerusalem*"' (Luke 24:45–47).

For Matthew 28:16, as in his presentation of Jesus' earlier Transfiguration on 'a high mountain' before the Three, 'the Eleven Disciples' go up 'to the mountain' in Galilee, where Jesus was supposed either to have first 'appointed them' or which he 'appointed for them' – the text is unclear here. The only problem is that there is no such 'mountain' where Jesus first 'appointed them' in Matthew, though there is in Mark and Luke (3:13 and 6:12). In Matthew, this '*mountain*' is rather associated with things like 'the Sermon on the Mount', other miracles (5:1), or 'the Transfiguration'. Notwithstanding, Jesus basically announces to them there what amount to the parameters of the Pauline Mission, i.e., '*making Disciples of all the Nations*' (*Ethne*) and something resembling *the 'Authority' to remit sins* (28:18–19).

However all of this may be, it should be appreciated that there is no individual appearance to 'Peter' on record in *any* of the Gospels. Therefore, there never could have been a *first* appearance to 'Peter' or '*Cephas*', no matter how he is referred to, that is, unless we were to identify '*Cephas*' with the '*Cleopas*' – to whom Jesus first appears in Luke 24:18. Strictly speaking, too, though Peter is pictured as *charging into Jesus' tomb* in Luke and John, even in these, he never actually *sees the risen Christ* only 'the linen clothes' lying there (Luke 24:12 and John 20:6).

John mentions these 'linen clothes' three times in three lines, though for him it is 'the Disciple whom Jesus loved' (one begins to suspect this really may be a linguistic evasion for *James, not John*) who outruns Peter into the tomb – a tomb, except for these *clothes, which is empty* (24:4–7). John also goes on to mention 'tw*o Angels in white*' who are then seen by 'Mary', but this is supposed to be 'Mary Magdalene' (20:12).

For the other Gospels, this matter of the Angel(s) and the various Mary's occurs before either Peter and the other Apostle – whoever he was – *charge into the empty tomb*. In fact, the language they use to describe the '*clothing*' of these Angels basically recapitulates that already encountered above in Jesus' Transfiguration, though without the comparison to the '*whiteness*' of the laundryman's washing.

Matthew says that the face of this '*Angel of the Lord*' was *as lightning* and his *clothing white as snow*' (28:3); in Mark, he is clothed, like our 'Essene' Daily Bathers '*in a white robe*'; for Luke, the clothes of these Angels – there are two in Luke – were '*shining*' (24:4). In fact, in the Synoptics, 'Mary Magdalene' and 'Mary *the mother of James*' – this is how Luke refers to her – never actually *see* Jesus but, rather, only these Angel(s).

For Mark, elaborating upon Matthew's laconic '*the other Mary*', this Mary is '*Mary the mother of James and Salome*' (16:1). Luke, to add to the confusion – and, seemingly, the obfuscation – even adds *a third woman* to these scenes – someone he now calls '*Joanna*' (24:10). In Luke 8:3, where she is also a companion of 'Mary Magdalene', this 'Joanna' – if it is the same individual – is actually *the wife of an Herodian Official*! Whatever one wishes to make of this, she is, in all events, never heard from again.

John, whose focus is strictly on 'Mary Magdalene', allows this 'Mary' alone and no other the *first* vision of the *resurrected Christ* (20:14–18). Still, this appearance, which is not part of the initial empty-tomb scenarios, is not paralleled in any of the other Gospels. For John, '*turning backwards*', she '*saw Jesus standing*' (the '*Standing*' allusion again)! Once again there is no '*first*' individual appearance to 'Peter' in Johannine tradition either.

As for the third point in Paul's testimony to the post-Resurrection appearances of Jesus here in 1 Corinthians – for us, the interpolated part, the appearance '*to five hundred brothers at once*' – there is no reference to an early appearance of such magnitude in any extant Gospel. Some might wish to see this as simply an extension of Jesus' appearance before '*the Eleven and those that were with them*' after the Emmaus road episode in Luke 24:34 – in Mark 16:14, simply '*the Eleven as they reclined*'.

For John 19:20, this appearance is simply to '*the Disciples*' (plural). Here again 'Jesus', *in the place they 'were assembled'* – 'the doors having been shut *for fear of the Jews* (oh no, not again – 'the Disciples', therefore, *were not 'Jews'*?) *came* and *stood in their midst*'. For perhaps the fourth time, we have the '*Standing*' allusion attached to Jesus' name – there will be more.

The First Post-Resurrection Appearance to James and the Last to Paul

If we now look at the second part of this famous testimony by Paul in 1 Corinthians 15:7–8, which basically recapitulates and parallels the first part about '*Cephas, then the Twelve*' (15:5–6), 'and after that (his death and resurrection 'according to the Scripture'), *he appeared to James, then to all the Apostles, and last of all, as (if) to an abortion, he appeared also to me*' and set aside the first part as not only inaccurate, but tendentious; one might at first glance assume that also here one has more dissembling or interpolation. But this is deceptive, as unlike the first part there is nothing inherently impossible or contradictory in the second part, except our preconceptions regarding it. If we discard these – which are rarely very well-founded or thought out anyhow – we find ourselves on *very* firm ground indeed.

For example, we do not have 'Twelve Apostles', when there are supposed to be only 'Eleven' – nor do we have an undocumented, *first appearance* to someone called '*Cephas*' or the obviously-inflated detail that 'then he appeared to over five hundred brothers at the same time'. Rather, the notice '*then to all the Apostles*', which follows the note about *this first appearance to James*, is indeterminate and in line with all Paul's other references to '*the Apostles*', which are always – except in this single instance of the interpolated first part – *general and unqualified*.

This would include the references in Galatians to '*the other Apostles*' – James and Peter presumably among them – and in Philippians to Epaphroditus, whom Paul also calls an 'Apostle' (2:25), as well as the structure of 'Apostles and Prophets' in general he outlines in 1 Corinthians 12:28–29 reiterated, as well, in Ephesians 2:20 and 4:11. This is not to mention Paul's repeated allusions to himself as '*an Apostle of Jesus Christ*' – in Romans 11:13: '*the Apostle to the Gentiles*' – and here in 1 Corinthians 15:9, '*the Least of the Apostles*' and '*the Last*' to whom 'Jesus' appeared.

Of course there is no actual, physical appearance by Jesus to Paul on record, only the vision recorded in Acts of '*a light appearing out of Heaven*' and a voice crying out to him as '*he drew near Damascus*' identifying itself as 'Jesus' (9:3–5). That being said, given Paul's constant communication with the Supernatural-style Figure in Heaven he identifies either as '*Christ Jesus*' or '*Jesus Christ*', one can assume that he took either one or all of these appearances as real.

In fact, as we have already suggested, his characterization of himself as being, not only the '*Last*', but '*the Least of the Apostles*' is very revealing, particularly as we saw, when one ranges it alongside favorite sayings attributed to Jesus in the Gospels, including '*the First shall be Last and the Last shall be First*' (Lk 13:30 and pars.), '*suffer these Little Ones to come unto me*' (Lk 18:16 and pars.), '*everyone that exalts himself shall be humbled and he who humbles himself shall be exalted*' (Lk 9:48 and 14:11), and the like.

Also this '*Last*' phraseology, Paul is using, has a clear parallel at Qumran which knows the language of '*the First*' *versus* '*the Last*', but with a completely different signification. In texts, such as the Damascus Document, '*the First*' are '*the Ancestors' to whom God first revealed the Law* and who *set down 'the boundary markers' which 'the Lying Spouter' is described as 'removing'*. '*The Last*' are those in the present age or '*the Last Days*' or '*Last Generation*' who, in '*the Faith*' or '*Compact of the New Covenant in the Land of Damascus*' rededicate themselves to the Old Covenant, namely, that of 'the First'. Of course, Paul has changed this into a completely new signification having to do with his own appointment as Apostle (belittled by some), Jesus' revelations to him personally, and his new converts.

It is possible to argue that we have in this notice about the order of these post-Resurrection sightings the actual notice about a post-Resurrection appearance by 'Jesus' to James. If one deletes the first part of this notice about appearances to 'Cephas', 'the Twelve', and 'five hundred brothers at the same time', leaving only the second about first '*to James, then to all the Apostles, and last of all*' to Paul, then *this is a first appearance to James*. Nor does the second half of this testimony, taken by itself, contradict previous notices in the letter about 'the brothers of the Lord', Barnabas, and Cephas traveling around with women, nor about James being reckoned '*among the Apostles*' in Galatians – nor, for that matter, the other brothers of Jesus as Apostles which, later we shall show to be the clear implication of Gospel 'Apostle' lists and other sources.

In fact, the evidence of a first appearance to James *does* exist in apocryphal Gospels, early Church testimony, and can be ascertained to some extent in Gospel presentations even as we have them. This is, of course, just what we would expect in light of the contention in the Gospel of Thomas about Jesus' *direct* appointment of James: '*Jesus said to them* ('the Disciples'), *in the place where you are to go* (paralleling John 20:19 above), *go to James the Just, for whose sake Heaven and Earth came into existence*' (*thus*!), or, for that matter, in the same vein as we saw in the Pseudoclementine *Recognitions*, that '*the Church of the Lord, which was constituted in Jerusalem, was most plentifully multiplied and grew, being governed with the most Righteous ordinances by James who was ordained Bishop in it by the Lord*' (1.43).

In addition to these, both Apocalypses of James from Nag Hammadi contain numerous allusions that, not only make this direct appointment implicit, but even a tradition of a first appearance to James '*on the mountain*' – called, for some reason Golgotha ('*Gaugelan*'), but meaning most probably the Mount of Olives. Here Jesus is not only presented as naming James '*the Just One*', but kissing him on the mouth (1 Apoc. Jas. 5.29–32), obviously a '*Disciple Jesus loved*' if there ever was one. This is just what we would expect if James was, indeed, the *first successor* to his brother in Palestine, 'the Bishop of the Jerusalem Church', and 'the Bishop of Bishops' of 'Christianity' worldwide – whatever might have been meant by this term at this point in its pre-Pauline embodiment. Actually, the Qumran documents would be a better approximation of what this was – at least in Palestine – than anything in the Pauline corpus or the Gospels and the Book of Acts dependent on this corpus.

But in Jerome's testimony to James in *Lives of Illustrious Men*, he is sentient as ever in understanding the implications of Paul's testimony in Galatians 1:19, to wit, '*none of the other Apostles did I see, except James the brother of the Lord*'. This Jerome actually quotes and he was the first to develop, in any systematic manner, the idea that the brothers of Jesus *were* Apostles which has become more or less received doctrine in Catholicism – at least for those informed of Jerome's works. In doing so, he quotes '*the Gospel according to the Hebrews*', which he claims to have translated in its entirety both into Greek and Latin and which he says Origen also used two centuries earlier.

This Gospel, which Jerome also calls '*the Jewish Gospel*', seems to have been called by others 'the *Gospel of the Nazoraeans*', but it is unclear if the two are really distinct. The same can be said about the Gospel Epiphanius identifies as being in use among '*the Ebionites*' which he also calls '*the Gospel of the Hebrews*'. Scholars generally refer to these as three distinct Gospels, but their relationship is impossible to determine on the basis of the data available to us – nor is it clear that they were ever really separate at all.

Jesus' First Appearance to James in the Gospel of the Hebrews

As Jerome reports it, this Gospel contained a slightly different picture of the baptismal scene than the one in Epiphanius. It should be observed that, despite the low opinion in which Epiphanius is usually held; in the matter of adoptionist baptism, the version he provides preserves *more original material* and, given the doctrines of these groups, *makes more sense* than that which one finds in orthodox Scriptures. Where the first appearance to James is concerned, according to Jerome's testimony, '*after the account of the resurrection of the Savior, it was recorded in the Gospel according to the Hebrews*':

> But the Lord, after he had *given his linen clothes* to the Servant of the Priest (i.e. the High Priest – for once, this is accurate!), *went to James and appeared to him.* For James had sworn that he would not *eat bread* from that hour in which he *drank the Cup of the Lord* until he should see him rising again from *those that sleep* (of course, this is something of the situation recorded in Luke's narrative of 'Jesus'' appearance '*on the way to Emmaus*' to '*Cleopas*' and an unnamed other – 24:13-27).[13]

Besides our '*linen clothes*' motif again, there are several important symbolisms here. One is the '*Cup*' symbolism, which we have already demonstrated to be in use at Qumran, particularly where *the description of the death of the Righteous Teacher and the retribution visited on the Wicked Priest* are concerned. This 'Cup' imagery is combined at Qumran with that of the 'Anger' or 'Wrath of God', so much so that playful word-play develops between the two words in Hebrew, 'Cup' (*Chos*) and 'Anger' or 'Wrath' (*Cha'as*), which God will '*pour out*' on those responsible for *the destruction of the Righteous Teacher and 'the Poor'* (*Ebionim*) *with him.*[14] This, in turn, is recapitulated in Revelation in terms of '*the wine of the Wrath of God* which is *poured out full strength into the Cup of His Anger*' (15:10). The '*pouring*' imagery, here, again inverts that being used relative to '*the Lying Spouter*' at Qumran – '*Spouter*', it will be appreciated, being based on the Hebrew root for '*pouring*'.

In this regard, one should recall, too, its use in Acts to denote the all-important '*pouring out upon them*' of the Pauline '*Holy Spirit*' at Pentecost (Acts 2:43 and 10:45). For Paul, too – and the Gospels – this language will also have implications for the '*pouring out*' of the blood of Christ, now to be drunk in '*the Cup of the New Covenant in (his) blood*'. '*Cup*' imagery, as used above, to signal death is also present in Gospel accounts of '*the Cup*' which *John and James* – 'the two sons of Zebedee' – *will drink* (Mt 20:22–23 and Mark 10:38–39).

Also note the Nazirite oath-style '*swearing*' not to *eat or drink* in the Gospel of the Hebrews account of James' behavior after Jesus' death which – aside from the 'Emmaus Road' episode, already noted above – is similar to that of the would-be assassins of Paul in Acts 23:12, who '*put themselves under a curse swearing not to eat or drink until they have killed Paul*'. These oaths '*not to eat or drink*' are important. After the fall of the Temple, many were taking such oaths in mourning for the Temple and putting themselves under a penance of some kind '*not to eat or drink*', presumably, *till they should see it rebuilt.* So concerned were the Rabbis about such '*Nazirite*'-style penances that, as we shall see, they attempted to discourage them in Judaism thereafter by designating those taking them as '*Sinners*'.

In doing so, they seem to be associating such oaths with the disaster of the destruction of the Temple and the fall of Jerusalem which had befallen the People. Still, a thousand years later, the Spanish-Jewish traveler, Benjamin of Tudela, not only claims there were large numbers of *Jewish Rechabites* in Arabia in '*Thema*' or '*Tehama*' north of Yemen – clearly 'Taima' in today's Saudi Arabia – who were in *a perennial state of fasting and wearing only black*, i.e., '*mourning for Jerusalem and mourning for Zion*'. As he describes it, these were taking oaths (in the *Jamesian* manner) '*to eat no meat and abstain from wine*' and '*living in caves or makeshift houses*'. This testimony is so unexpected and original it is hard to believe he just made it up out of whole cloth – one of the usual standards one applies for authenticity.

Jerome continues:

> And again a little later ('later' in this narrative of *a first appearance to James in the Gospel of the Hebrews*), it says, "'Bring a table and bread,' the Lord said.' And immediately it is added: 'He took the bread, blessed it, and breaking it, *gave it to James the Just*, saying to him, "*My brother*, eat your bread, for *the Son of Man is risen from among those that sleep.*"'

Again one should remark the similarity of this to 'Last Supper' narratives of Jesus announcing '*the New Covenant*' (Mt 26:26–29 and pars.), but also the appearance to the unnamed other in Luke's 'Road to Emmaus' narrative to say nothing of *the kind of vows reported of James* in all early Church sources above – of lifelong *abstinence from strong drink, animal flesh, and sexual activity*. These themes, centering around *abstention from 'food and drink'* or '*partaking of these with the Risen Christ*', will proliferate in stories relating to post-Resurrection appearances to Jesus' family members – particularly 'his brothers'.

Jerome directly follows this notice about Jesus '*breaking bread' and 'giving it to James the Just' to eat* to commemorate his '*rising from among those that sleep*' (the kind of expression also found in the Pseudoclementines) with his own details about how James '*was buried near the Temple, from which he had been cast down, his tombstone with its inscription being well-known until the siege of Titus and the end of Hadrian's Reign*'(which, of course, somewhat *gainsays the possibility of a 'James Ossuary*' in the present generation) In this context, Jerome contends James '*ruled the Church in Jerusalem for thirty years until the Seventh Year of Nero*', thereby dating James' rule from the early 30's and reinforcing, however circuitously, the impression that James was appointed by 'Jesus' himself and that *his succession was direct.*

Most commentators, embracing the picture of Peter's intervening Leadership in Acts, would allow James only a twenty-year reign from the early 40's. All of this, however, is dependent on an accurate date for the crucifixion of Jesus, which cannot be determined with any precision on the basis of the available evidence. Josephus even seems to imply a date of about 35–6 for Herod Antipas' execution of John which, in the Gospels, *precedes the execution of 'Jesus'*!

Aside from this additional motif of '*rising from among those that sleep*', one should remark the tell-tale use of the '*Son of Man*' terminology again – always interesting in view of its connection to James' like-minded proclamation of this conceptuality in the Temple at Passover in all early Church accounts of the run-up to his own death.

The Picture of the Orthodox Apostles as Fishermen in the Gospels

It is also useful to compare this account in the Gospel of the Hebrews of Jesus' *first appearance to James* with all the others in the Canonical Gospels incorporating this theme of '*breaking bread*' and '*eating with*' Jesus after his resurrection or his appearance to the Apostles while '*they were reclining*' or '*eating*' – or, in fact '*eating*' generally, which, as we discovered, is perhaps *the* crucial theme.

The most important of these – aside from that on '*the Emmaus road*' at the end of Luke – occurs in the Gospel of John following the famous '*doubting Thomas*' episode. Thomas '*called Didymus* (*the Twin*), *one of the Twelve*' (20:24) is *absent* from among '*the Disciples*', just as 'Judas *Iscariot*' is *absent from the conclaves of 'the Eleven' following Jesus' death* in the Synoptics, but for completely different reasons. 'Judas' is absent because he 'betrayed' Jesus (cf. John 13:2 and pars.) subsequently allegedly committing suicide!

These references to '*Judas*' have been understood as pejorative (the last notice about whom in John seems to be Jn 18:5: '*And Judas who betrayed him was standing with them too*' – here our '*standing*' vocabulary again – his place seemingly taken by '*Thomas called Didymus, one of the Twelve*' in 20:24 above), just as those to '*Thomas*' who is popularly referred to as '*doubting*'. The reason for this is because he '*will not believe*' until he has actually *put his finger into the nail holes in Jesus' hands* (John 20:25). This is accompanied by the aspersion ('Jesus' responding to 'Thomas') – again using Pauline vocabulary – 'You have (only) *believed* because *you have seen me*, Thomas, but *blessed are they that have not seen and still have believed*' (Jn 20:29).

Not only should one note, here, the emphasis on the Pauline ideology of how '*belief in Jesus saves one*', but it should be clear that this now retrospectively even confirms Paul's own 'belief' itself, not to mention that of his communities. Again, it should be appreciated that Paul *never actually saw Jesus* or, if he did, *saw him* as *Thomas is depicted as doing here* – *after his resurrection.*

It should be kept in mind that both '*Didymus Thomas*' ('Twin Twin') and 'Judas *Iscariot*' – who seems to give way to '*Thomas*' in John – are probably connected in some manner with the members of Jesus' family itself and, where 'Thomas' anyhow is concerned, tradition conserves the name of '*Judas*' for him too. Where '*Judas*' is concerned, not only does John at one point even call him '*the Iscariot*', making it clear that this has to be considered *a title not a name* (14:22 – the closest cognate being '*Sicarios*'); but, unlike the other Gospels, John four times refers to him as '*of Simon Iscariot*' (6:71, 12:4, 13:2 and 13:26).

This has always been interpreted as '*Simon Iscariot's son*', but we shall presently see the relationship of this to another '*Apostle*', around whose name confusion abounds, '*Simon the Zealot*' or '*Simon the Cananaean*' – with regard to whom, one should keep in mind the interchangeability of these 'son' or 'brother' allusions in the Greek, all equally implied by the genitive construction 'of'. This individual, too, we shall ultimately identify as *one of Jesus' brothers.*

However this may be, following this appearance to the so-called '*doubting Thomas*', Jesus next '*manifests himself again to the Disciples*' (Judas *Iscariot*, of course, now missing even in John) at what John – but not the other Gospels – calls '*the Sea of Tiberias*' (21:1). Here '*Thomas*' is among '*the Disciples*' *about to go fishing in the sea.* These include Simon Peter, Nathanael (never mentioned in the Synoptic Gospels), the sons of Zebedee, and '*two others of his Disciples*' (John 21:2). Just as Jesus had just '*stood among them*' in the room in the preceding episode, now '*Jesus stood on the shore*' and asked the Disciples – whom he also calls '*little children*' – for food, instructing them to '*cast* (*balete*) *the net to the right side of the boat*' (21:4–6 – both the '*net*' and '*casting*' vocabulary once more). Simon Peter, who '*was naked, put on his upper garment and cast himself* (*ebalen* – though why he would do this is hard to understand) *into the sea*' (21:7).

Not only do we have our '*casting out*'/'*casting down*' vocabulary repeated *three times* in as many verses, but now it is joined to that of the '*net*' – repeated *four times in six verses* (21:6–12). This is not to mention the references to the two 'sons of Zebedee' and the 'two' unnamed Disciples – who will be important for sorting out additional problems related to the issue of '*the brothers*' presently – nor the curiousness of why 'Peter' would '*put on his upper garment to cast himself into the sea*'!

It will be recalled that in the Damascus Document – not to mention its expansion in the '*Balaam*'/'*Balak*' episode in Revelation – it is Belial who '*casts a net*' before the Sons of Israel, catching them in the '*Three Nets*' of *fornication, Riches, and pollution of the Temple.* For Revelation, '*Balaam teaches Balak* – all variations of this *ba–la–'a*-language circle having to do with '*the Devil*' ('*Diabolos*' in Greek) or '*Devilishness*' – *to cast* (*balein*) *a net before the sons of Israel to eat the things sacrificed to idols and to commit fornication*' (Rev. 2:14). Both of these are the essence of

James' instructions to overseas communities – not to mention forming, perhaps, the central focus of the Qumran Letter(s) called '*MMT*'. By now, this should be clear.

All this language having to do with 'Devilishness' and 'casting', whether in Hebrew or Greek, has a strong pejorative tone. We have already seen this in the '*swallowing*' language in the Scrolls which is the Hebrew root of both the names, '*Belial*' and '*Balaam*' and the '*casting down*' language applied to James' death in our Greek sources. But when the New Testament playfully applies this language and its variations either to Jesus' choosing his core Apostles or to his post-resurrection appearances to them, or both, the result is to trivialize this language – reducing it to farce.

Thus '*the Apostles*', inverting the use of '*Belial*' in the Dead Sea Scrolls ('*Beliar*' in Paul – 2 Cor. 6:5), become peaceful '*fishermen*' on the Sea of Galilee '*casting down their nets*'. In other appointment episodes, as we have seen, they are given the '*Authority to cast out* (*ekballo*) demons' – like 'the Essenes' do backsliders or 'the Zealots' do to James' destroyer Ananus' body, when they '*cast it out*' (again *ekballo*) *naked from the walls of Jerusalem as food for jackals.*

In the Synoptic Gospels, however, this episode, depicting the principal Apostles as '*fishermen*', occurs *before* Jesus' resurrection – when 'Jesus' *calls two pairs of brothers along the Sea of Galilee* – not *after* it. These are '*Simon who is called Peter*' and '*his brother*', now denoted as '*Andrew*' (in Greek '*Andrew*' means '*Man*' – a variation of '*the First Man*' or '*Primal Adam*'-ideology once again?), and '*the other two brothers, James the son of Zebedee and John his brother*' (Mt 4:18–22 and pars.).

In Mark 1:16, 'Simon and Andrew *the brother of Simon* are *casting* (*ballontas*) *a net* into the sea', while in Matthew 4:21, 'James the son of Zebedee and John *his brother*' are *mending their 'nets*'. Here, not only do we have both these various permutations of the '*brother*' theme, but also of our '*casting down*' and '*nets*' vocabulary with a vengeance. Mark adds the charming little detail, missing from Matthew, that *Zebedee had 'hired servants' with him in his boat* (Mark 1:20).

This episode, as it is retold in Luke 5:1–11, almost perfectly parallels the post-resurrection episodes in John. Meticulous as ever, Luke even gets the name of the Lake right: '*Gennesaret*', not '*Tiberias*' as in John. For Luke, it is 'the fishermen' who are now '*washing their nets*' at the start of the episode – not the two brothers, 'James the son of Zebedee and John his brother' – not 'mending' them (5:2) and he, too, repeats the word 'net' or 'nets' *four times in five lines* before he is done!

According to his version, 'Jesus' goes out in Simon's boat and, is teaching the people from it, when he tells Simon '*to let down' his 'net'* (5:4). When it is all done – for they '*worked through the whole night*' – '*their net was breaking*' and filled almost two boats to the sinking (5:7)! For Luke, all then left their boats and followed him, Jesus uttering the now proverbial words that '*henceforth' he (Peter) 'would be catching men*' (5:10).

In Matthew and Mark, '*they left their nets and followed him*' and 'Jesus', addressing all four, utters the even more famous, '*I shall make you fishers of men*' (Mt 4:18 and Mk 1:17). Both clearly play on and invert the allusions in the Damascus Document about '*Belial*' ('*Balaam*' and '*Balak*' in Revelation) casting his '*net*' to deceive Israel (in Revelation, this is literally '*cast a stumbling block before the Sons of Israel*') or '*catch*' men. The writers of these Hellenized New Testament parodies could not have been unaware of this.

For his part, Matthew 13:1–53 again returns to this theme of '*casting a net into the sea and gathering together every kind' of fish* in his famous series of 'Jewish Christian' parables. These include the now-proverbial '*Parable of the Tares*' which condemns '*the Enemy*' who, *while all the men slept, 'came and sowed the tares* (i.e., weeds) *among the wheat*' (13:24–30). As in Luke, Jesus is *teaching from a boat* and now it is '*the crowd*' which '*stood on the shore*' (Mt 13:2). In Matthew, this comes right after the 'Gentile Christian' episode about Jesus' *curing a series of demonics* (12:22–45) and his rejection of his '*mother and his brothers standing outside seeking to speak to him*' in favor of his Disciples (12:46–50) – providing a good example of Matthew's schizophrenia and rather representing the layering of various contradictory sources.

In the largely 'Jewish Christian' parables that follow, Jesus is ostensibly explaining what 'the Kingdom of Heaven' is. In his final interpretation of this, '*the sower*' once again is '*the Son of Man*'; the good seed, '*the Sons of the Kingdom*'; and '*the Enemy who sowed the tares*', '*the Devil*' or '*Diabolos*' (Mt 13:36–42). Jesus goes on to picture – in the spirit of the War Scroll, the Letter of James, and James' proclamation in the Temple – how '*the Son of Man will send forth his Angels*' to gather out of the Kingdom '*the tares sowed by the Enemy*' and 'cast them into the furnace of Fire' (*balousin*).

After describing how 'the Righteous shall *shine forth as the sun* in the Kingdom of their Father', he compares the Kingdom of Heaven to '*a large net cast* (*bletheise*) *into the sea*', *catching all different kinds of fish* – this, a clear 'Gentile Christian' overlay. Nevertheless, the Parable ends on the same uncompromising 'Jamesian' note as the preceding one about '*the tares*'. Here, instead of 'breaking bread' with Jesus and 'sitting down to eat' – as in the majority of these episodes – the fishermen rather 'sit down and gather the good into containers, and the bad they *cast away* (*ebalon*)'. This is now followed by the words: 'So shall it be at *the Completion of the Age. The Angels will go out and separate the Evil from among the midst of the Righteous* and *cast them* (*balousin*) *into the furnace of the fire*' (Mt 13:49–50). This is an *authentic* Palestinian Christian tradition because everything in it reflects what we know about these native Palestinian movements.

These '*casting*'s, of course, undergo even further transformation and refinement into the '*casting out spirits*' (*ekballo*) or '*demons*' in the Gospels – an '*Authority*' or '*Power*' given to the Apostles on their appointment by 'Jesus'. In turn, they recall how Josephus portrays the Essenes as '*casting out*' (again *ekballousi*) *backsliders unwilling* or unready to *keep the practices of the Community or observe its secrets* – nor is this to mention how Josephus recounts the '*casting*' of James' nemesis Ananus' naked body '*out*' of the city without burial as food for jackals above; nor how he describes '*the Zealots*'' '*casting down*' the body of the '*Rich*' collaborator, 'Zachariah', as well, from *the Pinnacle of the Temple into the Kedron Valley below*, whom they also executed after a cursory trial, when they took over the City![15]

The first of these is, of course, reversed in Acts' portrayal of the '*casting out*' (*ekbalontes*) of its archetypical Gentile believer 'Stephen' from the city – itself inverting, as we have seen, *the stoning of James*. As we also saw, these are now further trivialized, as *per* the casting down of Belial's '*nets*', in episodes relating to 'the Power' Jesus gives his Apostles '*to cast out demons*' and *the supernatural accoutrements attached to this* – as, for instance, in Mark 3:15: '*and he appointed Twelve ... to have authority to cast out demons*' (*ekballein*) or Matthew 17:19's further elaboration of the same idea following Jesus' 'Transfiguration' on the mountain.

This last directly precedes another episode about how Peter '*casts*' (*bale*) his hook into the sea to get the money to pay the Roman tribute – an easy answer to the tax question – whose relation the Habakkuk *Pesher*'s exposition of Hab. 2:3-4, we have already expounded above. Here, '*the Disciples*' (the Central Triad of Peter, James, and John 'his brother'), who are portrayed as being unable – unlike Jesus – even *to cure a demonic boy*, ask Jesus, '*Why were we unable to cast out?*' (*ekbalein*). For perhaps the umpteenth time, Jesus gives the typical Pauline response, '*Because of your unbelief* (Matt. 17:20)!

In a parallel reversal, using now the subject matter of the '*Parable of the Tares*' and again showing the various layers of these inverted polemics, Mark 4:26–32, as we saw, has 'Jesus' *teaching the people from a boat*, but now 'the Parable' is that of 'the Mustard Seed'. Yet again, a man is '*casting* (*bale*) *the seed on the ground*', which grows into a quite gigantic tree with '*great branches*' (note, the Messianic '*Branch*' symbolism), '*larger than all the plants*'. Though the meaning here should be clear even to the non-specialist, the fiercely apocalyptic, indigenous Palestinian attitude has now been completely pacified in a haze of Hellenizing intellectualization.

In another funny adumbration of the way this kind of '*casting out*'/'*casting down*' language is used in the Gospels, directly after the 'Transfiguration' scene and the ensuing aspersion on the Central Three as being '*unable to cast out*', Matthew 17:24–27 varies Jesus' position on the tax issue. At the same time he employs the '*stumbling block*'/'*being scandalized*' language, that is, so as '*not to offend*' or '*scandalize them*' ('*them*' being the *tax collectors*!) and now he has Peter '*casting (bale) a hook*', as we have already signaled, into the sea to get a coin from a fish's mouth there in order to pay the Roman tax.

This is supposed to be serious, the point being, that 'Jesus' is portraying as doing this because he was, presumably, unwilling to pay the tax himself or, Essene-style, *did not carry coins on his person* – or both (though in the portrait here, he never actually 'touches' the coin Peter returns with). Notwithstanding, in typical Platonic repartee and following the ideology of Paul, Jesus is made laconically to conclude 'then the Sons are *truly free*'. Here, typically, '*freedom from Rome*' or '*foreign dominion*' or '*oppression*' is, as usual, *ever so subtly transformed* into Pauline *freedom from the Law*.

The conclusion has to be that, by looking into seemingly innocuous episodes about Jesus 'breaking bread' with his Apostles after his resurrection – relative to *the first appearance to James* hinted at by Paul in 1 Corinthians 15:7 – we are, once again, led to completely unexpected results about the whole '*Belial*'/'*Diabolos*'/'*casting out*' circle-of-language, now turned into stories about how the Apostles '*cast down their nets*' or have the Authority '*to cast out demons*', rather than how James was '*cast down*' from the Temple steps or Temple Pinnacle.

Nor could we have foreseen where the investigation of such language and examples would lead us. In another transmogrification of this language, that of the '*tares*' or the '*rotten fish*' being '*cast into a furnace of Fire*', we are led into a picture of the plight of '*Evil persons*' generally at '*the Last Judgment*' which does, in fact, parallel the Qumran response to how these same 'Evil' persons '*swallowed*' the Righteous Teacher. In turn, they themselves would '*be paid the Reward on Evil*' or '*be swallowed*' by '*the Cup of the Wrath of God*', which so parallels the Isaiah 3:10 verse, applied to James' death by the Second-Century testimony of Hegesippus: '*Wherefore they shall eat the fruit of their doings*'.

John's 'Net Full of Fishes' Again and Luke's Emmaus Road Sighting

To return to the Gospel of John's testimony to Jesus' appearance to his Disciples along the shore of the Sea of Galilee *after* his resurrection: after putting on his clothes '*to cast himself into the sea*' ('for he was naked') Peter is *swimming to shore*. Nor does he this time appear to 'sink' for 'lack of Faith' as when he tries to walk on the waters in Matthew or as the boats so '*full of fish*' are on the verge of doing in Luke. Rather, he was '*dragging the net full of one hundred and fifty-three large fishes to land but, though there were so many, the net was not torn*' (John 21:11).

Meanwhile in John, the other Disciples, too, were dragging their '*net of fishes*' to land (21:8–11 – the '*dragnet*' in Hab. 1:15 above?). 'Jesus then said to them, "Come and eat" ... and took the bread and gave it to them' (21:12–13). Here, of course, is the *pro forma* 'dining' and 'eating' scenario always part of these accounts and an integral element of Jesus' *first appearance to James* in Jerome's '*Gospel according to the Hebrews*' as we saw. Nor should the subtle play in 'Jesus'' constant command to '*eat*' and allusions in the Gospels, such as '*the Son of Man came eating and drinking*' (Mt 11:19 and Lk 7:34) on Paul's more over-arching and permissive understanding of the term '*eating*' be missed; nor, of course, the use of '*eating*' to mean '*Vengeance*' in these pesharim at Qumran.

More importantly, as we have also seen, all of these things relate to the allied usage in the Habakkuk *Pesher* – in exposition of Habakkuk 1:14–16 on '*taking up with a fishhook, catching them in a net, and gathering them in a dragnet ... and burning incense to his dragnet*' too – where '*eating*' is interpreted to mean '*tax collecting*'. In this manner, '*the Kittim*' ('*the Romans*') '*gather their Riches together with all their booty like fish of the sea', 'parceling out their yoke and their taxes, eating all the Peoples* (that is, '*the Ethne*' as in Paul) *year by year'.*

Not only is this delineated in terms of their '*portion being fat*' and their '*eating plenteous*'; but this is the same passage in which *their burning incense to their 'dragnet'* is interpreted in terms of their '*sacrificing to their standards and worshipping their weapons of war*' – perhaps the key dating parameter where the Habakkuk *Pesher* is concerned.[16] Its bearing, of course, on the related 'play' on this in Matthew 17:27, of 'Peter' – at 'Jesus'' request – '*casting a fishhook' into the Sea of Galilee to retrieve a 'silver coin from the mouth of the first fish he should see to pay the tax'*, should be patent.

As far as this episode in the Gospel of John is concerned, the words attributed to Jesus here are basically what the mysterious voice cries out to Peter in 'the Heavenly tablecloth' episode in Acts, legitimatizing 'table fellowship' with Gentiles and more – thus demonstrating that all these episodes are playing their small, but integrated part and being subjoined to Pauline theological arguments insisting on 'freedom from the Law'.

As John draws to a close, Jesus is not only presented as taking the bread and giving it to the Disciples, but – in light of its previous subject matter *about fishes* – he gives them '*some of the fish too*' (21:13). One is tempted to remark, yes and some big ones too – perhaps the biggest of all '*big fish*' stories! For his part, John remarks, again prosaically one might add in view of the far-reaching implications of the subject matter: 'This was now *the third time* that Jesus was manifested to his Disciples, after having been *raised from among the dead*' (John 21:14).

The Gospel of John closes with the mini-episode about how Jesus asks Simon Peter whether he 'loves' him – again *three times*! Aside from being the number here of Jesus' post-resurrection appearances, 'three' is always associated with the subject of Peter's lack of Faith and poor stewardship in the other Gospels in which, for instance, Peter *denies the Messiah three times on the eve of his crucifixion.* In Acts too, 'the Voice from Heaven' ('*Bat-Kol*') has to call out *three times* to Peter before he gets the message.

The theme of '*loving*' is, not only important *vis-à-vis* 'the Disciple Jesus loved' – purportedly the author of this Gospel, it is important across a whole spectrum of ideas and related to the central ideology of these 'Opposition' groups of Abraham being '*the Friend of God*' – in Hebrew, this is '*the Beloved of God*' – found in the Letter of James, the Damascus Document, and later moving directly into the basic ideology of Islam. As we shall see, this theme will be of particular import to the propagation of these ideas into the Northern Syrian framework of Antioch, Edessa, or Haran – Abraham's place of origin – and, of course, the reason for their ultimate transmission into Islam.

It is also related to the theme of '*loving God*', a motif to be encountered in all these documents – as, for instance, James 2:5 and Paul in 1 Corinthians 8:3 – and the basic definition of 'Piety'. This is the second part of the Righteousness/Piety dichotomy of 'loving your fellow man' and 'loving God' – also put into 'Jesus'' mouth in the Gospels (Mt 22:37–39 and pars.) and found in Paul's exposition of why *it is necessary to pay taxes to Rome* (Rom. 13:8–10).

Carrying on this '*love*' motif, John concludes with Peter seeing '*the Disciple Jesus loved*' and asking Jesus about him (21:20). In an aside, John identifies him as the Disciple 'who had reclined on his breast at the (Last) Supper, asking "Lord, who is it who will deliver you up?"' and 'the Disciple who bears witness to these things and writing these things' (21:20–24).

This brings us back to the pretence that James was the author of the Second-Century Infancy Gospel known as the Protevangelium of James, in which the doctrine of Mary's '*perpetual virginity*' was first announced and, in a kind of sardonic irony, *ascribed to James.* Presumably, James *should have known best about these things*, even though it was *he* and patently *not Mary* who was '*the perpetual virgin*' – another reversal of astonishing proportions. These matters just serve to increase the overlaps between 'the Disciple Jesus loved' and James. For

John, Jesus responds to Peter's query by, once again, lightly rebuking him: '*If I desire him to tarry until I come, what (is this) to you?*' (John 21:22–23) – again *repeated twice* for emphasis.

This allusion to '*tarrying till I come*' is normally interpreted to mean the 'Second Coming' or what is often called 'the *Parousia* of Jesus' or, if one prefers, *final eschatological Judgment*, meaning, something like the proclamation attributed to James in interpretation of Daniel 7:13's 'Son of Man' of *coming eschatological Judgment.* One should note, too, that in the run-up to the exegesis in the Habakkuk *Pesher* of '*the Righteous shall live by his Faith*' from Habakkuk 2:4, the previous verse, '*if it tarries, wait for it*', is also subjected to exegesis. It is important to note that the exposition both passages in the Habakkuk *Pesher* is circumscribed by its application: *only to 'Torah-Doers'*, the exegesis of 2:4 adding the additional qualification, '*Torah*-Doers *in the House of Judah*', meaning, it would appear, only '*Torah-doing Jews*'! The implication would appear to be, it does not apply to *non-Torah*-Doers *who are not Jews.*

The first part of Habakkuk 2:3, '*for there will be another vision about the time appointed for the Completion of the Age and it shall not Lie*' contains significantly both the allusion to the '*Completion of the Age*', paralleling Matthew in 13:29 and 28:20, and '*Lying*'. The commentary in the Habakkuk *Pesher* reads as follows:

> Its interpretation is that *the Last Age will be extended and shall exceed anything that the Prophets have foretold*, for *the Mysteries of God are astounding*. '*If it tarries, wait for it, because it will surely come and not be delayed*' (Hab. 2:3). Its interpretation concerns *the Men of Truth, the Doers of the Torah, whose hand will not slacken from the Service of Truth, though the Last Age is extended around them, because all the Eras of God will come to their appointed End, as He determined them in the Mysteries of His Intelligence. 'Behold, his (soul) is puffed up and not Upright within him'* (Hab. 2:4). Its interpretation is that *their sins will be doubled upon them and they will not be pleased with their Judgement.*[17]

'*The Men of Truth*' may be contrasted to its opposite, '*the Men of Lying*'; the same for '*the Service of Truth*' and '*the Service of Lying*' – cf. Paul's similar contrasts in 2 Corinthians 9–11. There is also an inverse parallel in the stress on being '*puffed up*' to Paul's attack on those '*measuring themselves by themselves and comparing themselves with themselves*' – '*the Highest Apostles*' who, according to 2 Corinthians 10:12, *write their own letters of recommendation* (cf. too '*those reputed to be important*' in Galatians 2:6).

In fact, Paul actually uses the very same allusion, '*puffed up*', to criticize the same sort of persons, i.e., obviously his enemies from James' 'Jerusalem Church', five times in 1 Corinthians 4:6–19 and 1 Corinthians 8:1. In the latter, he compares it, not insignificantly, to '*love*' which, he says, by comparison with the 'Knowledge' they pretend to have about '*things sacrificed to idols*', does not 'puff one up' but rather 'builds one up' and '*is patient*' – '*not vainglorious*' (1 Cor. 13:4)!

In this passage from the Habakkuk *Pesher*, there is absolutely no hint of any authority to 'remit sins'; nor can there be any doubt that it is speaking about a Final Judgment of some kind. The context, too, is clearly eschatological concerning '*the Last Times*'/'*Last Things*' and we are certainly in a framework of these New Testament allusions to '*the Completion of the Age*' as in Mt 13:49 above. This is how this important allusion to '*waiting for*' or '*tarrying*' is in this preamble to the exegesis of Habakkuk 2:4, '*the Righteous shall live by his Faith*' – the exegetical foundation piece of Christianity, as Paul understands it – this 'waiting' or 'tarrying' basically going by the name of '*the Delay of the Parousia*' in modern Christian parlance.

This allusion to 'tarrying' or 'remaining' also occurs in the pivotal Emmaus road post-resurrection appearance in Luke and is transformed into something different again – this time that the Apostles should '*tarry*' or '*wait in the city of Jerusalem*' (24:47). Not paralleled in the other Gospels: after Cleopas and an unnamed other Disciple encounter Jesus '*along the Way*', 'Jesus', as we saw, once again '*reclines*' and '*breaks bread*' with them (Lk 24:30). The ethos of this episode, despite its context, is basically clearly 'Ebionite' or 'Jewish Christian'.

In it, 'Jesus' is *only 'a Man, a Prophet ... mighty before God in work and Word*' and is '*delivered up*' – now, not specifically by Judas *Iscariot*, but by 'the Chief Priests' and 'Rulers' 'to Judgment of death' (Luke 24:19–20 – the words, one finds here, '*a Prophet*' and '*mighty before the Lord of the Throne*', are also exactly those the Koran uses to describe its Messenger, Muhammad, in *Surah* 81:19–21). Like the Teacher of Righteousness, '*to whom God made known all the Mysteries of His Servants the Prophets*' (also described as 'the Priest, in whose heart God placed insight *to interpret all the words of His Servants the Prophets, through whom God foretold all that would happen to His people*'), Jesus in this episode in Luke is essentially portrayed as an Interpreter of Scripture too (24:25–27 and 44–49).[18]

In Luke 24:35. these two 'Disciples' then return to Jerusalem and report '*to the Eleven*' and *those with them 'the things in the Way and how he was known to them in the breaking of the bread*'. At this point, 'Jesus' is portrayed as '*standing among them*'. What he now teaches this '*Assembly of the Eleven and those with them*', in the manner of an Interpreter of Scripture, is exactly what Paul says he received '*according to the Scriptures*' in 1 Corinthians 15:3–4, right before his testimony about Jesus' post-resurrection appearance to James: 'It behooved the Christ to suffer and rise from among (the) dead on the third day, and repentance and remission of sins should be proclaimed in his Name to all Peoples (*Ethne* again) beginning at Jerusalem' (Lk 24:46–47). In 1 Corinthians, Paul puts this: 'I transmitted to you in the first instance what I also received, that Christ died for our sins according to the Scriptures ... and that he was raised from the third day, according to the Scriptures.' One should also note here the Pauline cast of the proclamation, '*to all Peoples*' – already presaged in Matthew 12:21 above.

In this appearance by 'Jesus' in Jerusalem, as reported by Luke, the 'Doubting Thomas' material from John – where Jesus shows them the nail holes in his hands and feet – is once more combined in one and the same episode with the theme of '*eating*'; but instead of commanding the Disciples to 'eat' as in John – and by refraction, Peter's vision of the tablecloth in Acts where the Heavenly voice instructs 'Peter' three times to '*eat*' – Jesus asks, '*Have you anything that is eatable here?*' (24:41). They then produce '*a broiled fish and part of a honeycomb*'!

Not only is this immediately recognizable as the '*and some fish too*' of the episode following Jesus' appearance by the Sea of Galilee in John, where Jesus tells the Disciples to '*come and eat*'; but to this is then added, not only the note about the Apostles 'being witnesses of these things', but the command '*to tarry' or 'remain' in Jerusalem until 'you are clothed with Power from on High*' (again our 'Great Power' vocabulary – Lk 24:49). This is the third iteration of the 'tarrying' or 'remaining' theme, connected in John with 'the Disciple Jesus loved'.

Interesting enough, this is also basically the implication of the Gospel of Thomas text about Jesus' *direct appointment* of James as successor, i.e., '*in the place where you are to go* (presumably Jerusalem), *go to James the Just*'. In effect, 'Jesus' is telling his Disciples here, in going to seek James, *to return to Jerusalem and remain there.* Like these others, too, the statement in Thomas is essentially eschatological because it describes James as being of such importance that for his '*sake Heaven and Earth came into existence*'!

To conclude – instead of '*coming down from Heaven*' as James is pictured as proclaiming it in Hegesippus before the riot in the Temple that leads to his death; in Luke's denouement, Jesus is rather '*carried up into Heaven*' (24:51). As Mark would have it, he '*was received up into Heaven and sat down at the right hand of God*' (16:19). In Luke, however, all the Apostles then '*returned to Jerusalem with great joy and were continually in the Temple praising and blessing God*' (24:53).

This return to Jerusalem is not paralleled in the other Gospels, which are more interested in their view of the Pauline 'going forth' and 'making Disciples of all the Peoples' of Mt 28:19 and pars. Notwithstanding, it is paralleled by the sense of the notice from the Gospel of

Thomas above and, even more importantly, in how James' Community is pictured as *being in the Temple every day* in early Church testimony and by refraction in Acts. This note about *being continually in the Temple* is, once again, both striking and 'Jamesian' in ethos and probably true.

This post-resurrection appearance by 'Jesus' to his most well-known Disciples along the shores of Lake *Gennesaret* in John lends further weight, then, to the fact that all traditions – those of the early Church, Qumran, and New Testament raconteurs – are operating within the same *'B–L–°'/'Balaam'/'Belial'* parameters. In addition, the New Testament and early Church writers appear to have had full knowledge of both James' death scenario and the tradition of *a first post-resurrection appearance to him*, now altered and overwritten though, on the surface, sometimes seemingly playfully – in the end, always disparagingly whether in the tradition of the Synoptic or the Johannine Gospels.

Above: Qumran cliffs from across the Wadi, showing Cave Four, where the bulk of the Scrolls were found. The Dead Sea can be seen in the background.

Left: View of Qumran graves showing North–South orientation. The Dead Sea is in the distance.

Chapter 21
Last Supper Scenarios, the Emmaus Road, and the Cup of the Lord

Breaking Bread and *Eating* in Other Gospels

We should now return to other 'eating' and 'breaking-bread' scenarios in the Gospels. These not only incorporate the essence of this appearance by the Sea of Galilee in the Gospel of John in a more Jerusalem-oriented framework, but bear a direct relationship to Paul's 'Communion with the blood' of Christ, announced in 1 Corinthians 10:14–11:13 amid further allusions to 'eating and drinking' (11:29). In doing so, Paul addresses his discussion also to 'Beloved Ones' – this time his own (10:14).

In John, Jesus appears in Jerusalem preceding the appearance along the shore of the Sea of Galilee. This is reproduced to some extent in Mark's documentation of an appearance by Jesus in Jerusalem 'to the Eleven as they were reclining' (Mk 16:14). Another of these manifestations in Jerusalem is Luke's Emmaus Road appearance, which also incorporates yet another allusion to 'reclining' (Lk 24:30).

Circumscribed as it may be, Mark also alludes to this appearance in Luke to the two 'walking on their way into the country'. But, derogatory as ever, he emphasizes the lack of Pauline-style '*belief*'; for him, Jesus is, once again, censuring his core Apostles for '*their unbelief and hardness of heart*, because *they did not believe those who had seen him risen*' (16:11–13). In these appearances, Jesus also generally shows 'his hands and his feet' so, like Thomas, they can see the holes, or, as in Luke 24:41, when he asks for '*something eatable*', they give him '*a piece of broiled fish and a honeycomb*'!

Luke's description of Jesus' appearance on the Emmaus Road, preceding his '*standing*' in the midst of the Eleven as they were '*assembled*' in Jerusalem, not only parallels Paul's vision along another road – this, '*to Damascus*' – but actually ties all our themes together. It is that important and also almost completely paralleled by the description of the *first appearance* to James in the Gospel Jerome calls, 'according to the Hebrews'. This latter described how, '*after the Lord had given the linen clothes to the Servant of the Priest, he went to James and appeared to him. For James had sworn that he would not eat bread from that hour in which he drank the Cup of the Lord until he should see him risen again from among those that sleep.*'

Not only does this clearly play on James' seeming proclivity for Nazirite oath procedures (not to mention his Rechabitism), it appears to replace 'Last Supper' scenarios where the Gospels picture 'Jesus' announcing Paul's 'Holy Communion' doctrines. Here too 'the Servant of the Priest' clearly means 'of the High Priest' bearing out Qumran usage to similar effect. Curiously enough, this 'Servant of the High Priest' reappears in the Gospels as the one *whose ear Peter lops off* in the struggle when Jesus is arrested (Mt 26:51 and pars.)! Finally, the excerpt from the Gospel of the Hebrews continues in Jerome:

> And again, a little later, it says, 'The Lord said, "Bring a table and bread!"' And immediately it adds, 'He took the bread, blessed it, broke it, and *gave it to James the Just* and said to him, "My brother, eat your bread, for *the Son of Man is risen from among those that sleep.*"'

Not only do we have here a parallel to both 'Jesus'' *breaking the bread and giving it to 'Cleopas' and the unnamed other* along the Emmaus Road in Luke and *to his principal Disciples along the Sea of Galilee* in John; but something of the actual wording Paul uses in 1 Corinthians 11:24, in delineating his doctrine of '*Communion with' the body and blood of Jesus Christ* – the basis too of these Gospel presentations of 'the Last Supper'. Bringing all these allusions full circle, these

Gospel 'Last Supper' scenarios also incorporate the references to 'Judas *the Iscariot*' or 'Judas *("the son" or "brother") of Simon Iscariot*', which will be so telling when it comes to unraveling all these '*brother*' allusions.

Before returning to this appearance on the Road to Emmaus in Luke, it would be well to look at these 'Last Supper' scenarios in the Gospels – the language of which is paralleled both in Paul's 1 Corinthians and in this excerpt about James from the lost Gospel of the Hebrews. In the Gospels, these 'Last Supper' scenarios are always introduced by references to 'Judas *the Iscariot*' in the Synoptics (Mk 14:10) and 'Judas (the son or brother) *of* Simon *Iscariot*' in John 13:2. He, in turn, is almost always described as he '*who would deliver him up*' or '*betray him*' – language repeatedly recapitulated in the Scrolls, but always with a completely differing signification usually meaning God's '*Wrath*' on Israel for '*rebelliousness*' or '*Covenant-breaking*'.[1]

These descriptions of 'Judas *Iscariot*' also generally include a reference to '*Satan*' (Lk 22:3) or '*the Devil*' (*Diabolos* – Jn 13:2 – Jn 13:27 even interchanging both allusions in the same context). Characteristically, Luke also contains an attack on '*those who recline*' and does so in the context of evocation of '*the Kings of the Peoples*' (*Ethnon*) – a term in the Damascus Document almost undoubtedly denoting *Herodian Kings* – which again introduces another of these seemingly completely unjustified attacks on 'Simon' (that is, 'Peter') as someone '*Satan has claimed for himself*' (22:25–31).

Since this very phraseology, '*Kings of the Peoples*', also appears in Roman legal practice where it is used to denote puppet kings in the East of the genre of these Herodians and others, this is yet another concrete philological link between the Gospels and the Scrolls. One cannot help but think of the parallel allusion in Josephus' picture of Agrippa II '*reclining' while eating and watching the Temple sacrifices from his balcony*. In this connection, it should not be forgotten that it was the visit to the household of his father Agrippa I by the '*Simon*' in Josephus, *who wanted to bar him and Herodians generally from the Temple as foreigners*, that we believe is historical rather than some of the other visits and positions, the New Testament pictures the individual it is calling '*Simon*' as taking.

In Luke's picture of Jesus' repartee with and his aside to Simon at the Last Supper, contemptuously dismissing Simon's expressed willingness to be imprisoned and die with him, *Jesus rather throws up to Simon his coming denial.* This, according to Jesus, will occur *three times* or is it to be *the cock that crows three times* – another favorite piece of Gospel folklore (Lk 22:33–34 and 22:60)? Again, it is hard to conceive that in some esoteric manner all these citations are not connected. How ironic it would be if this favorite episode of Jesus at 'the Last Supper' teaching 'his Disciples' what amounts basically to the Greek Mystery Religion practice of consuming the body and blood of the living and dying god was connected in some manner to Agrippa II's eating and reclining while viewing the sacrifices in the Temple in a state of some kind of uncleanness in the Temple Wall Affair (which we have already specified as *leading directly and inexorably to the death of James*).

As Luke continues, he has Jesus swinging back to a more narrowly apocalyptic Jewish viewpoint: 'You may *eat and drink at my table* in my Kingdom *and sit on Thrones judging the Twelve Tribes of Israel*' (22:30–31). Here he, not only returns to the Apostles *participating in the Last Judgment*, an activity which the Habakkuk *Pesher* ascribes to *the 'Elect' of Israel,* themselves synonymous – according to Damascus Document definition – with *the Sons of Zadok 'called by Name who would stand in the Last Days*'[2] – to say nothing of the theme of '*eating and drinking*', now tied to the issue of table fellowship – but also to the '*Twelve Tribe*' scenario regarding these things as in Galatians.

In the Gospels, Jesus is portrayed as 'reclining' with 'the Twelve' at the Passover meal at the Last Supper (Jn 13:1–30). Luke, for instance, has Jesus saying: "'*I will not eat any more with you until it is fulfilled in the Kingdom of God*'" and (as in the Gospel of the Hebrews), *taking his Cup*, he gave thanks saying, "… I will never again *drink of the fruit of the vine until the Kingdom of God has come*'" (22:16–18 and pars.). Not only do we have here yet another play on the *Rechabite* or *Nazirite* theme of 'abstention from wine', but also James' oath in the Gospel of the Hebrews.

Furthermore, we again have in this statement by 'Jesus' at 'the Last Supper' in the Synoptics a variation on the '*eating and drinking*' theme – so important in early Church accounts of James' behavior and interactions with Paul – following which, Jesus announces almost a verbatim version of Paul's '*Communion with the blood of Christ*' in 1 Corinthians 10–11, the letter with which we began our discussion of all these post-resurrection sightings of Jesus in the first place.

Jesus' words here just about amount to a word-for-word recapitulation of those, the Gospel of the Hebrews attributes to James, also repeated to some degree in the sighting 'along the way' to Emmaus in the Gospel of Luke (24:30). It is not even clear whether this passage from the Gospel of the Hebrews about James – which obviously has nothing to do with any consumption, even symbolically, of *'the body' and 'blood' of Jesus* – is not the more primitive original of what 'Jesus' was supposed to have said at 'the Last Supper' in the Gospels; wherein *the Pauline symbolical consumption of 'the body' and 'blood' of Jesus* is, perhaps, *written over* an originally *more Jamesian core.*

Communion with the Blood of Christ in Paul and at the Last Supper

Paul launches into this subject of 'Communion with the body' and 'blood of Christ' in 1 Corinthians 10:16 after first announcing that '*if food scandalizes* (or '*offends*') *my brother, I will never eat flesh forever*' – this followed immediately by his reference to '*the brothers of the Lord and Cephas*' (8:13–9:5) – and elaborating on his philosophy of '*winning*' at all costs (9:18–27). When he does so, he addresses himself yet again to the '*Beloved Ones*', admonishing them to '*flee from idolatry*' (1 Cor. 10:14).

He says: 'The Cup of blessing which we bless, is it not Communion with the blood of Christ? The bread which we break, is it not Communion with the body of Christ?' (1 Cor. 10:16), and then goes on to allegorize on the Qumran language of 'the Many', denoting himself and 'the Many' as the 'body', by which he means both the body of the Church and the body of Christ (1 Cor. 10:17). At the same time he proceeds to invoke '*drinking the Cup of the Lord' and 'eating at the Lord's table*' (1 Cor. 10:21), both encountered in Jerome's account of Jesus' first appearance to James in the Gospel of the Hebrews. It is at this point that he starts to contrast 'Communion with the blood of Christ' and 'Communion with the body of Christ' with '*the sacrifices of the other Israel*' – the one '*according to the flesh*' – which '*eats the sacrifices in Communion with those at the altar*' (1 Cor. 10:18 – *thus*!).

In the peculiar manner in which his *allegorizing logic* works – and again showing it is James with whom he is arguing – Paul actually alludes now to these 'sacrifices in the Temple' in terms of the '*things sacrificed to idols*' prohibited in James' directives to overseas communities according to Acts' portrayal (15:29 and 21:25) – and *MMT* – *yet again reversing the original sense of this phrase.* It becomes clear he is, once more, talking about the more general theme of '*eating and drinking*', referring to it in terms of his characteristic language of 'causing offence'/ 'stumbling', and 'all things being Lawful' to him (1 Cor. 10:23–32).

Just so there can be no mistaking what he means here, he now *compares these sacrifices in the Temple to 'the Cup of demons' and 'the table of demons'* (1 Cor. 10:21). This would have been shocking in a Palestinian milieu, though the idea of the '*pollution of the Temple*' sacrifices was already widespread in the Qumran documents, particularly in the 'Three Nets of Belial' condemnations and *MMT*, paralleling James' directives to overseas communities as we have shown above. We have seen in the Pseudoclementine *Homilies* how Peter identifies this 'table of demons' with eating 'food sacrificed to idols'. Still, it is another excellent example of how Paul reverses the vocabulary of his interlocutors, using their own ideological posture against them.

He ends this discussion by, once again, alluding to the theme that characterizes his ideological position: '*to me, all things are Lawful*' (1 Cor. 10:23). Paul uses this to move directly on to the two specific permissions, '*eat everything sold in the marketplace' and 'eat everything set before you*', in connection with which he now cites a second time *James' prohibition on eating things 'sacrificed to an idol'* – with which, of course, he disagrees, *referring to it as 'a stumbling block*' (10:25 –32).

This leads to Paul's further discussion in chapter 11 of the '*eating and drinking*' theme, which he *specifically relates to 'eating the Lord's supper' and to 'drinking the Cup of the Lord*' (as in the Gospel of the Hebrews' 'breaking bread' scene with James above) and *the Cup of 'the New Covenant in (his) blood*' (11:20–29). Paul, for his part, puts this as follows: 'For *I received from the Lord*, that which I also delivered to you, the Lord Jesus, in the night in which he was delivered up, *took bread* and, after giving thanks, *he broke it and said, "Take, eat ...* "' (11:23–24).

Paul purposefully juxtaposes his first use of the word 'delivered' with that of his second, 'delivered up' – in the New Testament normally associated with 'Judas *Iscariot*' (a usage widespread, too, in the Dead Sea Scrolls but to entirely different effect) however, in Paul, no '*Judas Iscariot*' is ever mentioned! 'In the same manner also, (he took) the Cup after having eaten, saying, "*This Cup is the New Covenant in my blood* ... For as often as you *eat this bread* and *drink this Cup*, you announce *the death of the Lord until he comes*"' (11:25–26). We have already remarked and will further discuss in a follow-up volume how this '*New Covenant in my blood*' relates to the Dead Sea Scrolls' '*New Covenant in the Land of Damascus*' – '*Cup of blood*' in Hebrew and the Greek '*Damascus*' being homophones.

That Paul announces he '*received' this new insight 'from the Lord*' makes this claim even more curious. This is also true where his first enunciation of this 'Cup of blessing' as 'Communion with the blood of Christ' is concerned earlier in 1 Cor. 10:14–23 – itself preceded by his lengthy analyses of the two subjects from James' directives to overseas communities in Acts, '*fornication*' and '*things sacrificed to idols*'.

The implication of this claim preceding the list of 'Jesus'' post-resurrection appearances in 1 Corinthians 15 is that he 'received' these doctrines from the Apostles before him. In the case of 'Communion with the body and blood of Christ' here 11:23–27, the implication is clearly that he *did 'not receive this from any man' but rather as a direct 'revelation from Jesus Christ*' (Gal. 1:12). In fact, the implication of this, too, may be that no one else even knew of the doctrine. The Gospels, of course, make good this deficiency.

In fact, not only does Paul then proceed in 11:30 to cast aspersions on *the 'weak'* again, his favorite circumlocution for those in authority over him who cause problems regarding '*eating and drinking*', *circumcision*, table fellowship, etc. Here, Goebbels-like, he also calls them '*sickly*' while, again, repeating his '*many are fallen asleep*' allusion and tying all these things to another allusion to *the idea of being 'examined*' (11:31). Previously *being 'examined'* for him had to do with *his teaching credentials or lack of them*, however now he asserts *rather ominously*: 'For *he who eats and drinks* unworthily, not seeing through to the body of the Lord, *eats and drinks Judgment to himself*' (*thus* – 11:29).

Not only is the play on the language of 'eating and drinking' again self-evident, but now he is threatening those, who do not 'see' things in the manner he does, with '*Judgment*'. This clearly has to do not with a reversal once again of the kinds of '*Judgment*' his opponents would call down on him – as, for instance, that on '*Law-breakers' who 'do not keep the whole Law' and on those who claim their 'Faith will save them*' in James 2:10–14 – i.e., *Divine or eschatological Judgment*. Furthermore in regard to this '*Judgment*', he is using '*Cup*' imagery, in particular, '*drinking the Cup of the Lord*' – *imagery specifically employed in the Scrolls* to describe '*the Vengeance' God would take for the destruction of the Righteous Teacher and 'the Poor*'.

Of equal importance, this same Habakkuk *Pesher* – which described '*the Lying Spouter*' as having *'led Many astray to build a Worthless City upon blood and erect an Assembly on Lying for the sake of his Glory, tiring out Many with a Worthless Service* and *instructing them in works of Lying so that their works will be of Emptiness*' – calls down upon this '*Liar*'/'*Spouter of Lying*' and his associates the very same '*Fire with which they blasphemed and vilified the Elect of God*'![3]

In both of these quotations, the one from Paul and the one from Qumran, one should note the repetition of the allusion to '*Many*' and how Paul also uses the word '*Glory*' – also used here in this passage from the Dead Sea Scrolls – as part of his allusion to 'eating and drinking' in 1 Cor. 10:31 and repeatedly through Chapters 11 and 15. It should also be appreciated that throughout these passages concerning the destruction of 'the Righteous Teacher' in the Scrolls, the word '*drinking*' is being used to express both this and '*the Divine* Vengeance' that will be exacted because of it.

Before mentioning 'the other Apostles and Cephas and the brothers of the Lord' traveling around with women in Chapter 9, Paul protests: '*Am I not an Apostle? Am I not free? Have I not seen Jesus Christ our Lord? Are you not my work in the Lord? If I am not an Apostle to others, at least I am to you ... My defense to those who would examine me is, do we not have authority to eat and drink?*' (9:1–4). This, just after he had studiedly concluded, '*food (*literally, *'meat') does not commend us to God*' – '*neither, in not eating, do we fall short*' (8:1–11); but *his subtle plays on language* and *the way he turns the language his adversaries appear to be using against* him back on them are canny.

Basically what we have in Paul's reformulations in 1 Corinthians – ending in allusion to 'the Cup of the Lord', 'breaking bread', and 'Communion with the body' and 'blood of Christ' – is none other than a variation of the scenario portrayed in 'the Gospel of the Hebrews' where James 'swore *not to eat bread from the hour in which he drank the Cup of the Lord until he should see him risen again from among those that sleep*'. To this, Jesus, '*breaking the bread*' and '*giving it to James*', reportedly responds, '*My brother, eat your bread for the Son of Man is risen from among those that sleep.*'

This is especially true since Paul has quoted his '*Lord Jesus*' to the effect that, '*This Cup is the New Covenant in my blood ... For as often as you eat this bread and drink this Cup, you solemnly proclaim the death of the Lord until he comes.*' The only real difference is that now 'Jesus'' speech from 'the Gospel of the Hebrews' is expanded *to incorporate Paul's new scenario* of '*Communion with the body and blood of Jesus Christ*'.

The Negation of Paul's Mindset at Qumran

One can well imagine how, in particular, this would have infuriated those of a Qumran perspective, whose approach would appear to be at the heart of what Paul is responding to. Paul's direct allusion to the fact that he is not '*throwing down a net before them*' makes this about as clear as anything can. Paul knows full well what he is doing. Again, as we have pointed out often, on almost all these issues Paul is systematically allegorizing and turning the Qumran positions back against them. He is doing the same to James.

That Paul groups his positions regarding 'dining in an idol-temple' and 'Communion with the blood of Christ' under the heading of 'loving God' or 'Piety' would have only infuriated groups like those at Qumran all the more. One should note that in Josephus' descriptions of the Opposition or 'Zealot' positions from the disturbances of 4 BCE up to the events culminating in the Uprising against Rome, the constant demand on the part of all 'Opposition' forces is for *a High Priest of 'greater purity' and 'higher Piety'*. One also gets this demand reflected in Hebrews 4:15 and 7:26 even as it has survived.

As we have also noted, James 1:12 and 2:5 refers both to '*loving God*' or '*Piety*' – the first in Chapter One with reference to '*the Crown (Stephanon) of Life promised' those loving God*; the second in Chapter Two, to *the 'Beloved' or 'Poor' as 'Rich in Faith and heirs to the Kingdom promised to those that love Him*'. In the background to both, '*the Religion' of 'the one who cannot control his Tongue, but has Lying in his heart' is said to be 'Worthless*' (Jas. 1:26).

One should note as well that, in Josephus' picture of 'the Essenes', the Commandment of '*Piety towards God*' is mentioned twice – once in connection with their daily bathing in cold water, eating habits, and wearing white linen garments; and a second time, in connection with the oaths that such individuals take '*not to tell Lies*' and '*not to reveal any of their doctrines to others*', nor communicate their doctrines '*which they have received from their Forefathers*' ('*the First*' at Qumran) in any manner different from how they '*have received them*' themselves. Not only is this almost word-for-word the Pseudoclementine *Homilies*' picture of the fearsome impression – when responding to Peter's Letter – made by James' imprecations on the Elders; but it is also precisely the words Paul repeatedly uses when describing *the doctrines he 'has received'*.[4]

It is important to realize that in the Scrolls *the ban on the consumption of 'blood' is fundamental.* The same is true of James' directives to overseas communities and one should see this as pertaining to *symbolic consumptions of 'blood' as in Paul's 1 Corinthians* as well. In the Damascus Document, *the horror of 'blood'* ranges from the attack on those who '*lie with women during* the *blood of their menstrual flow*' to the charge of '*each man marrying the daughter of his brother or sister*' – which focuses both of these as *an attack on the Herodian family and those 'polluted' by their contacts with them* – to the connection of *the 'cutting off' of the Children of Israel in the wilderness* to the assertion: '*because they ate the blood*'. This last, occurring at the beginning of Column iii of the Damascus Document, precedes these sections on the definition of '*the Sons of Zadok*' and the exposition of '*the Three Nets of Belial*' charges in Columns iv-vi.

Just as we have had the allusion to '*keeping God's Commandments*' in Paul's discussion of '*fornication*' in 1 Corinthians 7:19; in Column iii of CD, leading up to the evocation of the ban on '*blood*', we have the references to Abraham being accounted '*Beloved*' or '*Friend of God*' because he '*kept the Commandments of God and did not choose the will of his own spirit*' nor 'do what seemed right in his own eyes and walk in stubbornness of heart' (one should compare this to James 2:21–23 on '*Abraham*'). As in James as well, one should note the emphasis on being both a '*Keeper*' and a '*Doer*'.[5]

Over and over in these passages about Abraham, Isaac, and Jacob being '*the Beloved*' or '*Friends of God*' in CD, the text repeats the phrase '*keeping the Commandments of God*' – *n.b.,* the parallel to Jeremiah's '*sons of Rechab*' (i.e., '*the Rechabites*') repeatedly being described as '*keeping the Commandments of their father*'. Nor is this to mention the description of these same Patriarchs in Surah 2 of the Koran and, therefore, in Islam as 'Friends' because they '*surrendered to God*' – meaning, they were the first '*Muslims*' too!.

For the Damascus Document, it is as a result of '*not keeping' God's Commandment that the Heavenly Watchers fell* – the allusion is to Genesis 6:2 where '*the Sons of God have intercourse with the daughters of men*'. Following this, the text evokes the Noahic 'Flood' and, finally then, how *the Children of Israel 'ate blood' in the wilderness* and, *therefore, 'were cut off*' (what would the Pauline 'Gentile Mission' make of this?) It is because of these things that, in CD's world-view, *God's 'Wrath' is 'kindled against' the Children of Israel* and they and '*their Congregation*' (or '*Church*') are continually '*being cut off*' or '*delivered up*'.[6]

From its very First Column, which describes how '*the Lying Scoffer*' arose and '*poured over Israel* (the same root as '*Spouting*' in Hebrew) *the waters of Lying … abolishing the Ways of Righteousness and removing the boundary which the First* (i.e., '*the Forefathers*') *had set down for their inheritance*'; CD '*calls down on them the curses of His Covenant*' and '*the avenging sword of the Covenant*' – meaning, *God's 'Wrath' and 'avenging sword*', not Rome's.[7] This is in line with '*curses*' and '*cursing backsliders*' and '*Enemies*' generally at Qumran which is never accommodating, gentle, or forgiving.[8]

For his part, Paul takes the opposite approach. A good example is in Romans 12:17, where he recommends '*not to return Evil for Evil*' and follows this up with the quotation, once again addressed to the '*Beloved*', '*Vengeance is mine. I will repay, saith the Lord*' and, following this, '*overcome Evil with Good*'. This includes the additional recommendation to *feed your Enemy 'when he is hungry and give him drink when thirsty'* (Rom. 12:19–21). It will be immediately apparent that what we have here is ideological and verbal sparring, back and forth – all being like the sayings attributed to 'Jesus' in the Gospels, the only question being which, historically speaking, came first. The reason Paul gives for such recommendations, however, is often a bit more cynical than in the Gospels, i.e., '*in so doing, you will heap coals on his (your enemy's) head*' (Romans 12:20).

This is almost exactly the kind of saying Josephus imputes to Paul's putative '*kinsman*' Herod Agrippa I who, Josephus says, '*was of a gentle and compassionate nature*'. Particularly, in relation to the episode about the 'Simon' above, *the Head of a 'Church' or 'Assembly' of his own in Jerusalem,* who wished to *bar this Agrippa from the Temple as a foreigner*, Josephus emphasizes that King Agrippa '*esteemed mildness a better quality in a King than intemperance, knowing that moderation is more becoming in great men than passion*'.[9] This is certainly very 'Christ'-like but, not only does Josephus record a similar saying attributed to this 'Agrippa', he does not hesitate to apply the characteristic to him or '*chrestos*' in Greek, meaning 'gracious'/'gentle'!

One should note in Romans, too, that after Paul discusses his doctrine of a '*Grace no longer of works*', God '*thrusting aside' the Jews* and how '*they killed' all the Prophets* – '*Salvation being granted to the Gentiles*', and the Jews now being '*zealous of*' or '*jealous over' this*; he, once again, employs the '*net*', '*snare*', and '*stumbling block'/'cause of offence'/'stumbling*'-language (11:1–11). He also refers to '*Riches*' here – the second of Belial's '*nets*' in the Damascus Document – e.g., it is now the Jews' '*stumbling*' that becomes both '*the Riches of the World*' and '*the Riches of the Gentiles*' (Rom. 11:11–12 – of course, the very opposite of how Qumran would see things). The final insult in all of this – at least as far as Qumran would see it – would be his characterization of his communities in the manner of the description of 'the Community Council' in the Dead Sea Scrolls, i.e., as '*living sacrifices, Holy and well pleasing to God*' (Rom. 12:1) so that '*the offering up of the Gentiles might be pleasing, made Holy by the Holy Spirit*' (Rom. 15:16 – *thus*!).

In describing himself as being '*the Apostle of the Gentiles* (*Ethnon*)', Paul actually uses the words, the Habakkuk *Pesher* uses to describe the '*Worthlessness of the Liar's Service*' in '*erecting*' or '*building an Assembly*' or '*Church upon Lying … and blood … for the sake of his Glory*', i.e., '*I glorify my Service*' (Rom. 11:13). From here Paul moves immediately into evocation of the Messianic '*Root*' and '*Branch*' imagery, again so dear to Qumran, but now applied to his new Gentile Christians as '*grafts*' or the new '*branches'* upon the tree and the '*members' of Christ's body* (Rom. 11:16–28); while at the same time (in the manner of 1 Thessalonians 2:16 accusing the Jews of '*killing the Lord Jesus and their own Prophets*' – a refrain picked *ad nauseum* in the Koran), characterizing the Jews as '*Enemies for your sakes*' (12:4–5) – itself parodying the terminology, theoretically, applied by many of the more-'zealous' to him).

It is interesting that this striking and relevant exhortation in the first three columns of the Damascus Document includes allusion to 'knowing Righteousness and understanding the works of God', 'breaking the Covenant', 'walking in Perfection', 'the Last Generation', and the Evil Ones who 'justify the Wicked and condemn the Righteous'. This last is the direct opposite of the paradigmatic activity of '*the Sons of Zadok'* who, two columns later, are rather described as '*justifying the Righteous and condemning the Wicked*'.[10] This, of course, is the parallel to New Testament notions of '*Justification*' though more in line with the 'Jamesian' (not the Pauline) exposition of Habakkuk 2:4: '*the Righteous shall live by his Faith*' – the Pauline riposte to which occupies a good part of Romans and Galatians as well.

These early lines of the Damascus Document also contain allusion to '*men called by Name*' as duly-designated instruments of Salvation. This is repeated in Column iv as part of the definition of '*the Sons of Zadok*' as '*the Elect of Israel… destined for life Eternal*', in the course of which it is announced that '*all the Glory of Adam would be theirs*'(again a seeming allusion to the

Ebionite '*Primal Adam*' ideology). Parallel language is repeated in the Community Rule in the midst of baptismal imagery and evocation of *the 'pouring out' the Holy Spirit.*[11] This idea of eternal life coupled with a curious sort of allusion to 'Adam' is the glorified state of Heavenly or Eternal being, to which Paul himself even makes reference in 1 Corinthians 15:22 and 47).

The phrase '*called by Name*', too, is often transformed into '*called by this Name*' or 'by *the Name of the Lord Jesus*' in Acts and Paul (1 Cor. 5:4 and 6:11). As opposed to this, however, one should note the more Qumran-style way in which James 2:7 evokes '*the Good Name by which you were called*' in conjunction, significantly, with allusion to '*not blaspheming*', that is to say, '*the Good Name*', and evocation – as in these passages in the Damascus Document, James, and Paul – of '*the Royal Law according to the Scripture*'.

It is interesting, that in the course of this allusion to '*being justified in the Name of the Lord Jesus and by the Spirit of our God*' in 1 Cor. 6:11, Paul also goes on to speak about '*being washed*' *and 'made Holy'* (the '*consecration' or 'sanctification*' in descriptions of James' 'Naziritism'), '*all things for me being Lawful', 'the body not being for fornication*', and the members of Christ's body (i.e., Paul's Communities) *not 'being joined' to the flesh of a prostitute.* The latter is contrasted, Qumran-style, with the more proper '*being joined to the Lord*' (1 Cor. 6:11–20).

Regardless of the way 'prostitutes' are referred to in the Gospels (who generally are portrayed as being acceptable to 'Jesus' – even '*keeping table-fellowship*' with him) and parallel plays on the language of '*fornication*' at Qumran, this also evokes the Qumran language of 'join' and 'Joiners'. This language cluster most particularly occurs in Column iv of the Damascus Document in exposition of Ezekiel 44:15's crucial '*Zadokite Covenant*' following the allusions in Columns ii-iii to '*God's Wrath*' against those '*walking in the stubbornness of their own hearts*', '*Law-breakers*', and how these would be '*cut off in the wilderness*' and/or '*delivered up to the sword*'.

Playing off the word 'Levites', based on a Hebrew root meaning '*to be joined to*' and the appositive of '*the Sons of Zadok*' in the underlying text; the exegesis that is developed has to do with '*and the Joiners with them*' – meaning, of course, in '*the Land of Damascus' or 'the wilderness camps'*. It should be appreciated that in both Esther and Isaiah, this expression literally applies to 'Gentiles joining themselves to the Jewish Community' (therefore, the use of the terminology '*joining*'/'*Joiners*' found at this point in the Damascus Document). It is for this reason we have postulated a cadre of Gentile '*Joiners*' ('*Nilvim*') attached to the Community at Qumran – in the closing columns of the Document referred to by the typical expression '*fearing God*' or '*God-Fearers*'

It is also important to appreciate that in the course of the first allusion to '*Justification*' in Column One, that is, the '*justifying the Wicked* (also possibly '*Sinners*') *and condemning the Righteous*'; an attack on '*the Righteous One*' (*ha-Zaddik* – probably alluding to '*the Righteous Teacher*' already alluded to earlier in the Column) is evoked – literally on '*the soul of the Righteous One*' usually meaning one's mortal quick (in this case, therefore, probably implying *a mortal attack*) – to wit: '*They (the Law-Breakers) banded together against the soul of the Righteous (One) and against all the walkers in Perfection,*[12] *execrating their soul (or 'being'), and* they *pursued them with the sword, attempting to divide the People.*'

One should note the use here of the verb '*pursuing*', also used in the Habakkuk *Pesher* in the matter of *the attack on the Righteous Teacher by the Wicked Priest 'in the House of his Exile'.* Where such '*pursuits*' were concerned, a death penalty was usually pronounced or involved. This, no doubt, '*the Wicked Priest*' had done; but, in the literature known to us '*the Zealots*', for their part, could and, no doubt, did turn this around as justification *for treating those, who had 'pursued' either their Leader* or *some of their fellows*, or both, *with intent to kill,* in the same manner.[13]

The use of the word '*soul*' here is widespread at Qumran, particularly when evoking *the suffering of 'the Meek'* or '*the Poor*' (always '*Ebionim*') in texts like *The Qumran Hymns* or the so-called '*Hymns of the Poor*'.[14] One also finds such an allusion to '*soul*' in Paul – as, for instance, '*every soul of man*' in Romans 2:9 used, there, in the context of *evocation of God's 'Wrath'* and the '*revelation of Righteous Judgment*' echoing the language of these introductory exhortations in the Damascus Document. Here, however, Paul is at his most circumspect. Notwithstanding, in these passages he again even alludes to the James-like *God* '*not being a respecter of persons*' but rather '*paying each according to his works*' (Rom. 2:5–2:11).

He also refers to '*soul*' in 1 Corinthians 15:45 in relation to '*the First Man Adam became a living soul*' above – an aspect of how the '*Primal Adam*'-ideology was understood. One also finds it in the last line of James, this time having to do with '*saving a soul from death*' (5:20).

This attack on '*the soul of the Righteous One*' and his followers by '*the Liar*' and his confederates in CD probably best parallels the one in the *Recognitions* by Paul on James – also called '*the Zaddik*' – above. It is important to appreciate that, following the allusion to this attack at the end of Column One in CD, the first allusion to '*raising up men called by Name*' occurs. It is in this context that God in Column ii is referred to as '*revealing His Holy Spirit to them by the hand of His Messiah*'.

One should realize that the allusion to '*Messiah*' here is singular not plural. One can see this by the singular verb and adjectival usages attached to and surrounding it despite some scholarly attempts – purposeful or otherwise – to obscure it. One well-known English translator even leaves out the next phrase: '*and in the explanation of His Name, their Names are (to be found)*' – presumably because of this conundrum.

These allusions, which are always *singular* – however obscure their meaning may be – are extremely important. In the first place, because they reinforce the impression of the *expectation of a singular Messiah at Qumran* and, in the second, reference to him – as in Christianity – is accompanied by the tell-tale allusion to the all-important '*Holy Spirit*'.[15]

Wounding Weak Consciences in Paul and More Damascus Document Parallels

'*Conscience*', too, is the catchword Paul uses to express his contempt for those who, under the twin rubrics of '*loving God*' and '*being weak*', make problems over '*meat*' or '*eating things sacrificed to idols*' (or, in other words, '*reclining at an idol-Temple*'). Here too, Paul vowed – disingenuously – '*never to eat flesh or meat again forever, so as not to cause the weak brother to stumble*' or '*wound his weak conscience*' (1 Cor. 8:3–13). Not only is Paul opposed to the 'Jerusalem Church' perspective, but he knows it so well that he can draw out and deride its every minute point. James and the rest of '*the Elders*' in Jerusalem must have been at a complete loss as to how to deal with him.

In Romans 13:5, not only does he reverse the normal Palestinian thrust of 'lo*ving your neighbor as yourself*', but also another allusion to '*conscience*', that is, 'fear' the Authorities (this, of course, his counterpart to the normal 'fearing God') and subject yourself to them, 'not only because of wrath (the Authorities' 'wrath' that is), but also for the sake of *conscience*'. Instead of being a euphemism for meticulous observation of the Law, '*conscience*' now becomes something that should impel the ordinary citizen to pay all the 'taxes' and 'tributes due' the State (13:6–10). The implied allusion here to 'Wrath of God' now becomes, rather, the vengeance the State will take upon Evil-doers, for 'he' or 'it' – there is a *double entendre* here – 'does not wear the sword in vain' (13:4). Again, not only do we have here much of the vocabulary of Qumran reversed, but a more anti-'Zealot' and, in particular, anti-'*Sicarii*' point of view could not be imagined.

Not only is this contradicted by the picture of 'Jesus' *instructing his Apostles* to 'purchase a sword' (and their showing that they already have two! – Lk 22:36–38), but we encountered a version of this vocabulary in the First Column of the Damascus Document in the picture of those 'seeking to divide the People ('the Liar', 'Covenant-Breakers', and 'Traitors to the New Covenant') *pursuing the Zaddik and all the 'Walkers in Perfection with the sword*'. Following allusion to the Children of Israel 'being cut off in the wilderness' because 'they ate blood', 'the sword' to which they 'are delivered up' becomes 'the avenging sword of the Covenant'![16]

The Damascus Document now goes on in Column Six to evoke what the Letter of James calls 'the Royal Law according to the Scripture', so disingenuously invoked by Paul in support of paying taxes to the Roman Authorities and submitting to foreign rule above: 'they shall each man love his brother as himself'.[17] The allusions that follow this include: 'not to uncover the nakedness of near kin, but keeping away from fornication according to Law'. 'Keeping away' here is expressed in terms of the Hebrew verb '*lehinnazer*' – the root of the word 'Nazirite' in English. Two columns earlier this was the rationale for the ban on niece marriage, also part of the 'Three Nets of Belial' prohibition of 'fornication'. In fact, one begins to see that this usage, '*lehinnazer*' in Hebrew, is the root of the expression 'keep away' or 'abstain from' *in James' directives to overseas communities in Acts*.[18]

Preceding the Righteousness Commandment at the end of Column Six of the Damascus Document was the admonition 'to separate between polluted and pure and to distinguish between Holy and profane', exactly the opposite of what Acts says Peter learned on the rooftop in Jaffa.[19] This also included the commandment to 'separate from the Sons of the Pit' and, in Column Seven, 'from all pollutions according to Law, so that a man will *not defile his Holy Spirit, which God separated for them*'. This last is basically an allusion to either temporary or life-long Naziritism and being 'consecrated' or 'set aside as Perfectly Holy'.

This passage ends with another admonition '*to do* according to the exact sense of the Law' – again the tell-tale Jamesian note on 'doing' – 'everyone walking in these (Commandments) in Perfect Holiness relying on all that was transmitted of the Covenant of God, promising them (here, a variation of the word, 'Faithfulness') to live for a thousand generations'.[20]

In the Damascus Document, this section also includes the allusion to 'the offspring of vipers' (Isa. 59:5), applied to those 'who defile their Holy Spirits, opening their mouth with a blaspheming Tongue against the Laws of the Covenant of God saying, "They are not sure." They speak an Abomination (or 'a blasphemy') concerning them.' This section of the Damascus Document draws to an end, following the allusion to 'separate from the Sons of the Pit', with the instruction 'to keep away from polluted or Evil Riches (acquired by) vow or ban and (to keep away) from the Riches of the Temple (meaning the Temple Treasury) and robbing the Poor of His People'.[21]

Towards the end, in the Eighth Column, those who 'have spoken wrongly against the Laws of Righteousness and rejected the Covenant and Compact ('the Faith') they raised in the Land of Damascus, the New Covenant' – including 'the Liar' – are condemned. Not only are such persons said to have 'put idols on their hearts' and 'walked in the stubbornness of their heart', but 'all the Holy Ones of the Most High' are described as having 'cursed him' and 'no one is to co-operate with him in regard to Riches (or 'purse') or work (in the sense of 'Mission' or 'Service')'.[22] These, as the Document puts it, 'shall have no share in the House of the *Torah*', a spirit, as should be plain, that could not be more different from the Pauline. Not only does reference to 'the Man of Lying' directly follow, but in addition, so do two allusions to 'fearing God' and 'fearing His Name', coupled with the pronouncement that 'to those that love Him' and 'reckon His Name', God would reveal Salvation (*Yesha'*) and Justification ... for a thousand Generations.[23]

That we have in the midst of these allusions by Paul to 'eating and drinking' and 'breaking the bread' in 1 Corinthians 10–11, evocation of 'taking the Cup' and 'the New Covenant in my blood' or 'Communion with the blood of Christ' (1 Cor. 10:16 and 11:25 – repeated in Matthew, Mark, and Luke in the context of the 'Last Supper'), is of the utmost importance. As Paul goes on to express it, 'for as often as you *eat this bread and drink this Cup*, you announce the death of the Lord until he comes' (11:26).

It should be appreciated further that the context in Paul is one of 'examining oneself' so as 'not to be judged' (1 Cor. 11:28–32), concepts that in the Letter of James come out in the context of subjecting yourself 'to God' (not the Roman State), and 'resisting the Devil' (*Diabolo* – Jas. 4:7–10), also seen as representing that State. The Letter of James puts it, 'He that speaks against a brother and judges his brother, *speaks against the Law* and judges the Law, but if you judge the Law, *you are not a Doer of the Law, but a judge*' (4:11). This could not agree more with the Damascus Document, which specifically mentions 'speaking erroneously against the Laws of Righteousness'. Even the expression, 'Doer of the Law', is to be found in two successive notices in the Habakkuk *Pesher*, fundamental both to the exposition of Habakkuk 2:3 on 'the Delay of the *Parousia*' and Habakkuk 2:4, 'the Righteous shall live by his Faith'.

For Paul the 'judging' in the Letter of James is now applied to the man who 'eats and drinks unworthily', by which he means, 'not seeing through to the body of the Lord'. Such a man is not only '*guilty of the body and blood of the Lord*', but moreover, '*eats and drinks Judgment to himself*' (11:27–29). Not only does this fly in the face of allusions like the one to 'putting idols on his heart' in the Damascus Document above and of the substance and spirit of the Letter attributed to James in the New Testament; '*abstention* ('*lehinnazer*') *from things sacrificed to idols and from blood*' – just as at Qumran – form the centerpiece of James' instructions to overseas communities, which Paul appears to be answering in these passages from 1 Corinthians.

One should note that in 1 Corinthians 10:5, when discussing these things, Paul actually alludes to the Children of Israel 'being cut off in the wilderness' – found at this same point in the Damascus Document – but without telling why. In fact, he even uses these words 'cutting off' to express the hope in Galatians 5:12 that the circumcisers disturbing his communities, like the 'some sent by James' earlier in the same letter, would 'themselves cut off' – meaning, as we have previously explained, their own privy parts.

It is almost inconceivable that this could be accidental or that these things could have been misunderstood, though they have been for the better part of two millennia, particularly since Paul is combining all these allusions in 1 Corinthians. The only difference is that instead of 'abstaining from things sacrificed to idols and blood', Paul's communities are now being encouraged (or at least not discouraged) *to partake*, certainly *to partake of the blood of Christ*. This flies in the face of the James-like vegetarianism and Rechabite-style aversion to wine of all these Nazirite extremist groups, who neither consumed wine, nor ate meat at all. It also flies in the face of James' proscription on the consumption of blood in the Book of Acts, even as we have it, not to mention Jewish legal restrictions generally.

It cannot be that Paul misunderstood the true thrust of James' instructions to overseas communities (if these are the same or parallel to those enshrined in *MMT*, all the more so). On the contrary, Paul reveals that he understands them very well. That these directives were *written down* in some manner is not only averred in Acts' account – such as it is – of an 'epistle' being sent down from James with two 'prophets', Judas (called by Acts) 'Barsabas', and Silas (15:22–23), but also by Paul in 1 Corinthians 10:11 (though, strictly speaking, this allusion more likely refers to these passages in the Damascus Document).

That in his delineation of these issues involving the 'Cup of blood', Paul is speaking figuratively and James literally is just the point. As we have repeatedly stressed, Paul allegorizes in the manner that Philo of Alexandria – his older contemporary – allegorized about the Old Testament. Only in Paul, everything emerging from a 'Jamesian' framework – and, as it were, the perspective of Qumran – is not only allegorized, but reversed.

It is no wonder that the world has for so long been confused about the true nature of what occurred at this crucial juncture in human history. But now that we have the Qumran documents to aid us (come down nineteen centuries after they were deposited as if to haunt us), it is no longer possible to be mistaken about the true nature of what occurred. Without these documents we could never have, using the words of Paul, 'seen through to it'.

The Cup of the Lord, Tombs that Whiten, and Linen Clothes Again

We can now return to this passage in the Gospel of the Hebrews with a clearer understanding of this process and of what is at stake in considering all these parallel and interlocking testimonies about 'breaking the bread', 'eating', and 'the Cup of the Lord'. We can now see that the language of this short passage, inadvertently preserved by Jerome, actually parallels Paul in 1 Corinthians 10–11 and, in turn, the Synoptic Gospels about 'eating and drinking' at the so-called 'Last Supper'.

But in the Gospel of the Hebrews, the episode, while including reference to 'the Cup of the Lord', is completely devoid of extrapolation into 'the Communion with' or 'the Cup of the New Covenant in' the blood of Jesus Christ, which nowhere did play or could have played a part in any *Palestinian* documents – only overseas or foreign ones. Whatever the redaction process involved, and however amazing it might at first seem, it is possible even to conclude that the Gospel of the Hebrews' version of the tradition about 'the Cup of the Lord', which James purportedly drank with Jesus, incorporating, as it does, a *first appearance* to James, represents an earlier version than orthodox Gospel ones – or even *the original one*. This was then inverted, in line with Paul's understanding of 'Communion' in 1 Corinthians 10:14–33 and 11:22–30, and retrospectively inserted into the history as it has come down to us.

In fact, this episode in this so-called 'Jewish Gospel' is not only paralleled in John's episode about Jesus' appearance along the Sea of Galilee, where in addition to 'giving them' some of the bread, *Jesus gives them* 'some of the fish too' (in Luke 24:42, this is turned around to '*they gave him* a piece of broiled fish and part of a honeycomb' and the locale is confined to Jerusalem); but even more completely in Luke's detailed story of a first appearance by Jesus to the 'two' outside Jerusalem on the Emmaus Road. If what we have just said is true, this would make the story about the first sighting by these two Disciples in Luke – one called 'Cleopas' – *later* than the one in the Gospel of the Hebrews – or at least the source on which it was based. To put this slightly differently, both are based on the same *Palestinian source about James*. This in our view is the proper conclusion to draw.

Though we have already described the basic outline of this episode above, it is worth considering it in more detail. This sighting is also noted in Mark, where characteristically (as in most other matters relating to the family of Jesus), it is for the most part erased (16:12–13). Whereas Luke only partially rubs out the identities of its protagonists, making it difficult to determine precisely what happened, Mark simply notes this initial appearance in the environs of Jerusalem and then moves on, as do Matthew and John, to Galilee (for some reason the preferred focus of these other Gospels). Luke, in line with the saying in the Gospel of Thomas about 'going to James the Just', never does get to Galilee – but rather has everyone stay in Jerusalem, which is more sensible. Just as Mark also retains the traces of an appearance 'to the Eleven' as they reclined – like Agrippa II on his dining patio – again, Paul-like, Jesus chastises even his core Apostles for their lack of 'belief or 'Faith' here.

Mark retains the traces of the appearance to the two on the Emmaus Road, which he places just before the appearance 'to the Eleven' in Jerusalem, noting that: 'After these things, he appeared in a different form'. This motif will reappear in all three mistaken-identity episodes in John, where Jesus is either portrayed as 'standing' in front of Mary Magdalene (20:14), 'standing among them' (20:26), and 'standing on the shore' (21:4), and will be the reason no one recognizes him.

The 'things' Mark is referring to are for a start the report of a *first appearance* – not paralleled in the other Synoptics – 'to Mary Magdalene, from whom he *cast out* seven demons' (Mark 16:9)! Here, of course, is the language of 'casting out', 'casting down', and even sometimes 'casting into', an additional adumbration. Wherever the phraseology occurs, its basic relationship to the 'nets' Belial or Balaam 'cast before Israel' in the Damascus Document or Revelation and to the deaths of both the Righteous Teacher in the Dead Sea Scrolls and James in early Church sources, should always be appreciated.

The variations on this '*ballo*'/'casting' theme are so widespread and insistent in the Gospels that these, in effect, begin to resemble divertimentos or excurses on this word. One particularly humorous example in Mark has to do with the Temple Treasury again – and, of course, by implication, its pollution. It is Jesus' Parable about 'the Poor widow's two mites' (Mk 12:41–44 and Lk 21:1–4).

In Mark, the 'Poor widow' – 'Poor' terminology again – 'casts into' the Treasury what appear to be her last 'two mites'. Here, the allusion, 'casting into' (*ebalen*), occurs *five times in just four lines*. The widow's contribution is not only favorably contrasted with what 'the Many' – the name, as we have seen, for the rank and file at Qumran – 'cast in' (*eballon*), but, significantly, also what 'the Rich cast in', a major theme of both the attack on the Establishment in the Letter of James and the parallel 'Three Nets of Belial' critique in the Damascus Document.

It should also be immediately apparent that this episode is but a further variation on Matthew's story of Judas *Iscariot* 'casting the thirty pieces of silver' he received for betraying Jesus 'into the Temple Treasury' (Mt 27:3–10) – itself an adumbration of the Talmudic story about Jesus' recommendation, attributed to the James-like 'Jacob of Kfar Sechania' in the *Talmud*, to use not 'the *Poor* widow's', but *the Rich prostitute*'s gifts to the Temple Treasury to build a latrine for the High Priest and the whole 'Rechabite'/'Potter'/'blood' and 'poverty' circle of motifs encountered in our discussion of this.

Also part of 'these things', referred to in Mark before the appearance to 'the two as they walked along the Way', are the experiences of 'Mary the mother of James and Salome' – obviously meant to be the mother of Jesus – who with Mary Magdalene witnesses the crucifixion and enters the empty tomb (Mk 15:40–16:8). Matthew simply calls her 'the other Mary', though five lines earlier, as a witness to the Crucifixion, he referred to her as 'Mary the mother of James and Joses and the mother of the sons of Zebedee' (Mt 27:56–61). For Luke, Mary is simply and, perhaps most tellingly, '*Mary the mother of James*' (24:10).

In Luke and Matthew, these women are not, strictly speaking, recipients of a post-resurrection appearance by Jesus at all. Rather they are only the *witnesses to the empty tomb* and the *bearers of the rumor of his resurrection*. References to any unnamed or partially named 'two' in these accounts should also always be remarked; for instance in Luke, the two unnamed 'men in brilliant white clothing', who suddenly 'stood beside' Mary Magdalene, Joanna, and Mary *the mother of James* in the empty tomb (24:4 – note the allusion to 'standing' again here, as we will also encounter it repeatedly in John). In Matthew and Mark the two become one – in Matthew, an 'Angel of the Lord'; in Mark, 'a young man'.

There are also the 'two', chosen at the beginning of Acts 'to become a *witness of his resurrection*' to fill Judas *Iscariot*'s 'Office' – 'from which he fell away' – the first supposedly called Barsabas, also 'surnamed Justus' (Acts 1:21–26 – one should keep an eye, too, on the use of the word 'witness' here). We have repeatedly encountered another of these Barsabases, but there he was 'Judas Barsabas'. One should also always remark, as in all these Gospel portrayals, the castigation of these central figures for their lack of 'Belief' or of the key Pauline requirement of 'Faith'.

In Matthew and Mark, the appearance of the single individual sitting in the tomb or on a rock outside it – as in the scene of Jesus' Transfiguration before the Central Three 'on the mountain' – 'was as *lightning* and his clothing was *white as snow*' (Mt 28:3). In Matthew's description of Jesus' Transfiguration before Moses and Elijah, it was Jesus' 'face, which *shone as the sun* and his clothing was *white as the light* (17:2). We have already connected these kinds of miraculous 'whitening' notices to the description in *Recognitions* of 'the tombs of the two brothers that *whitened of themselves* every year' following the escape of James' Community to Jericho.

One should remark the tell-tale number 'two' again in this seemingly innocuous sidelight, when the Community visits these tombs outside Jericho and thus escaped Paul pursuing Peter as far as Damascus. In *Recognitions*, the '*tombs of the two brothers whitened of themselves every year*', paralleling Luke's version of the empty tomb, which had, it will be recalled, the three women and 'some (others)' surprised by the appearance in the tomb of '*two men standing beside them in brilliantly shining clothing*' (Luke 23:1–4).

To carry this line of thinking a little further, in the very next sentence in *Recognitions*, where James sends out Peter on his first missionary journey to confront Simon in Caesarea (Ps. *Rec.* 1.71), Simon is identified as 'a *Samaritan* magician' – the accuracy of the Pseudoclementine description of Simon's geographical origins, as compared to the patent imprecision of Acts should always be remarked – who, to repeat: '*led Many* of our people *astray* (the typical language applied to the adversary at Qumran, who 'rejected the Law', and false teachers generally), by asserting that he was 'the Standing One', that is in other words, 'the Christ' and 'the Great Power of the High God', which is superior to the Creator of the world' (Ps. Rec. 1.72).

Not only do we have in these lines from the *Recognitions* an almost perfect description of the relationship of the 'Primal Adam' ideology to 'the Christ', but here the word 'standing' is applied in an ideological manner to Jesus and not simply as a narrative detail as in the Gospels.[24] That this series of allusions to 'whitening', the 'two', and 'the Standing One' in the Pseudoclementine *Recognitions* relates intrinsically and not just accidentally to these *empty tomb* scenarios in the Gospels should be growing more and more apparent.

At this point in Mark, for instance, it is the 'young man, *sitting on the right side clothed with a white robe*' (16:5) – in Matthew 28:2–3, it was 'an Angel of the Lord come down from Heaven', whose '*face was as lightning and his clothing white as snow*', *sitting on a stone*. Earlier in Mark on the mountain when Jesus transfigured himself, Jesus' '*clothes became brilliant, exceedingly white as snow, such as no fuller on earth would be able to whiten*' (9:3).

We have already seen this last echoed in the language of the 'fuller' beating out 'the Just One's' brains with 'the club that he used to beat out clothes' in parallel early Church accounts based on second-century sources, such as Clement and Hegesippus, of James' demise. But not only was the 'fuller' language from these early accounts of the death of James present in this description in Mark of Jesus' clothes on the Mount of his Transfiguration, but incredibly, so too, as we also saw, was this 'whitening' language from the Pseudoclementine description of James' Community's escape outside Jericho to view the tombs of the *two brothers* after the attack on James by Paul!

Once again, however hard at first to conceptualize, in our view this *proves* that the Gospel accounts are *later* than either of these, or at least the sources upon which they are based. The Gospels are certainly every bit as and even more fantastic. For its part, Acts 1:10, in its account of Jesus' Ascension forty days after his resurrection, now has the 'two men standing *beside them* in white clothes' – 'them' being now 'the Apostles'. Again there is the reprise of the 'standing' motif here – not to mention the number 'two' – followed in the very next line by the reference to the Apostles, now addressed as 'Men! Galileans!', also described as 'standing' once again and 'looking up at the Heavens' watching him go.

The picture of these 'two men' in white clothes in Acts repeats Luke's earlier picture of the 'two men standing *beside them*' – the 'them' now being the women and the ubiquitous 'some' again – and Gospel pictures generally of the 'resplendent white clothing' of these individuals, as it does the earlier words used in the Synoptics to describe Jesus' clothing, 'effulgent, exceedingly white as snow', on the mountain of his Transfiguration (Mk 9:3 and pars.).

For its part, the Gospel of John repeats Luke's scenario of 'two men' in 'star-like' clothing in the empty tomb, but these, incorporating a part of the motif in Matthew, are now simply 'two Angels in white'. Here, only Mary Magdalene sees them, no others, and this not till *after she* returns to the tomb a *second time* (Jn 20:12). Earlier in John, it was *she alone* who originally 'came to the tomb, while it was still dark and saw the stone taken away', but without any explanation of by whom or why (Jn 20:1).

At first she does not appear to enter the tomb. Rather she runs then to tell 'the Disciple Jesus loved' and Peter, who themselves run back and enter the tomb – first Peter, then the Disciple Jesus loved (Jn 20:2–6). For John, it is they who enter the tomb, not Mary Magdalene, Mary *the mother of James* and Joanna as in Luke. But instead of seeing the one or two men or Angels in the 'white' and 'brilliantly shining clothes standing there', as in Luke and the others, Peter and the Disciple Jesus loved only see 'the linen clothes lying there' with a 'napkin that had been about his head *neatly folded to one side*' (Jn 20:5–8)!

A separate episode then ensues in John after Peter and the Beloved Disciple go off, where Jesus then *actually* appears 'standing' behind Mary Magdalene alone (Jn 20:14), also reflected in the added material in Mark above. For John, this involves Mary Magdalene 'peeking into the tomb' *a second time* after Peter and the Beloved Disciple 'went on their way home again' (Jn 20:10–11). Several lines before, it had been 'the Disciple Jesus loved' who 'peeked' into the tomb, first seeing 'the *linen clothes lying there*, yet not going in' till Peter did (Jn 20:5).

It is during this second visit to the empty tomb in John, where it is now Mary Magdalene '*standing* at the tomb weeping outside' (20:11), that she sees 'the two Angels in white' – now 'sitting one at the head and one at the feet of where the body of Jesus was laid' (20:12) – replicating the 'two men *standing* beside them in brilliant white clothes' that the three women had seen in their first visit to the empty tomb in Luke. It is at this moment, 'turning around, she saw Jesus *standing there*, but she did not know it was Jesus' (Jn 20:14). Here, of course, it is Mary Magdalene seeing Jesus as 'the Standing One'. No wonder she could not recognize him!

This point about 'not recognizing' Jesus is common to several of these accounts as we have explained, usually accompanied by the 'standing' language. This is always the case in John. Here, however, it is Jesus himself who is described as 'standing' before her when she turned around, not the 'two men in brilliant white clothes', twice described earlier in Luke and in Acts as 'standing beside them'. A few lines earlier, it will be recalled, it was Mary herself. All of these allusions, even in the orthodox Gospels as we have them, should be seen as reflections of the Ebionite/Sabaean 'Standing One' ideology *par excellence.*

What the transmission mechanism could have been for combining these various concepts into a single narrative or narratives with slightly altered or trivialized signification is impossible to say. What is clear is that there were *earlier* traditions, which not only preceded the Gospels, as we now have them, but read *quite differently* – perhaps even like those underlying the parallel materials about 'tomb', 'servants', 'clothing', and 'whitening' in the First Book of the Pseudoclementine *Recognitions* or the tradition about the first appearance to James preserved in Jerome's 'Gospel according to the Hebrews'.

The note about the 'linen clothes' in the Gospel of John – now meant to be the grave clothes of Jesus – is also very important. Now those who see 'the linen clothes lying there' in John are not the two Marys and Luke's Joanna, or even Peter alone as in Luke, but now, first Peter and then 'the Disciple Jesus loved' (Jn 20:5–7). Even more to the point – and perhaps more accurately – they are *the 'clothes' Jesus is pictured as giving to 'the Servant of the (High) Priest'* in Jerome's Gospel of the Hebrews.

If 'the Disciple Jesus loved' in John, who with Peter first sees these 'linen clothes lying' there, has any connection with James, then here again we have additional material bearing on post-resurrection appearances possibly involving family members of Jesus. These also must be seen as not unconnected with the theme of 'linen clothes' – bathing or otherwise – repeatedly encountered in descriptions about 'Essene'/'Sabaean' ritual bathing practices. These are the several permutations of the circle of materials we are dealing with here.

The theme of these 'linen clothes' also reappears in the note about 'the clothes the witnesses laid at' Paul's feet in Acts' account of the Jewish mob stoning Stephen. But here the material probably owes as much to the stoning of James in all early Church sources and Josephus, 'the clothes' – again probably 'white linen' – of course, having been *James'* clothes which, as in all such stonings, were removed, *not the witnesses'*! In fact, here too, the stoning of James and the special 'linen clothes' he wore may have been the original core giving rise to these other variations.

Preceding his account of a *first* appearance to what appear to be members of Jesus' family on the Emmaus Road outside Jerusalem, Luke also refers to these 'linen clothes lying by themselves'. This small addendum, not paralleled at all in Matthew and Mark, has Peter 'running to the tomb' *alone* – not as in John *with* 'the Disciple Jesus loved' – after the report by the three women 'to the Eleven and all the rest' (repeated in the next line as 'to the Apostles' – Lk 24:9–10), which they took to be 'idle talk'. Then Peter, 'having risen up', ran to the tomb, because the other Apostles 'didn't believe them' (the 'not believing' theme in Mk 16:11 again). Now he, not Mary Magdalene, 'stoops down and seeing the *linen clothes lying alone*, went home wondering at what had happened' (Lk 24:11–12).

There is a certain parallel in the way Peter is the witness to these things, here, to the way Epiphanius in his version of Hegesippus has Simeon bar Cleophas as 'the witness' to the stoning of James. For his part, Eusebius, it will be recalled, rather describes this 'witness' as 'one of the Priests of the sons of Rechab, a son of the Rechabites spoken of by the Prophet Jeremiah'. Both allude to this in conjunction with the language of 'casting down' and the 'laundryman' and his 'club' allusion, we have been delineating above. For Eusebius, this is 'a club he used to beat out clothes'. For Jerome, describing this in slightly different language but nevertheless betraying the same source, 'such a club as laundrymen use to beat out clothes'.[25]

Acts' version also has Stephen being 'cast out of the city'. We have already identified this as a substitution for Paul's attack on James in the Pseudoclementine *Recognitions*, where not only the language of 'casting' occurs – now 'casting down' – but also that of 'whitening'. At this point in Acts, 'the *witnesses lay their clothes* (completely incomprehensibly) *at the feet of a young man* named Saul', thus combining our 'witness', 'clothes', and 'feet' themes, but now adding a new one, that of the 'young man' (Acts 7:58).

However convoluted it may seem, in Mark this 'young man' is now actually *in* the empty tomb, parallel to the 'two men' – plural in Luke – and the Angel, whose 'clothing was white as snow', 'sitting on' the stone in Matthew. Mark rather now describes him as '*sitting on* the right side, *clothed in a white robe*' (16:5). It is a not incurious coincidence that two lines before this reference to Saul as 'a young man' and Stephen being 'cast out of the city', Acts portrays Stephen as 'full of the Holy Spirit' and, like the witnesses to Jesus' Ascension earlier, 'looking into Heaven' and seeing 'Jesus s*tanding at the right hand* of God'.

Repeating this in the next line, but substituting the usage 'the Son of Man' for Jesus, Acts now has Stephen 'crying out' how he 'saw the Heavens opened and *the Son of Man* standing at the right hand of God' (7:55–56), a variation on what James is said to have proclaimed in the Temple in the early Church accounts before he 'was cast down' – even including the repetition of the words 'crying out', now attributed to Stephen.

Not only do we have here basically the language Mark combines to produce his version of the 'young man *sitting on the right*' *side* in the empty tomb (the 'clothing white as snow' in these pictures probably coming from Daniel 7:9's picture of 'the Ancient of Days', also evoked in these visions); but also that of our Primal Adam/Standing One ideology again, now identified directly with Jesus. It should not be forgotten, too, that this language, 'the Son of Man *sitting on the right hand of Power* and coming on the clouds of Heaven', actually appears in Matthew 26:64 and Mark 14:62.

Our purpose in presenting the multiple variations on these repeating historical motifs is to demonstrate the fertile manner in which the Gospel artificers felt free to improvise or enlarge on their themes. These also provide vivid illustration of the endlessly creative manner with which they allowed their imaginations to rove across the real or historical events before them, creating a host of scriptural parodies.

Luke's Picture of the First Appearance to James along the Way to Emmaus

Again, it should be emphasized that Luke's account of what occurred in the empty tomb contains no mention of an actual physical appearance to Mary Magdalene, Mary *the mother of James*, or Joanna. The women only see the 'two men *standing* beside them in effulgent astral-like clothing'. Nor one to Peter, as per the implication of Paul's testimony in 1 Corinthians 15:5 – which we have already designated as an orthodox interpolation – who in Luke and John sees only 'the linen clothes lying by themselves'. Instead, Jesus appeared to 'two of them' – presumably either 'Apostles' or 'Disciples' – who 'were going the same day to a village called Emmaus, sixty furlongs (about seven and a half miles) from Jerusalem' (Luke 24:13).

It is interesting that the only mention of Emmaus in Josephus comes in the *Jewish War* following *the fall of the Temple*. Here, in the same breath that he tells us that the two drachmas' tax formerly paid by Jews to the Temple – the 'two mites' paid by the Poor widow in Gospel parody in Mark and Luke! – were *now to be paid directly to Rome* and that Titus was leasing *out the whole country*, Josephus tells us that Emmaus was only 'thirty furlongs from Jerusalem', not the 'sixty' as here in Acts. What is more, it was now to be settled by *eight hundred Roman army veterans at Titus' express order*.[26]

One should immediately remark the parallel represented by this appearance 'in the Way' – as the two put it to each other when discussing 'these things' afterwards, their 'heart burning within' them (Lk 24:32) – to presumable family members of Jesus and an appearance 'in the Way' that Paul was supposed to have experienced as he chased those 'of the Way' to Damascus, albeit in a somewhat more visionary (literally, 'apocalyptic') manner (Acts 9:2–8). In Acts' picture of Ananias going to meet Paul in Damascus and 'laying hands on him', Ananias too for some reason – *not* Paul – announces that Jesus appeared to Paul 'in the Way in which' he came (Acts 9:17). Even here, there appears to be just a touch of parody of Jesus' words directly appointing James as successor, 'in the place where you are to go', in the Gospel of Thomas.

When Barnabas brings Paul to Jerusalem, he confirms once again how Paul 'saw the Lord in the Way' (Acts 9:27), which are, of course, the very words the two use here in Luke. In this sense, these are competitive, if antithetical, encounters with or visions of 'the Risen Christ'. In Luke's encounter, the two – one identified as 'Cleopas' – are conversing with each other along the way to Emmaus when 'Jesus draws near'; in Acts, Paul 'draws near to Damascus when suddenly a light from Heaven shone round about him' (9:3).

Again as is usual in these post-resurrection manifestations – in the Gospel of John and even Luke, usually associated with Jesus '*standing in their midst*' – they are unable to recognize him (Lk 24:15–18). This is a very important aspect of these encounters, usually signaling his otherworldly substantiality, but also his true nature as 'the Standing One' or 'Primal Adam'. The two then tell him all 'the things that had happened' (the language Mark later absorbs into his account), including the charge that 'the Chief Priests and our Rulers *delivered him up* to the death penalty and *crucified him*' (24:20).

However tendentious the author's intent in stating this last – the emphasis being on the word 'our' – it is still altogether more accurate than the repeated description of 'Judas *Iscariot*', the archetypical 'Zealot' or '*Sicarios*' of the kind of *Judas the Galilean* or *Judas Maccabee*, as 'delivering him up', or, for that matter, the equally misleading and malicious picture of the People crying out for Jesus' 'blood' and Pontius Pilate 'delivering Jesus up *to their will*' (Lk 23:24 and Matthew).

This formulation, 'their will', will reappear in the general 'delivered them up' formulae in Hebrew in the picture of the salvationary history of Israel in the Damascus Document. In it, 'delivering them up' is what God repeatedly did to 'those who walked in the *stubbornness of their heart*, deserting the Covenant', 'each choosing *his own will*' or 'doing what was right *in his own eyes*'. It is usually combined with the imagery of God's 'Visitation of the land' and, of course, 'delivering up to the sword' – the real origin of the repeated use of such words like 'delivering up' and, for that matter, giving him over 'to their will'.

Here too, along the way to Emmaus, Jesus castigates the two for their lack of 'belief' and elucidates for them the scriptural meaning of his suffering and death (Lk 24:25). The same is true to some extent in the Gospel of the Hebrews of his lecturing James. But the words Jesus is pictured here as using, 'slow of heart to believe', are also another variation of the words used in the above passages in the Damascus Document about 'delivering up His people' or 'cutting off their males in the wilderness' – 'stubbornness of their heart'. At Qumran, this is almost always used in regard to 'the Liar' and implies 'rejecting', 'not doing', or 'breaking' the Law, essentially the reverse of the more Pauline signification here of 'not believing'.

Jesus then goes on to 'expound to them the things about himself in all the Scriptures', this a seeming follow-up to what Paul says he received 'according to the Scriptures' prior to his version of post-resurrection appearances in 1 Corinthians 15:5–6. The Righteous Teacher, too, is described as 'interpreting all the words of His Servants the Prophets', God having put this 'Intelligence in his heart' and 'revealed to him all the Mysteries of the words of His Servants the Prophets'. Notice the parallel too in these kinds of notices to the language Hegesippus uses in his account of the death of James, whose cognomens, 'the Righteous One' and 'Protection of the People', 'the Prophets' were said to have 'declared concerning him'.[27]

'Drawing near to the village where *they were going*', Jesus now 'reclined with them'. 'Taking the bread, he blessed it, and breaking it, he gave (it) to them' (Lk 24:28–30). This is almost verbatim the language of the Gospel of the Hebrews' account of the *first appearance to James* – not to mention aspects of other accounts involving Jesus breaking bread and eating with his principal Apostles or Disciples in Luke again and in John. This is also the picture one gets in Paul in 1 Corinthians 11:23–27 about how the Lord Jesus 'taking the bread, and having given thanks, broke it and said, "Take and eat!"', as it is in the Gospel 'Last Supper' accounts as they have come down to us, in particular, echoing this last almost verbatim – the only difference being that in this appearance in Luke, as in the Gospel of the Hebrews, there is nothing about 'Communion with the blood of Christ' or 'the New Covenant in my blood'.

To put this in a somewhat different way, these two accounts – that of a *first appearance to at least one member of Jesus' family*, his uncle Cleopas, along the way to Emmaus and that embodying a *first appearance to James* after 'the Lord had given his linen clothes to the Servant of the (High) Priest' in the Gospel of the Hebrews – are exactly the same. The only difference is that Luke presents him breaking the bread and 'giving it to them' (Cleopas and the other), whereas in the Gospel of the Hebrews, Jesus 'breaks it and gives it *to James the Just*'.

It would be possible to conclude at this point that the unnamed other along with Cleopas in this account of a first appearance in Luke, to whom Jesus appears and with whom he breaks bread 'along the Way', erased for one reason or another or eliminated in the redaction process, is none other than *James the Just, the brother of Jesus*, himself, conveniently rubbed out in the Lukan redaction.

So here too – even in Luke's presentation then – we have the unmistakable traces, however obliterated, of the lost Palestinian tradition of *a first appearance to James* – confirmed for us by Paul in 1 Corinthians 15:7, when read in its uninterpolated form, which can now be read simply:

> For I delivered to you what in the first place I also received: that ... (first) he appeared to James, then to all the Apostles and last of all he appeared also to me, as if to an abortion. For I am the least of the Apostles, who am not fit to be called an Apostle, because I persecuted *the Assembly of God.*

Of course, this is also supported by all sectarian traditions featuring James, as, for instance, that at Nag Hammadi. There, James is clearly 'the Beloved Disciple' and Jesus, who 'sits down on a stone' with him (like the Angel in Mt 28:2), actually kisses him on the mouth, as we saw.[28] At this point the account in the Gospel of Luke becomes rather confused, since now that 'they recognize him', Jesus vanishes (Luke 24:31)!

Returning to Jerusalem, these two then 'relate the things in the Way' to the Eleven and those 'assembled' with them and how 'he was (made) known to them in the breaking of the bread' (24:35). Again, the difference is that in the Gospel of the Hebrews, it is James to whom 'these things' are made known, and it is he who learns, after Jesus breaks the bread and gives it to him, that 'the Son of Man is risen from among those *that sleep*'.

What Jesus says to James, 'My brother, eat your bread, for the Son of Man is risen from among those that sleep', finds an echo in Luke after the report of Mary Magdalene, Joanna, and Mary *the mother of James* about the empty tomb, preceding this episode of Peter, 'having risen up', running to the tomb only to find 'the linen clothes lying alone'.

We have also already remarked how this allusion to Jesus 'giving his *grave clothes* to the Servant of the (High) Priest' is refracted in Acts' account of the stoning of Stephen. Its presence here in the Gospel of the Hebrews not only inextricably links this account to those in John and Luke of the linen clothes 'lying by themselves' or 'piled neatly to one side' in the empty tomb – but to all these various accounts involving *linen clothing* of one kind or another, indirectly implying that Jesus too wore such garb.

There is another parallel in this testimony in the Gospel of the Hebrews, which once again bears on the subject of 'not *eating or drinking*' and Christ 'being raised *the third day* according to the Scriptures' in 1 Corinthians 15:4. That is the point about 'James *swearing not to eat bread* from that hour in which he had *drunk the Cup of the Lord* (nothing here about any blood) until he should see him risen from among those that sleep' and Acts' competitive picture of Paul's vision 'along the Way' to Damascus. One should also keep in mind with regard to the former the Rabbinic attempts after the fall of the Temple to discourage those taking like-minded oaths 'not to eat or drink' either mourning for Zion or till they should see the Temple rebuilt.[29]

In Acts, after 'hearing the voice but seeing no one', Paul's travelling companions bring him to Damascus. Then Paul's eyes were 'opened', but it is now *he* who 'sees no one' (basically, the inability to recognize Jesus again, but also note the repetition of the word 'see') and 'he was *three days there not seeing* and *did not eat or drink*'. The language overlaps with what amounts, in effect, to James' swearing *not to eat or drink* for three days – not to mention some of these other groups and with much more historical veracity – should be clear.

For Paul in 1 Corinthians 11:25–27, it will be recalled, 'the Cup of blessing, which we bless, is Communion with the blood of Christ' or 'the Cup of the New Covenant in (his) blood'; and the bread, 'Communion with the body of Christ'. In the Gospel of the Hebrews, this 'Cup' is simply 'the Cup of the Lord', which Paul also refers to in 10:21 and 11:27. But, as per his wont, Paul turns somewhat aggressive on this point, linking '*eating and drinking* the Cup of the Lord unworthily' to being 'guilty of the *body and blood of the Lord*' – notice the word 'Lord' here, as in the Gospel of the Hebrews, instead of the word 'Christ'.

He does the same two lines later, but in this instance he specifically defines 'eating and drinking unworthily', as '*not seeing through to the body of the Lord*' (11:29). For him, the person who does this then 'drinks Judgment unto himself'. Again, the implication of these two maledictions is that Paul is actually calling down the blood-libel accusation of being 'guilty of the blood' of Christ on his opponents, seemingly those within the Movement or 'Church' itself, even the very Leadership itself, including James, who do not interpret 'the Cup of the Lord' or 'see through to the body of the Lord' in the spiritualized manner he does. Again, note that repetition of the word 'seeing' occurs in all these accounts, even in the finale of the Damascus Document on 'seeing His *Yeshu'a*' or 'His Salvation'.

In the light of such an attitude, the blood libel in the Gospels against a whole people, most of whom actually opposed the very same rulers and foreign powers Jesus and his followers seem to have done, is not surprising. These died in the hundreds of thousands seemingly for the very same reasons, but Paul's belligerence in these passages – for example, as regards 'circumcision' – fairly takes one's breath away, the command 'to love one's enemies', except perhaps Romans, for him seemingly having long since gone by the boards.

This is the perspective one encounters at Qumran, as well, which also employs the imagery of 'the Cup of the Lord' Paul alludes to here and part of the language of James' last encounter with Jesus on earth – however curtailed the account of it we get in Jerome's fragment from the Gospel of the Hebrews. Notwithstanding, at Qumran, Habakkuk 2:16: 'the Cup of the right hand of the Lord', is very definitely a 'Cup of Vengeance' or 'the Cup of the Wrath of God' – again inverted from the general presentation of Paul and the Gospels. In the Habakkuk *Pesher*, for instance, it is directed against 'Covenant-Breakers' and backsliders generally – in particular, 'the Wicked Priest' described as not 'circumcising the foreskin of his heart' – not in support of those setting aside the Law, as it would appear to be in the Gospels and here in Paul.

As the Habakkuk *Pesher* expresses this, the Wicked Priest, who himself 'swallowed' 'God's Elect' – the Righteous Teacher and his followers, 'the *Ebionim*' or 'Poor' again – would himself be 'swallowed' or 'consumed' by 'the Cup of the Lord's Divine Vengeance', which 'he would drink to the dregs' or from which 'he would drink his fill'. As he tendered them this 'cup', so too would God tender him 'the Cup' of His Divine Wrath and 'he would be *paid the reward he paid the Poor*'.[30]

This symbolism, which is basically that of 'the Cup of wine' or 'the wine Cup of God's Fury', is omnipresent at Qumran, as it is in Revelation. In both, it is not 'the body and blood of Christ' being consumed in some symbolical or esoteric manner, but rather 'the wine of the Cup of the Wrath of God' consuming God's enemies. This, too, may be something of the implied meaning of this 'Cup of the Lord', which James drinks in this last encounter with Jesus here in the Gospel of the Hebrews.

The belligerence we have just seen, with regard to 'drinking Judgment to oneself' and 'guilt for the blood of the Lord' in Paul, is also refracted to a certain degree in the Habakkuk *Pesher*'s fulsome condemnation of 'the Spouter of Lying' – characterized, it will be remembered, as 'building a Worthless City on blood and erecting an Assembly (or 'Church') upon Lying'. This takes the form of expressing the wish that he would be 'subjected to the same Judgments of Fire, with which *he vilified and blasphemed the Elect of God*'.[31]

To return to the narrative in Luke: at this point either 'the Eleven and those assembled with them' or 'they' say, '*the Lord has indeed risen and appeared to Simon*' (24:34), and 'he was known to them in the breaking of the bread' (24:35). Here the text does not allow us to know whether 'the Jerusalem Assembly' – this implied by those 'assembled with them' – is doing the speaking or Cleopas and the unnamed other Disciple. Even more to the point, it is not even clear whether the reference is to 'Simon Peter' here or to some other 'Simon' – possibly even a 'Simeon'. Origen is so sure that the second unnamed person is 'Simon' that he even quotes this passage from Luke to this effect, but, even he does not tell us which 'Simon' this might be – Simeon bar Cleophas or Simon Peter. Again the words spoken, however, are a variation of the words Jesus is portrayed as speaking to James in the Hebrew Gospel, 'Eat your bread, my brother, for the Son of Man has indeed risen from among those that sleep.'

Of course, it has always been taken for granted in all orthodox circles without the slightest proof – the contrary as we have just seen – that the reference here in Luke to 'Simon', as the one to whom Jesus first appeared, is 'Simon Peter'. But at least in the logic of the narrative of Luke as we have just described it, it would make more sense if the reference here were to 'Simeon' or 'Simeon bar Cleophas'. At least, then, the garbled allusion to 'Cleopas' would be comprehensible.

The problem is that, as in the instance of the orthodox part of Paul's presentation of an appearance to 'Cephas', there is no reported instance of an appearance to Peter alone at all, to say nothing of 'the Twelve', not even in the Lukan episode preceding this of Peter running back to the empty tomb but seeing 'only the linen clothes'.

Even this appearance in Luke to 'the Eleven and those assembled with them' – not 'to the Twelve' – when Jesus himself suddenly 'stands in their midst', does not occur until after 'the two' report his appearance to them on the Emmaus Road and the Community praising 'the Lord' for his having 'appeared to Simon'.

Therefore, a way out of the conundrum is to look at the report that follows the appearance to the two on the Road to Emmaus, of an 'appearance to Simon', in a different way. If we take the reference to 'Simon' rather to refer to the sighting which has just occurred 'in the Way' to 'Cleopas' and another, then this 'Cleopas' – certainly meant to represent Jesus' 'uncle' but, as usual, not so stated in Luke – can with even more sense be seen as the son of this 'uncle', 'Simeon *bar Cleophas*', Jesus' 'cousin' and second successor in Palestine, and, according to Epiphanius, *the witness to the stoning of James.*

The second companion then, the unnamed other, who with 'Cleopas' *sits down and breaks bread with Jesus*, and then either *recognizes him* or *is recognized by him*, would or could be James, his 'cousin' and neatly rubbed out here in Luke. At the very least, it must be acknowledged that it is a *first appearance to family members.* Paul himself attests James was the recipient of a post-resurrection appearance by Jesus – perhaps even the *first to whom Jesus appeared.* Not only is such an appearance to James the Just also pictured here in Jerome's almost word-for-word copy of this appearance to 'the two along the Way' in this tiny fragment from the Gospel of the Hebrews; this episode would then, in effect, comprise the residue of *the native Palestinian appointment tradition*, confirming Jesus' two family members as his real successors in Palestine – not the clearly illusory overseas appointment episodes we get in the Gospels as we have them.

This is how we would interpret this curious *non sequitur* in the report of 'the two' to 'the assembled Eleven' in Jerusalem about an appearance to 'Simon' and the whole episode about Jesus' appearance to 'the two' – one of whom definitely his relation – 'along the Way' to Emmaus that precedes this in the Gospel of Luke. Interpreting these notices in this manner and linking them to the report in the Gospel of the Hebrews of a *first appearance to James* allows us, at least, to *begin* to approach convergence regarding many of these interlocking themes and the reality behind some of these very real Palestinian traditions.

Chapter 22
Jesus' Brothers as Apostles

Cleopas, Cephas, and Clopas the Husband of Mary's Sister Mary

Who then is this mysterious 'Cleopas' who appears without introduction in the crucial Emmaus-road sighting episode in Luke? Not only do we have in Jesus' appearance to two seeming unknowns in the environs of Jerusalem the wherewithal to attach a tradition of this kind to the person of James – thus, bearing out the second part of Paul's 1 Corinthians 15:6–7 enumeration of Jesus' post-resurrection appearances: 'he appeared to James, then to all the Apostles, and last of all, he also appeared to me' – but also, even perhaps the wherewithal to attach it to the 'Cephas' who appears in the first part.

Admittedly, the appearances 'to the Twelve' and the 'over five hundred *brothers* at the same time' cannot be borne out. This is to say nothing of the contradiction represented by the mention of the two separate and successive appearances to the Apostles – the first, 'then to the Twelve', and the second, 'then to all the Apostles'.

There is a reference to this 'Clopas' (*thus*) in John – not in John's version of the post-resurrection appearances, but in his presentation of the witnesses to Jesus' crucifixion preceding these (Jn 19:25). For John all these are called 'Mary': 'his mother, and his mother's sister, Mary the wife of Clopas, and Mary Magdalene', so instead of one Mary, we now have three! Aside from this ephemeral 'Mary Magdalene' – out of whom Jesus cast 'seven demons' – probably another of these fictional overwrites over something – one can imagine the contortions indulged in by theologians and apologists over the millennia to reconcile Mary having as her sister *another Mary* – and this, even more germane, the wife of that Clopas clearly meant to be the same individual as that 'Cleopas' or 'Cleophas' again!

For some, 'Mary *the wife of Clopas*' is Mary's half-sister; for Jerome, *her niece*. But there is really no way out of the conundrum presented by such evasions. Mary patently *did not* have a 'sister Mary'. There is a difference between historical truth and literature. The Gospels, like the Pseudoclementines, are *literature*. There may be a kernel of truth lurking here and there like a pebble beneath the surface of a stream, which it is the task of the historian to discover and decipher.

For a start, let us reiterate that the initial stories about the brothers of Jesus in the Gospels show no embarrassment whatsoever about the reality of the 'brother' relationship, that is, whatever and whoever Jesus was *he had brothers*. That he also had a mother should be self-evident. He also seems to have had a sister or sisters. The Gospel of John, for instance, after the Prologue and the choosing of three of his Disciples, speaks about how 'his mother and his brothers' joined him along with other Disciples at Capernaum very early in his Galilean career (2:12).

Matthew and Mark list Jesus' brothers quite straightforwardly as 'James and Joses and Simon and Judas' (13:55–56 and 6:3–5). The same goes for Jesus' mother Mary and 'his sisters', one of whom Mark identifies in his version of the witnesses to the Crucifixion as 'Salome' (15:40). At the Crucifixion, she is explicitly identified as the sister of 'James the Less and Joses'; at the empty tomb, simply '(the sister) of James' (16:1). In this 'Less' sobriquet, as already observed, one can see the pejoration at work.

In Matthew 13:55, for instance, when Jesus' mother, brothers and sisters are mentioned at the conclusion of the Parables about 'the Tares' and 'the Dragnet' unique to it, Jesus' father is straightforwardly identified as 'the carpenter' – 'is this not the *son of the carpenter*?' In Mark, the same statement turns into: 'is not this *the carpenter the son of Mary*?' (Mk 6:2), so that Jesus now becomes the proverbial 'Galilean' *carpenter* just as his principal Apostles became 'Galilean' *fishermen.* Luke and John wisely simplify this into 'Joseph's son' (Lk 4:22). Interestingly, Mark's version already shows traces of doctrinal deformation and this has gone, via St Augustine, directly into the Koran, where Jesus is always designated as 'the Messiah *son of Mary*' and nothing else.[1]

In John, the depiction of Jesus as 'the son of Joseph' also occurs by the Sea of Galilee – called now, quite incisively, 'of Tiberias' – and even more importantly, introduces his version of Jesus calling himself 'the living bread, which came from Heaven', and the concomitant conclusion, 'he *who eats my flesh and drinks my blood* shall have Eternal life' (Jn 6:42–58). Even more to the point, in John, when Jesus makes the statement 'unless you have eaten the flesh of the Son of Man and drunk his blood, you shall not have life in yourselves' (6:53), this ends with the extremely prescient: 'from that time Many of his Disciples fell back and did not walk with him any more' (6:66).

Jesus is also pictured in this extremely pregnant passage here in John as wondering aloud whether 'the Twelve' would 'turn aside as well'. It is here that Simon Peter is quoted as applying the pivotal identification of Jesus, 'You are the Christ, the Son of the Living God' (John 6:67–69), also applied to him by the voice from the cloud 'on the mountain' at his Transfiguration or, even more significantly, by Peter just preceding this in all the Synoptics (Mt 16:16–17:5 and pars.).

In John, Jesus is described as 'knowing from the beginning who they were *who did not believe and who would deliver him up*' (6:64). In the Synoptics, all these enumerations are accompanied by attacks on Jesus' family and countrymen, aimed in the typical Pauline manner at distinguishing Jesus from both. These generally circulate about the formula, 'A Prophet is not without honor, except in his own country and in his own house' (Lk 4:25 and pars.). In case we didn't get the polemical thrust of its meaning, Mark adds: 'and *among his own kin*' (6:4). These are paralleled, as well, in the episodes preceding these, when Jesus or his Disciples are 'casting out demons' and his mother and brothers come to see him and are described as '*standing outside*' *calling to him* (Mt 12:46–50 and Mk 3:31–35).

In Matthew 12:24–28 (paralleled in Mk 3:22–30), preceding this episode, this 'standing' language we have just highlighted in relation to it occurs *two* more times in two verses in the context of five more allusions in five verses to another weird circumlocution, 'Beelzebul Prince of the demons', 'casting out the demons' (*ekballei* again). This leads directly into the episode, basically disparaging Jesus' 'mother and his brothers', who were, as Luke puts it, 'unable to get to him *because of the crowd*' (Lk 8:19–21) – 'the crowd', patently symbolizing Paul's new Gentile Christian converts in the retrospective polemic this kind of invective represents.

When Jesus is told that his mother and brothers 'are standing outside', he responds in good Pauline style: 'Who is my mother and who are my brothers?' (Mt 12:48), this obviously being before the Mary cult gathered momentum in the second and third centuries. In all the Synoptics, Jesus is then pictured as adding, gesturing towards his Disciples, 'Behold *my mother and my brothers*, for whoever shall *do* the will of God *is my brother and sister and mother*' (Mk 3:35). The purpose of all this sectarian repartee is to divorce Jesus from his family – and by extension his own people – and attach him to all the people of the world.

The Jamesian emphasis on 'doing' in these parallels is interesting too. Just so that we should make no mistake about its more cosmopolitan aspects and that the doctrine of Jesus as 'Son of God' should be attached to whatever is meant by this word 'doing', Matthew formulates the proposition as 'whosoever shall *do the will of my Father who is in Heaven*, he is my brother and sister and mother' (12:50). Luke, pointing to the crowd, makes the Jamesian thrust of all this even clearer: 'My mother and my brothers are these which *hear* the word of God, and *do it*' (Lk 8:21).

It is also interesting that the context in the Synoptics here is one of 'doing mighty works and wonders', normally presented as including *raisings*, *healings*, *casting out demons*, and the like. In the War Scroll from Qumran, however, where these same 'mighty works and wonders' of God are referred to, these are the battles God has fought and the wonders He has done on behalf of his people as, for instance, overthrowing the chariots of the army of Pharaoh in the Red Sea and the like.[5] One is not making any value judgments here, as *healings*, *exorcisms*, *raisings*, and the like might be superior to military victories, depending on one's point of view, only showing how these terms were being used in Palestine in this period.

The Doctrine of the Perpetual Virginity of Mary (and James)

The embarrassment over the existence of Jesus' brothers, along with that about his paternity, develops later than these materials. For instance, in the Gospels we see little or no embarrassment over the matter of their actual *physical* relationship to Jesus – or to 'the Lord' as Paul would have it – only theological ones, in line with the aims and aspirations of the Pauline Mission to the Gentiles overseas, to downplay the perception of family members' proper doctrine – their 'Belief', as the Gospels succinctly term it – and the familial and national traditions upon which their status as successors was based.

But this is the case as well for attacks on Jesus' most intimate Apostles, particularly Peter, because of his role in the confrontation at Antioch – as Paul presents it in Galatians. These, like Jesus' family members and by extrapolation Jews generally, are described as 'weak in Faith' – 'weak' being a favorite aspersion Paul uses to attack his antagonists within the Movement who are supporting 'circumcision', 'the Law', and restrictive dietary practices and opposing 'table fellowship' with Gentiles, and those whose 'consciences are so weak', they eat only vegetables.

Paul, in 1 and 2 Corinthians, even goes so far in his histrionics as to attack these 'Hebrew' Archapostles as 'disguising themselves as Servants of Righteousness' – a term widespread too in the Scrolls. Not only are these 'Super Apostles' for him – like 'Judas the son of Simon *Iscariot*' in John 6:71 above – really 'Servants of the Devil' (also, 'the *Diabolos*'), he ends by proclaiming in one and the same breath, 'eat everything sold in the marketplace' and that grandiloquently, he 'will never eat meat again forever' so as not to 'cause his brother to stumble' or 'scandalize' him (1 Cor. 8:13 and 10:25).

Even at the end of the Second Century, Tertullian (*c.* 160–221 CE) is still assuming that 'the brothers of the Lord' are his true brothers and their mother is Mary, who generated them through normal conjugal intercourse.[2] It is Origen (185–254 CE), in the next century, who is the first really to gainsay this in line with the growing reverence being accorded Mary, citing a book he and his predecessor, Clement of Alexandria both saw. He does so, not surprisingly, in commenting on the passages from Mark 6 and Matthew 13 we just have been discussing above.

Origen calls this book '*The Book of James*' (but we have been referring to it as the 'Protevangelium of James') and states that though the Gospels imply his contemporaries considered Jesus to be *a man*, 'the son of Joseph and Mary', he 'was not a man, but something Divine'. Even more informative, he reveals the idea that 'the brothers of Jesus were the sons of Joseph by a former wife whom he married before Mary' was circulated by those 'who wish to preserve the honor of *Mary in virginity to the end*'.[3]

This idea of perpetual virginity – even after the birth of Jesus – was already circulating in two apocryphal works – one on the Old Testament, called the Ascension of Isaiah (11:9), and the other, as we have seen, called the Protevangelium of James. In the latter, which seems to have been written to glorify Mary and which was ascribed to James – hence its title, Joseph is an *elderly widower* (9.2)! The idea of such 'virginity' seems first to have been emphasized in the correspondence of Ignatius of Antioch at the end of the First Century.[4] Also Justin Martyr, in the middle of the second, was one of the first to accord Mary special prominence. He saw Mary as the good side of Eve, both of whom he considered virgins, giving rise to the idea that Mary brought life, but Eve, disobedience and death.

The idea of Mary's perpetual virginity also gained momentum with the growing vogue virginity was beginning to enjoy in ascetic circles, not to mention its possible tie-in with James' paradigmatic *lifelong virginity*. Still Jesus' rebukes in the Synoptics not only of Mary, but the 'brothers' and all the *Jewish* Apostles troubled early commentators. These grappled with the idea of Mary's sinfulness and, in particular, whether she – unlike her son – was subject to the Pauline concept of 'original sin'.[5] Many cited the words Luke attributes to Mary, 'all generations will henceforth count me blessed' (1:48), not to mention the very ambiguous prophecy – attributed to one Simeon in the next chapter – about a 'sword piercing her soul too' (Lk 2:35 – here the Qumran 'soul' and 'sword' language again).

This 'prophecy' is attributed to 'the Righteous and Pious Simeon' in Luke's infancy narrative, to whom 'the Holy Spirit' revealed that 'he would not see death until he had seen *the Christ* of the Lord' (Lk 2:25–26). Again these words echo the traditions about James' 'seeing the Lord' and, very possibly, his kinsman and successor, Simeon bar Cleophas, too.

Here in Luke, this is expressed in terms of 'seeing Your Salvation' (Lk 2:30), the very words used at the end of the exhortative section of the Damascus Document. Once again, just as this notice is accompanied in Luke by allusion to preparing for 'all Nations' a light 'to the Gentiles', the sense is completely the opposite of the concluding line of this section of the Damascus Document, which ends with the words: 'they will be victorious over all the Sons of the Earth ... and see His Salvation, because they took refuge in His Holy Name'.[6]

Epiphanius in the late 300s is still resisting this cult and holding on to the idea that Jesus was born by natural means, that is, that Mary's virginity had been interrupted at least by a natural birth, if not natural generation. Having said this, however, he completely accepts Origen's idea that 'James was Joseph's son by his first wife', whoever this wife may have been. Still for him, it was James and the rest of 'Joseph's sons who *revered virginity and followed the Nazirite life-style*' – the very important reversal of Mary's alleged status.[7]

It is Jerome, prescient as ever and often responding to the true implications of the data before us, who sets the pattern for the modern, doctrinaire or at least 'Catholic', approach to the 'brothers': that Jesus' brothers were not 'brothers' at all, but rather 'cousins'. He is, of course, taking off in this, without perhaps realizing it, from the fact that Cleophas was 'the brother of Joseph' and his son Simeon, therefore, the *cousin of Jesus*. However, it never seems to have dawned on him that this would make 'Simeon' the *brother of James* and, as we shall presently see below, *Jesus* as well!

Jerome arrives at this conclusion by a comparison of the Apostle lists and correctly appreciating that 'James the son of Alphaeus' (Mt 10:3 and pars.) – not to mention 'Judas (the brother) of James' (Lk 6:15–16) – had to be the son of that woman designated as Mary 'the sister of' Mary and 'the wife of Clopas' in John 19:15 ('Mary the mother of James and Joses and the mother of the two sons of Zebedee' in Mt 27:56, 'Mary the mother of James the Less and Joses and Salome' in Mk 15:40, and 'Mary the mother of James' in Lk 24:10).[13]

This would make 'Alphaeus' and 'Clopas' the same person, as they most certainly were, the mix-up here simply being the difference between a Greek letter *kappa* and an *alpha*.[9] Interestingly enough Levi, later identified as Matthew and depicted as 'sitting at the tax office' (Mt 9:9), is also designated as 'the son of Alphaeus' (Mk 2:14). This may provide the basis of Luke's later tie-in of 'Matthias' and the so-called 'Joseph Barsabas surnamed Justus' in the spurious election to replace Judas 'the *Iscariot*' (i.e., 'the *Sicarios*'), at the beginning of Acts.

It is left to Augustine, who corresponded with Jerome on the worrisome conflict between Peter and Paul in Galatians, to have the last word on the subject: 'The Lord was indeed born of woman, but he was conceived in her without man's co-operation':

> Begotten by the Father, He was not conceived by the Father. He was made *Man* in the mother, whom He himself had made, so that he might exist here for a while, sprung from her who could never and nowhere have existed except through His *Power* ... She in whose footsteps you are following had no human intercourse when she conceived. She remained a virgin when she brought forth her child. (Sermon 191)

While impressive for its rhetorical skill, this certainly is arcane. Augustine as well, while not denying that Mary was born subject to 'Original Sin', also championed the cause that she had been delivered of its effects 'by the Grace of rebirth'.[10]

Trajan's Executions of Simeon bar Cleophas and the Descendants of Jesus' Brother Judas

This brings us back to the question of Simeon bar Cleophas and Cephas. In both Eusebius and Epiphanius, 'Cleophas' is of course the father of Simeon bar Cleophas and the uncle of Jesus. Both are clearly dependent on Hegesippus. In two separate places Eusebius, in writing about Simeon bar Cleophas, the next to succeed among 'the Desposyni' (the family of Jesus), informs us that 'Hegesippus tells us that Cleophas was Joseph's brother'. This he tells us in the same breath as the fact that:

> After the martyrdom of James and the capture of Jerusalem which *immediately followed*, there is a *firm tradition* that those of the Apostles and Disciples of the Lord who were still alive, together with those who were related to the Lord according to the flesh, *assembled* from all parts ... to choose a fit person as *successor to James*. They *unanimously elected Simeon the son of Clopas, mentioned in the Gospel narratives*, to occupy the Episcopal Throne there, who was, so they say, *a cousin of the Saviour*.[11]

Not only does Eusebius in this testimony, taken from Hegesippus, display no embarrassment whatsoever at the kinship of these '*Desposyni*' to Jesus, once again we have another of these tell-tale 'elections'. Nor is it clear whether it is this 'Simeon' or his father, 'Clopas', the husband of Mary's sister Mary in the Gospel of John, who is the one 'mentioned in the Gospel narratives'. If Simeon, then we have already described where.

In referring to these '*Desposyni*' (literally, 'of the Lord'), Eusebius records – also on the basis of Hegesippus – how first of all Vespasian, after the capture of Jerusalem, issued an order to ensure that no one who was of royal stock should be left among the Jews, that all descendants of David should be ferreted out and for this reason a further widespread persecution was again *inflicted upon the Jews* (note, this 'persecution' is not 'inflicted upon' the Christians).[12] If this order can be confirmed, then it shows that Vespasian properly appreciated that the root cause of the Uprising against Rome from 66 to 70 CE and the unrest continuing thereafter was Messianic. This is the writer's view and we have already shown it to be the implication of Josephus' data.

It is also the implication of the data in the Dead Sea Scrolls, which are thoroughly Messianic. It also gainsays the view of early Church fathers like Eusebius, who, encouraged by the picture in the Gospels, repeatedly averred that the Jews suffered all these things, because they *rejected the Messiah*.[13] On the contrary, the Jews suffered the things they suffered, because they *were so Messianic* – a point the authors of the Gospels are at great pains to disguise – and, as things transpired, rejected the view of the Messianism disseminated by people like Eusebius! In addition, it again demonstrates the root cause of the problems that continued to plague Palestine and most of the Eastern region of the Roman Empire as well – even as far as Rome itself.

Eusebius gives no further information on this point, instead going on to document the attempts by Domitian (81–96 CE), Vespasian's second son, to do the very same thing he pictures Vespasian as doing – as remarked above, in the questioning of the descendants of Jesus' third brother 'Judas' he supposedly and, no doubt, apocryphally indulged in. Eusebius, in describing this new 'persecution', again prefaces it by the notice that 'Domitian issued an order *for the execution of all those who were of David's line*' – this may have indeed been the case – while at the same time claiming Domitian's 'father Vespasian planned no Evil against us'.[14] It is hard to reconcile the two accounts, and either the order to execute all Messianic claimants of David's line originated under Domitian or he simply renewed an order his father made a decade or so before at the conclusion of the First Jewish Revolt against Rome.

Whatever the truth here, Eusebius goes on then to quote Hegesippus' account of the arrest and examination of Jesus' brother Jude's *two* descendants – some versions even claiming to know their names: '*Zoker*' and '*James*' – on a charge of being '*of the family of David*'.[15] When Domitian discovered them to be common laborers and the Kingdom they professed, Heavenly and Angelic not temporal, he is pictured by Hegesippus as 'dismissing them as simpletons' and *rescinding* the decree – the reason being that an 'other-worldly' or spiritual Kingdom was clearly considered no threat to the power of Rome.

But the language used by Hegesippus here to describe this Kingdom 'at the End of the World, when he would come in Glory to judge the quick and the dead and *reward each according to his works*', recalls nothing so much as James' vision in the Temple of the Son of Man 'coming on the clouds of Heaven' with the Angelic Host, so vividly echoed as well in the picture in the War Scroll of the 'multitude of Heavenly Holy Ones mighty in battle', not to mention the Letter of James' picture of the 'cries of the reapers reaching the ears of the Lord of Hosts' and the 'coming of the Lord' – and the 'Jamesian' emphasis generally on 'works'.

Regardless of the truth or falseness of these reports, after discussing 'the Ebionites' – whom we have identified as holding James' name in such high regard – Eusebius then goes on to recount the martyrdom of Simeon bar Cleophas in the reign of Trajan (98–117 CE).[16] As will be recalled, these 'Ebionites', who reject the notion of the Supernatural Christ, 'still cling tenaciously to the Law', notions that Eusebius, playing on the meaning of their name in Hebrew (which he understands), dismisses as '*poverty-stricken*'.

Once again, he gives us the same story about Simeon being accused of being a 'descendant of David and a Christian' – whatever might be meant by this term at this time – and a search being made for those 'of the family of David' we just encountered twice before under Vespasian and his son Domitian. He notes that Simeon was 'the son of Mary the wife of Clopas', this time directly quoting Hegesippus to the effect that he was 'the son of the Lord's uncle'.[17] If nothing else, this demonstrates something very disconcerting to the Romans was going on in the Palestine region at this time.

It is this information Jerome also uses – this and the Gospel accounts of 'Mary the wife of Clopas' being 'the mother of James, Joses, and Salome' – to conclude that 'the brothers of Jesus' were actually his *cousins*. At the same time he neglects to point out that this would make Simeon bar Cleophas, the next in the line of these alleged '*Desposyni*', Jesus' *second brother* ('Clopas' and 'Cleophas' being identical) – probably the one called 'Simon' in the Gospels. Of course, this would make what was developing in Palestine, as we have already suggested, something of a family 'Caliphate' – 'Caliph' meaning 'Successor' in Arabic.

Eusebius claims there were fifteen in the line of these so-called '*Desposyni*' down to the time of Simeon or Shim'on Bar Kochba and the Second Jewish Revolt from 132 to 136 CE.

This sounds suspiciously similar to the number of the Community Council at Qumran, composed of – so it appears – 'Twelve Israelites' and 'three Priests', and not a list at all. Realistically speaking, fifteen 'Bishops' or 'Archbishops' – as the case may be – in some sixty–seventy years, sounds not a little hypothetical.

The first successor to Simeon bar Cleophas in these fictionalized lists of *Desposyni* is also someone Eusebius again portentously refers to as 'Justus', recalling the defeated candidate in the election to succeed 'Judas' in Acts. For his part, Epiphanius calls the individual who succeeds Simeon by the equally auspicious name of 'Judas'. Indeed, he may very well have been a descendant of Jesus' third brother 'Judas' or 'Judas of James' in Apostle lists and the Letter of Jude. For Eusebius, interestingly enough, 'Judas' is the name of the last or fifteenth on this list and we are back to where we started again.[18]

Regardless of the believability of Simeon bar Cleophas, 'the son of the Lord's uncle', being crucified at Moses' age of 'one hundred and twenty', again 'the witnesses' marvel that 'he could bear such tortures'. On top of this, Eusebius then describes how at the same time 'the descendants of one of those considered *brothers of the Lord, named Judas*' were re-arrested under Trajan – it will be recalled they had previously so been arrested under Domitian – and *executed in similar fashion.*

As to the descendants of Jesus' *third brother* Judas generally – again quoting Hegesippus – Eusebius says 'they came forward and presided over every Church *as witnesses* and *members of the Lord's family*'. Again this point is totally missing from Acts. Also characterizing Simeon as being '*among the witnesses who bore testimony to what had both been heard and seen of the Lord*' (again, not even a word about this in the orthodox Gospels or Acts, unless we take the story of the 'two' witnesses on the road to Emmaus, so equivocally identified in Luke, to relate to either Simeon or James, or both – which we do) and '*dying a martyr's death*', he concludes, still following Hegesippus:

> Until then, the Church remained as *pure and uncorrupt as a virgin* ... but when the sacred band of Apostles and the generation of those who had been *privileged to hear with their own ears* the Divine wisdom, reached the ends of their lives and passed on, then impious error took shape through the *Lying and deceit of false teachers* who, seeing that none of the Apostles were left, shame-facedly *preached, against the proclamation of the Truth, their false Knowledge.*[19]

Epaphroditus and the Sequence of Events Leading to the Martyrdom of James

To go back to the interesting sequence in these events where James' martyrdom is concerned, which helps illumine some of the factors behind his removal. In the first place, there is the *confrontation between Simon and Agrippa I over barring foreigners* – including Herodians – *from the Temple* which has as its counterpart, in the next generation, *the erection of the Temple Wall which triggered the stoning of James.* The purpose of this wall, as we have explained, was not simply to bar Agrippa I's son Agrippa II from the Temple, but to bar his view of the sacrifices in the Temple as he reclined dining on the terrace of his palace. This is indicative of the real atmosphere in Palestine in this period – Gospel portraiture of the pastoral 'Galilean' countryside notwithstanding – and overseas it would have been perceived, no doubt, as the epitome of recalcitrant malevolence.

This kind of intolerant 'zeal' is reversed, for instance, in the Pauline Letter to the Ephesians, which not only contains the doctrine of 'Jesus as Temple' – enunciated by Paul as well in 1 Corinthians 3:10 and 12:27 – but also the opposite position, that there should 'no longer be strangers or foreign visitors' (Eph. 2:19). For it and for Paul, all are 'fellow citizens in the Household' or 'Temple of God', of which 'Jesus Christ is the Cornerstone' (2:20–22).

This is also the picture in the Gospels. These are noble sentiments, to be sure, with wide appeal; but, in a Palestinian framework, they are historically inaccurate as the Dead Sea Scrolls now clearly testify – as did the Temple warning blocks threatening death for strangers or foreigners entering the central area around the Temple even inadvertently.

After this confrontation in Caesarea and those that follow between Greeks and Jews throughout the next decade there, comes the assassination of the High Priest Jonathan, accompanied by Josephus' introduction of 'the *Sicarii*' responsible for it. Josephus rails against the assassination of this Jonathan and the bloodshed that followed as 'polluting' both city and Temple. As Josephus puts it, once again reversing the 'Piety' language of 'loving God':

> This is the reason why, in my opinion, even God himself, out of *hatred for their Impiety, turned away from our city* and, because He deemed the Temple to be no longer a *clean dwelling place for Him*, brought the Romans upon us and *purified our city by fire*, while inflicting *slavery* upon us together with our wives and children, for He wished to *chasten us* by these calamities.[20]

This is a different kind of '*mea culpa*' confession from those one gets in the New Testament generally, which are, nevertheless, but a variation of it.

This is followed by the unlawful Sanhedrin trial Ananus 'pursued' against James at his new 'House' of sitting (his '*Beit-Galuto*'), succeeded by James' stoning, which clearly indicate that James was identified as the centre of the agitation behind many of these things. That this 'blasphemy' trial was undoubtedly trumped up by the Herodian Authorities in conjunction with the Temple Establishment, and that both Agrippa II and Ananus joined forces in it, further connects James to the source of both the Temple Wall Affair directed against Agrippa II and the assassination of Ananus' brother – Caiaphas' brother-in-law – Jonathan. This, in turn, leads to the fire in Rome, which Nero blamed on so-called 'Christians'. More sympathetic sources, however, perhaps prompted by some of these Christian 'friends' in high places we so often hear about, put the blame rather on Nero himself.[21]

Whatever the mechanism, Nero clearly seems to have decided to rid himself of Jews and Jewish agitation generally. He sends a Governor, Florus (64–66 CE), to Judea who by Josephus' own testimony seems *intentionally* to goad the population into revolt.[22] At the same time Nero kicks his wife Poppea – for Josephus, 'a worshipper of God', in other words, 'a God-Fearer' – to death, presumably agitated by concerns over her interest in causes of this kind and other things, not to mention her pregnancy.

In the midst of the war in Judea, Nero is assassinated. Among those accused of having a hand in this would appear to be Paul's associate Epaphroditus, a man whom he called 'his brother, co-worker, and fellow soldier', an 'Apostle' (Phil. 2:25), and who, Josephus tells us, had 'participated in many important events'. Though some, as signaled earlier, will object to this three-fold identification; not only do Suetonius and others affirm that he was Nero's secretary – which would make Paul's intimations about 'Saints' in 'the household of Caesar' even more meaningful (Phil. 4:18) – but this same Epaphroditus re-emerges some years later – survivor as he appears to have been – as *Domitian's secretary* as well.

Not long before Domitian too was assassinated in 96 CE, Epaphroditus appears to have run afoul of him purportedly over his behavior at the time of Nero's assassination, which Domitian used as a pretext, complaining that Epaphroditus dared to raise his hand against an Emperor, and had him executed. This is *very* peculiar indeed, coming from Domitian, and there would appear to be more behind these events than appears on the surface. Not only was this about the time that Domitian was rounding up all those of the family of David and possibly even the real year Simeon bar Cleophas was executed, but 96 CE was also the year

Flavia Domitilla, the wife or niece of Flavius Clemens, one of the consuls that year and Domitian's co-ruler, was, according to Eusebius, exiled for 'her testimony to Christ'.

In fact she was Domitian's niece and Flavius Clemens was his cousin. Domitian, who was apparently childless, had designated their two sons his heirs – he had renamed them Vespasian and Flavia – that is, before he had Flavius Clemens executed *the same year* as Epaphroditus.[23] Domitian was himself assassinated by Domitilla's *own steward*, 'Stephanos' or 'Stephen' – a familiar name. Suetonius, an individual who cannot be described as particularly philo-Semitic, describes Domitian's hatred, or at least cruelty towards Jews, attesting that he 'levied the tax against them' with the utmost vigor, even 'prosecuting those who, while not publicly acknowledging the Faith, yet lived as Jews, as well as *those who concealed their origins* and *did not pay the tribute levied against their people'*.[24] One such prosecution of a man 'ninety years old' – which may even have served as the model for the supposed prosecution of the *one hundred and twenty year-old* Simeon bar Cleophas – Suetonius himself acknowledges having witnessed as a boy, who 'was examined before the procurator to see whether he was circumcised' – not very different from more recent events in our purportedly modern world!

As we have already suggested, Epaphroditus would appear to be the same individual Josephus dedicates many of his works to, including the *Antiquities* and the *Vita*, and his words regarding him in the former – 'a lover of all kinds of learning, but principally delighted by the study of history' – are thoroughly modern, attesting to how little things have changed. Though the relationship to Domitian's Epaphroditus is contested – to say nothing of Paul's companion in touch with 'the Saints' in Nero's household – for Josephus, Epaphroditus was a man who had experienced many important political events. Had Epaphroditus not encouraged him, Josephus would not have made the effort 'to overcome his sloth' and pour out the *Antiquities*.[25]

Much depends, of course, on how Josephus himself died and when, which is unclear, since no Josephus remained to chronicle it, but he too seems to have disappeared about the same time Epaphroditus did and possibly for similar reasons – maybe even because of information contained in the newly published *Antiquities* or *Vita* (both of which encouraged by Epaphroditus) that some may have found offensive. Some even try to explain these inconsistencies by proposing there were two Epaphroditus' working under both Domitian and Trajan, but the writer considers this highly unlikely, though there may have been a father and son. This is the same genre of problem surrounding the overlapping Messianic round-ups under Domitian and Trajan.

Whatever the conclusion, the Julio-Claudians, represented by the last Emperor of that line Nero, gave way to the Flavians who, abetted by a host of Jewish turncoats such as Josephus and Tiberius Alexander, seem to have marketed their own version of Jewish Messianism, which at the very least was presented as submissive and deferential to the power of Rome and its emperors – this not to mention marketing a healthy dose of Greco-Alexandrian, Hellenistic anti-Semitism.

Epaphroditus and his Intellectual Circle

This brings us to another difficult subject: who could have written the original accounts upon which so many of our Gospel episodes are based? Though puzzling scholars for generations, this question may not be as difficult to gain a measure of insight into as most may think. One must keep in mind the attitudes, the orientation, or, if one prefers, the *polemics*, which are in fact quite straightforward. With rare exceptions the point of view is almost always anti-Semitic, pro-Gentile, anti-national, and pro-Roman.

While employing the warp and woof of Jewish Messianism, this is exploited basically to produce a pro-Roman, spiritualized, Hellenistic-style mystery religion. Here, one must understand that, while all the Gospels exhibit differences, the Synoptics are basically variations on a theme – with more or less material added. John, while differing markedly as to specific historical points and development, still comes from the same Hellenistic, anti-Semitic mindset – even more extreme.

What we are speaking about here is the original core of materials and the mindset they evince, not the endless variations, addenda, or accretions. The underlying mindset is on the whole consistent, while the variations are so complex and creative that even the modern techniques of form, redaction, or text criticism have not succeeded in elucidating these in any generally-acceptable manner – nor are they ever likely to do so to everyone's satisfaction. However, the central question must be, *who might have had an interest in the general thrust of the presentation of 'Messianic' events in Palestine which all more or less have in common* – to be sure, acquiring accretions as the original core went through manifold transformations and additions – *whose interests did the ideological thrust of this central core of material serve?*

We have already given numerous examples of the orientation we have in mind, despite the variations, perhaps the most important aspect of which was to lighten and deflect the fundamental embarrassment over the Roman execution of Jesus as a subversive and anti-Roman agitator. This, anyhow, has to some extent come to be recognized by scholars. Out of it proceeds the positive portrayal, where possible (it almost always was), of Roman officials and Herodian puppets.

Two of the most obvious of these were: 1) the patent fraudulence of portraying Pontius Pilate's *high regard for Jesus* and '*his* (Pilate's, that is) *wife*' – naturally unnamed and in a dream no less – as *recognizing 'Jesus' as 'a Righteous Man'* (again, it is difficult to suppress a guffaw – this, as we have been seeing, the most revered concept in Judaism of the time and, in particular, among what we have been calling '*Opposition groups*'); and 2) the henpecked '*Herod the Tetrarch*' (it was hard to whitewash him) hesitating to execute John the Baptist but, rather, *likewise recognizing him as a 'Righteous Man'* ('a *Zaddik*'! – again, the by-now *pro forma* guffaw) *while the majority of Jews could not – yet being forced to execute John because of a lascivious dance performed by his wife Herodias' daughter* (as few realize, in the Gospels anyhow – *unnamed*) *at his (Herod the Tetrarch's) birthday party* (a celebration usually honored by Romans and but hardly very many Jews – if any!). Almost *any fair-minded person would immediately recognize such portrayals as patent dissimulation* – even worse, *disinformation.*

We have also reviewed some of the other, more obvious *non sequiturs* in the core materials as we have them – all directed towards the same end – for instance, *the impossibility of a Jewish Sanhedrin, composed of High Priests, Elders, and Scribes, meeting in the middle of the night of Passover at 'the High Priest's House'* to hold a trial of someone for '*blasphemy*'; or the presentation of 'Peter' as *constantly misunderstanding the Master's teaching* – Paul, of course, *understands it* – *unable to walk on the waters of the Sea of Galilee because his 'Faith' was too weak* or *denying the Master* (this in all the Gospels) '*three times' on his death night*; or the Messiah incarnate *eating congenially with Roman tax collectors, prostitutes, and other 'Sinners'* while variously disparaging his own people and family.

How delicious all this must have been for those who created it and what good drama it made, but what poor history as the Dead Sea Scrolls now are able to play their part along with early Church history in amply demonstrating. Where the charge of '*blasphemy*' is concerned, this *should have been punished by stoning*, not *crucifixion*. However, what should be clear is that it *retrospectively assimilates the same charge as made against James* – in Establishment eyes with more cause; and this does seem to have *resulted in a stoning* or, at least, *a very intentional shove.*

Who then would or could have produced the basic core of this kind of material before, like a snowball rolling down a hill, it grew into a massive accumulation of generally like-minded tradition? In the first place, the writers were extremely able craftsmen, who knew their material thoroughly. For instance, as we have been explaining, they had to know all the traditions associated with the death of James – even those represented by the later

Pseudoclementine *Recognitions* and accounts in the early Church writers about James 'being cast down' from the Pinnacle of the Temple – and this at a very early time. They also probably knew the traditions about a first post-resurrection appearance to 'James, then to all the Apostles, and last of all, as if to an abortion, he also appeared to me', as Paul recounts it in 1 Corinthians 15:7–8. In fact, Paul says as much himself, implying there were already written documents or traditions relating to these things which he had 'received' (1 Cor. 15:3).

Paul did survive James, though by how many years must remain the subject of some debate. Still, after his final trip to see Nero – either the earlier one in Acts from 60-62 CE, preceding James' judicial murder, or – depending on the point of view – the later connecting him to Josephus' '*Saulus*' around 66 CE; one would have to observe that Paul or one or another of his associates – such as Titus ('Timothy'?), Silas ('Silvanus'?), Luke ('Lucius of Cyrene'?) or Epaphroditus himself – would have had time to produce a rough version of some of the key events, we have been calling attention to, *incorporating the principles of good Roman citizenship if not Palestinian Messianism.*

Epaphroditus, who must be seen as a prime candidate for the direction of this kind of activity, not only had a hand in the assassination of Nero, but was also Domitian's *Secretary for Letters*, before he too was executed by him on unspecified charges – probably, like his contemporary Flavius Clemens, for being a secret 'Christian'. One is not imagining these things. They *really* occurred, despite various attempts to obscure them.

The writers we are speaking about would also have known many of the works, we have since found in the caves near Qumran – particularly the Damascus Document but, also, the Community Rule and War Scroll – which they systematically (sometimes seemingly even gleefully) reworked or subverted. In passage after passage, as we have been signaling, they inverted fundamental Qumran imageries and orientations, turning them back upon their initial creators and reversing their import; thereby capitalizing on their obvious weak points from a 'public relations' standpoint and ridiculing their inward-looking, intolerant, and idiosyncratic nationalism (sincere as it may have been) with devastating results.

This was a substantial intellectual feat, which could only have been effected by extremely able and well-informed minds – but without the discovery of the Dead Sea Scrolls as we now have them, we could never have understood this – suspected it, yes, but never *known* it – which is why their discovery is of such primary historical importance. Even the Gospel of John, which differs so markedly from its Synoptic counterparts, exhibits a difference, as we noted, only in substance, not in kind. The orientation and playful inversion of Qumran themes are perhaps most glaringly and humorously illustrated by the almost total obfuscation of the report of a first appearance to James in the portrayal there of Jesus' post-resurrection appearance along the shore of the Sea of Galilee, and his principal Disciples as 'dragging their nets full of fishes'. Peter even had 'a hundred and fifty-three' 'large fishes' in his 'net', which 'though there were so many', yet 'was it not torn'.

This is particularly true when one is aware of what subsequently happened to the 'Galilean' fishermen around the shores of the Sea of Galilee under Titus and his colleague, Agrippa II, when, even as Josephus describes it, 'the whole sea ran red with their blood'. The old, the infirm, and the young were butchered and the rest given over to this same Agrippa to be sold as slaves. Titus, of course, kept back a few to cover his own expenses. Which returns us to our initial question, who could have written this kind of artful, yet nefarious material in its initial configuration, before it was elaborated upon and developed into a larger literature around the Hellenistic Mediterranean? Who would have had the knowledge to do so?

In the first place, there were quite a few well-educated and intelligent people, many of whom were very good writers, in the above circle of individuals. For instance, in the *Antiquities* Josephus tells us that Agrippa II made over to him some ninety-nine of his letters to help him rewrite his earlier work, the *War*. In addition, he tells us that, not only did this same Epaphroditus – to whom the *Antiquities* was dedicated – sponsor his work, but it was read appreciatively by Julius Archelaus. He may well have been Paul's nephew, mentioned in Acts 23:16–23's account of Paul's marvelous rescue by Roman troops from the furious Jewish mob at the Festival of Pentecost – so critical to Acts' portrayal of the parameters of the new Pauline Gentile Mission – who wanted to kill him for introducing Gentiles into the Temple. In this regard, it should be observed that this *same* mob was not interested in killing James, though it had ample opportunity to do so. On the contrary, James seems to have been killed by the Establishment precisely *because* he was held in such high regard by the people, in particular, these same 'Zealots for the Law'.

Paul already refers in the Letter to the Romans to his '*kinsman the littlest Herod*' who, in all probability, was the son of Aristobulus, King of Lesser Armenia, and the Salome who allegedly performed the lascivious dance ending up with the legendary portrait in Gospel tradition of John the Baptist's head upon the platter – which no one will ever forget. In addition to Josephus himself (who lived well into the 90's, if not beyond), there were all of Philo of Alexandria's kinsmen and heirs, thoroughly compromised by contacts with Romans and Herodians, who certainly knew the allegorical approach to Scripture that Philo himself had pioneered.

It would not have been a very great step for any of these or even Paul – who is already doing so in his letters – to apply this approach to the literature and conceptualities found at Qumran. In particular, Philo's kinsmen included, as we have seen, Tiberius Alexander, mentioned in Acts 4:6 – along with Caiaphas and Ananus the High Priests – *in one of the few honest portrayals of a Roman official.* He was, however, *a Jewish turncoat*, directly responsible for the execution of the two 'sons' of the Jewish Revolutionary Leader, Judas the Galilean, c. 47 CE. Later, as Titus' adjutant (c. 68-70 CE), *this same 'Tiberius' personally directed the siege of Jerusalem and the final destruction of the Temple.*

For good measure, the Romans even went on to destroy a sister 'Temple', that had been constructed in Heliopolis in Egypt in the Maccabean Period. Someone had to be giving them extremely good intelligence that they should remove *the several root-causes of so much of this anti-Roman agitation* so decisively. These events in Egypt were followed under Trajan around the time of or after the execution of Simeon bar Cleophas – as pictured in Christian sources – by the actual eradication of the entire Jewish population in Lower Egypt, perhaps numbering a million and a half souls. In addition in Rome, after the fall of Jerusalem, there were other individuals, either retired or there as hostages – all extremely well informed and cultivated – such as Antiochus of Commagene and his son, Epiphanes, *who had led 'the Macedonian Legion' on the Roman side in the recent War.*

Of course, where providing good intelligence was concerned, we have numerous candidates, Josephus himself being a self-admitted informant and interrogator of prisoners. Tiberius Alexander is identified by him as a Jewish backslider – the equivalent of the pot calling the kettle black. Then there are all the Herodians, including Bernice, the mistress of Titus the destroyer of the Temple and Tiberius Alexander's sister-in-law, from *two* marriages, not to mention the 'Saulus' who so mysteriously and ubiquitously keeps popping in and out of Josephus' picture of the last days of Jerusalem. There was also another 'Maccabean' Herodian resident in Rome in these years, Tigranes, who was sent by Nero to be King of Armenia. His father, also Tigranes, had been King of Armenia before him and his son became King of Cilicia. All of these, too, '*deserted the Jewish Religion and went over to that of the Greeks*'.[26]

Nor do we know what other clique might have been operating around the Roman Governor Felix – married to Bernice's other sister Drusilla – whose brother Pallas was Nero's favorite and who seems to have been involved in bringing Paul to Rome. Felix certainly seems to have been responsible for bringing Simon *Magus* to Rome (if there was a difference). There is also Gallio, the Roman Governor of Corinth and brother of Nero's adviser and major-domo, the famous Seneca. Acts revels in presenting this Gallio, a historical figure who can actually be identified as Governor of Corinth in 52 CE, as rescuing Paul from the anger of the Jewish mob and having the Head of the Synagogue there, it calls 'Sosthenes', flogged before 'the Judgment Seat' (18:17). To be sure, for Paul, significantly in 1 Corinthians 1:1, this same Sosthenes is one of his closest lieutenants 'and brother to the Church of God in Corinth'. This is to say nothing about Seneca himself, whose anti-Jewish feelings even Augustine feels constrained to remark and to whom a pseudepigraphic correspondence with Paul is attested.[27]

All of these were *very* literate men. Josephus even identifies his father, the priest 'Matthias' (Matthew), as a writer of great repute. Of course, one must always bear in mind that his father might have been the prototype for the renowned 'Matthew', to whom the traditions incorporated in the First Gospel are attributed. In Mark 2:14, for some reason, it will be recalled, he is called 'Levi the son of Alphaeus', that is, 'Cleophas' and another of these alleged 'tax collectors'!

However this may be, Josephus has very good contacts in Rome indeed. But with all his flaws, he could not have been responsible for the kind of materials upon which the Gospels as we have them were based – except tangentially – nor any other self-professing Jew, turncoat or otherwise. The rhetoric and drumbeat of anti-Semitic polemic are just too strong for that. Besides, Josephus is too inordinately proud of his heritage, as he repeatedly demonstrates in the *Antiquities*, to have done this. But the information he possessed *could* certainly have been used by someone, as could that possessed by Agrippa II and his sister Bernice, both smarting over the loss of their palaces in Jerusalem – not to mention their sister Drusilla married to Felix.

Julius Archelaus, too, who ended up in wealthy retirement reading Josephus' works in Rome (and who '*could vouch* – according to the latter – *for their accuracy*'), had previously been Bernice's brother-in-law. Julius was the son of the Temple Treasurer Helcias, whose father and grandfather (the genealogies are unclear here) had been Temple Treasurer before him and close associates of the earlier Herod. Another of his '*kinsmen*', '*Antipas*', had been a close associate of the '*Saulus*' mentioned in Josephus. He, too, also became Temple Treasurer before being executed by '*the Zealots*' as a 'Traitor' in the midst of the Uprising.

The best candidate among this group for producing or sponsoring the production of materials of this kind – if indeed it is possible to trace such materials to a given source – turning what was basically an aggressively apocalyptic Messianism into a more benign and pacifistic one, would be someone of the experience and talents of an Epaphroditus or, even perhaps, one or another of Paul's other traveling companions. The ascription of Acts to Luke basically says something of this kind and Luke himself – if, indeed, the author of the Gospel under his name and Acts were the same person – confirms this, telling us how knowledgeable he was in comparing sources. Epaphroditus was certainly very literate and probably more knowledgeable even than Luke. Plus he had all Josephus' works, which he had commissioned, to guide him. Then too, if he was a traveling companion of Paul, he probably knew Luke as well.

If he is, indeed, the same individual Paul mentions in Philippians (and elsewhere, possibly too, under the name of 'Erastus') as his *closest* associate (his 'Apostle') and 'fellow worker and fellow soldier' – and we can see no good reason for challenging this – then he knew Paul's mind intimately, better probably than just about anyone else. He would also appear to have been extremely adventurous and personally brave, as Josephus attests as well. In fact, Epaphroditus' execution by Domitian – to say nothing of Domitian's own assassination by Flavia Domitilla's servant 'Stephen', obviously in vengeance for something – not to mention Epaphroditus' involvement in the death of Nero, does raise serious questions as to just what was going on beneath the surface of these events so close to the source of Imperial Power in Rome.

These are some of the things we shall never know but the Gospels as we have them – whoever produced them – at their core are just too anti-Semitic to have been produced by anyone other than Gentiles. The animus against Jews – Jews of all stripes, even those representing the Leadership of the Jerusalem Church (represented as '*Pharisees*' in Acts, probably because of the perception of their legal hair-splitting) – is just too intense and unremitting to be otherwise. It is no wonder that the effects of this continue to be felt today and are grappled with by people who still argue over their cause.

It should not be forgotten, too, that both Philo and Josephus addressed works against Alexandrian anti-Semitic agitators, such as Apion, who himself led a 'Mission to Gaius' that apparently nullified the one led by Philo. An Apion-like character also makes an appearance in the Pseudoclementines, where he was an associate of Simon *Magus*! Apion was actually a known historian at the Museum in Alexandria, who invented the ritual murder accusation against Jews. His successor as grammarian there, Chaeremon, like Seneca, was also a tutor of Nero. Both had already completely falsified Jewish Old Testament history – falsifications that sent even Josephus into paroxysms of indignation.[28] Paul, too, as we have seen, was a master of such literary invective and allegorization.

This is, in fact, the circle of individuals (themselves having a very substantial knowledge of Josephus' works) to whom one might attribute the core of material that finally ends up – with numerous variations, expansions, and accretions – in what we call Gospels today, if, in fact, one can attribute such a core to anyone known, as opposed to unknown transmitters. It is certainly the circle that produced Acts. Any of these individuals, or combinations thereof, could have been involved. Though the core of the Gospel materials had to go back to someone very close to or knowledgeable about both the Qumran Community and 'the Jerusalem Community' of James, this could have been fleshed out and overwritten – as in Acts – some time after the momentous events of 95–6 CE, in the course of which so many individuals like Epaphroditus, Flavius Clemens, and possibly even Josephus himself, lost their lives. Nor is this to mention the martyrs in Palestine – reportedly under Trajan, but perhaps before – such as Simeon bar Cleophas and the two descendants of Jesus' third brother 'Judas'.

These are the problems and issues one must weigh in attempting to determine who might have been responsible for turning Palestinian Messianism on its ear and reversing its most precious and fundamental concepts and ethos into their mirror opposite.

The Traditions of the 'Pella Flight'

In the course of his discussion of the earlier 'calamities which at that time overwhelmed the whole nation in every part of the world' and estimating that by both famine and sword over 'one million one hundred thousand persons perished' in Judea alone as 'vengeance for *the guilt and Impiety of the Jews against the Christ of God*' (our tell-tale 'Piety' inversion again),[29] Eusebius makes one of his last references to James.

In doing so, he also delineates his sense of sequence in these matters, noting that:

> After the ascension of our Savior, the Jews had followed up *their crimes against him* by devising *plot after plot* against his Disciples. First *they stoned Stephen to death*, then *James the son of Zebedee and the brother of John* was beheaded, and *finally James*, the first after our Savior's Ascension to be raised to the Bishop's Throne there (in Jerusalem), lost his life in the way described, while the remaining Apostles in constant danger from

> *murderous plots*, were driven out of Judea … to teach their message of *the Power of Christ* in every land.

His lurid description of 'the calamities' that then befell the Jews which follows is lifted almost bodily from Josephus' *Jewish War*, which describes how the Jews during the siege of Jerusalem even ended up *eating their own children*. All of this is foreseen, as far as Eusebius is concerned, by Jesus 'weeping over' Jerusalem in Luke and his prediction that it shall be 'leveled to the ground, both you and your children, not a stone upon a stone' (19:41–44).

It is at the close of this sequence that Eusebius makes his first reference to the famous 'Pella Flight'. Pella he describes as 'one of the cities of Perea' – the area beyond Jordan we have already specified as being where John the Baptist was executed – to which 'the people of the Jerusalem Church removed before the War began, on account of *an oracle given by revelation to men considered worthy* there'. We shall have more to say about this oracle later, but connected as it is to the fall of Jerusalem, at this point it cannot be totally divorced from the counter-oracle Jesus was just pictured as making with more or less detail about the destruction of Jerusalem, 'stone upon stone' by Roman armies and the suffering of its inhabitants.

As Eusebius pictures this oracle, here and hereafter,

> Those who believed in Christ removed from Jerusalem, and when these Holy Men had utterly abandoned the Royal metropolis of the Jews and the whole Land of Judea, the *Judgment of God* finally overtook them for their *abominable crimes against the Christ and his Apostles*, entirely blotting out that Generation of Evil-Doers from among men.[30]

Eusebius appears almost gleeful here.

The Martyrdom of Simeon bar Cleophas and 'Drinking the Cup' Imagery in the Gospels and at Qumran

It should be appreciate that 'the Pella Flight', if credible, must have occurred under the stewardship of James' successor and putative 'cousin' or 'brother', Simeon bar Cleophas, concerning whom it would be well to look at a later statement of Eusebius that '*James the Just suffered martyrdom for the same reason as the Lord*'. In this, Eusebius is again dependent on Hegesippus and mentions *the universal demand that Simeon bar Cleophas be elected Bishop and 'be second, because he was a cousin of the Lord*' (*thus*!). Moreover, this parallels a statement he made earlier, again dependent on Hegesippus, about how 'Simeon *the son of Clopas, the second to have been appointed Bishop of the Church at Jerusalem … ended his life in martyrdom … suffering an end like that of the Lord … when Trajan was Emperor* and Atticus Consul'.[31]

Allied material in the Synoptics following allusion to 'the Son of Man sitting upon the Throne of his Glory' and allusion to his Apostles as 'sitting on Twelve Thrones, judging the Twelve Tribes of Israel' (Mt 19:28), have James and John the sons of Zebedee come to Jesus and ask to sit on Jesus' right and left hand in 'Glory' (Mk 10:35–38). In Matthew 20:20, however, it is rather 'the mother of the sons of Zebedee' (later at the Crucifixion, she is 'Mary the mother of James and Joses and the mother of the sons of Zebedee' – 27:56) who makes this request. Interestingly, this request is also preceded by the pat anti-family instruction 'to the Disciples' to leave 'house or brothers or sisters or father or mother or children or lands for the sake of the Kingdom of God' (Lk 18:29 and pars.).

Luke places these notices right before Jesus, 'drawing near Jericho', visits the house of the Rich Chief Tax Collector and midget Zacchaeus and, directly thereafter, 'drawing near' Jerusalem, weeps over it, predicting its coming demolition stone by stone (18:13–19:44). Mark and Matthew picture Jesus as quoting, in relation to his promise to those forsaking brothers, sisters, mothers, lands, etc., the clearly pro-Pauline, anti-Jerusalem Church, 'Many that are First shall be Last and the Last First' (Mk 10:31 and Mt 19:30). Both 'the First' and 'the Many' are favorite usages at Qumran, the latter the preferred nomenclature for the rank and file; the former, the beneficiaries of 'the First Covenant'. Where 'the Last' is concerned, one should bear in mind Paul's similar characterization of himself at the end of his list of post -resurrection appearances by Jesus in 1 Corinthians 15:8 above.

In these two episodes about *two* brothers, asking 'to sit', as James elsewhere proclaims it, 'on the right hand' in 'Glory', Jesus responds: 'Are you able to drink the Cup which I drink?' When they answer in the affirmative, Jesus is then pictured as responding, 'My Cup indeed you shall drink', at which point, 'the ten' are pictured as being 'offended concerning the *two brothers*' (Mt 20:20–24; Mk 10:35–41 adds their names, 'James and John').

But aside from the artificial designation 'sons of Zebedee', one must ask who these 'two brothers' really were. One should also note the same kind of imagery reappears in John, when Peter strikes off the ear of 'the High Priest's Servant' – the same 'High Priest's Servant' that seems to be the recipient of the linen 'grave clothes' in the Gospel of the Hebrews episode cited above – and Jesus tells him to put away his sword (Jn 18:10). Here Jesus is pictured as saying, 'Should I not *drink the Cup* which the Father has given me?' (18:11), thus making it unmistakably clear that this kind of 'drinking the Cup' imagery is being applied to martyrdom and death – not to mention God's retribution for these things in the Book of Revelation and the Scrolls.

This 'Cup' imagery for death and God's Vengeance is crucial in key passages in the Habakkuk *Pesher* dealing with the destruction of the Righteous Teacher and 'the Cup of God's Wrath'. Here too it is expressed in terms of 'the Cup of the right hand of the Lord' (Hab. 2:16), which the individual responsible for the 'destruction' or death of the Righteous Teacher and, as it were, 'the Poor' – would be forced to 'drink' or 'swallow' as well, and connected to the imagery of *ba-la-'a* or 'swallowing', which at Qumran is being employed to express both the ideas of being given this 'Cup to drink' and being 'destroyed'.

It should also be clear that it is inextricably tied up with 'the Cup of the Lord' allusion we have been discussing with regard to the Gospel of the Hebrews – uniquely reverberating too in Paul's version of what he reports Jesus said in his version of the 'Last Supper'. This shows that Paul, too, was well aware that this 'Cup of the Lord' symbolism was circulating among early Christian groups, but he was using it in a more esoteric way. It is this which is picked up in Gospel representations of this scenario, coupled with the betrayal by the archetypal 'Traitor', 'Judas *the Iscariot*' – only now minus the allusion 'of the Lord'.

This same imagery of '*the Cup of God's Vengeance*' and '*the Cup of God's Anger*' or '*Wrath*' (partially based on Hab. 2:16 above, but also on that of '*the Cup of Trembling*' in Isa. 51:17–22) is present as well in Revelation. This is the same imagery we have just encountered in Luke's version of Jesus' speech, which refers to this 'Anger' or 'Wrath' and '*the Days of Vengeance*' (in the Qumran Community Rule, the more '*Zealot*'-like '*Day of Vengeance*') in relation to Jerusalem being trodden underfoot and 'not even suckling mothers or babes being spared'.

As Revelation expresses this, more in the style of the Scrolls than Jesus in the Gospels, 'He also shall *drink of the wine of the Fury of God*, which is *poured full strength* ('*undiluted*' – the exact expression occurs in the Habakkuk *Pesher* as we have seen and, of course, Isa. 51:22) into *the Cup of His Wrath*' (14:10).[32] Here, plainly, is the more militant variation of the words Luke uses to characterize Jesus' speech at 'the Last Supper', phrased in terms of the Pauline '*Cup of the New Covenant in my blood, which is poured out* for you' (Lk 22:20) – but, of course, these do not mean the same thing at all.

But 'John and James the two sons of Zebedee' *do not drink this 'Cup'*. Perhaps this 'James' does, but he is conveniently removed as Acts unfolds to make room for the introduction of the other and, in our view, the *real* James. On the basis of the data, John – whoever he was – *does not.* This is true whether he is identified with the John of Patmos, who purportedly wrote the Book of Revelation, or John, the alleged author of the Fourth Gospel and 'Disciple Jesus loved', who in Eusebius was supposedly buried in Ephesus and, like James, *'wore the mitre' of the High Priest.*[33] So here we have a problem with the overt meaning of this episode.

But 'James his brother' – Jesus' brother not John's – and his 'cousin' Simeon bar Cleophas, or, as we shall presently demonstrate, his putative *second brother*, the successor to James in Jerusalem, *do* 'drink the Cup' that Jesus drank. Here, once again, our overlaps develop. Presumably too, a *third brother*, known variously as Judas, Judas of James, Judas *Thomas*, and, as we shall see below, even 'Judas the Zealot' and, perhaps, 'Judas *Iscariot*' 'the son' or 'brother of Simon *Iscariot*', does as well. He would also seem to have been known as 'Lebbaeus who was surnamed Thaddaeus' (Mt 10:3).

So does the character Josephus calls 'Theudas', who may have been 'Thaddaeus' or 'Judas *the brother of James*', beheaded according to Josephus at about the same time as the so-called 'James *the brother of John*', who in Acts turns out to present such a problem where the true succession to Jesus is concerned. So do 'the grandsons' of this 'Judas' under Trajan according to Hegesippus. So much for 'drinking the Cup of the Lord' and who drank it.

Eusebius reiterates these things several times in no uncertain terms, repeatedly quoting Hegesippus on all these round-ups and martyrdoms, which, as he puts it, occurred at a time when the Church was still 'a virgin, not yet corrupted by vain discourse'![34] For his part, Paul cynically contrasts *'the Cup of the Lord'* with *'the Cup of demons'*, by which he at first seems to imply 'the cup' Gentiles drink in their religious rites, but finally identifying it, as it appears in another disparaging aside, as that which 'Israel according to the flesh partakes of at the altar' (1 Cor. 10:18). This also parallels 'the Lord's table'/'table of demons' turnabout in 1 Cor. 10:14 – identified in the *Homilies* as James' 'food sacrificed to idols'.[35] As we saw, too, for him this *'Cup of the Lord'* now becomes the Cup *'of the New Covenant in (Christ's) blood'* – language, not surprisingly, faithfully echoed in Luke 22:20's picture of the Last Supper.

The Apostle Lists in the Synoptic Gospels and Acts

In order finally to answer this question about Jesus' brothers as Apostles, we must look at the Apostle lists in the Gospels and Acts, and compare them with the descriptions of Mary's descendants at the Crucifixion and in post-resurrection appearances. To take Mark first, which in this instance actually does appear the most primitive, Jesus 'went up into the mountain' and 'appointed Twelve that they might be with him' (Mk 3:13–14).

This trip up the mountain is basically the way Luke presents things too, only adding the additional point that Jesus also 'named' the Inner Twelve Disciples, 'Apostles', and 'went out into the mountain to pray' there (Lk 6:13). In Matthew, aside from a host of trips 'up into' and 'down the mountain' – for instance 'the very high mountain' where he was tempted by 'the Devil' (4:8) – Jesus does not 'go up' or 'out into' *any* mountain to appoint the 'Twelve' (as opposed seemingly to the implication of the notice about his post-resurrection instruction to 'the Eleven Disciples to go into Galilee to the mountain he had commanded' or 'appointed them' – meaning ambiguous here – Mt 28:16) – the 'mountain' scene having already taken place earlier in the famous 'Sermon on the Mount' (Mt 5:1–8:1).

For Mark these 'Twelve' are to be sent forth:

> to preach and to heal diseases and to have Authority to *cast out* demons (*ekballein* again). And he added to Simon the name 'Peter', and James (the son) of Zebedee and John the brother of James (the same expression used in the Letter of Jude). And he added to them (the) names *Boanerges*, which is 'Sons of Thunder' (the meaning of

> which is unclear, but there is a certain militancy to this description, and perhaps dissimulation), and Andrew and Philip and Bartholomew and Matthew and Thomas and *James* (*the son*) *of Alphaeus and Thaddaeus and Simon the Canaanite, and Judas Iscariot, who also delivered him up.* (3:14–19)

Despite the reversal of Acts' 'James *the brother of John*' into 'John *the brother of James*' and the militant 'rain' and 'cloud' imagery involved in the 'Sons of Thunder' definition for the mysterious '*Boanerges*', the most striking thing about this enumeration of the Twelve Apostles in Mark is how few of them have any real substance. Except for Simon Peter, Thomas, Judas *Iscariot*, and, of course, James and John 'the sons' either of 'Zebedee' or 'Thunder' themselves – problems associated with the actuality of *their* existence aside – they are for the most part insubstantial. Even core Apostles are insubstantial. True, there are a few traditions about Philip and Matthew – identified for some reason as 'Levi the son of Alphaeus' in Mark 2:14 – and a second 'Matthew' or 'Matthias' will be chosen, as per the picture in Acts 1:26 of the 'election' of the successor to replace Judas *Iscariot* which will confuse the situation still more.

But Bartholomew, Andrew, 'Simon the Canaanite', and 'James *the son of Alphaeus*' have little or no substance. As we shall presently see, 'Thaddaeus', a key figure, and Judas *Iscariot* (not to mention 'Simon the *Iscariot*') will overlap each other or other names on this list.

In Matthew, Jesus is rather portrayed as going back and forth across the Sea of Galilee or wandering around Galilee curing, raising dead persons, and 'casting out demons' generally (Mt 9:1–13). The actual scene of his appointment of 'the Twelve' occurs in good dramatic style after his debarking from a boat. He then dines with 'tax collectors and Sinners', repeating the proverbial 'think not I have come to call the Righteous (this is precisely what the Dead Sea Scrolls would have thought) but the Sinners' and that he will replace 'old clothes … with new cloth' and 'put new wine in new wineskins' (Mt 9:16–17).

In Matthew 10:1, Jesus 'calls his Twelve Disciples, and giving them *Authority over unclean spirits*, so as to *cast them out* (*ekballein*)' – not as 'the tares sown by the Enemy' and gathering the polluted fishes into baskets, 'to separate the Wicked from the midst of the Righteous and cast them (*balousin*) into the furnace of Fire' – but rather, the 'Authority' is now 'to *heal every disease and bodily weakness*', a distinctly more peaceful and less aggressive undertaking. Matthew now lists 'his Twelve Disciples' as follows:

> First Simon who is *called Peter* and Andrew *his brother*, James (the son) of Zebedee and John *his brother* (different from Mark above), Philip and Bartholomew, Thomas, and Matthew *the tax collector*, *James* (*the son*) *of Alphaeus*, and *Lebbaeus who was surnamed Thaddaeus*, *Simon the Canaanite* (or 'Cananaean'), and *Judas Iscariot*, who also delivered him up. (Mt 10:2–4)

The changes here are obvious. Now the 'brother' theme, attached to 'John the brother of James' in Mark or *vice versa* in Acts, is attached to 'Andrew *his brother*' too. It will be recalled that in Greek, 'Andrew', besides being the name of a later Jewish Messianic leader (who led the Uprising in Egypt and Cyrene in 115–17 CE),[36] also means 'Man' – in Hebrew or Aramaic, '*Adam*' or '*Enosh*'. This makes Peter – whether by coincidence or design – the *brother of 'Man'* as well. For his part, Andrew's place in Matthew moves up accordingly, though we never hear *a single additional word about him* in Matthew again – and hardly anywhere else either, except in John.

As with Andrew, Mark's 'John the brother of James' is also reduced to 'his brother' – whose, unspecified, though we are obviously to presume James', that is, 'James the son of Zebedee'. Now, however, a 'Lebbaeus' is included – never mentioned anywhere before and never to be mentioned again, except, for instance, in the *Recognitions*, where he takes the place not only of 'Thaddaeus' generally, but also the Apostle to be called 'Judas (the brother) of James' in Luke and Acts.

In Matthew's list, though missing from some recensions, 'Lebbaeus' is identified also with this mysterious Thaddaeus – now characterized, as we saw, as *Lebbaeus*' 'surname'! Matthew himself, as in 9:9 earlier and Mark 2:14 – where for some reason he was called 'Levi (the son) of Alphaeus' – is also, now, again called 'the tax collector' (Mt 10:3). This is obviously totally tendentious and, in view of the history we have been delineating above, not a little slanderous as well.

Not only will 'Lebbaeus surnamed Thaddaeus' be replaced in Luke's listings by 'Judas (the brother) of James', another individual about whom we shall never hear another word in the Gospels again, but, with whom the reader will become very familiar. Since 'Alphaeus' in these lists, for some reason mixed up in Mark with both 'Matthew' and 'tax collecting', always has to do in some manner with *James* – probably a variation or deformation of 'Cleophas' – we again are verging in these things on matters related to individuals connected to Jesus' family.

It is true that in John's version of 'the Last Supper', this other 'Judas, *not the Iscariot*' (thus) does appear again – since the 'Judas (the son) of Simon *Iscariot*' has already departed to '*deliver him up*' and his place, as we have seen, is rather taken by '*Didymus Thomas*'/'*Twin Twin*' (in apocryphal Gospels and early Church texts, '*Judas Thomas*' – much more accurate and likely) – and, for some reason, it is he who John represents as asking 'Jesus' the question concerning why he is revealing himself (14:21–22). But these may simply be Johannine substitutions for Matthew 26:25's portrait of Judas asking Jesus, when all the Apostles 'dip with' him, 'is it I?', or Synoptic portrayals generally of Judas 'kissing' Jesus at his arrest – more shades of 'kissing' portraits, like those at Nag Hammadi of *Jesus kissing James*, or *vice versa*, or of 'the Disciple Jesus loved' generally.

Luke's Apostle list – which he presents in both his Gospel and Acts – is probably the most edifying of all. As one would expect, these two lists agree in almost every respect, differing only in the place accorded the one named '*Andrew*' (as we have seen, '*Man*') – regarding which, Luke's Gospel follows Matthew and Acts follows Mark.

The latter enumeration takes place in 'the upper room' and follows the picture of Jesus himself '*commanding them*' (as in the Gospel of Thomas's appointment *logion* relating to James) '*not to leave Jerusalem*'. Then he ascends '*hidden by a cloud*' (1:4–9). Curiously enough in the picture of the Apostles looking up at him here, *as he 'ascends'*, the two men again – 'who *stood beside* them in *white clothing*' – address them all as '*Galileans*' and ask querulously, '*Why stand you looking into the Heaven?*'

Of course, '*Judas Iscariot*' is missing from the listing in '*the upper room*' as he is in the '*Didymus Thomas*' episodes in John 20-21. This is because we are, doubtlessly, supposed to assume *he has already committed suicide*. Let us quote the list in the Gospel. Again Moses-like, as in Mark, Jesus '*went out into the Mountain*' – this time ostensibly '*to pray*'. It reads:

> Simon, whom he also named Peter, and Andrew *his brother* (so far so good), James and John (the appellatives '*sons of Zebedee*', '*sons of Thunder*' or '*his brother*' are missing here in Luke as they are in Acts), Philip and Bartholomew, Matthew and Thomas, *James* (*the son*) *of Alphaeus, Simon who was called Zealot, Judas* (*the brother*) *of James*, and *Judas Iscariot who also became* (his/*the*) *Betrayer* (Lk 6:12–16; cf. Acts 1:13)

The only difference between the list in Luke's Gospel and the one in Acts, as we have said, is that Andrew's place is changed and Judas *Iscariot* literally 'falls away'.

But, there are two astonishing things about the list, as Luke presents it in both places. In the first place, there is no '*Thaddaeus*' at all. Rather, he is called, both here and in Acts, 'Judas (the brother) of James'. But additionally, in actual order, his place is simply that accorded in Matthew and Mark to *Judas Iscariot.* This is particularly clear in Acts, when the second Judas – 'the *Iscariot*' or the '*son of Simon Iscariot*' in John – simply 'falls' away.

In addition, the 'Simon' who now follows *James the son of Alphaeus* in the listings is now quite straightforwardly and without embarrassment '*called Zealot*', not '*Canaanite*'/'*Canaanite*'/'*Cananaean*' or some other obfuscation or mistaken transliteration. In Acts, now minus the curious additional 'Judas' called 'the *Iscariot*', this is even more clearly rendered, because the *Simon the Zealot* is now really characterized as '*the Zealot*' and not the '*called Zelotes*' of Luke 6:15 (Acts 1:13).

But in the Gospel of John, Judas *Iscariot* is on four separate occasions designated '(the son) of Simon *Iscariot*' (Jn 12:4, 13:26, etc.). John also specifically refers to the 'Judas *not the Iscariot*' (14:22). This reference to 'the *Iscariot*' side by side with 'the other Judas' – 'the brother of James' (elsewhere, as will become plain, 'Judas *Zelotes*') – preceded by the definite article, is just what we have been attempting to point up. Whether accidental or otherwise, it does parallel the allusion to 'Simon *the Zealot*' or 'called *Zelotes*' in Acts and Luke, with whose name we began this discussion. It will now be an open question whether the terminology '*Iscariot*' is a direct offshoot of the singular term in Greek '*Sicarios*' (plural, *Sicarioi*), as we have been signaling all along – the Greek *iota* and *sigma* simply being inverted – and its closest linguistic anagram.

For Josephus it is 'the *Sicarii*' who retreat from Jerusalem to the fortress Masada after one of their leaders, a son or grandson of Judas '*the Galilean*' named Menachem – who 'put on the royal purple' – is stoned by collaborating High Priests in the early chaotic events of the Uprising – the only other stoning apart from James' that Josephus records in this period.

Under the leadership of another descendant of this 'Judas the *Galilean*', Eleazar ben Jair, they participate in the famous final suicide at Masada in 73 CE, parodied in the Gospel presentations of its 'Judas the *Iscariot*'. One should note that not only has Eleazar's name been found on an actual shard surviving on Masada, but both his names are paralleled in Scripture in the names 'Lazarus' and 'Jairus'. With this connecting of Judas now with Simon and the use of the term 'the *Iscariot*' as a cognomen not a proper name, it now becomes an open question whether the two characters, Luke's 'Simon *the Zealot*' – also connected to 'Judas the brother of James' – and John's 'Simon *Iscariot*', are not to be equated. Both clearly show the revolutionary aspect of early 'Christians'.

In addition, one will now have seriously to consider whether the term 'Judas Zelotes', found in the *Epistula Apostolorum*, which may date to the early Second Century, should not be taken more seriously.[37] This Gospel, generally following terminology found in John, lists the Apostles as: John, Thomas, Peter, Andrew, James, Philip, Bartholomew, Matthew, *Nathanael, Judas Z–el–ot–es, and Cephas.*

The last three, as usual, are particularly interesting. 'Nathanael', who appeared in the early part of John with Philip in Galilee, was quoted there as saying, 'can anything good come out of Nazareth' – meaning undecipherable – and with '*Didymus* Thomas' and the others in the episode of Jesus' appearance at 'the Sea of Tiberias' at the end, is distinctly designated there as from '*Cana of Galilee*' (Jn 1:45–49 and 21:2). This last is not so different from the term 'Canaanite' in Gospel Apostle lists, nor the mysterious 'Kfar Sechania' in Rabbinic sources associated with James' curious stand-in 'Jacob'. In Synoptic reckonings, he is clearly taking the place of 'James the son of Alphaeus' (our James), which should surprise no one.

Even more to the point, Cephas in this reckoning is now obviously distinct from Simon Peter, yet reckoned among the Apostles not the Disciples as in some other later Church listings. In this reckoning, he occupies the same position as and is clearly equivalent to the individual being called 'Simon Z–el–ot–es' or 'Simon the Zealot' in Luke and Acts – 'Simon the Canaanite' in Matthew and Mark (note the play on 'Cana' and 'Cananaean' again) – or, as we shall finally conclude below, Simeon bar Cleophas, the second *brother* – not 'cousin' – of Jesus. This individual called 'Cephas', and coming last in the list in the *Epistula Apostolorum*, also plainly occupies the same position as the 'Simon *Iscariot*' in John, called 'the father' – or 'brother' – 'of Judas *Iscariot*'.

'Judas Zelotes' in the *Epistula Apostolorum* is clearly to be identified with that Apostle called 'Thaddaeus' in Mark or 'Lebbaeus surnamed Thaddaeus' in Matthew, the same individual that Luke calls, doubtlessly most accurately of all, 'Judas (the brother) of James'! Notice the same appellative in the first line of the Letter of Jude, now baldly calling himself 'Judas the brother of James' in clear expostulatory prose. It is important that Luke in Acts 21:20, when talking about the greater part of James' followers in the Jerusalem Church, gives the actual basis for the derivation of this name, '*Zealots*' or '*Zealots for the Law*' – also expressed as '*Zelotai*' – about which we shall have more to say presently.

We shall have more to say presently as well about this 'Jude' or 'Judas', who also appears to have had quite a few other names and whose grandchildren, according to Hegesippus, are so cruelly executed under Trajan. It is, however, also edifying to note that in Old Latin manuscripts of the Gospel of Matthew, the name of 'Lebbaeus surnamed Thaddaeus' is replaced by 'Judas the Zealot' as well. Where such perspicuity came from is impossible to say (possibly Syriac sources) – but these old medieval manuscript redactors certainly seemed to understand the gist of the traditions before them even better than many moderns do.

Much of the misinformation, circumlocution, and dissimulation turn on this 'Judas the brother of James' and on Simeon bar Cleophas/Cephas/Simon the Zealot – including Mark and Matthew's garbled 'Simon the Cananaean' – as should be becoming clear. We shall also now find these same tell-tale allusions to 'Judas the Zealot' and 'Simon the Zealot' in the Syriac sources we shall treat further below.

Ruins at Pella in the Decapolis across the Jordan, to which 'the Pella Flight' of the Jamesian Jerusalem Community allegedly occurred.

Chapter 23
Simeon Bar Cleophas and Simon the Zealot

Simon the Canaanite, Nathanael, and James

Actually the Simeon bar Cleophas/Simon *the Zealot*/Simon *Iscariot* complex is relatively easily untangled – or shall we say deciphered. 'Cananaean' is an attempt in Greek, as many scholars now realize, to transliterate a Hebrew word, which then ends up either purposefully or out of ignorance as 'the Canaanite'. But the word is based on the Hebrew word for 'zeal', that is, *kin'at-Elohim – zeal for God* or *kin'at ha-Hoq – zeal for the Law*, so that, even as Matthew and Mark understand this cognomen as applied to Simon – or rather misunderstand it – it is based on the Hebrew phrase 'zeal for the Law'.

This is based on the episode in the Book of Numbers from the Old Testament, in which the High Priest Phineas, the grandson of Aaron, receives 'the Covenant of an Everlasting Priesthood ... *to make atonement* over the Sons of Israel, because of his *zeal for God*' (Num. 25:12–13). This, in Numbers, is considered equivalent to the 'Covenant of Peace', simultaneously conferred upon Phineas for his 'exceedingly great zeal'. Phineas receives these two Covenants, really the same, on behalf of all his descendants 'forever', because of the 'exceeding great zeal' or 'burning zeal for God' he displayed in *killing backsliders* who were *marrying foreigners* (note the relation of this to Herodian family practice), *introducing pollution into the camp of Israel in the wilderness* (Num. 25:6–11).

All of these themes, as should by now be apparent, are basic to the period before us and James' place in it. This theme of '*zeal*' is also referred to in the Maccabean books, where Phineas' '*zeal for the Law*' and '*keeping the Covenant*' are now pictured as the rallying cry of Judas Maccabee's father Mattathias who – on the altar at Modein (*thus*) – kills the Seleucid Royal Commissioner and the collaborating Jew willing to follow instructions forbidding the practice of Judaism.

For 1 Maccabees 2:19–28, the latter's offence is described in terms of forsaking 'the Law' and 'customs of the Forefathers' and no longer 'keeping the Covenant of the First' – language pervasive at Qumran and echoed, sometimes polemically, in the New Testament. For 1 Maccabees 2:50, the implication is that Mattathias wins the High Priesthood in perpetuity for his descendants on account of his 'burning zeal for the Law' and willingness to sacrifice his life 'for the Covenant of the Forefathers'. This is stated explicitly in 1 Maccabees 2:54, where 'the Covenant of the Everlasting Priesthood' accorded Phineas, 'because he was exceedingly zealous for the Law', is once again evoked and obviously meant to be equivalent to the aforementioned 'Covenant of Peace'.

This is certainly the atmosphere in the time of Aristobulus II (*c.* 63 BCE), who is unwilling to debase himself before Pompey and whose supporters go about the sacrifices, while the Romans – outpaced in this by their Pharisee confederates – slaughter these exceedingly Pious Priests in the Temple as they continue the sacrifices. It is also the atmosphere among the assembled crowd, who weep when they see Jonathan, the younger brother of Herod's *Maccabean* wife Mariamme, don the High Priestly vestments upon coming of age at thirteen (36 BCE). Herod, thereupon, had him brutally murdered and, not long after that, his sister Mariamme too (29 BCE).

Aside from the notice in Acts about *the majority* of James' followers in Jerusalem being 'Zealots for the Law' (21:20), one should also note the portrait in John's Gospel of Jesus' 'zeal' – in good Maccabean fashion – for his 'Father's House' and the purification of the same (John 2:17). Here John even paraphrases the words of Psalm 69:9, 'zeal for Your House consumes me', applying them to Jesus driving out the sellers and overturning the tables of the money-changers *in the Temple, at Passover time.*

John never does list all the Apostles, though he does refer to Andrew as 'Simon Peter's brother', followed by Philip, who when Jesus 'wants to go into Galilee', finds Nathanael (1:40 –45). At first the Gospel of John – paralleling the 'two' along the Way to Emmaus later in Luke – only identities this first pair (one of whom turns out to be 'Nathanael'), as 'two of his Disciples', with whom John 'was again *standing*' (1:35). Nathanael then goes and gets 'his *own* brother Simon' – the sobriquet 'Peter' is now missing from the denotation. It is right after this that Jesus is pictured as renaming Simon, '*Cephas*, which interpreted means "Stone"' (1:42). Clearly, there is some very peculiar textual rewriting going on here.

John does, however, refer to 'the Twelve', and whatever attempt there seems to be at a listing occurs in the post-resurrection sighting by the Sea of Galilee, containing the ubiquitous 'net' and 'casting down' motifs. Simon Peter is now listed with 'Thomas called *Didymus*', whoever he is, instead of 'Andrew' and, once again, the omnipresent 'other two Disciples' appear this time alongside 'the sons of Zebedee' – both again unnamed.

Here, too, the mysterious 'Nathanael from Cana of Galilee' appears. It is interesting that this 'Cana of Galilee' – mentioned four times in John, but in no *other* Gospel – is mentioned in only one other place in the literature of this period. This is by Josephus in his *Vita* who calls it 'a village of Galilee', at which he claims he made his headquarters (though usually he claims his headquarters was at '*Asochis*').[1] In the one story John tells about Nathanael at the beginning of his Gospel, he is pictured as sitting 'under a fig tree' at or before the time Philip calls him. This, Jesus is supposed to have either 'seen' or 'foreseen' (Jn. 1:48–50).

This motif of 'sitting under a carob tree' or 'fig tree' is to be encountered as well in Rabbinic stories about Honi the Circle Drawer or Onias the Righteous, whom we identified earlier as the putative ancestor or, at least, forerunner of John the Baptist and James. In Talmudic tradition, Honi falls asleep under this omnipresent carob or fig tree, before awakening in the generation of his grandson – that is, either Hanan the Hidden, John, one Abba Hilkiah (who like James supposedly also made rain), or James himself – seventy years later when the fruit is ripened. Then, because no one recognizes him – a familiar motif – he prays for death and, in the abrupt manner of Judas *Iscariot* in Gospel tradition, dies.[2]

In John's story, Jesus sees Nathanael – whom he supposedly greets with the words: 'Behold, in truth, an Israelite in whom there is no guile' (clearly the product of a non-Jewish author) – sitting 'under a fig tree', implying that this was somehow of great moment or a visionary or prophetical recognition of some kind. Not only does Nathanael now call Jesus 'Rabbi' – as in Nag Hammadi sources above about James and Jesus – but he immediately designates Jesus as 'the Son of God' and 'King of Israel' (1:47–49) and is the first to do so.

Thereupon Jesus predicts, because *he* has 'seen' Nathanael, that *Nathanael* will, in turn, '*see* greater things than this'. He predicts Nathanael 'will see the Heaven opened' – the very words used in Acts to describe *Stephen*'s vision of 'the Son of Man standing at the right hand of God' – 'and the Angel of God ascending and descending on the Son of Man' (1:50–51). Whatever else it is supposed to mean, this last, of course, is just another variation of James' final apocalyptic vision of 'the Son of Man coming on the clouds of Heaven' with the Heavenly Host, in Hegesippus' tradition recorded in Eusebius, and one more element linking 'Nathanael' to James and, therefore, 'Cana' to 'Canaanite' or 'Cananaean', not to mention the whole Honi 'Hidden' tradition attaching itself to members of this family.

In Rabbinic tradition, Honi 'was hidden' for seventy years because the terrain was so rocky, another link with the 'Hidden' traditions surrounding him and John and Jesus. Where the confusion or overlap of either 'fig' or 'carob' trees associated with these stories is concerned, both were considered by tradition to grow apart in rocky places and produce a kind of 'honey' that was eaten – usually as *poor man*'s food. In Rabbinic sources the passages 'honey out of a crag' (Deut. 32:13) and 'honey out of a rock' (Ps. 81:16) were applied to these genera of trees.[3] Again, we have the overlap with the food ascribed in Christian sources to John.

One final link-up in all these traditions: Simeon bar Yohai, the eponymous founder of *Zohar* tradition and a central figure of Jewish Kabbalistic lore, was said to have '*hidden*' himself with his son – also named Eleazar – in a cave for some twelve years at the time of the Bar Kochba Uprising (132–36 CE), again surviving on the honey or fruit of carobs or fig trees growing in these rocky areas.[4] It is interesting that when John mentions this '*Cana of Galilee*', 'Jesus' mother' – again, as we have said, *always unnamed* in John – also suddenly materializes (as in the Synoptics, somewhat confrontationally – 2:1–2:4), as do 'his brothers' (2:12). Presumably she goes unnamed because for John, '*Mary*' is 'the wife of Clopas'.

Aside from the final reference to 'Nathanael from Cana of Galilee' at the end of John, it is in the context of the other three references to 'Cana of Galilee' that Jesus is said to 'make water into wine', 'manifesting his Glory, so that his Disciples believed on him' (Jn. 2:11 and 4:46).

'Zeal for Your House Consumes Me'

Psalm 69, which John applies to Jesus' 'zeal' for *his* 'Father's House', is itself also a completely Messianic psalm. It is also '*Ebionite*', in the sense that it contains positive allusions to 'the Poor' (*Ebionim* – 69:33). It was obviously very important to the exegetes of early Christianity, because not only does it contain this allusion attributed to Jesus about *zeal* for his 'Father's House', but another familiar-sounding motif about being 'alienated from my brothers and estranged from my mother's other sons' (69:8), just encountered to some extent in this 'Cana of Galilee' episode in John. It also contains the allusion to 'being given poison to eat and vinegar to drink' that is such a central element in Gospel Crucifixion narratives (69:21).

But the Psalm is also replete with Qumranisms like: 'let their table become a snare before them' – an important connotation for these various disputes (69:22) – 'swallowing' (69:15), 'the Righteous', 'the Meek', and 'the Pit' (69:29–32). It also contains reference to the Lord's 'Wrathful Anger' and his 'Fury being *poured out* upon them' – usually connected in the Scrolls to these 'drinking' and 'swallowing' motifs (69:24), but in a pro-Palestinian not a Hellenistic manner. In fact, it ends up on the thoroughly Zionistic note, despite the anti-Zionistic use made of several of these citations above in the Gospels: 'God will *save Zion* and *rebuild the towns of Judah*. They will be lived in, owned, inherited by His Servants' descendants, lived in by *those who love His Name*' (69:35–36).

It should be remarked that this episode in John evoking Jesus' 'zeal' for the Temple is slightly out of synch with the Synoptic Gospels, which place the Temple-cleansing and the clear note of violence it contains in the run-up to Jesus' last days in Jerusalem, thus making it appear that the Roman soldiers and Temple police had ample cause for arresting Jesus as a subversive disturbing the peace. This notion of 'zeal for the Law' and 'zeal for the Judgments of God' is also prevalent in the attitude of the Scrolls, making these last appear at once 'Zealot' as well as 'Messianic'.

Of course, Josephus shows that the 'Zealot' Movement also has its root motivation in the 'Messianic' or 'World Ruler Prophecy' found in these passages of Numbers leading up to this evocation of Phineas' *zeal* for the Law (24:17–25:15). At Qumran, 'zeal for the Judgments of Righteousness' is part of 'the Spirit of Truth' and 'the Way of Light' of 'the Sons of Righteousness' and the curses upon 'the men of the lot of Belial'.[5] The phrase 'zeal for the Law' occurs in the crucial exegesis of the 'Way in the wilderness' Prophecy from Isaiah 40, utilized in the Gospels to characterize the activities of John the Baptist there. The

Community Rule reads: 'He shall *separate* from every man who has not turned away from all *Unrighteousness*, and ... *Everlasting hatred* for the Men of the Pit in a Spirit of secrecy ... For he shall be like a man *zealous for the Law, whose time will be the Day of Vengeance*!'[6]

One should also remark the use of this word 'zeal' throughout the Pauline corpus. Since Paul actually seems to be playing on the language of his opponents – and these within the 'Movement' not outside it – its connotation is usually reversed. In 1 Corinthians, for example, Paul calls his communities 'zealous of spiritual things'. He uses the term there amid motifs of 'building up the Church' or 'Assembly' and, what would have infuriated Jerusalem more than anything, 'speaking in Tongues' (1 Cor. 14:12). In 2 Corinthians 7:11 he uses it, as here in the Community Rule, in connection with God's 'Anger' and 'Vengeance', but with exactly opposite signification.

He alludes twice to 'zeal' in Galatians, once in connection with the all-important allusion to 'being chosen' from his mother's womb, we have discussed above, even going so far as to imply that he himself had once been 'a Zealot' by pointing out how '*exceedingly zealous* for the traditions' of his Fathers he had been (thus – Gal. 1:14). Even more tellingly, he uses it in Galatians 4:17–18 three times, this after attacking the Law as bringing death, attacking circumcision, and attacking the Jerusalem Leadership. Just following his own evocation of the 'Enemy' and 'Lying' epithets ('So your Enemy have I become by speaking Truth to you?' – 4:16), he proceeds to accuse his opponents – here clearly *within* the Movement and the very *ones* using these epithets against him – of being, '*zealous after you to exclude you*, so that you will be *zealous after them*', though not '*zealous for the right things*'! The play on their central concept of 'zeal' is hard to miss.

Perhaps his most characteristic use of the term comes in chapter 10 of Romans. This follows his insistence that the Gentiles attained 'a Righteousness of Faith', as opposed to Israel's failure to attain 'a Righteousness of the Law ... because it was *not by Faith but by works of the Law*' (9:30–31 – note the play on the 'works' ideology normally associated with James). In turn the condemnation of the 'zeal for God' of the Jews in this passage, which we shall quote below, is followed in Romans 11:3 and 11:28 by variations of his accusations against the other Israel – 'the Israel according to the flesh' – of killing all the Prophets and being 'Enemies' of all men that we previously encountered in 1 Thessalonians 2:15.

In Romans 12:19, he plays off the emphasis in the Community Rule's interpretation of Isaiah 40:3 on zeal for '*the Day of Vengeance*' – a term vividly used in Isaiah 63:4 amid the imagery of '*making the Peoples drunk with My Fury*' – by quoting Deuteronomy 32:35's '*Vengeance is mine ... saith the Lord*'. Finally, he completely attacks the Zealots in Romans 13:1–7, where he recommends 'paying taxes', because the Authorities '*have been appointed by God*' and *the tax collectors are, therefore, 'Servants of God*'!

One should note, in addition, the admonition to 'feed your Enemy' in Romans 12:20 and the 'Community as Temple'/'Community as sacrifice' imagery, 'the Many being one body in Christ' in Romans 12:1–5 – imagery encountered in the Community Rule expounding Isaiah 40:3's 'Way in the wilderness' in terms of 'zeal for the Law' and 'the Day of Vengeance'. Here, quoting Isaiah 8:14, which in the original Hebrew ends with the important 'net' and 'Pit' imagery – which he significantly omits – he reverses the 'Cornerstone' imagery from Isaiah 28:16, not to mention that language of 'stumbling' used in James 2:9 to emphasize the crucial point about 'keeping the whole Law'.

Now 'the Israel, following after a Law of Righteousness' and 'works of the Law', 'stumble over the Stone of Stumbling', 'a Stone of Stumbling in Zion and a Rock of offence' (in Greek, '*Petra*', that is, '*Peter*', here); but instead of the words 'a net to the inhabitants of Jerusalem and a Pit' that follow in Isaiah 8:14, Paul substitutes the phrase 'and everyone that believes on him shall not be ashamed' that goes with the 'Cornerstone' and 'laying in Zion a sure Foundation Stone' imagery of Isaiah 28:16, with which he began, not Isaiah 8:14 (Rom. 9:32–33).

These too were the very words we just heard in the John 2:11 episode about the miracles Jesus did in Cana of Galilee, 'revealing his Glory so that his Disciples *believed on him*' – not to mention the thrust of Psalm 69, which John goes on to quote in 2:17, about 'loving God' and 'loving His Name' generally. In fact, as we have repeatedly seen, Paul uses the Commandment to 'love your neighbor as yourself' to justify his whole panoply of anti-Zealot instructions, such as 'rendering tribute to all those due tribute' and obeying the ruling Authorities, 'who are no terror to good works', but are rather 'appointed by God'. The former possibly even plays on the Habakkuk *Pesher*'s verdict of Vengeance on the individual responsible for destroying the Righteous Teacher and the Poor: 'he shall be paid the reward with which he rewarded the Poor', also reflecting the Isaiah 3:10–11 passage applied to James' death in early Church literature, 'the reward of his hands shall be rewarded him'.[11]

These are all matters retrospectively inverted and superimposed in the Gospel portrait upon Jesus, so much so that it would be proper to call the individual who therein emerges, not Jesus, but Jesus/Paul. Is it any wonder that the Gospels portray their 'Jesus', not only as '*eating and drinking*', but keeping 'table fellowship' with tax collectors? Wherever one finds allusions of this kind in Paul, retrospectively imposed on the portrait of 'Jesus' in the Gospels, the description 'Jesus/Paul' would be appropriate.

The complete passage, referred to above, from Romans 10:2–4 reads:

> For I bear witness to them (the Jews) that they have *zeal for God*, but *not according to Knowledge*, for *being ignorant of God's Righteousness*, but rather seeking to *establish their own Righteousness*, they failed to submit to *the Righteousness of God*. Because for Righteousness, Christ is the end of the Law for anyone that believes.

Paul ends this particular discussion with the conclusion: '*For there is no difference between Jew and Greek*, for that same Lord of all is *Rich* towards all who *call on Him*' (10:12) – here playing on Qumran allusions to '*Riches*' and '*being called by Name*' – both reversing and spiritualizing the outright attack one finds there and in James on '*the Rich*' or '*Riches*'.[8] Paul is at his allegorizing best here. It is small wonder that his opponents – again, those *within* the Movement not outside it – found him difficult to contend with.

All of these things are part and parcel of what it meant to have '*zeal for God*' or, for that matter, to be a part of '*the Zealot Movement*'. It is no wonder Mark and Matthew found these things confusing when it came to handling the cognomen of Jesus' possible cousin and putative *second brother*, '*Simeon*' or '*Simon the Zealot*', and, therefore, thought that in some manner we had to do with '*Canaanite*' or '*Canaanites*'. The reader will probably feel the same bewilderment trying to make his or her way through these interlocking metaphors and terminologies.

The 'Zealot' Essenes in Hippolytus' Josephus

One work from Hippolytus of Rome (*c.* 160–235 CE), a contemporary of Clement of Alexandria – it is clearly authentic, though perhaps not from Hippolytus – which literally connects both '*Zealots*' and "*Essenes*' (even '*Sicarii*' and '*Essenes*'), was found in the Nineteenth Century at Mount Athos Monastery in Greece. In saying these things, sometimes it is of the most astonishing clarity and perspicuity; and, though basically reproducing the gist Josephus' descriptions, according to it the '*four groups of Essenes*' differ from received Josephus' presentations.

For it, the original are the more peace-loving kind, many still associate with the term '*Essene*', one encounters in the received Josephus. These seek always 'to help the Righteous' and in addition to 'white garments' wear 'linen girdles' exactly in the manner all texts aver about James and, by implication, John the Baptist. Nor 'will they hate a person who injures them' – here the admonition in the New Testament attributed to Jesus, to 'love your enemies' (though at Qumran, it should be appreciated, the general position was 'hate the Sons of the Pit'). Paul-like, they seek to keep faith with Rulers, because their 'position of Authority cannot happen to anyone without God'. These may be early Essenes and are obviously the Essenes of Josephus, 'but after a lapse of time' – according to this work attributed to Hippolytus – 'they *split into four parties*'.[9]

There are those who will carry no coin, 'nor carry or look on any graven image', a position clearly reflected in the Gospels. These will not even enter a gate on which there are statues erected, considering it a violation of the Law – note the relationship of this to an incident, described by Josephus, where the two Rabbis encouraged their followers to pull down the eagle Herod had erected over one of the gates to the Temple 'contrary to the laws of their Forefathers' at the beginning of the disturbances leading to the establishment of the 'Zealot' Movement.[10]

But even more zealous than these, are those who, on hearing anyone *discussing God and His Laws*, if they suspect him to be an *uncircumcised person*, they will carefully observe him and when they meet a person of this description in any place alone, they will *threaten to slay him if he refuses to undergo the rite of circumcision*.[11] If he refuses to comply with this demand, they will not spare him, but rather execute him forthwith. Hippolytus now makes it clear that this more extreme group of Essenes 'were called *Zelotai* by some (that is '*Zealots*') and *Sicarii* by others'.

Taken at face value, this is absolutely devastating testimony, confirming the antiquity of the source, no matter to whom one wishes to attribute it (for ease of attribution we shall henceforth refer to it simply as 'Hippolytus'). Not only this, but it totally illuminates the situation in Palestine at this time and the real import of evoking Phineas' killing backsliders for introducing *pollution into the camp of Israel*.

'Hippolytus' now weaves this in with Josephus' account of 'Fourth Philosophy Zealots', by asserting, as Josephus does on two occasions, that they will '*call no man Lord* except the Deity, even though one should attempt to torture or even kill them'.[12] This is, of course, the 'freedom' and 'bondage' Paul reverses and allegorizes into freedom from the *very* Law these '*Zealot Essenes*' are dying to protect. For his part, Josephus describes the bravery and 'immovable resolution' of this group, which he is now calling not '*the fourth group of Essenes*', but '*the Fourth School of Jewish Philosophy*'!

These, he says, did not mind suffering tortures or deaths of every kind, nor 'could any such fear make them *call any man Lord*'. Their resolution 'was well known to a great many'. Josephus declines to say more for fear that, as he puts it, what he has described would 'be beneath the resolution they exhibit when undergoing pain'.[13]

This, clearly, is very similar to what goes by the name among early Christians of martyrdom. As a Roman interrogator of prisoners Josephus should certainly have known, 'for it was in the time of Gessius Florus' (also sent out by Nero at his wife Poppea's recommendation – this *after the fire in Rome*), 'who by his abusive and lawless actions caused the nation to grow wild with *this distemper*, provoking them *to revolt against the Romans*'.

Thus Josephus' description of 'the *fourth* school of Jewish Philosophy' in his *Antiquities*, where he did deign to discuss the Movement begun by Judas the Galilean and his mysterious colleague '*Saddok*' at the time of the Census of Cyrenius some seventy years before – the same Census the Gospel of Luke equates with the birth of 'Jesus'.

In the *Jewish War*, as we have seen, Josephus does begin his well-known description of the '*three* philosophical schools among the Jews' at the point he mentions that 'a *certain Galilean*, whose name was Judas (in the *Antiquities*, it will be recalled, Judas does *not* come from Galilee, but rather Gaulonitis – today's Golan) incited his countrymen to revolt, upbraiding them as cowards if they *submitted to paying a tax to Rome* and would *after God, submit to mortal men as their Lords*'.

But instead of now going on to describe Judas' sect – 'which was not at all like the rest' – Josephus at this point launches into his well-known description of the '*Essenes*'. At the same time, he cuts the above piece from his description of the Movement founded by Judas and *Saddok* in the *Antiquities* and adds it to that of '*the Essenes*' here in the *War*. He now says of these Essenes:

> *They are above pain* ... and as for death, *should it be for Glory* (we have encountered this '*Glory*' in notices about Jesus and in the Scrolls above), *they esteem it better than living a long time*. And, indeed, our War with the Romans *gave abundant proofs what immovable resolutions they have in enduring sufferings because, although they were tortured and dismembered, burned and torn to bits, going through every kind of instrument of torture* to make them *blaspheme the Name of the Law-giver* or *to eat what was forbidden them*, yet could they not be made to do either of these, nor at the same time even *to flatter their torturers or shed a single tear. Rather they smiled in their very pains and laughed scornfully at those inflicting these tortures on them, resigning their souls with great alacrity as expecting to receive them back again.*

Not only do we have here, once again, the very essence of what is normally understood as 'Christian' martyrdom, but these are the very words ascribed to the literary prototypes of the Maccabean Movement two centuries before, where the doctrine of Resurrection of the Dead is first enunciated in a straightforward manner. This is in the 'Seven Brothers' episode in 2 Maccabees 7, caricatured in Gospel discussions of Resurrection.[14] In the 'Seven Brothers' episode, the mother of the brothers urges each in turn to '*die for the Laws of his country*' encouraged by the doctrine of Resurrection from the Dead.

As the martyred teacher of the Law, Eleazar, who 'preferring to *die gloriously* rather than live a *polluted life*', is made to express it in the episode just preceding this one, to teach the young an example of '*how to make a good death, zealously and nobly for the venerable and Holy Laws*' (2 Macc. 6:28). The brothers are portrayed as disdaining life and limb '*for the sake of His Laws, hoping to receive them back again from Him*', since '*it is for His Laws we die*' (7:9–12).

For her part, the mother encourages the seventh brother to make a good death, averring that God, 'in His Mercy will most surely *raise you up to both breath and life, seeing you now despise your own life for the sake of His Laws* ... Fear not this brutal butcher, but prove yourself worthy of your brothers and *welcome death, so that in His Mercy I shall receive you back again in their company*' (7:23–29). This last is, surely, the explanation for the Masada suicide, to avoid pollution and to be reunited together again at the Resurrection – which is the reason that the '*bones*' passage from Ezekiel has been found buried under the synagogue floor there.

In the same book, Judas Maccabee, following these martyrdoms, after a particularly difficult battle, is portrayed as making a sacrifice on behalf of the fallen, in which '*he took full account of the Resurrection*, for if he had not expected the fallen to rise again, it would have been altogether silly and superfluous to pray for the dead. But since he had in view the splendid recompense reserved for those who make a good death, the intention was completely *Holy and Pious*' (12:45–46). As the second and fourth brothers put this, after being *skinned alive* and otherwise tortured, because they would not *break the Law*, 'The King of the Universe will raise us up to new and everlasting life ... whereas for you, there will be no Resurrection again to life' (7:9–14).

In the parody of these things in the Synoptic Gospels, 'some of the Pharisees *with* the Herodians' (this is an important addition) 'send out spies to *ensnare*' Jesus about whether or not 'it was Lawful to pay tribute to Caesar' (Mt 22:15–40 and pars.). Here not only do we have the ubiquitous 'net' and 'snare' language – of course, with reverse signification – but also the 'tribute' question again. In addition, there is the theme of 'spying', also encountered in Paul's complaints against 'those of the circumcision' in Galatians 2:4–12, who 'come in by stealth *to spy out the freedom*' that Paul and his companions 'enjoy in Christ Jesus, because they wish to *reduce us to bondage*', this a different kind of 'bondage' than that being referred to above where the tax question is concerned.

After this, a group identified as 'the Sadducees' comes, for whom 'there is no Resurrection' – the very words used in 2 Maccabees 7:14 above. Of course, the Sadducees are, also, the party Josephus identifies as denying the doctrine that the dead could enjoy immortal life, the knowledge of which Acts also portrays Paul as evincing (Acts 23:6–10). The situation being caricatured here in the Gospels also parodies the story of John the Baptist and the arcane Jewish legal custom of levirate marriage being alluded to there – in this episode relating to the 'Seven Brothers', each rather being portrayed as, in turn, 'leaving no seed behind' and, therefore, marrying the wife of the next (Mt 22:23–33 and pars.).

Thus, instead of *noble* encouragement to martyrdom on the part of the mother to her seven sons – a thing few Jewish mothers would encourage even today – to die for the Holy Laws of their country, taking note of the doctrine of resurrection, as in 2 Maccabees, here each brother is basically portrayed as marrying the wife of the previous brother and the tragic pathos of the original story turned into something resembling comic farce.

The 'Sadducees' then ask the nonsense question, which brother will get whose wife after the Resurrection (Mt 22:28 and pars.). Not only does this completely trivialize the basic Zealot Resurrection ideology, it shows clear knowledge of the direct connection of the 'Seven Brothers' story, as it was told here in 2 Maccabees, to the doctrine of resurrection – not to mention knowledge of Josephus' portrait of the 'Sadducees' generally. It also makes a mockery of the hope of resurrection being expressed in the willingness to undergo torture and the steadfast attachment to the Law described in Hippolytus' picture of his fourth group of 'Essenes' and Josephus' 'Fourth Philosophy' followers of Judas *the Galilean and Saddok* – that is, '*Zadok*'.

Hippolytus' Naassenes, Ebionites, and Elchasaites

It is following this attestation of the longevity of these 'Essenes', 'many living over a century' – echoing Epiphanius' picture of James 'dying a virgin at the age of ninety-six' and Simeon bar Cleophas 'a hundred and twenty', both following '*the Nazirite life-style*' – that Josephus gives the description about their willingness to undergo any kind of torture rather than 'blaspheme the Law-giver', 'eat what was forbidden them', or 'flatter their torturers', all clearly themes of this 'Seven Brothers' episode in 2 Maccabees above connected to its resurrection ideal.

As Josephus puts this point about their longevity, this is 'because of the simplicity of their diet (by which he appears to be implying, like Hippolytus, that they *ate only vegetables*) and the regularity of the life-style they observe'. This culminates in his description of their willingness to undergo torture and martyrdom like the early Christians, but again of course for the absolutely opposite reasons – those reasons expressed by 2 Maccabees not the Gospels and Acts.

Though Hippolytus is basically following Josephus' sequence again here, the language he uses is different. For the purposes of our identifications too this makes all the difference. He expresses this as follows: 'They assert, therefore, that the cause of this (their longevity) is their extreme devotion to Religion (this, of course, the very language James 1:26–27 is using) and condemnation of all excess in regard to *what they eat* and their *being temperate* and *incapable of anger*. And so it is that they despise death, rejoicing when they can *finish their course with a good conscience*' (here Paul's 'running the course' and 'conscience' language in 1 Corinthians 8:7–10:25).

Hippolytus continues: 'If, however, anyone would attempt to torture men of this description with the aim of inducing them *to eat, speak Evil of the Law or eat that which is sacrificed to an idol*, he will not effect his purpose, for these *submit to death and endure any torture rather than violate their consciences*.' Here not only is Hippolytus once again using the language of 'eating' and 'conscience' that Paul is using in 1 Corinthians 8:4–9:14 and 10:16–33 (in 8:12, referring to 'the *brothers*', '*weak* consciences', and eating only vegetables, Paul actually uses the *very* words, 'wounding their consciences'), but Hippolytus is also employing the language of James' directives to overseas communities Paul also exploits in his arguments with Community Leaders (principally James) who make problems over 'things sacrificed to idols' – 'a *stumbling block* to those who are *weak*' (8:9).

That Hippolytus here actually evokes the very directive incontrovertibly (and probably uniquely) associated with *James*' name in the New Testament, which Paul so rails against in 1 Corinthians and which Peter quotes too in the Pseudoclementine *Homilies*,[15] makes it absolutely clear whom and what we are dealing with here. It would be impossible, I think, to achieve a more perfect match and better convergence of themes than this. These '*Zealot*' Essenes are also *Jamesian*. Earlier in this section, in the aftermath of alluding to 'loving God', 'love building up', not 'Knowledge puffing up' (8:1–3) – all phraseologies encountered at Qumran – Paul even plays on all these conceptualities by ridiculing the 'Knowledge' of the 'some' (that is, those who 'came down from James'), who 'with conscience *of the idol* (the wordplay here works in the Greek only), eating as if of a thing *to* an idol', 'their "conscience", being weak, is *defiled*' (8:7). Paul is at his allegorical and polemical best here, again reversing the ideology of his opponents against them with spellbinding rhetorical artistry.

His conclusion is a model of facetious dissimulation: 'Yet, if anyone sees you, having Knowledge, eating in an idol Temple, will not the *conscience* of such a *weak being* be built up (meaning, in this context, 'strengthened'), causing him to *eat things sacrificed to idols*?' (8:10). Therefore, 'through your Knowledge, the weak brother will be destroyed ... so if meat causes my *brother to stumble*, I will *never eat flesh forever* that I should not *cause my brother to stumble*' (8:11–13).

He even goes on to use this word 'conscience' in Romans 13:5 to justify *paying taxes* to Rome – the same 'conscience' Hippolytus claims *these 'Zealot' Essenes 'would submit to death and endure torture rather than defile' by 'eating things sacrificed to idols*'. We can say here that Paul and Hippolytus are basically talking about the same group. One even might go so far as to claim that Paul was among those 'cast out' (*ekballo*) of such a group, one reason perhaps for the New Testament's focus on this kind of language and its trivialization into that of 'casting out demons', the Authority for which Jesus accorded his principal Apostles.

In view of Josephus' notice about Nero sending Florus as Governor in Palestine with the express purpose, seemingly, of goading the Jews into revolt, it begins to look as if the circle of people around Nero we have described above – who were neither unsophisticated nor unintelligent (including people like Epaphroditus, Seneca, Felix's brother Pallas, and on its fringes someone even Josephus calls '*Saulus*') – were willing even to wipe out a whole people. In the end, anyhow, their best general, Vespasian, was sent from Britain to rid the world of this pestilent Messianic agitation that was then disturbing the entire Mediterranean and inciting revolt against Roman Imperial Authority everywhere.

It is this then which, via the magic of literary re-creation, becomes converted in the traditions embodied by the Gospels and the Book of Acts into the picture of a pacifist, other-worldly 'Messianism' with politically-harmless '*Disciples*', such as '*Stephen*' and Paul, who basically approve of foreign or Roman Rule and do not oppose it. By the same token, their tormentors (as, for instance those '*Nazirite*'-style oath-takers who '*vow not to eat or drink until they have killed Paul*) are essentially the very people obliterated *en masse* because of their propagation of this form of more militant 'Messianism' – the more subversive '*disease-carriers*' of the '*Nazoraean heresy*' whom, as Acts 24:5 attests, were active around the Mediterranean, '*fomenting revolution among all the Jews in the inhabitable world*'.

It is to this description of their continent life-style, their unwavering willingness to undergo death or torture rather than *blaspheme their Law-giver* or *eat any forbidden things* that Josephus attaches his picture of the 'resolution' these 'Essenes' showed in the *recent War with the Romans*, thereby tying Essenes of this kind to the Uprising against Rome in the manner of 'Zealots'. This is missing from Hippolytus' description. For Josephus the point was simply 'eating *forbidden* things' or 'blaspheming the Law-giver', but the direct association here in Hippolytus of 'blaspheming' or 'speaking Evil against the Law' – the point is the same – with not eating '*things sacrificed to an idol*' ties this description *absolutely* to the Community of James.

At this point in Josephus' description of Essenes and, interestingly enough, in regard to what he calls their '*practicing Piety towards the Deity*' as well, Josephus uses the '*casting out*' language, but this now in regard to those '*cast out from the group*' or '*expelled*' (*ekballousi*). This language, as should be clear, is rife in both the Qumran Community Rule and Damascus Document. Since the probationer had already *sworn an oath only to eat 'the pure food' of the Community* – the '*eating and drinking*' theme again (this is exactly the same as at Qumran) – according to Josephus, he will, therefore, die unless he breaks his oath.[16]

The language Josephus uses to describe this, including '*not revealing secrets to others even if tortured to death*', '*swearing to transmit these exactly as he received them himself, and always being a lover of Truth and an exposer of Liars*', is almost word-for-word the language of the terrifying oath-taking required by James of the Elders of the Jerusalem Assembly, following Peter's Letter to him in the introduction to the Pseudoclementine *Homilies*. This is the kind of '*casting out*', that is, '*casting*' someone '*out*' of the Community or '*expelling*' him, that in the New Testament becomes, as we have now made clear, the Jews viciously 'casting Stephen out of the city' (*ekbalontes*) in Acts or the Apostles receiving 'the Authority to cast out Evil Demons' from Jesus in the Gospels (*ekballein*).

It also is interesting that in his description of those he calls 'the *Naassenes*', Hippolytus asserts that they received their ideas from numerous discourses which '*James the brother of the Lord handed down to Mariamne*'. Whatever confusion may be involved here, the same idea appears in the Second Apocalypse of James from Nag Hammadi, where this individual is now called '*Mareim one of the Priests*'. There he is associated with someone called '*Theuda, the father*' or '*brother of the Just One since he was a relative of his*',[17] and we are now on our way to solving the 'Thaddaeus'/'Theudas' problem as well.

One can assume that the discourses, which Hippolytus says James 'handed down', are basically the same as those which somehow reappeared in the Pseudoclementine literature – or what other early Church writers refer to as the 'Travels' and/or the 'Preaching of Peter' – or, for instance, Epiphanius' 'Ascents of James'. Curiously enough, Hippolytus considers these 'Naassenes' to have been the first '*heresy*' before even the Ebionites or Elchasaites, whatever Hippolytus might mean by '*heresy*' at this point – the same word used to describe early Christianity in Acts 24:14, where it is also called '*the Way*', and 28:22.

He says they believed 'the Christ' to be, in a kind of incarnationist or Islamic-style '*Imam*'ate doctrine, 'the Perfect Man' or 'the Primal Adam' – or simply 'Adam'. But these are just the ideas which in the Pseudoclementines come to be associated with Jewish Christianity or the Ebionites, as well as with 'the Standing One', not unrelated to all these allusions to 'standing' in the various Gospel accounts we have been looking at above. One can still find such teachings among groups called in Arabic 'the *Subba*' or 'the Sabaeans of the Marshes' – the 'Mandaeans' of Southern Iraq. Apparently 'Mandaean' was the name for the rank and file of such groups, the priestly élite being known as the *Nazoraeans*! '*Subba*', of course, meant to be baptized or immersed.[18]

For Hippolytus, this '*Christ*' or '*the Perfect Man*' – according to Mandaean doctrine '*the Demiurge standing above the cosmos*' – descended on numerous individuals. This is a quasi-Gnostic doctrine. For the latter, in the '*aeon*' we have before us, the descent of this '*Christ*' or '*Perfect Man*' on 'Jesus' occurred *in the form of a dove* – the picture disseminated in the Gospels. Hippolytus ascribes the same ideology to '*the Elchasaites*' who seem to be a later adumbration of such groups as well as to one, 'Cerinthus', referred to by all these heresiologists, who was said to have taught 'the Ebionites'.

This doctrine of 'the Perfect Man' or 'Standing One' is also abroad among Shi'ites in Islam even today, albeit in a slightly different nexus, which seems to have developed out of the persistence of many of these groups and the central notions they all seemed to share in Northern Iraq. In Epiphanius, some two centuries after Hippolytus, these 'Naassenes' are called 'Nazareans' or 'Nazrenes' – the 'Nazoraeans' who go into the élite Priest Class of Mandaeans. For him, *they exist even before Christ* – as do our so-called 'Essenes' at Qumran – and are coincident with other similar groups he calls Daily Bathers/Hemerobaptists and '*Sebuaeans*' (thus!).

It is clear that the majority of these groups do not differ markedly from each other as to basics and we are really only witnessing overlapping designations and the transference of terminology from one language into another in this region. In Arabic and to Islam they are what – via the Aramaic and Syriac – come to be called '*Sabaeans*', based on the word in those languages for baptism or immersion, '*masbuta*' – 'Masbuthaeans' according to some of Eusebius' reckonings. In Palestine, for example, one of the several names for them is 'Essenes'.

In the First Apocalypse of James from Nag Hammadi, where James is regarded as a kind of Supernatural Redeemer figure, James is encouraged to teach these things, firstly, to Addai and, secondly, to '*Salome and Mariam*', and in the Second Apocalypse, to '*Mareim one of the Priests*' – this obviously the '*Mariamne*' (also '*Mariamme*' elsewhere at Nag Hammadi) in Hippolytus' descriptions of what he is calling '*Naassenes*'. Like Matthew of Christian tradition – called in Mark, it will be recalled, 'Levi the son of Alphaeus' and, therefore, usually considered 'Priestly' or at least 'levitical' – he is described as doing the 'writing'.

We now can see where perhaps some of these criss-crosses between '*James the son of Alphaeus*' and Matthew as '*Levi the son of Alphaeus*' may have come from. Clearly we have a large measure of garbling and overlap here, but, whatever else these correspondences may imply, it is clear that as early as Hippolytus' time – Second–Third Century CE – many of these doctrines, 'Gnostic' or otherwise, were being ascribed to 'James the brother of the Lord'.

One should also note that in addition to teaching that 'the Christ' descended on Jesus in the form of a dove, Cerinthus is said to have taught that 'Jesus was *not born of a virgin*, but he sprang from Joseph and Mary similar to *the rest of men*', whom he only '*exceeded in Righteousness*, wisdom, and understanding'.[19] These are the doctrines, of course, that Eusebius, a century after Hippolytus, is ascribing to the '*Ebionites*' not Cerinthus. According to Hippolytus, these Ebionites not only saw Christ in the manner of Cerinthus, but 'live in all respects according to the Law of Moses, insisting that one could only be justified – that is, 'made Righteous' – in such a manner'.[20]

For Hippolytus, too, Cerinthus is already teaching the doctrine that 'Christ' did not suffer on the cross, but departed from Jesus at that moment. This reappears in slightly more developed form in the Gnostic texts at Nag Hammadi and, from there, the Koran.[27] For some of these 'Gnostics', it was rather Simon of Cyrene, who carried the cross in Gospel accounts, who thus suffered (one should always watch this usage, '*Simon of Cyrene*' because it may be that we have another mix-up with '*Simeon bar Cleophas*', who actually *was crucified*). For Hippolytus, the Elchasaites, whom we have already met, have the same doctrine. For them 'the Christ', who is superior to the rest, is transfused into many bodies frequently and was now in Jesus … likewise this Jesus afterwards was continually being transfused into bodies and was manifested in many at different times.[22]

This doctrine is, of course, simply that of Shi'ite or '*Imam*ate' Islam, only now, instead of '*the Christ*', the Supernatural incarnationist figure is called '*the Imam*' and considered to be 'Ali, Muhammad's 'first cousin'/'son-in-law'/and 'legitimate Successor'. Again, this term in Arabic bears some relationship to '*the Standing One*' doctrine – for other groups, as we have seen, '*the Primal*' or '*Perfect Adam*' – not only in kind, but because it actually derives from and means '*the One Standing before*'.

The Elchasaites follow a teacher called '*Elchasai*' – a name Hippolytus thinks translates as 'Righteous One'; for others, such as Epiphanius, as we saw, it is 'Great' or 'Hidden Power'. He is a contemporary in some respects to our Simeon bar Cleophas above – if the reports about Simeon's extreme longevity can be believed. These 'Elchasaites' are virtually indistinguishable from another group Epiphanius is later calling the 'Sampsaeans', another probable corruption or variation of the Syriac/Islamic 'Sabaeans' or 'Masbuthaeans', that is, Daily Bathers.

For Hippolytus, 'Elchasai' came in the third year of Trajan's reign (101 CE), the period of the latter's difficulties in the East with Parthia and the time both Eusebius and Epiphanius equate with Simeon bar Cleophas' martyrdom. It is also the time of Messianic unrest, as we have seen, in Egypt and North Africa under 'Andrew' or 'Andreas of Cyrene'. A book ascribed to '*Elchasai*' was apparently brought to Rome during the second year of Hadrian's reign (119 CE). This book included the important reference to 'the Standing One', already encountered above in the Pseudoclementines. There purportedly it was also a revelatory Angel 'standing' some 'ninety-six miles high' (in competing accounts this is the risen Christ), whose feet were approximately fourteen miles long![23]

The height of 'ninety-six' here, manifestly, is nothing but the number of years Epiphanius – two centuries later – considers to be *James' age* when he died. 'Elchasai', for Epiphanius, is 'a false prophet'. He joined the Ebionites, who it would appear – according to him – were already extant and no different from the 'Sampsaeans', 'Essenes', and the 'Elchasaites', again tying all these groups together. (In fact, for Epiphanius, who amid all the confusion and fantasy sometimes has extremely good, factual material, the 'Elchasaites' and 'Sampsaeans' – at least in 'Arabia' and 'Perea' – are equivalent.) These all taught the doctrine that 'Christ' and 'Adam' ('Man') were the same thing. As he puts it, 'the Spirit, which is Christ' put on 'Adam's body' or 'him who is called Jesus'.[24]

For Hippolytus, '*Elchasai*' received this doctrine from a group in Northern Mesopotamia or Persia called 'the *Sobiai*', clearly 'the *Sabaeans*' or 'Daily Bathers' we have already encountered in Islam – but these now in *the First or Second Century CE*. Elsewhere in Hippolytus, it is clear this area is not far from 'the country of the *Adiabeni*', whom we shall now presently meet in the story of the conversion to Judaism or 'Christianity' of Queen Helen of Adiabene. It is also clear that these Mesopotamian '*Subba*' or '*Sabaeans*' are no different really from Hippolytus' and Josephus' 'Essenes', the name simply being expressed in a different linguistic framework.

Conclusions as to James the son of Alphaeus, Simon the Zealot, and Judas the Brother of James

We are now getting to the point where we can draw some conclusions about these various overlaps, substitutions, and changes in Gospel lists where those called 'Apostles' are concerned. It is clear that the 'James the son of Alphaeus, Simon the Zealot, and Judas (the brother) of James' – also called in Greco-Syriac tradition 'Judas *Zelotes*', that is, 'Judas the Zealot' – are obviously those being reckoned in the picture of the Synoptic Gospels as 'the brothers of Jesus' and that, therefore, 'Alphaeus' and 'Cleophas' (or 'Clopas') must be identical. The same as far as the term '*Lebbaeus*' is concerned, which also may be a variation of another term we have seen applied to James, '*Oblias*'.

But one can go further. If one takes into account the witnesses to the execution and resurrection of Jesus – or, depending on the account, the empty tomb – it becomes quite clear that purposeful obfuscation or garbling of traditions is going on. Still, 'Mary the mother of James and Joses and the mother of the sons of Zebedee' in Matthew 27:56 and '*Mary the mother of James the less and of Joses and Salome*' in Mark 15:40 and 'Mary the mother of James' in Luke 24:10 are all, simply, *Mary the mother of Jesus*. I think we can take this as a *first* conclusion.

In the Book of Acts, after '*James the brother of John*' has conveniently been disposed of and the *real* James introduced, the 'Mary the mother of John Mark', to whose house Peter goes after escaping from prison to leave a message for '*James and to the brothers*' (12:12), is none other than this *same* Mary – either 'Mary the mother of Jesus' or 'Mary the mother of James', despite obfuscations stemming from Mary being '*a life-long virgin*' or James being *the son of Joseph by a previous wife*. In any event, this is precisely what she is called in Mark 16:1 and Luke 24:10.

'*James the Less*' is hardly James the less (Mk 15:40). Rather, *he is James the Great* – James *the Just* – the victim of more obfuscation, in this instance aimed at '*belittling*' him – literally. The same for '*James the son of Alphaeus*'. '*Mary the sister*' of Jesus' mother '*and the wife of Clopas*' in John 19:25 is, once again, simply James' or Jesus' mother Mary – if Jesus had a mother called Mary or if Mary had a son called Jesus (John doesn't know either point) – it being normally absurd for someone to have the same name as her own sister. Thus, the proliferation of all these Mary's diminishes.

'*Cleopas*' and '*Alphaeus*' are simply Jesus' father Joseph or, as the case may be, '*Clopas*' or '*Cleophas*' – ideological attempts to dissociate Jesus from his forebears notwithstanding. Garblings or mix-ups such as these might strike the Western ear as surprising, until the nature of oral tradition is understood. For instance, in the Middle East, the old Greek Constantinople has become, via the shortening '*Stanbul*', today's '*Istanbul*'. A city like Nablus on the West Bank of Palestine comes out of the Greek '*Neopolis*', there being, for instance, no letter equivalent to 'p' in the Arabic alphabet. Even the romantic and seemingly melodious name '*Andalusia*' for Spain comes via the Arabic from the less pleasing one '*Vandals*', that is, in Arabic, '*al-Andals*'/'*the* Andals', who sacked Rome in the Fourth Century and came via Spain to Tunisia in North Africa – where the Arabs first encountered them.

This raises the question of whether Jesus' father was ever really called 'Joseph' at all except via literary re-creation. The Gospel of John, once again, implies something of this tangle, when Philip tells the Disciple it calls 'Nathanael' – either Bartholomew or our old friend, 'James the Less' again, in the Synoptics and, in our view, James – at almost the first breath, that 'Andrew' and 'Peter' 'have found the one written of by Moses in the Law and the Prophets, "Jesus the son of Joseph from Nazareth"' (1:46). But if we take this statement at face value, there is, plainly, no 'Jesus the son of Joseph from Nazareth' written about in either the Mosaic Law (the five Books of Moses) or the Prophets.

At this point, too, John is anxious to mask the true thrust of the 'Nazoraean' terminology, which, as we have been discovering, means 'Keeper' – either 'Keeper of the Law' or 'Keeper of the Secrets' – transforming it into 'Nazareth'. Either this, or perhaps it relates to the 'Nazrene'/'Nazirite' usage, not to mention the 'Cana'/'Canaanite'/'Cananaean' terminologies. There is, however, the biblical 'Joshua the son of Nun', of the Tribe of Ephraim, a 'son of Joseph'. It is passages of this kind in 'the Law of Moses' that John appears to be evoking. To put this in the shortest manner possible, the biblical 'Joshua', the individual upon whom Jesus is typed – Jesus being the closest Greek homophone to the name '*Joshua*' or 'Yeshu'a' in Hebrew, which literally does mean '*save*' or '*Savior*' – really *was* a true '*son of Joseph*' through Ephraim. This does not mean that the actual 'Jesus' of history *was*.

In addition, because of overlaps in the biblical text between the Books of Joshua and Judges, there is another twist to the relationship of this name '*Jesus*' to '*Joshua*'. Joshua, who is pictured as having died at the end of the Book by his name (24:29) as well as in the first line of the next book Judges (1:1), is then depicted as being alive again and giving his final instructions to the tribes in Judges 2:6. Of course modern exegetes understand this as being a problem of composite sources; but here we have a scenario in that some over-zealous ancient biblical exegete might have interpreted in terms of a dead-alive '*Joshua*' or '*Jesus*' in these biblical books too – '*Joshua*' and '*Jesus*' being cognates.

In addition, in Jewish tradition or folklore, two Messiahs are often pictured, a '*Messiah ben Judah*' and a '*Messiah of Israel*', matching the dual nature of the Southern and Northern Kingdoms. The Northern Kingdom was, in effect, the Kingdom of the descendants of Joseph, these being the most numerous and the principal tribe there. This was of course the tribe of Ephraim, Joshua's tribe. Therefore in Talmudic allusion, the latter is often dubbed the '*Messiah ben Joseph*', that is, the '*Messiah the son of Joseph*'.

The story of Jesus' birth parentage may, in fact, be no more complex than this. These kinds of matters are perhaps also reflected to some extent in the Qumran notion of a dual or two Messiahs, if such a notion, in fact, exists at Qumran, which is questionable. The evidence is unclear and depends on the meaning of usages that may be idiomatic. All the same, the issue has to do with a priestly or a lay Messiah, as it does in Hebrews, or a combination of both, and has very little relevance to the question of Jesus' parentage, whether real or simply formulary.

The 'Papias' Fragment and Conclusions as to Jesus and Joses

However, there is a passage from the early Church father Papias (*c.* 60–135 CE) from Hierapolis in Asia Minor, a contemporary of the younger Pliny, that can help us tie all these passages together and resolve these difficulties. Papias is perhaps the oldest Church father, aside from Clement of Rome (*c.* 30–97) and Ignatius (c. 50–115), his older contemporary. Irenaeus (*c.* 130–200) calls Papias a friend of Polycarp (69–156) and a hearer of John, meaning the John of Ephesus to whom the Gospel is attributed.

It is to Papias that Eusebius owes the information that Mark, who never saw the Lord, but who was called in 1 Peter 5:13 Peter's 'son', was Peter's associate and disciple overseas – probably in Rome – and that 'Matthew put together the oracles in the Hebrew language, and each interpreted them as best he could'.[25]

This last is very important information, because it gives us a certain insight into the manner in which the Scriptures were put together – in the first place, by culling biblical Scripture for the prophecies and passages relevant to Messianism. Some call these '*Oracles of the Lord*', but it should be clear they are Old Testament prophecies or proof-texts. Then there was the interpretation – that is, the various stories developed upon these proof-texts.

A fragment from a medieval manuscript found at Oxford attributed to Papias has him saying that: '*Mary the wife of Cleophas or Alphaeus ... was the mother of James the Bishop and Apostle, and of Simon, Thaddaeus, and one Joseph*'.[26] This is very startling testimony! Not only does it unwaveringly confirm James' role as *both 'Bishop and Apostle*', but it also now affirms that one of these brothers – '*Judas*' in all other texts – is here simply and straightforwardly denoted '*Thaddaeus*'. This was the implication rendered by a comparison of Gospel Apostle lists anyhow, where '*Thaddaeus*' in Mark and '*Thaddaeus surnamed Lebbaeus*' in some of the versions of Matthew give way to '*Judas (the brother) of James*' in Luke.

Not only is this testimony startling, but it is exactly in line with what we shall be discovering from other sources. Our conclusion is that, whoever wrote it, it is *early, very early*, and *it is* authentic. Interestingly, it also goes on to identify another '*Mary Salome the wife of Zebedee*' as '*an aunt of the Lord*' and '*the mother of John the Evangelist and James*'. Again, this is really starting detail, but the same fragment then goes on to note, *ever so laconically*, that she was probably '*the same as Mary (the wife) of Cleophas*' – all this obviously alluding to the infuriating notice in John about '*Mary*' being *both* '*the wife of Clopas*' and '*the sister*' of Jesus' mother (19:25 – in most sources usually also *called 'Mary'*!).

The fragment (if it is genuinely from Papias and we think it is) already gives evidence that Jesus' '*brothers*' are slowly turning into his '*cousins*' – a doctrine finally made 'official' two centuries later by Jerome. To put it in a nutshell: '*mothers*' become '*aunts*' (not to mention finally turning into *their own sisters*!), '*Fathers*' become '*uncles*' and, if one really wants to go that far, '*Jesus*' himself turns into his own brother '*Joses*' (two letters in linguistic theory being sufficient to determine a loan – here there are three). All have to do in some sense with the developing doctrines of '*Jesus'' Divine birth* and *the Supernatural* '*Christ*' as well as its concomitant, the '*perpetual virginity*' *of Mary* as also concretized in the contemporary Second-Century *Protevangelium of James*. This '*Infancy Gospel*' ascribed, as it were, to James (therefore, how could anyone contradict it?) excludes all other births on Mary's part thereby *directly contradicting the Gospels even as we have them.*

It may be that some of this reflects later emendation, but still the notice as we have it provides us with the key to sorting out all these confusing relationships and basically echoes what we have already been delineating and have come to suspect. In the first place it avers that Cleophas and Alphaeus are identical. We did not need this fragment to suspect this, but it confirms it. It also makes it very clear that this Cleophas or Alphaeus ('Clopas' in Hegesippus) was also the father of James and that, *of course*, James the son of Alphaeus in Apostle lists *is* our James.

Finally, it confirms that Cleophas cum Alphaeus was actually *the husband of Mary*. Whether he was also called 'Joseph' or not will never be known, but it is beside the point. It, also, ever so gently points to further garblings between 'Joses' and 'Joseph', which bear on those between 'Joseph Barsabas Justus' and 'Judas Barsabas' above. But 'Joses' really does appear to be the name of the *fourth brother*. All sources are more or less in agreement on this. Mary and Cleophas (or Alphaeus) have *four sons* not five, to wit: James, Simon, Judas of James or Thaddaeus, and Joses. This Jude/Judas of James or Thaddaeus is also called Lebbaeus in some versions of Matthew, which possibly means '*Oblias*' or further garbles the name of the father of all these various children, Cleophas, Alphaeus, or 'Clopas'. This, of course, makes James and Simeon bar Cleophas *brothers* not 'cousins', as we have already come to suspect anyhow.

It is interesting that Tatian (*c.* 115–185 CE), a student in Asia Minor of Justin Martyr (c. 100–165), refers to James the son of Alphaeus also as 'James the *Lebbaean*' – again pointing to the basic overlap of this 'Lebbaeus' terminology with Eusebius' '*Oblias*' cognomen, also applied to James as we have seen. Once again, this confirms in the process that the latter is a type of surname or sobriquet applying not just to Judas, Judas Thomas, or Thaddaeus, but other members of the family as well – most notably *James.*

The disputed notice from Papias, also, tries to clear up the supposed parentage of James and John and the notice in Matthew about Mary being 'the mother of the sons of Zebedee' (27:56). These last are now described as 'sons of another aunt of the Lord's' not 'Mary the mother of James the Less and Joseph, the wife of Alphaeus' (thus), but someone he calls 'Mary Salome' or just plain 'Salome'.

It should be apparent by now that all these evasions circulating around the two 'sons of Zebedee' are really connected in some manner to the issue of James and his direct succession as Leader of the Jerusalem Community, which again we have suspected for a long time, and that 'Zebedee' is just another one of these nonsense names and one more stand-in for these 'Alphaeus'/'Lebbaeus' evasions. In fact the only real person by the name of John, other than John the Baptist and the individual Josephus designates as 'John the Essene', that ever really materializes in any of these sources is 'John the Evangelist', considered buried in Ephesus.

'James the brother of John' has no substance whatsoever, except in Gospel enumerations of the Central Three, where he is simply a stand-in for the *real* James. In Acts, where he is executed, he is also a stand-in for Jesus' *third brother*, Jude or Judas. It is the 'brother' signification that has the real substance here – albeit again completely obscured and transformed – and if one keeps one's eyes on it, one will never go far wrong.

The Gospels just cannot present the real James as an Apostle, brother, and principal successor of Jesus – despite the fact that this is absolutely attested to without embarrassment by no less a witness than Paul himself – because of their anti-family, anti-national, and anti-Jewish or Palestinian Apostle orientation, the family of Jesus already having been presented as distinct from Jesus' true followers and real believers and, therefore, the need for this fictional James *the brother* of John and the fictional nomenclature 'Zebedee'.

This will be further borne out, and to our thinking, definitively so, when we treat the person of this *third brother* of Jesus – Judas, Judas Thomas, Judas the brother of James, or Thaddaeus below. In the meantime it can be averred without reservation that *all* the brothers of Jesus have very *real* substance, including James, Simon/Simon the Canaanite/Simon the Zealot/Simeon bar Cleophas and very likely 'Simon *Iscariot* (the father or brother) of Judas', and Judas, also known as '*Zelotes*' – however highly refracted or obscured these may have become in the literature as we have it.

But 'James the son of Zebedee' does not have any substance. But the 'brother' theme connected to this 'James the brother of John' and the *beheading* do have real substance, and, as we have shown, simply relate to a *different brother of Jesus*.

Also '*Joses*', when considered *very* carefully, has *real* substance, even though we never hear a single word about him and this is not apparent on the surface. Moreover this is borne home, as we just saw, by looking at the form of the two words in Greek, '*IOSES*' and '*IESOUS*'. What becomes immediately apparent is their similarity and what Papias or his interpolator is telling us, in their straightforward enumeration of the names of Cleophas' and Mary's sons, is that there *were only four brothers*, *all of whom known*, *all of whom substantial*, and the fourth brother, as we just said, is simply '*IESOUS*' or '*Jesus*' himself!

In fact, what has happened in these early transmissions is that – to repeat – 'Jesus' has simply *turned into his own brother* just as 'Mary' has done *her own sister*; however, this should not be surprising. We cannot blame these early compilers or redactors, who may or may not have been aware of these transformations or substitutions, if they did not recognize these things, as almost all or most of them were foreigners. Nor do they seem to have recognized the conversion of Mary into her own sister Mary, nor the conversion of Jesus' father into his uncle. They do not even seem to be aware that Drusilla in Acts, the granddaughter of Herod, is not simply '*a Jewess*' – or were they?

In other words, just averred by Papias – as usual condemned by later theologians like Irenaeus or Eusebius – or the text attributed to Papias (one of the earliest theologians in the Church), there *were only four brothers* and *all were sons of Mary and Cleophas* (*Alphaeus*). Jesus is simply his own brother Joses. This is the reason why nothing substantial is ever really said about this fourth brother 'Joses' – though he is mentioned in the Gospels (which may tell us something about their dating) – in any of the other early sources, as opposed to the other three brothers. Nor does he appear in the Apostle lists as these other three do.

But how did this happen and why? When did Jesus become his own brother? When did fathers turn into uncles, brothers into cousins, and mothers into their own sisters? The answer is very simple and has been clear from the beginning. It is the growing concept of Jesus as the 'Son of God', not, as at Qumran and in other 'Ebionite' materials, only a symbolical or 'adoptionist' one – in the sense that all these 'Perfectly Righteous Ones' *become* 'Sons of God'. Not only have we now found this notion at Qumran, it is widespread even in the New Testament as we have it.

In other words, as the doctrine of Christ as a Supernatural Being and the 'only begotten' Son of God gained momentum, all these shifts in genealogies became necessary too. It was necessary that 'Joseph' – or Cleophas or another – no longer be the real father, but rather only the stepfather. Even the genealogies in the Synoptics show confusion on this issue, as does John.

Then Jesus' brothers could not have been his *real* brothers, but rather only half-brothers or brothers by a previous marriage of his father or even a different mother. By Jerome's time, they are simply his 'cousins'. Mary could not be the mother of these brothers. Therefore in the Gospel of John she gains a sister by the same name who becomes the *real* mother of the brothers – and all other absurdities and evasions follow accordingly.

Clearly, Jerome finds it impossible to admit for ideological reasons that this 'Mary the wife of Clopas' in John – in John, 'Jesus' mother' is not even called *Mary* – could be *Jesus' real mother*. This leads him into a series of self-evident contradictions and evasions, most notably about the relationship of Simeon bar Cleophas and Jesus. Simeon, it should now be appreciated, had to have been Jesus' *second* brother, equivalent to 'Simon the Canaanite/ Zealot', as well as being his second successor, at least in Palestine, if not perhaps worldwide as well, as some of our sources imply.

Of course, who the 'Peter' in the Gospels was, whether the same as 'Cephas' or different from him now takes on renewed significance. Are 'Cephas' and 'Cleophas' confused as well? Was Peter the same as this Simeon bar Cleophas or different from him? Was he the same as the 'Simon the Head of his own Assembly' in Jerusalem, who wanted to *bar* Herodians from the Temple as foreigners – and this, because they did *not* 'regularly observe the Law' – or different from him? These things will probably never be known, but the suspicion is strong that we have two 'Simon's or two 'Peter's, as the case may be – the traditions being somewhat crisscrossed.

How many of the traditions about the *real* character '*Simeon bar Cleophas*' – the putative Second Successor in the Church in Palestine – have become confused with those surrounding '*Peter*', '*the Rock of the Church*' in Rome? Certainly the idea of 'Peter' being a direct successor to Jesus is not borne out by any *real Palestinian* traditions. These have obviously been refurbished in Acts, where, for instance, they portray Peter as *learning to accept Gentiles* and *eat forbidden foods with them*. Not only are these straightforwardly gainsaid in the Pseudoclementine *Homilies*, they are clearly refuted by Paul's account of his own experiences with 'Cephas' in 'Antioch' – whichever 'Antioch' this will finally turn out to be. The idea, too, of Peter being 'Bishop of Bishops', the forerunner of the modern Popes and Leader of Christianity everywhere, owes much to the real position of this Simeon in Palestine – the putative second brother of Jesus. But the present state of our sources, overwritten and mythologized as they are, where Jesus' brothers and other family members are downplayed and all but written out of the tradition, do not allow us to proceed further or achieve finality on this matter.

Suffice it to say that many of the traditions regarding Simeon – including that of a first sighting on the road to Emmaus, to 'Cleopas' and another, and which may or may not have involved 'Simeon' and not simply his father 'Cleophas' (Origen thinks it involved both, and says so explicitly) and most certainly has something to do with *the first appearance to James* reported in all sources – either overlap with or have been absorbed into traditions regarding

'Peter', the successor in Rome and linchpin of Western Christian claims to the mantle of Jesus, to whom no separate appearance ever occurred (at least not in the Gospels).

These are the kinds of conclusions that can be arrived at by pursuing the question of what being a '*brother*' meant and the Apostolic relationship of James the Just, '*the brother of the Lord*', to Jesus. It is attention to detail and to the *real*, not spurious, *traditions about James* that led us to these insights.

The Mandaeans, a Sabaean baptizing group in Southern Iraq, laying on of hands.

Ritual immersion among the Mandaeans, Disciples of John the Baptist in southern Iraq.

Left: 'The Pool of Abraham' at Edessa ('Antioch-by-Callirhoe') in Northern Syria – 'the Land of the Osrhoeans'.

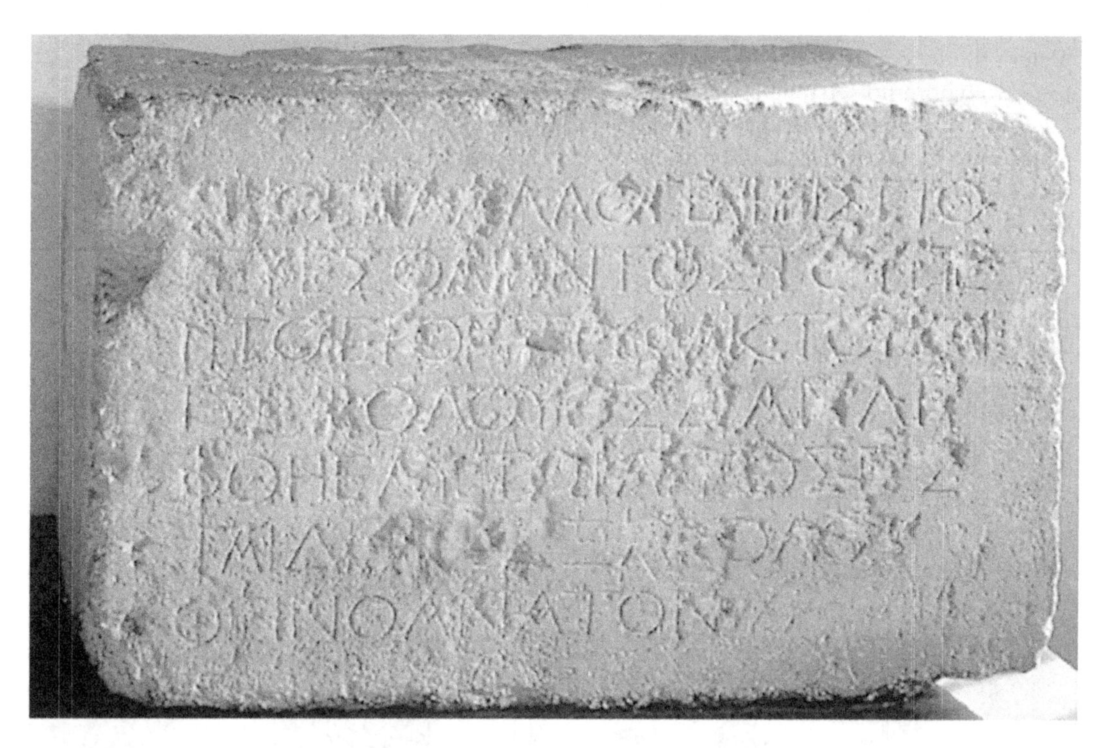

Greek warning block in the Temple, forbidding Gentiles to enter the Sacred Precincts or Inner Court on pain of death.

The Last Column of the Damascus Document at Qumran, referring to the reunion of the wilderness 'camps' at Pentecost, to curse all transgressing the Law.

PART VI

JAMESIAN COMMUNITIES IN THE EAST

Chapter 24
Judas the Brother of James and the Conversion of King Agbar

Judas the Brother of James, Thaddaeus, and Judas the Zealot

We can now turn to more extensive data relating to Jesus' putative *third brother*, Judas ('Judas *Thomas*'/'Thaddaeus'). The extant notices about him are particularly interesting. I think we can grant that he is the individual called 'Judas the brother of James' in the New Testament Letter of Jude, not to mention the individual in Apostle lists following 'James the (son) of Alphaeus' and 'Simon the Cananaean' ('Simon who was called *Zelotes*'), variously referred to as 'Thaddaeus' (Mk 3:18), 'Lebbaeus surnamed Thaddaeus' (Mt 10:3), and, most realistically, 'Judas (the brother) of James' (Lk 6:16 and Acts 1:14).

It should also be noted, and this is important, that he is always followed by reference to another 'Judas' – this time, Judas *Iscariot*, called in the Gospel of John either 'the *Iscariot*' or 'the son' or 'brother of *Simon Iscariot*'. Judas is related to 'Simon the Canaanite' or 'Zealot' in these lists and there is a notice in the *Epistula Apostolorum* calling him 'Judas Zelotes' or 'Judas the Zealot'. This too was immediately followed by reference to a 'Cephas' separate from 'Peter', who could be only either Simeon bar Cleophas or Simon the Zealot.

Now comes the rub. In an apocryphal text called the Apostolic Constitutions, when it comes to discussing the bequest of 'Lebbaeus surnamed Thaddaeus' – the clear nomenclature of the Gospel of Matthew only reversed – two variant manuscripts note he was also 'called *Judas the Zealot*'.[1]

The date of the Apostolic Constitutions, which comes to us from the Syriac, is contended. Some have it as a typical second-century document – others earlier; according to some scholars (depending on how conventional its conventionalities are thought to be) later. Like the Pseudoclementines, also attested in Syriac, this text refers to James quite straightforwardly as 'the brother of Christ according to the flesh' – simply that, no attempt being made at equivocation or evasion. In addition, as in the *Recognitions*, the point is stressed that James was 'appointed Bishop of Jerusalem by *the Lord himself*.[2]

In another interesting note in one of these variant manuscripts, following directly upon the one about 'Lebbaeus surnamed Thaddaeus' also being called 'Judas the Zealot', the claim is made that 'Simon the Cananaean', who directly follows 'James the son of Alphaeus' and 'Thaddaeus' in Matthew and Mark, was '*crowned with martyrdom in Judea in the reign of Domitian*'. This is very interesting, because it concurs with suggestions that the executions under Trajan of Simeon bar Cleophas and the grandsons of Jesus' brother Judas have been transposed in our sources – at least Simeon's has.

Since there were clearly Messianic troubles under Domitian – which were to be expected under such a Nero-like and seemingly demented Ruler – then the execution of Simeon bar Cleophas could be put under Domitian's rule not Trajan's, when it more likely occurred.

This neatly fits in with the possibility of Josephus transposing traditions about the family of Judas the Galilean with those of the family of Jesus in the New Testament or *vice versa*. Who, for instance, were these two '*Sons of Thunder*' who purportedly '*drank the Cup' that Jesus drank* (Mk 3:17 and 10:39)? The first pair of candidates that present themselves are, of course, James the Just 'the brother of Jesus' and this other brother, called, according to Luke, 'Simon the Zealot', but also possibly Simeon bar Cleophas. The second and even more appropriate possibility would be 'James and Simon, the two sons of Judas the Galilean'.

For some reason Josephus neglected to mention their crucifixion and Theudas' beheading preceding them in the *Jewish War*. Why? Nevertheless, in the *Antiquities* twenty years later, he *does* mention their execution, placing it under the Governorship of Tiberius Alexander, Philo's backsliding nephew, around 48 CE. In fact, he mentions it in the same breath he mentions 'the Famine' (*c.* 46–48 CE), directly following that of Theudas, whose beheading we have already remarked in connection with Jesus' *third brother* Judas and Acts' 'James the brother of John, with the sword' at about the same time.

As we already saw, too, the first pair of '*James and Simon*'s *did* '*drink the Cup*' *that Jesus drank*, since they really *were crucified* in a preventive execution – also seemingly around Passover time. One can see how excitable the Jewish crowds became at festivals of this kind, not long after under the Roman Governor Cumanus, from Josephus' account of the riot that ensued at Passover again when a Roman soldier, on the wall or portico of the Temple, exposed himself to the Jewish crowd – resulting in a stampede in which, according to Josephus (perhaps not without a little exaggeration), *'thousands' were killed.*

It is not incurious that it is the deletion of the mention of the execution of these two brothers in Acts that causes the anachronism regarding the note about Theudas coming *before* the Census of Cyrenius and the Revolt led by Judas the Galilean – all oddly put in the mouth of the *Pharisee* 'Gamaliel' as well (5:36–37 – should we rather read here the Pharisee 'Josephus' instead?). For Acts, the sequence, as will be recalled, was the deleted reference to the two brothers, 'James and Simon', and Theudas following the reference to Judas the Galilean. These proceed into the stoning of Stephen, Philip meeting the Treasurer of the Ethiopian Queen 'on the way to Gaza', Peter's visit to the Roman Legionnaire Cornelius in Caesarea, the 'prophet' called 'Agabus' coming down from Jerusalem to Antioch to predict the Famine 'that came to pass under Claudius', the beheading of 'James the brother of John', Peter's arrest, and finally the introduction of the *real* James.

For Josephus, the order is: the visit of Simon to Agrippa I in Caesarea, the beheading of Theudas, the Famine, followed by the mention of Queen Helen of Adiabene's Famine-relief efforts (which we shall treat below), the preventive crucifixion of Judas the Galilean's *two sons* 'James and Simon', the attack on the Emperor's messenger Stephen in the midst of problems between Galileans and Samaritans and Greco-Syrian Legionnaires and Jews at Caesarea, and the stoning of James – itself followed by the riot led by one Saulus, a 'kinsman of Agrippa', leading up to the War against Rome.

That there are confusions, overlaps, and evasions going on here should be evident, but what precisely is at the root of them is more difficult to discern. Just as Josephus seems to have transposed the riot led by Saulus in the 40's – as reported in the Pseudoclementines and reflected even in Acts – to the 60s, so Acts has transposed the stoning of James in the 60s, *refurbishing it into the stoning of Stephen* in the 40's. It is possible (though not very probable) that Josephus somehow transposed the crucifixions of Jesus' brother Jude's two grandsons and that of Simeon bar Cleophas either under Domitian or Trajan to an earlier period. It is impossible to say. Simeon bar Cleophas *does seem to have been crucified*, however fabulously Christian tradition seems to have exaggerated his lifespan.

If executions of this kind did take place under Domitian and not Trajan, Josephus would have been alive to see and record them, albeit anachronistically, just as for some reason he omitted the executions of Judas the Galilean's two sons and of Theudas in his earlier *War*. How could he have failed to record these things then? Is it Agrippa II, residing in Rome, giving Josephus this new information, or is it Tiberius Alexander, Agrippa II's brother-in-law and, as Titus' deputy, the destroyer of Jerusalem? However these things may be, this notice about 'the martyrdom of Simon the Cananaean' taking place under *the reign of Domitian* from a variant manuscript of the Syriac Apostolic Constitutions has an accuracy and prescience about it that belies mere creative imagination or hearsay.

The execution of Theudas immediately preceding these things is an important event to consider. The two variant notices about 'Lebbaeus surnamed Thaddaeus' in the Apostolic Constitutions read: 'Thaddaeus, *also called Lebbaeus* and who was *surnamed Judas the Zealot, preached the truth to the Edessenes and the people of Mesopotamia*, when Abgarus ruled over Edessa.'

One should note the reversal here of how this reference to 'Thaddeus' appears in Matthew and the normative Apostolic Constitutions text. The variant text is more logical, since 'Thaddaeus' would appear to be a name, while 'Lebbaeus' a title of some kind – possibly a garbling of 'Alphaeus', itself a garbling of 'Cleophas'. Directly following this, the notice also adds the interesting information that 'he was buried in *Berytus in Phoenicia*'.

We have already remarked the kind of fun and games that went on in this Berytus or Beirut after the destruction of Jerusalem in 70 CE and Titus' celebration of his brother Domitian's birthday there, and Berytus does seem to have been a favorite possession of both Agrippa I and II. The information about 'Thaddaeus' or 'Judas the Zealot' being buried – after perhaps being executed – there is very precise and not found in any other sources. It is stated very matter-of-factly and, to the author's ears, while admittedly prejudiced, does have the ring of truth.

The point about this putative *third brother* of Jesus – since he is distinctly called 'Judas (the brother) of James' in Luke and Acts – like the second brother, 'Simon the Zealot', being 'a *Zealot*', is extremely interesting. Of course, it accords with the notice in the 'We Document' narrative in Acts – James speaking to Paul – about the majority of James' 'Jerusalem Church' supporters being 'Zealots for the Law' and we have already heard the same thing about this 'Judas' in the *Epistula Apostolorum*. It is, in any event, something we would have expected from previous analyses, even if we had not encountered it so baldly and plainly presented in this variant manuscript of the Apostolic Constitutions.

But what does it mean? First of all it places all these individuals squarely in the 'Zealot' tradition. But secondly, it links up with a host of traditions – again mostly based on Syriac sources, but also summarized in Eusebius, writing in Greek and known throughout the Christian world – about one Thomas or, more accurately, 'Judas *Thomas*'. We have already encountered this Apostle in the Gospel attributed to his name from the so-called 'Gnostic' texts at Nag Hammadi. This Gospel begins quite matter-of-factly with the words: 'These are the *secret words*, which the Living Jesus spoke, and which *Didymus* Judas Thomas wrote down.' There are also Acts attributed to Thomas extant in Greek and Syriac, probably going back to a Syriac original, in which culture Thomas always bears the name of 'Judas' – 'Judas Thomas who is also called *Didymus*' – exactly as in the prologue to the Gospel of Thomas (1.1).[3] In fact in these Acts, in which Thomas is always the custodian of the mysterious or esoteric words of Christ, he is not only identified with this brother of Jesus; but, as the Aramaic '*Thoma*' – echoed by the Greek '*Didymus*' – implies, his *twin* brother as well.[4]

We can dismiss doubling and overlaps with '*Thaddaeus*', '*Lebbaeus*', and '*Judas the brother of James*' in the Synoptic Gospel lists. We can also dismiss dissembling, as in the Gospel of John's '*Twin Twin*' equivocations, themselves accompanied by the themes of 'doubting' and 'eating' with Jesus which overlap Luke's account about Jesus' appearance to Cleopas and the unidentified other 'in the Way' to Emmaus and to James in the Gospel of the Hebrews.

In fact, the traditional Gospel Apostle lists include few individuals of any real substance, and these lists with their variations have been transmitted into a plethora of other traditions, which occasionally provide additional bits of interesting information. For instance, in the Acts of Thomas, Thomas' burial scene contains elements of the empty-tomb scenario about Jesus in the Gospels, including the ever-present, tell-tale element of the 'linen clothes' again (Acts of Th. 12.168–70).

Of course, Thomas is not only important in Edessa and Mesopotamia in these variant manuscripts of the Apostolic Constitutions, but traditions about his activities go as far east as

India, the place of his supposed burial in these apocryphal Acts, even though we have already seen this to have been Berytus in some manuscripts of the Apostolic Constitutions above. This is also the case for the Acts of Thaddaeus. But aside from this kind of cultural imperialism, Thomas is almost always presented in association with '*his Disciple' Thaddaeus* (*thus!*) in connection with traditions about the conversion of someone called '*King Abgarus*' or '*Agbarus*' (possibly a title having something to do with the allusion '*Great One*' in Syriac or Aramaic) of the Edessenes or Osrhoeans – the last, a clear transliteration of *Assyrians.*

The 'Judas who Preached the Truth to the Edessenes'

This story is known as the conversion of King Agbarus. Actually in most sources he is called Abgarus, which is more correct, but in Latin the letters are often reversed, or replaced, with letters like 'u', 'r', or 'c', and we prefer this other version of the name for reasons that will eventually become clear. This legend is, interestingly enough, first recorded in an actual written document by Eusebius himself, who for a change does not claim to have had it from other writers, but literally to have transcribed and translated it himself from an original Syriac chancellery office document in the Royal Archives of Edessa! At the end Eusebius actually provides a Syriac date to it, approximately 29–30 CE.[5]

Whatever the veracity of his claim, the materials do appear very old, that is, before the time of Eusebius (c. 325 CE), who hardly ranks as a creative writer. We shall, in fact, be able to detect their reflection just beneath the surface of Acts. Though some scholars take a dim view of them, trying to accord them a *later* rather than an *earlier* date, they are very widespread in the Syriac sources with so many multiple developments and divergences that it is hard to believe they could all be based on Eusebius' poor efforts.

In all these sources, '*Thomas*' (i.e., '*Judas Thomas*') sends out '*Thaddaeus*' – here our original conjunction of the two names again – after 'the Ascension of Jesus' to evangelize the Edessenes (this is also the point about '*Judas the Zealot*' in the *Apostolic Constitutions*) and after this, joins him there himself, ultimately traveling further into Mesopotamia and then on to India, as in the Acts of Thomas – the source of Indian legends circulating around his name.[6]

Edessa is an important centre of early Christianity, probably more important than the centre Acts attributes to Paul and his colleagues in nearby Antioch (11:20–26). Its cultural heritage is claimed by both Armenian and Syriac Christians, as are its kings. In fact, there were originally numerous '*Antioch*'s, 'Antiochus' being the name of the father of the first Seleucid King following Alexander the Great in this region who apparently liked *honoring the memory of his father.* Edessa was one of these '*Antioch*'s, being called '*Antiochia-by-Callirhoe*' or '*Edessa Orrhoe*' – the source of its present name in Turkey, '*Urfa*'. So was another town at the southern tip of the Tigris and Euphrates, '*Antiochia Charax*' or '*Charax Spasini*', which will figure prominently in our story.[7] This will make for very interesting mix-ups indeed – as it does in the Paul being at '*Antioch*' story.

Aficionados of searches of this kind even trace the Shroud of Turin back to this city, carbon-dating notwithstanding. Indeed, it is claimed in the literature associated with the Agbar/Abgar Legend that Jesus sent his image to the city.[8] Out of this also has sprung up a lively literature circulating around the individual 'Addai', a name clearly not unrelated to 'Thaddaeus' or *vice versa*, and even the name Edessa would appear to be based on a not unsimilar phonetic root, not to mention the name of Adiabene just a *little further east.* In fact, Adi is a religious name endemic to this region, revered even today by the quasi-pagans extant in the area called '*Yazidis*'. We shall see how it is also picked up in Muhammad's stories about 'Ad and Thamud', and 'the Prophet' sent to the former, 'their brother Hud' (in Hebrew, 'Yehudah' or 'Judas'), not to mention the one called in Arabic, 'Salih' or 'the Righteous One', sent to the latter.[9]

Eusebius himself is already referring to Thomas as Judas Thomas.[10] While acknowledging that Judas Thomas was an Apostle, he is confused about 'Thaddaeus', whom he appreciates appears with 'Barnabas' and 'Cephas' as members of 'the Seventy' in Clement of Alexandria's *Hypotyposes*. This is also something of the case in the Apostolic Constitutions above, 'the Seventy' being the Seventy Disciples or Elders stemming from Jewish ideas of the Seventy Nations or language-groups of mankind, as well as 'the Seventy' it took to make up a proper 'Assembly' or 'Sanhedrin'.[11]

In fact, Eusebius seems to be presenting the exchange of letters between Jesus and Agbarus, the King of the Osrhoeans, as an answer to some other materials that had recently appeared from Roman chancellery records, called the '*Acti Pilati*' that he considered scurrilous. The extant Acts of Pilate – so-called because of their attribution to Pilate – are rather pro-Christian documents attesting to Pilate's recognition of Jesus, but these other so-called 'Acts', which appear to have represented themselves as the *actual* administrative records of Pilate's Governorship, upset Eusebius so much because they claimed a different date for the Crucifixion of Jesus – around 21 CE.

In truth the Romans did keep very careful administrative records, even in the provinces, and it would have been surprising if records such as these had not once existed, but the '*Acti Pilati*' Eusebius so rails against were obviously being circulated by enemies of Christianity. They claimed that Jesus was crucified in the seventh year of the reign of Tiberius *which commenced in the year 14 CE*. Eusebius counters with the statement from Josephus that Pilate came to Palestine in 26 CE and, in so doing, claiming these '*Acti Pilati*' to be fraudulent – but there is no real proof of this proposition other than this one remark about Pilate from Josephus who hadn't even been born yet.

Josephus himself might well have been mistaken about this and it would seem foolish to purposefully circulate something like these 'Acts' which could, on the surface anyhow, appear so patently fraudulent. If Pilate did come earlier, a 21 CE date for the Crucifixion of Jesus would help markedly in explaining why someone like Paul, who seems to have begun his career in the 30's, knows so little factually about him. It would also go a long way towards explaining the 'twenty-year' period of 'groping for the Way', referred to in the Damascus Document from the time of the death of the Messianic 'Root of Planting' to the rise of the Righteous Teacher.[12]

But however these things may be, for those who would dispute the age of traditions like that of the Agbarus legend, it should be appreciated that Hippolytus, a century before Eusebius, whose testimony about Josephus' 'Essenes' is so full of startling precision and extra detail, was already aware of the tradition concerning 'Judas the Zealot' and the Edessenes above, not to mention the one about 'Lebbaeus surnamed Thaddaeus' or 'Thaddaeus surnamed Lebbaeus' in the two variant editions of the Apostolic Constitutions being the same as 'Judas the Zealot'.

As another work attributed to Hippolytus puts this in a listing of the Twelve Apostles, it now combines both saying: '*Judas, also called Lebbaeus*, preached to the people of Edessa and to all Mesopotamia, and *fell asleep at Berytus and was buried there*.'[13] On the face of it, this is absolutely startling testimony, because the Hippolytus work – if authentic, it would be from the second–third centuries – now combines the note about 'Judas the Zealot being buried in Berytus' from the variant manuscripts of the Apostolic Constitutions with the one about 'Lebbaeus being surnamed Thaddaeus' in the tradition represented by the Gospel of Matthew.

But in its listing of the Twelve Apostles this work (again ascribed to Hippolytus) goes even further than this. Moving over to the matter of 'James the son of Alphaeus', obviously the first of our three brothers, it now by implication identifies him with James the Just, the brother of Jesus, saying: '*James the son of Alphaeus*, when preaching in Jerusalem, *was stoned to death by the Jews and was buried there beside the Temple.*' Nothing could be clearer than this, which is nothing but our tradition about James the brother of the Lord, called the Just One in all early Church sources. Whoever wrote this was unerringly prescient.

Clearly, by the end of the Second Century or the beginning of the Third Century, if this listing is authentic, Hippolytus as far away as Rome already knew that 'James the son of Alphaeus' was *the same* as the James called 'the brother of the Lord' but, as he was not yet privy to Hegesippus' traditions about the latter's death (being transmitted at approximately the same time), he does not put them all together as relating to the same person. But this is certainly very important testimony for identifying 'James the son of Alphaeus' – 'James the Less' at a later point in Mark – with James the brother of the Lord, and, no doubt too, because of the garbling inherent in the name 'Alphaeus', 'James the son of Cleophas'.

In addition, in another fragment ascribed to him, found together with the previous list, purporting now to be a catalogue of 'the Seventy Apostles', by which is clearly meant 'the Seventy' – 'the Elders' or 'Disciples' of other reckonings – Hippolytus is presented as listing the first four of these – clearly meant to approximate the names of Jesus' brothers – as: 'James the Lord's brother, Bishop of Jerusalem', the second being 'Cleopas Bishop of Jerusalem'.[14] The spelling here is the spelling Luke uses in the matter of the first Emmaus Road appearance by Jesus to 'Cleopas', and there can be little doubt that what Hippolytus is presented as meaning or implying here – if not Luke – is that the recipient of this appearance *is* 'Simeon bar Cleophas', the second Bishop of the Jerusalem Church according to all sources.

Then he lists, regardless of contradictions as to who is or is not an 'Apostle', 'Matthias who filled the vacancy in the number of the Twelve Apostles', and fourth, 'Thaddaeus, who conveyed the epistle to Augarus (*thus*).'[15] In other words – if this recording is accurate – Hippolytus has not yet put this 'Thaddaeus' together with 'Judas also called Lebbaeus' (whom he described 'as preaching to the people of Edessa and all Mesopotamia' in the listing of the Apostles attributed to him), even though the Gospels of Matthew and Luke (not to mention these variant manuscripts of the Apostolic Constitutions) have already done this for him – Luke quite straightforwardly calling him 'Judas the brother of James'.

But even more important than this, if we go back to the previous listing, this text attributed to Hippolytus now calls 'Simon the Cananaean' (or 'Zealot') '*the son of Clopas*, who is also (the brother of) Judas and *became Bishop of Jerusalem after James the Just* and fell asleep and was buried there at the age of 120 years'.

Aside from again stressing the matter of Simeon bar Cleophas' apparent longevity, this important notice clearly identifies Simon the Canaanite or Cananaean (that is, 'the Zealot') with Simeon bar Cleophas in a straightforward manner, as we have already done and the variant manuscript of the Apostolic Constitutions does as well. In addition, it affirms, as the fragment attributed to Papias quoted earlier, that 'Clopas' – regardless of what spelling one uses – was basically the father of these four children. It is hard to believe that all these fragments, whatever one makes of their origins, could be wrong on all these matters, especially since they make so much good sense!

The reference to 'Judas' here again links Simon the Zealot, the son of Cleophas, *the second successor to Jesus in the Church at Jerusalem*, with Judas, not only in the matter of both being 'Zealots' or 'Cananaeans' – this being the basic implication of the notice as it stands – but also as far as both having the same father, once more our ever-present Cleopas, Clopas, or Alphaeus. It also relates – as over and over again in these notices – to the two *Iscariot*s, both called in the Johannine tradition if not the Synoptic, 'Judas' and 'Simon'.

The Conversion of King Agbar according to Eusebius

Equally important, if authentic – and we think it is – this notice from Hippolytus on 'the Seventy Apostles' also provides vivid testimony that the Agbarus legend is a good deal older than Eusebius' recording of it and that the latter was not fantasizing or indulging in creative writing when he said he got it from the official archives of Edessa. Additionally, as in the case of Eusebius, it is already associating this tradition with the name of Thaddaeus (the 'Judas also called Lebbaeus') and our 'Judas *Thomas*' or '*Judas the brother of James*', 'who preached the truth to the Edessenes and all Mesopotamia'.

Equally important too, Hippolytus or a copyist has already begun garbling or mixing up Abgarus' or Agbarus' name, calling him here 'Augarus' (in some Latin manuscripts he is even called 'Albarus'). We shall see why this becomes so important below. For Eusebius, the whole is based on Syriac sources and, as Hippolytus before him, Eusebius quotes these as calling Thaddaeus both an 'Apostle and one of the Seventy' and directly involves him, in addition, with an individual, 'Judas', he too now admits 'is also *Thomas*'. Interestingly enough, Eusebius' source presents the courier in this correspondence as someone called 'Ananias', the same name as the individual Acts introduces as Paul's associate when the latter comes to Damascus (9:12–17). It should not be forgotten too that at this point Paul was staying at the 'house' of someone called '*Judas*' on a 'street called Straight' (9:11)!

As we shall see, Josephus too mentions an individual he calls 'Ananias', who plays an important role in the parallel conversion of Queen Helen at approximately the same time – whether to Judaism or Christianity is not always clear in our sources.[16] Though for Josephus this is Judaism, for Armenian sources, which are also interested in the matter of Helen's conversion, it is, as the conversion of King Abgar, to Christianity. What is even more interesting is that these sources, which see Abgar as an *Armenian* King (which may simply mean he spoke Aramaic; he certainly was King of Edessa), claim that he had allied himself to Aretas, King of Petra in Arabia, thus increasing the pan-Arab ties among these 'Arab' Kings.

Therefore, when Herod Antipas – that is, '*Herod the Tetrarch*' – repudiated Aretas' daughter to marry his niece Herodias, 'a circumstance in connection with which he had John the Baptist put to death' (this from Armenian historian Moses of Chorene in the Fifth Century – or perhaps later – echoing Josephus in the First), King Abgar gave Aretas military help in his defeat of Herod, by which Divine 'Vengeance was taken for the death of John the Baptist'.[17] However inflated such claims may at first appear, there may indeed be an element of truth in this idea of a link between these 'Arab' Kings, both as to history and in the light of the political axes developing here.

Later Herodian Kings, like Aristobulus, Herodias' nephew who was married to Herodias' daughter Salome, are put by the Romans in control of Lower Armenia. As opposed to them, the family developing around Helen of Adiabene, just a little further East, seems to have been highly esteemed in Palestine by opposition and resistance forces; and her son Izates, the convert to Judaism whom Josephus calls her '*only begotten*', seems to have preferred '*circumcision*'. On the other hand, Helen, responding to the teaching of Ananias and another unnamed companion – the doctrines of whom have a lot in common with Paul's (to say nothing about Acts portrait of his encounter with one 'Ananias' reputedly '*in Damascus*') – seems to have had *a horror of the practice* which, for her (thinking realistically, would put her favorite son Izates in ill-repute with his subjects.[18]

Izates has an older brother named, like their father, '*Monobazus*' – a name or hereditary title within the family, like 'Ceasar' in Rome or 'Herod' in Palestine and its analogue in Edessa, '*Agbarus*'/'*Abgarus*'/'*Augarus*'/'*Albarus*' – one perhaps in a Persian framework and the other, Semitic. In turn, one or the other of these brothers appears to have had a third-generation descendant or '*kinsman*', also named 'Monobazus'. Josephus calls him and another such '*kinsman*', his brother 'Kenedaeos' – both of whom later leaders in the Uprising against Rome – '*descendants of Queen Helen*'. We shall have more to say about these later two descendants of hers presently but, for the moment, suffice it to say that they fought on the Jewish/Revolutionary side and were the first martyrs in the War against Rome – leading the initial stand at the Pass at Beit Horon (shades of Leonidas at the Battle of Thermopylae?).

These same Syriac sources, being Semitic and talking about '*Agbarus*'/'*Abgarus*' in Northern Syria, '*the King of the Edessenes*' and all the '*Peoples beyond the Euphrates*' – as Eusebius and Moses of Chorene do. They even claim that Helen was one of '*Agbarus*'' or '*Abgarus*'' wives – like all 'Eastern Potentates' he kept a big harem which seems even to have included quasi-'sisters'.

For Josephus, the name of 'Helen's husband (who so much overlaps this '*Agbarus*'' in Edessa) was 'Bazeus' – that is, a cognate of 'Monobazus' above. Moreover, he adds the fact that she was his '*sister*' too, in consequence of which this original/first-generation 'Bazeus'/'Monobazus' – obviously identical with '*Agbarus*'/'*Abgarus*' in Edessene and Roman sources – allowed her '*the Kingdom of Adiabene*', roughly equivalent to present-day Kurdistan further East. It should be appreciated that Kings of this kind had numerous wives, some merely formal arrangements for the purposes of child-bearing or other alliances, and some even sisters or half-sisters as seems to be the case here.

This last arrangement is attested to in this region as far back even as in the Old Testament (cf. Genesis 20:12) aboriginal here, the legendary '*Abraham*' who, for it, purportedly married his half-sister Sarah. Probably even more to the point, Abraham also came from this area – '*Haran*' in Northern Syria (Haran and Edessa being contiguous and part of the same geographical framework) – what Eusebius and others are also calling at this point '*the Land of the Osrhoeans*' (meaning, of course, '*Assyrians*'). It is perhaps not simply coincidental that this is '*the Kingdom*', Josephus tells us, Izates received from his father '*Bazeus*' – the first and original '*Monobazus*'.

The association of this area with '*Abraham*' – real or legendary is immaterial – will also have great importance for Paul's constant evocation of Abraham in his writings, as well as James' – not to mention Muhammad's in succession to them, whom, as we shall assert below, is absorbing the traditions from this area six centuries later. If Helen was, indeed, the wife or wife-sister of this 'Abgarus'/'Agbarus' (i.e., Josephus' 'Bazeus'/'Monobazus') and Izates, too, his son, as Josephus contends; this would draw the stories of these two conversions – Agbarus' to 'Christianity' and Helen's and Izates' to 'Judaism' (depending on the observer) even closer still. We shall see how materials in Acts, by implication, give credence to much of this complex in a completely unexpected and very powerful way.

Before moving on, one should note again how the name of her Kingdom, 'Adiabene', incorporates a root phonetically parallel to the name perennially associated with this region and this omnipresent Apostle '*Addai*'. As later Syriac documents would have it, quoting Eusebius: 'Thomas the Apostle, one of the Twelve, by a divine impulse, sent Thaddaeus, who was himself also numbered among the Seventy Disciples of Christ (this in accord with our other materials), to Edessa to be a preacher and Evangelist of the teaching of Christ.'[19] These documents also incorporate the correspondence Eusebius says he translated from the chancellery records of Edessa, to wit, how 'after the Ascension of Jesus, *Judas who is called Thomas*, sent him *Thaddaeus the Apostle, one of the Seventy*'. Note how the confusion between Thaddaeus 'as an Apostle' and 'one of the Seventy', already evident in the Hippolytus fragment and here in Eusebius (not to mention the Gospels), continues.

Eusebius returns to this affair again at the beginning of the Second Book of his *History* immediately after his discussion of how – now quoting Clement of Alexandria – there were 'two Jameses, one called *the Just*, who was thrown from a wing of the Temple and beaten to death with a fuller's club, and another, who was beheaded'. Eusebius now repeats what he has just said earlier, also quoted in the Syriac sources: 'But *Thomas*, under a divine impulse, sent *Thaddaeus* as preacher and Evangelist to proclaim the doctrine of Christ, as we have shown from the public documents found there.'[20]

The sequencing of these events as Eusebius begins his Second Book, leading into Hegesippus' long presentation of the death of James is interesting. First he mentions the election to replace 'the Traitor Judas' and then the stoning of Stephen 'by the murderers of the Lord'. But immediately after this, he introduces James as 'the brother of our Lord' and 'the son of Joseph' – no 'cousin' relationship here, though Mary is called 'the Virgin' – it is, therefore, the previous-wife theory. Here Eusebius immediately adds that 'he was the first elected to the Episcopate of the Church at Jerusalem', only the point about being direct 'from Jesus' hand' is missing.

The implication, however, is that this event happened *directly* after Jesus' death, so if we discard the material from Acts about 'Judas *Iscariot*' and 'Stephen', then we do have roughly the proper sequence of events in the early Church. Eusebius, of course, does take the time to point out the translation of Stephen's name as 'Crown', associating it with his being 'the First' to 'carry off the martyrs' Crown', and we have already noted the relation of this to the *Nazirite* 'Crown' of the long hair worn by martyrs such as James. He then gives the notice from Clement about 'The Lord imparting the gift of Knowledge to James the Just, to John, and to Peter after his resurrection. These delivered it to the rest of the Apostles, and they to the Seventy, of whom Barnabas was one.' Then the notice about Thomas sending Thaddaeus to 'the King of the Osrhoeans' – the Assyrians. The proximity of all these matters, bunched so soon after the death of 'the Lord', is interesting and, after making the proper deletions, one does get a sense of the approximate history.

The Background of Agabus' Prediction of the Famine in Acts

Seven chapters further along, now following Acts as a source, Eusebius refers both to 'the Famine', because of which Paul and Barnabas were delegated by the brothers at the Church in Antioch to proceed to Jerusalem to bring Famine relief (Acts 11:28), and the martyrdom of James the son of Zebedee 'with the sword' (Acts 12:1).[21] At this point, Eusebius returns to Josephus as his source, quoting the passage about the 'impostor' or 'Deceiver called Theudas', who persuaded the multitude that 'he was *a prophet*' (it is from here that Acts takes its material about 'Agabus' being a 'prophet') and that he would take them to the other side of the Jordan – that is, Perea where John the Baptist had been executed – and repeat Joshua's miracle in the biblical Book under his name of 'dividing the Jordan at his command'. One should keep one's eyes on the parallels here with the miracles, he has already recited, done by 'Thaddaeus' – and in later Syriac sources, 'Judas *Thomas*' – in the Land of the Osrhoeans.

Eusebius, rather, immediately follows up these things with the story of Queen Helen, referred to in most title epitomes of Eusebius' work as 'the Queen of the Osrhoeans'. This is triggered by his mention at the end of the preceding Chapter Eleven (giving the citation about the miracle Theudas – who called himself 'a prophet', but whom Josephus rather calls 'an impostor' – undertook to do) of the Famine again 'that took place under Claudius'.

Eusebius does so, because his source, Josephus, also evoked this Famine directly following the story of Theudas' beheading and immediately preceding his mention of the crucifixion of James and Simon, the two sons of Judas the Galilean, 'who caused the people to revolt when Cyrenius came to make a census of the possessions of the Jews'.[22] As in Acts, where their deletion causes the anachronism of Theudas being described as coming *before* Judas the Galilean, Eusebius also declines to mention these two sons.

Of course, the reason Eusebius mentions Helen here is that Josephus did so as well at this point, describing how 'Queen Helen bought corn in Egypt at great cost and distributed it to those that were in need', because of 'the great Famine that happened in Judea'. The mention of this Famine at this point directly follows a brief aside about Tiberius Alexander, who succeeded Fadus (44–46), Theudas' executor, as Governor in 46 CE and whose 'Piety was not like that of his wealthy father (Philo of Alexandria's brother) the *Richest* among all his contemporaries'. Rather, as Josephus puts it, Tiberius Alexander 'did not continue in the Religion of his father'.[23]

Eusebius, following Acts once again, now turns to Barnabas and Paul and their Famine-relief mission 'to the Elders' (*Presbyters*) in Jerusalem taking the funds that were being sent up by 'the Disciples' at 'Antioch'. We are now patently in a contemporaneous situation. Eusebius had mentioned this mission and the Famine eight chapters before in Chapter Three in connection with 'Agabus' prophecy', the only problem being that Paul, in his corresponding description of these years in Galatians, *never* mentions such a journey or mission to Jerusalem. In fact, he is quite emphatic to the contrary, saying in a statement leading up to his introduction of Peter and James that has over two millennia become almost proverbial:

> When it pleased God ... by His Grace to reveal His Son in me that I should announce him as the Good News among the Nations, I *did not confer with people of flesh and blood*, nor did I go up to *those who were Apostles before me*, but rather went away *into Arabia* and again *returned to Damascus*. Then after three years I went up to Jerusalem to make the acquaintance of Peter, though of the other Apostles, I saw none except *James the brother of the Lord*. (Gal. 1:15–19)

Here Paul assures his respondents in his own inimical style, 'now the things that I write you, by God, I do not lie', continuing, 'then I came into the regions of Syria and Cilicia' – the regions of concern to us at this point in the discussion (Gal. 1:20–21).

To review the chronology: Paul points out that this was the reason he was 'unknown by sight among the Assemblies in Judea which were in Christ' ('they heard only that he who formerly persecuted us was now announcing the Good News'), before finally explaining, 'then after fourteen years I went up to Jerusalem again with Barnabas, taking Titus with me also' (Gal. 1:22–2:1). These 'fourteen years' put us somewhere into the early 50s, well past the time of 'the Famine' reported by Josephus.

Not only this, but in describing this *second* trip, Paul makes it clear it was not for Famine-relief activities, but rather he 'went up because of a revelation to lay before them the Good News which I announce among the Nations'. Paul says he did this 'privately' to 'those reckoned as important' – the same persons he goes on to speak of as 'those reputed to be something' or 'reputed to be Pillars', whose importance 'nothing conferred' – so that 'I should not be running or have run in vain' (Gal. 2:2–9).

Paul uses this 'running' imagery again in 5:7 to encourage his communities who were 'running well', not to fall back to 'circumcision' and 'the Law'. Paul returns to it again in the crucial section of 1 Corinthians 9:24–26, where he sets forth his philosophy of 'running the course to win', as opposed to the 'weak' people with 'their weak consciences' – including presumably James – who oppose him.

Interestingly enough, even this imagery of 'running' reappears in the Habakkuk *Pesher* (Hab. 2:2), where it is applied to the Scriptural exegeses of the Righteous Teacher of Habakkuk 2:3 on 'the Delay of the *Parousia*' and Habakkuk 2:4.[24] In 1 Corinthians, Paul mixes it with 'winning the Crown (*Stephanon*)' of stadium athletics generally, including boxing. Calculated to infuriate his opponents within the Movement, this is the imagery he uses generally in this letter in support of his position on eating 'things sacrificed to idols' and responding to 'those who would judge him' on the Authority he claims 'to eat and drink'.

In Galatians, Paul follows up these assertions with the problem about whether 'Titus who was with me, being a Greek, was obliged to be circumcised'. He grows extremely heated over this, virtually snarling at the 'some who came from James' and 'those of the circumcision' (2:12). This mounts to a crescendo, as he airs this problem in the next few chapters in his protestation 'so your Enemy I have become by *speaking the Truth to you*' (4:16) and his wish that 'those throwing you into confusion would *cut themselves off* – having the dual meaning of throw themselves out of the Movement, but also 'cut' their own sexual members 'off' (5:12).

Not only is this a pun on circumcising – which will bear heavily on the Queen Helen episode and the malevolent refraction of it we shall presently identify in Acts, showing that this was the issue that was so infuriating Paul, but also on the language in the Damascus Document about the Children of Israel being 'cut off in the wilderness' because 'they *ate blood*'.

In fact, in chapters 3–4 of Galatians, proceeding towards this climax, Paul, in delineating his new theology of how Jesus' death redeems us 'from the curse of the Law', arrives at how 'keeping days and months and times and years' – so important to the Qumran ethos, that they are called there the 'monthly flags and festivals of Glory' – are 'weak and beggarly elements' that reduce one to 'bondage' (Gal. 4:9–10).

In Acts' version of parallel events, which are at times so confusing as to be almost unfathomable, Stephen is stoned because of problems with so-called 'Hellenists' (6:9). Paul gets his vision 'in the Way' to Damascus, where Ananias meets him at the house of 'Judas'; Ananias then also abets him in 'confounding the Jews who dwelt in Damascus' (9:22). Then, because '*the Jews were conspiring together* to put him to death', Paul escapes 'down the walls of Damascus in a basket and flees to Jerusalem to join himself to the Disciples' (9:23–28), no mention of any intervening trip here 'into Arabia' as in Galatians 1:17. In Jerusalem, Paul is 'with them' in their comings and goings, that is, the Apostles and Barnabas, 'speaking boldly in the Name of the Lord Jesus' (9:28). Again this is totally opposed to the testimony in Galatians. The 'Hellenists', as in the case of Stephen previously – by now the code should be pretty clear (read 'Zealots') – now wish 'to put him (Paul) to death', but 'the brothers brought him down to Caesarea' and sent him away to Tarsus (9:29–30). The text adds at this point, 'Then, indeed, the Assemblies throughout all of Judea and Galilee and Samaria had peace' (9:31).

Now there intervene the episodes about Peter learning 'not to call any man (or 'thing') unclean' and to accept Gentiles – to the chagrin of '*those of the circumcision*' (10:14–11:2). After this, '*certain ones of them*, men from Cyprus and Cyrene (the same as those Hellenists from 'Cyrene', 'Cilicia', and 'Asia', persecuting Stephen above?) came to Antioch to announce the Good News to the Hellenists'. Previously 'they had spoken the word to *no one except Jews*' (11:19–20). This is the beginning of Acts' picture of the Church 'in Antioch', where 'the Disciples were first called Christians' (11:26).

Two chapters later, Acts lists the founding members of this 'Church' or 'Assembly' as 'Barnabas', who had supposedly gone back to Tarsus to get Paul, 'bringing him to Antioch' (11:25), 'Simeon who was called Niger' (note the doubling here for names like Niger of Perea, the leader of the prorevolutionary Idumaeans who dies such a Jesus-like death at the hands of 'the Zealots', not to mention our old friend 'Simeon bar Cleophas'), 'Lucius the Cyrenian' (possibly Luke), and someone called 'Manaen, Herod the Tetrarch's foster brother, and Saul' (13:1).

As we have suggested, concerning names such as 'James the brother of John', we have a possible 'shell game' going on and the appellative, 'Herod the Tetrarch's' or 'Herod Antipas' foster brother' may really be descriptive of Paul, not the semi-nonsense name 'Manaen'.

However this may be, at this point in its narrative Acts tells us that 'in these days prophets came down from Jerusalem to Antioch'. Here we are allegedly still talking about 'Antioch' *in Syria*, not 'Antioch-by-Callirhoe' of the Edessenes, some two hundred miles to the north-east (11:27). One of these, one '*Agabus*, rose up and predicted *by the Spirit* a Great Famine, that was about to be over the whole habitable world, which came to pass under Claudius Caesar' (11:28). This then triggers the notice about Barnabas' and Saul's Famine-relief mission to the Elders in Judea (11:29–30), which is immediately followed in 12:1 by the one about how 'at that time Herod the King stretched out (his) hands to mistreat some of the Assembly, and he put James the brother of John to death with the sword'.

Seizing Peter, too, because he saw this 'was *pleasing to the Jews*' (the opposite is more likely) – it was the time of the Passover again – 'he imprisoned him'. This is the point at which Peter escapes and leaves the message for '*James and the brothers*' at 'the house of Mary the *mother of John Mark*', the first mention of James in Acts' narrative (12:3–17). Peter then leaves to 'go to another place'. Of course, all of this is completely anachronistic because 'the Great Famine' occurred between 46 and 48 CE and the events Acts appears to be describing occur before 44 CE and Agrippa I's death, which Acts then apparently goes on to describe (12:19–23).

But all this was introduced by the mention of Barnabas' and Saul's mission on behalf of the Antioch Christian Disciples 'to the brothers living in Judea', because of the Famine purportedly predicted by *the prophet Agabus* (11:29–30), but nothing about what Paul and Barnabas actually did on this mission or where they went *is ever described*. Instead we get all this other intervening information and the section ends with the completely uncommunicative: 'Barnabas and Paul returned from Jerusalem, having completed their mission also bringing with them John Mark' (12:25), followed immediately at the beginning of the next chapter with the enumeration of the 'prophets and teachers of the Church at Antioch', which we have just described above.

Now Paul begins what are usually referred to as his 'missionary journeys', with a confrontation in Cyprus with a Jewish magician 'called *Bar-Jesus*', having much in common with Peter's confrontation with Simon *Magus* in Caesarea – in this regard, one should remember the confusion in our sources between 'Cyprus' and Simon's 'Cuthaean' origins in Samaria – and a sympathetic interview with the Roman proconsul there, 'Sergius Paulus' (13:6–12). It is at this point that 'John Mark' deserts them 'to return to Jerusalem' (13:13). After this, 'some Jews arrive from Antioch and Iconium', while Paul is teaching at Lystra 'and persuaded the crowds' – this still in Asia Minor – and Paul is stoned (14:19).

After this Paul and Barnabas return to Antioch. Then the ubiquitous 'certain ones came down from Judea' and taught the brothers: 'Unless you circumcise after the tradition of Moses you *cannot be saved*'. This triggers the famous 'Jerusalem Council', relating to 'the conversion of the Peoples' or 'the Nations', which is pictured as going to deal with the issue of whether it was 'necessary for them to circumcise and be charged with *keeping the Law of Moses*', but never really does so (15:3–5). This, of course, completely parallels Paul's obsession with these issues in Galatians, where he describes his return to Jerusalem after fourteen years, not because he was summoned, but as a result of 'a revelation', privately to explain the Gospel as he 'proclaimed it among the Gentiles', lest somehow he should have '*run in vain*'.

At the end of this 'Conference', as Acts pictures it, James makes the famous rulings, already amply described, the gist of which are carried down to Antioch in a 'letter' delivered by 'Judas (now 'Barsabas') and Silas', whom Acts describes as 'themselves prophets' (15:22–30). As far as Acts is concerned, everyone then 'rejoices at the consolation' and, supposedly, all 'go in peace' (15:31–33). Notwithstanding, 'after some days' Paul and Barnabas have a *violent quarrel*, ostensibly over 'John Mark', who had purportedly 'withdrawn from' their work in Pamphylia and 'would not co-operate with them' any more. It will be recalled, it was supposed to be *his* 'mother' Mary's house that Peter went to leave a message for 'James and the brothers' in Jerusalem. From 'John Mark', too, we never hear again. The language here is also significant, because of numerous parallels at Qumran.[25]

Paul now sets out for 'Syria and Cilicia' (at this point, allegedly with 'Silas'), never apparently to travel with Jewish companions again, while Barnabas parts company with him and 'sailed off to Cyprus' with John Mark (15:32–41). Finally – and, one might observe, blessedly – in chapter 16 the 'We Narrative' cuts in. Obviously very little of this jibes with Galatians, except the repeated motif and seeming core issue of whether new converts were going to be required to circumcise themselves or not. Judging from Paul's anger in Galatians over this issue, it is clearly not resolved by the time he writes this letter either.

Nor do those who come from James either in Galatians or Acts seem to have the same view of the so-called 'Jerusalem Council' as Paul does. In fact, these various messengers, who repeatedly 'come down from James' and 'from Jerusalem to Antioch' – one even called 'Judas' in Acts (namely 'Judas *Barsabas*') – have much in common with 'Judas *Thomas* sending out Thaddaeus' to Edessa, as reported in Eusebius' Agbarus correspondence and its variations – whoever these two individuals really were.

However this may be, the whole issue of an intervening trip to Jerusalem by Paul for the purposes of Famine relief – supposedly triggered in Acts' account by the coming down from Jerusalem to Antioch of 'a prophet called Agabus' (paralleling the notice about 'Theudas claiming to be a prophet' in Josephus) – is just not covered in the Letter to the Galatians at all. On the other hand, Acts does not treat what Paul was doing in the intervening 'fourteen years', between the time he stayed with Peter 'for fifteen days' in Galatians and met 'James the brother of the Lord' – before going off 'to the regions of Syria and Cilicia' – and the time he returned to put 'the Good News as he announced it among the Gentiles' before 'those reckoned as important'. The reference to 'Syria and Cilicia' *is*, however, mentioned at this point in Acts in conjunction with this new mission with this companion 'Silas' *after* the Jerusalem Council (Acts 15:41).

The 'prophet by the name of Agabus' does, of course, reappear – again fortuitously – in chapter 21 of Acts, just before Paul is about to go up on his last visit to Jerusalem to his final confrontation with James. Once more, the issue is Paul's teaching 'all Jews among the Nations *not to circumcise their children nor walk in our ways*' – probably the truth of the matter. This comes right after the notice about the majority of James' followers being 'Zealots for the Law' (21:20–21). Even in the speech Acts now pictures James as giving, there is no doubt as to which national grouping he belongs. He is certainly *on the side of the Jews* – not those teaching them to desert *their ancestral customs* – but, of course, we are now in the 'We Document' in these events.

In the episode at Caesarea preceding this, Paul is pictured as staying at 'the house of Philip the Evangelist, one of the Seven', who 'has *four virgin daughters who prophesied*' (21:8–9). It will be recalled that later in Acts Paul is also pictured as staying in protective custody in Agrippa II's palace (23:35). The Philip in Josephus, who was the head of Agrippa II's army, likewise lived in Caesarea. Josephus specifically notes his 'two daughters', who miraculously escaped the mass suicide at Gamala in the early days of the War.

Interestingly enough, like the Saulus in Josephus, this Philip too is sent to Nero in Rome to give an account of his actions in surrendering Agrippa II's Palace to the insurgents in Jerusalem, an event in which Josephus' 'Saulus' seems to have been involved as well. Unlike Saulus, however, Philip seems to have returned safely to Palestine after this mission, Nero being too preoccupied with his own troubles by this time to see him.[26] On the other hand, the 'prophet by the name of Agabus', once again described as 'a *somebody who came down from*

Judea', now came to Paul at this house and 'taking hold of his girdle and tying his hands and feet up' in it (*thus*), cried out: 'Thus says the Holy Spirit: *The Jews in Jerusalem* shall in this manner bind the man whose girdle this is and *deliver him up into the hands of the Nations*' (21:10–12). Not only do we have our tell-tale 'Gentile Christian' anti-Jewish animus again, but the same words, 'delivered up', used throughout the Gospels to describe Judas *Iscariot*'s treatment of Jesus and in the Scrolls to describe God's 'Judgment' or 'Visitation' for Vengeance on Jewish backsliders and Covenant-breakers. For Acts now, weaving in and out of the 'We Document', everyone present then begins to weep, begging Paul 'not to go up to Jerusalem', but he peremptorily dismisses these concerns, declaring he is 'ready to be bound and even die in Jerusalem for the Name of the Lord Jesus' (21:13).

Acts' Prophet Called Agabus and the Agbarus Legend

We are now in a position to sort out a good many of our threads and identify some further dissimulation in Acts – again at the expense of some favorite hagiographa in Christianity. At the same time, we shall be able to make clear just who this 'Thaddaeus' really was and, in the process, quite a few others. We shall return to the second prophecy that 'Agabus' is presented as making at the time of Paul's last visit to Jerusalem in Acts in our next volume, when discussing the mysterious oracle to leave Jerusalem given to *James' followers after his death* – presumably under the stewardship of Simeon bar Cleophas – which allegedly triggers 'the Pella Flight'.

This will also involve another mysterious oracle Josephus records *directly following James' death* about the fall of Jerusalem, given by 'one Jesus ben Ananias, a *simple field-worker*' (n.b. the 'field-working' theme again), who continued uttering it for seven and a half years until shortly before the fall of the Temple. The oracle 'Agabus' gives Paul here simply reverses that of the Pella Flight in the typical manner we have been observing, that is, instead of an oracle to *leave Jerusalem*, we have an oracle here that Paul should *not go up to Jerusalem*; the effect is the same.

But the first appearance of the prophet Agabus who 'came down from Jerusalem to Antioch' was to foretell 'the Great Famine that was going to grip the whole earth' in the time of Claudius. I think we can identify it with the story of Queen Helen's erstwhile husband, 'Abgarus' or 'Agbarus', according to Syriac sources, or, at least, the Agbarus Legend as it no doubt appeared in these and in Eusebius. In Acts the episode about Agabus' prophecy, introducing Paul's Famine-relief mission, occurs right before *the beheading of James the brother of John*.

The notice in Syriac texts about Queen Helen's relationship with Agbarus is, of course, disputed; but Northern Syrian Kings of this kind did not just have single wives, but extended harems. Nor did they live with each of them; on the contrary, they parceled out kingdoms or provinces to favorite wives and children in the manner hinted at in Josephus' account of Queen Helen's conversion – her husband is often suspiciously absent – and the place where her favorite son Izates lives will be quite different from that of her 'husband' (his supposed father) 'Bazeus' or 'Monobazus' (paralleling Abgarus or Agbarus in Aramaic/Syriac sources – 'Augarus' or 'Albarus' in Latin.

The key to all these matters is the notice in Acts about 'the Famine' and the reaction to it by 'the Antioch Community' of Paul and Barnabas and *Queen Helen's parallel Famine-relief activities in Josephus*, recapitulated in great detail in Eusebius' version of these matters. In fact Eusebius spends a considerable amount of time on these materials, as we saw, expounding them a second time in conjunction with his reproduction of Josephus' notice about the beheading of 'a certain impostor called Theudas'. He, as Josephus asserts even in what Eusebius reproduces, also 'claimed to be *a prophet*' with perhaps more reason than this 'Agabus' in Acts.

This note in Josephus' *Antiquities* is inserted in between the two notices about the beheading of Theudas and the crucifixion of Judas the Galilean's two sons, James and Simon, at the time of *the Famine*, emasculated but still recognizable in Acts' anachronistic version in 5:36–37. Though ignoring this second event, what Eusebius reproduces from Josephus, who also refers to it twice – both in relation to *Helen's grain-buying* activities not *Paul's* – is worth quoting: 'And at that time, it came to pass that *the Great Famine took place in Judea*, in which the Queen, Helen, having purchased grain i*n Egypt at great cost*, distributed it to the needy, as I have already related.'[27] In other words, there really was no 'prophet called Agabus', only our 'Agbarus Legend', the connection to which probably being that Queen Helen was probably one of Abgarus' wives, perhaps even his half-sister or sister.

We have already shown the way towards eliminating the second prophecy attributed to this 'Agabus' as well – the one in Caesarea right before Paul's last trip to Jerusalem. In the latter case, it will not relate to any 'Agbarus' or 'Abgarus', but rather also an 'Ananias' – a name playing an important part in all our stories, including Josephus' story of the conversion of Queen Helen and her son Izates, not to mention Acts' account of Paul's conversion in Damascus. This will be related to the 'Jesus ben Ananias' described at the beginning of this book.

Where the first prophecy ascribed to Agabus is concerned, Acts has gone to great lengths to erase the connection of the Famine to Queen Helen's conversion – not to mention the execution of another pseudoprophet, 'Theudas' – events fraught with significance where Jewish history and the Messianic Movement in Palestine are concerned. Instead, Acts overwrites these matters by what turns out to be childish nonsense. The writers of Acts certainly knew their audiences well.

The second prophecy ascribed to Agabus will also cover up another occurrence related to the life of James with equally childish storytelling. These incidents, in turn, also throw light on all the various goings up and down from Jerusalem, reflected in the Judas *Thomas*/Thaddaeus materials in the Agbarus Legend and paralleled in the 'some who came from James', 'Agabus', and 'Judas Barsabas' episodes – the last-named also sent 'with *an epistle from James*' (not from 'Thomas' or 'Jesus'), but always *from Jerusalem to 'Antioch'*. It should be observed that in the Syriac version of this correspondence and the headings of the Greek version of Eusebius, 'Ananias' plays a role as well, being the *courier between Agbarus and Jesus*.[28] It should be clear that the authors of Acts know all these materials and, in due course, we shall show the relationship of this correspondence with the 'letter(s)' known as *MMT*.

In fact, all of these insights come from a consideration of the life of James and how it has been overwritten and transformed in biblical warrant as it has come down to us. To be sure, modern scholars will object that 'the Agbarus Legend' *is* late, only beginning with Eusebius. That is because they have chosen to regard it as late and because the sources – except Hippolytus – concerning it are relatively late. But Eusebius doesn't consider it late, and on such matters he is usually pretty reliable, if at times demented. Nor do Syriac and Armenian sources consider it late, but, of course, these are depreciated as well.

But the fact of the matter is that this notice in the Book of Acts connecting the Famine to 'a prophet Agabus', which in Josephus is connected to the real-life Queen Helen, *proves* as almost nothing else can how early all these materials are. The notice also raises questions as to just what Paul's and Barnabas' relation to Helen was and who this Barnabas really was.

In our view, at least Paul – if not Ananias – was among Queen Helen's *grain-buying agents in Egypt and Cyprus*. The gateway to Egypt has always been '*Gaza*', a fact that will loom large in Acts' later overwriting of these materials. Again, as amazing as it may at face value appear, we are in Acts in a narrative *later* than the original for these others, whether in Josephus or some of these Syriac sources. Helen, of course, is depicted in Josephus as having sent her grain-buying agents out to conduct extensive Famine-relief activities, for which 'she won fame and widespread acclaim for herself and her family'.[29]

Aside from also identifying another town, Nisibis, very close to Edessa as 'Antioch' – this, along with other cities by this name, no doubt a contributing factor for so many of these confusions – Josephus also identifies Helen as having a relationship with a certain *Arab King* he calls 'Abennerig' in Southern Iraq, who harbors Izates from his brothers' hostility. We should pay close attention to the usage 'Arab' or 'Arabia' in these accounts and, here too, the town where Izates is given sanctuary, Charax Spasini, is known as 'Antiochia' as well.

But the general locale of most of these events is Northern Syria and Iraq up to the border of the Kingdom of the Medes in Persia. It is also what has come sometimes to be called Armenia, since Josephus specifically refers to the area in which 'the remains of that ark wherein it is related that Noah escaped the Flood … are still shown to such that are desirous of seeing them',[30] as part of it. This everyone knows to be Ararat in the part of North-Eastern Turkey formerly known as 'Armenia'. It is also the Kingdom Josephus says Izates later acquires from his father, though this is really further south in the region of *Abraham*'s Haran.

It should be noted, too, that just after considering the Elchasaites, whom he feels originated in this same area – at least in their incarnation as 'the *Sobiai*' or 'Sabaeans' – Hippolytus makes exactly this point, that 'the dimensions and relics of this (ark) are, as we have explained, shown to this day in the mountains called Ararat, which are situated in the direction of *the country of the Adiabeni* (that is, *Adiabene*)'.[31]

In fact, the Jewish traveler, Benjamin of Tudela (*c.* 1159–73), even went to visit this mountain, which he said stood above an island in the Tigris River, on his journey from Haran through Nisibis to Arbela and Mosul. For him, this is where Ararat was actually located – in the Land of Adiabene, just above the Tigris River, between Nisibis and Mosul – or *modern-day Kurdistan.* Here, he claims, Jews in the tens of thousands were still living. In Mosul, for instance, there were three synagogues, one headed by 'Nahum *the Elchasaite*', whom Benjamin doesn't even see as non-Jewish. In this area, too, he describes the recent Messianic Uprising of one 'David Alroy', who, he claims, 'called for a war with all Gentiles', 'called himself Messiah', and 'made the conquest of Jerusalem his final goal'.[32]

Left: Portrait bust of Nero's wife Poppea, whom Josephus visited in Rome and whom Nero kicked to death shortly before the Jewish Uprising of 66 CE.

Right: Jewish coin from the Revolt against Rome, showing 'the Cup', reading 'Year Three of the Redemption of Zion'. Others read 'Freedom of Zion'

Chapter 25
The Conversion of Queen Helen and the *Ethiopian Queen*'s Eunuch

Abraham's Homeland: Edessa to Adiabene

In order to understand these things, it is worth looking at the story of the conversion of Queen Helen as found in Josephus. The key issue which links this story to the other materials we have been attempting to delineate above is the one of 'circumcision'. This becomes the essence of the problem in the conversion of Queen Helen and her sons. Josephus presents the story at the beginning of the all-important Book Twenty of the *Antiquities*, which ends with his account of James' death. The story is obviously important, because he goes into great detail and it takes up the whole first part of this book.

Helen is pictured as the Queen of a country called '*Adiabene*'. It is important to note that for Muhammad in the Koran, ''*Ad*' is the name of an ancient Arab Kingdom, and the name of the 'prophet' sent to them is '*Hud*'.[1] The cities of this ancient kingdom are not very well documented. It is somewhere on the border with the Persians, at this point 'the Parthians', east of Asia Minor and Syria. The Rabbis speak of Helen in the same breath they do of Kurdistan, and, as with Hippolytus and Benjamin of Tudela, it is here that they would locate Ararat.[2]

Josephus also speaks of Ararat in this context, but he calls the area in which it is found 'Carron' – whether the same as '*Carrhae*' (Abraham's Haran) just south of Antioch Orrhoe or Edessa-by-Callirhoe is impossible to determine. This, he says, Helen's husband bestowed on Helen's younger son Izates, whom he seems hardly to know.[3] The area really is a buffer zone between the Romans in Syria and Armenia and the Parthians in Persia, and many armies have always passed back and forth through it. Therefore its importance.

As Josephus tells the story, Helen has two sons, Monobazus the older and Izates the younger – among myriad other sons of this '*Great King*'. These Kings (like the Saud family in Arabia today) had a plethora of wives and sons. It was customary to kill all the latter when one or another of these sons gained ascendance, a point on which the story of Izates' (and for that matter Helen's) conversion to some extent turns, because Izates, our hero, declines to do this. The key issue, 'circumcision' (or the lack thereof) where such 'conversions' are concerned, is also the key issue between those in the 'Jerusalem Church' following James and the 'Gentile Mission' following Paul, as per Paul's own testimony in Galatians – indirectly refracted through the portrait in Acts. It is also the key issue surrounding the '*Sicarii*' or, as Hippolytus terms them, '*Sicarii* Essenes'.

Not only is Izates' older brother called 'Monobazus' but Josephus also designates the father as being named 'Bazeus' or 'Monobazus' as well. So prevalent does this name appear to be that, like 'Herod' or 'Agbar', it is not clear whether it is a proper name or simply a title. In fact, another 'Monobazus', said to be a kinsman of Helen's son '*Monobazus King of Adiabene*', turns up among the 'Zealot' Revolutionaries at the start of the War against Rome, along with another of these 'kinsmen' of either Helen or the King, '*Kenedaeos*'. These two, along with Niger of Perea and Silas – formerly a member of King Agrippa II's army who 'deserted to the Jews' – are the really valiant fighters in the revolutionary army.[4]

Silas would appear to be the son of the previous Silas, who like Philip the son of Jacimus was commander of Agrippa I's army. Josephus calls 'Silas' a 'Babylonian' – whatever this means – as he does 'Philip', and they all seem to have been the descendants of a contingent of Babylonian horsemen the first Herod brought in from the plains region of Edessa and

Adiabene and settled in the 'Damascus' region to protect pilgrims coming from 'beyond the Euphrates' from local raiders.[5] Agrippa I had the elder Silas imprisoned, because, though his boon friend, Silas presumed to behave as an equal and would not sufficiently defer to him. After Agrippa's death, the Helcias ('Alexas') mentioned as the father of Paul's possible 'nephew', Julius Archelaus (Acts 23:16), whose forebear had been another intimate of Herod and whose family Herod used for that reason to oversee the Temple Treasury, acting on behalf of Agrippa I's brother, Herod of Chalcis, *executed* the elder Silas. In turn, Julius Archelaus' other uncle and Saulus' cousin, Antipas, was assassinated by another 'Zealot' known as 'John *the son of Dorcas*' in 68 CE.[6]

However these things may be – these four, Helen's two kinsmen, Monobazus and Kenedaeos,[7] and Niger and Silas lead the *initial assault* on the Roman Army on its way up to Jerusalem at the Pass at Beit Horon in the first heady days of the Uprising, the success of which touched off the feeling that the longer war (66–70 CE) could be won. In this assault, Monobazus and Kenedaeos were killed, but Niger, Silas, and 'John the *Essene*', not previously mentioned in Josephus, led a follow-up assault on the Romans at the southern sea-coast town, Ashkelon, near Gaza. If Josephus' testimony regarding the '*Essene*' bravery and indifference to pain while undergoing torture were not sufficient, this is further proof of the active role so-called '*Essenes*' took in the War against Rome.

Here at Ashkelon, Silas (does this name sound familiar?) and 'John *the Essene*' were killed and Niger given up for dead in a subterranean cave. However, 'Jesus'-like, *he emerges alive again*, much to the joy of his companions *who had been searching for him with lamentations on the battlefield for three days in order to bury him*.[8] This is not the only episode from Niger of Perea's life that appears retrospectively to have been absorbed into 'Jesus'' as, later, he too is dragged through Jerusalem by the 'Zealots' – the reasons for which are unclear – 'showing the scars of his wounds' as he went. Once outside the city, he is executed (possibly even crucified), but not before he calls down on them, again as Jesus is portrayed as doing upon the Jews in the 'Little Apocalypse's of the New Testament, 'famine, pestilence, and internecine slaughter'.

Josephus further clarifies who these two '*kinsmen of Helen*' are, martyred in the assault on the Roman army under Cestius at Beit-Horon – the traditional pass that had to be negotiated by invading armies on their way up to Jerusalem. Directly following the fall of Jerusalem, the sacrifice to their standards the Roman troops performed in the Temple facing eastwards, and their firing of the city, Josephus then describes how, when the fire reached Queen Helen's palace in the middle of the City's acropolis area, Titus took the surrender of many of the 'sons and brothers of Izates the King', who were all obviously *still living in Jerusalem in their grandmother's palace and those of her two sons*. These he took in bonds to Rome, having given them '*his right hand for (their) safety*', and, while still angry at them, kept them as hostages, because of their political importance, '*as surety for their country's fealty to the Romans*'.[9]

It is this group of individuals – namely, Idumaeans like Niger of Perea, pro-revolutionary Herodian Men-of-War such as Silas (Philip and Saulus would be examples of anti-revolutionary ones), and these descendants or brothers of Helen of Adiabene's son Izates – that we have suggested are alluded to at Qumran under the title of 'the Violent Ones of the Gentiles'. They may even be referred to as 'the Men of War' in the Damascus Document, 'who turned aside' and 'walked with the Man of Lying'.

Despite a certain tone of negativity in these references, 'the Violent Ones of the Gentiles', anyhow, are actually viewed with a certain amount of approbation, especially in the Psalm 37 *Pesher*, where they are credited with 'taking vengeance' for what had been done to 'the Righteous Teacher'/'the Priest', that is, 'the High Priest' or what we would consider to be 'the Opposition High Priest' of the sectarian alliance.[10]

In the Habakkuk *Pesher*, where they are simply referred to as 'the Violent Ones', they are also grouped with 'the Man of Lying', 'the Covenant-Breakers', and 'the Traitors to the New

Covenant and the Last Days' ('who defiled His Holy Name'), with whom they actually seem to take part in the scriptural exegesis sessions of the Righteous Teacher. Therefore, depending on the dating of these documents, they may even have been part of 'the New Covenant in the Land of Damascus' referred to in the Damascus Document. In other work, I have identified them, along with people like 'John the Essene', as, if not the moving force, at least *the fighting arm of the Uprising against Rome.*

Helen's son Izates must have been dead for some time before this Uprising, because Josephus describes his funeral along with Helen's and *the great monuments erected for them by Izates' older brother* – the *second 'Monobazus'* – outside the City. Eusebius, too, refers to these monuments and they were actually found in the last century near the present-day American Colony Hotel and are still splendid![12] For his part, Eusebius remarks that they were '*still being shown in the outskirts of Aelia*' in his time. Aelia Capitolina was the name given Jerusalem by Hadrian after his brutal suppression of the Second Jewish Uprising under Bar Kochba from 132-36 CE – '*Aelius*' being Hadrian's given name – after which Jews were forbidden either to approach within eyesight of or live in the City.[12]

In Josephus' story about Izates' conversion, Helen, as we saw, is just one of the King's many wives. She doesn't even appear to live with him. Rather, she is given this Kingdom further east on what would appear to be the outer edge of his dominions. Her son Izates is by this time living in a town at the southern tip of the Tigris–Euphrates Delta called Charax-Spasini.[13] This town would appear to be an important trading centre, which probably explains Izates' presence, not to mention the influences he encounters there. This would also appear to be true for the '*Jewish merchant Ananias*', he meets there – much the same as Paul or the '*Ananias*' Paul *also* met in 'Damascus' in Acts 9:10–17. Not only was Charax a centre for the Tigris River trade, but also areas further east. Two centuries later, Mani is said to have come from an 'Elchasaite' family there and 'the Mandaeans' ('the Sabaeans of the marshes') are still there today. Izates is the guest of another King called, as we saw, '*Abennerig*' – '*Abinergaos*' according to his coins[14] – whose daughter he marries. Her name, 'Samachos'/'Amachos'/'Symachos', is suspiciously similar to the name of the wife of '*Abgar Ukkama*' ('*Abgar the Great*') in Edessan chronicles – '*Abgar Uchama*' ('*Agbar the Black*') in Eusebius' presentation of his conversion.[15]

What is not generally appreciated about all these individuals with their strange-sounding names is that all of them are considered to be '*Arabs*' or '*Arabians*' by people *outside their cultural framework*. Tacitus, for instance, calls Agbar or Abgar, '*Acbar King of the Arabs*' and all the inhabitants around Edessa, '*Arabs*'.[16] For Strabo, Mesopotamia, for the most part, was inhabited by '*Arab Chieftains*' and '*the Osrhoeans*', to whom both Helen and Agbar appertain, according to Eusebius, and who occupied the country from Edessa to the Land of Adiabene, are also '*Arabs*'.[17] All of these points are extremely significant in attempting to determine just where Paul had in mind, when he informs us in Galatians that, after his conversion, first he '*went away into Arabia*' and only afterwards '*returned to Damascus*' (1:17–18).

For his part Eusebius calls Abgar, to whom Thaddaeus and ultimately Judas Thomas are sent, '*the Great King of the Peoples beyond the Euphrates*' as we saw – *exactly* the way Josephus describes *both Izates and his brother Monobazus*. These Kings would also appear to have had links to the 'Arabs' around Petra, somewhat confusingly called by modern scholars '*Nabataeans*', meaning descendants of Ishmael's firstborn son '*Nabaioth*' in the Bible (Gen. 25:13).

By Paul's time, these '*Arabs*' from Petra controlled Damascus, as he himself attests in 2 Corinthians 11:32, again after noting, he 'does not lie'. This also makes his notice about his mysterious three-year sojourn in 'Arabia' and, afterwards, 'Damascus' – again in the context of protesting he 'does not lie' – so interesting (Gal. 1:17–20). Does Paul mean by 'Arabia' here only 'Petra' and possibly 'Damascus' – where in Acts he supposedly links up with Ananias – or has he been further afield, to Charax Spasini, for instance, Edessa, or even

Adiabene? Aside from the 'Fertile Crescent' of cities extending from Damascus around to these Northern parts of Syria and Mesopotamia, and the legendary city of Palmyra on the direct caravan route to these areas – this trade being the source of the city's legendary wealth – these areas were mostly desert.

In fact, the fifth-century Armenian historian, Moses of Chorene – which some see as a pseudonym for a later ninth-century author – claims that Abgar helped his fellow 'Arab' King Aretas of Petra in his mini-war against Herod Antipas to avenge John the Baptist's murder – and John does, however indirectly, seem to be supporting Aretas' position on Herod's divorce of Aretas' daughter. In addition, this work attributed to Moses of Chorene makes it *very* clear that Helen was 'the first' of Abgar's wives, comparing her 'Piety' and her conversion to Abgar's. At the same time, by remarking her wheat distributions to 'the Poor' and her 'truly remarkable tomb, which was still to be seen before the Gate of Jerusalem', he makes it very clear she is Josephus' Helen![18]

To some extent Josephus turns this around, claiming that the Arab Kings from Petra were involved in some manner in the conflicts that broke out over Izates' succession to *his father*. For his part, Moses of Chorene records the defeat suffered by one of Herod's 'nephews' at Abgar's hands in Northern Syria. After this, he claims, Edessa was founded. The specificity of this information, in turn, does tally to some degree with material in Josephus about these same 'nephews' – the sons of Herod's brothers, Phasael, Joseph and Pheroras, and his sister Salome and their various marriages to his *own daughters*.[19]

While Paul does tell us in a notice that must date from around 35–37 CE, the year Aretas probably gained control of Damascus, that he (Paul) escaped from Aretas' Ethnarch by being 'let down from a window in the wall in a basket'; unfortunately, he does not tell us why the *Arab* King Aretas was chasing Paul, nor what he was doing in Damascus in the first place. Acts transforms this – much as the Gospels do the story of Jesus – into a plot *by 'the Jews'* in Damascus 'to kill Paul', none of which makes any sense, since he was supposedly sent there in the first place on a mission on behalf of the Jewish High Priest.

Of course, if Paul were a relative of Herod Antipas or his wife Herodias – who later sought the Kingdom for her new husband even over her brother Agrippa I – then there would have been reason enough for Paul's activity in this area, since Herod Antipas' Tetrarchy extended from Galilee across Jordan into Perea. In addition, *all* Herodians were related to the Arabian King of Petra, because Herod's mother seems to have been either a member of or related to that family.

Even more interesting, when considering Josephus' terminology of '*Idumaean*', Herod's sister had married one 'Costobarus', whom Josephus in turn identifies as an '*Idumaean*' or '*Edomite*'. This seems to be the line from which Paul's *Herodian* namesake 'Saulus' descended, since 'Saulus' is always linked in these notices in Josephus, two or three generations further along, with the two names 'Antipas' and 'Costobarus', the latter of whom Josephus identifies as Saulus' brother.[20] Political motives aside, many of these so-called petty 'Kings of the Nations' or 'Peoples' (*Ethnon*) – as the Romans referred to them – were little more than minor 'Arab Chieftains' as Strabo correctly points out. Pliny even refers to Charax Spasini, the town where Izates resided on the Persian Gulf, as 'a town of Arabia' and its inhabitants also, therefore, as simply 'Arabs'.[21] It should be remarked that even in the Koran some six centuries along, we have an echo of these matters in the stories of ''Ad and Thamud' and the fact that Muhammad regards all these 'Tribes' or 'Peoples' and the messengers who were sent to them as '*Arab*' or '*Arabs*'.

His '*'Ad and Thamud*', as suggested above, are clearly simply further garblings of the names '*Addai*' and '*Thomas*' and his stories, featuring them, are little more than echoes of these events centering about both Edessa and Adiabene. In claiming they '*denied the Messengers*', Muhammad identifies the first of these as the *Arabian* prophet *Hud* '*the brother of*

'Ad'. *'Hud'* in Hebrew is nothing but *'Yehudah'* or *'Judah'* and, therefore, our old friend *'Judas the Zealot'* or *'Judas the brother of James'* (or even *'Judas Barsabas'*) again – *'sent to teach the Truth to the people of Edessa'* – all this now in the Koran!

To *'Thamud'*, which is always paired with "Ad' in the Koran and basically replicates it, was sent *'their brother Salih'*, which simply means *'Righteous One'* in Arabic; so, once again, we have both the themes of the *'Righteous One'* and *his 'brother'*! For Muhammad, *'Thamud'* is an area abounding in 'hills, springs, plains, and date palms' (Koran 7.75 and 26.148–9), which is a very good description of the area around Edessa and Haran, Abraham's homeland. It fits well the description Josephus gives of the Kingdom he calls *'Carron'* (probably Edessa Carrhae – which he elsewhere identifies with Haran), that Izates' father gave him, wherein allegedly was found the ark. Though Muhammad confuses the area *'Thamud'* with the individual *'Hud'*, that he is dealing with the story of the evangelization of these areas by the individuals Judas *Thomas* and *Addai* (themselves confused in early Church sources), should be clear.

But Muhammad too repeatedly connects *''Ad'* and *'Thamud'* with *'the People of Noah'* and with Abraham (Koran 7.65–79 and 14.10 – this, the *Surah* entitled *'Abraham'*). This is a very important conjunction, as both of these individuals were considered to be connected to these lands and the traditions about them. He also repeatedly mentions the ark (11.38–50, in the chapter dedicated to *'Hud'*, not to mention *'Salih'* and 26.106–20). The conjunction of *'Hud'* with *'Salih'* is, of course, the conjunction of 'Judas' with 'his brother, the Righteous One' (probably James).

In Hippolytus' version of these things, Noah's ark is identified as landing *'in the Land of Adiabene'* – in Josephus, these are the lands Izates' father gives him. A final note – in these stories, Abraham's city of origin, *'Haran'*, is usually connected in some manner with either the conversion of Helen or her sons, or that of *'King Agbar'* correlating with it. This to some extent explains Paul's concentration on 'Abraham' in his letters – not to mention Muhammad's similar emphasis succeeding to him – and, by extension, James 2:21's brusque response about the sacrifice of Isaac, an important matter in Hebrews 11:17–20 as well (also echoed in the Koran – 37.101–14). This will also be seen to be the focus of both the admonitions and comparisons in the Letter(s) known as *'MMT'*.

The Conversion of Queen Helen and Her Son Izates in Josephus

As Josephus then tells this story, 'a certain Jewish merchant, whose name was Ananias, got among the women that belonged to the King and taught them to worship God according to the Jewish Religion'. Again one should remark the custom of multiple wives. The note here about Ananias being 'a merchant' is not surprising and adds to its authenticity, since certainly Charax Spasini, and Palmyra further north, were commercial centers. In this manner, Ananias 'was brought to the attention of Izates, whom he similarly won over through the *co-operation of the women'*.[22]

'At the same time another Jew' (unnamed), instructed Helen, who 'went over to them … and when he (Izates) perceived that his mother was very much pleased with Jewish customs, he hastened to convert and embraced them entirely.' It is hard to decipher where all this action is taking place, as even in Josephus there are two different versions of Izates' conversion. The first is at this Charax at the mouth of the Tigris on the Persian Gulf, but in this second note, Josephus portrays Izates as hurrying north where his mother seems to be.

This is the legendary conversion of Queen Helen and, aside from the romantic elements, it must be opined that the two conversions – Paul's and Helen's – have much in common, particularly as Acts relates the former. For his part, Josephus is anxious to point out that Izates brought this Ananias with him 'to Adiabene', when he was *summoned by his father to come into his Kingdom.* Who the 'other Jew' was, who converted Izates' mother Helen, is impossible to say, but the reader should be apprised that in Josephus, anyhow, we are in the same time frame as Ananias' purported conversion of Paul in Acts – at a time Paul by his own testimony had supposedly 'gone away into *Arabia*' (Gal. 1:17).

At this point in Josephus' narrative – as in Acts and Paul's letters – the issue of 'circumcision' arises. After Izates went back to Adiabene to take over from his brother Monobazus, whom Josephus portrays as holding his Kingdom for him after the death of his father 'Monobazus' (there would appear to be a few too many Monobazuses here), he finds the other sons of the King, 'his brethren', in bonds waiting to be executed as was the custom. Thinking this a barbarity and good politician that he is, Izates sends 'them and their children as hostages to Claudius Caesar in Rome' and the Persian King Artabanus 'for the same reason'. This is the same kind of situation that Josephus describes thirty years later, when Titus decides not to punish these 'sons and brothers of King Izates' for rebellion, but returns them rather to their previous state of being surety for fealty to Rome.[23]

However, it now turns out that, Talmudic sources notwithstanding, Helen's conversion is not quite what it appeared to be and she has, according to Josephus, been taught an imperfect form of Judaism by her teacher – *whoever* he was. Another teacher comes 'named Eleazar' ('Lazarus' in the New Testament), this now, the third teacher, who is specifically identified as 'coming from Galilee' – 'a Galilean', therefore, as the New Testament calls such types. Here we must be very insistent on reminding the reader about the name of those who followed Josephus' 'Fourth Philosophy' of Judas the Galilean and *Saddok*, who opposed paying the tax to Rome, have 'an inviolable attachment to liberty saying that God is their only Ruler and Lord' and, therefore, will 'not call any *man* Lord'.

Though at times Josephus is willing to apply the name of 'Zealot' to this group, particularly after the start of the Uprising against Rome and the destruction of the collaborating High Priests responsible for the death of James, and most particularly the group following one 'Eleazar' who take control of the Temple, others – such as those following the direct descendant of Judas above, Eleazar ben Jair, holed up on Masada – he also calls '*Sicarii*', because of the Arab-style curved dagger they carried under their garments. With this – according to Josephus – they *assassinated backsliders*, as, for instance, persons of Josephus' or Paul's ilk, not to mention the High Priest Ananus and his brother Jonathan or Herodians of the kind of Agrippa II and Bernice. (According to others, they used it *to circumcise*.)

Even people like Niger of Perea, a hero of the early stages of the War, fell afoul of such groups in some manner and was considered deficient. But not people like the 'kinsmen' or 'brothers' of Kings like Izates and Monobazus of Adiabene, who, just as obviously, met with their approval. As we saw, quoting Hegesippus, Eusebius applies the name 'Galileans' to this group when enumerating the various parties 'of the circumcision',[24] and even Josephus, when speaking of Izates' final decision to circumcise himself, mentions such 'zeal'.

This Eleazar is described by Josephus as very strict when it came to the ancestral Laws, and Izates, after encountering him, as 'feeling that he could not *thoroughly be a Jew unless he was circumcised* and ready to act accordingly'. Helen however is horrified, because she feels he will be rejected by his subjects if he is circumcised. With the help of 'Ananias', described now in Josephus' account as her son's 'tutor', she talks him out of it.

It will be recalled that in Eusebius' version of the conversion of King Agbarus, '*Ananias*' *was 'the courier'* who delivered the King's letter to Jerusalem and returned with Jesus' response. In Josephus, '*Ananias*' now argues that Izates might *worship God without being circumcised*, even though he did resolve to be a '*zealous practitioner of Judaism, worship of God being superior to circumcision*'. Paul, in Galatians 1:14, describes himself similarly, as once 'progressing in Judaism beyond many contemporaries in my race, being more abundantly *zealous for the traditions of my fathers*'.

These Edessenes of the country around Haran or those of Adiabene, the area to which some thought the ancient Israelites were exiled after the Assyrian conquest at the end of the 700's BCE, probably did consider themselves '*Children of Abraham*', as many in these areas still do today, as those following the later revelation of Muhammad did – also someone considered *as once having been a merchant plying the caravan trade in these areas*. It should be appreciate, however, that Paul, while calling himself an '*Israelite of the Tribe of Benjamin*' and even at times '*a Hebrew*', never actually calls himself a '*Jew*'. In fact, the opposite – he makes it clear that he is not '*of the Tribe of Judah*' and, as we have already argued, people of '*Herodian*' or '*Idumaean' Arab* extraction may well have and probably did consider themselves '*Children of Abraham*' (as Muslims do to this day), *though not 'Jews' per se.*

One should also keep in mind the problems over '*circumcision*' centering around these kinds of royal families generally. Josephus describes the problems *Herodian* Princesses, such as Agrippa II's sisters Bernice and Drusilla, were having in contiguous areas of Asia Minor and Syria. Antiochus, the son of the King of Commagene (later, as we saw, '*Head of the Macedonian Legion*' in the Jewish War), an area in between Paul's reputed homeland of Cilicia and Edessa and 'the Osrhoeans' of Adiabene (an area not a city), had been promised Drusilla by her father Agrippa I.

In the end Drusilla's marriage to Antiochus did not take place, because of *his refusal to be circumcised* – something Agrippa I, though not Agrippa II, seems to have insisted upon (*therefore, Agrippa I's more 'Pious' reputation*). Drusilla was then given to Azizus King of Emesa (present-day Homs, not far from Damascus) '*on his consent to be circumcised*' at around the time Felix was sent to Palestine by Claudius. Claudius seems to have given Drusilla's brother, Agrippa II, Philip's Tetrarchy in Galilee and further territories of his around Damascus as a reward for this.[25]

It was at this point that Drusilla was convinced by a '*Magician*' called Simon or '*Atomus*' (this last, as already remarked, clearly reflecting '*the Primal Adam*' ideology attributed to Simon *Magus* in the Pseudoclementines and other early Church heresiologies), '*by birth a Cypriot*' (here, of course, the usual confusion between '*Cyprus*' and '*Samaria*' – note, too, Paul's confrontation with the parallel 'Elymus *Magus*' *on Cyprus* in Acts 13:8) to divorce her husband and marry Felix, a thing that would have infuriated those like the '*Zealot*'-style writers at Qumran and, no doubt, this '*Galilean*' Eleazar in Josephus' story about King Izates' circumcision.

For her part, Bernice, Drusilla's sister, after she had been accused of incest with her brother Agrippa II, married Polemo, King of Cilicia (for Acts, anyhow, *Paul's reputed place of origin*), after he agreed '*to be circumcised*'. She did this, as Josephus admits, '*to prove the libels – namely the one about her and her brother – false*'. For his part, *Polemo was prevailed upon to circumcise himself 'chiefly on account of her Riches'*.[26] Bernice, it will be recalled, *had previously been married to her uncle*, Agrippa I's brother Herod of Chalcis in contravention, of course, of just about all of CD's '*Three Nets of Belial*' charges which included: '*Riches*', '*fornication*', '*niece marriage*', *and* '*divorce*'!

Finally Bernice, '*giving up all pretences of Judaism, forsook Polemo too*', that is, *even after he had specifically circumcised himself to marry her* – ultimately taking up with Titus who burned Jerusalem and the destroyer of the Temple. It is doubtful whether Agrippa II demanded circumcision on behalf of Bernice and Drusilla from their Roman consorts, Titus and Felix, which was, no doubt, the original issue dominating Peter's confrontation with Simon *Magus* in the first place – at least where Felix was concerned if not Titus.

To return to Izates, he does *finally circumcise himself*, as we have seen, much to the chagrin of his mother – for Jews, the *heroic* Queen Helen of Adiabene. Josephus' description of this is extremely informative and it appears fairly factual. When the '*Galilean*' teacher Eleazar entered into (Izates') palace to pay him his respects and finding him *reading the Law of Moses*, he said: 'Shouldn't you consider, O King, that you *unjustly break the principle of these Laws and bring offence to God himself*. For you should, *not only read the Law*, but all the more so *do what they command you to do*. How long will you remain uncircumcised? If you have not read *the Law about circumcision, and do not know the great Impiety you do by neglecting it, then read it now*.

This story will be fleshed out further in Rabbinic sources, which actually give the passage from Genesis 17:9–14 Izates was purportedly reading – importantly one of the chief Commandments '*Abraham*' received from God.

In Josephus' version of these events, one should note the omnipresent theme of '*doing all that the Law commands*', so much a part of the Jamesian approach and so prevalent at Qumran. Moreover, it will appear in the final admonitions in the correspondence known among scholars as *MMT*, or '*Two Letters on the Works that will be Reckoned for you as Righteousness*', which are also *addressed to a King and end up by evoking 'Abraham'*. In fact, one should always note the theme of being '*commanded to do*' so central to 'Rechabite' texts above, not to mention this constant thread of the theme of '*circumcision*' running through all the episodes noted above. Obviously this was *the* problem, as it was for Hippolytus' second group of so-called '*Essenes*', those he calls either '*Zealots*' or '*Sicarii*', whom he even describes as being willing to *forcibly circumcise people* – a practice also carried out in the '*Zealot*' War against Rome as we saw and probably during the Bar Kochba Uprising as well.

Queen Helen's Naziritism and the Suspected Adulteress in Rabbinic Tradition

This episode has not failed to leave its impression in Rabbinic sources as well, as it has in Acts' account of the conversion of the *Ethiopian eunuch*, '*the Treasurer of the Ethiopian Queen Kandakes*' (*thus*). Let us look at the former first. In Rabbinic sources, Helen's conversion is to Judaism and she is praised for her generosity. She is credited with giving *the golden candelabra to the Temple which stood its entrance*; and her son, Monobazus, *the golden handles for the vessels used on the Day of Atonement* – always an important ritual when discussing James' role as 'Opposition High Priest'.[27]

These sources specifically recount that she *donated a golden tablet to the Temple*, too, with the passage from Numbers 5:11–31 about '*the suspected adulteress*' inscribed on it.[28] This is a startling point and one has to ask why because this passage is, not only coupled with the one about the '*Nazirite*' oath for both men or women which follows it in Numbers 6:1–21, but Helen's own '*Naziritism*' is also made much of in these same sources – that is, Helen *was very much concerned about accusations such as adultery* or *fornication* and, in addition, cared about *Naziritism* and obviously *the Temple* generally. This is in marked contrast to the endless series of adulteries and like-minded legal infractions reported of Herodian Princesses above, who hardly seem to have evinced any embarrassment over these offences at all.

It is possible to conceive that Helen may have been accused of similar offences and, therefore, *the penances imposed upon her described in Rabbinic sources under the heading of* '*Naziritism*'; but the implication is that, aside from undertaking a series of these penances, *she also challenged these accusations*. It is a not incurious coincidence that 'Simon *Magus*' – implicated in this matter of the 'fornication' or adulteries of Herodian Princesses above – also appears to travel at this time with *another 'Helen'*, whom he represented as a '*Queen*' of some kind and with whom he seems ultimately to have appeared in Rome. As far as early Christian sources are concerned, *he picked her up* '*in a brothel in Sidon*' – certainly a malicious sort of characterization and meaning, at least, that she was *no better than a prostitute*.

Where Helen is concerned, there may have been some questions about her marriage and, if this marriage was to 'Agbarus' as it seems, there was also the additional issue of the nature of their relationship. For his part, as we saw, Josephus represents it as *being between a brother and sister* and we have also noted how Genesis pictures 'Abraham' – from a similar venue – as being in a similar relationship with his 'sister' - in this instance Sarah.

According to Rabbinic sources, Helen took a '*temporary Nazirite oath*' – similar, as it were, to the picture in Acts of *the penance James requires of Paul at Pentecost in the Temple*. In Rabbinic practice, this is normally taken for a periods of a month but, in Helen's case, this is stated *as being for seven years*, after which, she is supposed to have *gone on pilgrimage to Jerusalem*.[29] At this point, these same Rabbinic sources claim that the hero of many of their accounts, Hillel, *imposed another 'seven years' on her* – this in spite of the fact that, by this time, the Hillel (who appears to have been Herod's favorite rabbi and Sandhedrin Chief, *was long since dead*!

These sources are quick to claim credit for Queen Helen, too, even though her sons or their descendants *participated in the War against Rome* and, even, may have been among its chief instigators while the archetypical founder of Rabbinic Judaism, Yohanan ben Zacchai, did not. Rather, in an act of astonishing cynicism, he applied '*the Messianic Prophecy*' – that a '*World Ruler*' would come out of Palestine – to the *Roman Emperor-to-be* Vespasian, the destroyer of Jerusalem and the Temple. In so doing, R. Yohanan won for himself and his followers, according to Talmudic sources, the Academy at Yavneh where Rabbinic Judaism was born.

The reason given for the extraordinary back-to-back penances is supposed to be that Hillel did not consider residence outside the Land of Israel applicable for such 'Nazirite'-oath procedures because *such residence rendered one ritually unclean*. Not only is this a quite incredible explanation but, according to these same sources, after the second penance a *third* seven-year period was prescribed for her – this time, purportedly because she *had contracted some additional impurity by approaching a dead body* (*thus* – Izates' perhaps?). On the other hand, one can also imagine additional financial motivations having to do with her legendary philanthropy for extending these '*penances*' (and, in our view, if Helen was following the form of Judaism as that at Qumran, then the installation situated there, too, might have benefited substantially from her largesse not to mention that of her sons).

More to the point however, for our purposes, these claims are so extraordinary because these are *exactly the procedures that Acts 21 climactically pictures James as demanding from Paul* and *to pay the expenses, associated with Nazirite oath-type procedures in the Temple of four others* too – also, supposedly, *for various infractions overseas*. In Paul's case, as we have seen, these had to do with *his laxness in 'regularly observing the Law'* and, as it transpires in the riot in the Temple that follows, *teaching 'Jews in Asia' to break the Law and 'not to circumcise their children', nor any longer 'to walk in the Ways' of their Ancestors*, not to mention *'polluting the Temple' by introducing 'Greeks' into it* (Acts 21:20–29)!

Acts' account here – as we have repeatedly noted and clearly more historical than usual – even emphasizes *that James' followers were 'zealous for the Law'*, a denotation *Josephus twice uses* in explaining *why Izates' subjects would not submit to a man 'who was zealous (zelotes) for foreign practices'* and which the teacher Eleazar '*from Galilee*', *who demanded Izates circumcise himself*, most certainly was.[30] As usual, Josephus is always a *little more precise* and more fully-developed than the Rabbinic sources.

It is also interesting here that – according to these last – following the fall of the Temple, the Rabbis try to discourage those taking such '*Nazirite oaths*' not to '*eat or drink*' again. According to these, so distraught was the surviving population over what had transpired, that large numbers – this in a Rabbinic text – '*vowed not to eat meat or drink wine*' and '*became ascetics until they should see the Temple rebuilt*'![31] As we have alluded to, according to Benjamin of Tudela, '*Rechabite*'-*style ascetics*, living in lean-tos and caves, were still taking such oaths over a thousand years later in the Northern Arabian Desert out of '*mourning for Zion*' and '*mourning for the Temple*'.

In Acts 23:12, of course, the same kind of '*Nazirite*'-oath-taking individuals '*vow not to eat or drink till they have killed Paul*'. Not only are these the very characteristics we are hearing about in the various situations above but, in all the reports about James' life-style, they are precisely the points we continuously hear about as well. This is particularly true of the post-Resurrection appearance of 'Jesus' to James in the 'Ebionite' Gospel of the Hebrews who, according to the view of our tradition, had '*vowed not to eat or drink*' until he should 'see the Son of Man risen from the dead'. Of course, in the normative 'Christian' view of these matters in the Gospels, one should not forget the further consolidation of this theme in the notion of '*Jesus as Temple*' presented there and in Paul.

This theme of '*eating and drinking*' has been, of course, omnipresent in the Letters of Paul, we have considered above too; and this tradition, associating *refusal* '*to eat and drink*' not only with Nazirite-oath procedures, but also with *grief over the destruction of the Temple by the Romans*, just draws these parallels that much closer. Not only did the followers of James seem to have a particular predilection for this type of oath-taking and/or abstinence, but the '*eating and drinking*' motifs – connected in most accounts to the post-Resurrection appearances of 'Jesus' whether around Jerusalem or in Galilee – are transmogrified in other contexts, as we have also seen, into more complex ideologies like Paul's '*eating this bread* and *drinking this cup*' and *being in 'Communion with the body and blood of Christ*' (1 Corinthians 11:27).

These, in turn, bring the complex of this imagery full circle, because, as just signaled, for the authors of the Gospels and for Paul in several places too, 'Jesus'' body as we saw is the Temple! Here the parallel with these post-fall-of-Jerusalem Zealots, who take Nazirite oaths '*not to eat or drink*' until they should see it '*risen again*', is complete.

To crystallize further the circularity of this point in our sources about 'Jesus' or *his body being the Temple*, we also saw that Josephus, in writing *The Jewish War*, tried to exculpate the Romans of blame for the burning and subsequent destruction of the Temple – particularly his patrons, the Flavians, to whom he owed his survival. Likewise, those responsible for writing the Gospels are anxious to *relieve the Romans of any guilt in the crucifixion of 'Jesus'*. These themes of '*the destruction of the Temple*' and '*the destruction of Jesus*' parallel each other in our literature.

Though Rabbinic sources also connect Helen's Naziritism with an oath she took that she would become a Nazirite *if her son returned safely from battle* (a possibility that can be made sense of in Josephus as well), *they connect such vows with* '*adultery*' *too* – therefore the connection of the two passages from Numbers about '*the adulterous wife*' and '*Naziritism*'. At the conclusion of such a vow, one was obliged to make a sin offering, as Paul and the other four are pictured as doing in the Temple in Acts, in connection with which the head was shaved (21:24–26 – being the 'We Document', as we saw, Acts is *very* accurate here).

Paul performs another of these peculiar head-shavings, normally done at the completion of a Nazirite oath – as Muslims even now do at the conclusion of their Pilgrimage or *Hajj* to Mecca – at Cenchrea in Greece (the Aegean sea port of Corinth) according to Acts 18:18. But head-shaving of this kind seems to have been recognized only *in the Temple* – the hair being consumed on the altar – and what Acts seems to be doing here is either confusing another trip to Jerusalem Paul made for the purposes of a Nazirite oath or misplacing the later one just discussed above.

Helen's '*Naziritism*', in Rabbinic literature anyhow, ultimately leads her to Jerusalem to build a strategically-located palace for herself and her kinsmen to live,[32] her and her sons' famine relief efforts, and finally her burial there, over which stood such magnificent funerary monuments that no commentator has failed to remark them. Moreover, all of these things are clearly connected to her sons' decision to *circumcise themselves* and their, if not her, *outright conversion*. None was seemingly done for the purposes of monetary gain – which was generally the case with the tax-collecting Herodians – but for '*spiritual*' reasons, as Paul himself would put it in his '*I teach things spiritually*' (1 Cor 2:6-16).

Izates' Circumcision and his Famine-Relief Expenditures

As Rabbinic sources too describe this circumcision, both Izates *and* his brother Monobazus *are reading Genesis* and come upon the passage '*and you shall circumcise the flesh of your foreskin*' (Gen. 17:11–12.). God gives this command to Abraham not long after the passage about Abraham's '*Faith being reckoned for him as Righteousness*' or '*justifying him*', so important to the polemics of this period as we have shown (Gen. 15:6 – it should be remembered that a variation of this passage even turns up in the conclusion of *MMT* from Qumran as already remarked).[33] In Genesis, the Commandment *to circumcise is considered to apply to all males in his household*, including '*any foreigner not one of your descendants*'.

Once again, as in the Letter of James involving the sacrifice of Isaac and Paul's use of the example of Abraham's '*Faith counting for him as Righteousness*', we have examples connected with the name of 'Abraham' being used for the benefit of persons living presumably in *the area of Haran*, considered to be *the homeland of the Abrahamic family*. Just like the story of Agrippa I reading the *Torah* in the Temple on *Succot* and weeping over the matter of the Deuteronomic King Law, when both Izates and his brother Monobazus come to this passage, they begin to weep and immediately decide, without consulting their mother, *to circumcise themselves*.[34]

This is the story as Rabbinic literature would have it. It not only fleshes out Josephus' version further – for a change both agreeing on the essence of the contents – in addition, it adds Izates' brother Monobazus to the equation, actually insisting that both brothers knew about the necessity of these things, which from the perspective of later events in Palestine makes sense.

It is not only peculiar, but passing strange that the letter (or letters), called *MMT*, which became so controversial in disputes related to the Dead Sea Scrolls, appear to be *addressed to a King*. The first part of this 'letter(s)' actually focuses on the theme of the *uncleanness of Gentile sacrifices in the Temple*, particularly *grain offerings*, and does so in the course of actually mentioning the very words 'things sacrificed to an idol' (1.3–1.9), so important to all our discussions of James so far!

To review: in the first part of this correspondence, too – the 'First Letter'[35] – for the purposes of such sacrifices or offerings, Jerusalem is designated as 'the Holy Camp' and 'principal of the camps of Israel' (1.68–69). The 'Second Letter', which actually mentions a previous letter having been sent, outlined: 'the works of the *Torah* that would be reckoned for your own welfare and that of your people, because we saw that you had the intelligence and the Knowledge of the *Torah* to understand all these things'. (2.30–31) These are the actual words used and follow the admonition 'to remember David, for he was a *Man of Piety* (here the actual words used in Josephus' description of Eleazar's more 'zealous' conversion of Izates above) and he, too, was saved after many sufferings and forgiven' (2.28–29) – points Josephus also refers to in his descriptions of the trials and tribulations of Izates and his mother.

But even more importantly, it ends on the note, quoting Genesis from 15:6 on Abraham, and in direct contradiction to Paul, with the assurance 'that then at the Last Days, you will find some of our words to be true' and 'these are *the works*' that 'will be *reckoned as justifying you*' (1:2 and 2:33).

One should compare this with Paul in Galatians 4:16, also a *letter*, who 'by speaking Truth to you', against 'those who were *zealous after you*', but improperly so, since they were '*zealous to exclude*', has become 'your Enemy'. All of what we have just quoted from the two parts of this

MMT letter(s) above is also in *direct agreement* with the Letter of James, which in addition to citing this passage about Abraham above (2:23), evokes 'the Last Days' as well (5:3).

The constant reiteration of Abraham in all these contexts is important, too, as we have explained. Were it not for the technicality of the *two* letters – though, in fact, most see only one here – one would almost assume that one has here the actual Qumran version of the correspondence, delivered by 'the courier Ananias', between 'Jesus' or, as the case may be, 'the Teacher of Righteousness' or James, and 'the Great King'.

In fact, in view of the evocation of these very Jamesian 'things sacrificed to idols', in the first part, the very basis of James' instructions to overseas communities as depicted in Acts, reproduced in the Pseudoclementines and wrestled with so disingenuously by Paul in 1 Corinthians, and the second ending on the very note of the dispute between Paul and James of whether it was Abraham's 'works' or 'Faith' that 'were reckoned to him as Righteousness' and 'saving him', it does begin to make more and more sense – especially as one reads all the above-mentioned exchanges of 'correspondence'. Here at Qumran, we may have the actual record of the original correspondence, which was then changed by the magic of historical recreation into the stories about the new 'Messiah' as we have them today.

If this is true, then the main lines of what has occurred take shape. Izates' and his mother's conversion to this more zealous form of Judaism in the end also contributed to the Uprising against Rome, in which Izates' brave 'sons' or 'kinsmen', Monobazus and Kenedaeos, sacrificed their lives in the first engagement, giving others 'a splendid example' of how to 'make a good death' and a 'Pious end'.[36] Not only did Helen and her two sons, Izates and Monobazus, have the finances to undertake their illustrious Famine-relief efforts and build the splendid burial monuments accorded them in Jerusalem, they probably also had the finances to undertake far more.

So frightening was this form of Judaism (which was, not only revolutionary, but also comprised this form of '*Sabaean*' or *daily-bathing* type of Nazirite extremism or asceticism) that all has been transformed – including even the doctrine of '*the Standing One*' – in the various stories we have both in the Gospels and the Book of Acts and those about '*King Agbarus*' or '*the Great King of the Peoples beyond the Euphrates*'.

We have already suggested that Paul and 'Barnabas', whose 'Antioch' Community is made so much of in Acts, were originally among Helen's grain-buying agents. So probably was the fabulous 'Ananias' in Acts, Josephus, and the 'Agbarus' stories. Those who undertook this transformation had the highest knowledge of texts and sources. They also knew the incendiary nature of the ideas that were involved and were intent on transforming them into something a little less inflammatory that could live under the aegis of Roman Authority and which Rome itself could live with. This was an important literary task, for which those who achieved it were eminently qualified.

As we have suggested, it was perhaps the most successful literary rewrite enterprise ever undertaken, *and accomplished*. By means of it, not only did Rome defeat its enemies militarily, which was the successful first step, but also then *literarily*. By it, we have new religious mythologization of a Hellenizing kind taking place on top of an originally native Palestinian core.

Helen goes to Jerusalem to fulfill her vow 'to worship at the Temple of God and offer her thank-offerings there'. Izates enthusiastically consents to her going and 'bestowed upon her a great deal of money'! This is in the year 45 or 46 CE around the time of the Theudas episode and the beginning of the Famine. As Josephus describes Helen's arrival, 'it was of very great advantage to the people of Jerusalem', who were at that time 'hard-pressed by Famine, so that many perished for want of money to purchase what they needed' (45–48 CE). It is not unlikely that Theudas' attempt – as a kind of Joshua *redivivus* – at 'miracles' and to cross the Jordan in reverse, were connected with it, and there is material in Qumran sources about just such reverse exoduses across Jordan.

Helen then 'quickly sent a number of her attendants *to Alexandria* and *others to Cyprus* with large sums of money to buy grain and bring back large quantities of dried figs', and when her son, too, 'was informed of this Famine, he sent a great sum of money to the principal men of Jerusalem'. The beneficence of this family is a constant theme of our sources. 'She thus left a most excellent memorial behind her by this benefaction which she bestowed on our whole nation.'

When Izates died around 55 CE, Helen appears to have returned to Adiabene from her extended residence in Jerusalem – possibly still observing her extended Nazirite vows, as Rabbinic sources would have it. Here she too died suddenly, apparently out of grief for her son. It is at this point Josephus tells of the splendid funerary monuments erected by Monobazus in Jerusalem for Helen, as well as for Izates, who also seems to have been buried there, monuments Josephus himself claims to have seen. These external monuments are nowhere extant today, but the underground tombs with their majestic staircase are, and these are indeed very impressive.

Helen's behavior during this Famine is in marked contrast to people like the Roman Governor Fadus and Tiberius Alexander who, while himself doubtlessly 'fabulously Rich' and from Egypt, hardly appears to have gone to Alexandria to *buy grain for the people*. On the contrary, like Herod of Chalcis and Fadus, he executed the heroes of the people.

As will be recalled, Acts more or less couples its reference to 'Herod the King' putting 'James the brother of John to death with the sword' (12:2) with the prophecy by an unknown prophet called 'Agabus' – another of these persons who 'came down from Jerusalem' – of 'the Famine that would then overtake the civilized world' (11:28). This, in turn, paves the way for the introduction of James the Just directly thereafter in the same chapter, whose sudden intrusion into the text seems, as we have seen, either to assume that he had already been introduced previously or that we should know who he is (Acts 12:17).

'Agabus', 'Agbarus', and Helen's and Paul's Parallel Grain-Buying Activities

We are now able to put all our sources together. What is Paul's relationship to Helen's grain-buying activities? Acts claims that he and Barnabas were sent by the Church in 'Antioch' – where Christians 'were first called Christians' – to bring funds to Jerusalem; but in Galatians Paul nowhere refers to this mission, rather saying he 'went away into Arabia and then returned to Damascus' for three years. This is normally taken to mean the area around Petra but, as we have explained as well, it may have wider implications.

Then there is the second teacher in Josephus with the peculiarly Pauline approach, who teaches Queen Helen a form of Judaism in which '*the worship of God was more important than circumcision*' – but whom, for some reason, Josephus declines to name. This teacher seems to share this more easy-going approach to Jewish Law with the first teacher, Ananias, whom Josephus identifies as Izates' 'tutor' and *close associate*, who seems to follow Izates about wherever he goes. Of course in Eusebius and other Syriac versions of the King Abgar conversion, 'Ananias', as we saw, is the 'courier' to Jerusalem from 'the Great King of the Peoples beyond the Euphrates'. It should also not be forgotten that this 'Edessa', to which according to Syriac/Armenian sources Helen also appertained, was also known as 'Antioch' – 'Antioch-by-Callirhoe' or 'Edessa Orrhoe' – not to mention being the location probably of Paul's original '*Antioch Community*' above. It was only one of several 'Antioch's.

Moreover, according to Acts' account, Paul, too as we have seen, was associated in his conversion with someone named '*Ananias*' – this time 'in Damascus'. Thereafter Ananias drops out of Acts' version of these events altogether – itself very strange.[37]

In Eusebius' account of the conversion of this 'Abgarus' and the missions of 'Judas Thomas' and/or 'Thaddaeus' to 'the Land of the Edessenes' or 'Osrhoeans' and further elaborations in Syriac and Armenian sources, Ananias is obviously meant to be the same person as in the Queen Helen story. Here, again, is something of the letter-carrying scenario of Acts' picture of James sending out 'Judas Barsabas' after the Jerusalem Conference or the 'courier' connection between the 'Agabus' story in Acts and these 'Ananias' scenarios, not to mention the 'letter(s)' known as *MMT* and probably the work of 'the Righteous Teacher' at Qumran.

For instance, in the fourth- or fifth-century Syriac work known as the Doctrine of Addai – said to have been based on Eusebius, but much more extensive than anything he seems to have had access to – Ananias is Abgar's 'secretary' (in Josephus, as we saw, he was Izates' 'tutor'). Reference is distinctly made in the Doctrine of Addai to the story of the portrait Ananias had made of Jesus 'in choice paints', which he brought 'to his Lord King Abgar', the basis of present-day theories relating the fabulous Shroud of Turin to the city of Edessa, where Crusaders were thought to have come into possession of it.

Even more convincing, the collection of Syriac works, of which this one is a part, repeatedly refers to 'Simon Cephas', at one point even identifying him as 'Simon *the Galilean*'. He is said to have laid the foundation for the churches in Syria, Galatia, and Pontus, before going to Rome for further confrontations with Simon *Magus*.[38] Once again, here we have our two 'Simon's, Simon Peter and Simeon bar Cleophas, combined as in more orthodox works, such as Acts, into a single person. Nevertheless the identification of at least the second with 'Simon Zelotes' or 'Simon the Canaanite' (here now 'Simon the Galilean') stands. In fact, this second Simon may have been the person who really was involved in all these things – at least in eastern communities like Alexandria, 'Antioch', Edessa, and beyond in Adiabene.

What are we to make of all these sources? I think, first of all, we can say definitively that this mysterious 'prophet' called 'Agabus' is nothing more than a stand-in for 'Abgarus' or 'Agbarus' in the legends going under his name and their elaborations in works by Syriac authors and the overwriting going on here in Acts. Moses of Chorene, it will be remembered, even knows that Westerners have trouble pronouncing 'Abgarus'' name, which he anyhow simply sees as *a title* meaning 'Great One'. This derivation of the name also reappears to some extent in Eusebius' original translation of the correspondence.

The overwriting of whatever was meant by 'the Agbarus Legend' at this time, and the courier named 'Ananias' involved in it, by the nonsense name of the pseudo-prophet 'Agabus' – who certainly *never* existed and later reappears at another crucial juncture of Acts' story of the further adventures of Paul and his 'loin-cloth' or 'girdle' – would be in line with Acts' working method, as we have been delineating it above with regard to quite a few other historically documentable events: that is, to distort, to dissimulate, to confuse, and to delete – sometimes even simply, to have fun, or, if one prefers, a more malevolent intent, to *make fun*!

There is only one problem with identifying 'Agabus' in Acts with this 'Agbarus' or 'Abgarus' in the legends going by his name. This would mean that Acts knows 'the Agbarus Legend', whereas many scholars think the first indication we have of this story is from Eusebius, that is, they give Eusebius credit for being a creative writer – a dubious proposition! Scholars are simply wrong on this point and it is the account we have before us here in Acts that *proves it* – in connection with which, Helen (and/or her son, 'the Great King' Izates) sends her representatives on her more real grain-buying expeditions *to Egypt and Cyprus* (the importance of which in Acts' narrative we shall also see momentarily) – its linking 'Agabus'' name with 'the Famine' being altogether *too coincidental* to be accidental.

In any event, the fragments of the listings of 'the Twelve' and 'Seventy Apostles', attributed to Hippolytus in second-century Rome, already know the traditions connecting 'Judas called *Lebbaeus surnamed Thaddaeus*' with the evangelization of 'the Edessenes *and all*

Mesopotamia' and sending a letter to an individual called 'Augarus' – in the latter, it is 'Thaddaeus' who *conveys the letter*.[39] So do the two variant manuscripts of the Apostolic Constitutions, only now this individual is '*Thaddaeus called Lebbaeus ... surnamed Judas the Zealot*, who preached the Truth to the Edessenes and the people of Mesopotamia when Abgarus ruled over Edessa'. Then there is also the relationship of all these matters to the contemporary beheadings of '*Theudas*', who claimed to be 'a prophet' but was really a 'Deceiver', and 'James *the brother of John*', which we shall unravel below.

But this really would make Helen a 'wife' of King Agbarus, as Syriac sources and Moses of Chorene claim. The matter of the sizeable harems these monarchs kept has already been pointed out and Helen's marital status even in Josephus' account is extremely vague. As well, 'Monobazus' or 'Bazeus' are – like 'Caesar', 'Herod', and even 'Abgarus' – probably titles, reappearing as husband, son, grandson, and even *great-grandson*, if we are to take Rabbinic accounts seriously. Moreover, Helen is given territory within what seem to be her husband's domains (whoever he was) and seems to function in an independent manner as a kind of local grandee there, as her son Izates does elsewhere in his 'father's' domains – most notably the area around *Abraham's Haran*.

The whole area is referred to in all these sources as that of 'the Osrhoeans' – in Roman sources all considered 'Arabs', 'Acbar' being 'the King of the Arabs' – the relationship of Edessa to Adiabene further east being unclear, their being at least contiguous. What is clear, however, is that both areas have something to do with the archetypal prophetical figure 'Addai', who in our sources is associated either with 'Thomas' or 'Thaddaeus' (also related to this root '*'Ad*' or, in the Koran, '*the Land called 'Ad*').

The final confirmation of all these things, despite the doubts of many scholars, is the note that a future Edessene king, Abgar VII (109–116), probably the grandson of the Abgar or Agbar in our stories, was known as 'Abgar bar Ezad', that is, '*Abgar the son of Izates*' (not to mention the fact that in Josephus Izates' is sometimes '*Izas*').[40] Here the relationship of 'Abgar' to 'Izates' is made concrete.

In fact, as already suggested, in this fairly dubious relationship with her husband – and other perhaps even more scandalous rumors – may lie the source of Helen's documented interest in the 'suspected adulteress' passage from Numbers 5:11–31, which precedes the one about Nazirite oaths in that book – another of her evident passions.

Since her attitude and that of her sons – even her grandsons – would appear to have been a competitive one to Herodians, it is possible that the plaque she contributed represented *an attempt to embarrass the latter or rebuke them*. Just as the Herodians were the Roman puppet kings in Palestine seemingly sponsored by and championing the Pharisees, so those in the Royal House of Adiabene seemed to have carried with them the hopes of Nazirite-style, more extreme Zealot and *Sicarii* groups. In fact, the financing they provided Palestinian affairs probably did not just end with Famine relief activities, though this is nowhere as clearly documented as their grain-buying.

They may even have had something to do with the support of installations, as at Qumran – 'bathing' activity of this kind being quite popular among other 'Sabaeans' and 'Elchasaites' at the headwaters of the Euphrates contiguous to their domains, as already remarked. Buffer state as they were, to some degree their interest in Palestinian affairs can be seen as a proxy for the even more formidable and inimitable enemies of the Romans, such as the Parthians further east.

This state of affairs can be seen under the Roman Emperor Trajan who, once more, began to make and unmake kings in this area and stamp out all Messianic disturbances, but whose career was probably cut short because of it. In 115–16, he actually put an end to the Kingdom of Adiabene, marching down the Tigris to take the Parthian capital Ctesiphon, and then to the head of the Persian Gulf at Charax Spasini. As if on signal, Messianic revolts broke out among the Jews in his rear around the Mediterranean at Cyrene, Egypt, Cyprus, and Crete, sparking other revolts in Armenia, Syria, and Northern Mesopotamia, suppressing which Trajan suddenly died in 117 CE.

The interest in '*harlots*' and '*adulteresses*' is also keen in Gospel accounts about their 'Jesus' as it is at Qumran, providing yet another of these thematic circles; but in the Gospels, 'Jesus' is depicted, as we have on several occasions remarked, as keeping '*table fellowship*' with '*Sinners*' of this kind. Such behavior, if it were true – *which it undoubtedly was not!* – would have sent groups like those represented by the literature at Qumran into paroxysms of 'Righteous' indignation. Of course, according to Acts' distorted historiography, there were believers who were 'of the *sect of the Pharisees*, who rose up (at 'the Jerusalem Council') and said, it was *necessary to circumcise* them (meaning, Gentiles) and that they *be obliged to keep the Law*' (Acts 15:5).

As we have several times had occasion to point out, the use of the term '*Pharisees*' in the New Testament – as in this instance – is often a polemical code for attacks on Leaders of the Jerusalem Community like James because of the perception of their 'nit-picking' attitude over points of the Law – an attitude amply demonstrated in '*MMT*'. On the other hand, there were *real* 'Pharisees' as well, but these were more like – politically anyhow – the kind, pictured in Scripture as harassing teachers like John the Baptist or Jesus. This picture is doubtlessly true, but 'Pharisees' of this kind were basically Herodian/Roman clients.

To be sure, all this is very confusing for the newcomer, as it is for the veteran scholar, but attention to *political* attitudes towards Roman power and the Herodian Establishment, as we have been emphasizing, will soon put one right in sorting out these conflicting code names.

It is impossible to say what the intricacies of Helen's marital or sexual relations were and who was the father of which of her children. Even today, the institution of 'temporary marriage' is a recognized one in areas of Iran and Iraq, where Shi'ism has a hold and it seems to have been in widespread practice among 'Arabs' before the coming of Islam. There is also the issue of whether Helen's husband, 'Bazeus' or 'Monobazus', was her brother. Much as in the instance of her younger contemporary, the Herodian Bernice, that questions arose centering around the issue of 'fornication' concerning Helen's behavior seems almost undeniable.

In addition, in Helen's case, there was the inordinate *love* she lavished upon her 'only begotten' Izates, as opposed to her other children – Izates' 'brother' Monobazus, for instance. For this love, she was apparently well requited by the stipend Izates bestowed upon her and the relative splendor in which she seems to have lived in Jerusalem, rivaling, if not surpassing in some respects, that of *Herodians*. Of course, that Izates supplanted his older brothers and other relatives would lend further credence to his having had a more important forebear, as does the fact of his descendant, Abgar VII, becoming the *Edessan King* from 109 to 116, the period, in which Trajan *put an end* to the separate 'Kingdom of Adiabene'.

Paul may have had a relationship with Royal circles of this kind, as he did with Herodians before his mysterious trip to Rome at the end of Acts. It should be noted that if Paul is connected in any way with the enigmatic 'Saulus, a relative of Agrippa', in Josephus, then the note the latter provides that this Herodian Saulus was sent to Nero in Achaia (Corinth) to brief him on the state of affairs in Palestine is extremely interesting.

This is the year 66 CE and the last one hears about Josephus' mysterious 'Saulus', who had earlier been the intermediary between 'the Peace Party' in Jerusalem – consisting of Herodians, Chief Priests, and principal Pharisees – and the Roman Army and that of Agrippa II outside it. This is the coalition of forces that finally calls in the Roman troops *to suppress* the Revolution then in progress. This notice about Saulus in Josephus also fits in very nicely with Paul's own claims of important contacts in 'the household of Caesar', most notably

Epaphroditus – also Josephus' putative publisher, and secretary to both Nero and Domitian and the former's accused assassin (Phil. 2:25 and 4:18).

As we have seen, Paul does not speak of any intervening trip to Jerusalem to deal with anything resembling Famine relief before the one resulting in the 'Jerusalem Council', where Acts pictures James as making his rulings on what was required of foreign proselytes, including, most notably, where *MMT* is concerned, abstention from 'things sacrificed to idols'; where Helen is concerned, abstention from 'fornication', and where Paul is concerned, the ban on 'blood', implying presumably, too, 'Communion' with it. But Helen also sent representatives to Egypt and Cyprus 'to buy grain and figs', and Paul does seem to have been associated with a variety of people ostensibly from Cyprus as, for instance, the ubiquitous 'Joses Barnabas'.

The similarity of this name to 'Joseph Barsabas Justus', who doubled for James in the improbable election to replace 'the Twelfth Apostle' in Acts 1:22, should also be recalled. He, in turn mysteriously transmogrifies into 'Judas Barsabas' in the story of the two messengers who carry James' 'letter' with his instructions to overseas communities down to 'Antioch' in Acts 15:22. In Acts 4:36 this 'Joses surnamed Barnabas' is 'a Levite of Cypriot origins', while in Mark 2:14 the individual the other Gospels are calling 'Matthew' is called 'Levi the son of Alphaeus'. But, as we have seen, these 'Barnabas'/'Barsabas'/'Barabbas' names often have to do with writing over and the elimination of the members of Jesus' family from Scripture.

In Acts 21:16, before Paul goes up to Jerusalem to be mobbed by the Jewish crowd for allegedly bringing *Greeks* into the Temple (21:28), Paul has to do with another curious individual from Cyprus, this time named 'Mnason'. He is called 'an old Disciple' (meaning aged) and, once more, we are probably dealing with obfuscation. The 'Manaen' we have already met, the 'foster brother of Herod the Tetrarch', was grouped alongside 'those from Cyprus and Cyrene', including 'Lucius the Cyrenian' (Paul's putative travelling companion) as one of the five founding members of the 'Antioch' Community in Acts 11:20 and 13:1. These also include one 'Simeon', now mysteriously called 'Niger', a name we have previously, also, met under slightly different circumstance in Josephus above.

These 'men of Cyprus and Cyrene', who according to Acts' completely skewed narrative had scattered in the wake of the stoning of Stephen (that is, the attack by Paul on James in the Temple in the 40's), now speak to 'the Hellenists' (now '*Hellenistas*') at Antioch – whoever these might have been in such a context – about 'the Gospel of the Lord Jesus', at which point 'the Assembly in Jerusalem' sends down Barnabas to Antioch to deal with this situation there (where 'the Disciples were first being called Christians' – Acts 11:22–26) – yet another reverberation of the story of Thomas sending down Thaddaeus, 'as an Apostle, one of the Seventy', to the Land of the Edessenes and Mesopotamia when Abgarus ruled in Edessa – not to mention James sending down 'Judas Barsabas' with the 'epistle' containing his directives.

One can say that here these inverted notices about 'Cyprus and Cyrene' are nothing other than the contrapositive of the notices in Josephus about Helen sending her grain-buying agents to 'Egypt and Cyprus'. In continuing mix-ups involving so-called 'Cypriots', 'Simeon', and Samaritans, Simon *Magus*, the double of Elymus *Magus* from Cyprus in Acts, is also in some texts – most notably Josephus – said to have come from *Cyprus* not Gitta in Samaria. Hippolytus, the Pseudoclementines, and Eusebius, quoting Justin Martyr, put this right.

Queen Helen and the Supposed *Ethiopian Queen* Kandakes in Acts

However, it is the material in Acts about Philip in Caesarea that clinches in an unequalled manner our identification of 'Agabus' as a stand-in for or rub-out of 'Agbarus', becoming the ultimate example of Acts' working method. The material about Philip is peculiar anyhow, and tradition is never quite sure whether he is *an Apostle* or only *one of the Seventy*.

'Philip', not insignificantly, participates in John 6:5's version of the 'miracle of the loaves' – like the first account of this miracle, before 'five thousand', but now at *Passover*. Instead of the 'dates' added to the grain in Josephus' descriptions of Queen Helen's grain-buying activities in Egypt and Cyprus, it is, of course, now the 'fish' of the various versions of Jesus' 'breaking bread' with his Disciples in his post-resurrection manifestations to them above, added to the 'loaves'. In John, in answer to Jesus' question, 'where shall we buy loaves that these may eat?' (6:6), Philip is represented as responding in the language and manner of all these 'grain-buying' agent notices: 'two hundred pieces of silver's worth of loaves is not sufficient for them even for a little to eat' (6:7). Other than these few points and the story of his confrontation with Simon *Magus* in Samaria, after which he makes his way, *via the road to Gaza in the South* to *Caesarea in the North*, the New Testament knows next to nothing about 'Philip'.

Acts places the episode of Philip's circuitous trip – wherein he will finally meet *the Treasurer of the Ethiopian Queen Kandakes* – after the stoning of Stephen and Paul ravaging the Jerusalem Community, dragging people out of their houses and 'delivering them up', Judas *Iscariot*-like, to prison (8:1–3), but before his reported 'Damascus Road' vision and meeting with Ananias in Damascus in chapter 9. Acts presents Philip as something of a stand-in for Peter, who in any event comes to Samaria after him to rebuke Simon – that is, *Simon Magus* – for supposedly offering 'Riches' to Philip, himself, and John, the Samaria locale reflecting the 'Gitta' notices about Simon's origins in these other sources.

One should note how, in all these episodes, the theme of money, 'Riches', or being someone's 'Treasury' or grain-buying agent, is played upon in various ways – usually negatively. This totally intrusive episode in Acts 8:4–40, in between the two episodes about Paul's activities in Jerusalem and 'Damascus', has Peter speaking James-like to Simon *Magus* – in the context, totally incomprehensibly: 'May *the money you have with you* be destroyed, because you thought the gift of God could be *acquired by Riches*' (Acts 8:18–20). Peter's anger here is out of place and completely uncharacteristic, but it does echo the attacks on Paul for *profiteering by his ministry* that Paul responds to so emotionally in 1 Corinthians 9:3–12.

Acts' plot line then for some reason follows Philip, who is told by an 'Angel of the Lord' to go south, that is, *towards Gaza and Egypt*, even though his real destination seems to be north or west and *Caesarea on the Palestine coast* – where Paul later encounters him (8:26). 'On the way', he meets 'an Ethiopian man, a eunuch, one in power', as it turns out 'over all her Treasure' or *the Treasurer* of someone called 'Kandakes, the Queen of the Ethiopians' (8:27). Not only is the fact of this man being *the Keeper of the Treasure* noteworthy, but that he serves one *Kandakes, Queen of the Ethiopians*, even more so.

This is just our old friend, *Queen Helen of Adiabene*, again intruding into the text of Acts just where one would expect her to, but now concealed almost – but not quite – beyond all recognition. The masquerade has sufficed for almost two thousand years. Such is the power of mind-numbing devotion and dissimulation.

Though there was a Sudanese/Ethiopian Queen called Kandakes, defeated by Rome in 22 BCE, there were no longer any others in 45 CE, none certainly who *sent their agents or messengers to Jerusalem*. What, anyhow, would the 'Treasurers' of such 'Queens' be doing in Jerusalem in this period? But no matter; the point is that the name 'Kandakes' is but a thinly disguised variation on or overwrite of the name of Queen Helen's kinsman 'Kenedaeos' – probably her *grandson*. We have already encountered this Kenedaeos, probably one of Izates' numerous sons who, together with *his* brother – the third Monobazus – was killed in the forefront of the assault by Jewish freedom-fighters on the Roman troops coming up the Pass at Beit Horon in the opening days of the War against Rome and whose 'valor' even Josephus is forced to remark.[41] As with the confusion of *Iscariot* with *Sicarios* or 'Alphaeus' and 'Cleophas' – if we exchange the *iota* with the *sigma* here, i.e., '*sic*' for 'isc', then we probably come very close to the truth.

In the matter of 'Kandakes', '*Ethiopian'* has simply replaced the denominative '*Arab*'. For the Hellenistic/Roman mindset, all dark-skinned peoples would have been alike anyhow – and what fun! This transmutation, to which both the references to 'Treasure' and 'the *Queen of the Ethiopians*' should have already alerted us, is quite astonishing and of the same order as the one concerning 'Agabus', which follows a few chapters later. This '*Prophet called Agabus*' will appear, in a rather humorous fashion too, later in Acts in connection with Philip – in the story of Paul's *staying at 'Philip's house' in Caesarea.*

In addition, this *substitution* or *overwrite* shows substantial knowledge, not only of texts and traditions – in this case, the story of the conversion of Queen Helen and her Famine-relief efforts (the 'Treasurer', here, being nothing but one of Queen Helen's grain-buying agents) and probably the main lines of the 'Agbarus' story (*the real one, not the legend*), but also of history and the fact that one of Helen's descendants or kinsmen, a *heroic one* at that who distinguished himself in the opening engagement of the War against Rome, was named 'Kenedaeos'. Of course, all of these are being rubbed out and overwritten, probably just because of this *heroism* and the relationship of this family with *Revolutionary Forces in Judea*!

That the story of Kandakes found in Strabo and Pliny relates to 22 BCE and not Claudius' time demonstrates the deliberate artificiality of this episode. Moreover, in focusing on the story of this legendary 'Queen of Sheba', there is a *very real* play upon the kind of 'Sabaean' religious practices *Queen Helen* no doubt supported – 'Sheba' and 'Sabaean' being based on very close linguistic roots in Hebrew and other Semitic languages as well. In fact, the same confusion between 'Sabaean' meaning 'Daily Bather' and 'Sabaean' meaning 'South Arabian' or 'Ethiopian' has crept into the Koran and Islam as well.

Here someone is overwriting with *definite* knowledge. Such is the 'playfulness' of the writers of Acts' *pseudo*-history. In these materials, too, as if we had not already suspected it, 'Philip' begins to take, historically speaking, a giant nose-dive. But that these dissimulators have not scrupled to satirize the name of one of the holiest martyrs of the Jewish people – '*Kenedaeos*' – a hero and a convert at that, who has, in the process, been forgotten *even by the Jews themselves*. Such is the power of successful rewriting and the consequences of widespread and an almost congenital ignorance.

To take the name of this non-Jew and convert, who none-the-less was a *valiant freedom-fighter* and *real martyr* for his adopted people, and disembody and ridicule it in this way might not be upsetting for the general reader, but to anyone valuing that cultural heritage or tradition involved – particularly as these words have been taken by endless numbers of people, including even Muslims, as 'the Word of God' for the last almost twenty centuries – it will be seen as offensive in the extreme.

For the final and definitive proof, not only of the knowledgeability, but also the cynicism of those responsible for such transformations, one has only to continue the story as it is presented in Acts. Even though this Ethiopian 'eunuch' – the story, of course, is playing on 'circumcision', just as Paul is in Galatians 5:12 above – and 'the man over all the Queen's Treasure', is sitting in his chariot on the road returning from *Jerusalem to Gaza*, he is *reading the Bible* (as no doubt our author was) – in this case 'the Prophet Isaiah'. 'The Spirit' now counsels Philip to creep up on him and 'join himself' to his chariot (Acts 8:29).

At this point, of course, Philip hears the eunuch reading Isaiah, and then asks him, 'do you then know what you are reading?' (Acts 8:30). But this is nothing other than *the story from Josephus* about 'the Galilean' teacher Eleazar going into *Queen Helen's favorite son Izates* and finding him reading – not Isaiah – but the Law of Moses, namely the Genesis passage *commanding Abraham to circumcise all the males in his entourage* '*and any stranger not of his seed*' *that was with him* (Gen. 17:10–27). In Josephus' story, Eleazar then asks *Izates whether he understood what he was reading* – these, it will be recalled, were the precise words – and informing him of his *Impiety in neglecting this Commandment.*[42]

The substitution of the Prophet Isaiah here for the Book of Genesis on God's command to Abraham to *circumcise himself and those traveling with him – even the stranger* – is significant, Isaiah being perhaps the fundamental Christian biblical proof-text. The maliciousness in substituting 'a *eunuch*' for Izates is equally clear. If there were any doubts about what we have been saying previously concerning Acts' working method, these can now utterly be laid to rest. As obscure and inconsequential as this episode may seem to be, all our observations about Acts' rewriting activity can now be thought of as confirmed. The reader will also begin to appreciate that what we have been saying about Acts' sources and its manner of treating them is true too – all too true – many much older than previously supposed, and, because of Acts' extremely successful if tendentious methodology, *older, in fact, than Acts itself.*

But this is no longer simply humorous rewriting or overwriting. The disparaging caricature of *Izates' circumcision* puts paid to this idea. We are now in the realm of outright forgery aimed at disinformation of a most insidious kind. Unfortunately, the methods of our other documents do not differ to any extent from what we are seeing here, and the whole foundational edifice of 'Gentile Christianity' must be seen as derivative and tendentious. This is not the case for 'Jamesian' *Nazirite* or *Nazoraean* 'Christianity', if we can call it this.

Of course in Luke's version of this story, now *the Ethiopian eunuch and Treasurer of Queen Kandakes* – not *Izates the son of Queen Helen* – is reading the key exegetical passage of Christian theology on the death of Jesus, Isaiah 53:7–8, the 'Suffering Servant', at which point Philip asks him if he understood 'to whom the Prophet was referring', and proceeds 'to evangelize him' – for which reason he is, no doubt, known as 'the Evangelist' when Paul encounters him some thirteen chapters further along in Acts, with his 'four virgin daughters *who prophesied*' (*thus*: 21:9) – or, 'beginning with *this Scripture*, preaches to him the Gospel of Jesus', as well he might have (Acts 8:34).

Coming to some water 'along the Way', he now baptizes the 'eunuch' when he agrees that 'Jesus Christ is the Son of God' – all perfectly good Gentile Christian theology. The stand-in of this 'Ethiopian Queen's eunuch' for the Izates story should be patent, Philip now taking the place of Izates' 'Zealot' teacher Eleazar.

When they 'went down in the water', for both apparently then enter the water, 'the Spirit of the Lord took Philip away' and '*the eunuch never saw Philip again*' (Acts 8:39). One might add, neither do we, because Philip is then miraculously transported to Azotus on his way to 'evangelize all the cities' on the way to Caesarea in the opposite direction to which he had previously been going (8:40) – in time presumably to meet Paul there a decade and a half later.

The narrative immediately returns, this interruption out of the way, to 'Saul breathing threat and slaughter against the Disciples of the Lord', getting letters from the High Priest '*to the synagogues of Damascus*' (Acts 9:1–2) – wherever these may have been – and we are on our way to his vision on the road to Damascus. But what is the point of all this? One point, anyhow, is that the reason Philip and the Ethiopian eunuch are on their way from Jerusalem to Gaza and not Caesarea is that Gaza is *the gateway to Egypt* and this is where Helen's Treasury agents were, doubtlessly, going to buy grain.

There is unquestionably a lot of truth in this episode lying just beneath the surface, including whatever relationship Paul, Barnabas, or Philip might have had to these grain-buying operations and, no doubt, to Helen's Treasury agents, but one cannot proceed further along this line – only to observe that, without a thorough grasp of the Queen Helen materials, one would never have suspected the resemblance of this episode to the conversion of Queen Helen's son Izates and Queen Helen sending her representatives on Famine relief to Egypt and Cyprus thereafter.[43]

The Lukan author of Acts obviously knows the Queen Helen materials thoroughly, including her relationship to 'Agabus'. That he sees fit to affix Paul and Barnabas to these matters relating to the Famine, when Paul himself does not even refer to it in his letters, is further proof that Paul was in some manner involved (with some of his 'Cypriot' and 'Cyrenian' colleagues) not only in Queen Helen's Famine-relief efforts, or those of her son, but also perhaps her conversion. Josephus opines that Izates also sent relief, this time in the form of 'money' or 'coin', much like the 'eunuch who had power over all the Treasure of the Ethiopian Queen' – read here, '*Arabian Queen*' or '*Sabaean Queen*'.

Though Josephus promises us a further account of 'the good works of this royal pair', he never provides it, but Talmudic materials also deal with this aspect of the activities of Helen's son – now called Monobazus. When his brother asks him why he has impoverished himself in such activities, he replies, how good it was to store up 'Riches' in Heaven in place of those on earth, which his ancestors stored up, favorite allusions in the New Testament as we have seen – not to mention the Damascus Document – and the gist of Peter's rebuke to Simon *Magus* in the first part of the Philip materials in Acts.[44]

As to the reference to this 'Treasury' official as a 'eunuch', this, of course, has *nothing whatever to do with 'Ethiopia'*, but rather the practices of the Parthian court and those within the Persian sphere of influence generally, as Adiabene most definitely was. Even more to the point, it relates to the perception of 'circumcision' – as in the Roman '*Lex Cornelia de Sicarius*' – as a kind of sexual mutilation. In his full account of Izates' efforts to remain viable in a Persian buffer state, in addition to showing us how Izates' father originally gave him a Kingdom around Haran, Josephus gives us a vivid picture of Izates' struggles, for which his mother no doubt took her famous 'Nazirite' oaths or promised to. This 'eunuch' status also suits the purposes of the authors of the Book of Acts in inverting Qumran materials such as they are, which would rather ban all classes of such persons – cripples, lepers, diseased persons, those with running sores or 'founts' (as it is expressed), and most certainly *eunuchs* – from the Temple, and, as a 'eunuch', he would hardly 'have come to Jerusalem to worship' in those days (8:27). Acts' authors knew this.

Those responsible for these materials had an uncanny control over them, as well as a highly developed – albeit derisive – sense of humor. This was much more developed than many of their medieval or modern heirs, who normally see nothing funny in these materials and *almost never laugh at them*, regardless of how preposterous, outrageous, or ribald what is being recounted really is. Rather they take everything extremely seriously, some even to the extent of swearing by their mortal souls on them. The authors of Acts would, doubtlessly also, have been very pleased by the success of their poor efforts, the materials having almost as much power today as they did two millennia ago. They would, however, not perhaps have been very surprised at the credulity of mankind or by its tendency towards self-hypnosis or even mass hysteria over such a long expanse of time, as they seem already to have understood this.

Scroll Fragment: "The Community Council Cursing Belial," relating to 1QS, ii and echoing all Paul's allusions to "cursing" and "being accursed".

Chapter 26
Judas Thomas and Theuda the Brother of the Just One

Judas Thomas and *Thaddaeus* among the Edessenes

According to Syriac sources and Eusebius, 'Thomas' or 'Judas Thomas' sent out Thaddaeus to evangelize the Edessenes; in the List of the Seventy attributed to Hippolytus, Thaddaeus is sent with 'the letter to Augarus'. As Eusebius presents this tradition, which he claims to have found in the Royal Archives of Edessa: 'After the Ascension of Jesus, *Judas, who is also called Thomas, sent Thaddaeus the Apostle, one of the Seventy*, to him.' 'Him' is 'King Abgar the Great, King of the Peoples beyond the Euphrates' (Abgar *Uchama* – 'Acbar, King of the Arabs' in Tacitus); 'the Seventy' is clearly a variation on the Jerusalem Assembly (*Seventy* being the traditional number making up such Assemblies in Judaism). In Hippolytus, this 'Thaddaeus who carried the letter to Augarus' is clearly this same Judas, who preached the Truth to the Edessenes and to all Mesopotamia and died at Berytus (Beirut).

The story of the conversion of Queen Helen and her son to Judaism, found in Josephus and Talmudic tradition, has become in Eusebius and Syriac sources *the conversion of King Abgar to Christianity*. This is not to say that one can definitively identify Agbar with either Izates or Monobazus. One can't. But it is to say that Acts has transformed or obliterated *very old* materials, so embarrassing were they felt to have been. We can also say that the form of Judaism to which Queen Helen converted was not completely normative, despite Rabbinic claims and attempts to take it over, but more 'Zealot' or 'Jamesian'. This is implied by the extreme Naziritism associated with it even in Rabbinic sources, which do not really understand it any more than orthodox Christian sources do, because it is so alien to them. In fact, both the former and the latter show extreme hostility to this form of Judaism, particularly after the fall of the Temple.

Judas the Brother of James, *Thaddaeus*, and *Theuda*

This brings us to the third brother of Jesus, the individual called Judas of James or Thaddaeus/'Lebbaeus surnamed Thaddaeus' in Gospel Apostle lists or the Papias fragment. Regardless of confusions of this 'Judas of James' or 'Thaddaeus' with Thomas, that is, 'Judas Thomas', we would identify this individual with the third brother of Jesus, Judas or Jude. The 'Lebbaeus surnamed Thaddaeus' in some manuscripts of Matthew and the Apostolic Constitutions most likely represents a garbling of 'Alphaeus' (his father) and/or 'Cleophas', though one must always keep in mind the linguistic relationship of '*Lebbaeus*' to James' additional mysterious cognomen *Oblias*.

There can be little doubt that what Matthew and the Syriac sources echoing him are trying to say (or not to say as the case may be) is that Thaddaeus is the son of Alphaeus or the brother of James too, or that he bore the same cognomen *Oblias* as James did (in the end it is the same). We should leave 'Joseph' as Jesus' father out of this equation as a gloss, as Islam does. How puzzling it must have seemed to the author or redactor of some manuscripts of Matthew to have seen a tradition that Thaddaeus, who comes after 'James the son of Alphaeus', was also 'the son of Alphaeus'. He produced 'Lebbaeus who was surnamed Thaddaeus', whatever he thought this was supposed to mean.

Thus in two variant manuscripts of the Apostolic Constitutions, following Matthew, 'Thaddaeus, also called Lebbaeus and surnamed Judas *the Zealot*, preached the truth to the Edessenes and the people of Mesopotamia when Agbarus ruled over Edessa and was buried in Berytus in Phoenicia'. The Apostle list attributed to Hippolytus basically says the same thing, though now he becomes '*Judas who is also Lebbaeus*'. For Papias, '*Thaddaeus*' is *one of the four brothers of Jesus*' whose mother was '*Mary the wife of Cleophas*' or '*Alphaeus*'. Again, the conjunction of his name with that of '*Judas the Zealot*' is made clear.

'Berytus', as we saw, is the city where Titus continued his birthday celebrations – begun earlier in Caesarea *in honor of his brother Domitian after the fall of Jerusalem in 70 CE* – where upwards of 2,500 prisoners perished in games with animals and gladiatorial fights! At the time of the burial there of this '*Thaddaeus*' or '*Judas the Zealot*', Berytus was attached to the Kingdom of Herod of Chalcis in Syria; however, we have already implicated this same 'Herod of Chalcis' in the beheading of '*Theudas*', c. 45 CE! Apart from the parallel tradition in Syriac sources about the burial of 'Addai'/'Thaddaeus' in Edessa, this is a startling bit of information because it confirms what we have been thinking all along.

Where 'Thomas' is concerned, Eusebius, following Origen, would limit his activities to Mesopotamia and Parthia (Persia). However, since the sphere of influence of the latter extended further East, traditions developed which took his activities even as far as India – traditions surviving to this day.[1]

As far as Thomas' death is concerned, there is little information though these Acts of Thomas echo, to some extent, the picture of Stephen's death in Acts – only now this martyrdom occurs '*outside the city*' of some far-off Indian Kingdom not '*outside of Jerusalem*'; and, instead of being beheaded as with 'Theudas' or 'James the brother of John', 'Thomas' is run through by four spearmen (*thus*)! However, like *Addai*/Thaddaeus in Syriac tradition, *his bones* are transferred to Edessa, though Indian traditions contest this.[2] These Acts, plus documents from Nag Hammadi such as the Book of Thomas the Contender, make no bones about the fact that Thomas was not only a brother of Christ, but his twin brother – therefore the appellation.[3]

Regardless of the reliability of this 'twinning', once we draw the connection between Judas Thomas and Theudas which we have been suggesting, then the individual in these traditions does function as *Jesus redivivus* or, if one prefers, a *Joshua redivivus.* As in the case of John the Baptist and Elijah, but with more cause, Theudas attempts to part the River Jordan as Joshua did, though in the reverse direction, to leave not to enter. But before he could do so, Fadus the Roman Governor, ruling jointly with Herod of Chalcis, slew many of his followers and, taking him prisoner, ultimately beheaded him. Theudas was not the only one of these 'impostors' to attempt to re-create the miracles of Joshua in this period. Josephus describes someone active during the governorship of Felix (52–59 CE) whom he calls 'an Egyptian', who also 'claimed to be a prophet'.[4] Josephus calls these kind of individuals 'impostors', 'Brigands', and 'Deceivers' as we have seen. These 'banded together, inciting large numbers to revolt, encouraging them to claim their freedom and threatening to *kill any who submitted to Roman Rule*', the opposite of 'Jesus' in the Gospels. These, 'under the pretence of Divine inspiration, fostering Innovation and change in government, persuaded the masses to act like madmen and *led them out into the wilderness* in the belief that there God would show them *the signs of their impending Salvation*'.

We have related these 'signs' to those Jesus was supposed to have done in the Gospels at '*Cana of Galilee*' or out 'in the wilderness', multiplying the loaves and the fishes 'so that his Disciples believed on him', or murmur, 'this is truly the Prophet who is coming into the world'. But for Josephus, these men '*plundered the houses of the Rich* … till all Judea was consumed with the effects of their frenzy, the flames of which were fanned ever more fiercely till it came to out-and-out warfare'.[5]

Both 'Theudas' and this 'Egyptian' are Joshua *redivivuses* (revived or reborn); Josephus even calls Theudas 'an impostor' or 'magician'.[6] For Acts 5:36, he 'claimed to be somebody', which may be imbued with more significance than at first appears. This may be what was meant by this notion of 'twinning' in these various early Church sources so sympathetic to Thomas. None show any hesitation to identify Thomas as 'Judas *Thomas*', that is Judas the Twin, alias '*Didymus* Thomas' or 'Twin Twin'. We get the point.

The final proof of all these propositions comes in the two Apocalypses of James from Nag Hammadi. These not only relate one 'Theuda' to James, but to another individual, the 'Addai' one finds in Syriac texts (our Thaddaeus again), in both Apocalypses playing parallel roles, recipients of information from James. In the Second Apocalypse of James, Theuda is called 'of the Just One and *a relative* of his', meaning in this case 'his brother'. Here is *direct* testimony, which we did not have from any other source previously, linking the name Theuda or Theudas to Jesus, James, or 'the Just One' in a familial manner. It was already clear that Thaddaeus alias 'Lebbaeus' alias 'Judas, the brother of James' was related in a *direct* family manner to James. Now we can see that probably 'Theudas' was too.

Where this 'Judas the brother of James' or Thaddaeus is concerned, we have various sources that identify him, in the manner of his second brother Simon, as 'Judas the Zealot'. Again, this places him squarely in the Zealot/*Sicarii* tradition, which accords nicely with Acts' understanding of James' followers in Jerusalem as '*Zealots for the Law*'. Not only was James himself *exceedingly* zealous, but like the Righteous Teacher of the Scrolls we see him as the axis about which these Messianic and Revolutionary Movements turned in their desire to bring about the kind of *religious and social change* mentioned by Josephus.

That this individual – call him Theudas, call him Thaddaeus, call him Judas of James or Judas the Zealot, or call him Judas *Thomas* – also at some point *went to Edessa*, concentrates all our sources still further. In these, traditions about one 'Addai' begin to assert themselves, both in fourth-century documents like the 'Doctrine of Addai' or in Syriac sources generally – not to mention the Koran. But all these individuals begin to coalesce, including the individual known as Thomas or Judas Thomas, who, in addition to sending out Addai or Thaddaeus to King Agbarus, seems to have gone down to Edessa himself at some point, after which Mesopotamia and Parthia become the spheres of his activities. Since we can now place this 'Judas the brother of James' in 'Mesopotamia and Parthia', I think we can say he went to Adiabene as well – though probably not as far as India! This perhaps more appertains to Mani.

The Judas Who Taught the Truth to the Edessenes and James' Brother

If we now return to Acts' story about James sending down an individual called 'Judas Barsabas' with a letter to Antioch (*cum* Edessa or Adiabene) containing directives to overseas communities, particularly as related to *conversion of Gentiles*, while all the time keeping the 'brother' theme in mind and all the tricks and turns relating to it, a synthesis of sorts begins to emerge.

Recall how in Acts at the time supposedly of filling Judas' *Office*, Judas Barsabas had an *alter ego* 'Joseph called Barsabas who was surnamed Justus'. If we now identify Judas Thomas/ Thaddeaus/Jude the brother of James/Judas Barsabas with Theudas, our problems and redundancies begin to disappear. Not only are Theudas and Thaddaeus homophones, this brings us to a clearer understanding of just who was involved in this evangelization of the Edessenes and, by extension, Adiabene – and events implied by these stories as well.

The individual in Acts 12:2, 'beheaded by Herod with the sword', is not actually 'James the brother of John' – more of our 'shell game' again. Nor is the individual, sent with the letter to Antioch in the 'Agbarus' conversion story in Eusebius, sent down by Judas *Thomas*. Rather he is sent down by '*James the brother of Jesus*' – though this individual *is James' brother*. This is 'Thaddaeus' whom, as we have been seeing, is basically a double for '*Judas the brother of James*', '*Theudas*', and '*Judas the Zealot who preached the truth to the Edessenes*'. He also appears as

'Judas Barsabas' in Acts, that is, James *sent his brother, 'Judas the brother of James'* down to Northern Syria (Edessa) and Mesopotamia (including Adiabene) for religious and/or revolutionary activity.

Then the individual beheaded in Acts at the time of the Famine is simply *'Jude the brother of Jesus'* or *'Juda*s *the brother of James'* too. Not only is it chronologically in synch, but it also makes the 'Zealot' nature of all these episodes abundantly clear – *'Theudas'* obviously being another one of these *'Zealot'*-type *'Deceivers'* against whom Josephus so rails. It also accords with the notices from Hegesippus about Jesus' *third brother* 'Judas' having already been executed at the time his descendants are interviewed by Vespasian in the wake of the fall of the Temple and the collapse of the resistance against Rome after the *Sicarii suicide on Masada.*

There really is, therefore, a *'brother'* killed around the time of the Famine, but it is not *'James the brother of John'*. It is *'Theudas', 'Thaddaeus'*, or *'Judas the brother of James'*. 'Judas' is *the brother killed* and, just as there was no *'Stephen'* who was stoned *'by the Jews'* (though there was one in Josephus beaten outside the walls of Jerusalem by Revolutionaries), there was no *'James the son of Zebedee'* who was, as such, 'beheaded with the sword'. Again this is and was, more likely, 'Theudas'/ 'Judas'. All this is patent dissimulation but dissimulation with a clear goal – to *downplay the role of* and *finally eliminate 'James the Just' ('the brother of Jesus') from Scripture.*

Nor was there any Central Leadership of James, John *his brother* (the shell game continues), and Peter, as the Gospels portray it – this to displace the Central Leadership as enumerated straightforwardly by Paul in Galatians of James, Cephas, and John. These, as Paul says, were 'the Pillars' of the 'Jerusalem Assembly' (not that their importance meant anything to him, as he says). There may have been another 'John', possibly John the *Essene,* who along with Silas and Niger of Perea led the Zealot assault on Ashkelon on the Palestinian seacoast. But there was no *second* James, just as there was no *second* Mary – not Mary 'the mother of the sons of Zebedee'; nor 'Mary the wife of Clopas', Jesus' mother's sister; nor, for that matter, was there an 'Agabus'. There are many such substitutions, too numerous to list. We can now transform all these stories about someone called 'Judas Thomas' sending someone called 'Thaddaeus' to 'Augarus' or 'Albarus' or 'Abgarus' into James *sending his brother* 'Judas *the Zealot'* to Edessa and Adiabene to *evangelize the Edessenes and Osrhoeans.*

In this context, one should recall the third teacher who comes to Adiabene – whom Josephus says *came 'from Galilee'* and whose teaching about *the necessity of 'circumcision' for conversion* so contrasted with that of Ananias and his unnamed companion/Paul(?) who *'get in among the King's women'* but *'do not insist upon circumcision'*. This also puts into stark relief the Naziritism of Queen Helen, whom we have identified as a wife of this Ruler. He has perhaps given her a kingdom of her own from among his possessions further east, just as in Syriac sources Abgarus *divides his kingdom* between his two sons; one called 'Sannadroug' gets the area around Haran, Abraham's birthplace – this would clearly be 'Izates' in Josephus' version. This Abgarus would appear to have died around the time that Theudas was beheaded in 45–46 CE. Armenian sources claim that he was in alliance with Aretas, King of Arabian Petra, and actually sent forces to aid him in his mini-war with the Herodian Tetrarch Herod Antipas, husband of Herodias, after John the Baptist's death.

In approximately the year 49 CE, the Romans appear to have carved up parts of this area and given them to Herod of Chalcis' son Aristobulus, the *second* husband of Herodias' infamous daughter Salome; these two advertise themselves on their coinage as 'Great Lovers of Caesar'. This gave Herodians a foothold in these domains and was in exchange for Agrippa II succeeding to his father's Kingdom, which his uncle Herod of Chalcis had been holding for him. It is this Herod we consider to be alluded to in the execution of 'James the brother of John' in Acts and ultimately responsible for the beheading of *'Theudas'*.

Not only do the conditions of Izates' circumcision concur perfectly with the outlook of James, as expressed by refraction either in Paul's Letters or the Letter of James, but the whole episode harmonizes with the theme of Helen's extreme Naziritism from Rabbinic sources. For the new *Galilean* teacher, Izates 'was guilty of breaking the Law and bringing offence to God himself', and he is advised 'not only to read the Law, but to *do what was commanded in it*'. For James, as at Qumran, '*doing what was commanded*' is paramount and the point was, 'whoever shall keep the whole of the Law, but stumble on one (small point) is guilty of breaking it all'. It should be clear that, according to the parameters of the Letter of James, Izates' teacher is 'Jamesian'.

James' Naziritism and the Poor

Helen's 'Naziritism' is also exactly in conformity with this aspect of James' person and behavior, as we have been observing it in early Church sources. The terms of such Naziritism are laid out in the chapter on Naziritism following that on the suspected adulteress in Numbers 5–6. This Naziritism is also expressed in the penance James imposes on Paul, before Paul is finally mobbed by the Jewish crowd in the Temple and rescued by Roman troops stationed there. These last were perhaps already on the alert to intervene in this manner following Paul's convenient stopover in Caesarea – the Roman administrative centre in Palestine – where Acts pictures the 'prophet Agabus' as warning him not to go up to Jerusalem.

In the case of Paul and the 'four others', whose expenses Acts informs us he must pay, it is a temporary form of Naziritism. Here mythologization does seem finally to have gone by the boards, because Paul is obviously perceived of as being 'Rich' and capable of paying for these others. He himself avers the pains he went to in order to collect funds before going up to Jerusalem, presumably so that he could make a claim on the basis of such collections (1 Cor. 16:1–9 and 2 Cor. 8:1–9:15). In the case of Helen, too, her Naziritism was supposed to have been temporary, though in Rabbinic sources, however exaggerated, it was to last for *twenty-one years*. So in their own queer way these claims do begin to verge on life-long Naziritism of a Jamesian kind.

So we are entitled to say that Jamesian Christianity and the approach reflected in the Dead Sea Scrolls, which put so much emphasis on the 'Perfection of Holiness' and the 'wilderness Way', involved a stress on Naziritism. This included abstention from 'eating and drinking' – as Paul or Rabbinic literature would express it and, as both also appear to imply, abstention from eating meat. This last Paul confirms in Romans 14:2 and 1 Corinthians 8:13, when talking about the 'weakness' of his opponents whom he declines to name, though they are obviously important because Paul calls them 'Hebrews', 'Servants of Righteousness', and 'Apostles of the Highest Rank'. Not only does the theme of this abstention from eating and drinking get turned around in the Gospels into its mirror opposite, but finally this emphasis on Naziritism, too, becomes transmuted into something involving a *geographical location* – the same way that the Galilean terminology does. In this case, the phrase, 'He shall *be called a Nazirite*', in this instance literally 'Nazoraean' – attributed to 'the Prophets' (Mt 2:23), becomes Jesus came from 'Nazareth' or that Jesus is a 'Nazrene'.

In both Judaism and Islam, Christians are called either '*Nozrim*' or '*Nasrani*'s, emanating of course from this '*Nazirite*' ideology or the related play on it in Hebrew hinted at here, 'the Nazoraeans'. This, too, derives from a Hebrew root, meaning 'keeping', namely, 'keeping the commands of their father' or 'keeping their secrets'. The Nazirite, of course, was just an extreme example of this, but even here the wordplay is homophonic, 'Nazirite' carrying the meaning of 'abstain' or 'keep away from' – the language of James' directives to overseas communities, as Acts reproduces them. In fact, in Hebrew, these would actually have been expressed in terms of the Hebrew verb, '*lehinnazer*' or '*lehazzir*' – as they are in the Damascus Document – the Hebrew root of the word 'Nazirite' in English.[7]

In addition to this usage 'keep away from', based on the Hebrew root *N–Z–R*, the terminology *'linzor et ha-Brit'* ('to keep the Covenant') actually exists in the Scrolls and is a synonym for a parallel usage found there, 'the Sons of Zadok'. The latter, as we have seen in the Community Rule, are defined as 'the Keepers of the Covenant' (the '*Shomrei ha-Brit*'); the former is found throughout the Damascus Document.[8] It will also be recalled that the latter are defined in the Damascus Document as 'those who will *stand in the Last Days*'. The 'keeping' aspect of this terminology is exactly the definition emphasized by modern-day offshoots of this orientation, 'the Sabaeans of the marshes' in Southern Iraq, who still hold the memory of John the Baptist dear and call their Priests, 'Nazoraeans'.[9]

This kind of wordplay, of course, moves into a further adumbration of the 'Sons of Zadok' terminology at Qumran, the '*Moreh ha-Zedek*' or the 'Teacher of Righteousness', and we have come full circle. This is *exactly* the role James played in all early Christian literature, evinced by his cognomen or title 'James the Righteous', so called because of the *extreme Righteousness* he practiced, both in his uncompromising Naziritism and the *doctrine of Righteousness* he presumably taught.

The term, as we have seen, develops out of following the 'Righteousness' Commandment, 'You shall love your neighbor as yourself', to its absolute limits, that is, that you cannot be completely Righteous towards your fellow man if there is economic inequality. At Qumran, this is expressed in the Damascus Document as follows:

> (You shall) *separate between polluted and pure and distinguish between Holy and profane* . . . according to the Commandment of those entering *the New Covenant in the Land of Damascus* to set up the Holy Things according to their precise specifications, *to love each man his brother as himself, to strengthen the hand of the Meek, the Poor, and the Convert* ... *to keep away from fornication* ... *to separate from all pollutions according to Law*. And no man shall *defile his Holy Spirit*, which God separated for them. Rather all should *walk in these things in Perfect Holiness* on the basis of all they were instructed in of the Covenant of God, Faithfully promising them that they *will live for a thousand Generations*.[10]

This is also exemplified in the Gospel picture of Jesus by favorite sayings like 'sooner would a camel go through the eye of a needle than a Rich Man to Heaven' (Mt 19:24 and pars.) or, better still, in the denunciations of 'the Rich' found in the Letter of James.

Of course these denunciations of the Rich and Riches are also strong in the Qumran documents and run the gamut of almost all Josephus' notices about 'Deceivers' and 'impostors' leading the people astray by going out in the wilderness, there to show them 'the signs of their impending freedom' or 'Salvation'. In fact, at the actual moment of burning the palaces of the most hated and Richest of the High Priests, Ananias, and also the Rich Herodians, Bernice and Agrippa II (Queen Helen's palace and those of her two sons are spared until the Romans put them to the torch at its conclusion),[11] Josephus says these partisans and extreme *Sicarii* '*turn the Poor against the Rich*' and, in the process, *burn all the debt records*.

Hillel, the proverbial leader of Pharisaic Judaism, whose descendants became, after the destruction of the Temple, the Roman Patriarchs of Palestine, responsible among other things for collecting taxes – is, in fact, reputed to have made the continuation of these debts possible even past Sabbatical years by a legal device known in Rabbinic literature as 'the *Prozbul*' when, in theory, they were supposed to be forgiven.[12] James 5:1–5, by contrast, rails against '*the Rich*' in the most apocalyptic and uncompromising manner threatening them, as we have seen, with *the coming Vengeance 'of the Lord of Hosts*'. Immediately following this, James 5:6 blames '*the Rich*' for '*putting the Righteous One to death*' – presumably 'Jesus', but possibly even James himself – in contrast to Paul who, in 1 Thessalonians 2:14–15, rather blames (in his usual fashion) '*the Jews*'.

Indeed, in all materials associated with James and the Scrolls' Righteous Teacher, we inevitably hear about this antagonism to 'the Rich' and not making economic distinctions between men – therefore, the injunction given to Paul, not to forget to 'remember the Poor' in Galatians 2:10. This Paul claims he was 'most anxious to do', but whether he did or not is an open question. He certainly always made sure that, when he came to Jerusalem, he came with sufficient funds, which is why, no doubt, James says these things and, according to Acts, set him the penance of a Nazirite oath – usually thirty days, but in Acts 21:27, seven – and paying the expenses of four others under similar vow. At this point Paul is mobbed in the Temple, yet James, not surprisingly, is not!

Helen – someone with whom Paul was possibly connected – did show, according to all sources, her anxiety to *remember the Poor*, as did her sons, Izates and Monobazus. She did so at the sacrifice of a considerable amount of personal wealth, for which, says the *Talmud*, she won for herself and her sons a great name for ever more. Josephus says Izates too 'sent great sums of money to the leaders in Jerusalem', which was 'distributed among the Poor' delivering Many, and one wonders just which 'Jerusalem leadership' this could have been. It is also the kind of thing being played off, not a little disingenuously, in Acts' picture of the complaints brought by 'the Hellenists' against 'the Hebrews' regarding the 'daily distribution', leading up to the stoning of Stephen (6:1).

Helen and Izates' sons or kinsmen were clearly part of the 'Zealot' orientation, which, in our view, is indistinguishable at this point from the 'Messianic' one. They give themselves valiantly for the cause against Rome, even though they are only recent converts. This is mocked in Acts' presentation of the *Ethiopian* 'eunuch' (that is, someone who is *castrated*), who 'oversees the Treasure of the *Ethiopian Queen* Kandakes' and learns 'the Gospel of Jesus' from one 'Philip', thereafter wishing immediately to be *baptized not circumcised* – the 'Gospel', that is – among other things – clearly that of *peace with the Romans*.

Ben Kalba Sabu'a and the Nicodemus who Prepared the Body of Jesus

The *Talmud* also knows these problems of conversion either via baptism or circumcision and the issue still remains in Judaism today. For it, one Eliezer ben Hyrcanus – the Rabbi to whom Jacob of Kfar Sechania expounded Jesus the Nazorean's point about 'the High Priest's outhouse', considers that 'circumcision is the *sine qua non* of conversion'. Another rabbi, called Rabbi Joshua, is generally presented as holding the view that only baptism was necessary, though in some versions of his discussion with R. Eliezer on the subject, he is rather quoted as having the view that, *in addition* to circumcision *also* baptism was required.[13] This is all very interesting in view of the problems surrounding the conversion of Helen's sons and the character called 'Eleazar' in Josephus.

In fact the *Talmud* knows another character, one '*Ben Kalba Sabu'a*', who was also known for his generosity, fabulous wealth, and never turning away 'the Poor' from his home hungry. During the Roman siege of Jerusalem, he supposedly promised – along with two other colleagues (one called '*the Treasurer*') – to supply Jerusalem with food '*for twenty-one years*'.[14] Not only are we getting here clear reflections of the details of the stories about Queen Helen's conversion, Famine-relief, and possible '*twenty-one year*' *Nazirite* oath; but this name '*Sabu'a*' in Hebrew conserves a clear echo of the term '*Sabaean*' in other Semitic languages like Aramaic and Arabic – '*Sobiai*' in the Greek of Hippolytus. There is, also, just the slightest hint in all of these of the noun '*Sheba*' in Hebrew here (though the root is slightly different) and, in this regard, one should note the confusion in Luke's Acts of '*Ethiopian*' (in Hebrew, '*Sheba*') with '*Sabaean*' (in the sense of '*Daily-Bather*') or '*Edessene*' when the matter of '*famine relief*' is at issue.

The link-ups, too, with Luke's 'Treasury agent' story are obvious and one should remark that Josephus himself conserves a note about the fabulous palace of Queen Helen, not to mention those of her descendants, who stayed in Jerusalem during the War against Rome and did not leave it (which the Revolutionaries spared and did not burn).[15] In fact, '*Ben Kalba Sabu'a*''s name is traditionally associated in Jewish sources with the tomb built by Queen Helen's son Monobazus for her and his brother Izates in Jerusalem (called in these sources, '*Kalba Sabu'a*'s cave'). It can actually be translated – with a little creative ingenuity – to read, 'the son of the *Sabaean* Bitch', '*Kalbah*' bearing the meaning '*female dog*' in Hebrew (even if one does not allow this female sense for '*Kalba*' in Aramaic – it still translates as 'the son of the Sabaean dog' and where the confusion with 'Ethiopian' came from should be clear).

Not only did the daughter of this 'Ben Kalba Sabu'a' (who would then be a caricature of Izates or Monobazus, or their relatives) supposedly marry the 'Zealot' Rabbi of the next generation, Akiba (also executed by Rome for sedition or Insurrection), one of whose most ardent students was named 'Monabaz'; but Ben Kalba Sabu'a supposedly bequeathed to this 'Poor' Akiba half his wealth, when he finally came to marry his daughter with a huge following of twelve thousand Disciples![16] All of this is admittedly extremely abstruse, but Talmudic materials very often are.

Aside from an individual called in these sources '*Ben Zizit*' – like '*Ben Kalba Sabu'a*' surely another pseudonym of some kind – and often associated with him, Ben Kalba Sabu'a has another friend called 'Nakdimon ben Gurion'. He, too, is considered to be fabulously wealthy and is also credited with the scheme to supply the city with grain for *twenty-one years*! It is these stores which the *Talmud* claims 'the Zealots' either burned or despoiled by *mixing them with mud*!

One should note the curious conjunction of 'twenty-one years' with either the period of time between Theudas' revolutionary attempt at a reverse Exodus and the Famine in 45 to the outbreak of the Uprising in 66 and the 'twenty-one years' involved in Helen's repeated Nazirite oaths. These notices also add to the suspicion of a role of these agents of Helen or Izates in encouraging this war. As the *Talmud* presents it, at one point this friend of Ben Kalba Sabu'a, Nakdimon ben Gurion, after promising to pay twelve talents of silver to fill the water cisterns of the Temple, *prays for rain* and performs a 'rain-making' miracle equivalent to James'.[17]

Whatever one may think of these stories, Nakdimon does seem to reappear in the Gospel of John as Nicodemus, who *prepares the body of Jesus for burial* – again, in the tomb of the '*Rich*' *merchant* 'Joseph of Arimathaea'. The connection with the above tradition about 'Kalba Sabu'a' should be clear. He also would seem to appear in Josephus, who apparently reverses his name into 'Gurion the son of Nicomedes' (thus). In this episode, 'Nicomedes' is one of those attempting to save the Roman garrison in the Citadel, which wishes to surrender at the beginning of the Uprising and whose commander, it will be recalled, later *circumcised himself*. His associate in this attempt is, again, one '*Ananias* the son of Zadok'.[18]

We associate Saulus, Philip, and Antipas (whom Josephus not only identifies as the son of a Temple Treasurer and ultimately even, Treasurer himself) with this attempt to save the Roman garrison. In the later stages of the Uprising, when the Zealots take control and slaughter High Priests like James' executioner Ananus, this namesake of Nicodemus is executed as a collaborator along with Niger – as is Saulus' apparent cousin Antipas and another Rich collaborator, Zachariah. It is very likely this Zachariah's 'blood' that the Gospels of Matthew and Luke are accusing the Jews of shedding 'between the Temple and the altar', not the original Prophet Zechariah's.[19]

Not only does Josephus describe how the Zealots trumped up a Sanhedrin trial, summoning 'the Seventy' to try this 'Zachariah the son of Bareis' or 'Bariscaeus' (in the New Testament this is 'Barachias') on a charge 'of betraying the state to the Romans and holding treasonable communications with Vespasian'; but also how they 'slew him in the midst of the Temple', '*casting* him out of the Temple into the ravine below') which is the probable source of the legend about the Tomb of Zachariah next to the Tomb of St James in the Kedron Valley beneath the Temple Pinnacle. In this story, too, we probably have the contrapositive (and likely as not the source) of the story of James being 'cast down' from the Temple Pinnacle – reflected too in the tomb attached to his name in this Valley.

In John 7:50, Nicodemus, like Gamaliel in the Pseudoclementine *Recognitions* and Acts, is a *secret believer* who comes to Jesus 'in the night' (Jn 3:1–21). It is he who brings the ointments to anoint the body of Jesus in the tomb provided by the Rich Joseph of Arimathaea (19:38–42). We have come full circle and back to the stories about Queen Helen's wealth – to say nothing of her tomb. Not only are these stories related to the activities of Helen's Treasury agents in Palestine, but also possibly to James.

Queen Helen and her sons cannot really be conceived of as converts to Pharisaic or Rabbinic Judaism as such. Nor can we really say that Helen and her sons were converted to Christianity as we know it – at least not the Pauline variety. More probably they were converted to *Jamesian Christianity* or the kind of Zealotism evinced in the Scrolls or the Judaism of extreme Naziritism.

To show that the Messianic activity identified with her and her family continued down to the next century and the Bar Kochba affair, we have only to search through Talmudic records. Not only did the famous Rabbi Akiba – who would not preach *compromise with Rome* and for his pains was ultimately reputed to have been drawn and quartered by the Romans – have one of Helen's descendants called '*Monabaz*' as his student, but he was also married to *the daughter of Ben Kalba Sabu'a*, half of whose wealth he supposedly inherited! I think this is sufficient to bring Rabbi Akiba into some sort of association with this family as well.

It is worth noting that, at first, Akiba supported the Second Jewish Uprising against Rome, the one of 'Simeon bar Kosiba' or 'Simon Bar Kochba', that is, '*the Son of the Star*' – in fact, designating him as '*the Messiah*', for which he was laughed at by his Rabbinic confrères.[20] This Uprising was every bit as fierce as the earlier one but there was no Josephus around to document it. It resulted in the Jews being finally barred from Jerusalem altogether, even from viewing it from a distance except once a year – the legendary '*9th of the Month of Ab*', the traditional date for the fall of the Temple.

It is these sorts of 'revolutionary' things that, in our view, 'Judas *the Zealot*' or '*Judas the brother of James taught the Edessenes*'. In Syriac sources, this '*Judas*' is connected to one '*Addai*' – in the Koran, as we have seen, '*'Ad*' – just as in the Gospels and Papias he is indistinguishable from '*Thaddaeus*'. He is also, as we have shown, virtually indistinguishable from *Judas Thomas.* Our identification of him with the 'Theudas' in Josephus, whose 'imposture' precedes the note about Helen's 'Famine Relief', brings us full circle. It eliminates the problem of the 'beheading' of another *brother* named 'James', as it does that of the competitive Leadership Triad of John and James the two sons of Zebedee and Peter and is finally verified in the two 'Apocalypses of James' from Nag Hammadi.

It is also possibly verified elsewhere – in the Jewish catacombs of Rome where, not only is 'Justus' a name being used for 'Zadok', which has important ramifications for tying James to the individual referred to in this manner at Qumran, but mix-ups and overlaps of various letters and misspellings are commonplace. For instance, *alpha* is confused with *lambda*, which may account for some of our Cleophas/Alphaeus/Lebbaeus mix-ups, and *chi* is regularly interchanged with *kappa* as in '*Sicarii*', which again may bear on the transposition of '*Christian*' with '*Sicarios*'. Where Judas/Theudas is concerned, the *Y* or *I* in 'Yehuda' or 'Judas' is often confused with *T*, which can move into *Th* as in 'Theodore' or, as it were, 'Theudas'.[21] The point is that these kinds of confusions in transliterations of phonemes are widespread.

Theuda and Addai in the Two Apocalypses of James from Nag Hammadi

The two Apocalypses of James from Nag Hammadi are to some degree attributed to James. This James is clearly intended to be James 'the brother of the Lord', because Jesus is presented as addressing him as 'James my brother' (24.15), but that is as far as both documents are willing to go in admitting any *actual* 'brother' relationship. In fact, both try to deny it, the First adding, though 'not my brother materially'; the Second turns it around and has James greet Jesus as 'my brother'. Then, somewhat in the manner of the Protevangelium, Mary avers that he is rather a *step-brother* (50.19–2.0). Jesus then ultimately concludes, 'Your father is not My Father, but My Father has become a Father to you' (51.20). It then goes on to evoke the word 'virgin' three times, but it is not clear which 'virgin' it means, James or 'Mary mother of God' (51.27–52.1).

This is evidently playing off some very old materials and obviously in the thick of some of the disputes on these issues as they were developing. Continuing in the context in which these greetings are exchanged, the First Apocalypse then goes on not only to announce that he (Jesus) will be 'seized the day after tomorrow', but also that James will be 'seized' (25.10–15), making it clear that the James who, in the words of Matthew 20:22 and Mark 10:38, will 'drink the Cup' that Jesus has drunk will be *James the brother of the Lord* not some other James. Interestingly, it then goes on to speak of Jerusalem giving 'the Cup of Bitterness to *the Sons of Light*' (25.17). This is clear Qumran phraseology, as it is the phraseology of Revelation, and carries with it the sense of martyrdom or Vengeance as we have seen (14:10, 16:19, and 18:6).

What is important for our purposes is that in the First Apocalypse the only other person of any substance who is mentioned, apart from Jesus the Rabbi and James his brother, is 'Addai'. This is the individual who is always presented as the Apostle or Evangelist sent out by 'Judas *Thomas*' to the Edessenes/Osrhoeans. Addai is called 'Thaddaeus', as we have seen, in the 'Abgarus' materials presented by Eusebius, and a lively apocrypha has developed about him in Syriac tradition. It is to him that James is instructed to reveal what he has learned from his master and putative brother Jesus (36.15–20). Here, therefore, not only do we have James evidently being appointed successor by Jesus himself, but we have James (not Thomas) clearly involved with Addai/Thaddaeus.

James' death is just as clearly alluded to in the traditional manner of Origen, Eusebius and others (following either Hegesippus or Clement of Alexandria, or both), 'When you depart (or 'are killed'), immediately War will be made upon this land. (Weep) then for him who dwells in Jerusalem' (36.20). These words seem to embody something of the mysterious oracle to leave Jerusalem that the early Christian Community supposedly received following James' death, just prior to the appearance of Roman armies surrounding Jerusalem. It is also almost word-for-word from the prophecy of doom uttered by the mysterious Jesus ben Ananias following James' death in 62 CE and which he did not cease from proclaiming until his own death shortly before the fall of the Temple in 70 CE.

The text continues, making it plain what it intended to say about Addai anyhow, though it is fragmentary: 'But let Addai take these things to heart. In the Tenth Year, let Addai sit and write them down, and when he writes them down …' (36.21–25). There is also an echo here of 'the epistle' James supposedly dictates or gives to 'Judas surnamed Barsabas' – Addai's or Thaddaeus' double – to take to Antioch at the conclusion of the Jerusalem Council in Acts, not to mention the one supposedly taken by Thaddaeus on the part of Judas *Thomas* to Abgarus in other variations of this story. This we have already seen echoed in *MMT* or the two Letters on Works Righteousness, mysteriously found in so many copies at Qumran, the only letters of this kind extant there.

At the end of the First Apocalypse, James' death is clearly referred to, including something of the gist of the *Zaddik* citation from Isaiah 3:10 associated with it in Eusebius via

Hegesippus – not to mention Jesus' death in Scripture: 'They arose, saying, "We have no part in this blood, for a Righteous Man will perish through Unrighteousness". James departed …' (46.17–22). The text breaks off here. If nothing else, what is apparent in this text is that Addai is being presented as James' Apostle or messenger in much the same way that Thaddaeus is presented, in more orthodox treatments, as the Apostle or messenger of Judas *Thomas* – whom we have already presented as that brother of James known as Jude, not to mention, being identical with 'Theudas'.

But this is exactly the sense of the Second Apocalypse, told in the form of a discourse of James, in which Addai's place is basically taken by 'Theuda' – namely *Theudas*. This document over and over again focuses on James being called 'the Just One' and even, it would appear, 'the Beloved' or 'my Beloved' (49.9 and 56.17). It also mentions 'the fifth flight of steps' (45.25), though it is not always clear whether it is James being spoken of or Jesus, and quotes the verse from Isaiah 3:10 in the Septuagint version we have mentioned (61.12–20), associated with James' death via Hegesippus.

But most importantly, the individual there to whom James dictates his discourse and who clearly takes the place of Addai in the First, is called 'Theuda (the 'father' or 'brother') of the Just One, since he was a relative of his' (44.19) – this, and 'the steps', upon which either James or Jesus 'stands' or 'sits' in order to deliver his discourses (45.25). Here we are clearly in the milieu both of the Ascents of James – the *Anabathmoi Jacobou* evoked in Epiphanius – and the Pseudoclementine *Recognitions*' presentation of the debates on the Temple steps, also refracted in various passages in the Book of Acts in connection with the other Apostles and *even at one point Paul* (Acts 21:40) – but not James!

I think that we can again state at this point that our case is proven. Here we have the corroboration necessary to show that this Theudas – also called Addai, also known as Thaddaeus – who 'was a relative of his', was a *kinsman* or *brother of* Jesus or James, in fact, *his third brother* – 'the brother of the Just One' – known variously as 'Judas of James', 'Judas the brother of James', and 'Judas the Zealot'. It was the grandsons of this Judas who are interviewed by Domitian because of their *Messianic lineage*. Finally they were martyred (also according to Hegesippus) along with another relative of Jesus, Simeon bar Cleophas – also variously 'Simon the Zealot'/'Simon the Canaanite'/'*Cananaean*'– in the time of Trajan (in Simeon's/Simon's case, rather than Domitian's). It only remains to straighten out one or two last confusions centering about 'Judas *Iscariot*'.

Judas *Iscariot* and Simon *Iscariot*

The traditions about Judas *Iscariot* are malevolent on several counts, and this is, no doubt, what the creative writers of these materials intended. These writers also play on traditions about Jewish heroes from this period, namely Judas Maccabeus and Judas the Galilean, the latter the founder of what Eusebius via Hegesippus – if not Josephus – calls the '*Galilean*' Movement. This has to be what they are implying by this name, because Judas did not come from Galilee, but rather the area adjacent to it known as Gaulonitis (today's Golan) – unless we are involved in confusions like those in the Gospels, where, for instance, a geographical name like 'Nazareth' (undocumented in Galilee in Second Temple Times except in Scripture) is substituted for the very real concept of a 'Nazirite' or 'Nazoraean'.

A great deal of trouble is taken by these writers to get Jesus *to Galilee*, even though they rather have him *coming from Bethlehem*, the seat of the Davidic family of old. Nathanael again (a seeming stand-in for James in the Gospel of John), for instance, asks 'Philip' – when the latter announces that 'Jesus *the son of Joseph* who is from *Nazareth*' has been found, 'Can any good thing *come out of Nazareth*'? (1:46). A few chapters later, this question is reprised after 'Many' in the crowd apply the Ebionite 'True Prophet' ideology to Jesus. Others in the crowd then say, 'This is *the Christ*', to which still others respond, 'Does the Christ then come out of Galilee? Did not the Scriptures say that the Christ comes from the seed of David and from Bethlehem, the city where David lived?' (7:40–42)

This means that Jesus does not come from Bethlehem, nor was he born there, and, 'Galilean', meaning 'to come from Galilee', is preferred to 'Galilean' as an ideological designation, meaning to follow the Movement started by Judas and *Saddok* around the time of 'Jesus'' alleged birth. This episode ends with our Nicodemus again, intervening and asking whether the Law 'judges a man without first hearing from him and knowing what *he does*'. Whereupon the crowd responds, 'Are you also of Galilee? Search and see that no Prophet has arisen out of Galilee' (7:52).

The simultaneity of the birth of Jesus and that of the Fourth Philosophy is perhaps not merely coincidental, as both are 'Zealots' in the *true* sense of the word. But the animosity involved in these sleights of hand regarding the name Judas is also related to the fact that *all Jews* – in fact, the very name 'Jew' itself – come from the 'House of Judah', as the Habakkuk *Pesher* at Qumran knows, that is, 'Judas' or 'Jude' in Greek.[22] Therefore, a slur on the name of the one ends up a slur on the *whole people*. In some sense it is also related to the traditions surrounding Jesus' family members themselves. It is this we would like to focus on here, in order to part the cloud of unknowing and lift the fascination heightened by the allure of scandal hovering over the people as a whole.

In orthodox Apostle lists the individual known as Judas *Iscariot* either follows 'Simon the Cananaean' or 'Judas (the brother) of James'. This title *Iscariot* is almost always further accompanied by the epithet, 'who *delivered him up*', most often translated as 'who betrayed him'. For Luke, 'Simon the *Canaa*nite' is 'Simon the *Zealot*', '*kana*' in Hebrew translating into the word '*zelos*' in Greek, another bit of Gospel *sleight-of-hand*. Luke also puts the name 'Judas of James' in between this 'Simon' and 'Judas *Iscariot*'.

That is, the name *Judas Iscariot* always follows three others, namely, 'James the son of Alphaeus, Thaddaeus, and Simon the Cananaean', those we have identified as Jesus' brothers. This, Jerome had already come to realize, because he had intelligence, and used it – the only problem being the use he put it to. The names at the end then read (omitting 'James the son of Alphaeus'): 'Lebbaeus who was called Thaddaeus, Simon the Canaanite, and Judas *Iscariot* (Mt 10:4), or simply, 'Thaddaeus and Simon the Canaanite and Judas *Iscariot'* (Mk 3:18), or 'Simon who was called *Zelotes* and Judas of James and Judas *Iscariot*' (Lk 6:15–16). Acts 1:13 differs only in calling Simon simply 'Simon *Zelotes*' or 'Simon the Zealot'.

However, the Gospel of John, which contains no Apostle list, calls Judas, in four different places, 'of Simon *Iscariot*' or 'Simon *Iscariot*'s son' or 'brother' (6:71, 12:4, 13:3, and, most importantly of all, 13:26, where Jesus 'breaks the bread' and gives it to 'Judas of Simon *Iscariot*'. This is paralleled in the Gospel of the Hebrews above by Jesus 'breaking the bread and giving it to' *his brother James*.) At one point, John is at pains to distinguish this 'Judas' from *another* Judas, 'not the *Iscariot*', among the Apostles, whom he has not mentioned before in the Gospel (14:22).

It would appear to be plain that 'Judas *Iscariot*' is indistinguishable from Jesus' brother 'Judas of James', also called Thaddaeus, Lebbaeus (that is, 'Judas the son of *Alphaeus*' or '*Cleophas*'), Judas the Zealot, itself moving into Thomas/Judas Thomas appellations. Nor is this so-called 'Simon *Iscariot*' in John to be distinguished from Simon the Zealot, Simon the Canaanite, and probably also Simeon bar Cleophas, Jesus' purported *first* cousin – the multiplication of these Judases being not very different from the multiplication of Marys, Simons, and Jameses, but to even more deleterious effect. This is because, historically speaking, the calumny involved in calling Judas 'the Traitor', with all its implications, has echoed down the ages and hardly ameliorates even today.

But in expositions of key biblical texts at Qumran, those called 'the Traitors' just about always have something to do with the individual we have identified as Paul's *alter ego*, 'the Liar and the men of his persuasion', including 'the Violent Ones'. Even in Scripture, it will be recalled, Paul is originally portrayed as using *violence with the people*. These 'Traitors' are portrayed as 'rejecting' both the Law and the scriptural exegesis of the Righteous Teacher and being 'Traitors to the New Covenant in the Land of Damascus'.[23] This is not to mention the reversal of the 'delivering up' language associated with 'Judas *Iscariot*' throughout the Damascus Document, in the sense of 'delivering up' backsliders or Covenant-Breakers to 'the Avenging Wrath of God' or 'the sword'.

In Johannine tradition, the 'missing Apostle' at the time of Jesus' post-resurrection appearance is 'Thomas surnamed *Didymus*' (Jn 20:24) – elsewhere 'Judas *Thomas*' (more obfuscation). So here, just as in the Synoptics, the 'missing' Apostle is basically someone called 'Judas', again associated *with the family of Jesus*. In John, this Thomas will 'not believe' unless he can put his finger into the actual 'print of the nails' and 'his hand into his side' (*thus* – 20:25) – therefore, the still proverbial pejorative appellation, 'Doubting Thomas'.

In the Gospel of the Hebrews, James 'will not eat' until he has 'seen' Jesus or 'the Son of Man risen from among those that sleep' – more overlaps or transformations having to do basically with James and Judas. Eight days later in John, Thomas supposedly gets this additional appearance, which involves not eating or breaking bread but rather 'putting his finger' *into Jesus' side*. The effect is essentially the same. Another appearance occurs by the Sea of Galilee with Nathanael and others and, here, Jesus' 'taking the bread and giving it to them' does finally occur – and 'some of the fish too'. (In the story of Queen Helen and her son Izates' efforts, it will be recalled, it was 'grain (the bread) and dried figs'!)

The Synoptic accounts, of course, know nothing of all of this. Only Matthew and Mark have any real appearances along the Sea of Galilee. Though the 'breaking bread' and 'eating' are missing, the 'doubting' theme is present, at least in Matthew, perhaps Mark as well. But in all of these, including Luke, the *missing Apostle* is now 'Judas *Iscariot*', not John's '*Thomas* called *Didymus*', i.e., 'Judas' or 'Judas *Thomas*'. In Luke's version of the appearance to 'the Eleven' in Jerusalem, they give Jesus broiled fish to eat and he shows them his hands and feet, this after having appeared to at least *one* family member on the Emmaus Road, with whom he 'broke bread', as in the Gospel of the Hebrews.

It is difficult to avoid these confusions or overlaps in the traditions between Jesus' family members – particularly 'Jude' or 'Judas *Thomas*' – and Judas *Iscariot*. In turn, these overlap traditions having to do with James. The note about 'breaking bread' with Jesus in Last Supper scenarios in the Synoptics, incorporating the Pauline overwrite about 'Communion with the body' and 'blood of Christ' – missing from the 'Last Supper' narrative in the Gospel of John – just reinforces these overlaps. John only has Jesus 'dipping the morsel and giving it to Judas (the son or brother) of Simon *Iscariot*' in a clear parody of Jewish Passover scenarios. No Communion. This comes much earlier in conjunction with the 'multiplication of the loaves and the fishes' after turning *water into wine* at 'Cana' in 'Galilee'.

The Synoptics, of course, do not have Jesus actually 'give the bread' to Judas *Iscariot*, as Jesus does *James* in the Gospel of the Hebrews, though they do have Judas 'dipping his hand' with Jesus, as we saw (Mt 26:23 and Mk 14:20), and put heavy stress on the 'eating and drinking' theme tying it to the theologically even more difficult, *Communion with the blood of Jesus Christ*. This last, even when taken symbolically, flies in the face of Jamesian prohibitions to overseas communities, forbidding the consumption of blood, not to mention those at Qumran, which found it abhorrent. We already noted the reversal in this regard of *Nazirite*-oath abstentions from 'eating and drinking', but even more telling, *Rechabite*/Jamesian abstention from 'drinking wine' altogether (also parodied in the 'Cana' miracle of 'turning water into wine' above).

But we have been watching overlaps and confusions of this kind with traditions relating to James the Just the *brother of Jesus* – always reproduced with a kind of negative or inverted effect – throughout the book. For instance, we have seen how Judas' kiss of betrayal in the Synoptics (Mt 26:49 and pars.) simply inverts the kiss that Jesus gives *his brother James* or *vice versa.* This is not to mention the affection Jesus is pictured as feeling for *the Disciple he loved*, whom John portrays as lying on Jesus' bosom even as Judas is about to betray him (13:23). We have also seen how the election to replace Judas as the 'Twelfth Apostle' in Acts is probably little else than a substitution for the election of James as Overseer of the early Church.

It is hard to avoid the conclusion that the identification of the Apostle who 'betrayed' Jesus with Judas *Iscariot* – which has become such a set piece and one of the iconographies of Western Civilization – is, once again, just another of these malevolent addenda to tradition that has *no historical foundation whatsoever* – except further disparagement of the successors to and family of Jesus in Palestine. On the contrary, it is the product of some of the most successful historical rewriting ever accomplished.

James *sometimes becomes* Judas, just as in the Book of Acts, Judas at one point *even becomes James.* Even more revealing, though scholars have attempted to find the basis of the word '*Iscariot*', none have succeeded in showing any origin for this word other than *Sicarii*, that is, the extreme wing of the Zealot Movement, which Josephus repeatedly blames for assassinations and disturbances in Palestine, ending with the destruction of the Temple – note the additional play here on the *Sicarii causing the destruction of the Temple* and Judas *Iscariot, the destruction of Jesus.*

That, for John anyhow, Judas is also related to someone called Simon *Iscariot* – missing from the Synoptics – corroborates this still further. Nor should we forget that it is the last hold-outs among the followers of Judas the *Galilean* – the author along with '*Saddok*' of the Zealot Movement – under the leadership of another of this Judas' descendants, 'Eleazar ben Jair', who commit suicide on Masada in pursuance of this creed. These are, in fact, the last remnants of these *Sicarii*, against whom Josephus so rails. We have just mentioned the parody of this suicide implicit in Judas' actions as portrayed in Matthew and Acts, not to mention the additional note of betrayal 'for money'. How satisfying all this must have been for the authors of these accounts – and how diabolically successful.

Cave entrance in Wadi Murabba'at, south of Qumran, where Bar Kochba ("Son of the Star" and 2nd Jewish Revolt Leader) Letters were found

Epilogue

In *James the Brother of Jesus and the Dead Sea Scrolls* II: *The Cup of the Lord, the Damascus Covenant , and the Blood of Christ*, we shall continue where this book leaves off on the subject of the Jamesian Communities in the East, the Pella Flight, Agabus' second prophecy, and the oracle of Jesus ben Ananias in the Temple from 62 to 70 CE – all connected with the death of James. We will treat James' rain-making and direct confrontations between Paul and James more systematically, and explain *MMT* as a 'Jamesian' Letter to '*the Great King of the Peoples beyond the Euphrates*'.

Finally we will explore the confrontations between the Righteous Teacher and the Liar in the Scrolls, going through the parallels between James and the Righteous Teacher at Qumran in meticulous detail. We will show the Habakkuk *Pesher* in any event – and by implication, all documents related by sense and nomenclature to it – to be First Century. This will be a proof based on the clear sense of the internal data not the external. We will also treat the parallel '*Cup*' imagery in both it and the New Testament, showing the intimate relationship between the Scrolls' '*New Covenant in the Land of Damascus*' and the Pauline '*Cup of the New Covenant in the blood*' of Christ.

In the present book Part I, however, we thought it best to confine ourselves to arguments essentially delineating the parameters of James' existence, his importance for his time, and what he personally represented from the vantage point of New Testament and early Church sources, the Scrolls being used peripherally for purposes of external comparison and verification only. This was because, whereas the dating of early Christian documents is not the subject of inordinate differences of opinion, with the Scrolls it is different. Therefore, we have relegated such matters to the second volume, not wishing to impinge on the clear conclusions of the first based exclusively on New Testament documents, early Church sources, and Josephus.

In it, we have shown how information in the Book of Acts relating to the life and death of James was erased or overwritten. The rather staggering loopholes in the New Testament were systematically and painstakingly set forth. This was true of the election of James and its transformation in Acts into the election of the Matthias to replace 'the Traitor Judas *Iscariot*'. It is also true of the stoning of 'Stephen', executed (according to Eusebius) by '*the murderers of the Lord*' (sic).

The attack by 'Jews' on Stephen – identified by some scholars as a stand-in for the stoning of James – is paralleled in Josephus by the robbery and beating of the 'Emperor's Servant Stephen' by 'Zealot' Revolutionaries outside Jerusalem in 49 CE. It is also intimately related to the assassination by 'Stephen', Flavia Domitilla's servant, of the Emperor Domitian in 96 CE, itself probably in retaliation for Domitian's execution of *real* Christians like Flavius Clemens, her husband, and Epaphroditus, Josephus' putative publisher.

It is even more true of the relatively obscure passage having to do with Philip converting 'the eunuch of the Ethiopian Queen Kandakes', probably an overwrite of material relating to Queen Helen of Adiabene and her descendant 'Kenedaeos', killed in the assault on Roman troops at the Pass at Beit Horon in the first days of the Uprising against Rome in 66 CE. The conversion of Queen Helen's two sons, Izates and Monobazus, is a pivotal event. Its refurbishment had the additional benefit of heaping abuse on a favorite conversion episode of the Jews involving 'circumcision' – in the process vividly exemplifying the derisive invective involved.

Likewise, we have repeatedly shown how historical events were refurbished and changed in the history of early Christianity as represented in Acts. For instance, the visit of Peter to Caesarea to the 'Pious' Roman Centurion Cornelius – where Peter learns to accept Gentiles and not reject them – is a rewrite of the visit of Simon (who wished to bar Herodians from the Temple as foreigners, not admit them) to King Agrippa I in Caesarea in 44 CE in Josephus; and the beheading of '*James the brother of John*' is a rewrite of the beheading of the Messianic Leader 'Theudas' – presumably 'Thaddaeus' alias 'Judas the brother of James' (also 'a relative of his' – Jesus').

The 'prophet' Agabus, who in Acts predicts the Famine in Claudius' time (*c.* 45 CE), was but a thinly disguised substitute for even more important events about the history of early Christianity overseas in this time, namely the conversion of 'King Abgarus' of Edessa. The episode is but another related to the conversion of Queen Helen of Adiabene – in Syriac/ Armenian sources Abgarus' putative wife and probably one of his extensive harem – and her two sons.

We also suggested that the second prophecy attributed to 'Agabus', warning Paul not to go up to Jerusalem (Acts 21:11), was an overwrite of the prophecy of one 'Jesus ben Ananias' documented in Josephus, who for seven and a half years, immediately following the death of James, prophesied the coming destruction of Jerusalem until he was killed by a Roman projectile shortly before its fall. At the same time, it parodied and inverted the early Christian oracle connected to it, also following the death of James, warning the Jerusalem Community followers of James to flee Jerusalem.

In the process, we showed how abundant wordplay and parallel polemics were involved in these kinds of reformulations as well. For example, ideological notations, such as 'Nazirite', 'Nazoraean', 'Galilean', and '*Sicarios*', were turned into geographical locations. The 'casting down' language applied in all early Christian texts to James either being 'cast down headlong' from the Temple Pinnacle or Paul 'casting him down headlong' from its steps (not to mention to Stephen's being 'cast out of the city' or Judas *Iscariot*'s 'headlong fall') comes in for further expansion and variation in the 'casting down' metaphor employed in the New Testament's 'fishermen' and 'nets' allusions, relating to Jesus choosing his Apostles on the Sea of Galilee.

In the Habakkuk *Pesher* the '*casting*' and '*dragnets full of fish*' imagery from Habakkuk 1:14-16 is definitively interpreted in terms not only of taxation by the *Kittim* (in this context, the Romans), but also their *tax farming*, i.e., their '*parceling out*' their sovereignty and *tax collecting* among various petty rulers in the East (including, quite obviously, Herodians). This whole exercise is pointedly characterized in the Habakkuk *Pesher* as 'their plenteous eating' – all developed in terms of the innumerable '*fish of the sea*' they catch in '*their dragnets*'.

The New Testament reverses this language, showing its awareness that it was being applied to Roman taxation, by having Jesus recommend 'casting a hook into the sea' of Galilee to get the money to pay Roman taxes or tribute, or, reversing this again and returning to the original Jewish apocalyptic cast, 'casting the tares' or 'the polluted fish' into 'a furnace of Fire'.

In a further adumbration of this 'casting' language, the Gospels describe the 'Power' Jesus has and the 'Authority' he gives his disciples 'to cast out Evil demons'. Not only can this be seen as parodying what groups like those responsible for the documents at Qumran do to backsliders – 'cast them out' – but in Acts, 'the Jews' cast out *James' double* Stephen to be stoned, not to mention Josephus' Zealots 'casting out' the naked body of James' nemesis, the High Priest Ananus, without burial from Jerusalem, thereby desecrating it.

Determinations of this kind were made solely on the basis of early Church sources, both in and outside the New Testament, and on the basis of Josephus – with peripheral verification and illustration only, where ethos was concerned, from the Dead Sea Scrolls. These, in turn, led to the question about how and why such incredible lacunae occurred and who could have been responsible for or benefited from them.

For instance, James and his Jerusalem Assembly are able to go on functioning relatively without disturbance in the Jerusalem of the 40's to the 60s CE, while an individual like Paul can hardly set foot in the city without being mobbed – this because of fear of the Jewish populace as a whole, among whom individuals like James, John the Baptist, and presumably Jesus (if he was anything like them), appear to have been *very* popular. Paul's escape from the representatives of the Arab King Aretas down the walls of Damascus in a basket, by his own testimony in 2 Corinthians 11:32–33, also bears this out (for Acts' picture of parallel events, it is *the Jews* from whom Paul is escaping). This is the same 'Arab King' whom, according to Josephus, the Jewish common people saw as taking vengeance on the Herodians for the death of John the Baptist in the mid-30s, the same period in which Paul admits to having 'persecuted' those of 'the Way' even 'unto death'.

All this rather is lumped together in Scripture, as it has come down to us, under the general heading of the perfidy of 'the Jews'. This becomes frozen in early Church theology by the time of the works of Clement of Alexandria, Tertullian, Irenaeus, Origen, and Eusebius as the 'guilt of the Jews for their crimes against the Christ of God'.

But this was hardly the case in the Palestine of the time. This is to mistake sectarian strife for strife with foreigners. Though John, Jesus, and James may have run afoul of sectarian strife, that is strife with other Jewish Establishment groups or Herodians; it was not the mass of Jews *per se* who were their enemies. Rather, the opposite is more likely the truth.

Finally, we have placed James at the centre of sectarian and popular agitation ending up in the fall of Jerusalem and we have identified the basic issues involved in such strife, particularly as these related to gifts from Gentiles and their admission into the Temple (considered 'pollution of the Temple' at Qumran) – reflected too in *MMT* and its hostility to 'things sacrificed to idols'. We have been able to use these parameters to point out Paul's connections to the Herodian family and the kind of code that was being applied to such relationships – at Qumran and in Revelation, 2 Peter, and Jude involving 'Balaam', 'Belial', and 'Devilishness'.

It is these things that the Dead Sea Scrolls put in sharp relief. Without the Scrolls we would only have suspected them, because of the mutually contradictory information in the New Testament and early Church documents. With the Scrolls for use as control, we get an entirely different picture of events in Palestine than either the New Testament or the documents of Rabbinic Judaism – now normative Judaism – provide. Whether James is to be identified with the Righteous Teacher at Qumran or simply a parallel successor is not the point – the Scrolls allow us to approach the Messianic Community of James with about as much precision as we are likely to have from any other source.

One hopes that the arguments put forth in this book and its successor will lift some of the cloud of unknowing and misrepresentation surrounding these issues. Once James has been rescued from the oblivion into which he was cast, abetted by one of the most successful (and fantastic) rewrite enterprises ever accomplished – the Book of Acts – it is necessary to deal with the new constellation of facts which the reality of his being occasions. It will also no longer be possible to avoid the obvious solution to the problem of the Historical Jesus – the question of his actual physical existence as such aside – the answer to which is simple. *Who and whatever James was, so was Jesus.*

Trajan who fought in Judea and destroyed the Jews of Egypt and Medallion supposedly depicting Paul and Peter.

Chronological and Genealogical Charts

MACCABEAN PRIEST KINGS

Mattathias, 167–166 BC
Judas Maccabee, 166–160
Jonathan, 160–142
Simon, 142–134
John Hyrcanus, 134–104
Alexander Jannaeus, 103–76
Salome Alexandra, 76–67
Aristobulus II, 67–63
Hyrcanus II, 76–67 and 63–40
Antigonus, 40–37

HERODIAN KINGS, ETHNARCHS, OR TETRARCHS

Herod, Roman–supported King, 37–4 BC
Archelaus, Ethnarch of Judea, 4 BC – 7 CE
Herod Antipas, Tetrarch of Galilee and Perea, 4 BC – 39 CE
Philip, Tetrarch of Trachonitis, 4 BC – 34 CE
Agrippa I,Tetrarch and King, 37–44
Herod of Chalcis, 44–49
Agrippa II, 49–93

ROMAN EMPERORS FROM 60 BC TO 138 CE

Caesar, 60–44 BC
Mark Anthony and Octavius, 43–31 BCE
Octavius (Augustus), 27 BCE – 14 CE
Tiberius, 14–37
Caligula, 37–41
Claudius, 41–54
Nero, 54–68
Galba, 68–69
Otho, 69
Vitellius, 69
Vespasian, 69–79
Titus, 79–81
Domitian, 81–96
Nerva, 96–98
Trajan, 98–117
Hadrian, 117–138

ROMAN EMPERORS FROM 60 BC TO 138 CE

Caesar, 60–44 BC
Mark Anthony and Octavius, 43–31 BC
Octavius (Augustus), 27 BC – 14 CE
Tiberius, 14–37
Caligula, 37–41
Claudius, 41–54
Nero, 54–68
Galba, 68–69
Otho, 69
Vitellius, 69
Vespasian, 69–79
Titus, 79–81
Domitian, 81–96
Nerva, 96–98
Trajan, 98–117
Hadrian, 117–138

EARLY CHURCH AND OTHER SOURCES

Philo of Alexandria, *c.* 30 BC –45 CE
Clement of Rome, *c.* 30–97 CE
Josephus, 37–96
Ignatius, *c.* 50–115
Papias, *c.* 60–135
Pliny, 61–113
Polycarp, 69–156
Justin Martyr, *c.* 100–165
Hegesippus, *c.* 90–180
Tatian, *c.* 115–185
Lucian of Samosata, *c.* 125–180
Irenaeus, *c.* 130–200
Clement of Alexandria, *c.* 150–215
Tertullian, *c.* 160–221
Hippolytus, *c.* 160–235
Julius Africanus, *c.* 170—245
Origen, *c.* 185–254
Eusebius of Caesarea, *c.* 260–340
Epiphanius, 367–404
Jerome, 348–420
Rufinus of Aquileia, *c.* 350–410
Augustine, 354–430
St Cyril of Jerusalem, 375–444

The Maccabeans

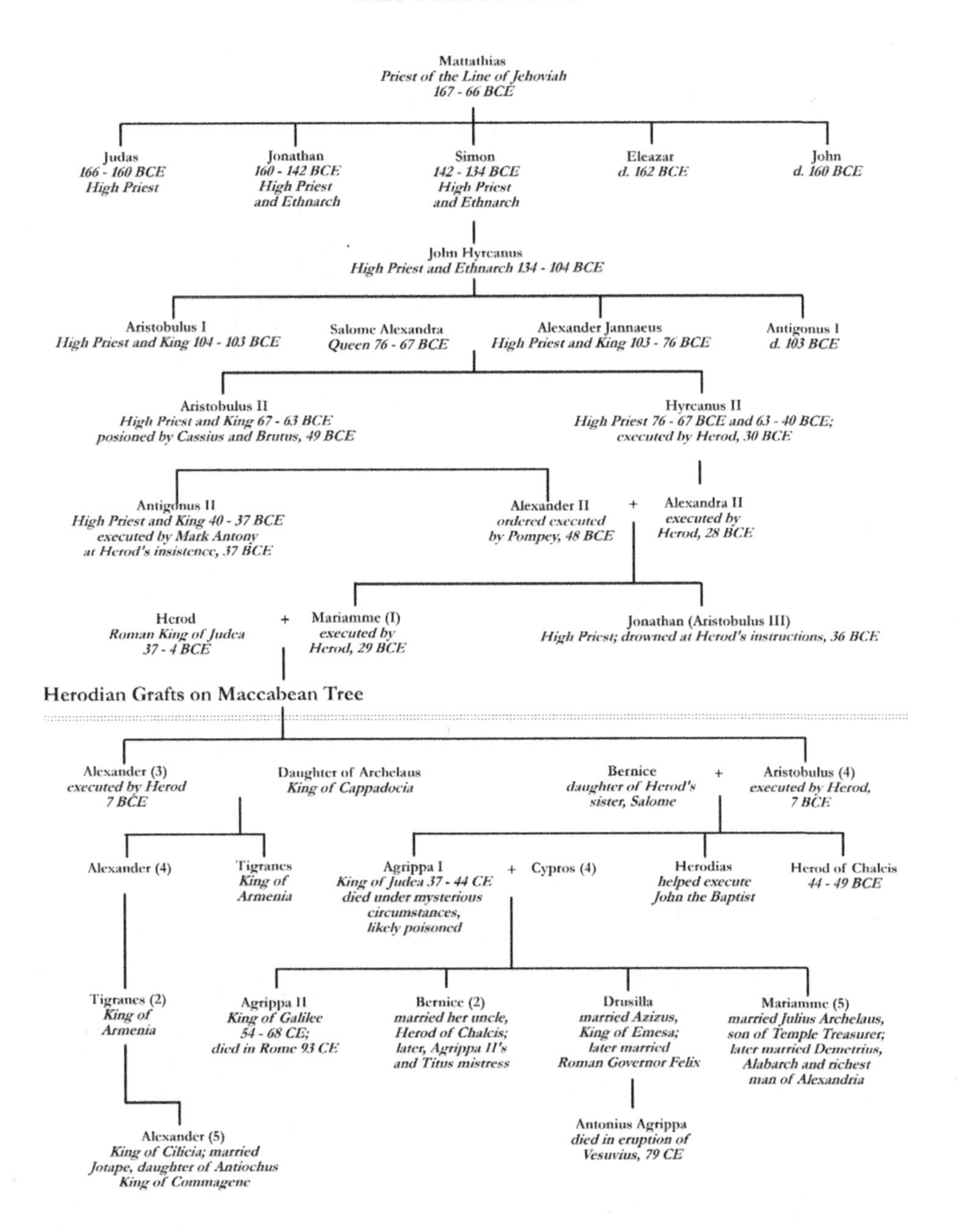

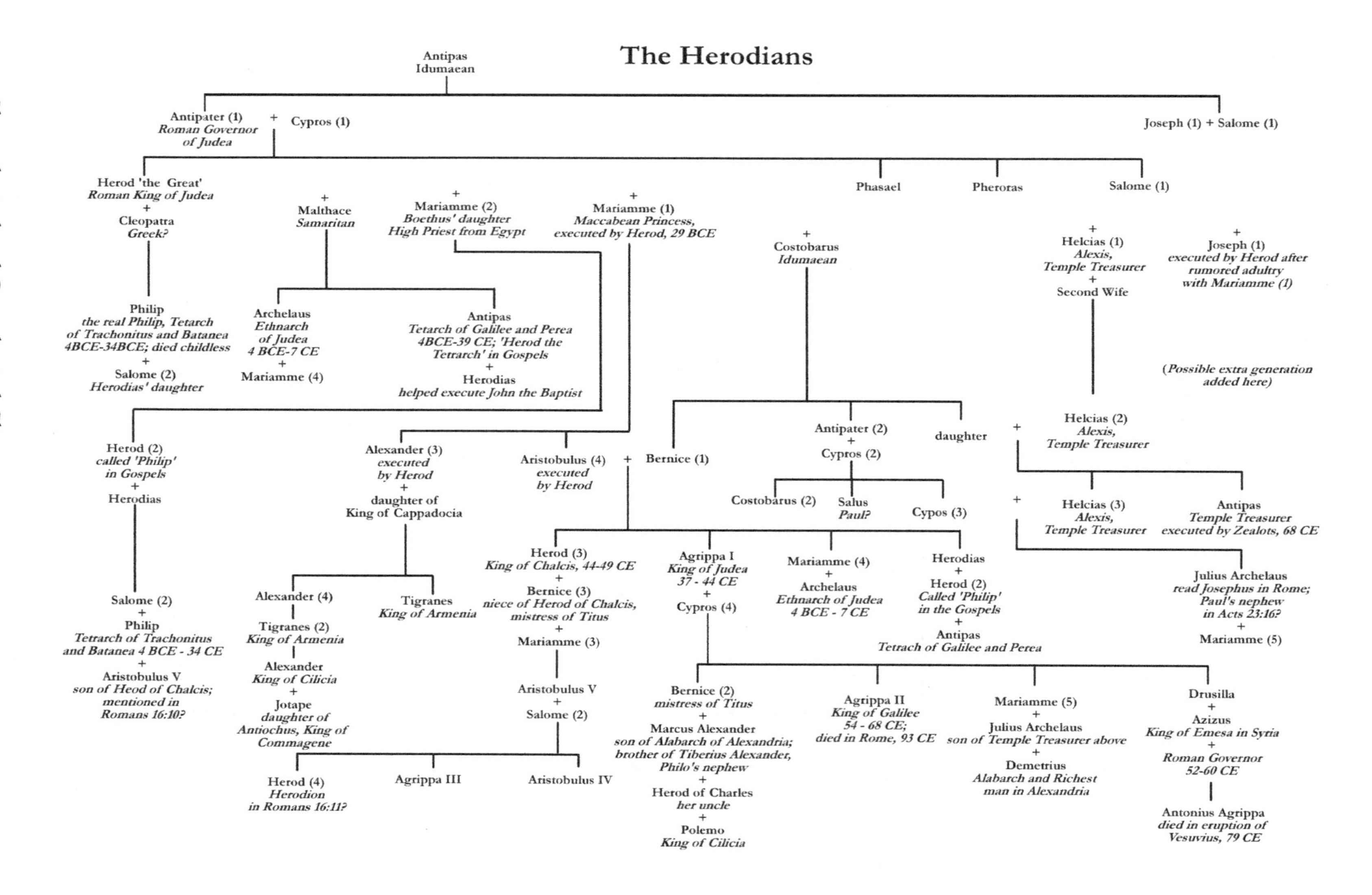

The Herodians
Antipas
Idumaean
Antipater (1)
Roman Governor
of Judea
+ Cypros (1)
Joseph (1) + Salome (1)
Herod 'the Great'
Roman King of Judea
+
Cleopatra
Greek?
+
Malthace
Samaritan
+
Mariamme (2)
Boethus' daughter
High Priest from Egypt
+
Mariamme (1)
Maccabean Princess,
executed by Herod, 29 BCE
Phasael
Pheroras
Salome (1)
+
Costobarus
Idumaean
+
Helcias (1)
Alexis,
Temple Treasurer
+
Second Wife
+
Joseph (1)
executed by Herod after
rumored adultry
with Mariamme (1)
Philip
the real Philip, Tetarch
of Trachonitus and Batanea
4BCE-34BCE; died childless
+
Salome (2)
Herodias' daughter
Archelaus
Ethnarch
of Judea
4 BCE-7 CE
+
Mariamme (4)
Antipas
Tetarch of Galilee and Perea
4BCE-39 CE; 'Herod the
Tetrarch' in Gospels
+
Herodias
helped execute John the Baptist
(Possible extra generation
added here)
Helcias (2)
Alexis,
Temple Treasurer
Antipater (2)
+
Cypros (2)
daughter
+
Herod (2)
called 'Philip'
in Gospels
+
Herodias
Alexander (3)
executed
by Herod
+
daughter of
King of Cappadocia
Aristobulus (4)
executed
by Herod
+ Bernice (1)
Costobarus (2)
Salus
Paul?
Cypos (3)
+
Helcias (3)
Alexis,
Temple Treasurer
Antipas
Temple Treasurer
executed by Zealots, 68 CE
Herod (3)
King of Chalcis, 44-49 CE
+
Bernice (3)
niece of Herod of Chalcis,
mistress of Titus
+
Mariamme (3)
Agrippa I
King of Judea
37 - 44 CE
+
Cypros (4)
Mariamme (4)
+
Archelaus
Ethnarch of Judea
4 BCE - 7 CE
Herodias
+
Herod (2)
Called 'Philip'
in the Gospels
+
Antipas
Tetrach of Galilee and Perea
Julius Archelaus
read Josephus in Rome;
Paul's nephew
in Acts 23:16?
+
Mariamme (5)
Salome (2)
+
Philip
Tetrarch of Trachonitus
and Batanea 4 BCE - 34 CE
+
Aristobulus V
son of Heod of Chalcis;
mentioned in
Romans 16:10?
Alexander (4)
Tigranes (2)
King of Armenia
Alexander
King of Cilicia
+
Jotape
daughter of
Antiochus, King of
Commagene
Tigranes
King of Armenia
Aristobulus V
+
Salome (2)
Herod (4)
Herodion
in Romans 16:11?
Agrippa III
Aristobulus IV
Bernice (2)
mistress of Titus
+
Marcus Alexander
son of Alabarch of Alexandria;
brother of Tiberius Alexander,
Philo's nephew
+
Herod of Charles
her uncle
+
Polemo
King of Cilicia
Agrippa II
King of Galilee
54 - 68 CE;
died in Rome, 93 CE
Mariamme (5)
+
Julius Archelaus
son of Temple Treasurer above
+
Demetrius
Alabarch and Richest
man in Alexandria
Drusilla
+
Azizus
King of Emesa in Syria
+
Roman Governor
52-60 CE
Antonius Agrippa
died in eruption of
Vesuvius, 79 CE

List of Abbreviations

Acts Th	Acts of Thomas
Ad Cor	Clement of Alexandria, Letter to the Corinthians
Ad Haer.	Irenaeus, *Against Heresies*
Ad Rom.	Ignatius, Letter to the Romans
Adv. Hel.	Jerome, *Against Helvidius*
Adv. Marcion	Tertullian, *Against Marcion*
ANCL	Anti–Nicene Christian Library (1867–71 edition)
Ant.	Josephus, *The Antiquities of the Jews*
Apion	Josephus, *Against Apion* (*Contra Apion*)
1 Apoc. Jas.	First Apocalypse of James
2 Apoc. Jas.	Second Apocalypse of James
Apoc. Pet.	Apocalypse of Peter
Apost. Const.	Apostolic Constitutions
APOT	*Apocrypha and Pseudepigrapha of the Old Testament* (ed. R. H. Charles)
ARN	*Abbot de Rabbi Nathan*
As. Moses	Assumption of Moses
b. Git.	Babylonian Talmud, Tractate *Gittin*
b. San.	Babylonian Talmud, Tractate *Sanhedrin*
b. Yoma	Babylonian Talmud, Tractate *Yoma*
BAR	*Biblical Archaeology Review*
BASOR	*Bulletin of the American Scholls of Oriental Research*
CD	Cairo Damascus Document
Comm. on Gal.	Jerome, Commentary on Galatians
Comm. on John	Origen, Commentary of John
Comm. in Matt.	Origen, Commentary on Matthew
de Carne	Tertullian, *On the Body of Christ*
de Mens. et Pond.	Epiphanius, *De Mensuris et Ponderibus*
de Monog.	Tertullian, *On Monogamy*
de Verig. vel.	Tertullian, *On the Veiling of Virgins*
Dial.	Justin Martyr, *Dialogue with Trypho*
DSSU	*The Dead Sea Scrolls Uncovered* (ed. R. Eisenman and M.Wise)
EH	Eusebius, *Ecclesiastical History*
Enarr. in Ps. 34:3	Augustine, *Discourses on the Psalms*
Eph.	Ignatius, Letter to the Ephesians
Epist. Apost.	Epistle of the Apostles
Epist. B.	Epistle of Barnabas
Gen. R.	*Genesis Rabbah*
Gos.Th.	The Gospel of Thomas
Haeres.	Epiphanius, *Against Heresies* (*Panarion:The Medicine Box* in Latin)
H.N.	Pliny, *Natural History*
Haer.	Tertullian, *Against Heretics*
Hennecke	*The New Testament Apocrypha* (ed. E. Hennecke and W. Schneemelcher)
Hipp.	Hippolytus, *Refutation of all Heresies*
Hom. in Luc.	Origen, *Homilies on Luke*
HUCA	*Hebrew Union College Annual*
JJHP	*James the Just in the Habakkuk Pesher* (R. Eisenman)

j.Ta'an	Jerusalem Talmud, Tractate *Ta'anith*
Lam. R.	*Lamentations Rabbah*
M. San.	*Mishnah Sanhedrin*
Mur.	Wadi Murabba'at, Cave 1
MZCQ	*Maccabees, Zadokite, Christians and Qumran* (R. Eisenman)
Opus imperf. C. Iul	Augustine, *Opus Imperfectum contra Secundum Juliani*
pars.	parallels
Protevang.	Protevangelium of James
Ps. *Hom.*	Pseudoclementine *Homilies*
Ps. Philo	Pseudo Philo
Ps. *Rec.*	Pseudoclementine *Recognitions*
Quod Omnis	Philo, *Every Good Man is Free*
4QD	The Qumran Damascus Document (Cave 4)
1QH	The Qumran Hymns
1QM	The Qumran War Scroll
11QMelch	The Qumran Melchizedek Text
4QMMT	The Qumran Letter(s) on Works Reckoned as Righteousness from Qumran
1QpHab	The Qumran Habakkuk *Pesher*
4QpIs	The Qumran Isaiah *Pesher*
4QpNah	The Qumran Nahum *Pesher*
4QpPs 37	The Qumran Commentary on Psalm 37
1QS	The Qumran Community Rule
11QT	The Qumran Temple Scroll
4QTest	The Qumran Testimonia
Suet.	Suetonius, *The Twelve Caesars*
Tos. Kellim	*Tosefta Kellim*
Trall.	Ignatius, Letter to the Trallians
Vir. ill.	Jerome, *Lives of Illustrious Men*
Vita	Josephus, *Autobiography of Flavius Josephus*
War	Josephus, *The Jewish War*

Ceremonial stairs leading to the Tomb of Queen Helen of Adiabene and her sons. Author and wife descending the steps.

Notes

Introduction

1. *Maccabees, Zadokites, Christians and Qumran*, Leiden, 1983, p. xvii.
2. *War* 1.1.
3. *War* 2.259 and 2.264/*Ant.* 20.168.
4. *War* 2.261-3/*Ant.* 20.169-71.
5. Cf. Koran 3.45, 4.156–7, and 19.20–21 with Augustine, Sermon 191.

Chapter 1

1. Augustine's Letters 28 (394 CE), 40 (397), and Jerome's response, Letter 72 (404).
2. *EH* 3.27.1.
3. Matt. 5:20, Luke 6:20, and Jas. 2:2–6. For Paul, Gal. 2:10.
4. See 'Wall', 'Fortress'/'Bulwark' and 'Rock' symbolism in 1QH 3.35, 5.39, 6.25–9, 9.298, 1QS 8.7–8, and *EH* 3.7.8–9.
5. For 'Enemy', see Paul in Gal. 4:16, the Parable of the Tares in Matt. 13:25–39, Ps. *Rec.* 1.70–71, and Jas. 4:4.
6. *EH* 2.1.4.
7. Gos. Th. 12 and Ps. *Rec.* 1.43.

Chapter 2

1. I Macc. 8:1–31, 12:7, and 14:16–24.
2. *War* 3.399–407. Cf. Suetonius, *The Twelve Caesars*, 10.4; Tacitus, *The Histories*, 2.78ff. and 5.13.
3. ARN 4.5, *b. Git.* 56a–b, *Lam.* R. 1.5.31 and *b. Yoma* 39b.
4. Cf. *Vita* 13–16 with *War* 3.346–9.

Chapter 3

1. See, for instance, the picture of these 'camps' in 1QM 7.3–7, 12.6–7, 19.1, CD 12.22–14.8, and *MMT*, Lines 2.66-70 in *DSSU*, p. 195.
2. *Haeres.* 19, 29.1.1–7, and 30.3.2.
3. *On the Contemplative Life* 2.
4. See, for instance, *Ket.* 30b, where a man sentenced to stoning 'falls down from the roof' or *M. San.* 9.6 on 'the *Kanna'im*' killing a priest serving at the altar in a state of ritual uncleanness by splitting open his head with clubs and compare with *E.H.* 2.23.16–18 or 2 Apoc. Jas 61–2.
5. Cf. Phil. 2:25 and 4:18–22 with *Ant.* 1.8, *Vita* 430, and *Apion* 1.1, 2.1, and 2.296.
6. Cf. Jas. 5:1–7 with 1QpHab 12.3–10, 4QPs 37 2.9–3.10 ('The Church of the Poor'), and the 'Hymns of the Poor' (4Q434–6) in *DSSU*, pp. 233–41.
7. *War* 1.535–7/*Ant.* 16.121–7 and 356.

Chapter 4

1. *Ant.* 20.97–8. Acts 12:2 refers only to 'Herod the King', but in the New Testament all Herodians were known as 'Herod'.
2. Gal. 2:2–9, I Cor. 8:1–13, 2 Cor. 3:1–9, 5:12, 10:12–16, 11:5–22, and 12:11.
3. *EH* 2.6.3–8 and 3.5.1–3.7.7.
4. Matt. 19:30 and 20:16/Mark 10:31/Luke 13:30.
5. Matt. 13:57/Mark 6:4/Luke 4:24.
6. Matt. 12:46–50/Mark 3:31–5/Luke 8:19–21.
7. Matt. 11:21/Luke 10:13.
8. *Historia Sacra* 2.30–31.

Chapter 5

1. See fragments in ANCL and *EH* 2.15.2 and 3.39.
2. Matt. 13:55/Mark 6:3.
3. *EH* quoting Justin Martyr, *Apology* 1.26, who came from Samaria, and Ps. *Rec.* 2.7 and *Hom.* 6.7.
4. For a detailed analysis of this topic, see *MZCQ*, pp. 28–31 and 78–89.

5. 4Q394-99, which Prof. Wise and I called 'Two Letters of Works Reckoned as Righteousness' in *DSSU*, pp. 182 –200.
6. 1QS 9.13–16 and 9.17–25.
7. 1QS 4.2–5.23 and 8.1–9.6.
8. See 1QpHab 5.12–6.11.
9. Ps. *Rec.* 1.71–2.
10. CD 9.17–22, 13.15–17, 14.8–12, 15.7–14, and 4QD266 1–16; also 1QS 6.12–20.

Chapter 6

1. 28 BCE. Mariamme's sons were executed in 7–6 BCE, two years before Herod's own death; *Ant.* 15.247–52/ *War* 1.550–51.
2. Cf. Matt. 9:10–13, 11:19, 21:31–32, and pars.
3. *Ant.* 20.145. For the ban on niece marriage see CD 4.17–5.11, 7.1–2, 8.6–7, and 11QT 66.11–17.
4. 11QT 56.12–57.18 (cf. Deut. 17:15–17).
5. *War* 1.185 and 357/*Ant.* 14.125, 140, and 20.245 (also see *War* 1.154, for Pompey earlier in 63 BCE after storming the Temple.
6. *War* 2.119–66/*Ant.* 18.11–25.
7. Mark 3:18; in Matt. 10:3 also 'Lebbaeus who was surnamed Thaddaeus'.
8. *EH* 3.19.1–20.7 and 3.32.1–8; cf. Hippolytus 9.21's 'Zealot Essenes' (*War* 2.150–51).
9. 2.15.1–2, 3.39.15 (as do Clement and Papias), and 6.14.6–7.

Chapter 7

1. In 1QpHab 11.3, the received version of Hab. 2:15's 'looking upon their privy parts' (*'me'oreihem'*) has been transmuted into 'looking upon their festivals' (*'mo'adeihem'*), but the sense re-emerges in 11.13 , when the Wicked Priest is characterized as 'not circumcising the foreskin of his heart'.
2. CD 6.15, 7.1–2, and 8.8.
3. 1QH 6.25–9, 7.6–10, and 9.24–9.
4. See *Zohar* 3.218a–b on 'Phineas'.
5. See *b. San* 97b.
6. 1QS 8.1 – also the possible reference in 4Q251, the *Halakhah* A text, 'A Pleasing Fragrance', *DSSU*, pp. 200–205, to 'fifteen men' composing the council, which may solve the problem.
7. 1QS 8.3–10and 9.3–6.
8. Cf. Gal. 2:9 with Matt. 17:1/Mark 9:2/Luke 9:28.
9. See Origen, *Comm. in Matt.* 17 and Fragment 10, attributed to Papias in ANCL and listed as 'James the Bishop and Apostle, Simon, Thaddaeus, and one Joseph', the sons of 'Mary' and 'Cleophas' or 'Alphaeus'.
10. Origen, *Contra Celsus* 2.62, assumes the appearance on the Road to Emmaeus was to 'Simon and Cleophas', meaning obviously, 'Simeon bar Cleophas'.
11. Cf. Ps. *Rec.* 1.70–71, Peter's Epistle to James, Ps. *Hom.* 2, and the Parable of the Tares in Matt. 13:19–50. The reflection of this terminology in Gal. 4:16, preceded by allusion to 'telling the Truth', vividly shows its currency even in the 50s.
12. Rom. 1:16–25 on Hab. 2:4, Rom. 3:1–8 on circumcision, Rom. 9:1, Gal. 1:20, 2 Cor. 11:31, Col. 3:9, 2 Thess. 2:2–12, I Tim. 2:7, 4:2, and Titus 1:1–11.

Chapter 8

1. Acts 15:20, 15:29, and 21:25.
2. *EH* 3.27.2–6. In Eusebius' words, Paul 'they reject' as a heretic and 'an apostate from their Law' and 'they use the Gospel according to the Hebrews only'.
3. Cf. *EH* 2.23.18–19 for those associating James' death with coming of armies and Jerusalem's fall.
4. Cf. Jas. 2:8–10 on 'keeping the whole Law'.
5. 1QS 8.22–9.
6. 1QS 8.11–18, 9.6–11, CD 5.7–11, and 6.17–7.9.
7. In exegesis of Isa. 40:3.
8. *DSSU*, pp. 182–200, in particular 1.1–10 of the first part or First Letter.
9. CD 5.7–11, recapitulated in 7.1–9.
10. *EH* 2.1.2 and cf. 'Forefathers' with 'the First' in CD 1.4–2.6, 3.10, 8.16–17, etc.
11. *EH* 1.12.1–3.
12. *EH* 1.13.1–22.
13. *Ant.* 12.414, 419, and 434.

14. Matt. 21:8–10 and pars.
15. *War* 2.8/*Ant.* 17.207–8.
16. *War* 4.154–7.
17. For 'cursing' and 'Deceitfulness' ('*Remiyyah*') as applied to the Liar, see 1QS 2.4–18, 4.9–23, and 8.22–9.8. Also see 4QpNah 2.8, in conjunction with 'Lying, a Tongue full of Lies', and 'deceiving Many'. For the 'blaspheming Tongue' in James, see 3:5–15.
18. CD 1.7, 5.15–16, 7.9, 7.21, 8.2–3, 8.25, 13.24, 1QS 3.14–18, and 4.12–26; for its use regarding 'the *Mebakker*' and 'the High Priest Commanding the Many', see CD 14.6–7, 15.8–10, and 1QS 5.22–4.

Chapter 9

1. See Moses of Chorene, 2.30–35, the Acts of Thomas, and the Doctrine of Addai the Apostle.
2. Moses of Chorene, 2.35, calls her 'the first of Agbar's wives', to whom he gave the town of Haran. For Josephus, her son Izates receives this town from *his* father. Eusebius appears, also, to think Helen Agbar's 'Queen'.
3. *Ant.* 20.18.
4. *Ant.* 20.39–41.
5. Mark 3:17–19 and Luke 6:15–16. In some versions of Matt. 10:3, he is also identified with 'Lebbaeus' – another of these obvious garblings, probably meant to stand also for 'Alphaeus', i.e., 'Cleophas'.
6. *Ant.* 20.49–53 and 101.
7. *EH* 2.12.1–3. Josephus also mentions these at the end of his story; 20.95. He says her son Izates also sent up relief, and Cyprus too is added to these stories – important for other notices in Acts.
8. *EH* 7.19; see also 3.7.8.
9. 20.22–34.
10. 2.23.3–4.
11. *Vir. ill.* 2.
12. Ibid.
13. 78.1.7; also 66.19.6.
14. 78.7.7.
15. Ps. *Rec.* 1.60.
16. *EH* 2.23.7–11.
17. *EH* 2.23.12–13.

Chapter 10

1. *Tosefta Hul.* 2:22–3. Also *b. A.Z.* 27b, *j. Shab.* 14:4, and *A.Z.* 2:2, 40d.
2. 1QpHab 2.3–4, CD 6.19, and 8.35–45.
3. Gen. 9:4–7.
4. *Haeres.* 30.2.3 and 78.14.3.
5. '*Ger-nilveh*' in 4QpNah 2.9 and 3.5; '*Nilvim*' in CD 4.3 and 1QS 5.6.
6. CD 5.7–12.
7. See *B.B.* 91b on 'Potters' and *Yalkut* Jeremiah 35:8ff., followed by the tradition in the *Yalkut* on Jer. 35:12, that the grandsons of the Rechabites served in the Temple and their daughters married the sons of the Priests.
8. 1QS 6.1–9.2, CD 13.7–14.11, etc.
9. CD 3.6–11.
10. *E.H.* 2.13.27.
11. See, for instance, Jerome's Letters 81, 82, 84, and his Preface to Ezekiel against Rufinus; also Rufinus' response in Letter 80 and his two *Apologies* attacking Jerome.
12. 2.23.20.
13. *Comm. in Matt.* 10.17; *Contra Celsum* 1.47 and 2.13.
14. *Vir. ill.* 2.
15. See *Ant.* 18.117 on John and *War* 2.128 and 139 on 'Essene' 'Piety towards God'/'Righteousness towards men'. For James see 2:5–8.
16. For instance, compare CD 6.21 and 1QM 11.9–13 with Jas. 2:2–10 and 5:1–8.
17. *Dial.* 23, 47, and 93.
18. Jas. 2:8 and CD 6.20.
19. 2.23.5.
20. Jerome, *Comm. on Gal.* 396 (1:19). For fringes, see Num. 15:38–9.
21. 29.5.7.
22. 30.1.3 and 78.13.2–14.3.
23. Exod. 13:2.

24. 29.5.6.
25. 29.1.3–5.3.
26. 1QS 8.13–14 and 9.9–24.
27. See *War* 2.56/*Ant.* 17.261.
28. *EH* 1.7.14.
29. 30.2.7 and 30.18.1.
30. 1QM 11.6–17, CD 7.18–8.5, and 4Qtest 9–13, preceded in 5–8 by Deut. 18:18–19 – 'the True Prophet'.
31. *B. San.* 105a–106b.
32. See *Lam.* R. 11.4.
33. *War* 6.310–15.
34. 2 Cor. 3:1–4:18 and 10:4–12:11.

Chapter 11

1. 1QpHab 10.9–12.
2. R. Eisler, *The Messiah Jesus and John the Baptist*, New York, 1931, pp. 236 and 614–15 points up confusions between the Hebrew/Aramaic word for 'locusts' and 'carobs'.
3. 30.13.4–5.
4. These were placed around the two Inner Courts of the Temple in both Hebrew and Greek, and read, 'Let no foreigner pass the railing and enter the platform around the Temple. Whoever is caught will have himself to blame for his ensuing death' or 'the responsibility for his ensuing death will be upon him'.
5. Ben Sira 52:9.
6. ARN 2.45 (referring to Gen. 6:9).
7. See Acts 3:14, 7:52, and 22:14.
8. CD 2.9–24.
9. Ben Sira 45:24. Cf. 50:24, *Zohar* 1.59b on Noah, and 1QM 12.3.
10. 4.218a–b on 'Phineas'.
11. *B. San.* 56a–60a.
12. CD 3.10.
13. 4QpNah 2.1–2 and 1QpHab 10.9–12.
14. 15:20, 15:29, and 21:25.
15. See also Rom. 1:16, 10:12, and Col. 3:11.
16. *Ant.* 19.332–4.
17. *Ant.* 20.145.
18. Acts 23:17–32.
19. *Ant.* 20.189–200.
20. *War* 2.427–8.
21. *Ant.* 20.216–18.
22. CD 8.42–44 and 11QT 46.11.
23. CD 6.12–7.5.
24. *EH* 2.23.4–5; *Haeres.* 78.14.1–2.
25. 78.14.5–6, deleted from *EH* 23.2.16–17.
26. 1QS 5.9–11.
27. 1QpHab 7.10–8.3.
28. 29.1.3–5.5.
29. See *Yalqut Shim'oni* on Jer. 35:12, *Siphre Num.* 78 on Num. 10:29, and *B.B.* 91b on 'Potters'. Also see Eisler, pp. 234–45, for a full presentation of 'the *Saleb*'.
30. Benjamin of Tudela, *Travels.*

Chapter 12

1. 2.23.5–6.
2. 11.2–8.
3. *Ant.* 20.216–18.
4. *Ant.* 20.160–61 and *War* 2.253. One should note that the word '*Lestes*' for 'Brigand' is the same as that of 'thief' in Matt. 27.38.
5. *War* 2.58–9.
6. War 2.264–6.
7. *Ant.* 20.173–8 and *War* 2.266–70.
8. CD 1.17–2.1.
9. *War* 2.454–5.

10. *EH* 3.3.5, the description of which continues to 3.8.2.
11. *Ant.* 20.180.
12. *Ant.* 20.181.
13. See 1QpHab 8.11–9.6 and 12.7–10 on 'stealing riches'.
14. *War* 2.155 and Hippolytus 9.21.
15. *EH* 3.31.1–4 and 4.22.4–5.
16. 29.15.1–4.
17. 78.14.1.
18. 78.1.3.
19. *EH* 3.18.5.
20. Cf. 9.16 with *War* 2.129, 132, and 161.
21. *Haeres.* 30.13.4.
22. *Vita* 11–12.
23. *Ant.* 18.116–19.
24. 1QS 3.3–12 and 20–23.
25. *War* 7.270–74.
26. 9.21. *War* 2.150–51 quickly brushes by this point.
27. *Ant.* 15.373 and *War* 2.139–42.

Chapter 13

1. 2.23.7.
2. 78.7.5–9; see also 29.7.1–4.
3. 1QH 2.32–4, 3.25, and 5.13–18. 'Soul' here does not refer exactly to what it might mean in Greek, but something more like the 'quick of life' or 'being'.
4. CD 1.20–21.
5. 1QH 2.15–31, 5.22–4, etc.
6. 6.24–7.
7. 7.6–9.
8. 1QpHab 12.2ff., 4QpIs[c] on 14:8ff. and on Zech 11:11/Isa. 30:1ff., 4QpNah. 1.7, and 4QpIsa[a] on 10:33f.
9. Cf. Dan. 7:13–14 with 1QM 11.17–12.10, 19.1–2, Matt. 24:30/26:64 and Mark 13:26/14:64.
10. 8.5–14, 9.3–6, and 19–24.
11. Ben Sira 50:24.
12. CD 7.13 and 8.3–24.
13. *Ant.* 14.22–5.
14. *Ta'an.* 23b.
15. 1.63a and 67b.
16. *Ta'an.* 23a.
17. CD 4.19–20 and 8.12–13.
18. 78.14.1.
19. 1QM 7.6–7.
20. 78.13.3–5; see also 29.4.1.
21. 29.3.3–7 and 51.22.21.
22. 1 Apoc. 29.20, 35.5, 2 Apoc. 55.15–18, 56.16, and 59.25.
23. See 1QH 9.29–35 and 11.9–14.
24. Acts 4:1–5:17, *Ant.* 20.199, and Ps. *Rec.* 1.54.
25. *War* 1.68–91/*Ant.* 13.300.
26. 4Q322–24, *DSSU*, pp. 119–27.
27. Probably Herod's Sanhedrin heads; *Pirke Abbot* 1.2–1.15 and ARN 4–13.
28. *Ant.* 14.28.
29. *Ant.* 14.22–3.
30. Koran 19.22–3.
31. *Ta'an.* 23a.
32. *Ant.* 18.25–8.
33. *War* 1.131–2.
34. *War* 1.148.
35. *Ant.* 14.176 and 15.3.
36. 1.47, 2.13, and *Comm. in Matt.* 10.17.
37. *Vir. ill.* 2.
38. Luke 21:6, 20–24 and pars.
39. 2.13 – the same section in which he attests that '*Sicarii*' are immediately put to death.

40. *Contra Celsus* 1.47.
41. Ibid.
42. 2.17.
43. *EH* 2.23.20.
44. Cf. *War* 2.651 abd 4,314–25 with *Vita* 74–76, 189–261, 309–10.
45. *War* 4.319–20.
46. *War* 6.378–86.
47. *War* 4.324–5.

Chapter 14

1. 2.1.4–5.
2. 2.23.2–3.
3. *Vir. ill.* 2.
4. 4.20.7–8.
5. *Ta'an.* 23a–b.
6. *Ant.* 18.6–10 and *War* 6.3130–15.
7. 1QpHab 9.4–7.
8. 12.14–13.4.
9. 1QM 6.6 and 7.3–7 (as opposed to '*the uncircumcised in heart and body*' of Ezek. 44:7).
10. 7.7–10 and 9.8–9.
11. 10.8–14 and 11.3–10.
12. 11.4–12, as is the exegesis in the Damascus Document.
13. In Acts 7:56, this is 'standing'.
14. 1QM 11.9–13; see also *Zohar* 4.19a on 'Balak and Balaam'.
15. CD 7.19–20.
16. See Koran 73.12, 74.26 and 46, 82.8–19, etc.
17. 1QM 11.11–14.
18. 1QM 11.17–12.3.
19. 12.4–9.
20. 18.12–19.4.
21. 1QpHab 7.1–14.
22. CD 9.1.
23. 1QpHab 5.8–12.
24. 4QpNah 1.11f.
25. 1QpHab 11.2–12.10.
26. 1QpHab 11.2–15.
27. Ps. *Rec.* 1.70.
28. *Vir. ill.* 2; cf. *EH* 2.23.18.
29. *Ant.* 15.320–32.
30. CD 5.7, Matt. 26:28 and par, and I Cor 10:16 and 11:25.
31. CD 5.13–15, 6.14–17, and 8.3–13.
32. 4QpNah 3.1 and 1QpHab 10.8–11.
33. 4QpNah 3.2–10 and 4.4–5.
34. Rom. 12:1–5, I Cor. 3.9–17, and 12:12–27.
35. *Dial.* 136–7; so does Hegesippus in Palestine, more or less contemporary with him, but rather to *James*. For 1QpHab 12.2–3 and 4QpPs 37 4.8–11, its language is being applied to the death or destruction of *the Righteous Teacher*.

Chapter 15

1. *Haeres.* 78.13.2 and 14.5.
2. 78.14.6 (*EH* 2.23.27).
3. *Haeres.* 30.3.1.
4. Cf. I Apoc. Jas. 34.15 with *EH* 3.5.3 and *Haeres.* 29.7.7–8.
5. Epist. B. 6 (also alluding to the 'Primal Adam').
6. 63,15–30.
7. 63.15 (Ps. *Rec.* 1.70–71).
8. *Vir. ill.* 2; also *Adv. Hel.* 21, in which, developiing Epiphanius 78.14.3's theme of the 'sons of Joseph following the virgin life-style', he maintains *both* Mary *and* Joseph were virgins.
9. *Vir. ill.* 2.

10. *Ant.* 20.197–8.
11. *Ant.* 20.10–16.
12. Ps. *Rec.* 1.54.
13. *MZCQ*, pp. 41–5.
14. Acts 11:27 and 13:1.
15. *Ant.* 14.83–96 and 18.116–19.
16. ARN 5.2.
17. *Ant.* 20.180 and 205–8.
18. *Ant.* 20.215.
19. *Vita* 65.
20. *Ant.* 20.251.
21. Cf. 1QpHab 11.6–12.10 and CD 1.19–21.
22. *War* 2.243–47/*Ant.* 20.137.
23. Cf. 1QpHab 12.6 with 1QH 4.10.
24. *Vita* 343–4.
25. *Ant.* 20.204–7.
26. *War* 2.255–7.
27. *War* 4.323–4.
28. *Ant.* 20.166.
29. *War* 6.312–15.
30. *War* 6.288–9.
31. *War* 7.407–53.
32. *War* 2.411–14.
33. *Ant.* 20.205–10.
34. *Ant.* 20.118–33.
35. *Ant.* 20.167; also *War* 2.259 and 2.264–5.
36. *War* 2.261–3/*Ant.* 20.169–72.
37. *Ant.* 18.85–7.
38. *Haeres.* 20.3.4 and Ps. *Hom.* 2.23.
39. *Ant.* 20.173–81.
40. *Ant.* 20.183–4.
41. *Ant.* 20.178.
42. *Ant.* 20.14.
43. *War* 2.253.
44. *Ant.* 20.131–6/*War* 2.242–6.
45. *Ant.* 20.181.
46. *Ant.* 20.206–7.
47. *Ant.* 20.188.
48. *Ant.* 15.252–66/*War* 1.486–7.
49. *Ant.* 20.189–91.
50. 11QT 46.9–18, referring to lepers; also see 4QMMT 1.47–62, referring to the blind and deaf.
51. *War* 1.401, 5.36–8, *Ant.* 15.380–425, 19.326, and 20.219–20.
52. *War* 2.225.
53. *War* 2.224.
54. 2.254–7.
55. For Poppea, see *Ant.* 20.195; regarding Helcias, and *Vita* 16, and see the allusions to 'Joiners'/'joining' in CD 4.2 and 4QpNah 2.9 and 3.5, denoting 'resident aliens'.
56. Phil. 4:18–22, also mentioning Epaphroditus.
57. The observation is Josephus'; *Ant.* 20.252–7.
58. *Vita* 13.
59. *Vita* 360.

Chapter 16

1. Acts 23:2.
2. *Ant.* 20.211–12.
3. *Ant.* 20.214.
4. 1QpHab 8.8–13.
5. 1QpHab 12.6–10.
6. *Ant.* 18.138, suggested to me by Nikos Kokkinos of London in 1986.
7. *War* 2.449–56.

8. *War* 4.140–365.
9. *Ad Cor.* 5 (attributed to Clement of Rome), Tertullian, *Haer.* 36, *EH* 2.25.5, and 3.1.2, quoting Origen's *Commentary on Genesis.*
10. Jerome, *Vir. ill.* 11 considers them authentic, as does Augustine.
11. *Ant.* 20.141–4.
12. *Ant.* 20.143.
13. Acts 13:1–12. It is in the aftermath of this that John Mark breaks with Paul and returns to Jerusalem (13:13).
14. *Ant.* 19.332–5.
15. *War* 4.319–20.
16. Cf. 1QS 8.21–4, CD 8.28–36, and 4QD266.14–16. Also see *War* 2.143–4 on those 'expelled from the (Essene) Community'.
17. *War* 2.270/*Ant.* 20.182–4 and *Ant.* 20.193–6 – 'the Temple Wall Affair'.
18. 1QpHab 5.8–12.

Chapter 17

1. *Vir. ill.* 2.
2. *B. San.* 45b–446b, 49b–50b, 53a–56b, etc., Lev. 24:14–16, and Deut. 17:2–5.
3. *EH* 3.33.
4. *EH* 3.20.1–4.
5. 2 Apoc. Jas. 62.10.
6. Appanius, *Civil Wars* 1.120. For beheading in the *Talmud*, see *San.* 37b, 49b–56b, and *Ket.* 30b.
7. *San.* 45a–b and *Ket.* 30a–b.
8. *B. San.* 56a–b and 60a.
9. 4Q246, *DSSU*, pp. 68–71.
10. Cf. Mark 11:15–18 and pars. With John 2:13–22.
11. Cf. Gen. 4:26 (Enosh), 12:8 and 14:4 (Abraham) with Exod. 3:14–15 (Moses).
12. T. Zahn in H.-J. Schoeps, *Paul: Theology of the Apostle in the Light of Jewish Religious History*, Philadelphia, 1961, p. 67.
13. *War* 2.7/*Ant.* 17.207–8.
14. Cf. CD 4.3–7 with 1QS 5.2 and 5.9.
15. 1QpHab 4.14–5.5 (also 10.3–5 and 13).
16. CD 6.5; cf. 1QS 8.13–14 and 9.19–24.
17. CD 14.8–11, 15.8–15, 1QS 6.12, etc.
18. Cf. 4QpPs 37 3.13–17 and 1QpHab 11.8 with Jas. 2:10, Rom. 13:13–23, and 1 Cor. 8:7–13 on 'things sacrificed to idols'.
19. *Ant.* 20.202.
20. 1QpHab 11.4–8.
21. 1QpHab 11.9–15.
22. *Ket.* 30b.
23. *B. San.* 81b–82b; *Tos. Kelim* 1.6.
24. *B. Tam.* 29a–b and *Men.* 21b.
25. *B. San.* 44a–b, *Sota* 8a, and 23a.
26. *War* 6.288–301.
27. *War* 6.288–301.
28. Ps. *Rec.* 1.70–73.
29. Ps. *Rec.* 1.10.5.
30. I am indebted to my colleague F. S. Jones for the basis of this translation.
31. *Ant.* 20.51–3 and 101. For Helen as Nazirite, see *b. Naz.* 19b and *Ket.* 7a.
32. Ps. *Rec.* 1.73–4.
33. For Helen and her son's 'Riches' and 'Piety', see *Ant.* 20.51–3 as well as *Yoma* 37a–b and *B.B.* 11a.

Chapter 18

1. CD 8.21–38.
2. Epistle of Peter to James 4.1–4.
3. Cf. *Ant.* 20.97–102 with Acts 5:36–8.
4. *Ant.* 20.214; cf. Acts 9:1 on 'Saulus'' riotous behavior.
5. *Ant.* 20.101.
6. *E.H.* 1.13.1–2.1.8 and 2.12.1. Cf. *Ant.* 20.17–96 and Moses of Chorene 2.30–33.
7. E.g. 1QpHab 11.4–16 and 1QH 9.8–9.

8. *War* 2.143.
9. Matt. 13:47, John 21:6–8, etc.
10. 1QS 8.5 and 9.4–6.
11. *Ant.* 1.8; cf. *Vita* 430, *Contra Apion* 1.1, 2.1, and 2.296.
12. *Ant.* 20.144 and 147.
13. Cf. Dio Cassius, 68.14.5–33.3 and 69.12.1–15 with EH 4.2.1–4.7.4 on the one led by 'Andreas'/'Man' or 'Adam' in Cyrene.
14. Suetonius, 12.15–17 and Dio Cassius, 67.14.1–18.2.
15. 3.32/1–6.
16. *E.H.* 3.12.1.
17. *E.H.* 3.19.1–20.9.
18. *E.H.* 3.20.5.
19. *E.H.* 3.32.3–8.

Chapter 19

1. 1QpHab 8.9 and 9.4–5 on the Community Council as a 'pleasing odor and sweet fragrance', including 'spiritualized Temple' imagery and making an atonement through suffering; also Rom. 15:16, 'the offering up of the Peoples' as 'a pleasing sacrifice' and Phil. 4:18, Epaphroditus' efforts, the same.
2. 1QpHab 10:11–12 – even 'of Emptyness'; cf. Jas. 2:20's 'Empty Man', relating to Gen. 15:6 and Hab. 2:4.
3. *Contra Apion* 1.51.
4. *War* 7.199–209.
5. *War* 7.32–4.
6. 4.9–11.
7. 1QpHab 10.10.
8. 1QM 12.8 and 19.1–2 (cf. Jas. 5:4–9).
9. John 1:21–7, however, specifically denies this.

Chapter 20

1. 1QS 8.1.
2. 1QS 8.5–9.4.
3. 1QS 9.4–5 and 9.20–24.
4. Cf. Matt. 20:20–28/Mark 10:35–45 with 1QpHab 5.3.
5. CD 4.10–12 and 1QpHab 8.1–3 in exegesis of Hab. 2:4.
6. Epistle of Peter to James 4.1–3.
7. 1QpHab 8.1–3 and 10.10–12.
8. Koran 2.61, 3.21, 3.183, 4.155, etc.
9. CD 4.7 (reversing 1.19), 1QS 3.2–3, 1QH 13.16–17, 16.11, etc.
10. A. v. Harnack, 'Die Verklarungsgeschichte Jesu, der Gericht des Paulus (I Kor. 15,3ff.) under die Beiden Christusvisionen des Petrus', *Sitzungsberichte der Preussischen Akademie*, 1922, pp. 62–80 – the first to point this out.
11. 1QS 2.22 (also 1.12).
12. Cf. Clement of Alexandria, 1.29, 2.15, *EH* 3.3.2, and Jerome, *Vir. ill.* 1.
13. *Haeres.* 30.13.7.
14. 1QpHab 11.2–12.6.
15. *War* 4.324 and 4.343.
16. 1QpHab 5.12–6.11.
17. 1QpHab 7.7–16.
18. 1QpHab 2.7–10, showing 'the Priest' (i.e., the High Priest) and 'the Teacher' are identical; cf. 1QpHab 7.4–14 – also beginning with the words, 'the Last Generation'.

Chapter 21

1. See CD 1.4, 'delivered them up to the sword'; 1.5–6, 'to be destroyed'; 1.17, 'to the avenging sword'; etc.
2. CD 4.3–7, 1QpHab 6.4–5, etc.
3. 1QpHab 10.6.
4. Cf. *War* 2.128–9 and 141–2 with Epistle of Peter to James 4–5 and Paul in 1 Cor. 15:3.
5. Cf. CD 3.2–6 with Jas. 1:16–25, 2:5–13, and 4:11.
6. CD 2.8, 3.1–9, etc.
7. CD 1.3–5, 1.14–2.1, 3.8–11, 5.13–21, 8.1, etc.
8. Cf. CD 8.14–36, 1QS 2.4–18, and 9.21–24, not 'loving' but 'Eternal hatred for the Sons of the Pit'.

9. *Ant.* 19.334, following his encounter with 'Simon'.
10. CD 1.1, 1.12, 1.19–21, 2.4, and 4.4–7.
11. CD 3.18–20 and 1QS 4.20–23.
12. CD 1.20–21.
13. 1QpHab 11.4–5.
14. *DSSU*, pp. 233–41 – 4Q436 2.1.
15. Cf. CD 2.12–13.
16. Cf. CD 1.20–21 with 1.17–18, 3.9–11, 7.81, and 8.49.
17. 6.20.
18. The usage, found in CD 6.15, 7.3, and 8.8, is exactly the same as that in Acts 15:20, 29, and 21:25.
19. Cf. 6.17–18 with Acts 10:14–15, 10:28, and 11:9.
20. 7.6–7 and 8.43–5.
21. CD 5.11–7.12; in 1QpHab 12.5–10, this is also '*Ebionim*'.
22. 8.18–36; cf. 1QS 8.19–24.
23. 8.31–6 and 42–5.
24. Matt. 12:46, Luke 24:36, John 20:14, 19, 26, 21:4, and Acts 1:10.
25. *EH* 2.23.17–18, *Vir. ill.* 2, and *Haeres.* 78.15.5–6.
26. *War* 7.217–18.
27. Cf. 1QpHab 2.8–10 and 7.4–5 with *EH* 2.23.7.
28. 1 Apoc. Jas. 31.5–32.17 and 2 Apoc. Jas. 56.15.
29. *B.B.* 60b.
30. 1QpHab 12.2–3.
31. 1QpHab 10.12–13.

Chapter 22

1. Cf. Sermon 191 with Koran 3.45, 4.157, and 19.19–23.
2. *Adv. Marcion* 4.19 and *de Verig. vel.* 6; also see *de Monog.* 8 on Jesus as Mary's first-born son.
3. *Comm. in Matt.* 10.17; cf. too *Hom. In Luc.* 7.
4. *Ad Eph.* 18–19 and *Ad Trall.* 9.1.
5. Cf. Irenaeus, *Ad Haer.* 3.16.7 and Tertullian, *de Carne* 17.
6. CD 8.56–7/20.33–4.
7. *Haeres.* 29.4.1–7.1, 66.19.7–8, 78.8.2–9.6, 14.3, and 18.1–24.4.
8. *Vir. ill.* 2 and *Adv. Hel.* 12–21.
9. Cf. in H. J. Leon, 'The Names of the Jews of Ancient Rome', *Transactions of the American Philological Association*, 1928, p. 208, with how the stonecutters frequently confused *alpha* and *lambda* in inscriptions.
10. *Opus imperf. c. Iul.* 4.122; cf. *Enarr. in* Ps. 34:3.
11. *EH* 3.11.1.
12. *EH* 3.12 (cf. 3.20.1–4).
13. Cf. *EH* 2.6.8, 3.5.1–4, 3.5.6, etc.
14. *EH* 3.17.
15. *EH* 3.19.1–20.7.
16. *EH* 3.32.1–6.
17. *EH* 3.32.3–6; cf. *Haeres.* 66.19.8 and 78.7.5.
18. Cf. *EH* 3.35 with *Haeres.* 66.20.1.
19. 3.32.7–8.
20. *Ant.* 20.166–7.
21. Tacitus, *Annals* 15.39–44, Suet. 6.38, and Dio Cassius 62.16–18.
22. *Ant.* 20.257.
23. *EH* 3.18.4.
24. 12.2.
25. *Ant.* 1.8–9.
26. Ant. 18.140; also see Tacitus, *Annals* 14.26.
27. See Augustine, *City of God* 6.11 and cf. Tertullian, *De Anima* 20 and 42, who calls him 'on our side'.
28. *Apion* 2.8.
29. 3.5.3–7.9.
30. *EH* 3.5.3.
31. Cf. 4.22.4 with 3.32.1–4 – date unclear, but elsewhere Eusebius implies it is 106–7 CE.
32. Cf. 1QpHab 11.2–15 on Hab. 2:15–16.
33. *EH* 3.31.2–3 and 5.24.3, quoting a letter from Polycrates (*c.* 190 CE).
34. *EH* 3.32.7.

35. These passages from Ps. *Hom.* 7.3–8 not only make it clear that James' 'strangled things' in Acts 15:18–30 and 21:25 is 'carrion', both here and in the Koran; but that Paul's rhetorical gamesmanship over 'eating in an idol temple'/'the table of demons' and James' 'things sacrifices to idols' in 1 Cor. 8:7–13 and 10:19–23 are just that – dissimulation.
36. Dio Cassius 68.32; Eusebius 4.2.4–5 calls him 'Lucuas', so this 'Andrew' does, in fact, seem to be a title.

Chapter 23

1. *Vita* 86.
2. *B. Ta'an.* 23a/*J. Ta'an* 66b.
3. *B. Sota* 11b; cf. *Ta'an.* 23a for the rockiness of the locale.
4. *B. Shab.* 33b.
5. 1QS 2.15.
6. 1QS 9.20–23. This is a direct quote from Isa. 63:4, where it comes amid 'cup' imagery of 'making the Peoples drunk with My Fury'.
7. 1QpHab 12.2–3/*EH* 2.23.14–15.
8. Cf. 1QS 9.22–3 and CD 2.11 and 4.4.
9. 9.16–28.
10. *War* 1.648–55/*Ant.* 17.149–57.
11. Cf. *War* 2.454 with *Contra Celsus* 2.13.
12. Cf. 9.21 with *War* 2.18 and *Ant.* 18.23.
13. *Ant.* 18.23–4.
14. Matt. 22:25–33 and pars.
15. Cf. Hipp. 9.21 with Ps. *Hom.* 7.3–4 and 8.
16. Cf. *War* 2.143–4 with 1QS 5.7–20, 7.17–25, etc.
17. Cf. Hipp. 5.2 and 10.5 with 2 Apoc. Jas. 44.15–20.
18. E. S. Drower, *The Secret Adam*, pp. xvi and 92–9.
19. Hipp. 7.21/10.17; also Irenaeus, 1.26.
20. *EH* 3.27.
21. Cf. 7.21/10.17, Apoc. Pet. 81.4–24, 2 Seth 56.6–19, and Acts of John 88–101.
22. 10.25.
23. 9.8; cf. Luke 3:16 on John and Jesus' 'shoes'.
24. 30.3.1.
25. *EH* 2.15.1–2 and 3.39.15–16.
26. ANCL Papias Frag. 10.

Chapter 24

1. See ANCL, note to Apost. Const. 8.25.
2. Apost. Const. 8.35.
3. Acts of Thomas 1–11, but particularly 139–70.
4. Acts of Thomas 11 and 39.
5. *EH* 1.13.5 and 22.
6. Cf. Acts of Thomas 16–170.
7. *Ant.* 1.145, 20.22, 20.34, and M. Grant, *From Alexander to Cleopatra*, New York, 1982, pp. 50–60.
8. Cf. *EH* 1.13.14–15 with Acts of Thaddaeus and Moses of Chorene 2.32.
9. Cf. Koran 29:39, 69:5–7, etc.
10. *EH* 1.13.11.
11. *EH* 1.12.1–3 and Apost. Const. 2.55.
12. CD 1.9–11.
13. ANCL Appendix to Hippolytus: 'Hippolytus on the Twelve Apostles', also found in the two codices of the Coislinian or Seguierian Library.
14. ANCL: Codex Baroccian, 206.
15. The spelling here is the same as Dio Cassius 68.18–21.
16. *Ant.* 20.34–48; cf. *EH* 1.13.9.
17. 2.29.
18. *Ant.* 20.39–40; for 'only-begotten', 20.20.
19. Syriac manuscripts from the Nitrian Monastery in Lower Egypt in ANCL.
20. *EH* 2.1.6.
21. *EH* 2.8–9.
22. *Ant.* 20.101–2; cf. *EH* 2.11.1–12.1.

23. *Ant.* 20.100.
24. 1QpHab 7.1–14.
25. 1QS 8.16–9.21, CD 6.14–7.4, 8.25–36, etc.
26. *Vita* 407–9.
27. *EH* 2.11–12.1 (*Ant.* 20.101–2).
28. Cf. Acts of Thaddaeus, ANCL Syriac Eusebius, Moses of Chorene 2.32, and Acts of Addai.
29. *Ant.* 20.51–2. Cf. *b. Yoma* 37a and *Naz.* 19b–20a.
30. *Ant.* 20.25–6.
31. 9.8 and 10.26.
32. See Benjamin of Tudela, *Travels*, years 1163–65 CE.

Chapter 25

1. Koran 7.65–84, 11.50–89, 26.124–55, 41.13–28, etc.
2. *Targum Onkelos* Gen. 8:4.
3. *Ant.* 20.24–6.
4. *War* 2.520; also 2.566 and 3.11–28.
5. *Ant.* 17.23–31.
6. *War* 4.14.
7. Cf. Ps. Philo 25.9–28.10 celebrating 'Kenaz' as a quasi-Messiah.
8. *War* 3.26–8.
9. *War* 6.355–7.
10. 4QpPs 37 2.18–25 and 4.7–12; cf. 1QpHab 9.1–2.
11. *EH* 2.12.3 and *Ant.* 20.95–6.
12. *EH* 2.12.3 and 4.6.4.
13. *Ant.* 20.17–23 and 34–7.
14. Cf. Segal, *Edessa the Blessed City*, p. 67.
15. Ibid., pp. 12 and 68–71.
16. *Annals* 6.44 and 12.12.
17. *Geography* 16.1.28.
18. 2.29–35.
19. Cf. Moses of Chorene 2.29 with *Ant.* 17.12–18.
20. Cf. *Ant.* 15.252–66 with 20.214, *War* 2.418, and 2.556.
21. *H.N.* 6.31.136–9.
22. *Ant.* 20.34.
23. Cf. *Ant.* 20.36–7 with *War* 6.356.
24. *EH* 4.22.4.
25. *Ant.* 20.137–41.
26. *Ant.* 20.145–6.
27. *B. Yoma* 37a and *Tosefta Pe'ah* 4:18.
28. *B. Git.* 60a and *Yoma* 37a.
29. *Naz.* 19a–20b; cf. Moses of Chorene 2.35.
30. *Ant.* 20:41 and 47.
31. *B.B.* 60b.
32. *War* 4.567, 5.253, and 6.355.
33. 4QMMT 2.33 (*DSSU*, pp. 196–200).
34. Cf. *Gen.* R. 46.10 with *Ant.* 20.43–8.
35. *DSSU*, pp. 182–96.
36. Cf. 2 Macc. 6:19–31, 12:44–5, and *War* 1.648–53.
37. Acts 13:1.
38. ANCL: 'The Teaching of Simon *Cephas* in Rome', attached to 'The Doctrine of Addai' and 'The Teaching of the Apostles'.
39. Cf. ANCL: Hippolytus on the Twelve Apostles and Codex Baroccian 206.
40. J. B. Segal, *Edessa the Blessed City*, p. 15; cf. Josephus' designation of Helen's son as 'Izas' (*War* 4.567).
41. Strabo, *Geography*, 17.1.54; Pliny *H.N.* 6.35.
42. *Ant.* 20.43–6.
43. *Ant.* 20.53.
44. *B.B.* 11a, quoting Isa. 3:10!

Chapter 26

1. Cf. Mani Fragment M 4575 with Manichaean Psalm Book 194–13.

2. Acts of Thomas 163–70.
3. Acts of Thomas 39, Thomas the Contender 138.10–13, etc.
4. *Ant.* 20.167–72/*War* 2.258–63.
5. *War* 2.264–5.
6. *Ant.* 20.97.
7. Cf. CD 6.15, 7.1, and 8.8.
8. Cf. 4Qtest 17 (Deut. 33:9), '*Britcha yinzor*'/'he kept Your Covenant'.
9. E. S. Drower, *The Secret Adam*, ix, xiv, and *The Mandaeans of Iraq and Iran*, pp. 1–17.
10. CD 6.17–7.3; cf. 4QpPs 37 3.1–2 and 4.2–3.
11. *War* 6.354–63.
12. *M. Sheb.* 10:3–7, *M. Git.* 4:3, *b. Arak.* 31b–32a, etc.
13. *B. Yeh.* 46a.
14. Cf. ARN 6.3 with *Git* 56a.
15. *War* 6.355–8.
16. *B. Ket.* 62b–63a and *Ned.* 50a.
17. Cf. ARN 6.3 and *Ta'an.* 19b–20a with *Haeres.* 78.14.1.
18. *War* 2.451, 628, and *Vita* 197–332.
19. *War* 4.335–44.
20. *Lam. R.* 2.2.4.
21. H. J. Leon, 'The Names of the Jews of Ancient Rome', pp. 207–12.
22. 1QpHab. 8.1–2.
23. 1QpHab. 2.2–6, 5.8–12, and CD 8.4–36.

Columns 4-5 of the Community Rule describing ritual immersion and "Holy Spirit" baptism

About the Author

Robert Eisenman is the author of *The New Testament Code: The Cup of the Lord, the Damascus Covenant, and the Blood of Christ* (2006), *James the Brother of Jesus: The Key to Unlocking the Secrets of Early Christianity and the Dead Sea Scrolls* (1998), *The Dead Sea Scrolls and the First Christians* (1996), *Islamic Law in Palestine and Israel: A History of the Survival of Tanzimat and Shari'ah* (1978), and co-editor of *The Facsimile Edition of the Dead Sea Scrolls* (1989) and *The Dead Sea Scrolls Uncovered* (1992).

He is Emeritus Professor of Middle East Religions and Archaeology and the former Director of the Institute for the Study of Judeo-Christian Origins at California State University Long Beach and Visiting Senior Member of Linacre College, Oxford. He holds a B.A. from Cornell University in Philosophy and Engineering Physics (1958), an M.A. from New York University in Near Eastern Studies (1966), and a Ph.D from Columbia University in Middle East Languages and Cultures and Islamic Law (1971). He was a Senior Fellow at the Oxford Centre for Postgraduate Hebrew Studies and an American Endowment for the Humanities Fellow-in-Residence at the Albright Institute of Archaeological Research in Jerusalem, where the Dead Sea Scrolls were first examined.

In 1991-92, he was the Consultant to the Huntington Library in San Marino, California on its decision to open its archives and allow free access for all scholars to the previously unpublished Scrolls. In 2002, he was the first to publicly announce that the so-called 'James Ossuary', which so suddenly and 'miraculously' appeared, was fraudulent; and he did this on the very same day it was made public on the basis of the actual inscription itself and what it said without any 'scientific' or 'pseudo-scientific' aids.

Made in the USA
Las Vegas, NV
27 November 2024